Cambridge IGCSE™

Information and Communication Technology

Third Edition

Graham Brown
David Watson

HODDER
EDUCATION
AN HACHETTE UK COMPAN

The Publishers would like to thank the following for permission to reproduce copyright material.

Photo credits

p.x c © 2020 World Wide Web Consortium, (MIT, ERCIM, Keio, Beihang). http://www.w3.org/Consortium/Legal/2015/doc-license; **p.1** © peshkov/stock.adobe.com; **p.4** tl © peno/Fotolia, tr © Mykola Mazuryk/Fotolia, tcl © Devyatkin/Fotolia, tcr © vetkit/Fotolia, tbl © Devyatkin/Fotolia, tbr © anmalkov/Fotolia, tb © rocksunderwater/istockphoto.com; **p.14** b © Denis Rozhnovsky/stock.adobe.com; **p.16** t © Kaspars Grinvalds/stock.adobe.com; **p.17** t © Scanrail/stock.adobe.com; **p.19** c © Scanrail/stock.adobe.com; **p.20** bl © Ian Dagnall/Alamy Stock Photo, bc © Jacek Lasa/Alamy Stock Photo, br © Jacek Lasa/Alamy Stock Photo; **p.21** cl © franz12/stock.adobe.com, cc © Seventyfour/stock.adobe.com, cr © Cepren Cochnuknn/Alamy Stock Photo; **p.26** c © Ingram Publishing/Alamy Stock Photo, b © Dmitriy Melnikov/Fotolia.com; **p.27** b © George Clerk/istockphoto.com; **p.28** c www.purestockx.com; **p.29** t © Dmitry Vinogradov/istockphoto.com, c © Mariano Ruiz/istockphoto.com, b © Drive Images/Alamy Stock Photo; **p.30** c © kmit/Fotolia.com, b © jerges/istockphoto.com; **p.31** c © George Dolgikh/Fotolia.com, b Thinkstock/Jupiterimages/Getty Images; **p.32** c © Martin Firus/istockphoto.com; **p.33** c © maksim masalski/stock.adobe.com; **p.36** b Courtesy Internet Archive/NASA Ames, © Gado Images/Alamy Stock Photo; **p.37** c Brand X/Getty Images; **p.38** t © Piotr Adamowicz/123RF; **p.40** c © bonnontawat/stock.adobe.com; **p.41** t © IvanSemenovych/stock.adobe.com; **p.42** t © thumb/istockphoto.com, c © Donald Gruener/iStockphoto.com; **p.44** b © Ingram Publishing/Alamy Stock Photo; **p.47** c © Andrey Turchaninov/istockphoto.com; **p.48** c © Konstantin Shevtsov/Fotolia.com; **p.49** t © Murat BAYSAN/Fotolia.com; **p.50** t © Ted Foxx/Alamy Stock Photo, b © Geppe/Alamy Stock Photo; **p.51** c © Miguel Navarro/Getty Images, b © space_expert/stock.adobe.com; **p.61** t © Nomad_Soul/stock.adobe.com; **p.62** t © rocksunderwater/istockphoto.com; **p.66** b © imageBROKER/Alamy Stock Photo; **p.70** c ©Tatiana Popova/istockphoto.com; **p.72** c © Alex Hinds/Alamy Stock Photo; **p.78** c © hadkhanong/Fotolia.com; **p.79** t © Savone/Alamy Stock Photo; **p.80** t © Alexandr Malyshev/iStock via Thinkstock, c © Sheval/Alamy Stock Photo; **p.89** b © Malcolm Haines/Alamy Stock Photo; **p.91** t © Paolese/stock.adobe.com; **p.92** c © ONOKY/Photononstop/Alamy Stock Photo; **p.102** t © Pasta/stock.adobe.com; **p.104** t © Ico Maker/stock.adobe.com; **p.105** t © Monica Wells/Alamy Stock Photo; **p.120** c © iurii/Shutterstock.com; **p.121** t © alan/stock.adobe.com; **p.122** t © Naeblys/stock.adobe.com; **p.126** b © Baloncici/iStock via Thinkstock; **p.141** t © Piero Cruciatti/Alamy Stock Photo, b © xiaoliangge/stock.adobe.com; **p.142** b © Iryna Khabliuk/123rf.com; **p.154** b © tournee/Fotolia.com; **p.158** t © Albert Lozano-Nieto/stock.adobe.com; **p.206** tl © George Clerk/istockphoto.com, tr © alswart/stock.adobe.com; **p.208** t © A. T. Willett/Alamy Stock Photo; **p.251** © Funtap/stock.adobe.com; **p.287** t, **p.290** t, c and b, **p.294** cr, **p.295** t © Alexey Kljatov/stock.adobe.com

t = top, b = bottom, l = left, r = right, c = centre

Acknowledgements

Every effort has been made to trace all copyright holders, but if any have been inadvertently overlooked, the Publishers will be pleased to make the necessary arrangements at the first opportunity.

Although every effort has been made to ensure that website addresses are correct at time of going to press, Hodder Education cannot be held responsible for the content of any website mentioned in this book. It is sometimes possible to find a relocated web page by typing in the address of the home page for a website in the URL window of your browser.

Hachette UK's policy is to use papers that are natural, renewable and recyclable products and made from wood grown in well-managed forests and other controlled sources. The logging and manufacturing processes are expected to conform to the environmental regulations of the country of origin.

Orders: please contact Hachette UK Distribution, Hely Hutchinson Centre, Milton Road, Didcot, Oxfordshire, OX11 7HH. Telephone: +44 (0)1235 827827. Email: education@hachette.co.uk Lines are open from 9 a.m. to 5 p.m., Monday to Friday. You can also order through our website: www.hoddereducation.com

ISBN: 9781398318540

© Graham Brown and David Watson 2021

First published in 2010

This edition published in 2021 by
Hodder Education,
An Hachette UK Company
Carmelite House
50 Victoria Embankment
London EC4Y 0DZ

www.hoddereducation.com

Impression number   10 9 8 7 6 5 4 3 2 1

Year   2025 2024 2023 2022 2021

Cover photo © Julien Eichinger – stock.adobe.com

Illustrations by Aptara Inc.

Typeset by Aptara Inc.

Printed in Slovenia

A catalogue record for this title is available from the British Library.

Contents

1, 2, 3, 4, 78, 16, 17, 18, 19, 20

Introduction

Aims

This book has been written for students of Cambridge IGCSE® Information and Communication Technology (0417/0983) for examination from 2023. It fully covers the syllabus content, provides guidance to support you throughout the course and helps you to prepare for the examination.

Assessment

The information in this section is taken from the Cambridge IGCSE Information and Communication Technology 0417/0983 syllabus for examination from 2023. You should always refer to the appropriate syllabus document for the year of examination to confirm the details and for more information.

The syllabus document is available on the Cambridge International website at:

www.cambridgeinternational.org

There are three examination papers:

	Paper 1 Theory	Paper 2 Document Production, Databases and Presentations	Paper 3 Spreadsheets and Website Authoring
Duration	1 hour 30 minutes	2 hours 15 minutes	2 hours 15 minutes
Marks	80 marks	70 marks	70 marks
Syllabus sections examined	1–21	11–16, 17, 18, 19	11–16, 20, 21

Papers 2 and 3 assess practical skills using a range of different software applications.

How to use this book

Organisation

The content is organised into 21 chapters, corresponding to the syllabus. The content is generally in the same order as the syllabus, although the material within practical chapters is presented in a natural teaching order to aid both teaching and learning, so may deviate slightly.

The material directly relevant to practical skills are covered in the practical chapters 11–21.

Features

Learning outline

Each chapter opens with an outline of the subject material to be covered. The practical chapters 11–21 also state required prior knowledge and source files used.

In this chapter you will learn how to:
*   ★ locate stored files
*   ★ open and import files of different types
*   ★ save files in a planned hierarchical directory/folder structure
*   ★ save files using appropriate file names
*   ★ display file details in a directory/folder
*   ★ save, export and print files in a variety of formats
*   ★ understand the need for, characteristics and uses of generic file formats
*   ★ understand the need to reduce file sizes for storage or transmission
*   ★ reduce file sizes for storage or transmission using file compression.

For this chapter you will need the source file **remora.jpg**.

Exercise

Chapters 1–10 contain short exercises to help recap and confirm knowledge and understanding of the concepts covered.

> ### Exercise 1a
>
> Name a number of devices in the home that contain embedded microprocessors, which can be controlled by smartphones, tablets or phablets using an app and the internet.
>
> What are the advantages and disadvantages of using smartphones, tablets or phablets to control these devices?

Exam-style questions

Chapters 1–10 conclude with exam-style questions, to provide practice with theory questions. Where these are taken from past papers, the details of the specific past paper appear at the end of the question. Any questions without this reference have been written by the authors of this book.

1 TYPES AND COMPONENTS OF COMPUTER SYSTEMS

Exam-style questions

1   There are a number of different types of computer. Write down the type of computer that best fits the following descriptions.
   a A computer that is difficult to move and has a separate monitor and keyboard. [1]
   b A portable computer that includes a physical keyboard. [1]
   c A thin portable computer that has a touch screen and a battery in a single unit, and normally used to make phone calls. [1]
   d A mobile phone that can be used as a computer. [1]

Cambridge IGCSE Information and Communication Technology 0417/12 paper 1
February/March 2016, Question 1

Task

Chapters 11–21 contain tasks throughout. Each task is a step-by-step worked example of a practical examination-style question. They often include the use of source files. The text demonstrates techniques used to solve the task using easy-to-follow step-by-step instructions, along with numerous screenshots, so that practical skills are developed alongside knowledge and understanding.

Task 11a

Create a new folder to store your work for this chapter in. Call this folder **Chapter 11**. Create two new sub-folders called **Source Files** and **Worked**. Open the file **remora.jpg** in a graphics package. Save the image **remora.jpg** in your Source Files folder.

Activities

These are examination-style questions in the practical section, usually at the end of a chapter or section. These often include the use of source files. Answers and mark schemes are available on *Boost:*

Activity 12a

Open the image **snowangel.png** in a suitable package. Rotate the image 90° clockwise. Save the image as snowangel1.png. Save the image again as snowangel1.jpg. Show evidence of the finished image, the filenames and file sizes.

Advice

These provide helpful tips and background throughout the book.

Advice

In some schools, network managers may have disabled some of these methods of opening files. This is to help increase the network security and keep your work safe. If this is the case use one of the other methods to open files.

Links

Numerous topics in ICT are connected together. The Links feature states where relevant material is covered elsewhere in the book.

Link

Importing files will be covered in other chapters as different programs use different methods.

Colour codes and symbols used

Some words or phrases within the text are printed in **red**. Definitions of these terms can be found in the glossary within the Teacher Resource on *Boost.*

Read-only memory (ROM) is a memory used to store information that needs to be permanent. It is often used to contain, for example, configuration data for a computer system. Chips used for ROM cannot be altered and can only be read from (hence their name). One of the main advantages is that the information stored on the ROM chip is not lost, even when power is turned off to the computer. They are often referred to as non-volatile memories. This was fully defined in Figure 1.1.

It is worth noting that that ROM also contains some coding known as the **boot file**. This code tells the computer what to do when it first starts up; it is often referred to as the **BIOS (basic input/output system)**.

In the practical section, words that appear in blue indicate an action or location found within the software package. Blue text that is in chevrons <like this> indicated that this is a key to be pressed on the computer's keyboard, for example:

> Type Chapter 11 (the name for the new folder) then press <Enter>. Open this new Chapter 11 folder and use this method to create two new sub-folders called Source Files and Worked.

In Chapter 18 Databases, words in orange show field names, for example:

> For this task, the descriptions help you to work out meaningful field names. These should always be short enough to allow printouts to fit easily on to as few pages as possible. The first example is Who manufactured the car?; this could be shortened to Manufacturer or even Make. Make is short, meaningful and appropriate, so use that. Price that we bought the car for could be changed to Purchase Price, Purchase, P Price, P_Price or just PPrice. Although *Access* will allow any of these, do not use field names with spaces in as they may cause problems if you try to do more complex operations with the database. You could use any of the other three options, as all would be acceptable. For this task, use PPrice. Similarly, the next field can be called SPrice. Consider the final field, Does the car need cleaning?. Simply using the fieldname Clean could give the wrong idea, as it could mean 'Does the car need cleaning?' or 'Is the car clean?'. It is sensible to plan this and make the changes in the .csv file before importing the data into *Access*.

In Chapter 20, words in green show the functions or formulae entered into the cell of a spreadsheet, for example:

> If we chose to change cell B5 to =$B$2+B3, then replicate this cell down, the cell below would now contain =$B$2+B4, as the absolute reference has been fixed yet the relative reference changes with each row/column.

In Chapter 21 all HyperText Markup Language (HTML) is shown is a blue proportionally spaced font and Cascading Stylesheets appear in a cerise proportionally spaced font, for example:

HTML markup

```
<!DOCTYPE html>
<html>
<!-- Markup created on 06/01/2022 -->
<head>
<title>Task 21a</title>
</head>
<body>
<p>My first web page by MY NAME HERE</p>
<h1>This is style h1, the largest heading style</h1>
<h2>This is style h2</h2>
<h3>This is style h3</h3>
<h4>This is style h4</h4>
<h5>This is style h5</h5>
<h6>This is style h6, the smallest heading style</h6>
<p>This is style p, the paragraph style</p>
</body>
</html>
```

CASCADING STYLESHEETS

```
h1      {color:#ff0000;
         font-size:14px;}
```

Hardware and software used

The practical elements of the syllabus can be undertaken on any suitable hardware platform and using any appropriate software packages. For the purposes of giving examples in this book, we have chosen specific software packages – but the functionality of many other packages is very similar. Many of the skills demonstrated in Chapters 11 to 21 are transferable and can be adapted for other hardware and software platforms.

All the tasks and activities within the practical chapters have therefore been created using a PC platform with *Microsoft Windows 10* operating system and include the use of *Notepad*. Independent packages used for the practical sections include packages from *Microsoft 365*, including *Word, Excel, Access* and *PowerPoint*. *Google Chrome* has been used as the web browser, although we would recommend testing all web pages in at least three different web browsers. For the website authoring section of the book (Chapter 21), all work has been produced in HTML code without the use of a What You See Is What You Get (WYSIWYG) package such as *Adobe Dreamweaver* and *Microsoft Expression Web*. Although you may have a WYSIWYG package, it is important to realise that you are expected to have knowledge of underlying HTML and CSS. All HTML written within this chapter is written in HTML version 5, and is W3C validated (at the time of going to print). All cascading stylesheets used have been W3C validated.

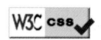

Using source files

Source files that are required for the practical chapters can be found at: www. hoddereducation.co.uk/cambridgeextras and will need to be downloaded onto your local machine or network drive in order to use them. Copy them and give them read/write access. This is essential to ensure that you can use some of the file types included.

Changing the source files to match your regional settings

Before attempting any of these processes, back up all source files. The .csv (comma separated value) files have commas as separators between fields and full stops within currency values. If your regional settings for these values are different (for example, if you use commas within currency values rather than full stops and your software settings require you to use semicolons for separators between fields), then the source data files will need to be edited for use with the regional settings for your software. You can do this in many different software packages, but the easiest (at this level) is *Word*.

Open the .csv file in *Word* using FILE and Open. Select the file from the list to open the file, which will look similar to this:

```
Who manufactured the car?;Model;Colour;Price that we bought the car
for;Price that we will sell the car for;Year;Extras;Does the car need
cleaning?
TVR;Tuscan;Black;18000;20305;2006;Alloy Wheels   Air Conditioning;N
Mercedes;C200;Silver;4995;5995;2003;Air Conditioning;N
Toyota;MR2 roadster;Electric blue;13995;15895;2005;Leather Seats   Air
Conditioning;N
```

Select the HOME tab, then the Editing section followed by the Replace icon.

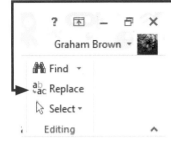

Enter a , (comma) into the Find what: box and a ; (semicolon) into the Replace with: box, then click on [Replace All].

Repeat this process, replacing a . (full stop) with a , (comma). All the characters will have been replaced within the file like this:

```
Who manufactured the car?;Model;Colour;Price that we bought the car
for;Price that we will sell the car for;Year;Extras;Does the car need
cleaning?
TVR;Tuscan;Black;18000;20305;2006;Alloy Wheels   Air Conditioning;N
Mercedes;C200;Silver;4995;5995;2003;Air Conditioning;N
Toyota;MR2 roadster;Electric blue;13995;15895;2005;Leather Seats   Air
Conditioning;N
```

Save the file with the same file name using the File tab and Save. This will ensure that the file is saved in .csv format.

Additional support

The *Theory Workbook* and *Practical Workbook* provide additional opportunity for practice. These write-in workbooks are designed to be used throughout the course.

Command words

Command word	What it means
Analyse	examine in detail to show meaning, identify elements and the relationship between them
Compare	identify/comment on similarities and/or differences
Contrast	identify/comment on differences
Define	give precise meaning
Demonstrate	show how or give an example
Describe	state the points of a topic/give characteristics and main features
Discuss	write about issue(s) or topic(s) in depth in a structured way
Evaluate	judge or calculate the quality, importance, amount, or value of something
Explain	set out purposes or reasons/make the relationships between things evident/provide why and/or how and support with relevant evidence
Give	produce an answer from a given source or recall/memory
Identify	name/select/recognise
Justify	support a case with evidence/argument
State	express in clear terms
Suggest	apply knowledge and understanding to situations where there are a range of valid responses in order to make proposals/put forward considerations

Disclaimers

SECTION 1

Theory

Chapters

Types and components of computer systems

In this chapter you will learn about:
★ hardware
★ software
★ analogue and digital data
★ central processing unit (CPU)
★ internal memory (RAM and ROM)
★ input and output devices
★ backing store
★ operating systems
★ types of computer – desktop computers and mobile computers (laptop, smartphone, tablet and phablet)
★ emerging technologies – artificial intelligence (AI) and extended reality (virtual and augmented).

Computer systems are now commonplace in every part of our daily life. This first chapter introduces the basic components that make up these computer systems; most of which will be described in much greater depth in later chapters. Basic components, including hardware (both external and internal) and software (both applications and system), are all briefly introduced in the following sections.

Comparing books with computers is a good analogy: the actual pages and the ink used on the pages are equivalent to the hardware used to make up computers; the words written on these pages are equivalent to the software. Without the words, the book is useless. Similarly, without software, computers would be of little use to any of us.

1.1 Hardware and software

1.1.1 Hardware

Hardware is the general term for the physical components that make up a typical computer system. For example:

>> keyboard ⎤
>> mouse   ⎬ input device
>> camera   ⎦
>> monitor ⎤
>> printer ⎬ output device
>> plotter ⎦

Hardware falls into two categories: internal and external. The list above are examples of external hardware, which is discussed in detail in Chapter 2. Figure 1.1 considers the following internal hardware devices:

>> motherboard
>> central processing unit (CPU)/processor
>> random access memory (RAM)

» read-only memory (ROM)
» graphics card
» sound card
» network interface card (NIC)
» internal storage devices (hard disk drive and solid-state drive).

Because it is not always possible to see the internal hardware devices, the photographs in Figure 1.2 will give you some idea of the physical appearance of the components described in Figure 1.1.

Motherboard
The motherboard is a printed circuit board found in all computers. It allows the processor and other computer hardware to function and communicate with each other. One of the major functions of a typical motherboard is to act as a kind of 'hub' which other computer devices connect to. A typical motherboard consists of a sheet of non-conductive material, such as hard plastic. Thin layers of copper or aluminium are printed onto this sheet. These form the circuits between the various components. In addition to circuits, a motherboard contains several sockets and slots to connect the other components.

Random access memory (RAM)
Random access memory (RAM) is an internal chip where data is temporarily stored when running applications. This memory can be written to and read from. Since its contents are lost when power to the computer is turned off, it is often referred to as a volatile or temporary memory.
RAM stores the data, files or part of the operating system currently in use.

Read-only memory (ROM)
Read-only memory (ROM) is a memory used to store information that needs to be permanent. It is often used to contain, for example, configuration data for a computer system. These chips cannot be altered and can only be read from (hence their name). One of the main advantages is that the information stored on the ROM chip is not lost even when power is turned off to the computer. They are often referred to as non-volatile memories.

Central processing unit (CPU)/processor
A central processing unit (CPU) or processor is an electronic circuit board in a computer that can execute instructions from a computer program. The two main components are:
• arithmetic and logic unit (ALU) where arithmetic and logical operations are carried out
• control unit (CU) which takes instructions the decodes and executes the instructions.

INTERNAL COMPUTER HARDWARE

Network interface card (NIC)
A network interface card (NIC) is a component that allows a computer or any other device (for example, a printer) to be connected to a network (for example, the internet); it can be wired or wireless.
Each NIC is hard-coded with a unique MAC (media access control) address code – refer to Chapter 4)

Graphics card
A graphics card allows the computer to send graphical information to a video display device such as a monitor, television, or projector. It usually connects to the motherboard (see above). Graphics cards are usually made up of:
• a processing unit
• memory unit (usually RAM)
• a cooling mechanism (often in the form of a heat sink since these cards generate a lot of heat)
• connections to a display unit (monitor, TV or projector).

Sound card
A sound card is an integrated circuit board that provides a computer with the ability to produce sounds. These sounds can be heard by the user either through speakers or headphones. Sound cards also allow a user to record sound input from a microphone connected to the computer, and manipulate sound stored on a disk.

Internal hard disk drive/solid-state drive (HDD/SSD)
These two devices are covered in considerably more depth in later chapters of this book. Basically, hard disk drives (HDDs) are magnetic in nature and are one of the main methods for storing data, files (text, photos and music) and most of the system and applications software. More modern computers (and all tablets) use the newer storage systems which make use of solid-state (SSD) technology and are replacing HDDs in many cases. Their function is the same as an HDD.

▲ **Figure 1.1** Internal computer hardware

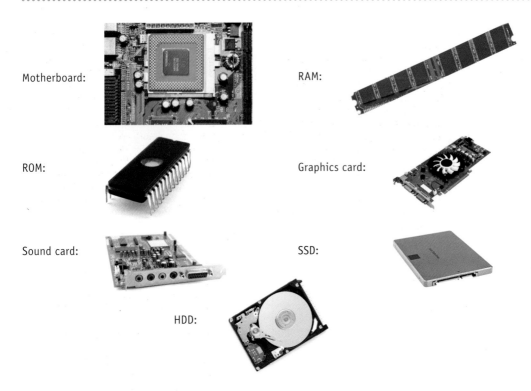

Motherboard:

RAM:

ROM:

Graphics card:

Sound card:

SSD:

HDD:

▲ **Figure 1.2** Examples of internal hardware

1.1.2 Software

Software is the general term used for the programs that control the computer system and process data. The software considered in this book falls into two categories: applications and system.

Applications software provides the services that the user requires to solve a given task. For example:

- » word processing
- » spreadsheet
- » database (management system)
- » control and measurement software
- » apps and applets
- » video editing
- » graphics editing
- » audio editing
- » computer-aided design (CAD).

(Refer to Figure 1.3 for more details.)

System software is the software designed to provide a platform on which all other software can run. For example:

- » compilers
- » linkers
- » device drivers
- » operating systems
- » utilities.

(Refer to Figure 1.4 for more details.)

Word processing
Word processing software is used to manipulate a text document, such as an essay or a report. Text is entered using a keyboard and the software provides tools for copying, deleting and various types of formatting. Some of the functions of word processing software include:
- creating, editing, saving and manipulating text
- copy and paste functions
- spell checkers and thesaurus
- import photos/images into a structured page format
- translation into foreign language.

Spreadsheet
Spreadsheet software is used to organise and manipulate numerical data (in the form of integer, real, date, and so on). Numbers are organised on a grid of lettered columns and numbered rows. The grid itself is made up of cells, and each cell is identified using a unique combination of columns and rows; for example: B6. Some of the functions of spreadsheets include:
- use of formulae to carry out calculations
- ability to produce graphs
- ability to do modelling and 'what if' calculations.

Database (management system)
Database software is used to organise, manipulate and analyse data. A typical database is made up of one or more tables. Tables consist of rows and columns. Each row is called a 'record' and each column is called a 'field.' This provides the basic structure for the organisation of the data within the database. Some of the functions include:
- ability to carry out queries on database data and produce a report (DBMS)
- add, delete and modify data in a table.

Apps and applets
Applets are small applications that perform a single task on a device (they are usually embedded in an HTML page on a website and can be executed from within a browser).
Apps refer to software which can perform a fairly substantial task (such as, video and music streaming, banking application or social media). The term originally referred to software that ran on a smartphone and could be downloaded from an 'app store'.

Control and measurement software
Control and measuring software is designed to allow a computer or microprocessor to interface with sensors so that it is possible to:
- measure physical quantities in the real world (such as temperatures)
- control applications (such as a chemical process) by comparing sensor data with stored data and sending out signals to alter process parameters (for example, open a valve to add acid and change the pH).

APPLICATIONS SOFTWARE
Programs that allow the user to do specific tasks

Computer-aided design (CAD) software
This is software used to help in the creation, manipulation, modification and analysis of a drawing/design.
It can be used to produce 2D or 3D diagrams which:
- can be rotated to view the drawing from any angle
- can produce full dimensions
- can be used to estimate manufacturing costs of the final product
- predict any structural problems.

Audio editing software
Audio editing software allows a user to edit, manipulate and generate audio data on a computer. It allows the user to alter:
- length of track
- start/stop time of track
- conversion between audio file formats
- volume of track
- fading in/out
- combine multiple sound tracks
- noise reduction
- to create another version of the sound track (for example, a continuous loop or phone ring tone).

Video editing software
Video editing software allows a user the ability to manipulate videos to produce a new video. It enables the addition of titles, colour correction and altering/adding sound to the original video. Essentially it includes:
- rearranging, adding and/or removing sections of video clips and/or audio clips
- applying colour correction, filters and other video enhancements
- creating transitions between clips in the video footage.

Graphics editing software
Graphics editing software allows bitmap and vector images to be changed. Bitmap images are made up of pixels which contain information about image brightness and colour. Bitmap graphics editors can change the pixels to produce a different image. Vector graphic editors operate in a different way and do not use pixels. This type of software manipulates lines, curves and text to alter the stored image as required. Both types of editing software are chosen depending on the format of the original image.

▲ **Figure 1.3** Applications software

Compiler
A compiler is a computer program that translates a program written in a high-level language (HLL) into machine code (code that is understood by the computer) so that it can be directly used by a computer to perform a required task. The original program is called the **source code** and the code after compilation is called the **object code**. Once a program is compiled, the machine code can be used again and again to perform the same task without recompilation. Examples of high-level languages include Java, Python, Visual Basic, Fortran, C++ and Algol.

Linkers
A linker (or link editor) is a computer program that takes one or more object files produced by a compiler and combines them into a single program that can be run on a computer. For example, many programming languages allow programmers to write different pieces of code, called modules, separately. This simplifies the programming task since it allows the program to be broken up into small, more manageable sub-tasks. However, at some point, it will be necessary to put all the modules together to form the final program. This is the job of the linker.

Device driver
A device driver is the name given to software that enables one or more hardware devices to communicate with the computer's operating system. Without drivers, a hardware device (for example, a printer) would be unable to work with the computer. All hardware devices connected to a computer have associated drivers. As soon as a device is plugged into the USB port of a computer, the operating system looks for the appropriate driver. An error message will be produced if it cannot be found. Examples of hardware devices that require drivers include printers, memory sticks, mouse, CD drivers, and so on.

Operating systems (OS)
The operating system (OS) is essentially software running in the background of a computer system. It manages many of the basic functions. Without the OS, most computers would be very user-unfriendly and the majority of users would find it almost impossible to work with computers on a day-to-day basis. Operating systems allow:
- input/output operations
- users to communicate with the computer (for example, *Windows*)
- error handling to take place
- the loading and running of programs to occur
- managing of security (for example, user accounts, log on passwords).

SYSTEM SOFTWARE
Programs that allow the hardware to run properly and allow the user to communicate with the computer

Utilities
Utility programs are software that has been designed to carry out specific tasks on a computer. Essentially, they are programs that help to manage, maintain and control computer resources. Examples include:
- antivirus
- anti-spyware
- backup of files
- disk repair
- file management
- security
- screensavers
- disk defragmenter.

▲ **Figure 1.4** System software

1.1.3 Analogue and digital data

Computers can only understand data which is in a binary format (that is, a base 2 number system where only the values 0 and 1 can be used). This is often referred to as **digital data** (because it can only have discrete, discontinuous values). However, data in the real world is actually **analogue** in nature. Analogue data is physical data that changes smoothly from one value to the next, and not in discrete steps as with digital data.

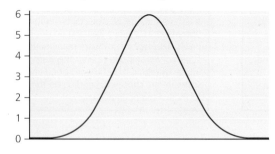
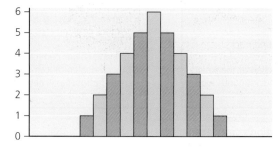

▲ **Figure 1.5** Analogue and digital data

In Figure 1.5, the graph on the left shows analogue data; an infinite number of values can exist between 0 and 6 (for example, 2.5, 4.652, and so on) because the curve is smooth in shape. The graph on the right shows digital data; notice **only** the **exact** values of 0, 1, 2, 3, 4, 5 or 6 can be taken.

If analogue data is being sent to a computer, it must first be converted into digital data; this is done by hardware known as an **analogue to digital converter** (ADC). If the computer is controlling a device (such as a motor) then the digital output from the computer needs to be converted into analogue form. This is done by a **digital to analogue converter** (DAC).

1.2 Main components of computer systems

As already mentioned in Section 1.1, a typical computer system is made up of hardware and software. The diagram in Figure 1.6 shows an example of a computer system consisting of input devices, output devices and secondary storage. These will be discussed in more detail in Chapter 2, but some examples are listed in Table 1.1.

▼ **Table 1.1** Examples of input, output and secondary storage devices

Device	Examples
Input devices	keyboard, mouse, camera, microphone, sensor, scanner
Output devices	monitor, printer, speakers, projector, (graph) plotter
Secondary storage devices	hard disk drive, solid-state drive, pen drive

The internal hardware devices were shown in Figure 1.2 – these consist of four key components:

» the central processing unit (CPU) (contained on the motherboard)
» internal hard disk drive or solid-state drive
» random access memory (RAM)
» read-only memory (ROM).

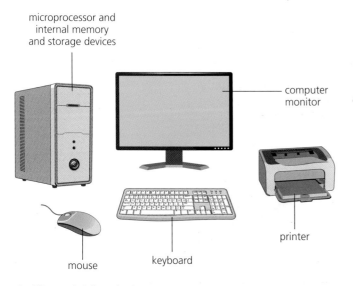

▲ **Figure 1.6** A typical computer system

1.2.1 CPU

The **central processing unit** (CPU) is the part of the computer that interprets and executes the commands from the computer hardware and software. It is normally part of the computer motherboard.

CPUs used to be made up of discrete components and numerous small integrated circuits; these were combined together on one or more circuit board(s). However, due to modern manufacturing techniques, the CPU is now referred to as a **microprocessor.** This is a single integrated circuit which is at the heart of most PCs and is also found in many household devices and equipment where some control or monitoring is needed (for example, the engine management system in a car).

The CPU/microprocessor is made up of a control unit, which controls the input and output devices; an arithmetic and logic unit (ALU), which carries out calculations and makes logical decisions, and small memory locations called registers.

1.2.2 Internal memory

Random access memory (RAM) is an internal chip where data is temporarily stored when running applications. This memory can be written to and read from. Because its contents are lost when power to the computer is turned off, it is often referred to as a volatile or temporary memory. This was fully described in Figure 1.1.

Read-only memory (ROM) is a memory used to store information that needs to be permanent. It is often used to contain, for example, configuration data for a computer system. Chips used for ROM cannot be altered and can only be read from (hence their name). One of the main advantages is that the information stored on the ROM chip is not lost, even when power is turned off to the computer. They are often referred to as non-volatile memories. This was fully described in Figure 1.1.

It is worth noting that that ROM also contains some coding known as the **boot file.** This code tells the computer what to do when it first starts up; it is often referred to as the **BIOS (basic input/output system).**

When the computer is turned on, the BIOS carries out a hardware check to find out if all the devices are present and whether they are functional. Then it loads the **operating system** into the RAM.

The BIOS stores the date, time and system configuration in a non-volatile chip called a **CMOS (complementary metal oxide semiconductor)** – this is usually battery powered.

Table 1.2 provides a summary of the main differences between RAM and ROM.

▼ **Table 1.2** RAM and ROM differences

RAM	ROM
Temporary memory device	Permanent memory device
Volatile memory	Non-volatile memory device
Can be written to and read from	Read-only, data stored cannot be altered
Used to store data, files, programs, part of operating systems (OS) currently in use	Used to store BIOS and other data needed at start up
Can be increased in size to improve operational speed of a computer	

1.2.3 Input and output devices

Input devices are hardware that allows data to be entered into a computer (these are covered in detail in Chapter 2). They use either manual entry (such as a keyboard or a mouse) or direct data entry (such as sensors or optical character readers). Essentially, these devices turn input into a form the computer can understand – for example, a mouse turns hand movements into cursor movements on the screen. As mentioned earlier, sometimes the data has to go through an ADC before the computer can make any sense of it.

When a computer processes data, and the human operator wants to see the results of the processing, then the computer sends the data to an output device. An output device shows the computer's output in a form that is understood by a human – for example, as text on a printer or moving images on a monitor.

Some devices can act as both input and output. For example, a touch screen can do both, as can a DVD writer/player; but most devices are only capable of **either** inputting data into a computer **or** displaying the results of computer processing (output device).

Table 1.3 summarises the differences between input and output devices.

▼ **Table 1.3** Comparison of input and output devices

Input devices	Output devices
An input device is any hardware device that allows a user to enter data or instructions into a computer directly.	An output device is any hardware device that takes the output data from a computer and puts it into a human-readable format or uses it to control another device.
An input device can send data to another device, but it cannot receive data from another device.	An output device is capable of receiving data from another device in order to generate an output, but it cannot send data to another device.
Input devices are necessary for a computer to receive commands from its users and data to process; the devices are under the control of the user or can be direct data entry.	Output devices are needed by a computer so it can share the results of its processing with a human; output devices are under the control of the computer.
Input devices can be fairly complicated because they have to ensure that the user can interact with the computer correctly.	Output devices are less complex than input devices because they only have to turn computer signals into an output.

1.2.4 Backing storage

The main memories in a computer are RAM and ROM. However, to permanently store large amounts of data it is necessary to use backing storage. This normally takes the form of the internal **hard disk drive (HDD)** or **solid-state drive (SSD)**. This is the computer's main internal storage where the applications software, disk operating system and files (for example, text, photo or music) are stored. A key feature of a backing store is that it must store data permanently – that is, it must be non-volatile.

Unlike RAM and ROM, backing storage is not directly addressable (that is, it cannot be read directly by the CPU). The data access time for RAM and ROM is much shorter than it is for backing storage. Backing storage is considerably larger than RAM because it is considerably less expensive per byte.

Backing storage can either be fixed (very often internal to the computer) or removable. The advantage of removable backing storage is that it can be used as a backup in case of data loss or corruption. Data from the main HDD or SSD can be copied onto another device (such as a pen drive or portable HDD) and then stored in a separate location. If the original data on the HDD/SSD has been lost or corrupted, it can be restored from the backup device.

Examples of removable storage include external hard disk drives (HDD), external solid-state drive (SSD) and Blu-ray discs.

Table 1.4 summarises the differences between backing storage and internal memory.

▼ **Table 1.4** Comparison of internal memory and backing storage

Internal memory	Backing storage
RAM contents are lost when computer is powered down; ROM contents are readable only.	Backing storage devices hold their contents permanently, even when powered down.
RAM and ROM are much smaller memories than backing storage.	Have considerably larger capacity to store data than RAM or ROM.
Data access time on RAM and ROM is extremely fast.	Has much slower data access time than RAM and ROM.
Much more expensive per byte than backing storage devices.	Is much cheaper per byte than RAM or ROM.
RAM and ROM are fixed inside the computer (internal memories).	Backing storage can either be fixed (external or internal) or it can be removable.
RAM and ROM can be read directly by the CPU.	Before data on a backing storage device can be read by the CPU, it must first be moved into RAM; this means backing storage is not directly addressable by the CPU.

1.3 Operating systems

Reference to operating systems has already been made earlier on in this chapter (see Figure 1.4).

To enable computer systems to function and to allow users to communicate with computer systems, special software, known as **operating systems (OS)**, have been developed. The general tasks for a typical operating system include:

» control of the operation of the input, output and backing storage devices
» supervising the loading, running and storage of applications programs
» dealing with errors that occur in application programs
» maintaining security of the whole computer system
» maintaining a computer log (which details computer usage)
» allowing communication between user and the computer system (user interface).

1.3.1 User interfaces

Operating systems offer various types of user interface. We will consider four different types:

» command line interface (CLI)
» graphical user interface (GUI)
» dialogue-based user interface
» gesture-based user interface.

Command line interface (CLI)

A **command line interface (CLI)** requires a user to type in instructions to choose options from menus, open software, etc. There are often a number of commands that need to be typed in, for example, to save or load a file. The user has to learn a number of commands just to carry out basic operations. It is also slow, having to key in these commands every time an operation has to be carried out. However, the advantage of a CLI is that the user is in direct communication with the computer and is not restricted to a number of pre-determined options.

For example, *Windows* has a CLI called the 'command prompt'. The following command opens the desktop folder in *Windows Explorer*:

%windir%\explorer.exe C:\Users\YourName\Desktop

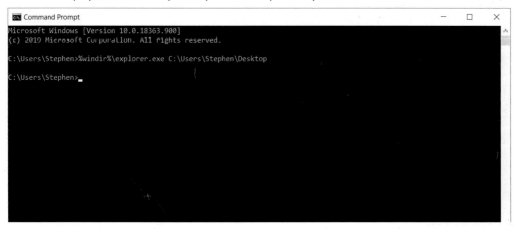

```
Command Prompt                                                    —    □    ×
Microsoft Windows [Version 10.0.18363.900]
(c) 2019 Microsoft Corporation. All rights reserved.

C:\Users\Stephen>%windir%\explorer.exe C:\Users\Stephen\Desktop

C:\Users\Stephen>_
```

▲ **Figure 1.7** Sample of CLI code

The statements in Figure 1.7 show how complex it is just to carry out a fairly straightforward operation using CLI.

Graphical user interface (GUI)

A **graphical user interface (GUI)** allows the user to interact with a computer (or MP3 player, gaming device, mobile phone, etc.) using pictures or symbols (**icons**) rather than having to type in a number of commands. For example, the whole of the CLI code in Figure 1.7 could have been replaced by clicking on the Desktop icon within Windows Explorer.

Simply selecting this icon would automatically execute all the commands shown in Figure 1.7 without the need to type it in.

GUIs use various technologies and devices to provide the user interface. One of the most common is **WIMP (windows icons menu and pointing device)** which was developed for use on personal computers (PC). Here, a mouse is used to control a cursor and icons are selected to open/run windows. Each window contains an application and modern computer systems allow several windows to be open at the same time. An example is shown in Figure 1.8 (here, a number of icons can be seen on the on the bottom of the screen 'window'):

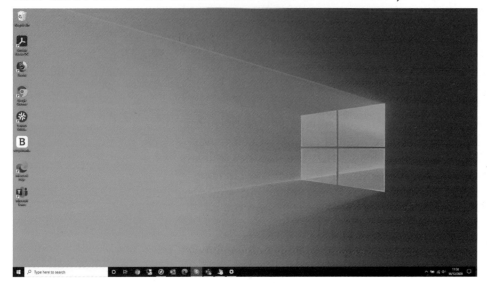

▲ **Figure 1.8** Screen image showing icons

A window manager looks after the interaction between windows, the applications and window system (which handles the pointing devices and the cursor's position).

In recent years, devices such as **touch screen** smartphones and tablets use **post-WIMP** interaction, where fingers are in contact with the screen allowing actions such as **pinching** and **rotating**, which would be difficult to do using a single pointer and device such as a mouse.

Table 1.5 summarises the main advantages and disadvantages of CLI and GUI.

▼ **Table 1.5** Advantages and disadvantages of CLI and GUI interfaces

Interface	Advantages	Disadvantages
Command line interface (CLI)	The user is in direct communication with the computer. The user is not restricted to a number of pre-determined options. It is possible to alter computer configuration settings.	The user needs to learn a number of commands to carry out basic operations. All commands need to be typed in, which takes time and can be error-prone. Each command must be typed in using the correct format, spelling, and so on.
Graphical user interface (GUI)	The user does not need to learn any commands. It is more user-friendly; icons are used to represent applications. A pointing device (such as a mouse) is used to click on an icon to launch the application – this is simpler than typing in commands.	This type of interface uses up considerably more computer memory than a CLI interface. The user is limited to the icons provided on the screen. Needs a more complex operating system, such as *Windows*, to operate, which can be slower to execute commands.

Who would use each type of interface?

CLI: a programmer, analyst or technician; basically, somebody who needs to have direct communication with a computer to develop new software, locate errors and remove them, initiate memory dumps (contents of the computer memory at some moment in time), and so on.

GUI: the end-user who does not have to (or does not need to) have any great knowledge of how the computer works; a person who uses the computer to run software, play games or store/manipulate photographs, for example.

Dialogue-based user interfaces

Dialogue-based user interfaces use the human voice to give commands to a computer system. An example of its use is in some luxury modern cars, where voice activation is used to control devices such as the in-car entertainment system or satellite navigation system. By speaking certain commends, such as 'Hey BMW, drive me to the nearest airport', the system allows natural speech to enable the driver to intuitively interact with the car. The satellite navigation system will automatically direct the driver to their chosen destination (in this case, the nearest airport). This type of interface could also be used in the home; by using voice commands, it is possible to switch on/off lights, operate electronic equipment and so on. In recent years, devices such as Amazon Alexa, Google Now, Apple Siri and Microsoft Cortana have all been developed to interact with a human by recognising verbal commands. These devices act as a personal assistant.

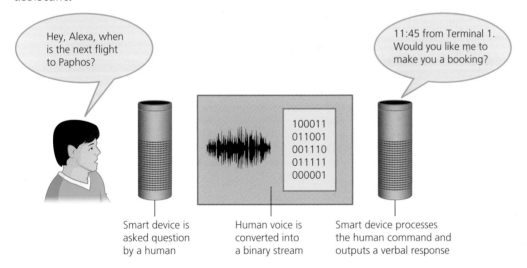

▲ **Figure 1.9** Smart voice activated devices

Gesture-based interfaces

Gesture-based interfaces rely on human interaction by the moving of hands, head or even the feet. Gesture recognition allows humans to interface with a computer in a more natural fashion without the need for any mechanical devices. This type of interface uses techniques known as **computer vision** and **image processing**. For example, using our car example again, the following gestures can be used to carry out certain functions:

» rotating a finger clockwise near the radio will increase the sound volume (rotating the finger anti-clockwise will reduce the sound volume)

» opening the thumb and next finger will change the track being listened to (for example, in a playlist)
» moving the foot under the rear bumper of the car automatically opens the boot lid
» moving a hand near a window switch automatically opens a window.

There are many other examples. Either a sensor or a camera is used to pick up the gesture and a signal is sent to an on-board computer to carry out the required action. It eliminates the need for an array of buttons and dials on the dashboard.

Table 1.6 summarises the main advantages and disadvantages of dialogue-based and gesture-based interfaces.

▼ **Table 1.6** Advantages and disadvantages of dialogue-based and gesture-based interfaces

Interface	Advantages	Disadvantages
Dialogue-based interface	» no need for a driver to take their hands off the steering wheel » in a home, very useful for people with disabilities, because many tasks can be carried out by the spoken word only » possible to use as a security feature, because voice recognition could be used to identify a person	» still unreliable, with many commands not being recognised or needing to be repeated several times (especially if there is background noise) » can be quite complex to set up » user needs to know which commands can be used
Gesture-based interface	» replaces mechanical input devices » no physical contact required » very natural interface for a human operator » no training needed to interface with the computer	» possible for unintentional movement to be picked up » only works fairly near to the camera or sensor (maximum of 1.5 metres) » may only accept a limited number of movements (for example, it may take several attempts to find out exactly what finger movements are recognised)

1.4 Types of computer

There are many types of computer systems in existence. The following summarises some of the more common types currently available:

1.4.1 Desktop computers

Desktop usually refers to a general-purpose computer that is made up of separate monitor, keyboard, mouse and processor unit. It is distinguished from, for example, a laptop computer by the fact that it is made up of a number of separate components, which makes them not very portable.

Because laptop and desktop computers tend to be used for very similar purposes, it is worth making a comparison between the two types of computer.

▲ **Figure 1.10** Desktop computer

The advantages of desktop computers over laptop computers are:

➤ Spare parts and connections tend to be standardised, which usually results in lower costs.
➤ Desktop computers are easier, and less expensive, to upgrade or expand.
➤ The desktop tends to have a better specification (for example, faster processor) for a given price (often due to size and construction constraints in laptops).
➤ Power consumption is not critical because they usually plug straight into a wall socket, and the larger casings allow a better dissipation of any heat build-up.
➤ Because they are usually fixed in one location, there is less likelihood of them being damaged or stolen.
➤ Internet access can be more stable because a desktop computer is more likely to have a wired internet connection (the user will always have the same data transfer rate); however, due to their portability, laptop computers usually use wireless internet connectivity where the signal can be very variable (giving variable data transfer rate).

They do have disadvantages when compared to laptop computers:

➤ The most obvious is that they are not particularly portable because they are made up of separate components.
➤ They tend to be more complicated because all the components need to be hooked up by wiring, which also clutters up the desk space.
➤ Because they are not particularly portable, it is necessary to copy files on, for example, a memory stick, when you want to do some work elsewhere (for example, doing office work at home); although cloud storage has diminished this disadvantage recently, it still may not be possible to save sensitive data files on the cloud.

Link

For more on cloud storage see Section 4.1.

The main uses of desktop computers include:

➤ office and business work (word processing, spreadsheets, finance software and databases being the main use)
➤ educational use (using interactive software to teach or learn from)
➤ use as a gaming device (for example, games such as chess, crossword puzzles, fantasy games, and so on)
➤ general entertainment (for example, live or 'catch-up' streaming of television programmes).

1.4.2 Mobile computers

Mobile computers, by their very name, suggest a group of computers which are considerably more portable than desktop computers. Such computers fall into four categories:

➤ laptop computers
➤ smartphones
➤ tablets
➤ phablets.

Laptop (or notebook)

Laptop (or notebook) refers to a type of computer where the monitor, keyboard, pointing device and processor are all together in one single unit. This makes them extremely portable.

Key features you would expect to find in a laptop:

>> lightweight (to aid portability)
>> low power consumption (and also long battery life)
>> low heat output (cooling is very important).

Laptop computers do have advantages when compared to desktop computers:

▲ **Figure 1.11** Laptop computer

>> The most obvious advantage is their portability; they can be taken anywhere because the monitor, pointing device, keyboard, processor and backing store units are all together in one single unit.
>> Because everything is in one single unit, there are no trailing wires (only one single cord is used).
>> They take up much less room on a desk, so they can be used anywhere (for example, in a café).
>> Their portability allows them to take full advantage of Wi-Fi features.
>> Because they are portable, they can link into any multimedia system.

Laptop computers also have disadvantages when compared to desktop computers:

>> Because they are easily portable, they are also easier to steal!
>> They have limited battery life so the user may need to carry a heavy power adaptor.
>> The keyboards and pointing devices can sometimes be more awkward to use.
>> It is not always possible to upgrade them, for instance by adding more RAM.

The main uses of laptop computers include:

>> office and business work (word processing, spreadsheets, finance software and databases being the main use)
>> educational use (using interactive software to teach or learn from)
>> used as a gaming device (for example, games such as chess, crossword puzzles, fantasy games, and so on)
>> general entertainment (for example, live or 'catch-up' streaming of television programmes)
>> used in control and monitoring (because they can be operated anywhere using their internal battery, it is possible to use laptops to gather data directly from the environment – for example, they can be plugged into a gas boiler during maintenance to monitor its performance).

Smartphones

Smartphones allow normal phone calls to be made, but also have an operating system (such as iOS, Android or Windows) allowing them to run a number of computer applications (known as apps or applets). They allow users to send/receive emails, use a number of apps, use a camera feature (to take photos or videos), MP3/4 players (for music and videos), and so on. Smartphones communicate with the internet either by using Wi-Fi hot spots or by using 3G/4G/5G mobile phone networks.

▲ **Figure 1.12** Smartphone

Some of the typical features of smartphones include:

>> high-definition, anti-glare displays
>> front- and back-facing cameras (which are used to take photos, videos or act as a webcam when doing video calls over the internet)
>> lower weight and longer battery life than laptops
>> use Bluetooth for connection to printers and other devices
>> make use of flash (solid state) memory and cloud storage facilities to back up and synchronise (often just referred to as 'sync') data sources
>> they use a number of sensors to carry out the following functions:
    - proximity sensors to detect if the device is close to, for example the ear, which allows it to block unintended 'touches'
    - accelerometers, which detect movement and orientation of the device (for example, move the display from portrait to landscape to view videos, or allow it to be used as a 'steering wheel' in-car racing games)
    - can use sophisticated speech recognitions systems (such as Siri) to enable the user to ask the device to look for things (such as search the address book).

The new generation of smartphones are becoming even thinner and lighter, because they make use of OLED (organic light emitting diode) touch screens.

Future smartphones will also use OLED touch screens that are coated with a crystalline layer that allows the phones to be partially solar powered; this allows them to use Li-Fi (similar to Wi-Fi, except communication uses visible light rather than radio waves). Communication using Li-Fi is considerably faster than with Wi-Fi (much higher data transfer rate); it is also more secure (by stopping internet 'piggybacking'). The Li-Fi system can also be used during aeroplane flights because it does not use radio waves and therefore does not interfere with flight control systems.

Advantages of smartphones:

>> They are very small in size and lightweight – therefore they are very easy to carry and have on your person at all times (this is more difficult with laptops because they are much bulkier and much heavier).
>> You can use them to make phone calls, but also connect to the internet while on the move.

>> Because they use Wi-Fi and mobile phone networks they can be used almost anywhere (this is not the case with laptops or desktops; although tablets also use the same technology).
>> They have apps which make use of sensor data provided by the smartphone, for instance location data for maps – this can provide services that are not available on desktops or laptops.
>> They have a reasonable battery life compared to laptops.

Disadvantages of smartphones:

>> The small screens and keyboards make pages difficult to read.
>> It is more difficult and slower when typing things in (laptops and desktops have much bigger screens and much larger keyboards).
>> Web browsing and photography can quickly drain the battery.
>> Memory size in most phones is not very large when compared to laptops and desktops – although it is comparable with tablets (however, the latest generation smartphones come with 1 TiB memories).
>> Not all website features are compatible with smartphone operating systems.
>> Because of their small size, it is much easier to lose a smartphone or for it to be stolen compared to laptops or desktops.
>> The data transfer rate using mobile phone networks can be slower than with Wi-Fi – this makes streaming of video or music, for example, less than satisfactory at times.

Tablets

Tablets are becoming an increasingly used type of mobile computer. They work in a similar way to a smartphone. Tablets use touch screen technology and do not have a conventional keyboard. The keyboard is **virtual**; that is, it is part of the touch screen and keys are activated by simply touching them with a finger or a stylus. However, it is possible to buy tablet cases which contain a normal-sized keyboard. Internet access is usually through Wi-Fi or 3G/4G/5G (mobile phone) connectivity. Like smartphones, tablets are equipped with a series of sensors which include camera, microphone, accelerometer and touch screen.

▲ **Figure 1.13** Tablet

The typical features of tablets are identical to those of a smartphone (described earlier).

Advantages of tablets compared to laptops:

>> very fast to switch on (no time delay waiting for the operating system to load up)
>> fully portable – they are so lightweight that they can be carried anywhere
>> touch screen technology means they are simple to use and do not need any other input devices
>> can use several apps as standard (such as built-in camera, MP3/4 players and so on)

>> not much heat – they use solid-state technology
>> battery life of a tablet is a lot longer
>> when the power button is pressed, it goes into standby, but remains connected to the internet so the user still hears alerts when emails or other 'events' are received.

Disadvantages of tablets compared to laptops:

>> tend to be rather expensive when compared to laptops (but this will probably change with time as they become more common)
>> they often have limited memory or storage when compared to a laptop (although some of the latest devices have 1 TiB memory capacity)
>> if 3G/4G/5G mobile phone networks are used, they can be expensive to run if the internet is being accessed frequently
>> typing on a touch screen can be slow and error-prone compared to a standard keyboard
>> transferring of files often has to be done through an 'application atore'; this lack of 'drag and drop' facility can prove to be irritating to users
>> laptops tend to support more types of file format than tablets and are also better equipped to run different types of software.

Some of the latest smartphones have been designed as a hybrid between a tablet and a smartphone; these are referred to as a **phablet**. They have much larger screens than a smartphone but are smaller than a tablet. All the features of a smartphone (described earlier) also apply to phablets together with the typical features of a tablet.

Smartphones	Phablets	Tablets
up to 5.1 inches in size (that is, 13 cm)	between 5.1 inches and 7 inches (that is, 13 cm to 18 cm)	over 7 inches in size (that is, over 18 cm)

▲ **Figure 1.14** Comparison of smartphone, phablet and tablet

19

The main uses of smartphones, tablets and phablets include:

» entertainment (streaming of music, videos and television programmes)
» gaming (including group games)
» as a camera or video camera (the quality of videos and photos now matches a good digital cameras)
» internet use (online sales, social networks, using QR codes, and so on)
» sending/receiving emails
» global positioning system (use of maps to navigate to a location)
» calendar functions
» telephone banking (sending and receiving money using the banking apps)
» Voice over Internet Protocol (VoIP) – telephone network using the internet which also allows video calling
» instant access to social networks (social contact with friends no matter where you are in the world)
» instant messaging
» office and business management (particularly the features that allow rapid voice and video communication)
» education use (using interactive software to teach or learn from)
» remotely control devices (it is possible to remotely operate devices in the home, such as microwave ovens, which contain embedded microprocessors; by using internet-enabled smartphones or tablets, it is possible to start/stop the oven even while several kilometres away from home by using an App and the internet).

> ### Exercise 1a
> ....
> Name a number of devices in the home that contain embedded microprocessors, which can be controlled by smartphones, tablets or phablets using an app and the internet. | What are the advantages and disadvantages of using smartphones, tablets or phablets to control these devices?

1.5 Emerging technologies

1.5.1 Impact of emerging technologies

Artificial intelligence

There are many definitions of **artificial intelligence (AI)**. Essentially, AI is a machine or application which carries out a task that requires some degree of intelligence. For example:
- the use of language
- recognising a person's face
- the ability to operate machinery, such as a car, aeroplane, train, and so on
- analysing data to predict the outcome of a future event, for example weather forecasting.

AI duplicates human tasks which require decision-making and problem-solving skills. Eventually, many tasks presently done by humans will be replaced by robots or computers, which could lead to unemployment. However, the positive side includes improvements in safety and quality of services and products. Some examples are detailed below.

The impact of AI on everyday life

Whenever AI is mentioned, people usually think of science fiction fantasies and think of **robots**. The science fiction writer **Isaac Asimov** even went as far as producing his three laws of robotics:

» robots may not injure a human through action or inaction
» robots must obey order given by humans without question
» a robot must protect itself unless it conflicts with the two laws above.

Many science fiction movies continue to fuel people's imagination with slightly sinister interactions between humans and machines. However, AI goes way beyond robotics and covers many areas, such as those shown in Figures 1.15–1.11

▲ **Figure 1.15** An autonomous (driverless) vehicle – we already have driverless trains and autopilots on aeroplanes, but future developments include driverless cars.

▲ **Figure 1.16** Robotic research is leading to improvements in technology to help amputees and people with disabilities.

▲ **Figure 1.17** Robots are used to help people carry out dangerous or unpleasant tasks – for example, bomb disposal, welding of car bodies, entering nuclear disaster areas (such as Chernobyl or Fukushima) where the radiation would kill a human in under two minutes.

There are many more examples and the list becomes longer and longer with time.

Negative impacts of AI

All of the above examples give a very favourable view of the effect of AI on our everyday lives. However, in any balanced argument, we should also consider the drawbacks of the new technology:

» could lead to many job losses in a number of areas (although it is true to say that new technical jobs would also be created); many jobs could be lost in manufacturing, but other roles are likely to be affected (such as bus, taxi, lorry and train drivers)

>> dependency on technology and the inability to carry out tasks done by robots, for example, could be an issue in the future
>> loss of skills – even now, skills from previous generations have been lost as humans have been replaced by machines and software applications.

Extended reality

Extended reality (XR) refers to real and virtual combined environments, and is a 'catch all' term for all immersive technologies. The three most common examples at the moment are:

>> augmented reality (AR)
>> virtual reality (VR)
>> mixed reality (MR).

All these immersive technologies extend the reality we experience by either blending the virtual and real worlds or by creating a fully immersive experience.

In this chapter, we will only consider the first two examples.

Augmented reality (AR)
The features of augmented reality include:

>> allow the user to experience the relationship between digital (virtual) and physical (real) worlds
>> virtual information and objects are overlaid onto real-world situations
>> the real world is enhanced with digital details, such as images, text and animation
>> the user can experience the AR world through special goggles or via smartphone/phablet screens
>> the user is not isolated from the real world and is still able to interact and see what is going on in front of them
>> examples include the Pokémon GO game which overlays digital creatures onto real-world situations.

In the future, augmented reality will have an impact on all the following areas:

>> safety and rescue operations (for example, it is possible to provide 3D images of an area where a rescue mission is to take place, giving the team the opportunity to interact with the environment and try out rescue procedures before doing the real thing)
>> entertainment (for example, AR takes users into a virtual environment where it is possible to interact with the characters; imagine the characters of your favourite film interacting with you at home)
>> shopping and retail (this is one of the big areas – for example, using your smartphone camera you can try out make-up and see how it looks on you before buying it, or you can experience a virtual tour of a new car where you can 'sit' in the interior and try out the driving experience before buying the car)

» healthcare (doctors can make use of AR to have a better understanding of a patient's body; software, such as *Echopixel* enables doctors to use CT scans from patients to build up a 3D image of their body to help with surgery and diagnosis).

Virtual reality (VR)
The features of virtual reality include:

» the ability to take the user out of the real-world environment into a virtual (unreal) digital environment
» in contrast to AR, the user is fully immersed in a simulated digital world
» users must wear a VR headset or a head-mounted display which allows a 360° view of the virtual world (this 'fools' the brain into believing they are walking on an ocean bed, walking in an alien world or inside a volcano)
» this technology can be used to good effect in: medicine (teaching operation procedures), construction, engineering and the military.

In the future, virtual reality will have an impact on all the following areas:

» military applications (for example, training to operate a new tank)
» education (for example, looking inside an ancient building as part of a history lesson)
» healthcare (for example, as a diagnostic tool to recommend treatment)
» entertainment (for example, games where gloves, goggles or helmets are worn to fully immerse players and make it seem very real)
» fashion (for example, to do fashion shows before doing the real thing – see the clothes on people, check out the venue and so on)
» heritage (for example, allowing users to walk around and close up to monuments like Stonehenge)
» business (for example, training courses and role-playing scenarios for staff)
» engineering (for example, seeing how new designs like bridges will look in an existing environment)
» sport (for example, a golfer trying to improve his swing can use this technology and get feedback to improve his game)
» media (for example, interactive special effects in movies)
» scientific visualisation (for example, part of a molecular structure in chemistry, or a cell in biology).

Exam-style questions

1 There are a number of different types of computer. Write down the type of computer that best fits the following descriptions.

   a A computer that is difficult to move and has a separate monitor and keyboard. *Desktop*   [1]

   b A portable computer that includes a physical keyboard. *Laptop*   [1]

   c A thin portable computer that has a touch screen and a battery in a single unit, not normally used to make phone calls. *Tablet*   [1]

   d A mobile phone that can be used as a computer. *Smartphone*   [1]

   Cambridge IGCSE Information and Communication Technology (0417) Paper 12 Q1, February/March 2016

2 Tick (✓) whether the following are features of operating systems containing a command line interface (**CLI**) or a graphical user interface (**GUI**).   [2]

	CLI (✓)	GUI (✓)
Instructions have to be typed.	✓	
Applications are represented by icons.		✓
Options are chosen from a menu.		✓
Many instructions have to be memorised.	✓	

   Cambridge IGCSE Information and Communication Technology (0417) Paper 12 Q2, February/March 2016

3 Most smart phones can carry out many functions which, until recently, only a computer could perform. Explain why computers of all types are still needed.   [7]

   they
   other types of computers have more storage *Cambridge IGCSE Information and Communication Technology (0417) Paper 12 Q10, February/March 2015*
   & are more convient to work with

4 Computer operating systems have developed since early computers used Command Line Interfaces (CLI). Many computers now use Graphical User Interfaces (GUI), some of which are capable of using touch screen technology.

   Compare and contrast CLI and GUI.   [8]

   Cambridge IGCSE Information and Communication Technology (0417) Paper 11 Q14, May/June 2017

5 Nine statements about random access memory (RAM) and read-only
memory (ROM) are given below. By putting a tick (✓) in the appropriate
box, indicate whether each statement refers to RAM or ROM. [9]

	RAM (✓)	ROM (✓)
Data on a chip is stored permanently and cannot be deleted		
It is not possible to alter or delete the data stored on the chip		
Data on the chip is stored temporarily and can be deleted by the user		
Data is retained even when the computer is powered down		
Stores data, files or part of the operating system which is currently in use		
Data is lost when power to the computer is turned off		
It contains the basic input/output system used to boot up the computer when it is first powered up		
It is a form of volatile memory		
It is a form of non-volatile memory		

6 a Describe what is meant by augmented reality and virtual reality. [4]
  b Describe how augmented reality and virtual reality could affect
      society in the near future. [4]

7 Six descriptions are shown on the left and six computer terms are
  shown on the right.
  Draw lines to link each statement to its correct computer term. [6]

Method whereby a person uses their voice to carry out a function	output device
Physical component that allows data to be entered into a computer system	analogue
Physical component, such as a monitor, printer or projector under the control of the computer	computer-aided design
Small application that carries out a single task; usually embedded in the html page on a website	dialogue-based interface
Software used to help in the creation, manipulation, modification and analysis of a drawing	input device
Physical data that changes smoothly and is not step wise; has an infinite number of possible values	applet

Input and output devices

As the name suggests, these are hardware devices that allow data to be input into a computer. Many such devices exist, ranging from the more common ones, such as the keyboard, through to more specialist devices, such as barcode readers. Some of these are described in this section.

2.1 Input devices and their uses

2.1.1 Keyboards

Keyboards are by far the most common method used for data entry. They are used as the input device on computers, tablets, mobile phones and many other electronic items.

▲ **Figure 2.1** Keyboard

The keyboard is connected to the computer through a USB or wireless connection. In the case of tablets and mobile phones, the keyboard is often **virtual** or a type of **touchscreen** technology (see later).

When the character on the keyboard is pressed, it is converted into a digital signal, which the computer interprets.

They are a relatively slow method of data entry and are also prone to errors. But keyboards are probably still the easiest way to enter text into a computer. However, frequent use of these devices can lead to injuries, such as **repetitive strain injury (RSI)** in the hands and wrists.

Ergonomic keyboards can help to overcome this problem – these have the keys arranged differently, as shown in Figure 2.2. They are also designed to give more support to the wrists and hands when doing a lot of typing.

Figure 2.3 and the following description summarises how the computer can recognise a letter pressed on the keyboard:

>> There is a membrane or circuit board at the base of the keys.
>> In Figure 2.3, the 'H' key is pressed and this completes a circuit as shown.

▲ **Figure 2.2** Ergonomic keyboard

» The CPU in the computer can then determine which key has been pressed.
» The CPU refers to an index file to identify which character the key press represents.

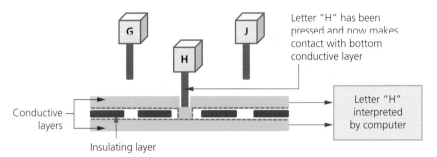

Conductive layers

Insulating layer

Letter "H" has been pressed and now makes contact with bottom conductive layer

Letter "H" interpreted by computer

▲ **Figure 2.3** Diagram of a keyboard

Uses of keyboards

» Input of data into applications software (for example, text into word processors, numbers into spreadsheets, and so on).
» Typing in commands to the computer (for example, Prnt Scrn, Ctrl+P to print out, and so on).

Advantages of keyboards

» Fast entry of new text into a document.
» Well-known method.
» Easy to use for most people.
» Easier to do verification checks as data is entered (can immediately compare the source document with typed data on the screen).

Disadvantages of keyboards

» Can be difficult to use if the user has limited arm/wrist use.
» Slow method when compared to direct data entry (for example, Optical Mark Recognition – see Section 2.2).
» Fairly large device that uses up valuable desk space.

> ## Exercise 2a
> Find out about a number of applications that use input/output devices and discuss the reasons why they were chosen (that is, their advantages and disadvantages).

2.1.2 Numeric keypads

A **numeric keypad** is used to enter numbers only (although some have a function key to allow alphabetic characters to be input).

Uses of numeric keypads

» **Automatic teller machines (ATMs)**, where the customer can key in their PIN, amount of money, etc.
» Mobile phones to allow phone numbers, etc. to be keyed in.
» **Point of sale terminals (POS)** in case the barcode reader fails to read the barcode – the number has to be keyed in manually by the operator.

▲ **Figure 2.4** Numeric keypad

» Chip and PIN devices when paying by credit/debit cards (key in PIN, amount of money, etc.).
» Fast entry of numeric data into a spreadsheet.

Advantages of numeric keypads

» Faster than standard keyboards when entering numeric data.
» Because many are small devices (for example, mobile phones) they are very easy to carry around.

Disadvantages of numeric keypads

» Sometimes have small keys which can make input more difficult.
» Sometimes the order of the numbers on the keypad is not intuitive.

2.1.3 Pointing devices

Mouse

The **mouse** is an example of a **pointing device**. The user controls the position of a pointer on the screen by moving the mouse around. There are usually two buttons which have different functions; the left button is used to select items by double clicking, while the right button brings up drop-down menus.

▲ **Figure 2.5** Mouse

Many also have a scroll button, which speeds up the process of moving through a document.

The **optical mouse** (where movement is detected by reflected light rather than the position of a moving ball) and the **cordless** or **wireless mouse** (which transmits signals to a USB wireless receiver plugged into the computer) are in use on modern computers. The advantage of an optical mouse is it has no moving parts and it also does not pick up any dirt. This makes it more robust and improves its performance because the older type of mouse can 'skid' on certain surfaces reducing the control of the pointer.

▲ **Figure 2.6** Example of a drop-down menu

Uses of a mouse
Almost anything, depending on the software, but includes:

» opening, closing and minimising software
» grouping, moving and deleting files
» image editing, for example, controlling the size and position of a drawing pasted into a document
» controlling the position of a pointer on the screen to allow selection from a menu or selecting an icon, and for scrolling up and down/left and right.

Advantages of a mouse

» Faster method for choosing an option rather than using a keyboard.
» Very quick way of navigating through applications and the internet.
» Does not need a large desk area when compared to a keyboard.

Disadvantages of a mouse

» Can be more difficult for people with restricted hand/wrist movement than using a keyboard for data entry.
» Easy to damage, and the older type of mouse quickly becomes clogged up with dirt.
» Difficult to use if no flat surface readily available (for example, on an aeroplane).

Touchpad

Touchpads are used as a pointing device in many laptop computers. The pointer is controlled by the user moving their finger on the touchpad and then gently tapping it to simulate the left-hand button of a mouse (that is, selection). They also have buttons under the touchpad which serve the same function as the left and right buttons on a mouse.

▲ **Figure 2.7** Touchpad

Use of a touchpad

Their uses are the same as those of a mouse.

Advantages of a touchpad

» Same as the mouse (faster than a keyboard for choosing options, used to navigate applications and the internet, etc.).
» Because the touchpad is integrated into the laptop computer there is no need for a separate mouse – this aids the portability and is a big advantage if there are no flat surfaces available.

Disadvantages of a touchpad

» People with limited hand/wrist movement find the device difficult to use.
» Can be more difficult to control the pointer when compared to a normal mouse.
» More difficult to use when doing certain operations such as drag and drop.

Trackerball

Trackerballs are similar to a mouse, except that a ball is on the top or the side of the device; the user controls the pointer on the screen by rotating the ball with their hand. It is easier to use for people with limited hand/wrist movement. Some trackerballs have two buttons, which have the same function as the left- and right-hand mouse buttons. If they have a third button, it is equivalent to a double click. Because trackerballs do not physically move, there is no need for a large amount of desk space.

▲ **Figure 2.8** Trackerball

Uses of a trackerball

» Can be a good alternative to a mouse for people with conditions such as RSI.
» Used in an industrial control room environment where it is faster than a mouse to navigate through process screens.
» Used in some luxury cars to select functions such as radio, telephone, music, satnav and so on.

▲ **Figure 2.9** Trackerball used in a luxury car

Advantages of a trackerball

» Does not need the same fine control as a mouse.
» Easier to use than a mouse if the operator has problems with their wrist or hand.
» More accurate positioning of the pointer on screen than a mouse.
» They are more robust than a mouse.
» Needs less desk space than a mouse or keyboard.

Disadvantages of a trackerball

» Not supplied with the computer as standard, therefore more costly.
» User may need training because it is not standard equipment.

2.1.4 Remote control

A **remote control** is used for the operation of other devices using infrared signals.

The buttons on the keypad are used to select options (such as television channels, sound levels on a Hi-Fi, timings on a DVD recorder, etc.).

Uses of a remote control

» Televisions, satellite systems, DVD/Blu-ray players and Hi-Fi systems all use remote controls to alter functions such as sound volume, on/off, change channels, open the disc drawer, and so on.
» Used to control multimedia systems.
» Used in industrial applications to remotely control processes, stop and start machinery, etc.

▲ **Figure 2.10** Remote control

Advantages of a remote control

» Can be operated from any reasonable distance, unlike, for example, a wired mouse which is restricted by the length of the wire. Some industrial processes are hazardous, so it is a big advantage to be able to select operations from a distance.

Disadvantages of a remote control

» Difficult to use if the operator has limited hand/wrist movement.
» It is easier to block the signal if, for example, the walls in the building are very thick.

2.1.5 Joysticks and driving wheels

Joystick

Joysticks have similar functions to a mouse and a trackerball. By gripping the stick, a pointer on the screen can be controlled. Buttons are used to make selections. Often they have another button on the top of the stick that is used for gaming purposes for example to fire a weapon.

▲ **Figure 2.11** Joystick

Uses of a joystick

» Used in video/computer games.
» Used in **simulators** (for example, flight simulators) to mimic actual controls.

Advantages of a joystick

» Easier than a keyboard to navigate the screen.
» Control is more realistic for some applications than, for example, using a mouse.

Disadvantages of a joystick

» More difficult to control the on-screen pointer than with other devices, such as a mouse.

Driving wheel

A **driving (steering) wheel** is an example of an input device that is similar to a joystick in many ways. It connects to a computer (or games machine), usually through a USB port. The wheel allows you to simulate the turning of a steering wheel, and there are associated devices (such as buttons or pedals) which allow you to accelerate and brake. Sensors are used to pick up left/right movement so that the user gets the sensation of steering a car around a circuit or on the road.

▲ **Figure 2.12** Driving wheel

Uses of a driving wheel

» Used in video/computer games (for example, car racing games).
» Used in **simulators** (for example, car-driving simulators) to mimic actual vehicle controls.

Advantages of a driving wheel

» Easier than a keyboard or joystick to control steering movements; it is more natural.
» The 'driving experience' is nearer to how an actual steering wheel and other controls operate in real life.

Disadvantages of a driving wheel

» It can be a rather expensive input device compared to mouse or joystick.
» Movements in the steering can be too sensitive, giving an unrealistic 'feel'.
» Unless it is an expensive simulator, feedback to the driving wheel is non-existent.

2.1.6 Touch screens (as an input device)

With a **touch screen** the user can choose an option by simply touching a button/icon on the screen. The selection is automatically made without the need for any pointing device.

Uses of touch screens

» Self-service tills, for example, petrol stations, where the user just touches the screen to select the fuel grade and payment method.

▲ **Figure 2.13** Touch screen

» Automatic teller machines (ATMs) to choose from on-screen options.
» Point of sale terminals such as in restaurants.
» Public information systems at airports, railway stations, tourist offices, etc.
» Mobile phones, tablets and satellite navigation systems.
» Interactive white boards in education.
» Computer-based training (CBT) where answers are selected during on-screen testing.
» They can obviously also be used as an output device because they also work as a flat-screen monitor (see Section 2.3.2).

Advantages of touch screens

» Faster entry of options than using keyboard or mouse.
» Very easy method for choosing options.
» User-friendly method – no training necessary in its use.
» Option to expand the size of the display if necessary.

Disadvantages of touch screens

» Limited number of input options available.
» Can lead to problems if an operator has to use the system frequently (straining of arm muscles, RSI, etc. are all possible).
» The screen can get very dirty with constant touching (giving a risk of spreading infections, and reduce its responsiveness which makes it more difficult to read in strong sunlight).

2.1.7 Scanners

Scanners are used to enter information from hard copy (for example, text documents, photographs) into a computer. The most common type is the flatbed scanner (see Figure 2.14), which is made up of a glass panel and lid. The hard copy document or photo is scanned by a light source and produces a computer-readable image.

The subsequent image can then be manipulated using a drawing package. Images of text can also be used with optical character recognition (OCR) software to produce editable text documents (see Section 2.2). There are also specialist scanners which are designed to carry out a specific task, for example, barcode scanners (see later).

▲ **Figure 2.14** Flatbed scanner

Uses of scanners

» Scan in documents and convert into a format for use in various software packages.
» Scan in old/valuable documents/books, thus protecting the originals, as well as producing records in case the paper copies are lost/destroyed (this is also known as archiving).
» Scan in photographs (not all cameras are digital and therefore photographs are still printed on paper, requiring conversion to computer format for storage).
» Scan in barcodes at POS terminals.

Advantages of scanners

- » Images can be stored for editing at a later date.
- » When used with OCR, much faster and more accurate (no typing errors) than typing in documents again.
- » It is possible to recover damaged documents and photographs by scanning in and then using appropriate software to produce an acceptable copy.

Disadvantages of scanners

- » Quality can be limited depending on how good a resolution the scanner is capable of (most scanners have a range of resolutions you can choose from).
- » They can be fairly slow at scanning, especially if the colour scanning mode is chosen or if the chosen scanning resolution is high.

2.1.8 Digital cameras

Digital cameras have largely replaced traditional film-based cameras. The images are stored on a memory card (solid-state memory) and can be transferred to a computer by:

- » directly reading the memory card (by slotting it into a card reader attached to a computer or a printer)
- » connecting the camera to the computer using a USB port
- » using wireless data transfer (Wi-Fi or Bluetooth).

▲ **Figure 2.15** Digital camera

The images are uploaded from the camera and stored in a file in the computer; the user can select which photos to upload and which to discard. The images are then available for printing out as photos, can be used in a 'slide show', imported into software such as a word processor, or uploaded on to the internet.

Uses of digital cameras

- » Taking photographs; they still take better photgraphs than smartphones or tablets due to the use of expensive lenses and dedicated software.
- » Used as a data-capture device; for example, as a reversing aid in a car where small cameras (in the bumpers) help the driver to see their immediate surroundings.
- » Dentists use digital cameras to take photos of a patient's teeth to help them diagnose any problems; they are also used to improve colour matching when doing dental fillings.
- » The creation of virtual reality tours around houses, historical buildings, industrial plants, and so on.

Advantages of digital cameras

- » Easier to produce better-quality photographs than with a traditional camera.
- » Easier and faster to upload photographs to a computer rather than having to scan in hard copies when using traditional methods.
- » No need to develop film and print out photographs anymore – this saves money and is also environmentally more acceptable (saves paper and reduces the use of the chemicals used in developing traditional film).
- » Memory cards can store many thousands of photographs.

Disadvantages of digital cameras

» Need to be computer literate to use the cameras properly; also, the transferring, storing and manipulating of the images via a computer requires some understanding of how computers work.
» There is some artistry lost because clever software now corrects errors in the photographs (for example, incorrect exposure, removal of red eye, etc.).
» Images often need to be compressed to reduce the amount of memory used (a single image can use more than 12 MB of memory, for example).

Many smartphones and tablets are now capable of taking photographs of a very high quality. Some of the latest smartphones are essentially making cameras almost obsolete for the casual photographer. Because the quality of the lens is an important feature, professional photographers will continue to use digital cameras for a number of years. However, it is now possible to get special attachments for many smartphones to allow special effects, zooming functions and even light filters.

2.1.9 Microphones

Microphones are either built into the computer or are external devices connected through the USB port or using Bluetooth connectivity. Figure 2.16 shows how a microphone can convert sound waves into an electric current. The current produced is converted to a digital format so that a computer can process it or store it (for example, on a CD).

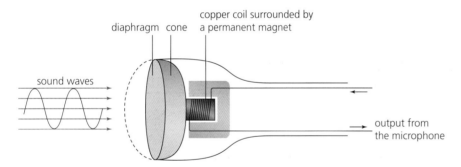

▲ **Figure 2.16** Diagram of how a microphone works

» When sound is created, it causes the air to vibrate.
» When a diaphragm in the microphone picks up the air vibrations, the diaphragm also begins to vibrate.
» A copper coil is surrounded by a permanent magnet and the coil is connected to the diaphragm using a cone. As the diaphragm vibrates, the cone moves in and out causing the copper coil to move backwards and forwards relative to the magnet.
» This forwards and backwards motion cuts through the magnetic field around the permanent magnet, inducing an electric current.
» The electric current is then either amplified or sent to a recording device. The electric current is analogue in nature.

The electric current output from the microphone can also be sent to a computer where a sound card converts the current into a digital signal which can then be stored in the computer.

Uses of microphones

»   To input speech/sounds to be used in various applications, for example, in presentations, sampling (in films, music, etc.) and special effects (films).
»   Input in voice-recognition software:
    –   the software converts the speech into text that can be used in, for example, a word processor or to input commands into a computer
    –   to recognise commands; for example, some cars now have voice-activated systems to switch on the lights, turn up the radio volume, etc. (see Chapter 1).
»   Microphones can also be used as a sensor to pick up sound (for example, in an intruder alarm system).
»   Used in video-conferencing or Voice over Internet Protocol (VoIP) applications.

Advantages of microphones

»   Faster to read in text than to type it in using a keyboard.
»   It is possible to manipulate sound in real time using special software rather than work on a recording done at some earlier stage.
»   If used in a voice activation system, it has the advantage of improving safety (because the car driver, for example, does not need to take their hands off the wheel to operate a switch or alter the radio station, etc.).

Disadvantages of microphones

»   Sound files can use up a lot of computer memory.
»   Voice-recognition software is not as accurate as typing in manually (for example, the software cannot distinguish the difference between 'their' and 'there').

2.1.10 Sensors

This section deals with **analogue sensors**. A sensor is a device that inputs data to a computer; the data is a measurement of some physical quantity that is continuously changing (for example, temperature, light, moisture, etc.). These physical quantities are analogue in nature. Because computers only understand digital data (1s and 0s), the information from the sensors needs to be converted; this is done using an **analogue to digital converter (ADC)**.

Sensors are used in monitoring and control applications – various types of sensors are used depending on the application (see Table 2.1). When monitoring, the data sent to the computer is often transferred directly to a spreadsheet package (for example, taking measurements in a scientific experiment, measuring atmospheric pollution, etc.).

> **Link**
> ....
> For more on the differences between analogue and digital data see Section 1.13.

Uses of sensors

▼ **Table 2.1** Uses of sensors

Type of sensor	Applications
Temperature	Used in automatic washing machines, central heating systems, automatic glasshouses, ovens
Pressure	Used in intruder alarm systems, washing machines, robotics, environmental monitoring
Light	Used in automatic glasshouses, automatic doors, intruder alarm systems, street lighting control
Sound/acoustic	Used in intruder alarm systems, monitoring liquid and powder flow in pipes
Humidity/moisture	Used in automatic glasshouses, environmental monitoring, in factories where moisture levels are crucial (for example, manufacture of microchips, paint spraying)
pH	Used in automatic glasshouses, chemical processes, environmental monitoring

Advantages of using sensors

>> More accurate readings taken when compared to human operators.
>> Readings are continuous – no break in the monitoring.
>> Because it is a continuous process, any necessary action (control system) or warning (monitoring system) will be initiated immediately.
>> Systems can be automatic, removing the need for human intervention (very important if the process is hazardous or needs precise control/monitoring).

Disadvantages of using sensors

>> Faulty sensors can give spurious results – for example, sensors on the rear bumper of a car that monitors obstacles; if these become dirty, they may either not identify an obstacle or give a continuous alarm.
>> Most sensors are analogue, therefore they require conversion using an ADC.

2.1.11 Light pens

Light pens are used with computers as an input device. They contain sensors that send signals to a computer whenever light changes are detected. The devices only work with CRT monitors (see Output devices section as they rely on the screen image being built up row by row by an electron beam. The screen is refreshed 50 times every second; because of this, the computer is able to determine the pen's position by noting exactly when the device detected the electron beam passing its tip. Systems to allow light pens to operate with LCD monitors are still at the development stage.

▲ **Figure 2.17** Light pen

Uses of light pens

>> Selecting objects on CRT screens.
>> Drawing on screen (for example, with CAD packages).

Advantages of light pens

>> Greater accuracy than touch screens.
>> Small (can be used where space is an issue).
>> Easy-to-use technology.

Disadvantages of light pens

>> Problems with lag when drawing on screen.
>> Only works with CRT monitors (at the moment).
>> Not that accurate when drawing.
>> Rather dated technology.

2.2 Direct data entry (DDE) devices

Direct data entry (DDE) devices are used to input data into a computer without the need for very much, if any, human interaction. For example, barcode readers are DDE and the only human involvement is to point a reader at the barcode. The transfer of the data to the computer is done automatically.

2.2.1 Card readers

Magnetic stripe readers

These are used to read information on the **magnetic stripe** found on, for example, the back of a credit or debit card. The stripe contains useful information, such as: account number, sort code, expiry date and start date.

Uses of magnetic stripe readers

>> On credit/debit cards for use at ATMs or EFTPOS (electronic funds transfer at point of sale) terminals.
>> Security devices to allow entry to buildings, hotel rooms, etc.

Advantages of magnetic stripe readers

>> Fast data entry, rather than keying in with a keyboard or keypad.
>> Error-free (because no typing is involved).
>> Secure (information not in human readable form and, because there is no typing, removes the risk of somebody observing your key strokes).
>> Prevents access to restricted/secure areas.
>> Not affected by oil, water, moisture, etc.
>> No moving parts – so physically very robust.

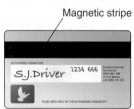

Magnetic stripe

▲ **Figure 2.18** Magnetic stripe reader

Disadvantages of magnetic stripe readers

>> If the magnetic stripe gets damaged (for example, due to exposure to a strong magnetic field) the data is lost.
>> Does not work at a distance (card needs to be in close contact with reader).
>> Because the information is not human readable, this can be a disadvantage in some applications.

Contactless debit card readers

Contactless debit or credit cards allow customers to pay for items worth up to a certain amount of money without entering their PIN. All contactless cards have

Chip

▲ **Figure 2.19** Contactless debit card

a small chip that emits radio waves embedded in them. The card is held within a few centimetres of the payment terminal to pay for an item; the terminal picks up the signal from the chip and allows the transaction to be processed.

The steps taken are:

1 Customers look out for the contactless symbol (((on the payment terminal.
2 The shop assistant enters the amount for payment.
3 The card reader informs the customer to present their contactless card.
4 The customer holds their card close to the front of the card reader.
5 The terminal display will indicate that the card has been read successfully.

Advantages of using contactless cards

▲ **Figure 2.20** Contactless card reader

›› Faster transactions (typical transaction takes 10 seconds as opposed to 30 seconds using magnetic stripe reader).
›› The contactless card system uses 128-bit encryption systems to protect the data.
›› Customers do not have to worry about typing errors (such as incorrectly typing in a PIN).
›› Retailers no longer have access to the customer's credit/debit card information.
›› The chip in the contactless credit card responds to the payment terminal reader with a unique number used for that transaction only; it does not simply transmit the consumer's account number; this number is also encrypted.

Disadvantages of using contactless cards:

›› They are more expensive than normal credit/debit cards.
›› A thief with a suitable reader could monitor your contactless card transaction while standing at the counter with you, or just behind you (the third point above reduces this risk considerably however; because you do not have to type in a PIN, somebody standing behind you could not steal your PIN and use it).
›› Can take money twice if the customer uses it as a chip and PIN card (one is contactless and the other is chip and PIN).
›› Transactions are usually limited to a small maximum value (for example, $50).
›› Transactions have been carried out, in some countries, without the card holder being aware of this while they were just standing in the payment queue (although it should be pointed out that this is much rarer today with new technologies in most countries).

Chip and PIN readers

Chip and PIN readers are similar to smart card readers but are used at EFTPOS terminals. The device has a slot into which the card is placed and the chip is read; the PIN is entered using the keypad. The reader also has a small screen which gives instructions to the operator. They are similar to the contactless system, except for two points:

1 The customer has to key in their PIN to make a transaction.
2 These cards do not make use of radio frequency technology.

Uses of chip and PIN readers

» Where payments are made using cards (restaurants, supermarkets, travel agents, etc.).

Advantages of chip and PIN readers

» More secure system than contactless payments (PIN typed in must match up with PIN stored on chip).
» More robust system than magnetic stripe cards.

Disadvantages of chip and PIN readers

» Fraud – need to be careful to ensure PIN is not read by somebody else while typing it in.

2.2.2 Radio frequency identification (RFID) readers

Radio frequency identification (RFID) readers use radio waves to read and capture information stored on a tag. In some applications, the **tag** can be read from a distance of several metres, which is one of its advantages over the barcode system. The RFID tag is made up of two components:

» a microchip that stores and processes information
» an antenna which is used to receive and transmit data/information.

The tags can be passive or battery-powered. Passive tags use the reader's radio wave energy to relay back the information; battery-powered tags use a small embedded battery to power the RFID.

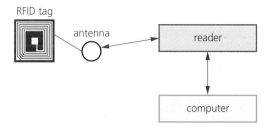

▲ **Figure 2.21** RFID

Uses of RFID

» Livestock tracking (so that the whereabouts of each animal on a farm is known; it also identifies which farm owns the animal).
» Retail (it is similar to barcodes, but does not require any scanning; details such as price can be stored on the tag and then automatically read at a checkout – a big advantage is that several tags can be read at the same time, thus speeding up the checkout process).
» Admission passes (for example, in theme parks RFID cards eliminate the need to scan or swipe people before 'rides', reducing the waiting time; it also allows the tracking of people in the theme park and certain information, such as height or age, can be stored to prevent entry to certain rides on safety grounds).
» Libraries (books can be tracked in and out automatically by readers at the library entrance; no need to scan barcodes or use magnetic stripe cards, making the process quicker and more accurate).

Advantages of RFID

» No line-of-sight contact is necessary; the tags can be read from a distance.
» It is a very robust and reliable technology.
» Very fast read-rate (typically less than 100 milliseconds to respond).
» Bidirectional data transfer (that is, it allows read and write operations to take place).
» Bulk detection is possible (that is, it can detect several RFID tags at the same time).

Disadvantages of RFID

» Tag collision (this is when the signals from two or more tags overlap, interfering with each other).
» Because RFID uses radio waves, they are relatively easy to jam or interrupt.
» It is relatively easy to hack into the data/signal transmitted by the tag.
» RFID is more expensive than a comparable barcode system.

2.2.3 Optical mark recognition/reader (OMR)

Optical mark recognition (OMR) is a device which can read marks written in pen or pencil on a form. The places where the pen or pencil marks can be made are clearly shown on the form, for example:

▲ **Figure 2.22** OMR

In this example a pencil mark has been made between the dots on option 1. The position of the mark is stored in the computer's memory after being read by the OMR device.

Uses of OMR devices

» Used to read questionnaires, multiple-choice examination papers, voting papers and many other types of form where responses are registered in the form of lines or shaded areas.

Advantages of OMR devices

» Very fast way of inputting the results of a survey, etc. The documents are fed in automatically and there is no user input.
» Because there is no typing, they are more accurate than keying in the data.
» They are more accurate than OCR methods.

Disadvantages of OMR devices

» The forms need to be carefully designed to make sure the marks/shading are correctly positioned to gather accurate information.
» There can be problems if they have not been filled in correctly; sometimes they have to be manually checked before being read, which is both time consuming and expensive.

2.2.4 Optical character recognition/reader (OCR)

Optical character recognition (OCR) is the name given to a device that converts the text on hard copy documents into an electronic form. OCR software converts this electronic data into a form that can then be used in various application packages, such as word processors or presentation software.

Uses of OCR

» One of the most recent uses is the processing of passports and identity cards.
» Converting hard copy documents into electronic form which can be stored on a computer.
» Used in automatic number plate recognition (ANPR) systems in car parks.
» Digitising historic newspapers and rare books so they can be archived and used by researchers, preventing damage to the originals.

▲ **Figure 2.23** Using OCR to process a passport

Advantages of OCR

» It is a much faster data entry system than manually keying in data.
» Because there is no manual data entry, the number of errors is also reduced.

Disadvantages of OCR

» The system still has difficulty reading some handwriting.
» Still not a very accurate technique.

Comparison of OMR and OCR features

A company has decided to produce a questionnaire to gain information from customers. What features of OCR or OMR need to be considered when designing the data-capture form? This comparison is needed before the form is designed and the appropriate input method chosen. Table 2.2 summarises the features of both methods.

▼ **Table 2.2** Comparison of OCR and OMR

OCR	OMR
Because this method reads handwriting, it is possible for customers to extend their answers to questions	Because this involves shading in lozenges to answer set questions, the information obtained is limited to the choices offered in each question
This method can read handwriting – but if the handwriting is poor it may cause reading errors	OMR relies on simply detecting where marks have been made on a page; the position of the marks is compared to a template stored in memory
OCR is used for converting printed documents to an editable electronic format	OMR simply reads the position of marks so it is ideal for multiple-choice exam papers
OCR requires a complex recognition system	This method requires complex (and expensive) forms to be completed; but the recognition system is simpler than OCR
Fewer 'how to fill in' instructions are needed for forms designed to be completed and then read by OCR	While this method requires more 'how to fill in' instructions, it is easier and faster for customers to complete OMR forms than to complete OCR forms
While OCR is more accurate than data entered into a computer by keyboard, there are still problems recognising all types of handwriting leading to inaccuracies	OMR is essentially a more accurate method for reading data than OCR

2.2.5 Barcode readers

Barcode readers are used to read information in the form of a bar code (see barcode example in Figure 2.24).

The readers are usually in the form of a barcode scanner and are often built into POS terminals in supermarkets. **Handheld scanners** or **wands** (as shown in Figure 2.25) are also very common for reading barcodes if portability is required (for example, if the barcodes are on large or fixed objects).

Uses of barcode systems

>> Used in supermarkets and other shops where the goods are marked with a barcode; the barcodes are used to give information about the product which enables automatic stock control, itemised billing, etc. to take place.
>> Used in libraries to keep track of books on loan.
>> Used as a safety function in many companies to ensure that electrical equipment is checked on a regular basis (barcodes are placed on an item to identify it and a database holds all the information related to that barcode so it is possible to interrogate the system as part of a safety audit).

Advantages of barcode systems

>> Much faster than keying in data manually and fewer mistakes will be made.
>> If used as a way of recording safety testing of components (for instance electrical components) they can help improve safety.
>> They allow automatic stock control.
>> They are a tried and trusted technology.

Disadvantages of barcode systems

>> Relatively expensive system to administer.
>> Not fool-proof (barcodes can be swapped around on items).
>> Can be more easily damaged than RFID tags or magnetic stripes.

2.2.6 Quick response (QR) code scanners (readers)

Another type of barcode is the **quick response (QR)** code. This is made up of a matrix of filled-in dark squares on a light background. For example, the QR code in Figure 2.26 is a website advertising rock music merchandise. It includes a web address in the code.

QR codes can hold considerably more information than the more conventional barcodes described earlier.

Description of QR codes

A QR code consists of a block of small squares (light and dark) known as pixels. It can presently hold up to 4296 characters (or up to 7089 digits) and allows internet addresses to be encoded within the QR code. This compares to the 30 digits which is the maximum for a barcode. However, as more and more data is added, the structure of the QR code becomes more complex.

▲ **Figure 2.24** Sample barcode

▲ **Figure 2.25** Portable barcode reader (scanner)

▲ **Figure 2.26** Sample QR code

The three large squares at the corners of the code function as a form of alignment; the remaining small corner square is used to ensure the correct size and correct angle of the camera shot when the QR code is read.

Because of modern smartphones and tablets, which allow internet access on the move, QR codes can be scanned anywhere. This gives rise to a number of uses:

>> advertising products (for example, the QR code in Figure 2.26)
>> giving automatic access to a website or contact telephone number
>> storing boarding passes electronically at airports and train stations (Figure 2.27).

▲ **Figure 2.27** Sample boarding pass

By using the built-in camera on a mobile smartphone or tablet and by downloading a QR app (application), it is possible to read QR codes on the move using the following method:

>> Point the phone or tablet camera at the QR code.
>> The apps will now process the image taken by the camera converting the squares into readable data.
>> The browser software on the mobile phone or tablet automatically reads the data generated by the apps; it will also decode any web addresses contained within the QR code.
>> The user will then be sent to a website automatically (or if a telephone number was embedded in the code, the user will be sent to the phone apps 📞).
>> If the QR code contained a boarding pass, this will be automatically sent to the phone/tablet.

Uses of QR codes

>> Used in advertising to contain data such as business addresses, phone numbers, email addresses and website addresses; scanning the QR code gives all the necessary data on the smartphone screen, or the user is sent automatically to the website embedded in the QR code.
>> Contain links to apps (for example, they can be found in app stores to enable the appropriate apps to be quickly downloaded onto a user's device).
>> Wi-Fi authentication; QR codes can be used to store Wi-Fi network authentication (proof of identity) details, including passwords and type of encryption used – when the QR code is scanned using a smartphone/tablet, it will be able to automatically join that network.
>> QR codes can be used to deliver **augmented reality** (see Chapter 1) experiences, by helping an AR system to determine the positions of objects in three-dimensional space.
>> QR codes have been used to establish **virtual online stores**, where a gallery of product information and QR codes are presented to the customer, for example, on a train station wall. The customers scan the QR codes, and the products are automatically delivered to their homes.

Advantages of QR codes

>> They can hold much more information than normal barcode.
>> There will be fewer errors than with barcodes; the higher data capacity of the QR code allows the use of built-in error-checking systems; normal barcodes

contain almost no data redundancy (that is, data which is duplicated) therefore it is not possible to guard against badly printed or damaged barcodes.

» QR codes are easier to read; they do not need expensive laser or LED (light emitting diode) scanners like barcodes – they can be read by the cameras used on smartphones and tablets.

» It is easy to transmit QR codes either as text messages or images.

» It is also possible to encrypt QR codes, which gives them greater protection than traditional barcodes.

Disadvantages of QR codes

» More than one QR format is available.

» QR codes can be used to transmit malicious codes; known as **attagging**. Because there are a large number of free apps available to a user for generating QR codes, that means anyone can do this. It is relatively easy to write malicious code and embed this within the QR code. When the code is scanned, it is possible the creator of the malicious code could gain access to everything on the user's smartphone/tablet (for example, photographs, address book, stored passwords, etc.). The user could also be sent to a fake website, or it is even possible for a virus to be downloaded.

2.3 Output devices and their uses

As the name suggests, these are devices that usually show the result of computer processing in a format that can be understood by a human (for example, on a monitor or printed on paper). However, some output devices are part of a control system. In these examples, the computer is controlling a process and sends signals to these output devices.

2.3.1 Monitors (screens)

In this section we will consider two types of monitor:

» the cathode ray tube (CRT) monitor

» LCD (or TFT) screen (TFT means 'thin film technology'; a general term for modern thin screens).

While CRT monitors have just about been phased out everywhere, they are included here because these are the only type of device which allows the use of light pens (see Section 2.1.11). Consequently, some companies using CAD still use large CRT monitors to enable the use of light pens as part of the drawing environment.

▲ **Figure 2.28** CRT monitor

CRT monitors

Cathode ray tube (CRT) monitors are the least expensive type of monitor, although they are becoming increasingly rare as LCD monitors are now taking over. They come in various sizes and make use of an electron gun firing against a phosphor screen. The picture is made up of tiny dots which are coloured red, green or blue – the intensity of each coloured dot makes up the vast range of colours interpreted by the eye.

Uses of CRT monitors

» They are only used in specialist areas, such as computer-aided design (CAD); the screens are usually very large to enable complex diagrams to be created or modified.
» They are used with light pens to allow designs to be created on screen.

Advantages of CRT monitors

» The screen can be clearly seen at a wider range of viewing angles than with most LCD monitors.
» They allow the use of light pens in, for example, CAD/CAM applications.

Disadvantages of CRT monitors

» They tend to be rather heavy and present a weight hazard if not supported properly; they also have a very large footprint on a desk (they cover about ten times the area of an LCD monitor).
» They run very hot and can cause fires if left unattended (especially as they get older).
» They consume considerably more power than LCD monitors.
» They can flicker, which can lead to headaches and eyesight problems with prolonged use.

LED and LCD screens

LED screens
An LED screen is made up of tiny light emitting diodes (LEDs). Each LED is either red, green or blue in colour. By varying the electric current sent to each LED, its brightness can be controlled, producing a vast range of colours.

This type of screen tends to be used for large outdoor displays, due to the brilliance of the colours produced. Recent advances in LED technology have led to the introduction of OLED (organic LED) screens.

Many monitors and television screens are advertised as LED when in fact they are LCD screens which are *backlit* using LEDs.

LCD screens
LCD screens are made up of tiny liquid crystals. These tiny crystals make up an array of pixels which are affected by changes in applied electric fields. How this works is outside the scope of this book, but the important thing to realise is that for LCD screens to work, they require some form of backlighting.

Modern LCD screens are backlit using light emitting diode (LED) technology and must not be confused with pure LED screens. When LEDs are used, a matrix of tiny blue-white LEDs is used behind the LCD screen. The use of LED backlighting gives a very good contrast and brightness range.

Before the use of LEDs, LCD screens used cold cathode fluorescent lamps (CCFL) as the back lighting method. Essentially, CCFL used two fluorescent tubes behind the LCD screen to supply the light source.

The reason that LEDs have become increasingly more popular as the method of backlighting is due to a number of advantages over older CCFL technology:

» LEDs reach their maximum brightness almost immediately (there is no need to 'warm up' before reaching full efficiency).

>> LEDs give a whiter light, which sharpens the image and makes the colours appear more vivid; CCFL had a slightly yellowish tint.
>> LEDs produce a brighter light which improves the colour definition.
>> Screens using LED technology are much thinner than screens using CCFL technology.
>> LEDs last almost indefinitely; this makes the technology more reliable and makes for a more consistent product.
>> LEDs consume very little power which means they produce less heat as well as using less energy.

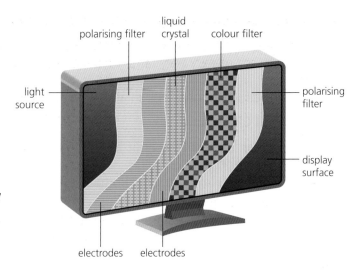

▲ **Figure 2.29** Inside an LCD screen

Uses of LCD screens

>> Used as the main output device for most modern computers.
>> Many LCD screens offer touch-screen input.
>> Mobile phones, tablets, laptops and portable video games all use LCD screens.

Advantages of LCD screens

>> Very efficient, low power consumption.
>> Lightweight devices.
>> Unlike CRT monitors, do not suffer from screen image burn-in (that is, a permanent image burned into the screen due to unchanging images over a period of time).
>> Screens can be made in large variation of sizes.
>> Do not suffer from a flickering image, unlike CRT monitors.
>> Very sharp image resolution (allow a vast range of colours).
>> Produce low electromagnetic fields compared to CRT monitors.

Disadvantages of LCD screens

>> Colour and contrast from various viewing angles can be inconsistent.
>> Motion blur is a common issue.
>> Lower contrast than CRT monitors, because it is harder to produce a deep, rich level of black.
>> LCDs can have weak or stuck pixels, which are permanently on or off; some pixels may be improperly connected to adjoining pixels, rows or columns.
>> The LCD panel may not be uniformly illuminated by the back light, resulting in uneven intensity and shading over the screen.

2.3.2 Touch screen (as an output device)

Touch screens can work as both an input device (see Section 2.1.6) and as an output device. This is one of the few devices that can be used in this way. When options appear on the screen, for example a food selection at a fast food outlet, a user can make a selection by touching the screen (this is the input). Another set of options then appear on the screen, such as choosing another drink – this is the output produced based on the previous input.

Uses of touch screens (acting as both input and output)

»» Smartphones and tablets (allowing interaction with apps).
»» ATMs at banks (where screen options displayed depend on previous input response).
»» Ticket collection machines at theatres, cinemas and railway stations (again on-screen outputs will depend on previous inputs).
»» Information kiosks at museums or art galleries.

Advantages of touch screens

»» Faster entry of options than using a keyboard or mouse.
»» Very easy method for choosing options.
»» User-friendly method – no training necessary in its use.
»» Option to expand the size of the display if necessary.

Disadvantages of touch screens

»» Limited number of options available.
»» Not very good if large amounts of data are being input or output because they are not very accurate and the interface is not fast.
»» The screen can get very dirty with constant touching (giving a risk of spreading infections, as well as reducing its responsiveness and making it more difficult to read in strong sunlight).
»» Easier for a third party to track a user's interactions, which is a security risk (for example, entering credit card details).

2.3.3 Multimedia projectors

Multimedia projectors receive signals that can be either analogue or digital (although most modern projectors only work with digital inputs). The signal source is usually from a computer, television or DVD player. The image from the source is magnified and projected onto a large screen. The devices work with a remote control which acts like a cordless mouse when interfacing with the screen. It is then possible to direct the computer presentation without being tied to the computer (another feature of the virtual mouse is the laser pointer). Most multimedia projectors take input from various types of video format.

▲ **Figure 2.30** Multimedia projector

Uses of multimedia projectors

»» Training presentations (to allow the whole audience to see the images from a computer).
»» Advertising presentations (large images showing product features, for example a new car; can be shown at exhibitions, shopping malls, etc.).
»» Home cinema systems (projecting the images from a DVD or television).

Advantages of multimedia projectors

»» Enables many people to see a presentation rather than crowding around a small computer screen.
»» Avoids the need for several networked computers (for example, when looking at a video clip on an internet site, everybody can see the video on the large screen rather than logging on to a number of computers).

Disadvantages of multimedia projectors

» Images can sometimes be fuzzy.
» Expensive to buy.
» Setting up projectors can be a little difficult.

2.3.4 Printers

This section will consider the use of the three most common types of printer:

» laser printer
» inkjet printer
» dot matrix printer.

Laser printers

Laser printers produce very high-quality hard copy output. The print rate per page is very quick if a large number of pages are being printed. They rely on large buffer memories where the data for the whole document is stored before pages can be printed out.

Let us briefly consider how a page is printed:

» The start of the printing process involves a printing drum being given a positive charge; as this drum rotates, a laser beam is scanned across it removing the positive charge in certain areas; this leaves negatively charged areas which exactly match the text/images of the page to be printed.
» The drum is then coated with positively-charged toner (powdered ink); because the toner is positively charged, it only sticks to the negatively charged parts of the drum.
» A negatively-charged sheet of paper is then rolled over the drum.
» The toner on the drum now sticks to the paper to produce an exact copy of the page sent to the printer.
» To prevent the paper sticking to the drum, the electric charge on the paper is removed after one rotation of the drum.
» The paper finally goes through a fuser, which is a set of heated rollers; the heat melts the ink so that it fixes permanently to the paper.
» At the very end, a discharge lamp removes all the electric charge from the drum, making it ready to print the next page.

▲ **Figure 2.31** Laser printer

Uses of laser printers

» They are used where low noise is required (for example, in an office).
» If fast, high-quality, high-volume printing is required then laser printers are the best option.

Advantages of laser printers

» Printing is fast (unless only a few pages are to be printed, in which case they are little faster than inkjet printers).
» They can handle very large print jobs.
» The quality is consistently high.
» Toner cartridges last for a long time (and the printers can sometimes be a cost-effective option, particularly if colour outputs are not required).

Disadvantages of laser printers

» Only really fast if several copies are being made.
» Colour laser printers tend to be expensive to run (four-colour/black cartridges are needed, plus diffuser kits, which are expensive to purchase).
» They produce ozone and volatile organic compounds because of their method of printing and type of toner/ink used (these have been linked to health hazards in the office).

Inkjet printers

Inkjet printers are used to produce good-quality hard copies. Unlike laser printers, inkjet printers do not have large buffer memories, therefore printing is done a bit at a time. This is why printing is sometimes paused – the whole print job cannot be stored in the buffer, and it has to wait for the computer to send more data.

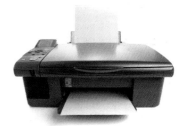

▲ **Figure 2.32** Inkjet printer

Inkjet printers are essentially made up of:

» a print head, which consists of nozzles which spray droplets of ink on to the paper to form characters
» an ink cartridge or cartridges; either one cartridge for each colour (blue, yellow and magenta) and a black cartridge, or one single cartridge containing all three colours plus black (note: some systems use six colours)
» a stepper motor and belt, which moves the print head assembly across the page from side to side
» a paper feed which automatically feeds the printer with pages as they are required.

The ink droplets are produced using two different technologies:

» **Thermal bubble** – tiny resistors create localised heat which makes the ink vaporise. This causes the ink to form a tiny bubble; as the bubble expands, some of the ink is ejected from the print head onto the paper. When the bubble collapses, a small vacuum is created which allows fresh ink to be drawn into the print head. This continues until the printing cycle is completed.
» **Piezoelectric** – a crystal is located at the back of the ink reservoir for each nozzle. The crystal is given a tiny electric charge which makes it vibrate. This vibration forces ink to be ejected onto the paper; at the same time more ink is drawn in for further printing.

Uses of inkjet printers

» Used where low-output volumes are required (high-volume jobs are difficult to do because the ink cartridges tend to be used up very quickly).
» If high-quality printing is required for single pages (or only a small print job) then these printers are ideal; for example, they are very good at producing photo-quality printouts.
» 3D inkjet printers are now being used in industry to produce prototypes (see Section 2.3.6).

Advantages of inkjet printers

» High-quality output.
» Cheaper to buy than laser printers.

» Very lightweight and have a small physical footprint.
» Do not produce ozone and volatile organic compounds, unlike laser printers.

Disadvantages of inkjet printers

» Slow output if several copies are needed (little buffer capacity to store the pages).
» Cannot do large print jobs (ink cartridges run out too quickly).
» Printing can 'smudge' if the user is not careful.
» Can be expensive if used a lot (original ink cartridges are expensive to buy).

Dot matrix printers

Dot matrix printers are a type of impact printer where a print head (made up of a matrix of pins) presses against an inked ribbon. They tend to be slow, noisy and the output is not that good compared to inkjet and laser printers. They are still useful, however, where multi-part stationery (carbon copies) or continuous rolls of paper (rather than individual sheets) are being used. They also work well in dirty atmospheres (such as on a factory floor), unlike inkjet or laser printers.

▲ **Figure 2.33** Dot matrix printer

Uses of dot matrix printers

» They can be used in noisy or dirty environments (for example, garage workshops) and in applications where print quality is not that important.
» They are used in applications where multi-part stationery or the fact that they are an impact printer is of value (for example, when producing physical 'carbon copies' such as when producing wage slips).
» Still widely used in till receipts.

Advantages of dot matrix printers

» They can be used in environments which would be a problem for laser or inkjet printers (for example, dusty/dirty or moist atmospheres).
» Carbon copies or multi-part outputs can be produced.
» Very cheap to run and maintain.
» Easy to use if continuous stationery is required (for example, long print jobs such as wages slips).

Disadvantages of dot matrix printers

» Very noisy – not good in an office environment.
» Actually cost more than an inkjet printer to buy initially.
» Very slow, poor-quality printing.

2.3.5 (Graph) plotters

A (graph) **plotter** is an output device. Although they print on paper, they work very differently to printers. Instead of toner or ink cartridges, plotters use a pen, pencil or marker pen to draw multiple continuous lines, rather than a series of dots like a printer. The size of the paper can be anything from A4 up to several metres. They produce vector graphic drawings and are often used in conjunction with CAD and CAM (computer aided manufacturing).

▲ **Figure 2.34** (Graph) plotter

Some plotters are used to cut out material by replacing the pen with a cutting blade. However, in general, plotters are being phased out, as wide-format inkjet printers are being produced at lower cost.

Uses of plotters

» Producing architectural drawings.
» Producing engineering drawings.
» Drawing animation characters (cartoon characters).

Advantages of plotters

» Very high-quality output.
» Able to produce large, monochrome and colour drawings to a high accuracy.
» Able to print on a variety of materials (for example, aluminium, cardboard, plastic, steel and wood) as well as paper.

Disadvantages of plotters

» Very slow at printing.
» Expensive equipment (and software) to purchase initially; although running costs are low once purchased.
» Have a very large physical footprint compared to a printer.

2.3.6 3D printers

3D printers arc primarily used in **computer-aided design (CAD)** applications.

They are primarily based on inkjet and laser printer technology and can produce solid objects that actually work. The solid object is built up layer by layer using materials such as powdered resin, powdered metal, paper or ceramic.

The alloy wheel in Figure 2.36 was made using an industrial 3D printer.

It was made from many layers of powdered metal (0.1 mm thick) using a technology known as binder 3D printing.

▲ **Figure 2.35** 3D printer

Other examples are discussed below.

The following information describes some of the features of 3D printing:

» Various types of 3D printers exist; they range from the size of a microwave oven up to the size of a small car.
» 3D printers use **additive manufacturing** (i.e. the object is built up layer by layer); this is in sharp contrast to the more traditional method of **subtractive manufacturing** (i.e. removal of material to make the object). For example, making a statue using a 3D printer would involve building it up layer by layer using powdered stone until the final object was formed. The subtractive method would involve carving the statue out of solid stone (i.e. removing the stone not required) until the final item was produced. Similarly, **CNC** (computer-controlled machine – a type of lathe) removes metal to form an object; 3D printing would produce the same item by building up the object from layers of powdered metal.

▲ **Figure 2.36** Alloy wheel made by 3D printing

» **Direct 3D printing** uses inkjet technology; a print head can move left to right as in a normal printer. However, the print head can also move up and down to build up the layers of an object – each layer being less than a tenth of a millimetre (less than 0.1 mm).

» **Binder 3D printing** is similar to direct 3D printing, but this method uses two passes for each of the layers; the first pass sprays dry powder, then, on the second pass, a binder (a type of glue) is sprayed to form a solid layer.

» Newer technologies are using lasers and UV light to harden liquid polymers; this further increases the diversity of products which can be made.

Uses of 3D printers

3D printing is regarded as being possibly the next 'industrial revolution' because it will change the manufacturing methods in many industries. The following list is just a glimpse into what we know can be made using these printers; in the years that follow, the applications list could probably fill an entire book:

» Prosthetic limbs can be made to fit exactly on the injured body part.

» Making items to allow precision reconstructive surgery (for example, facial reconstruction following an accident); the parts made by this technique are more precise in their design as they can be made from an exact scan of the skull.

» In aerospace, manufacturers are looking at making wings and other aeroplane parts using 3D technology; the bonus will be lightweight, precision parts.

» Fashion and art – 3D printing allows new creative ideas to be developed.

» Making parts for items no longer in production, for example, parts for a vintage car.

How to create a solid object using 3D printers

The steps in the process of producing an object using 3D printers is summarised in Figure 2.37.

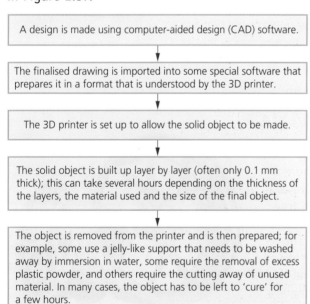

▲ **Figure 2.37** Creating a solid object using 3D printers

Advantages of 3D printers

» The manufacturing of items has become much easier than ever before. It is now theoretically possible to manufacture any product a user wants using only a 3D printer. This has led the way for customised products, as it allows a user to create their own designs in 3D and have them printed in solid form.

» Because 3D printers can manufacture items relatively quickly, it allows rapid prototyping. This means that it will take a really short length of time for designs to be converted into working prototypes.

» Even though the cost of 3D printing is very high, it is still less when compared to labour costs and other costs involved in manufacturing a product in the more conventional way. The fact that the cost of manufacturing using 3D printers is the same for both small-scale and mass production is also a very useful benefit.

» Medical benefits are emerging, such as producing artificial organs, prosthetics and precision-made items for reconstructive surgery.

» Parts for machinery that are no longer made could now be manufactured using 3D printers. A car made in the 1930s, for example, will no longer have parts available off-the-shelf. By scanning the broken part (using a 3D scanner), or by obtaining its blueprint, it will be possible to simply email the file to a company and have the part made on an industrial 3D printer. This clearly has many benefits in a number of applications.

Disadvantages of 3D printers

» The biggest possible drawback of 3D printers is the potential to make counterfeit items or items that infringe others' copyright. 3D printing technology essentially turns every owner of one of these printers into a potential manufacturer. Thus, it could become very difficult to trace the source of fake items; copyright holders would also have great difficulty in protecting their rights.

» All new technologies in the hands of the wrong people can lead to dangerous or illegal activities. With the possibility of creating almost anything with the use of a 3D printer, this technology could be used to manufacture dangerous items by almost anyone.

» There is the potential for job losses if this technology takes over from some types of manufacturing. Of course, this could also be seen as a benefit by some companies as it could lead to lower manufacturing costs for certain items.

2.3.7 Speakers

Speakers (or **loudspeakers**) are output devices that produce sound. When connected to a computer system, digitised sound stored on a file needs to be converted into sound as follows:

» The digital data is first passed through a **digital to analogue converter (DAC)** where it is changed into an electric current.

» This is then passed through an amplifier (because the current generated by the DAC will be very small); this creates a current large enough to drive a loudspeaker.

» This electric current is then fed to a loudspeaker where it is converted into sound.

The schematic in Figure 2.38 shows how this is done.

▲ **Figure 2.38** Digital to analogue conversion

As Figure 2.38 shows, if the sound is stored in a computer file, it must pass through a digital to analogue converter (DAC) to convert binary (digital) data into an analogue form (electric current) which can then drive the loudspeaker. Figure 2.39 shows how the loudspeaker converts the electric current into sound.

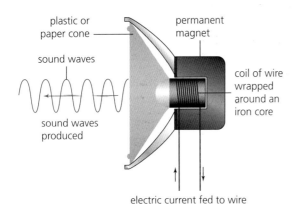

▲ **Figure 2.39** Diagram showing how a loudspeaker works

» When an electric current flows through the coil of wire that is wrapped around an iron core, the core becomes a temporary electromagnet; a permanent magnet is also positioned very close to this electromagnet.
» As the electric current through the coil of wire varies, the induced magnetic field in the iron core also varies. This causes the iron core to be attracted or towards or repelled from the permanent magnet and as the current varies this will cause the iron core to vibrate.
» Because the iron core is attached to a cone (made of paper or thin synthetic material), this causes the cone to vibrate, producing sound waves.

Uses of speakers

» Used in all phones and built in to most computers.
» Outputs sound from multimedia presentations.
» Helps visually impaired people (together with speech generation software) through reading aloud text on the screen.
» Plays downloaded sound files.

Advantages of speakers

» Sounds amplified through speakers can be much louder than the original sound – this is important whenever more than a few people need to listen to something.
» Everyone in a conference, for example, can hear the output from a computer.
» It can create a good atmosphere when making a presentation.

» They can help visually impaired people as discussed.
» Very simple technology.

Disadvantages of speakers

» Speaker output can be disturbing to others in, for example, an office environment.
» To get high-quality sound, the required speakers can be quite expensive.
» Speakers can take up a lot of desk space.

2.3.8 Actuators

When a computer is used to control devices, such as a conveyer belt or a valve, it is usually necessary to use an **actuator** to, for example, start/stop the conveyer belt or open/close the valve. An actuator is a mechanical or electromechanical device such as a relay, solenoid or motor. We will consider a solenoid as the example; this converts an electrical signal into a magnetic field producing linear motion:

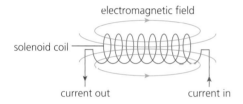

▲ **Figure 2.40** Solenoid

If a plunger (for example, a magnetised metal bar) is placed inside the coil, it will move when a current is applied to the coil (see Figure 2.40). This would allow the solenoid to operate a valve or a switch, for example. There are also examples of rotary solenoids, where a cylindrical coil is used. In this case, when a current is supplied to the coil, it would cause a rotational movement of the plunger.

Uses of actuators

» They are used to control motors, pumps, switches, buzzers and so on.
» They allow a computer to control physical devices that normally require analogue inputs.

Advantages of actuators

» They allow remote operation of many devices (for example, pumps in a nuclear reactor where remote operation is a big safety factor).
» They are relatively inexpensive devices.

Disadvantages of actuators

» They are an additional device in the system that could go wrong.
» Because they are usually analogue devices, computer signals need to converted using a DAC to enable computer control.

Exam-style questions

1 a State one suitable application for each of the following printers.
A different application should be given in each case.
   » inkjet printer
   » 3D printer   [2]
   b Name another type of printer and describe one way in which it is
   different from the two printers named in part **a**.   [3]

2 Contactless debit cards are replacing standard debit cards. Some
countries are introducing contactless debit card transactions at ATM machines.
Give **three** disadvantages to the customer of using these cards at an ATM.
                                                                                   [3]

Cambridge IGCSE Information and Communication Technology (0417) Paper 12 Q12,
October/November 2017

3 In each of the following questions, only one of the responses is
correct. Choose one of the five options given.   [10]
   a Which one of the following is the most suitable device for inputting
   a short report into a computer?

a	trackerball
b	scanner
c	keyboard
d	optical mark reader (OMR)
e	joystick

   b Which one of the following would you use to produce a digital
   image of a hard copy photograph?

a	touch screen
b	keyboard
c	optical character reader (OCR)
d	scanner
e	QR scanner

   c Which one of the following is **NOT** a suitable use for an optical mark reader?

a	reading barcodes
b	multiple-choice exam papers
c	choice of candidate in voting forms
d	opinion poll survey
e	data collection with limited options

   d Which one of the following is the most appropriate device for printing out
   wage slips, where carbon copies are also required?

a	laser printer
b	(graph) plotter
c	inkjet printer
d	actuator
e	dot matrix printer

e Which one of the following devices could be used to produce a very large drawing on plastic sheeting?

a	(graph) plotter
b	laser printer
c	dot matrix printer
d	3D printer
e	touch screen

f Which one of the following printers is most suitable for printing a very large number of high-quality black and white leaflets?

a	(graph) plotter
b	laser printer
c	dot matrix printer
d	inkjet printer
e	computer-aided design (CAD)

g Which one of the following **cannot** be **directly** measured using a sensor?

a	temperature
b	light intensity
c	heat
d	air humidity
e	pressure

h Which one of the following devices allows the use of a light pen?

a	CRT monitor
b	LCD monitor
c	barcode reader
d	QR reader
e	touch screen

i Which one of the following cannot be used as an output device?

a	touch screen
b	(graph) plotter
c	actuator
d	speaker
e	mouse

j Which one of the following cannot be used as an input device?

a	touch screen
b	3D printer
c	optical mark reader (OMR)
d	QR reader
e	(graph) plotter

4 Five devices are shown on the left and five descriptions are shown on the right. By drawing lines, connect each device to its correct description. [4]

Inkjet printer	Display that uses light modulating properties of crystals
LCD screen	Image from a source is magnified and shown on a large screen
3D printer	Droplets of ink are ejected onto a sheet of paper
Digital projector	Electrically-charged powdered toner is melted onto paper
Laser printer	Produces solid objects using CAD software

5 Which ten computer terms are being described below? [10]

a A matrix of filled-in dark squares on a light background; read using a smartphone camera or tablet using an app.

b A device that can read marks written in pen or pencil; the pencil or pen marks must be made in the correct position.

c An input device that takes physical readings from the surroundings and sends the data back to a computer.

d An input device that converts sound into electric signals that can be stored digitally on a computer.

e A device that converts a photograph or document into a computer-readable file.

f A device used to control the operation of other electronic devices using infrared signals.

g A direct data entry device that uses radio waves to read and capture information stored on an electronic tag.

h A device that produces very high-quality hard copy output; uses dry ink cartridges and an electrically charged drum.

i A device that prints by impacting a print head made up of an array of pins against an inked ribbon.

j A pointing device that moves around on a surface in an X–Y direction to control a cursor on a computer screen.

6 a i Describe how a QR reader works.
  ii What are QR codes used for? [4]
  b Give two advantages and two disadvantages of using QR codes. [4]
  c A touch screen can be used as both an input device and an output device. Explain how this is possible. [2]

7 Give a use for each of the following input and output devices. [10]

a	Keyboard	**f**	Touch screen
b	Driving wheel or joystick	**g**	3D printer
c	QR code reader	**h**	Dot matrix printer
d	Barcode reader	**i**	RFID
e	Microphone	**j**	chip and PIN reader

8 A home is fitted with a microprocessor-controlled burglar alarm system.
It is not connected to a police station.
Tick (✓) **three** sensors which would be used in such a system. [3]

	(✓)
Pressure sensor	
Oxygen level sensor	
Wind speed sensor	
Sound sensor	
Body sensor	
Moisture sensor	
Infra-red sensor	
Touch sensor	

Cambridge IGCSE Information and Communication Technology (0417) Paper 11 Q7 a,
May/June 2015

9 A school is holding an athletics competition. The timings of each running event will be measured electronically using sensors at the start and finish. Runners begin a race in starting blocks. When the starting pistol is fired the electronic timing starts. The winner of the race is the first to break the light beam at the end of the race.

a Complete the table using the most appropriate words from the list below.

Infra-red sensor   Light sensor   Moisture sensor   Motion sensor
pH sensor   Pressure sensor   Sound sensor   Temperature sensor

	Device
Data from the starting pistol is read by this device	
This device detects that the athlete has left the starting block	
When the light beam is broken the data is read by this device	

[3]

Cambridge IGCSE Information and Communication Technology (0417) Paper 12 Q3,
October/November 2017

b A member of the sports department will use a computer to produce a magazine of the competition. He will include photographs stored in a digital camera as well as printed photographs.

Identify the methods he would use to transfer the photographs to the computer.

[2]

10 Tick (✓) whether the following statements are True or False. [2]

	True (✓)	False (✓)
Answers to multiple-choice examination papers can be read using an optical mark reader (OMR)		
The PIN is stored on the magnetic stripe on a credit card		
The chip on a credit card is read by a PIN reader		
An RFID chip can be used to track stock		

3 Storage devices and media

In this chapter you will learn about:

★ storage devices:
  - magnetic (hard disk drive (HDD) and magnetic tape drive)
  - optical (CD, DVD and Blu-ray read/write devices)
  - solid state (solid-state drive (SSD), pen drive and flash drive)
★ storage media:
  - magnetic media (magnetic disks and magnetic tape)
  - optical (CD, DVD and Blu-ray discs)
  - solid state (including SD, XD and CFast).

Secondary storage includes all non-volatile devices that are not part of primary memory. They allow data to be stored as long as required by the user. This type of storage is much larger than RAM and ROM (primary memory), but data access time is considerably longer. All applications, the operating system, device drivers and general files (for example, documents, photos and music) are stored in secondary storage. There are three different categories of secondary storage which are based on technology that uses the following media:

● magnetic
● optical
● solid state.

It is very important to distinguish between the terms **storage media** and **storage device**. Media is the hardware on which the data is actually stored (for example, a CD or a DVD); whereas the storage device is the hardware used to read from or write to the media (for example, a CD/DVD reader or writer).

3.1 Magnetic media and magnetic storage devices

Using the properties of magnetism is one of the oldest known methods for the electronic storage of data; its roots go back to the nineteenth century.

Today, magnetic media rely on the property that an iron oxide coating can be magnetised to represent a binary 1-value and demagnetised to represent a binary 0-value. Because each magnetised area is very small, this allows a huge amount of data to be stored. One of the big advantages of this technology is that the magnetic state of the iron oxide is permanent unless it is written over again. The two most common devices that use these magnetic properties to store data are magnetic tape drives and hard disk drives (HDD).

3.1.1 Magnetic tape drives

A **magnetic tape** is a very thin strip of plastic which is coated in a magnetic layer (iron oxide). They are read from or written to by a read/write head in a magnetic tape storage device. The data is stored as a magnetised area (which represents a 1) or demagnetised area (which represents a 0). Data is read from the tape using serial access (in other words, data can only be read in the same order that it was written). This type of storage is useless in real-time or online applications (due to the very slow data access speeds) and is best suited to offline or batch processing. However, due to their vast storage capacity, magnetic tapes are still used on large industrial or university computers.

▲ **Figure 3.1** Magnetic tape drive

Uses of magnetic tape

» Use in applications where batch processing is used (for example, clearing bank cheques, utility billing (gas, electricity, water), and producing pay slips). In these applications there is no need for any specific processing order and speed of data access is not essential).
» Used as a backup media where vast amounts of data need to be stored.
» Used in long-term archiving of data; magnetic tapes have huge data storage capacities and are known to be very stable, which makes them ideal for long-term storage.

Advantages of magnetic tapes

» They are generally less expensive (per byte) than the equivalent hard disk drive.
» It is a very robust technology (they do not deteriorate much over time and remain stable).
» They have a huge data storage capacity.
» The **data transfer rate** is actually fast (this should not be confused with data access time which is very slow for magnetic tapes).

Disadvantages of magnetic tape

» Very slow **data access times** (they use serial access, which means all the previous data needs to be read until the required data is found) - whilst magnetic tape data access time is slow, the data transfer rate is still high.
» When updating, another tape is needed to store the final updated version; this requires the use of a master tape (the original tape) and a transaction tape (which contains all the changes to be made) to produce a new master tape. This is clearly a slow way of updating data, and can also introduce errors, which is why magnetic tapes are no longer a common method of storing data).
» They are affected by magnetic fields; a strong magnet (for example, one found in a loudspeaker) can corrupt data stored on the tape.

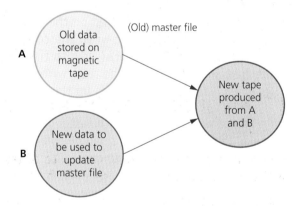

▲ **Figure 3.2** Updating a magnetic tape

Advice

Data transfer rate is the rate at which data can be sent from a storage device to a computer (or vice versa). **Data access time** is the time it takes to locate specific data stored on the storage media.

3.1.2 Hard disk drives (HDD)

Hard disk drives (HDD) are still one of the most common methods used to store data on a computer. Data is stored in a digital format on the magnetic surfaces of the hard disks (or platters, as they are usually called). A hard disk drive will very often have more than one platter depending on its capacity. A number of read/write heads can access all of the platter surfaces in the disk drive (normally each platter will have two surfaces where the data is stored). These read/write heads can move very quickly – typically they can move from the centre of the disk to the edge of the disk (and back again) 50 times a second. Data on an HDD can be read using direct access – this means, unlike magnetic tape, earlier data does not have to be read first before the required data is found. We will now look in more detail at how HDD works:

▲ **Figure 3.3** Hard disk drive – the hard disk (platter) is the media and the hard disk drive (HDD) is the storage device

» Actuators are used to move the read/write heads (voice coils are used as the actuators; these are similar to the electromagnets used in speakers – hence their name).
» A read/write arm swings the read/write head back and forth across the platter; the platter is rotating at up to 10 000 rpm (revolutions per minute).
» Each read/write head contains a tiny magnet which allows the data on the platter to be read.
» Platters are made from glass, ceramic or aluminium which are coated in iron oxide.
» There are two read/write heads per platter (one for the top surface and one for the bottom surface).
» Data is stored in concentric, circular tracks; each track is broken up into sectors (see Figure 3.4).
» A map of the sectors is stored on the HDD and is known as a file allocation table (FAT); when the computer wants to store new data, it looks at the FAT map to find out which sectors are free and then moves the read/write heads to the correct location – this greatly speeds up the writing process.

While hard disk drives have much faster data access times than magnetic tape, there are still small delays. Many applications require the read/write heads to constantly seek the correct blocks of data; this means a large number of head movements. The effects of **latency** then become very significant. (Latency is defined as the time it takes for a specific block of data on a data track to rotate around to the read/write head). Users will sometimes notice the effect of latency, especially if many different applications are open, when they see messages such as: 'Please wait' or, at its worst, 'not responding'. HDDs can be either fixed or portable.

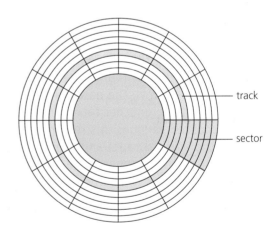

track

sector

▲ **Figure 3.4** Hard disk platter (showing tracks and sectors)

Uses of fixed hard disk drives

>> To store the operating system, systems software and working data/files.
>> Storing applications software.
>> Used in real-time systems (for example, robots, control of a chemical plant) and in online systems (for example, booking airline tickets, automatic stock control (using EPOS)).
>> Used in file servers for computer networks.

Advantages of fixed hard disk drives

>> They have a very fast data transfer rate and fast access times to data.
>> They have very large memory capacities.

Disadvantages of fixed hard disk drives

>> They can be fairly easily damaged (for example, if the correct shut-down procedure on a computer has not been correctly carried out, it is possible to sustain a head crash).
>> They have many moving parts which can affect their overall reliability.
>> Their read/write operation can be quite noisy when compared to solid-state drives.

3.1.3 Portable hard disk drives

Portable hard disk drives are essentially HDDs external to the computer and can be connected to the computer using one of the USB ports. In this way, they can be used as a backup device or another way of transferring files between computers.

Uses of portable hard disk drives

>> They can be used as backup systems to prevent loss of data.
>> They can be used to transfer data/files/software between computers.

Advantages of portable hard disk drives

>> The data access time and data transfer rate are very fast.
>> They have a large memory capacity.
>> They can be used as a method of transferring information between computers.

Disadvantages of portable hard disk drives

>> As with fixed disk drives, they can be easily damaged if the user accidentally drops it or does not correctly shut down the drive after use.
>> Data transfer rate is not as fast as for fixed hard drives.

3.2 Optical media and optical storage devices

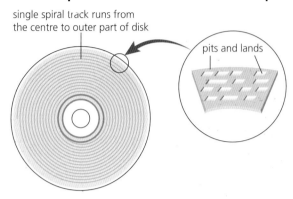

single spiral track runs from
the centre to outer part of disk

pits and lands

▲ **Figure 3.5** Optical media

3.2.1 CD/DVD optical disks

CDs and DVDS are described as **optical media** and are read from or written to by **optical storage devices**. Optical storage devices can be built in to a computer or connected externally via a USB cable. They rely on the optical properties of laser light, which is used to read data and to write data on the surface of the disk.

CDs and DVDs can be designated as: 'R' (write once only), 'RW' (can be written to or read from many times) or 'ROM' (read-only).

Both CDs and DVDs use a thin layer of metal alloy or a light-sensitive organic dye coating to store the data. As can be seen from the diagram in Figure 3.5, both systems use a single, spiral track, which runs from the centre of the disk to the edge. When the disk spins, an optical head in the drive unit moves to the start of the track. The laser beam then follows the spiral track from the centre outwards. The read/write head does not actually touch the CD or DVD surface. As with an HDD, a CD/DVD is divided into sectors, allowing direct access of data. Also, as in the case of HDD, the outer part of the disk runs faster than the inner part of the disk.

The data is stored in **pits** and **lands** on the spiral track (lands are the gaps between pits). A red laser is used to read and write the data. The depth of these pits is only about 20 per cent of the wavelength of the laser light used to read the disc. This means the wavelength of the reflected laser light is slightly different to the original laser light, causing **destructive interference**. This allows the pits and lands to be read and then be converted into binary data.

DVD technology is slightly different to that used in CDs. One of the main differences is the potential for **dual-layering** which considerably increases the storage capacity. Basically, this means that there are two individual recording layers. Two layers of a standard DVD are joined together with a transparent (polycarbonate) spacer, and a very thin reflector is also sandwiched between the two layers. Reading and writing of the second layer is done by a red laser focusing at a fraction of a millimetre difference compared to the first layer.

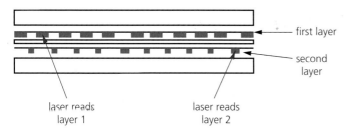

first layer

second
layer

laser reads
layer 1

laser reads
layer 2

▲ **Figure 3.6** Dual-layering in a DVD

Standard, single-layer DVDs still have a larger storage capacity than CDs because the 'pit' size and track width are both smaller. This means that more data can be stored on the DVD surface. DVDs use lasers with a wavelength of 650 nanometres; CDs use lasers with a wavelength of 780 nanometres. The shorter the wavelength of the laser light, the greater the storage capacity of the medium.

Uses of CD-R and DVD-R

» Home recordings of music (CD-R) and films (DVD-R).
» Used to store data to be kept for later use or to be transferred to another computer.

Advantages of CD-R and DVD-R

» Cheaper medium than RW disks.
» Once burned (and finalised) they behave like a ROM.

Disadvantages of CD-R and DVD-R

» Can only be recorded once; if an error occurs then the disk has to be thrown away.
» Not all CD/DVD players can read CD-R/DVD-R.

Uses of CD-RW/DVD-RW

» Used to record television programmes which can be recorded over, time and time again (although increasingly replaced by HDD recording systems).
» Used in CCTV systems.
» Can be used as a backup device for files and data.

Advantages of CD-RW/DVD-RW

» Can be written over many times.
» Can use different file formats each time it is used.
» Not as wasteful as R format because the files/data can be added at a later stage (with CD-R/DVD-R it is only possible to do a write operation at the time and you cannot come back a few days later to add more files).

Disadvantages of CD-RW/DVD-RW

» Can be relatively expensive media.
» Possible to accidentally overwrite data.

Uses of CD-ROM/DVD-ROM

» These optical disks are read-only memory (ROM) which means they cannot be written over and can only be read. They are a permanent method of data storage.
» CD-ROM is used to store music files and to store software, computer games and reference software (such as an encyclopaedia).
» DVD-ROM has much larger storage and is used to store films; but now it is increasingly used to store computer data and the evermore sophisticated games.
» CD-ROMs and DVD-ROMs are used in applications where there is a real need to prevent the deletion or overwriting of important data.

Advantages of CD-ROM/DVD-ROM

» They are less expensive than hard disk drive systems.

Disadvantages of CD-ROM/DVD-ROM

» The data transfer rate/data access time is slower than for hard disks.

It should also be noted that there is another type of DVD, called DVD-RAM. It is constructed and operates differently to the other DVD formats and has been used as RAM in computers and camcorders. The format is now quite old.

3.2.2 Blu-ray discs

Blu-ray discs are another example of optical storage media. However, they are fundamentally different to DVDs in their construction and in the way they carry out read/write operations. Blu-ray discs are read from or written to using a Blu-ray optical storage device.

Note: it is probably worth mentioning why they are called Blu-ray rather than Blue-ray; the simple reason is it was impossible to copyright the word 'Blue' and hence the use of the word 'Blu'.

The main differences between DVD and Blu-ray are:

» A blue laser, rather than a red laser, is used to carry out Blu-ray read and write operations; the wavelength of blue light is only 405 nanometres (compared to 650 nm for red light).
» Using blue laser light means that the **pits** and **lands** can be much smaller; consequently, Blu-ray can store up to five times more data than normal DVD.
» Single-layer Blu-ray discs use a 1.2 mm thick polycarbonate disk; however, dual-layer Blu-ray and normal DVDs both use a sandwich of two 0.6 mm thick disks (i.e. 1.2 mm thick).
» Blu-ray disks automatically come with a secure encryption system which helps to prevent piracy and copyright infringement.
» The data transfer rate for a DVD is 10 Mbps and for a Blu-ray disc it is 36 Mbps (this equates to 1.5 hours to store 25 GB of data).

▲ **Figure 3.7** Blu-ray disc

Because Blu-ray discs can come in single-layer or dual-layer format it is probably also worth comparing the differences in capacity and interactivity of the two technologies.

Comparison of the capacity and interactivity of DVDs and Blu-ray discs

» A standard single-layer DVD has a storage capacity of 4.7 GB (enough to store a two-hour standard definition movie).
» A single-layer Blu-ray disc has a storage capacity of 27 GB (enough to store a two-hour high definition movie or 13 hours of standard definition movies).
» A dual-layer Blu-ray disc has a storage capacity of 50 GB (enough to store 4.5 hours of high definition movies or 20 hours of standard definition movies).
» Blu-ray devices allow greater interactivity than DVD devices. For example with Blu-ray, it is possible to:
  – record high definition television programmes
  – skip quickly to any part of the disc
  – create playlists of recorded movies and television programmes
  – edit or re-order programmes recorded on the disc
  – automatically search for empty space on the disc to avoid over-recording
  – access websites and download subtitles and other interesting features.

Finally, Table 3.1 summarises the main differences between CDs, DVDs and Blu-ray discs.

▼ **Table 3.1** Comparison of CD, DVD and Blu-ray

Disk type	Laser colour	Wavelength of laser light	Disk construction	Track pitch (distance between tracks)
CD	red	780 nm	single 1.2 mm polycarbonate layer	1.60 µm
DVD (dual-layer)	red	650 nm	two 0.6 mm polycarbonate layers	0.74 µm
Blu-ray (single-layer)	blue	405 nm	single 1.2 mm polycarbonate layer	0.30 µm
Blu-ray (dual-layer)	blue	405 nm	two 0.6 mm polycarbonate layers	0.30 µm

(NOTE: nm = 10^{-9} metres and µm = 10^{-6} metres.)

(Blu-ray can currently go up to six-layer technology, but this is outside the scope of this book.)

Uses of Blu-ray discs

» Home video consoles.
» Storing and playing back movies (one high definition movie of two hours duration uses up 25 GB of memory).
» Computers can use this technology for data storage or backing up hard drives.
» Camcorders can use this media (in cartridge form) to store movies.

Advantages of Blu-ray discs

» Very large storage capacity, therefore ideal for storing high definition movies.
» Very fast data transfer rate.
» The data access speed is also greater than with other optical media.
» Blu-ray discs automatically come with a secure encryption system, which helps to prevent piracy and copyright infringement.

Disadvantages of Blu-ray discs

» Relatively expensive discs.
» Encryption problems (which are used to stop piracy) when used to store video.
» Introduction of HD (high definition) DVD players has reduced the advantages of using Blu-ray disc technology.

► Exercise 3a

Review all of the uses, advantages and disadvantages of optical media. Produce a table comparing CD formats, DVD and Blu-ray. Once you have completed the table, choose which optical media could you use for the following (include a reason for your choice):
a Supplying software for use on a computer.
b Backing up your files at the end of the day.
c Recording or playing back a high definition movie.
d Saving data that you do not want to be changed for any reason.
e Saving word-processing files.

3.3 Solid-state media and solid-state storage devices

Latency is a major issue in HDDs as described earlier. **Solid-state technology** removes this issue because all the data is retrieved at the same rate. Solid state does not rely on magnetic properties and they have no moving parts. The most common type of solid-state technology stores data by controlling the movement of electrons within NAND chips. The data is stored as 0s and 1s in millions of tiny transistors (at each junction one transistor is called a floating gate and the other is called a control gate) within the chip. This effectively produces a non-volatile rewritable memory. Devices that use solid-state technology in this way are often referred to as flash memories or flash drives.

3.3.1 Floating gate and control gate transistors

Floating gate and control gate transistors use CMOS (complementary metal oxide semi-conductor) NAND technology. Flash memories make use of a grid; at each intersection on the grid there is a floating gate and a control gate arranged as follows:

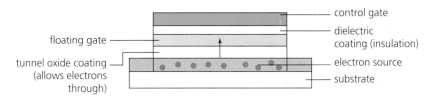

▲ **Figure 3.8** Floating gate and control gate (solid-state memory)

A dielectric coating separates the two transistors, which allows the floating gate transistor to retain its charge (which is why the memory is non-volatile). The floating gate transistor has a value of 1 when it is charged and a value of 0 when it is not. To program one of these 'intersection cells' a voltage is applied to the control gate and electrons from the electron source are attracted to it. But due to the dielectric coating, the electrons become trapped in the floating gate. Therefore, we have control over the bit value stored at each intersection. (Note: After about 12 months, this charge can leak away which is why a solid-state device should be used at least once a year to be certain it will retain its memory contents).

3.3.2 Solid-state drives (SSD)

Uses of SSDs

Solid-state drives have revolutionised computers over the last few years, and they are rapidly taking over from HDDs as the main type of backing storage. As the name suggests, they use solid-state media and can be used in the same way as an HDD (that is, as a storage device to store files, applications, operating system, and so on). They have enabled laptop computers to become thinner and much lighter. They have given rise to the development of smartphones and tablets; without solid-state technology, these devices simply would not exist.

Advantages of SSDs

So, when developing a new computer or electronic device (such as a phone or tablet), what are the main benefits of using an SSD rather than an HDD? The main benefits of SSDs are:

» they are more reliable (no moving parts to go wrong)
» they are considerably lighter (which makes them suitable for laptops)
» they do not have to 'get up to speed' before they work properly
» they have a lower power consumption
» they run much cooler than HDDs (both these points again make them very suitable for laptop computers)
» because of no moving parts, they are very thin
» SSD data access time is only 0.1 milliseconds compared to 10 milliseconds for HDD
» data transfer speed for SSDs is also much faster than for HDDs.

Disadvantages of SSDs

The main drawback of SSDs is the longevity of the technology (although this is becoming less of an issue). Most solid-state storage devices are conservatively rated at only 20 GB write operations per day over a three-year period – this is known as **SSD endurance.** For this reason, SSD technology is still not used in all servers, for example, where a huge number of write operations take place every day. However, the durability of these solid-state systems is being addressed by a number of manufacturers to improve them, and they are rapidly becoming more common in applications such as servers and **cloud storage** devices.

3.3.3 Pen drives

Pen drives (memory sticks) are small portable devices that make use of solid-state technology.

They connect to the computer through a USB port. Their main advantage is that they are very small, lightweight portable devices which make them very suitable as a method for transferring files between computers. They can also be used as small backup devices for music or photo files, for example. Pen drives are examples of USB flash drives which draw their power from the computer via the USB connection. Some devices combine the functionality of a **portable media player** with USB flash storage; such devices require a battery to play music on the go.

▲ **Figure 3.9** Pen drive/memory stick

Note: The terms pen drive (memory stick) and flash drive are often incorrectly used to mean the same thing. Essentially, any device that uses solid-state technology can be referred to as a flash drive; a pen drive (memory stick) is a flash drive with a USB connector. In other words, a pen drive is a type of flash drive with a particular purpose. However, flash drives can be used inside many devices to carry out a number of different tasks. These devices may be acting as the controller for a microwave oven, for example, which is certainly a very different task to a pen drive.

Uses of memory sticks/pen drives

>> Transporting files between computers or using as a backing store.
>> Used as a security device to prevent software piracy (known as a dongle).

Advantages of memory sticks/pen drives

>> Very compact and portable media.
>> Very robust.
>> Does not need additional software to work on most computers.
>> They are not affected by magnetic fields.

Disadvantages of memory sticks/pen drives

>> Cannot write protect the data/files by making it 'read-only'.
>> Easy to lose (due to the small physical size).
>> The user needs to be very careful when removing a memory stick from a computer – incorrect removal (for example, while it is still doing a read/write operation) will corrupt the data on the memory stick and make it useless.

3.3.4 Memory cards

A memory card makes use of solid-state technology. They can be inserted into a device which can read the card or allow data to be written to the card. The cards come in various memory sizes. There are many available memory card formats, for example:

» SD cards (**s**ecure **d**igital card)
» XD cards (e**x**treme **d**igital card)
» CFast card (**c**ompact**fast** card).

The XD card is a type of removable memory card designed for use in digital cameras. They can be written to or read from the camera or other suitable XD card reader (the card readers can often be attached to a computer to allow the memory card to be read directly).

The SD card is a type of very small card with a very high-capacity memory. SD cards are primarily used in portable devices such as digital video recorders, digital cameras, audio players, smartphones and tablets.

A CFast card is a memory card format which was developed to allow solid-state technology to be used in a very small portable device. It has no moving mechanical parts and does not need a battery to retain data. CFast cards are primarily used as removable memory for higher-end digital photo and video cameras.

Uses of memory cards

» Storing photos on digital cameras.
» Used as mobile phone memory cards.
» Used in **MP3** players to store music files.
» Used as a backing store in hand-held computer devices.

Advantages of memory cards

» Very compact – can be easily removed and used in another device or for transferring photos directly to a computer or printer.
» Because they are solid-state memories (and have no moving parts) they are very durable.
» They can hold large amounts of data.
» Digital devices, such as compact cameras and smartphones, are able to read and write to memory cards, allowing the user to transport large collections of photographs, songs or information with them.

Disadvantages of memory cards

» Expensive per gigabyte of memory when compared to hard disk drives.
» Have a lower storage capacity than hard disks.
» Have a finite life regarding number of times they can be read from or written to.
» Memory cards, specifically the micro SD card, are the smallest storage devices available; this means they are more likely to be lost, stolen or damaged.
» Not all computers come with memory card readers built in; users will often be required to purchase a card reader or USB converter to view the data on a memory card.

3.4 The future of storage devices

In recent times, both the CD and DVD are showing signs of becoming obsolete. Many computer systems now come only with USB connectors and no internal DVD or CD drive. The main method of transferring files between devices has become the flash memory. Many people now store all their music in the following ways:

» on hard disk drive systems (set up as sound systems, as shown in Figure 3.10)
» in MP3 format on:
  - a computer/tablet
  - their mobile/smartphone
  - a portable music player (such as an iPod)
» using the **cloud** to store all their files so they can access their music from anywhere in the world
» by **streaming** their music from the internet; provided the user has an internet connection, they can access music through a laptop computer, smartphone, tablet or any other receiving device.

▲ **Figure 3.10** Sound system

It is also a similar story for movies, where streaming is becoming increasingly more common. Many television sets are now set up as **smart televisions** – this means it is now possible to simply stream movies or television programmes **on demand** without the need for any DVD or Blu-ray players. In effect, the television set has become the central computer with a link to the internet using a wireless connection.

Exam-style questions

1 CD, DVD and Blu-ray are types of optical storage media.
Tick (✓) the most appropriate optical storage medium for each of the statements. [4]

	CD (✓)	DVD (✓)	Blu-ray (✓)
Stores lower quality audio files			
Has the highest storage capacity			
The RAM version of this medium is used to record and play recorded images at the same time			
Stores high definition movies			

Cambridge IGCSE Information and Communication Technology (0417) Paper 12 Q4,
February/March 2018

2 Tick (✓) whether the following are optical, magnetic or solid-state storage media. [4]

	Optical (✓)	Magnetic (✓)	Solid state (✓)
SSD			
Blu-ray			
Pen drive			
Portable hard disk drive			

3 **a** Explain what is meant by the term optical media. [2]
 b Hard disk drives (HDD) are being replaced by solid-state drives (SSD). Give four reasons why this is happening. [4]

4 Six descriptions are shown on the left and six computer terms are shown on the right.
By drawing lines, connect each description to its correct term. [5]

Areas on a DVD surface where 1s and 0s are stored		Serial access
Two individual recording layers sandwiched together to form a single DVD		Pits and lands
Technology that makes use of floating gates and control gates		Memory cards
Device that uses solid-state memories and plugs into the USB port of a computer		Solid-state memory
Media that comes in XD, SD or CFast formats		Dual-layering
System whereby all the previous data needs to be read before the required data is found		Pen drive

5 Fifteen words or phrases are listed below:

- » actuator
- » Blu-ray discs
- » cards
- » data access time
- » data transfer rate

- » direct access
- » flash drives
- » latency
- » media
- » memory sticks

- » platters
- » serial access
- » SSD endurance
- » storage device
- » three-year period

Use words or phrases from this list to complete the following paragraph. Note that each word or phrase can be used once, more than once or not at all.

_____ is used by magnetic disks, optical disks and solid-state media when locating data. _____ is the name given to the hardware on which the data is actually stored. Magnetic disks in an HDD are better known as _____; the time taken for a specific block of data on a data track to rotate around to the read/write head is called _____. _____ is the time taken to send data from a device to a computer's memory. _____ is how long it takes to locate data on any type of media. Some optical media use laser light of 405 nm; this media is called _____. Solid-state drives are rated at 20 GB write operations per day over a _____; this is known as _____. Solid-state devices that plug into a computer USB port are known as _____. [10]

6 Indicate whether the following ten statements are True or False by putting a tick (✓) in the appropriate box. [10]

Statements	True (✓)	False (✓)
Both DVDs and Blu-ray discs can make use of dual-layering technology		
CD-RW can act as the same as a ROM chip		
Solid-state drives wear out very quickly due to rapid electron movements in the transistors that make up the memory matrix		
Cloud storage makes use of Blu-ray disks to store customers' music and photo files		
Platters on an HDD can be recorded on both the bottom and top surface		
HDDs suffer from latency due to the time taken for a specific block of data on a data track to rotate around to the read/write head		
Magnetic tapes make use of serial data access		
The data transfer rate is the time taken to locate data on an HDD platter		
The areas on a DVD where 1s and 0s are stored are called pits and lands		
A memory stick is another name for a flash drive		

7 a i Blu-ray and DVD are two types of optical media.
Give **three** differences between Blu-ray and DVD. [3]

ii Give one application that uses Blu-ray discs and one application
that uses DVD disks. [2]

b i Hard disk drives (HDD) and solid-state drives (SSD) are two types
of storage device.
Give **three** differences between HDDs and SSDs. [3]

ii Give **one** application that uses an HDD and **one** application that
uses an SSD. [2]

8 a Describe the changes in technology which have led to the disappearance
of the hard disk drive (HDD) as the main backing store on a computer. [4]

b Describe the changes in technology which have led to the reduction
in the use of CD and DVD drives being installed on modern laptop
computers. [4]

Networks and the effects of using them

In this chapter you will learn about:

★ networks:
  - routers
  - common network devices – NICs, hubs, switches, bridges and
  - Wi-Fi and Bluetooth
  - cloud computing
  - intranets, extranets and the internet
  - LANs, WLANs and WANs
★ network issues and communication:
  - security (including passwords, types of authentication)
  - anti-malware
  - electronic conferencing.

Most computer systems are now connected in some way to form a network. This ranges from a basic home network of only a few devices to very large networks, often set up to share resources, such as printers or software. The largest network is the internet itself.

4.1 Networks

4.1.1 Common network devices and terms

We will begin this section by defining four important terms you will often come across in this chapter:

» network interface card (NIC)
» media access control (MAC) address
» internet protocol (IP) address
» data packet.

Network interface card (NIC)

A **network interface card (NIC)** is needed to allow a device to connect to a network. An NIC turns binary data into an electrical signal that allows access to a network. The NIC is usually integrated into the motherboard on most modern computers.

Each NIC is given a unique hardwired (or hard-coded) media access control (MAC) address at the manufacturing stage. When installed in a device, this uniquely identifies that device.

Wireless network interface cards (WNICs) are the same as NICs in that they are used to connect devices to the internet or other networks. However, they use wireless connectivity, utilising an antenna to communicate with networks via microwaves. They would normally plug into the USB port or be part of an internal integrated circuit.

Media access control (MAC) address

The **media access control (MAC) address** is a number which uniquely identifies a device when it is connected to a network. The MAC address is made up of 48 bits which are shown as six groups of hexadecimal digits with the general format:

NN   NN   NN   DD – DD – DD
manufacturer's code   device serial number

For example,   00 – 1C – B3 – 4F – 25 – FF   , where the first six hex digits identify a device made by Apple and the second set of six hex digits are the unique serial number of the device itself. If the NIC card is replaced, the MAC address will also change. The MAC address is sometimes referred to as the **physical address** because it uniquely identifies a device. MAC addresses are useful when trying to identify network faults because they never change, which makes it a more reliable method of identifying data senders and data receivers on a network.

Internet protocol (IP) addresses

Whenever a computer connects to the internet it is given an **internet protocol (IP) address.** This is usually assigned to the computer by the internet service provider (ISP). Because the operation of the internet is based on a set of protocols (rules), it is necessary to supply an IP address. Internet protocols define the rules that must be agreed by senders and receivers of data communicating through the internet. An IP address essentially identifies the location of a device on a network.

This means that if you are using your laptop at home, it will have been given an IP address when it connected to the internet. If you now take your laptop to a coffee shop, and log into the internet again, it will be assigned a new IP address. Unlike the MAC address which remains constant, the IP address changes each time you log in at different locations.

There are two versions of IP: IPv4 and IPv6. IPv4 is based on 32 bits and the address is written as four groups of eight bits (shown in denary format); for example:

254.25.28.77

Because there are now so many devices connected to the internet, and this number is growing, in the future 32 bits will no longer be enough to give each of them a unique address. Therefore, a newer version called IPv6 is now being used. This uses a 128-bit address, which take the form of eight groups of hex digits; for example:

A8FB:7A88:FFF0:0FFF:3D21:2085:66FB:F0FA

Note the use of colons (:) and hexadecimal numbering. IPv6 has been designed to allow the internet to grow in terms of the number of hosts and potential increase in the amount of data traffic.

Data packets

Data is moved around networks in the form of data packets. Whenever a user sends some data, it is split up into a number of packets and each packet is transmitted separately. Packets of data will usually have a header which contains:

» the sender's IP address
» the receiver's IP address
» the sequence/identity number of the packet (this is to ensure that all the packets can be reassembled into the correct order once they reach the destination)
» the packet size (this is to ensure the receiving station can check if all of the packets have arrived intact)
» how many data packets make up the whole message.

When a router (see later) receives a packet of data, it checks the destination IP address against the stored routing table, which allows the router to determine the packet's next step in the path. A data packet will pass through a number of routers before it reaches its final destination. All the information in the data packet headers allows the data packets to be reassembled in their correct order, according to the sequence/identity number, by the receiving station.

> ## Exercise 4a
> Try finding and running a program called 'tracert' which shows the 'hops' data packets take from sender to receiver. The screen printout will show the routers used in the path and the 'hop' numbers. (You can find 'tracert' utilities using a search engine.)

Hubs

Hubs are hardware devices that can have a number of other devices connected to them. They are used primarily to connect devices together to form a **local area network (LAN)**, often in the same building. A hub will take a data packet received at one of its ports and broadcast it to **every** device connected to it.

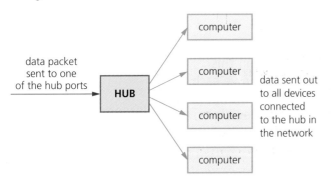

▲ **Figure 4.1** Hub

▲ **Figure 4.2** Hub network connections

Because data packets are delivered to every device on the network:

» hubs are not very secure because every device will receive every data packet
» there will be unnecessary traffic on the network, which results in reduced bandwidth.

Switches

Switches are 'intelligent' versions of hubs. As with hubs, they connect a number of devices together to form a LAN. However, unlike a hub, a switch stores the MAC addresses of all devices on the network. Each port on the switch connected to a device will have a matching MAC address (called a look-up table) as shown in Table 4.1.

▲ **Figure 4.3** Switch

▼ **Table 4.1** Switch MAC address table

Port number	MAC address
1	a4-00-22-a4-fe-d1
2	00-1c-b3-4f-25-ff
3	33-11-ad-6f-f1-00
4	a4-00-22-b2-24-11
5	00-1c-b3-44-ff-02
6	0d-3e-4f-1a-22-00

Using the look-up table, a switch matches the MAC address of an incoming data packet arriving at one of its ports, and directs it to the correct device. None of the other devices will see this data packet. Thus, if a data packet arrives at port 2, and the MAC address in the data packet is a4-00-22-b2-24-11, then the switch will connect the data packet to port 4 only.

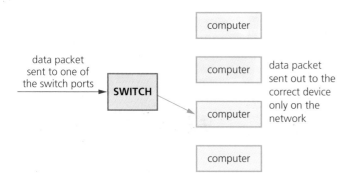

▲ **Figure 4.4** Switch network connections

Consequently, switches are more secure than hubs (because only the intended device is sent the data) and do not waste bandwidth (because network traffic is reduced).

In conclusion, hubs and switches are used to exchange data **within** their own local area networks. They are unable to exchange data with outside networks (such as the internet). To exchange data outside their own LAN, a device needs to be able to read an IP address. Therefore, we need another device to allow communication with external networks.

In summary:

» both a hub and a switch are used to connect devices in a LAN
» both hubs and switches use data packets
» hubs send data packets to every device on the network; whereas switches send data packets to a specific device only

» security is lower with hubs than with switches
» a switch uses a look-up table to determine the destination device
» switches use MAC addresses to locate the destination device.

Bridges

Bridges are devices that connect one LAN to another LAN that uses the same protocol (communication rules). They are often used to connect together different parts of a LAN so that they can function as a single LAN.

▲ **Figure 4.5** Bridge

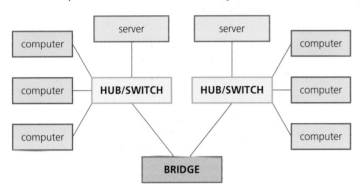

▲ **Figure 4.6** Use of a bridge to connect two LANs together

Unlike routers, bridges cannot communicate with other external networks, such as the internet.

4.1.2 Routers

Routers are used to route data packets from one network to another network, based on IP addresses. It can do this because each router has its own IP address. Routers are used to join a LAN to the internet.

▲ **Figure 4.7** Router

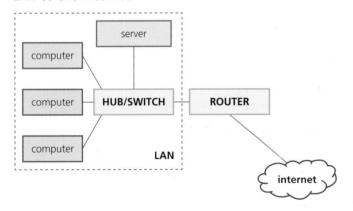

▲ **Figure 4.8** Router used to connect a LAN to the internet

When a data packet is received at one of its ports, the router inspects the IP address and determines whether the data packet is meant for its own network or for another, external network. If the data packet is meant for its own network, then the data packet is routed to the local switch or hub. Otherwise, the data packet is transmitted to a different router (and therefore to an external network).

Routers know where to send data packets by consulting a routing table (stored on the router's RAM). The routing table will contain information about the router's immediate network (such as computer addresses) and information about other routers in its immediate vicinity. When a data packet reaches a router, it examines the IP address. Because the routing table contains computer addresses of all the computers/devices on its network, it will be able to work out that the data packet is intended for a computer on its network. Routers however, do not store the MAC addresses of devices (only IP addresses of all computers and devices are stored). The router does not need the MAC address because the data packet will be sent by the router to the switch on the recipient local network. The switch can then use its look-up table to send the data packet to the correct device.

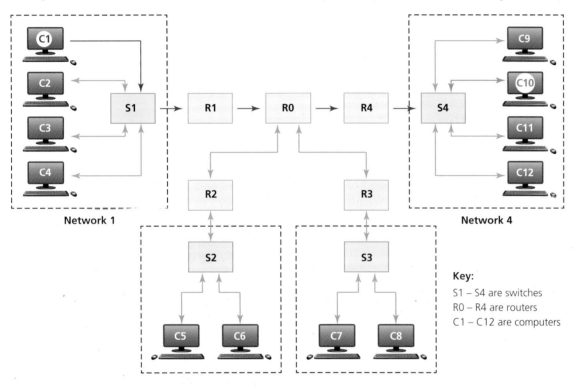

▲ **Figure 4.9** Routing of data from **C1** to **C10**

Suppose, in Figure 4.9, computer **C1** wishes to send data to computer **C10**:

» Data packets are sent from C1 to R1.
» R1 checks the IP addresses and notes the data packets are not intended for any devices on Network 1.
» The data packets are then forwarded onto the internet (R0).
» The IP address (in the header of the data packet) matches that of R4; this ensures that each data packet is eventually forwarded to R4.
» R4 recognises that the IP address of each data packet refers to Network 4, and forwards them to S4 which then directs each data packet to C10.

Many modern broadband 'routers' actually combine the functions of a router and a switch – this means that they store MAC addresses and IP addresses to enable data packets to be sent to the correct network and then to the correct device on the network.

Table 4.2 summarises the differences between bridges and routers.

▼ **Table 4.2** Comparison of routers and bridges

Router	Bridge
The main objective of a router is to connect various types of network together	The main objective of a bridge is to connect LANs together
Routers scan a device's IP address	Bridges scan a device's MAC address
Data is sent out using data packets	Data is sent out using data packets
Connected networks will use different protocols	Connects networks together that use the same protocols
A routing table is used to direct data packets to the correct device	Bridges do not make use of routing tables
A router has more than two ports	A bridge has only two ports

4.1.3 Wi-Fi and Bluetooth

Both **Wi-Fi** and **Bluetooth** offer wireless communication between devices. They both use electromagnetic radiation as the carrier of data transmission.

Bluetooth sends and receives radio waves in a band of 79 different frequencies (known as channels). These are all centred on a frequency of 2.45 GHz. Devices using Bluetooth automatically detect and connect to each other, but they do not interfere with other devices because each communicating pair uses a different channel (from the 79 options).

When a device wants to communicate, it picks one of the 79 channels at random to pair with another device. If the channel is already being used, it randomly picks another channel. Once paired, to minimise the risks of interference with other devices, the devices constantly change the channels they are using (several times a second). This is known as **spread-spectrum frequency hopping**. Bluetooth uses key encryption to create a secure **wireless personal area network (WPAN)**.

Bluetooth is useful:

» when transferring data between two or more devices which are very close together (less than 30 metres distance)
» when the speed of data transmission is not critical
» for low-bandwidth applications (for example, when sending music files from a mobile phone to a headset).

Wi-Fi sends and receives radio waves in several different frequency bands – 2.4 GHz and 5 GHz are the most common at the moment. Like Bluetooth, each band is also further split into channels. The 5GHz band has a faster data transfer rate but a shorter signal range.

Wi-Fi is best suited to operating full-scale networks because it offers much faster data transfer rates, better range and better security than Bluetooth. A Wi-Fi-enabled device (such as a computer or smartphone) can access, for example, the internet wirelessly at any **access point (AP)** or **'hot spot'** up to 100 metres away. Table 4.3 summarises some of the differences between Wi-Fi and Bluetooth.

▼ **Table 4.3** Comparison of Wi-Fi and Bluetooth connectivity

Feature	Bluetooth	Wi-Fi
Transmission frequency used	2.4 GHz	2.4, 3.6, 5.0 GHz
Data transfer rate (maximum)	25 Mbits/second (~3.1 Mbytes/second)	250 Mbits/second (~31 Mbytes/second)
Maximum effective range (metres)	30 metres	100 metres (but can be obstructed by walls, etc. reducing effective range to only a few metres)
Maximum number of devices connected	Up to 7	Depends on the router used (can be one device or many devices)
Type of data transmission security	Key matching encryption	WEP (wireless equivalent privacy) and WPA (Wi-Fi protected access) are the most common security systems)

4.1.4 Cloud computing (storage)

Cloud computing is a method of data storage where data is stored on remote servers – there may be thousands of servers in many different locations. The same data is stored on more than one server in case of maintenance or repair, allowing clients to access data at any time. This is known as **data redundancy**. The physical environment of the cloud servers is owned and managed by a hosting company.

There are three common cloud storage systems:

» Public cloud – this is a storage environment where the customer/client and cloud storage provider are different companies.
» Private cloud – this is storage provided by a dedicated environment behind a company firewall; customer/client and cloud storage provider are integrated and operate as a single entity.
» Hybrid cloud – this is a combination of the two previous environments; some data resides in the private cloud and less-sensitive/less-commercial data can be accessed from a public cloud storage provider.

Instead of, or in addition to, saving data on a local hard disk or other storage device, a user can save their data 'in the cloud'.

Advantages of cloud computing (storage)

» Customer/client files stored in the cloud can be accessed at any time, from any device, anywhere in the world, as long as internet access is available.
» There is no need for a customer/client to carry an external storage device with them, or even use the same computer, to store and retrieve information.
» The cloud provides the user with remote backup of data, with obvious advantages in the event of data loss/disaster recovery on their own computer.
» If a customer/client has a failure of their hard disk or backup device, cloud storage will allow recovery of their data.
» The cloud system offers almost unlimited storage capacity (at a price!).

Disadvantages of cloud computing (storage)

» Security aspects of storing data in the cloud (see comments later on).
» If the customer/client has a slow or unstable internet connection, they could have many problems accessing or downloading their data/files.

>> Costs can be high if a large storage capacity or high download/upload data transfer is required.
>> The potential failure of the cloud storage company is always possible – this poses a risk of loss of all backup data.

Several computer manufacturers (especially tablets and laptops) and mobile phone manufacturers are encouraging customers to store or backup all their files on to cloud storage. Users purchase cloud storage and can then access all their files (for example, photos, videos, music or e-books) from any device anywhere in the world. This has obvious advantages:

>> You do not need to carry memory sticks around with you if you want to access your files away from home.
>> You do not have to pay for large storage capacity on your computer/tablet or mobile phone.
>> Because the cloud is controlled by external companies, they will ensure that your files are backed up and therefore reduce the possibility of losing irreplaceable data.
>> The ability to synchronise (sync) files ensures they are automatically updated across all devices; this means that the latest version of a file saved on a desktop computer, for example, is also available on other devices, such as a smartphone.
>> Cloud storage is also ideal for collaboration purposes; it allows several users to edit and collaborate on a single file or document – there is no need to worry about tracking the latest version or which user made the changes.

In spite of all these obvious advantages, there are still security worries about using cloud storage. The main fears are data security and data loss.

Data security using cloud storage/computing

Companies that transfer vast amounts of confidential data from their own systems to a cloud service provider are potentially relinquishing control of their own data security. This raises a number of questions:

>> What physical security exists regarding the building where the data is housed?
>> How good is the cloud service provider's resistance to natural disasters or power cuts?
>> What safeguards exist regarding personnel who work for the cloud service company? Can they use their authorisation codes to access confidential data for monetary purposes?

Data loss

There is a risk that important and irreplaceable data could be lost from cloud storage facilities. Actions from hackers (gaining access to accounts or pharming attacks, for example) could lead to loss or corruption of data. Users need to be certain that sufficient safeguards exist to overcome these potentially very harmful risks.

In 2019, there were a number of breaches of cloud security. We will briefly mention two of these breaches:

>> On 2 April, a Mexican digital media company (called Cultura Colectiva) exposed 540 million Facebook accounts stored on one of their cloud servers; the data included user profiles, user IDs, account names, likes and comments.

» On 29 July, Capital One Bank (in the USA) had some of their cloud-based data hacked exposing 80,000 bank account numbers, 140,000 social security numbers and over one million government ID numbers.

4.1.5 Common network environments

Extranets, intranets and the internet

Extranets, intranets and the internet are all common types of network environment. You will find these types of network covered in some depth in Chapter 10.

Link

See Section 10.2 for more on extranets, intranets and the internet.

4.1.6 Network types

This section will cover the following types of network:

» local area network (LAN)
» wireless local area network (WLAN)
» wide area network (WAN).

Local area network (LAN)

Local area networks (LANs) are usually within one building or geographically near each other. A typical LAN will consist of a number of computers and devices (for example, printers) which will be connected to hubs or switches. One of the hubs or switches will usually be connected to a router to allow the LAN to connect to external networks, such as the internet.

There are advantages of networking computers together using LANs:

» they allow the sharing of resources such as hardware (e.g. printers and scanners) and software (e.g. word processors and photo editing software)
» they permit easy communication between users of the LAN (e.g. by using simple text messaging between computers on the network)
» they use a network administrator that ensures security and use of the LAN is constantly monitored (e.g. the administrator can maintain passwords and also monitor data traffic within the network).

There are also disadvantages of networking computers using LANs:

» easier spread of viruses throughout the whole network
» queues for shared resources (such as a printer) which can be frustrating
» slower access to external networks
» increased security risk when compared to stand-alone computers
» if the main server breaks down, in many types of network structures, the network will no longer function properly.

Wireless local area network (WLAN)

Wireless LANs (WLANs) are similar to LANs, but there are no wires or cables. In other words, they provide wireless network communications over fairly short distances using radio or infrared signals instead of using cables.

Devices, known as **access points (APs)**, are connected into a wired network at fixed locations. Because of the limited range, most commercial LANs (for example, a college campus or an airport) need several APs to permit uninterrupted wireless communications. The APs use either **spread-spectrum**

technology (which is a wideband radio frequency with a range of about 30 to 50 metres) or **infrared**, but this has a very short range (about 1–2 metres) and is easily blocked, and therefore infrared has limited use.

The AP receives and transmits data between the WLAN and the wired network structure. End-users access the WLAN through wireless LAN adapters which are built into their devices.

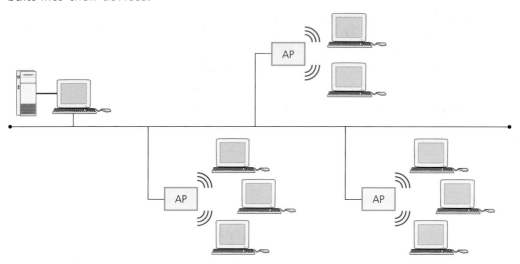

▲ **Figure 4.10** Wireless LAN set-up

Wired versus wireless

Table 4.4 compares wired LANs and wireless LANs.

▼ **Table 4.4** Wired versus wired LAN

Wireless networking	Wired networking
It is easier to expand the networks and it is not necessary to connect the devices using cables	Using cables produces a more reliable and stable network; wireless connectivity is often subject to interference
This gives devices increased mobility, as long as they are within range of the APs	Data transfer rates tend to be faster and there will not be any 'dead spots'
No cabling, so there is a safety improvement and increased flexibility	
There is an increased chance of interference from external sources	Setting up cabled networks tends to be cheaper overall in spite of the need to buy and install cable
Data is less secure than with wired systems; it is easier to intercept radio waves and microwaves than cables; it is essential to protect data transmissions using encryption	However, cabled networks lose the ability for devices to be mobile; they must be close enough to allow for cable connections
Data transmission rate is still slower than for cabled networks although it continues to improve	Having lots of wires can lead to a number of hazards, such as tripping hazards, overheating of connections (leading to potential fire risk) and disconnection of cables during routine office cleaning
It is possible for signals to be stopped by thick walls (for example, in old houses) and there may be areas of variable signal strength leading to 'drop out'	

Advice

Wi-Fi is a series of protocols that enable a WLAN to be set up.

Wide area networks (WANs)

Wide area networks (WANs) are used where computers or networks are situated a long distance from each other geographically (for example, in a different city or country). As mentioned earlier, if a number of LANs are joined together using a router, then they can form a WAN. The network of ATMs (automated teller machines) used by banks is one of the most common examples of the use of a WAN.

Because of the long distances between devices, WANs usually make use of some public communications network (such as telephone lines or satellites), but they can use dedicated or leased communication lines, which can be less expensive and also more secure (less risk of hacking, for example).

A typical WAN will consist of end systems and intermediate systems (Figure 4.11).

In Figure 4.11, **1**, **3**, **7** and **10** are known as end systems and the remainder are known as intermediate systems. The distance between each system can be considerable, especially if the WAN is run by a multinational company.

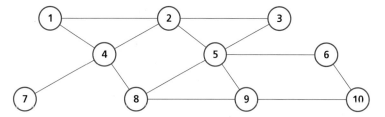

▲ **Figure 4.11** WAN end systems and intermediate systems

The following is used as a guide for deciding the 'size' of a network:

» WAN: 100 km to over 1000 km
» MAN: 1 km to 100 km
» LAN: 10 m to 1000 m (1 km)

Advice

Metropolitan area networks (MANs) is outside the syllabus; this is included here for comparison purposes only.

4.2 Network issues and communication

4.2.1 Security issues regarding data transfer

Many aspects of security (such as hacking, phishing, pharming and viruses) are covered in depth in Chapter 8 (Section 8.3). This section covers some of the more general aspects of internet security, together with how we use networks to communicate.

4.2.2 Passwords

Passwords are used in many instances when accessing the internet. For example:

» when accessing your email account
» when carrying out online banking
» accessing social networking sites.

There are many more instances when you might need to type in a password and, in many cases, a user ID. It is important that passwords are protected. Some ways of doing this are described below:

» Run anti-spyware software to make sure that your passwords are not being relayed back to whoever put the spyware on your computer
» Change passwords on a regular basis in case it has come into the possession of another user illegally or accidentally.
» Passwords should not be easy to crack (e.g. your favourite colour, name of a pet or favourite rock group); passwords are grouped as either strong (hard to crack or guess) or weak (relatively easy to crack or guess).
» Strong passwords should contain:
  – at least one capital letter
  – at least one numerical value
  – at least one other keyboard character (such as @, *, & etc.).

An example of a strong password is: Sy12@#TT90kj=0

An example of a weak password is: GREEN1

> ### Exercise 4b
> ....
> Which of the following are weak passwords and which are strong passwords?
>
> Explain your decision in each case.
> i   25-May-2000
> ii   Pas5word
> iii ChapTer@15
> iv   AbC*N55!
> v   12345X

4.2.3 Other authentication methods

Passwords are one of the most common types of authentication (that is, a way of proving your identity). This section will look at a number of other types of authentication:

» zero login
» biometrics
» magnetic stripes
» smart cards
» physical tokens
» electronic tokens.

Zero login and biometrics

The Fast ID online (FIDO) Alliance and WWW Consortium (W3C) announced a new technology standard that allows users to login to computer systems without the need to type in a password. The mishandling of personal data over the years now means we can no longer regard data, such as passwords, as being secret or protected.

Zero login essentially relies on devices being smart and secure enough to instantly recognise a user by a number of features based on:

» biometrics
» behavioural patterns.

Instead of using passwords, the zero login system builds up a complex user profile based on the above two features. Biometrics is already used on many smartphones as a way of logging into the phone. By placing your finger on the screen, a fingerprint recognition system recognises the user and unlocks the phone. Newer systems allow the user to simply look at their smartphone screen (using face recognition) to unlock it.

Behavioural patterns include: how you walk, your typing speed, your normal location, how you swipe the screen, and so on. These behavioural patterns, coupled with biometric data, should be enough to uniquely identify a user, and allow them into a system without actually supplying any passwords or other security information. The advantages of zero login are fairly clear: enhanced security (it is difficult to copy biometrics and behavioural patterns) and an easier and much quicker way to login to a system. But there are certain disadvantages that need consideration:

» How do users know when they are being monitored?
» How do you know if and when you have been logged out?
» How well protected is it in reality?

Link

Biometrics, which includes fingerprint recognition, face recognition and voice recognition, are covered in detail in Sections 6.10 and 8.3.

Magnetic stripe cards

Magnetic stripe cards are also covered in Chapters 2 and 6. The cards have a magnetic stripe on the reverse side (made up of tiny magnetic particles on a plastic film). Each particle can act as a north-pole or a south-pole (which corresponds to the two binary values of 0 and 1).

The stripe is read by swiping it through a card reader. Data such as name, ID number, sex, and date of birth may be contained on a magnetic stripe when used as a security device to allow entry to a building, for example. Access will only be allowed if the scanned data matches data in a database.

Some ID cards also use a **holographic image (hologram)**. These are designed to make forgery of the card more difficult. Holographic images change colour or appear to have a moving object as the image is viewed from different angles. Because these are difficult to copy, it prevents somebody simply photocopying a card and using it illegally.

Another form of security is to have a photographic image of the card user printed onto the card surface. This prevents a stolen card from being used, because the image etched into the card will not match the perpetrator.

▲ **Figure 4.12** Sample holographic security images

Advantages of magnetic stripe cards

» They are easy to use.
» It is not an expensive technology.
» Magnetic cards can be remotely deactivated (if lost or stolen).
» The cards can be multi-purpose (for example, door key cards, network access cards or used in vending machines to buy food or drink).

Disadvantages of magnetic stripe cards

» Less secure than, for example, biometric methods (no encryption is used and the stripe contents can be copied fairly easily).
» The cards wear out with a lot of use.
» Magnetic readers often fail to read the cards on first attempt.

Smart cards

By inserting a tag (chip and antenna) into a security card, it can act as a smart **contactless card** (that is, it can be read from a distance and does not have to be swiped through a card reader). The chip on the smart card can store data such as name, security number, sex, date of birth and a PIN. Smart cards can therefore be used as a security device. If the card is in a wallet or a pocket as the owner of the card walks up to a security gate, readers on either side of the gate quickly scan the security data stored on the RFID tag embedded in the card. The user will then be invited to enter a PIN on the keypad. If all details match, then access will be allowed.

Physical tokens

A physical (or hardware) token is a form of authentication in the form of a physical, solid object. The user's interaction with a login system is used to prove that the user has possession of the token. Physical tokens contain internal clocks and when a PIN and other authentication details are entered, then a one-time password (OTP) is generated. The OTP is shown on a small screen. The code changes on a regular basis and is usually only valid for less than a minute.

We will use banking as our example of its use. A customer has logged on to the bank's website. They get to a web page which requires some form of authentication to prove who they are. To do this, they need to use a physical token supplied by the bank:

» The customer inserts their debit card into the top of the token device (first authentication step) and the device either recognises the card as genuine or rejects it.
» The device then asks the customer to press 'IDENTIFY' and then enter their PIN (second authentication step).
» A one-time password is then shown on the device screen – this is usually an eight-digit code.
» The customer now goes back to their bank web page and enters the eight-digit code.
» They are now given access to their account.

This clearly enhances security, because a thief needs to have in their possession: the token device, a cloned card and the PIN to allow them to gain access.

<div class="sidebar">

Link

For more on smart and contactless card technology, and RFID, see Chapters 2 and 6.

</div>

▲ **Figure 4.13** Example of disconnected physical token device used in banking

This is a classic example of a multi-factor authentication method. There are two types of physical tokens:

1 a **disconnected physical token** – this is the type described above, where a separate device is used, requiring the user to key in data manually using a keypad
2 a **connected physical token** – this type of token transmits the generated one-time password directly to a computer through a USB connection; the user does not need to manually enter data.

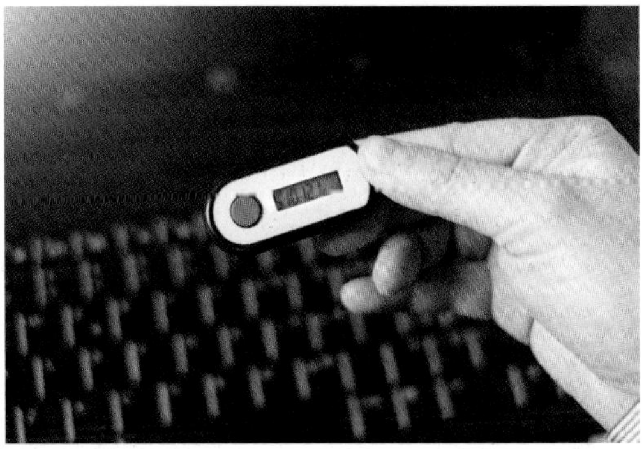

Electronic tokens

Electronic (software) tokens are software installed on a user's device, such as a smartphone. Suppose a user wishes to log on to a website using their tablet computer. This website requires electronic tokens to be used to authenticate the user. The user has already installed the electronic token app on their smartphone. When the website requests the user to authenticate who they are, the user opens the app on their smartphone. The app generates a one-time password (OTP) which is valid for less than a minute. The user enters this OTP when prompted by the website, together with some other form of authentication, such as PIN, touch ID or face ID.

▲ **Figure 4.14** Connected physical token

The website server runs the same software as the app. Because both the server and smartphone have synchronised clocks, they will generate the same numbers. Once the OTP and other form of authentication are verified by the website, the user will be allowed access.

4.2.4 Anti-malware software

Refer to Chapter 8 for further information on the running of anti-malware software. In this section, we will concentrate on the use of a type of anti-malware software, known as anti-virus software, to protect devices against a potential virus attack.

Anti-virus software should be loaded onto a computer and then run to allow all software and devices to be scanned for viruses. Whenever data or software is downloaded or being transferred to another device, it is essential that a virus check is carried out on that other device too.

> **Link**
> ....
> For more on malware see Section 8.3.

Running **anti-virus software** in the background on a computer will constantly check for virus attacks. Although various types of anti-virus software work in different ways they all have the following common features:

>> They check software or files before they are run or loaded on a computer.
>> Anti-virus software compares a possible virus against a database of known viruses.
>> They carry out **heuristic checking** – this is the checking of software for types of behaviour that could indicate a possible virus; this is useful if software is infected by a virus not yet on the database.
>> Any possible files or programs which are infected are put into **quarantine** which:
  – allows the virus to be automatically deleted, or
  – allows the user to make the decision about deletion (it is possible that the user knows that the file or program is not infected by a virus – this is known as a **false positive** and is one of the drawbacks of anti-virus software).

>> Anti-virus software needs to be kept up to date because new viruses are constantly being discovered.
>> Full system checks need to be carried out once a week, for example, because some viruses lie dormant and would only be picked up by this full system scan.

4.2.5 Electronic conferencing

This section will consider three types of electronic conferencing:

>> video conferencing
>> audio conferencing
>> web conferencing.

Link

There is further information on video calls and VoIP in Section 6.1.

Video conferencing

Video conferencing is a communication method that uses both video and sound. It is a substitute for face-to-face conferences between a number of people, who may be in a different part of the country or live overseas. It is carried out in real time and makes use of some form of network.

The basic hardware includes:

>> webcams
>> large monitors/television screens
>> microphones
>> speakers.

There are a few items to consider when a conference is about to begin:

▲ **Figure 4.15** Video-conferencing room

>> It is essential to agree a time and date for the conference to take place.
>> The delegates in each conference room must log into the video-conference system.
>> The video-conference set-up needs to be checked before the meeting goes live.
>> Webcams need to be placed in the correct position so that all the delegates in the room are within visual contact (the webcams will capture the images and then transmit them to the other delegates – they will see the images on their own large screens).
>> Microphones need to be placed centrally so that all of the delegates can speak – the sound is picked up by the microphones and is transmitted to the other delegates (they hear the voices through speakers in their own conference room).
>> It is important for one person to be the main contact in each conference room to make sure each delegate is able to be heard; this is particularly important if more than two video-conference rooms are linked up at the same time.

In addition to the hardware items described above, it is also important to realise that software plays an important role in a successful video conference.

▼ **Table 4.5** Software used in video conferencing

Software	Description
Webcam and microphone software drivers	It is vital that the correct software is used to ensure that the webcam and microphone transmit their images and sound to the other delegates (these are sometimes referred to as hardware drivers).
CODEC	**CODEC** can stand for **CO**der-**DEC**oder or **CO**mpression-**DEC**ompression. The first is used to encode or decode the digital data stream to allow data to be transmitted (encoded) and played back (decoded). The second is used to compress the data before it is transmitted and then decompress it again at the receiving conference room.
Echo cancellation software	**Echo cancellation software** allows talking to take place in real time and permits the synchronisation of communication. Microphones can pick up sound from the speakers (creating an echo); this software copies received signals and checks for parts of the signal that reappear but are delayed slightly. The reappearing parts are removed from the signal (the echo is removed).

Advantages of using video conferencing

» As people are in their own building, it is much easier to access important documents or bring in 'experts' at key parts of the conference – this would be difficult if they were a long way away from their office.
» It is possible to hold conferences at short notice (a conference date can be set up within a few hours as no person needs to travel very far).
» Not travelling physically to meetings reduces costs:
    – reduced travelling costs
    – no need to pay for hotel accommodation or venue hire
    – it also reduces the cost of taking people away from their work for two or three days to travel – people are still paid their wage even though they are not in the office, so this is a large 'hidden' cost.
» It may be better to use video conferencing than have delegates travel to potentially unsafe places around the world.
» It is better for the environment – less travel means less pollution.
» It connects people in an organisation who might be otherwise left out, for example, people not based at the headquarters.

Disadvantages of using video conferencing

» There is potential time lag in responses/delays when talking.
» Images can jerk – usually due to poor internet/network performance or poor bandwidth.
» It can be very expensive to set up in the first place (both the hardware and the software are expensive to purchase and get set up correctly).
» There can be problems if the delegates live in different countries where the time zone differences are large.
» Training people to use the system correctly can be both costly and time consuming.
» It can be demotivating for staff if they believe that one of the 'perks' of their job is international travel.
» The whole system relies on a good network connection – if it breaks down or the signal strength is diminished in any way, then the video conference can be almost unusable.

Audio conferencing

Audio conferencing refers to meetings held between people using audio (sound) equipment.

Audio conferencing can be done over the standard telephone network (often referred to as **a phone conference**). The procedure to be carried out during a phone conference is detailed below.

1 The organiser of the phone conference is given two PINs by the phone company. One PIN is the personal PIN (e.g. 2151) given to the organiser and the second PIN is the participant's PIN (e.g. 8422).

2 The organiser contacts all of the participants and informs them of their PIN and the date and time of the phone conference.

3 When the phone conference is about to start, the organiser dials the conference phone number and, once they are connected, keys in their personal PIN (2151 in this case).

4 The participants then call the same conference number to join in – once they get through they each input the PIN given to them by the organiser (8422 in this case). Without this PIN, it would be impossible to join the phone conference.

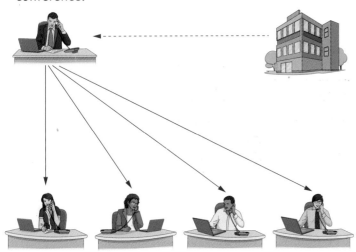

▲ **Figure 4.16** Audio conferencing

The equipment required for an audio conference over a standard telephone network normally just includes a standard telephone.

It is also possible to hold an audio conference using a computer, as long as a microphone and speakers are connected. This makes use of Voice over Internet Protocol (VoIP). It is also possible to connect an internet telephone, which usually plugs into the router or other internet device.

In this case equipment can include:

» a computer (with built-in microphones and speakers)
» external microphone and/or speakers
» an internet phone
» a standard phone.

> **Link**
> ....
> For more on VoIP see Section 6.1.

Using VoIP allows an organiser to create a group of people to take part in the conference call. The group is created by dragging and dropping user details into the group. When the conference is to take place, the organiser clicks on the required group and the conference is initiated.

Using VoIP allows communication using voice, instant messaging and video (by using an attached webcam). If some of the users do not have an internet connection or do not have access to a computer, it is possible to add actual telephone numbers (landline or mobile) to the created group. The only real drawback is the quality of the sound when using this technique because it is totally reliant on a fast, stable broadband connection – otherwise 'drop out' (loss of voice on occasions), echoing (when the user can hear their own voice being echoed back as they speak) or a very noisy line can happen, making it difficult to understand.

Web conferencing

Web conferencing (often referred to as a **webinar** or **webcasts**) uses the internet to permit conferencing to take place.

Multiple computers are used with this system, all connected over the internet. As with video conferencing, it is carried out in real time and allows the following types of meeting to take place:

>> business meetings to discuss new ideas
>> presentations
>> online education or training.

The only requirement is a computer and a high-speed, stable internet connection. To carry out web conferencing, each user either downloads an application or logs on to a website from a link supplied in an email from the conference organiser.

Delegates can leave or join the conference as they wish. The organiser can decide on who can speak at any time using the control panel on their computer. If a delegate wishes to speak, they raise a flag next to their name. Delegates can post comments using instant messaging for all delegates to see at any time.

Some of the main features include:

>> Slide presentations using presentation software can be posted on the conference website in advance of the meeting.
>> The host's computer screen can be shared for live presentations, or other live demonstrations.
>> It is possible for any delegate to draw or write on a 'whiteboard' using their own keyboard or mouse.
>> It is possible to transmit images or videos using the webcam throughout the conference.
>> Documents can be shared by first uploading them to the website before the conference begins.
>> As described earlier, it is possible to chat verbally or by using instant messaging throughout the conference.

As indicated earlier, there is cross-over between web conferencing, video conferencing and audio conferencing through the use of webcams and the built-in microphone and speakers. It is possible to have a conference using any device which allows these functions (for example, tablets and smartphones would both permit this type of group communication).

Exam-style questions

1 A company is setting up a video conference.
  a Name **three** computer hardware devices they would need. [3]
  b The company could have set up a web-conference rather than a video-conference.
    Describe what is meant by a web-conference. [4]

Cambridge IGCSE Information and Communication Technology (0417) Paper 11 Q8, May/June 2017

2 Both Wi-Fi and Bluetooth can be used to enable devices to communicate wirelessly.
  Describe the differences in how Bluetooth and Wi-Fi both operate. [6]

3 Hubs and switches are both used to enable devices to communicate with each other in a network.
  a Describe the differences and similarities in the use of hubs and switches in a network. [4]
  b A bridge is another device used in network connectivity.
    Describe the function of a bridge. [2]
  c Routers are used to allow local area networks to connect to external networks. Local area network 'A' is in Europe and local area network 'B' is in India.
    Describe how routers are used to enable a computer on network 'A' to send data to a computer on network 'B'. [3]
  d Describe the main differences between routers and bridges. [3]

4 Authentication is an important part of network security.
  Explain the meaning of the following three types of authentication.
  In each case, also give an example of its use.
  a Zero login
  b Physical token
  c Electronic token [9]

5 Six features of network devices are given in the table below.
  For each feature, tick (✓) the appropriate box to indicate whether it refers to a router, hub or switch. [6]

Feature	Router (✓)	Switch (✓)	Hub (✓)
Used to connect devices together to form a local area network (LAN)			
The destination MAC address is looked up before the data packet is sent to the correct device			
Used to connect LANs to other, external networks			
Uses both MAC and IP addresses to enable data packets to be sent to the correct device on another network			
All data packets are sent to all the devices on the network			
Data packets are sent only to a specific device on the same network			

6 a Describe what is meant by a virus.   [2]
   b Describe **three** of the features you would expect to find in any
      anti-virus software.   [3]

7 a Explain how magnetic stripe cards could be used to control
      the entry and exit to a security building.   [4]
   b Describe how these magnetic stripe cards could be improved
      to increase the security of the building.   [3]

8 Seven descriptions are shown on the left and ten computer
   terms are shown on the right.
   By drawing arrows, connect each description to the correct
   computer term.   [7]

Descriptions	Computer terms
Form of authentication in the form of hardware devices; uses periodically changing random numbers to log in to a secure system	Password
	Zero login
Type of network that covers a huge geographical area, such as a country or different continent	Physical token
	Wide area network
Devices used to connect two LANs together that use the same protocols, but cannot communicate outside the two LANs	Internet
Authentication software installed on a user's smartphone that generates a one-time password	Network interface card
Type of login authentication that relies on biometrics and behavioural patterns	Hub
Devices that connect computers together to form a LAN; directs data packets to a specific device or computer only	Bridge
	Electronic token
Hardware needed to connect a device to a network; a MAC address is hardwired or hard-coded into the device at manufacture	Switch

9 a Explain what is meant by cloud computing.   [3]
   b Give **three** advantages of storing data on the cloud.   [3]
   c Give **three** disadvantages of storing data on the cloud.   [3]

10 Name each of the **six** network devices labelled 'A' to 'F' in the diagrams below: [6]

a

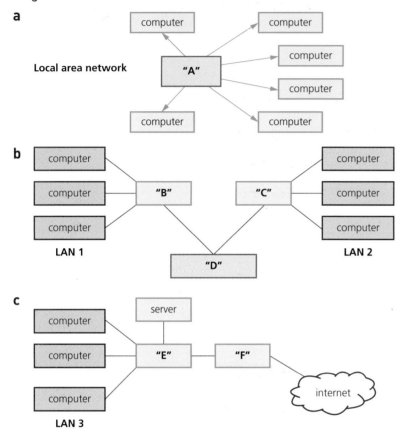

Local area network

b

c

5 The effects of using IT

In this chapter you will learn about:
- ★ microprocessor-controlled devices:
  - – their positive and negative effects on various aspects of everyday life in the home
  - – positive and negative effects in monitoring and controlling transport
- ★ health issues from using a computer:
  - – such as RSI, back and neck problems, eye problems and headaches
  - – causes of health issues and ways of preventing them.

The introduction of microprocessor-controlled devices into our everyday lives has had a profound effect in a number of ways. Some of these are positive and some are negative. This chapter will consider the effects of devices used in the home and elsewhere, and how they have changed how we live. We will also consider the health risks posed by prolonged use of computers at home and at work.

5.1 Microprocessor-controlled devices

5.1.1 Effects of using microprocessor-controlled devices in the home

Using microprocessor-controlled devices in the home can have positive and negative effects on our:

- ›› lifestyle
- ›› leisure time
- ›› physical fitness
- ›› data security
- ›› social interaction.

Many common household devices are now fitted with microprocessors to control a large number of their functions. The devices fall into two main groups:

Labour-saving devices (group 1):

- ›› automatic washing machines
- ›› microwave ovens
- ›› cookers
- ›› automatic dishwashers
- ›› robotic vacuum cleaners
- ›› bread-making machines
- ›› smart fridges and freezers.

Other devices (group 2):

- ›› alarm clocks
- ›› television sets
- ›› central heating and air-conditioning systems
- ›› home entertainment systems
- ›› mobile phones and tablets.

Essentially, a microprocessor-controlled labour-saving device allows people to get on with other things while the device carries out their tasks. Microprocessors within the second group of devices make them easier to use and gives them additional features, such as 'intelligent tuning' in television sets.

Lifestyle, leisure time and physical fitness

Table 5.1 summarises the effects of microprocessor-controlled labour-saving devices on a person's lifestyle, leisure time and physical fitness.

▼ **Table 5.1** Advantages and disadvantages of microprocessor-controlled labour-saving devices

Advantages	Disadvantages
» People no longer have to do manual tasks at home. » They give people more time for leisure activities, hobbies, shopping and socialising. » There is no longer a need to stay home while food is cooking or clothes are being washed. » It is possible to control ovens and automatic washing machines, for example, using smartphones – a web-enabled phone allows devices to be switched on or off while the owner is out. » Automated burglar alarms give people a sense of security and well-being as they give a very sophisticated level of intruder warning at all times. » Smart fridges and freezers can lead to more healthy lifestyles (they can automatically order fresh food from supermarkets using their internet connections) as well as prevent food waste.	» Labour-saving devices can lead to unhealthy lifestyles (because of the lack of exercise) – people can become less fit if they just lie around at home while the devices carry out many of the previous manual tasks. » They tend to make people rather lazy because there is a dependence on the devices. » There is a potential to lose household skills. » As with any device which contains a microprocessor and can communicate using the internet, there is the risk of cybersecurity threats (this is discussed in more depth later).

Table 5.2 shows some of the more general ways in which **all** microprocessor-controlled devices can affect our lives. This table includes devices which are not necessarily labour-saving, and simply use microprocessors to improve their functionality.

▼ **Table 5.2** General advantages and disadvantages of using all microprocessor-controlled devices

Advantages	Disadvantages
» Microprocessor-controlled devices save energy because they are far more efficient and can, for example, switch themselves off after inactivity for a certain time period. » It can be easier 'programming' these devices to perform tasks rather than turning knobs and pressing buttons manually (for example, QR codes on the side of food packaging can simply be scanned and the oven automatically sets the cooking programme).	» The devices lead to a more wasteful society – it is usually not cost effective to repair circuit boards once they fail; the device is then usually just thrown away. » They can be more complex to operate for people who are technophobes or who are not very confident around electronic devices. » Leaving some devices on standby (such as televisions or satellite receivers) is very wasteful of electricity.

Data security issues

As mentioned in Table 5.1, having a microprocessor-controlled device connected to the internet can lead to cybersecurity issues. If you are able to communicate remotely with devices in your home, then so can a hacker. Any household device which can be remotely-controlled could allow a hacker to gain personal data about you. These devices are often set with a default (or no) password, making it easy for cybercriminals to obtain personal details. For example, by hacking into a central-heating controller (or the app used to communicate with the controller) it is possible to find out holiday dates, which then makes a home an easy target for break-ins. If the fridge/freezer automatically orders food from a supermarket, then it is possible for a hacker to gain key data, such as credit card numbers. It is therefore important to manage passwords (and have a different password on each device) and also install software updates, which often contain new security features.

Social interactions

There are both positive and negative impacts of microprocessor-controlled devices on social interactions to consider. While some devices leave people with more time to do things outside their home, other devices encourage people to stay at home. Devices, such as smartphones, smart televisions or tablets allow people to communicate from home using VoIP (a type of video conferencing), emails or chat rooms. The positive aspects include:

»» easier to make new friends using chat rooms
»» easier to find people who share similar interests/hobbies
»» less expensive to keep in touch using VoIP technology.

But the negative aspects include:

»» people do not meet face-to-face as much (social isolation)
»» a lack of social interaction may make people more anxious of meeting people in real life
»» people behave differently when interacting online – sometimes they can be ruder or more aggressive, and cyberbullying is a real problem, particularly for young people.

It is a balance that each individual needs to make. Please refer to Chapter 8 for further discussion on electronic communication methods.

5.1.2 Monitoring and controlling transport

The use of microprocessors in transport systems is becoming more and more widespread. Examples of where they are currently used include:

»» monitoring of traffic on motorways
»» congestion zone monitoring
»» automatic number plate recognition (ANPR)
»» automatic control of traffic lights
»» air traffic control systems
»» railway signalling systems.

As with any device containing a microprocessor, security is a big issue.

Control of smart road systems and smart signs

Many modern motorways are now called **smart motorways**. This is because the monitoring and control of the traffic and/or the information displayed on the motorway signs is controlled by a central computer system.

If there has been an accident or there is considerable traffic congestion, then smart motorway signs can control the traffic to keep it moving or redirect it to avoid the accident. Even the traffic lights in cities are now computer-controlled systems.

However, imagine the chaos that would be caused if any of these systems were hacked. Somebody could then have control over a chosen section of the road network. That has huge safety and security implications.

▲ **Figure 5.1** Smart motorway signs

Rail and airline network control systems

Safely coordinating the large number of trains and aeroplanes entering and leaving stations and airports is a complex task, but computerised monitoring systems make this possible. It is possible to run a more efficient timetable under total computer control.

Train and aeroplane journeys are also safer, because human error is removed – many rail accidents are caused by drivers making mistakes.

Advantages and disadvantages of these monitoring and control systems are summarised in Table 5.3.

▼ **Table 5.3** Advantages and disadvantages of transport monitoring and control systems

Advantages	Disadvantages
Smart motorways constantly adapt to traffic conditions, reducing traffic jams and minimising everyone's journey time.	A hacker could gain access to the computerised system and cause disruption.
Transport systems are more efficient – more cars, trains and aeroplanes can use the transport network, allowing for more regular services.	If the computer system fails then the whole transport system could be brought to a standstill.
Traffic offences (for example, driving in the wrong lane) can be automatically penalised using ANPR.	Poorly designed systems could compromise safety.
Stolen cars and criminals can be spotted using ANPR.	ANPR systems mean that innocent people's movements can easily be tracked. Who has access to that data?
Computerised control systems minimise human error, which reduces the rate of accidents.	

Autonomous vehicles in transport

Driverless (autonomous) vehicles are increasing in number every year. These are very complex robots, but the big problem is not really the technology (because problems will be solved over time) – it is human perception. It will take a large leap of faith for humans to ride in an autonomous car or an aeroplane with no pilot. We are already used to autonomous trains, as these are used in many cities throughout the world. These systems have been generally accepted; but that is probably because trains do not overtake other trains and have a very specific track to follow (see later).

Autonomous cars, buses and vans

In this section, we will consider autonomous cars as our example. Autonomous cars use sensors, cameras, actuators and microprocessors (together with very complex algorithms) to carry out their actions safely. Sensors (radar and ultrasonics) and cameras allow the control systems in cars to perform critical functions by sensing the dynamic conditions on a road. They act as the 'eyes' and 'ears' of the car.

Microprocessors process the data received from cameras and sensors and send signals to actuators to perform physical actions, such as:

» change gear
» apply the brakes
» turn the steering wheel.

Cameras catch visual data from the surroundings, while radar and ultrasonics allow the vehicle to build up a 3D image of its surroundings (very important when visibility is poor, such as in heavy rain, fog or at night).

Suppose an autonomous car is approaching a set of traffic lights which are showing red. The first thing the control system in the car needs to recognise is the road sign, and then check its database as to what action to take. Because the traffic light shows red, the microprocessor must send signals to actuators to apply brakes and put the gear into 'park'. Constant monitoring must take place until the light changes to green. When this happens, the microprocessor will again instruct actuators to put the car into first gear, release the brakes and operate the throttle (accelerator). This is a very complex set of operations because the microprocessor must constantly check all sensors and cameras to ensure moving off is safe (for example, has the car in front of it broken down or has a pedestrian started to cross the road, and so on). To go any further is outside the scope of this book.

Security and safety when using autonomous vehicles

Autonomous vehicles use sensors, cameras and microprocessors to 'understand' their immediate environment. These vehicles run using complex software systems and a large number of external sensors. This makes such vehicles rather vulnerable to cybercriminals. A hacker may not even have to break into the vehicle's control system; they may be able to cause many problems by blocking sensor information or sending false information back to the vehicle. There are many reasons why this would be of benefit to a hacker, but it is outside of the scope of this textbook. However, the hacker probably is not really interested in gaining control of the vehicle; they may be more interested in knowing where the car is, where it is going and finding personal information about the owner of the vehicle. Remember, these vehicles could be a car, a train or even an aeroplane – so the potential security and safety risks are vast.

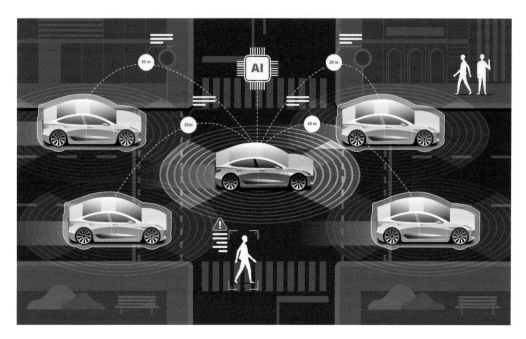

▲ **Figure 5.2** Autonomous car sensors

However, there are many positive sides to autonomous transport. If the security issues can be resolved, all forms of transport will become safer by removing the human element. Vehicles will be able to drive in cities or on the open road, for example, and be totally aware of their environment, thus removing many of the current safety issues (both to vehicle occupants and to pedestrians).

Table 5.4 considers some of the advantages and disadvantages specific to autonomous vehicles.

▼ **Table 5.4** Advantages and disadvantages of autonomous vehicles

Advantages	Disadvantages
Safer because human error is removed, leading to fewer accidents	Very expensive system to set up in the first place (high technology requirements)
Better for the environment because vehicles will operate more efficiently	The ever-present fear of hacking into the vehicle's control system
Reduced traffic congestion (humans cause 'stop-and-go' traffic known as 'the phantom traffic jam' – autonomous vehicles will be better at smoothing out traffic flow, reducing congestion in cities)	Security and safety issues (software glitches could be catastrophic; software updates would need to be carefully controlled to avoid potential disasters)
Increased lane capacity (research shows autonomous vehicles will increase lane capacity by 100% and increase average speeds by 20%, due to better braking and acceleration responses together with optimised distance between vehicles)	The need to make sure the system is well-maintained at all times; cameras need to be kept clean so that they do not give false results; sensors could fail to function in heavy snowfall or blizzard conditions (radar or ultrasonic signals could be deflected by heavy snow particles)
Reduced travel times (for the reasons above) therefore less commuting time	Driver and passenger reluctance of the new technology
Stress-free parking for motorists (the car will find car parking on its own and then self-park)	Reduction in the need for taxis could lead to unemployment (imagine New York without its famous yellow cabs!)

Autonomous trains

As mentioned earlier, autonomous (driverless) trains have been around for a number of years in a number of large cities. As with other autonomous vehicles, driverless trains make considerable use of sensors, cameras, actuators and on-board computers/microprocessors. Autonomous trains make use of a system called **LiDaR** (Light Detection and Ranging); LiDaR uses lasers which build up a 3D image of the surroundings. Other sensors (such as proximity sensors on train doors) and cameras (including infrared cameras) are all used for various purposes to help control the train and maintain safety. The control system in the

▲ **Figure 5.3** Autonomous train (London Transport)

train also makes use of global positioning satellite technology, which allows accurate changes in speed and direction to be calculated. Again, actuators pay a huge role here in controlling the train's speed, braking and the opening and closing of the train doors. The safety improvements made by these autonomous systems are fairly obvious.

Table 5.5 considers some of the advantages and disadvantages specific to autonomous trains.

▼ **Table 5.5** Advantages and disadvantages of autonomous trains

Advantages	Disadvantages
Improves the punctuality of the trains	The ever-present fear of hacking into the vehicle's control system
Reduced running costs (fewer staff are required)	System does not work well with very busy services (at the moment)
Improved safety because human error is removed	High capital costs and operational costs initially (that is, buying the trains, expensive signalling and control equipment and the need to train staff)
Minimises energy consumption because there is better control of speed and minimal delays (trains stuck in stations still use energy)	Ensuring passenger behaviour is acceptable, particularly during busy times (for example, jamming doors open on trains, standing too near the edge of platforms, and so on)
It is possible to increase the frequency of trains (automated systems allow for shorter times between trains)	Passenger reluctance of the new technology
It is easier to change train scheduling (for example, more trains during busier times)	No drivers mean there will be a need for CCTV to monitor railway stations

Autonomous (pilotless) aeroplanes

Aeroplanes have used auto-pilots for many years to control flights. Human pilots only take over during take-off and landing. Autonomous (pilotless) aeroplanes would make even more extensive use of sensors, actuators and microprocessors to control **all** stages of the flight. Some of the main features of a control system on a pilotless aeroplane would include:

» sensors to detect turbulence to ensure smooth flights
» an increase in self-testing of all circuits and systems
» sensors that would automatically detect depressurisation in the cabin, therefore allowing for quick stabilisation of the aeroplane
» use of GPS for navigation and speed calculations
» use of actuators to control, for example, throttle, flaps (on the wings) and the rudder.

Table 5.6 considers some of the advantages and disadvantages specific to pilotless aeroplanes.

▼ **Table 5.6** Advantages and disadvantages of pilotless aeroplanes

Advantages	Disadvantages
Improvement in passenger comfort (reasons given earlier)	Security aspects if no pilots on-board (for example, handling terrorist attacks)
Reduced running costs (fewer staff are required)	Emergency situations during the flight may be difficult to deal with
Improved safety (most crashes of aeroplanes have been attributed to pilot-induced errors)	Hacking into the system (it could be possible to access flight control via the aeroplane's entertainment system)
Improved aerodynamics at the front of the aeroplane because there would no longer be the need to include a cockpit for the pilots	Passenger reluctance to accept the new technology
	Software glitches (recent software issues with modern aeroplanes have highlighted that software glitches sometimes only surface a few years later, causing devastating results)

5.2 Potential health problems related to the prolonged use of IT equipment

Using IT equipment for long periods of time can impact on a user's health. Table 5.7 considers the most common health risks and shows ways to eliminate or reduce the risk.

▼ **Table 5.7** Health risks of using IT equipment

Health risk	Causes of health risk	Elimination or reduction of health risk
Back and neck strain	Caused by sitting in front of a computer screen for long periods of time	» Use fully adjustable chairs to give the correct posture » Use foot rests to reduce posture problems » Use tiltable screens, raised to the correct height, to ensure the neck is at the right angle
Repetitive strain injury (RSI)	Damage to fingers and wrists caused by continuous use of a keyboard or repetitive clicking of mouse buttons, for example	» Ensure correct posture is maintained (for example correct angle of arms to the keyboard and mouse) » Make proper use of a wrist rest when using a mouse or keyboard » Take regular breaks (+ exercise) » Make use of ergonomic keyboards » Use voice-activated software if the user is prone to problems using a mouse or keyboard
Eyestrain	Caused by staring at a computer screen for too long or by having incorrect lighting in the room (causing screen reflections)	» If necessary, change screens to LCD if older CRT screens are still used » Take regular breaks (+ exercise) » Make use of anti-glare screens if the room lighting is incorrect (or use window blinds to cut out direct sunlight) » Users should have their eyes tested on a regular basis (middle vision glasses should be prescribed if the user has a persistent problem with eye strain, dry eyes, headaches, etc.)
Headaches	Caused by incorrect lighting, screen reflections, flickering screens, and so on	» Make use of anti-glare screens if the room lighting is incorrect (or use window blinds to cut out reflections which cause squinting, leading to headaches) » Take regular breaks (+ exercise) » Users should have their eyes tested on a regular basis (middle vision glasses should be prescribed if the user has a persistent problem with headaches)
Ozone irritation	Caused by laser printers in an office (symptoms are dry skin and respiratory problems)	» Proper ventilation should exist to lower the ozone gas levels to acceptable values » Laser printers should be housed in a designated printer room » Change to using inkjet printers where possible

Exam-style questions

1 The use of microprocessor-controlled devices in the home affects an individual's leisure time, social interaction and the need to leave the home.

    a Give **three** advantages to the individual when microprocessor-controlled devices are used in the home. [3]

    b Give **three** disadvantages to the individual when microprocessor-controlled devices are used in the home. [3]

Cambridge IGCSE Information and Communication Technology (0417) Paper 13 Q15,
October/November 2014

2 You use a computer to do your homework. You are concerned about the health issues of using a computer.

Discuss the advantages and disadvantages of different methods you could use to help minimise the health problems of using the computer. [6]

Cambridge IGCSE Information and Communication Technology (0417) Paper 11 Q15,
May/June 2017

3 a There are potential security issues when using microprocessor-controlled devices in the home.

      Describe these issues and explain how they can be mitigated. [4]

    b Indicate which of the following statements are True or False by ticking (✓) the appropriate box. [5]

	True (✓)	False (✓)
Using microprocessors has increased the longevity of devices in the home, therefore reducing waste		
Microprocessor-controlled devices are far more energy efficient		
Smart televisions are an example of a labour-saving device		
Microprocessor-controlled devices in the home are not vulnerable to attack by viruses or hackers		
Microprocessor-controlled devices, such as smartphones, have no impact on social interactions		

4 Five statements are shown on the left and eleven ICT terms on the right.
Draw arrows to connect each statement to its correct term. [5]

Monitor

Name given to driverless vehicles, such as cars, vans and buses

Cybercriminal

Autonomous

A type of 'intelligent' road sign used to monitor and control road traffic

Regular

Smart

Name given to hackers and other people who try to break into ICT systems

Restorative

Automatic

Name of the type of risk associated with ozone gas reaching high levels

Repetitive

Clever

Health

Meaning of the letter 'R' in RSI

Control

5 a Describe the advantages of having major roads controlled and monitored by smart road signs. [3]
b Describe the risks of having smart road signs under computer control. [3]

6 ICT applications

This chapter will cover a number of different applications associated with the use of ICT. Many of the applications bring together notes from earlier and later chapters in this book. There are many more examples of the use of ICT, and you may wish to investigate other uses within the framework of syllabus requirements.

Exercises throughout the chapter, and exam-style questions at the end of the chapter, will allow you to test your understanding of the various ICT applications which have been covered.

6.1 Communication

There are several communication systems that make use of ICT technology. For example:

» newsletters and posters
» websites
» multimedia presentations
» media streaming
» e-publications.

6.1.1 Communication media

Newsletters and posters

Newsletters and posters can be produced very easily using, most commonly, a **word processor.** Often, the newsletter or poster will have photos which have been taken specially or have been downloaded from the internet (with the permission of the copyright holder). The following sequence is fairly typical of how such a document would be produced on a computer system. The sequence is not always necessarily in the order shown; it can vary depending on what already exists or what needs to be created):

» First a word-processor application would be opened
» Photos could be obtained by:
  – using a digital camera and taking photos
  – searching for images/photos on the internet, or suitable photos could already be stored on the hard drive or cloud
  – using hard copy photos, which could be scanned in.
» If necessary, camera images would then be uploaded (either by connecting the camera or camera memory card) to the computer via a USB port, or by using Bluetooth connectivity).
» Photos from all selected sources would then be saved to a file on the HDD or SSD.
» When the user is finally ready to produce the document, the photos would be imported from the file stored on the HDD/SSD.
» Once imported, photos would need to be cropped, edited and/or resized.
» Text would be typed in using a keyboard.
» Alternatively, any previously saved text would need to be imported.
» Photos need to be placed in their correct position and the text wrapped.
» Finally, the whole document would need to undergo proofreading for errors and then saved, ready for printing.

Very often, other features, such as a spell checker, would be used to make sure no mistakes had been made. Care needs to be taken when using a spell checker for the following reasons:

» The language used in checking the spelling could be different; for example, British English and American English often have different spellings of words.
» Names or proper nouns might be highlighted as an error by the spell checker, but may be acceptable.
» Similar sounding words need to be checked; for example, where, were or wear all sound the same but have very different meanings – these will not be picked up by the spell checker (but might be picked up by a grammar checker).
» The (correct) highlighted word may not exist in the spell checker dictionary.

> **Exercise 6a**
>
> Find out what other word-processing features would need to be used when producing a newsletter or poster. For each feature identified, write down how you would use it to produce a professional-looking document.

Link

Other word-processing features could be used when producing the newsletter or poster; refer to Chapter 17 for more information.

A **newsletter** is a very useful method for getting important information to a target group. If, for example, you are doing a fundraising exercise, a well-presented newsletter to accompany the fundraising would be invaluable. Newsletters can be either printed out or available online as an e-publication (see later in this chapter); the method used depends on who the target audience is. With a printed document handed personally to somebody, you can be certain they have seen the newsletter – but in both cases it is nearly impossible to be certain that they have read it!

A few of the common guidelines to produce an attractive newsletter include:

» Do not try and squeeze too much information onto one page.
» Use very clear, easy-to-read fonts (for example, Arial or Trebuchet MS) and use a suitable font size (11-, 12- or 14-point font size).
» Decide on whether to use columns (a useful feature if there are diagrams and photos).
» Avoid using capital letters as this appears to be 'shouting'!
» Use bold text in headings rather than underlining text.
» Use real photos rather than clip art to make the newsletter more interesting.

Posters are a good way of publicising, for example, a sporting event or an advertisement for a forthcoming movie. A sporting event poster would need to include at least the following information:

» what the event is and where it will take place
» date, time and place of event
» admission fees (if any)
» contact details
» other information (such as whether there will be a crèche or facilities for people with disabilities).

The movie poster would need to include:

» an image taken from the movie to give some idea of the type of movie (that is, comedy, horror, science fiction, and so on)
» the date of release
» a list of the main characters.

Exercise 6b

Using a word processor, produce two posters for the following:

a an upcoming charity event where there will be stalls selling food and gifts

b a music band advertising the release of their new song.

Refer to chapters in the second half of this book wherever necessary.

▲ **Figure 6.1** Examples of posters

As with newsletters, posters can be printed out using high-quality printers or can be posted online. Printed posters can be any size. Large posters have the advantage that they are eye-catching and usually very difficult to miss. They are used in many countries on the sides of roads so motorists see them on their way to work. By placing the posters in strategic positions, it is possible to target certain people rather than the general public (for example, advertising expensive cars by placing the posters on buildings or advertising hoardings in financial districts in big cities). The drawback is the cost of display (the advertising areas can only be rented) and that they are subject to weather conditions, so only have a limited life.

Websites

Rather than producing newsletters and posters by printing them out, it is possible to use websites for advertising. This method of advertising requires a company to either develop their own website or pay another company to advertise on their website.

Using the first option may require the company to either employ a team of web designers or go to a specialist company with experience in website design. It may also be necessary to buy hardware and software to develop and store the website. This method can therefore be expensive, but the cost does not stop there. It will be necessary to use programmers to make sure that their website is safe from hackers and from pharming attacks.

It has, however, become much easier and cheaper for individuals or small organisations to create and host their own website, using off-the-shelf content management systems to organise content, and pay hosting fees to rent space on a **web server**.

The big advantage to websites is that they offer worldwide advertising capability and there is no need to buy paper and other consumables, or pay people to deliver newsletters or flyers. Before deciding which is the best way to advertise their goods or services, companies have to weigh up the advantages and disadvantages of both methods.

Websites tend to be used to advertise goods or services which require national or international coverage. They can cover almost anything from car sales to advertising a musician's forthcoming album. The main reasons for using websites, rather than newsletters or posters for advertising products and services, are summarised in Table 6.1.

▼ **Table 6.1** Advantages and disadvantages of using websites for communication

Advantages	Disadvantages
» sound/video/animation can be added » links to other pages and websites can be added in hyperlinks and hot spots » buttons to navigate/move around the website, leading to more information » 'hit counters' allow the owner to see detailed information about how many people have visited the website » can be seen by a global audience » cannot be defaced or thrown away » it is much easier to update a website (and there is no need to do a reprint and then distribute the new version)	» websites can be hacked into and modified or viruses introduced » risk of potential pharming » it is necessary for the potential customers to have a computer and internet connection » it is not as portable as a paper-based system (although with modern smartphones and phablets this is fast becoming untrue) » possible for customers to go to undesirable websites (either by accident or as a result of a pharming attack) – this can lead to distrust from customers » there is a need for the company to maintain the website once it is set up – this can be expensive » because it is a global system, it is more difficult to target the correct audience using website advertising » still need to find a way for people to find out about the website

Multimedia presentations

Presentations that use animation, video and sound or music are generally much more interesting than static presentations done on slides or paper.

Presentations are produced using one of the many software packages on the market and then used with a **multimedia projector** so that the whole audience is able to see the presentation. There are many advantages and disadvantages for this type of presentation, with some examples listed below.

Advantages of multimedia presentations

» use of sound and animation/video effects which are more likely to grab the attention of the audience, and can make the presentation easier to understand
» possible to have interactive hyperlinks built into the presentation; this means the presentation could access a company's website or even key files stored on the cloud (such as video footage, images, spreadsheets and so on)
» use of transition effects allow a presentation to display facts in a key or chronological order
» can be interactive
» more flexible; because of the links to websites and other external systems (for example, the cloud), the presentation can be tailored to suit a particular audience.

Disadvantages of multimedia presentations

» a need to have special equipment which can be expensive
» danger that equipment could fail while giving multimedia presentations
» there may need to be internet access
» danger when using multimedia in presentations that the focus is on the medium (that is, the multimedia presentation) rather than the message or facts
» very easy to make a bad presentation with too many animation effects and too much text or images.

> **Link**
> Refer to Chapter 19 for more information on producing presentations.

Media streaming

Media **streaming** is when users watch movies/videos or listen to music on devices connected to the internet. When using media streaming there is no need to actually download and save the video or audio files.

Streaming is a continuous transmission of video or audio files from a remote server where the files are stored. This means data is transmitted and played in real time. In contrast, when downloading it is necessary for the user to store the entire file on the computer's HDD or SSD before they can watch the video or listen to the music. This uses up valuable storage space and download times for a two-hour video can be up to one hour, depending on the internet speed and the video quality.

With streaming, the file is sent as a series of packets of data. Each packet is interpreted by the web browser. Streaming only works well if the internet speed is stable, and at least 25 Mbits/second (for an HD video).

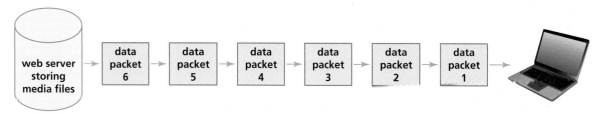

▲ **Figure 6.2** Media streaming data packets

Because the playback of the media files is usually much faster than the rate at which data is received over the internet, data packets are buffered in the computer. **Buffering** makes sure the video plays back smoothly without freezing. While the buffer is receiving data packets, it will be sending the data from the previous data packets to the playback device. In this way, there appears to be no gaps in the received data. Obviously, having a large buffer will considerably reduce the possibility of freezing the play back.

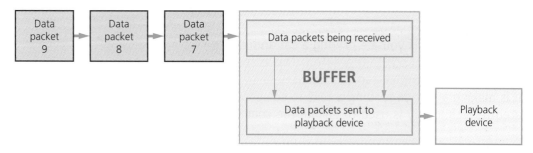

▲ **Figure 6.3** Buffering of media stream

e-publications

Most material which is published on paper is also available in an electronic format. For example:

» e-books
» digital magazines
» digital newspapers
» digital libraries.

In all cases, the publication can be downloaded to a device connected to the internet where it can be read. Moving between pages is usually done by swiping a finger across the screen. E-publications also have the advantage that pages can be expanded in size and it is possible to include media, which would be impossible with the more traditional paper-based publications. Specific devices, such as the *Kindle*, have been developed to allow a library of e-books to be stored on the device. These devices use a white background with black text to fully replicate reading a normal book. Because no printing costs are incurred, e-publications are usually cheaper than their paper-based counterparts.

> ## ▶ Exercise 6c
> Write down as many advantages and disadvantages you can think of for offering customers e-publications rather than paper-based publications. Write a paragraph describing each advantage and disadvantage.

6.1.2 Mobile communication

Mobile phones communicate by using towers inside many cells networked together to cover large areas. The towers allow the transmission of data throughout the mobile phone network.

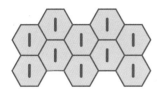

Cell showing tower at the centre. Each cell overlaps giving mobile phone coverage

▲ **Figure 6.4** Each cell overlaps, giving mobile phone coverage.

Each tower transmits within its own cell. If you are driving a car and get to the edge of a cell, the mobile phone signal starts to weaken. This is recognised by the network and the mobile phone then picks up the signal in one of the adjacent cells. If a person is making a call or sending a text to somebody in a different country, then satellite technology is used to enable the communication to take place.

Mobile devices either use a **SIM (subscriber identity module) card** to allow it to connect to the mobile phone cellular network, or they use wireless internet connectivity. Together they allow all of the following features:

» SMS (short message service) messaging
» phone calls
» Voice over Internet Protocol (VoIP) communication
» video calling
» internet access.

SMS (text) messaging

SMS or **text messaging** allows a very quick way of communicating with another person by typing on a keyboard (the keyboard is often virtual on a mobile phone or tablet). Its advantage is that the other person does not need to be available, and can pick up the message as and when they want. SMS/text messaging between phones using the same cellular network may be free-of-charge. Some of the features of SMS/text messaging include:

» quicker and less expensive than making phone calls
» can be sent at any time of the day even if the recipient's phone is switched off
» predictive texting, where the system completes a word from the first few letters keyed in; for example, key in 'preci' and the phone completes the word as 'precious'; predictive texting also allows the system to remember frequently used words – together they increase typing speed.

Phone calls

Probably the most obvious use of a mobile phone is its ability to make a phone call on the move. Because mobile phones are so small and they have their own power source, they are an ideal way of keeping in touch anywhere, provided there is a network signal. Mobile phone networks are still not as stable as landline systems and for that reason alone, landline phones are still in common use.

Using mobile phones to make phone calls has the following advantages:

- » There is no need to look for an operational public telephone in an emergency.
- » It is possible to conduct business or personal phone calls on the move.
- » It is easier to keep in contact with co-workers at the office no matter where you are.

Voice over Internet Protocol (VoIP) and video calling

One of the most common forms of internet telephony (that is, having a telephone conversation via the internet) is **Voice over Internet Protocol (VoIP)**.

Voice over Internet Protocol (VoIP) is a method used to talk to people using the internet. VoIP converts sound, picked up by the mobile device's internal microphone, into discrete digital data packets that can be sent to their destination via the internet. The internet can be accessed via a mobile phone network or a broadband network and the voice calls are sent over the internet using VoIP technology.

One of the big advantages is that phone calls themselves are free, no matter where in the world the caller and receiver are (there may be a cost to send lots of data over the internet via a mobile phone network, however).

The main problems are usually sound quality (echo and 'weird sounds' are both common faults). Security is also a main concern with VoIP, as it is with other internet technologies. The most prominent security issues over VoIP are identity theft, viruses and malware (malicious software), spamming (unwanted emails) and phishing attacks (the act of sending an email to a user, falsely claiming to be an established legitimate enterprise, in an attempt to scam the user into surrendering private information that will be used for identity theft).

One of the big advantages of using VoIP is that the device's built-in cameras can also be used so that it becomes a type of video call. While this does not have the sophistication of a true video conference, it is much cheaper (no need for special software and additional hardware items – VoIP uses built-in microphones, speakers and cameras). This relies on good broadband or mobile phone network coverage.

Video calling uses software such as *FaceTime* or *Zoom*. Both these options require the user to download an app. *FaceTime* makes use of the built-in smartphone cameras and microphone/speakers. A split screen allows you to see a number of people at the same time; although the small screen size limits the potential of this feature. *Zoom* is a cloud-based video calling service that allows live video chatting on any device. It is also possible to record sessions to be played back at a later date. Cloud-based video calling prevents the need for users to invest in expensive infrastructure; users can simply dial into a virtual meeting room which makes it much cheaper than conventional video conferencing.

> **Link**
>
> For more information on the features of mobile phones, refer back to Chapter 1.

> **Link**
>
> For more on security threats see Section 8.3.

Video calls permit:

» live video and audio chat
» screen-sharing during the call
» recording during sessions.

Internet access

Access to the internet from a mobile device is another valuable feature. Any mobile device can connect to the internet either using a wireless broadband connection or via the mobile phone network. Due to the use of smaller screens, internet pages displayed on mobile phones are often different to those on desktop or laptop computers. Software detects which type of device is connecting to a website, which then sends out the web page optimised for that device. Mobile devices also have a built-in feature which automatically selects wireless broadband connectivity (if possible), instead of the mobile phone network, when connecting to the internet. This has the following advantages:

» less expensive (mobile phone company 'data plans' often have a cap on how much data can be downloaded, and charge for exceeding this maximum)
» lower power consumption (Wi-Fi routers are usually much closer than the mobile phone towers; the longer the range, the greater the power consumption)
» quality of service (Wi-Fi usually offers greater bandwidth than the mobile phone network giving the possibility of downloading more data more quickly).

▲ **Figure 6.5** Cloud video calling

> **Link**
> ....
> See Chapter 4 for more on Wi-Fi networks.

6.2 Modelling applications

6.2.1 Computer modelling

A **simulation** is the creation of a model of a real system in order to study the behaviour of the system. The model is computer-generated and is based on mathematical representations.

The whole idea is to try and find out how a system behaves, predict the behaviour of the system in the future and see if it is possible to influence this future behaviour.

Advantages of using models

» Using computer models is less expensive than having to build the real thing (for example, a bridge!).
» On many occasions it is safer to use a computer model (some real situations are hazardous, for example, chemical processes).
» Computer modelling allows you to try out various different scenarios in advance.
» It is nearly impossible to try out some tasks in advance in real life because of the high risk involved or the remoteness (for example, in space, under the sea, in nuclear reactors, when crash testing cars, etc.).
» It is often faster to use a computer model than do the real thing (some applications would take years before a result was known, for example, climate-change calculations, population growth, etc.).

Disadvantages of using models

» A model is only as good as the programming or the data entered; the simulation will depend heavily on these two factors.
» Although building the real thing can be expensive, sometimes computer modelling is also a very costly option, and the two costs need to be compared before deciding which to use.
» People's reactions to the results of a simulation may not be positive; they may not trust the results it produces (there will always be a difference between the results from modelling and reality).

Examples where computer modelling is used include:

» personal finance
» bridge and building design
» flood water management
» traffic management
» weather forecasting.

Personal finance

Figure 6.6 uses a spreadsheet to model the sales of a tuck shop in a school.

	A	B	C	D	E	F	G
1	Item	Price	Selling	Profit	Weekly	Number	Total Profit
2		each ($)	price ($)	per item	shop cost	sold per	item ($)
3					($)		
4	chew	1.00	1.50	0.50		35	17.50
5	chox	2.00	2.50	0.50		45	22.50
6	gum	3.00	3.50	0.50		30	15.00
7	crisps	1.00	1.50	0.50		45	22.50
8	cake	2.00	2.50	0.50		40	20.00
9							
10					200.00	profit/Loss: $	-102.50

The formulae behind this spreadsheet are:

	A	B	C	D	E	F	G
1	Item	Price	Selling	Profit	Weekly	Number	Total Profit
2		each ($)	price ($)	per item	shop cost	sold per	item ($)
3					($)		
4	chew	1.00	1.50	= (C4-B4)		35	= (C4*F4)
5	chox	2.00	2.50	= (C5-B5)		45	= (C5*F5)
6	gum	3.00	3.50	= (C6-B6)		30	= (C6*F6)
7	crisps	1.00	1.50	= (C7-B7)		45	= (C7*F7)
8	cake	2.00	2.50	= (C8-B8)		40	= (C8*F8)
9							
10					200.00	profit/Loss: $	=sum(G4:G8)-E10

▲ **Figure 6.6** Personal finance modelling using a spreadsheet

By varying the values in column C or in column F, it would be possible to model the shop's profit or loss. This example is a very simple model, but it shows the principal of using spreadsheets to carry out any type of modelling that can be represented in a mathematical form. Spreadsheets are often used in some form to carry out financial modelling.

Bridge and building design

When an engineer or architect designs a new building or bridge, it is necessary to test the design long before any construction work is started. 3D computer modelling is used to try out a number of scenarios to ensure the final design meets critical criteria. Simulation of the final structure is often done as a combination of computer modelling and wind-tunnel tests on scale models of the final designs. For example, when building a bridge, the modeller has to consider a number of scenarios:

» the amount of traffic that might be caught in a traffic jam on the bridge in the event of an accident; this could lead to very heavy loading on the bridge structure
» the effects of strong winds; can the bridge design withstand the worst-case scenario?
» the effect of earthquakes; is the bridge earthquake-proof?
» the effect of tidal waves and ice floes during extreme weather conditions; can the pillars supporting the bridge withstand these conditions?
» the effects of vibrations – there have been cases over the years where bridges have collapsed due to, for example, wind causing the bridge to sway at its 'natural frequency'.

▲ **Figure 6.7** Wind-tunnel tests on a new bridge design

All of these scenarios can be tested using a computer model. The design can then be modified on the computer if any of the above scenarios caused the bridge to fail. After a number of modifications, a final design will be decided on. To ensure the computer model gives good results, a scale model of the bridge would then be constructed and subjected to wind-tunnel (and other) trials.

Similar methods are used when designing new buildings, particularly skyscrapers. Again, computer models are used, often in conjunction with wind-tunnel tests on a scale model. When testing the building using a computer model, a number of scenarios need to be considered:

» what is the effect of natural phenomena, such as hurricane winds, flooding, earthquakes and any other potentially damaging phenomena (wind movement is a key issue with tall buildings; a 100-storey building may sway one metre to the left and then one metre to the right, cycling every ten seconds, in strong winds – can the building survive such movement, will such movement be unpleasant or frightening to human occupants, and so on)
» the effect of a disaster, such as a fire – how does the structure stand up to such scenarios?
» how is it possible to move people around the building efficiently (some large structures have over 5000 people working in them and there is a need to model elevator movements to move people efficiently)?

All of these scenarios can be tested using a computer model. The design can then be modified on the computer if any of the above scenarios caused the building to fail to meet any of its design criteria. After a number of modifications, a final design will be decided on. To ensure the computer model gives good results, a scale model of the building is then constructed and it is subjected to wind-tunnel trials:

▲ **Figure 6.8** Scale models are used to test buildings.

Computer modelling provides the following features:

» It is possible to zoom into images so that fine details can be seen.
» The design can be rotated in a number of different ways to allow different views of the design to be made.
» Building a bridge or building is expensive and dangerous if the final design had a serious flaw; modelling should allow any potential design flaws to be detected before any construction starts.
» Various scenarios can be tried out to see the effect on the design (see earlier list of scenarios).

Flood water management

Flood water management uses computer modelling to perform a risk assessment to identify sources of potential flooding, the extent of flooding and how any mitigation or protection measures could work.

Computer models are used to predict water levels, water flows and potential flood depths. Input to the system could include:

» cross-section of rivers and sea inlets (for example, bottlenecks)
» dimensions of any bridges, weirs or sluices in the flood area
» factors that can affect water flow rates (for example, tides are affected by the time of year and by strong winds)
» boundary conditions (for example, upstream flows into rivers and downstream water levels)
» the start and finishing date for the simulation
» calibration data (observation of actual flooding in the past).

Once a model exists which simulates the area where there is potential flooding, a plan can be put forward to guard against future flooding. Data is continuously added to the model once the flood defences have been put into place. This could result in further flood defences being built, or modifications to the existing system.

Figure 6.9 shows the management of the flood protection system in the city of Venice as an example.

Flooding of the city over many years has led to the building of a number of flood barriers. It is useful to use computer models to understand how these flood barriers will react to a range of possible flooding scenarios. It is possible to try out several different solutions, using the model, before actually building any flood defences. Following the computer modelling results, Venice decided to develop a computer-based system rather than build a manual flood defence system. The main advantages of doing this are:

▲ **Figure 6.9** Flood management barriers

» Sensors could be used out in the bay area to monitor sea height and wave height (and possibly other factors, such as wind speeds); using sensors would give a much faster response to any deteriorating conditions in the bay.
» Using a computer system is safer, since using humans to monitor conditions could potentially put them at risk.
» Data collection is continuous and more accurate than manual measurements (readings can also be taken more frequently).
» Because of the faster response to changing conditions, city dwellers can be warned well in advance of any flooding actually taking place.
» Data from the sensors could also be fed into the simulation modelling the flood area; this could lead to further improvements as more data is gathered, which means the simulation becomes closer to reality.

Traffic management

Computer modelling can be used in traffic management. We will consider two different situations.

Closure of motorway lanes

Repairs need to be made to part of the central barriers on an eight-lane motorway. The company given the task of carrying out these repairs needs to model the impact of the roadworks on the traffic flow. They have decided there are two ways of controlling traffic which need to be modelled. The two models shown in Figure 6.10 will appear on the computer screens, representing the motorway lanes.

The company will run model 'A' and model 'B' using different traffic densities at different times of the day to see which one allows for the best traffic flow. The

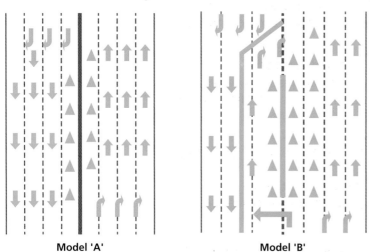

Model 'A'   Model 'B'

▲ **Figure 6.10** Motorway closures model

model will also try out the effect of different speed limits through the roadworks. They will also simulate the effects of a breakdown to see how this would impact on the traffic flow. By changing conditions in the simulation, it becomes possible to find an optimum design which allows the traffic to flow freely, but also allows the repairs to be done as quickly as possible. This is considerably safer, cheaper and much quicker than trying out different traffic closures on a real motorway.

Traffic light simulation

Figure 6.11 shows a second use of computer modelling in traffic management – a set of traffic lights are to be modelled at a Y-junction.

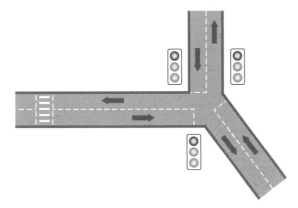

▲ **Figure 6.11** Traffic light simulation

In this simulation it is necessary to consider:

1 how and what data needs to be collected
2 how the simulation is carried out
3 how the system would work in real life.

How and what data needs to be collected?

Because the success (or failure) of a model depends on how realistic it is, data needs to be collected by watching traffic for a long period of time at the Y-junction. This is best done by using induction loop sensors which count the number of vehicles at each junction. Manual data collection is possible, but is prone to errors and is difficult to do over an 18-hour period per day (for example). The following data is an indication of what would need to be collected:

» the number of vehicles passing the junction in all directions
» the time of day needs to be recorded along with a vehicle count
» how many vehicles build up at the junction at different times of the day
» data should cover weekends, bank holidays, etc. as this can alter how the data needs be interpreted
» how long it takes a vehicle to clear the junction
» other data needs to be considered (for example, pedestrian crossings nearby, as shown in Figure 6.11)
» how long it takes the slowest vehicle to pass through the junction
» consider other factors (for example, left turns, right turns, filtering, etc.).

How is the simulation carried out?

Data from the above list is entered into the computer and the computer model is run. Once the designers are satisfied that the model simulates the real situation accurately (that is, by comparing the model's results with actual traffic flow data) then different scenarios can be tried out. For example:

» varying the timing of the lights and observing how the traffic flow was affected
» changing the number of vehicles stopped at part of the junction and then changing the timing of the lights to see how the traffic flow is affected
» increasing or decreasing traffic flow in all directions
» considering how emergency vehicles affect traffic flow at different times of the day.

How would the system work in real life?

» Sensors in the road gather data and count the number of vehicles at the junction.
» This data is sent to a control box or to a computer (it will need to be converted first into a form understood by the computer).
» The gathered data is compared to data stored in the system (the stored data is based on model/simulation predictions which were used to optimise the traffic flow).
» The control box or computer 'decides' what action needs to be taken.
» Signals are then sent out to the traffic lights to change their timing if necessary.

Weather forecasting

Weather stations are set up to automatically gather data from the environment. They are usually automatic and use a variety of sensors to measure:

» rainfall
» temperature
» wind speed
» wind direction
» barometric pressure (air pressure)
» humidity.

The data needs to be gathered every hour of every day of the week. This data can then be input into a model which simulates weather patterns. By running the computer model, weather forecasters can predict the weather for the next few days or even longer. The foundation for weather models are complex mathematical equations that represent air movement and how heat and moisture are exchanged in the atmosphere. In a model, the atmosphere is divided up into a three-dimensional grid. The data from the weather stations is input into the appropriate grid and the model is run forward in time to make predictions.

» Data is input into the model and a prediction of the weather for the next few days is made.
» At the end of the weather forecast period, the model compares its weather forecast with the actual weather that occurred.
» The model 'learns' from previous weather situations; improvements to how it predicts weather are constantly made.
» The new data is then input into the model, and a weather forecast for the next few days is made.
» A very powerful computer is needed to run this model, since it has to 'number crunch' vast amounts of data.

Weather modelling is often shown in animated format where cloud, rain, sun and wind are projected on top of a map of the country and shown in real time (Figure 6.12).

> **Link**
>
> Also refer to Section 6.10, which describes the use of automated number plate recognition (ANPR) systems – another way to carry out traffic management.

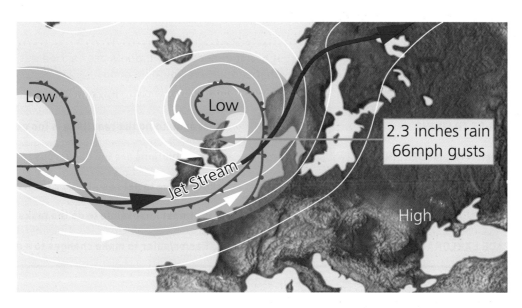

▲ **Figure 6.12** Animated weather forecast

> ## Exercise 6d

Create a spreadsheet to do some personal financial modelling. Include the monthly income in one row and then show all the monthly outgoings. For example:

	A	B	C	D	E	F	G
		Month 1	Month 2	Month 3	Month 4	Totals	
Income ($):							
Outgoings:	food						
	cinema						
	clothes						
	other						
	savings						

Extend the list as much as you want or change the outgoings to be more realistic if necessary. Insert some values into the spreadsheet and then change a few values to see the effect on your finances. Add extra columns or extra outgoings to extend the spreadsheet. Finally, try creating a graph of your income against outgoings for each month and for a year (do a prediction for the year after four months, for example).

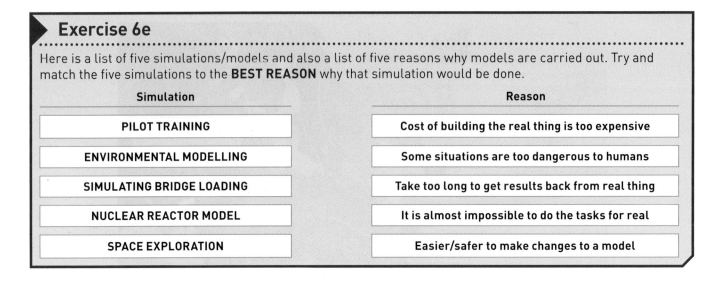

▶ **Exercise 6e**

Here is a list of five simulations/models and also a list of five reasons why models are carried out. Try and match the five simulations to the **BEST REASON** why that simulation would be done.

Simulation	Reason
PILOT TRAINING	Cost of building the real thing is too expensive
ENVIRONMENTAL MODELLING	Some situations are too dangerous to humans
SIMULATING BRIDGE LOADING	Take too long to get results back from real thing
NUCLEAR REACTOR MODEL	It is almost impossible to do the tasks for real
SPACE EXPLORATION	Easier/safer to make changes to a model

6.3 Computer controlled systems

6.3.1 Computer controlled systems

Robotics in manufacturing

Robots are used in many areas of manufacturing, from heavy work right through to delicate operations. Examples include: paint spraying of car bodies, welding bodywork on cars, manufacturing of microchips, manufacturing electrical goods and stock movement in automatic warehouses.

Control of robots is either through embedded (built-in) microprocessors or linked to a computer system. Programming of the robot to do a series of tasks is generally done in two ways:

1 The robot is programmed with a sequence of instructions which allow it to carry out the series of tasks (for example, spraying a car body with paint).
2 Alternatively, a human operator manually carries out the series of tasks; this can be done in two ways:
  i The robot arm is guided by a worker when spraying the object; each movement of the arm is stored as an instruction in the computer.

  OR
  ii The worker straps sensors to his own arm and sprays the object; each movement is stored as a set of instructions in a computer; the sensors send back information such as position relative to the object, arm rotation, and so on – this information forms part of the instructions stored in the computer.

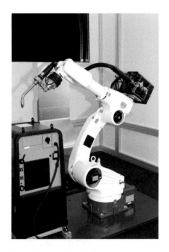

▲ **Figure 6.13** This robot arm is equipped with a spray gun 'end effector'. Different end effectors allow the robot arm to carry out many different tasks.

Whichever method is used, once the instructions have been saved, each series of tasks can then be carried out by a robot arm automatically. Each instruction will be carried out identically every time (for example, assembling parts in a television) giving a consistent product.

Robots are equipped with sensors so they can gather important information about their surroundings and prevent them from doing 'stupid things'; for example, stopping a robot spraying a car if no car is present, or stop the spraying operation if the supply of paint has run out, etc.

Robots are very good at repetitive tasks. However, if there are many different tasks to carry out (for example, making specialist glassware for some scientific work), then it is often better to use human operators.

Advantages in using robots

» They can work in environments harmful to human operators.
» They can work non-stop (24/7).
» They are less expensive in the long term (although expensive to buy initially, they do not need wages).
» They have higher productivity (do not need holidays, etc.).
» They provide greater consistency (for example, **every** car coming off a production line is identical).
» They can do boring, repetitive tasks, leaving humans free to do other more skilled work (for example, quality control or design work).
» They can carry out different tasks by fitting them with different end-effectors (attachments); for example, a spray gun, a welding gun, and so on.

Disadvantages in using robots

» Robots find it difficult to do 'unusual' tasks (for example, one-off glassware for a chemical company).
» They can cause higher unemployment (replacing skilled labour).
» Because robots do many of the tasks once done by humans, there is a real risk of certain skills (such as welding) being lost.
» Because robots are independent of the skills base, factories can be moved anywhere in the world (again causing unemployment).
» The initial set-up and maintenance of robots can be expensive.

Production line control

Production line control using robots is used extensively in industry. For example:

» filling bottles with a liquid, capping the bottle and applying a label
» filling metal cans with baked beans, sealing the cans and applying labels.

The production line will be continuous, with various robots at each station given a specific task. Using robots in this way leads to:

» faster operations (the number of cans of baked beans filled is 120 per minute)
» much greater productivity (the production can run 24 hours a day for every day)
» greater consistency (every can contains exactly the correct weight of baked beans)
» built-in quality control (automatic testing for foreign material, such as metal filings, which would result in automatic rejection from the production line)
» reduced cost to the consumer (although initial robot arms are expensive, there are far fewer staff in the factory who would need wages).

Let us take a closer view of how robots could be used in a bottling plant.

» Sensor 1 (a pressure sensor, light sensor or camera) detects the presence of a bottle; this sensor is constantly sending signals back to the computer.
» When the signal from sensor 1 indicates a bottle is present, the computer sends a signal to an actuator which opens a valve allowing liquid to flow into the bottle.
» Sensor 2 (a level sensor) is used to detect the correct liquid height in the bottle; this sensor sends continuous signals back to the computer.

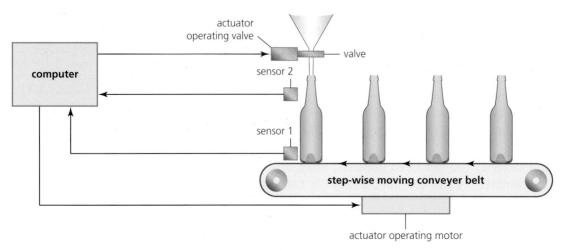

▲ **Figure 6.14** Bottling plant

» When the signal from sensor 2 indicates the bottle is full, the computer sends a signal to an actuator to close the valve.
» The computer then sends another signal to a second actuator which operates a motor to move the conveyer belt to allow the next empty bottle to take its correct position.
» The whole process is continuous until stopped for maintenance, errors occurring or a change in the process.

> ### Exercise 6f
>
> Find out about five industrial processes that use production line control.
>
> In each case, find out the functions of robots at each stage in the process.
>
> In each case, find the advantages and disadvantages of using robots on the production line

6.4 School management systems

6.4.1 School management systems

Schools have to manage a number of different tasks in their day-to-day running. These tasks include:

» registration and attendance records of students
» student performance
» computer-aided learning.

Registration and attendance records of students

The traditional way to record the registration and attendance of a student was to complete daily registers. This was very time consuming because it required a ten-minute session at the beginning and end of each day. It was also prone to error if a student's name was missed at some point during the registration process.

There are a number of possible ways of automating the registration process using hardware and software, some of which are included below.

Method 1

Issue each student with an ID card. These contain a magnetic stripe (shown in black) on the rear of the card. The student would have to sign the card and also write their unique student ID on the back of the card. The magnetic stripe would contain the name of the school, the name of the student, the student's data of birth and their unique ID (registration) number.

▲ **Figure 6.15** Student registration card

Each morning the student would arrive at school and swipe their ID card through a magnetic card reader. The data read would identify the student and the time and date they entered the school's premises. This data would now be stored on a database. On leaving the school (either at lunchtime or at the end of the day), the ID card would again be swiped. This would now record the leaving time and date on the database. This would give a very comprehensive record of when the student attended the school and the number of hours they attended. It would also be a more secure method in the event of, for example, a fire. Using the paper-based system, a student could register then just go home, but with an ID card system, the student's attendance would be known at all times. The school would now be able to account for every student on the school premises. At the end of a semester (or school year), the database could be interrogated and it would give an accurate attendance record for the student. This attendance record could then be sent out to parents or checked by teachers on a regular basis.

There are further functions that could be used such as:

» the use of a PIN to stop another student swiping in with the wrong card
» the use of GPS tracking (see Section 6.11) so the exact whereabouts of a student would be known; this would require the addition of a chip in the ID card so that the tracking system could identify them (see Section 6.11 for information on RFID) – however, there are privacy concerns surrounding location tracking.

Method 2

A second method could make use of biometrics. Each student would have their fingerprints recorded. Their personal details (as in Method 1) plus fingerprints would be stored on a database. When a student entered the school premises, they would be asked to put their hand on a scanner which would read their fingerprints. Because each student has unique fingerprints, this system would be very secure. As with Method 1, the date and time of entering or leaving the school would be accurately recorded on the database.

Advantages of this method compared to use of magnetic ID cards

» Fingerprints are unique, so it would be impossible for a student to sign in pretending to be someone else (with magnetic cards, a student could give their card to a friend and ask them to sign in for them) – this gives more accurate data and improved security.
» ID cards could easily be lost – fingerprints are 'part of you' so cannot be lost.
» ID cards could be affected by magnetic fields (for example, by being placed close to a mobile phone) which would stop them working properly.
» It is much easier to 'clone' (make copies of) ID cards than it would be to copy fingerprints (not impossible but very difficult).

Disadvantages of this method compared to use of magnetic ID cards

» It would take a long time to collect the fingerprints for every student in the school.
» The equipment needed to take and read fingerprints is more expensive than magnetic stripe reading equipment.
» If a student cuts a finger, the fingerprint may not be identified by the system (which would prevent entry to the school).
» There are invasion-of-privacy issues and a number of students and parents may object to having fingerprints stored on a database.

Student performance

Teachers could make considerable use of spreadsheets to monitor the performance of their students. Essentially, spreadsheets could record the test results of each student over a term/year. This would allow a teacher to easily see how they were performing against other students in the same subjects. It would also be easy to import data into a report, for example, summarising a student's performance over the academic year.

School management systems are used to record the performance of students. Performance can consist of both academic achievement and behaviour. To produce an end-of-term or end-of-year report, the system would need to have access to the following data:

» student's exam and test results in all subjects studied over the term/year
» behavioural data (this would include attendance records and, for example, number of times the student was in detention)
» CAT scores (these are standardisation test results to enable each student to be measured against a standard).

After processing this data, the system could produce:

» the average grades for all students in a class
» class and year group reports showing academic and behavioural performance.

Computer-aided learning

Computer-aided learning (CAL) is the use of computer-based systems to assist in the academic teaching of students. They are designed to enhance, and not replace, traditional classroom teaching. Students would use computers as part of their learning and complete online tests to monitor their performance. If a student encounters a problem, CAL is not always able to help the student, however, and in those cases, students would need to take steps to find additional help.

Advantages of using CAL to enhance the learning process

» Students can learn when they want to and at their own pace.
» It allows virtual reality (VR) learning to be used; with VR, the student is fully immersed into the learning environment.
» The student can stop at any point and return later to continue where they left off.
» It is possible to re-take tests until the student reaches the required skills level.
» CAL can make learning more interactive.
» CAL makes use of various multimedia (for example, short video clips, animation, music and interactive learning methods).

» The real goal of CAL is to stimulate student learning and not actually replace teacher-based learning; CAL, if used properly, should be an integrated part of the student's learning process.
» CAL can make use of multiple-choice questions (MCQs) which can be marked immediately by the computer system, giving instantaneous feedback to the student; other assessment methods can be used, such as fill in the missing words, crossword puzzles, linking correct terms to descriptions and gaming.
» It can deliver micro-learning; this is where a topic is broken down into small modules which are easy to learn, and is when CAL is most effective.

Disadvantages of using CAL to enhance the learning process

» CAL cannot give students the experience of handling laboratory equipment; for example, experiments shown in CAL are virtual in nature.
» It is expensive and time consuming to integrate CAL properly into the learning environment.
» Students can easily be distracted while online; for example, going on to social media sites, visiting websites or even playing online games.
» It can lead to the isolation of a student because they are spending their time on their own in front of a computer screen; this needs to be carefully managed.
» CAL cannot answer unusual questions, and the student will need to seek out guidance from a teacher; in other words, CAL is not a self-contained learning system.

6.5 Booking systems

6.5.1 Online booking systems

Online booking systems rely on the ability to update files immediately, thus preventing double-booking, which could happen if the system response time was slow. Online booking systems are used in:

» the travel industry
» for concerts (theatre and music events)
» for cinema tickets
» when booking sporting events.

Before we start looking at specific examples, it is worth considering some of the advantages and disadvantages of using online booking systems.

Advantages

» They prevent double-booking.
» The customer gets immediate feedback on the availability of seats and whether or not their booking has been successful.
» The customer can make bookings at any time of the day.
» The customer's email allows the booking company to connect 'special offers' to their email and inform them of such offers automatically.
» It is usually easier to browse the seating plans (particularly on flights) to choose the best seats available at the price.
» It is possible to 'reserve' a seat for a period of time – this allows a customer to 'make up their mind' before finalising the booking of the seat (this was difficult to do with the older paper-based systems).

» Very often there are no printed tickets, which saves postal costs and also allows 'impulse' bookings only a few hours in advance.

» Online booking allows the use of modern smartphone and tablet Apps technology; the customer is sent a QR code which contains all the booking information necessary (this QR code is stored on the smartphone or tablet and only needs to be scanned at, for example, the theatre or airport on arrival).

▲ **Figure 6.16** Example of a booking QR code

Disadvantages

» The setting up and maintenance of online booking systems is expensive.

» All customers using this service need access to a computer or mobile phone and a reliable internet connection.

» It is often more difficult to cancel the booking and get your money back using online systems.

» If the server is down for maintenance, or if the systems breaks down, it becomes impossible to book seats by any method (temporary paper-based systems cannot be used in case of the risk of double-booking occurring).

» If the websites are not well designed, it can be difficult to make exactly the booking you want or can lead you to make mistakes; this is a particular issue with flight bookings where correcting an error can cost the customer an additional fee.

» Booking online does not allow you to build a personal relationship with a travel agent who might offer free upgrades or special offers which may not be available to online bookings.

The travel industry

As an example, we will consider booking a flight online. A form similar to the one shown in Figure 6.17 would appear on the screen. The user only needs to fill in the appropriate fields and the system will automatically search for available flights, make bookings and transfer the funds from their bank account. Unless something goes wrong, there will be no need to talk to a human operator at any stage of the booking process.

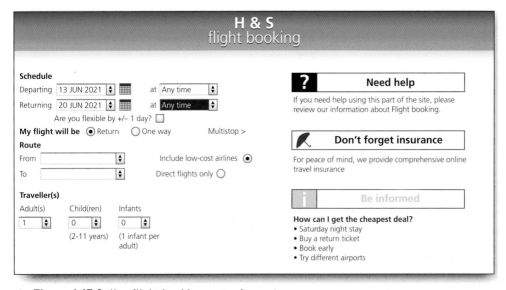

▲ **Figure 6.17** Online flight booking example

Exercise 6g

Using the screenshot in Figure 6.17, describe the stages when a person logs on to a flight booking website and makes a booking. Describe how the seats are booked, how double-booking is prevented, how the customer's tickets are produced and how payment is made.

Also investigate the latest ways of creating e-tickets, such as using apps on smartphones, and so on. Why are these new methods better than printing out a confirmation email to act as the e-ticket?

Events such as concerts, theatres and cinemas

We will now consider the online booking system when trying to book a concert, theatre or cinema performance. Because all three examples involve booking seats inside a building fitted with seats, we will use the same booking system for all three. With the example chosen, we have assumed that the customer has already logged on to the events booking website (and the event is a music concert at a seated venue).

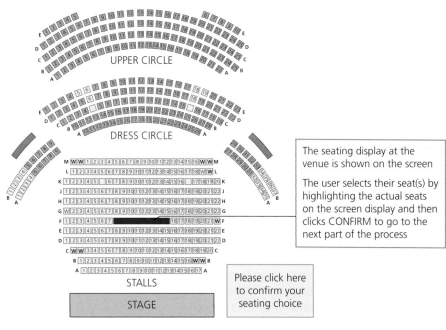

The seating display at the venue is shown on the screen

The user selects their seat(s) by highlighting the actual seats on the screen display and then clicks CONFIRM to go to the next part of the process

Please click here to confirm your seating choice

▲ **Figure 6.18** Event booking screen display

» The customer clicks on the performance they wish to see.
» A date and time is typed in.
» The required number of seats is also entered.
» The seating display at the venue is shown on the screen.
» The user selects their seat(s) by highlighting the actual seats on the screen display and then clicks CONFIRM to go to the next part of the process.
» The database is then searched to check the availability of the selected seats.
» If the seats are available, the total price is shown plus the seat numbers; this shows on another screen on the web page.
» If the customer is happy with this, they select CONFIRM on the screen.
» The seats are now temporarily held and set by the system as NO LONGER AVAILABLE – this stops anyone else from booking them.

» The customer then enters their personal details or indicates that they are a returning customer (in which case the website being used will already have their details).
» Payment method is then selected and payment made.
» The theatre seats are then booked in the customer's name.
» The final details are again shown on the screen.
» An email is sent to the customer which may contain a QR code which contains all their booking details (this acts as their **e-ticket**); the QR code is then scanned at the venue.
» The database is finally updated with the booking transaction and the seats are permanently confirmed as no longer available.

Booking sporting events

Booking a sporting event is very similar to the example above. Again, depending on the event, the online booking system will show a seating plan.

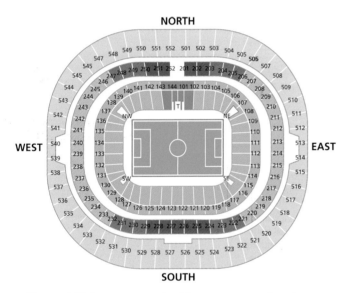

▲ **Figure 6.19** Sports venue booking system seating plan

The customer will need to select the event, the required day(s), number of people and preferred seats. Because the seats are often sold in blocks, the database will be searched to see if there are any seats available on the chosen date. Available seats will not show on the booking map, which is different to the concert/cinema booking system. If there is availability, the customer will be offered seats in the block. If the customer is happy with the option, they simply confirm the booking and payment is made online. Confirmation will be sent via email and/or possibly a QR code, which can be downloaded to the customer's smartphone; this QR code will act as their event ticket(s). Some sporting events do not book seats (such as a golf tournament) in which case the booking will simply be entry to the event.

The advantages and disadvantages of booking sports events online are the same as for online booking of concert and cinema tickets.

One additional feature often offered with sporting events, is the ability to also book flights and hotels if the event takes place overseas.

6.6 Banking systems

6.6.1 Banking applications

The use of computer technology has revolutionised how we all do our banking transactions. In this section, we will consider:

» the use of automatic teller machines (ATMs)
» electronic funds transfer (EFT)
» credit/debit card transactions
» cheque clearing
» internet banking.

Automatic teller machines (ATMs)

Automatic teller machines (ATMs) allow the customer to:

» withdraw cash
» deposit cash
» deposit cheques
» check the balance of their account
» see a mini bank statement
» pay a bill
» do a money transfer.

▲ **Figure 6.20** An automatic teller machine (ATM)

Table 6.2 shows a typical ATM process; withdrawing cash.

▼ **Table 6.2** Withdrawal of money from an ATM

Sequence for withdrawing cash	What goes on behind the scenes
Customer puts card into ATM	Contact is made with bank's computer
PIN is entered using the keypad	PIN is checked to see if it is correct; if not correct, customer is asked to retype PIN
	The card is checked to see if the card expiration date is exceeded or if the card has been stolen
	If card is stolen or if number of PIN attempts exceeds three, card is retained and transaction closed
A number of options are given: » change PIN » account balance — on screen — printed out » pay in cheques » get a mini statement » pay a bill » make a money transfer » deposit cash » withdraw cash	
The customer selects to withdraw cash	
A number of cash amounts are shown	

▼ **Table 6.2** (*Continued*)

Sequence for withdrawing cash	What goes on behind the scenes
The customer accepts one of the cash options or types in a different amount	Customer's account is checked to see if they have sufficient funds
	A check is then made to see if the daily cash limit has been exceeded
	If limit not exceeded and all other checks are OK, then the transaction is authorised
	The cash is then counted out by the machine
The customer is asked if they want a receipt	
The card is returned	
Money is dispensed	Customer's account is updated

We will now look at a second example; depositing cheques at an ATM:

» The user is asked to insert their debit card and type in the PIN.
» A message will then appear asking the customer which service they require.
» The customer chooses to deposit a cheque.
» A drawer will then open and the customer inserts the cheque.
» The drawer will then close and an OCR device will read the cheque details including the amount of money.
» The amount appears on the screen and the customer confirms the amount.
» The customer's account is updated with the amount on the cheque (pending cheque clearance within 24 to 48 hours).
» A printed receipt of the cheque is then given to the customer.
» If they do not require another service, the card is returned to the customer.

> **Link**
> For more about OCR (optical character recognition) see Section 2.2.

Advantages of using ATMs

» It is possible to withdraw cash at any time of day.
» They offer many banking services without the need to go into the bank – such as statements, account balance and bill paying – which helps people to manage their money more easily.
» It is possible to access an account from anywhere in the world.
» It usually provides quicker service than waiting in a queue in a bank.

Disadvantages of using ATMs

» They are often in places where theft can take place at night.
» There is potential for shoulder-surfing and card-cloning scams.
» Some banks charge customers for using ATMs.
» Cash withdrawal limits are often imposed on customers.
» If the debit card is faulty then no transaction can take place.
» There is a loss of the personal touch, which some customers will not like.

> **Link**
> See Chapter 8 for more details on card cloning.

Electronic funds transfer (EFT)

Electronic funds transfer (EFT) is a system that allows money transfer instructions to be sent directly to a bank's computer system. No actual money is transferred; the whole system relies on electronic transfer of money between accounts. When an EFT instruction is received, the computer system automatically transfers the specified amount from one account to another.

One common use of EFT is the payment of salaries to the staff of a company. On the day when payments are made, the company informs the bank to transfer money from their account into the bank accounts of their employees.

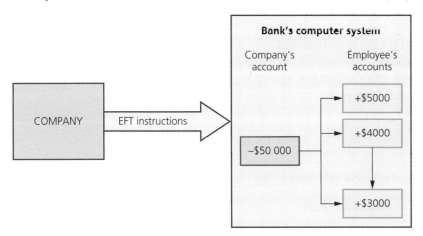

▲ **Figure 6.21** EFT example

Another example of EFT in use is when a credit/debit card is used to pay for a purchase in a store, the payment is made using a system called **electronic fund transfer at point-of-sale (EFTPOS)**.

Advantages of EFT

» It is a very secure payment method.
» It is a very quick payment method.
» It is less expensive than, for example, using cheques.
» The customer has the right to dispute an EFT payment for up to 60 days.

Disadvantages of EFT

» Once an amount has been transferred the bank cannot reverse a transaction (requires a full dispute investigation).
» The customer needs to have funds available immediately (unlike when using a cheque).
» It cannot guarantee the recipient (someone with a fake ID could collect the money).

Credit/debit card transactions

Many credit/debit cards are equipped with a chip as well as a magnetic stripe – the chip contains key information such as the PIN.

This system is designed to enhance security because it is better than relying only on a signature. Paying for items using a chip and PIN card is a form of electronic funds transfer (EFT). In this example, suppose a customer goes into a restaurant to pay for a meal using a chip and PIN card:

» The PIN is entered using a keypad.
» The card is checked to see if it is valid (check on expiry date, whether stolen card, etc.).
» The PIN is read from the chip on the card and is compared to the one just keyed in.
» If they are the same, then the transaction can proceed.

Link

See Section 6.9 for more details on EFTPOS.

Chip

▲ **Figure 6.22** Example of credit/debit smart card

>> If different, the transaction is terminated.
>> The restaurant's bank contacts the customer's bank.
>> A check is made on whether they have enough funds.
>> If the card is not valid or there are not enough funds available, then the transaction is terminated.
>> If everything checks out OK then the transaction is authorised.
>> An authorisation code is sent to the restaurant.
>> The price of the meal is then deducted from the customer's account.
>> The same amount of money is then debited to the restaurant's bank account.
>> A receipt is produced as proof of purchase.

The advantages and disadvantages of credit cards and debit cards are shown in Table 6.3.

▼ **Table 6.3** Advantages and disadvantages of credit cards and debit cards

Type of card	Advantages	Disadvantages
Credit	>> there is customer protection if a company stops trading or goods do not arrive >> internationally accepted method of payment >> interest-free loan if money paid back within agreed time period >> can buy items online	>> can be charged high interest rate >> annual fees often apply >> easy to end up with credit damage as sums mount up >> security risks when using credit card online (see Chapter 8)
Debit	>> money comes from customer's current account, therefore no interest charges >> safer than carrying cash >> can buy items online	>> less customer protection than credit card if goods do not arrive or company goes out of business >> no credit allowed; customers must have the funds available >> security risks when using debit card online (see Chapter 8)

Cheques

Cheques are one of the oldest ways of paying somebody for services or goods. Because it is a relatively expensive, slow and less secure way of making payments, cheques are slowly being phased out.

The advantages and disadvantages of using cheques are shown in Table 6.4.

▼ **Table 6.4** Advantages and disadvantages of using cheques

Advantages	Disadvantages
>> more convenient and safer than cash >> it is possible to stop payments if necessary >> a cheque can be drawn any time (up to six months after it was dated and signed) >> cheques can be post-dated >> cheques can be traced if they are 'lost'	>> cheques are not legal tender and can be refused >> it is a slow method of payment >> easier for fraudsters than credit card or debit card payment methods >> relatively expensive payment method

Centralised clearing of cheques

This method was first introduced around 2017 and has now been adopted by many banks worldwide. It is a much quicker system than the previous method used to clear cheques.

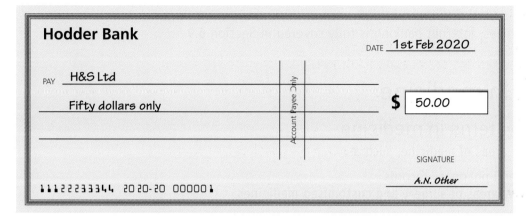

▲ **Figure 6.23** A typical cheque

In this method, cheques are cleared using an image-based system that speeds up the cheque clearing process considerably.

When a cheque is paid in to a bank, an electronic image is made of the cheque using OCR software. All of the bank details plus the sum of money to be paid are read.

So, suppose someone uses a bank called Hodder Bank and they pay a cheque for $50 to a company called H&S Ltd, who bank with the Smith Bank. How is the H&S bank account credited with $50?

» The first step is called **out clearing**. At this stage, when Smith Bank are presented with the cheque, a camera takes an image of the cheque and OCR software turns this image into an electronic data format.
» Smith Bank uses this electronic data to create a digital record of the money to be paid, the sort code on the cheque and the account number on the cheque.
» The cheque image and digital record are added to a file of other cheque images paid in that day. There are a number of files made. Each file contains all the cheque images and digital records for a particular bank. Therefore, there will be a file for Hodder Bank created by Smith Bank containing cheque data referring to Hodder Bank only; other banks will have their own files created containing cheque data referring to their bank only.
» Smith Bank now sends all the files to a central facility. One of the files contains all cheques relating to Hodder Bank. The central facility processes this file in the following way:
  – It breaks the file down into individual payment messages.
  – It does a payment validation.
  – It creates and sends a 'request to pay' message to Hodder Bank. This includes a copy of the cheque images as well as the encoded information (sort code, account number and payment amount).
» Hodder Bank receives a stream of 'request to pay' images and carries out the transactions. A 'no pay' decision will be made if the person paying has insufficient funds, if their account is blocked, if the cheque has not been signed or if there is suspected fraud.
» Once a 'pay' or 'no pay' message has been received, the central facility routes the 'pay/no pay' response to Smith Bank.
» All of this happens usually in less than 24 hours; still slow compared to card payments, but much faster than the older paper-based method.

Internet banking

Because of the many similarities, internet banking is fully covered in Section 6.9 along with online shopping.

6.7 Computers in medicine

6.7.1 Information systems in medicine

Computers are used in many areas of medicine, such as:

» keeping patient records and pharmacy records
» use of 3D printers in many areas of surgery and customised medicines.

Patient and pharmacy records

Doctors and hospitals need to keep accurate records of all their patients. This is essential to ensure correct diagnosis and treatment. An up-to-date medical history is part of the diagnosis process. Databases are kept by doctors and hospitals so that data can be shared between medical practitioners and pharmacies (for example, to ensure no drugs are prescribed which interact with each other in an unsafe manner).

Databases also allow a quick and easy search for patient records – this could be very important in an emergency, when accessing the patient's medical history could mean the difference between life and death. It also means that medication can be prescribed without issuing paper prescriptions – an email could be sent to the pharmacy instead.

The sort of data which would be required on a patient database is as follows:

» a unique identification number
» name and address
» date of birth
» gender (male or female)
» medical history (for example, recent medicine/treatment)
» blood group
» any known allergies
» doctor
» any current treatment
» any current diagnosis
» important additional information such as X-rays, CT scans, and so on.

Use of 3D printers

3D printers were first introduced in Chapter 3. Their use in a number of fields is rapidly progressing. One of the most innovative uses is in the field of medicine. The following is just a small insight into the many developments taking place across the world.

Surgical and diagnostic aids

It is possible to print out anatomical parts using 3D printers. These are used as an aid towards diagnosis and surgical procedures. The patient is scanned using:

» **CT (computed tomography)** – which involves producing images of the internal parts of the body in a series of thin slices less than 0.1 mm thick, or
» **MRI (magnetic resonance imaging)** – this uses strong magnetic fields and radio waves to produce a series of images of the internal organs in the body.

A 3D printer can then produce a three-dimensional representation of a patient's internal organs, blood vessels, major arteries, tumours and so on. The doctor or surgeon can use this to show the patient exactly what is wrong and then show them what procedures are required. This allows for patient engagement which would be missing from the more traditional consultation methods. It can also help the surgeons when planning surgical procedures because they can see exactly what is required well in advance of the operation. In this way, 3D printing systems can be used for diagnostic, pre-surgical aids.

Some 3D printers produce hard nylon objects which are used in certain pre-surgical planning. If a patient has suffered a bone break, for example, surgeons can physically test and position screws and plates in the '3D bone nylon image' prior to the surgery taking place. This reduces the chance of any errors when the actual procedure is carried out.

▲ **Figure 6.24** This is an example of prosthetic arm produced by 3D printing. Such technology can be life-changing to an amputee.

Prosthetics
3D printers are now being used to print out prosthetics (false arms, hands and legs). While state-of-the-art myoelectric prosthetics cost tens of thousands of dollars, the price for 3D-printing a prosthetic arm or hand can be as little as $100.

There is still much research needed in this field. However, the results to date are very encouraging, with many more people now having a chance to replace missing limbs at a fraction of the cost compared to existing methods.

Tissue engineering
Recent advances have allowed the 3D printing of bio-compatible materials, cells and supporting structures. This has enabled the viability of producing artificial cells and tissues within a 3D printed object. 3D bio-printing (using **bio-inks**) is a very complex process and requires input from biologists, medical engineers, physicists and other engineers. It has already been used successfully to produce multi-layered skin tissue, bone tissue, heart/artery grafts and tracheal splints.

There is still much research to do, but the goal of growing replacement organs, using cells from the actual patient, is getting ever closer thanks to 3D printing technology.

Artificial blood vessels
One particular type of tissue engineering is the 3D printing of artificial blood vessels using human cells. These bio-printed tissues work in much the same way as natural blood vessels. Biomimetic blood vessels can be fabricated using 3D printing and bio-inks.

> ### Advice
> 'Biomimetic' refers to the imitation of elements that occur in nature (such as human cells) to create solutions to human anatomy problems.
>
> 'Bio-inks' are biological inks developed to work with 3D inkjet printers. By using 3D layering, they produce artificial live tissue. These biological inks are made up of human cells and other materials (usually biopolymer gels).

▲ **Figure 6.25** Artificial blood vessels produced using 3D printing technique

Figure 6.25 shows a photograph of artificial blood vessels created from a 3D printer.

Customised medicines

3D printing techniques now allow scientists to customise medicines to suit the individual. This is known as patient-centric medicine. 3D printed medicines are sometimes referred to as **printlets** (**print**ed tab**lets**). As newly developed medicines are now very potent, and can have different effects on different people, there is now a need to review the manufacturing methods used to produce them. 3D printing offers the possibility of creating personalised medicine which allows automatically controlled release of the medicine into the patient. It even allows multiple medicines, within a single printlet, to make fixed-dose combinations and allows for the optimum release of each medicine into the body.

3D printing achieves all this by adopting a new 3D inkjet technology, known as vapour printing. This is a new technique where layering of multiple medicines can be done by spraying them as a fine gas. The vapour printing process works by evaporating a powdered medicine and then combining it with nitrogen gas. The resultant gas is then sprayed onto a cooled surface where it crystallises to form a thin film. The building up of several of these thin films (using 3D printing) forms the desired tablet with a carefully controlled geometry. Traditional medicines, in tablet form, are formed by compression of the powder; each compressed tablet has the same shape. By exploring the connection between geometry of the tablet and the release of the medicine, it is possible to create the most effective medicine release profile for each patient. Some of the advantages of this technology include:

» tailor-made medicines to suit the individual
» better control of medicine release into the body
» saves money (many modern medicines are very expensive)
» better targeting of the medicine so its effects can be optimised
» less chance of an overdose of the medicine, thus reducing harmful side-effects (for example, chemotherapy medicines can have very unwelcome side-effects; by reducing the release of the medicine to suit the individual, it will not only work better but also cause fewer harmful side-effects).

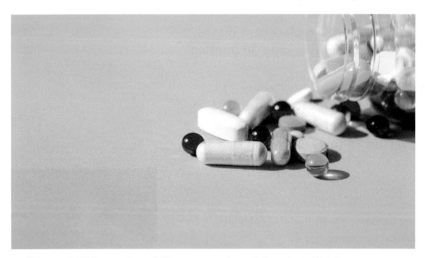

▲ **Figure 6.26** Examples of 3D generated medicines in tablet form

In the future it should be possible to send medicines to local pharmacies in the form of a blueprint; each blueprint would be custom-made for a patient. By supplying the necessary materials, it would then be possible to print out the customised medicines for each patient using the blueprint.

Link

Refer to Figure 2.36 in Chapter 2 to see how 3D printing uses CAD or blueprint designs.

6.8 Expert systems

6.8.1 Expert systems

Expert systems have been developed to mimic the expertise and knowledge of an expert in a particular field. Examples include:

» prospecting for oil and minerals
» diagnostics (finding faults in a car engine, finding faults on a circuit board, etc.)
» medical diagnosis
» strategy games (e.g. chess)
» tax and financial planning
» route scheduling for delivery vehicles
» identification of plants, animals and chemical compounds.

Before we describe how expert systems work, it is worth considering their advantages and disadvantages.

Advantages of expert systems

» They offer a high level of expertise.
» They offer high accuracy.
» The results are consistent.
» They have the ability to store vast amounts of ideas and facts.
» They can make traceable logical solutions and diagnostics.
» It is possible for an expert system to have multiple types of expertise.
» They offer a very fast response time (much quicker than a human expert).
» They provide unbiased reporting and analysis of the facts.
» They indicate the probability of any suggested solution being correct.

Disadvantages of expert systems

» Users of the expert system need considerable training in its use to ensure the system is being used correctly.
» The set-up and maintenance costs are very high.
» They tend to give very 'cold' responses which may not be appropriate in certain medical situations.
» They are only as good as the information/facts entered into the system.
» Users sometimes make the very dangerous assumption that they are infallible.

Figure 6.27 shows the typical make up of an expert system.

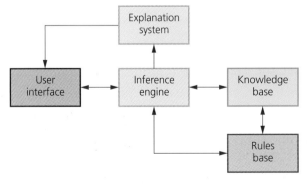

▲ **Figure 6.27** Expert system structure

User interface

- » This is the method by which the expert system interacts with a user.
- » It allows interaction through dialogue boxes, command prompts or other input methods.
- » The questions being asked usually only have yes/no answers and are based on the responses to previous questions.

Explanation system

- » This informs the user of the reasoning behind the expert system's conclusions and recommended actions.
- » For example, suppose the user was investigating a series of symptoms in a patient and the expert system gave the diagnosis of mercury poisoning; the explanation system would explain its reasoning with a statement such as 'impaired vision, lack of coordination, weak muscles, slurred speech and the patient used to work in a paint factory'. The user could then probe deeper if necessary.
- » The expert system will supply a conclusion and any suggested actions to take; the important thing is it will also give the percentage probability of the accuracy of its conclusions (for example, the following statement could be made: 'Based on the information given to me, the probability of finding oil bearing rocks in location 123AD21G is about 21%').

Inference engine

- » This is the main processing element of the expert system.
- » The inference engine acts like a search engine examining the knowledge base for information/data that matches the queries.
- » It is responsible for gathering information from the user by asking a series of questions and applying responses where necessary; each question being asked is based on the previous responses.
- » The inference engine is the problem-solving part of the expert system, which makes use of **inference rules** in the rules base.
- » Because the knowledge base is a collection of objects and attributes, the inference engine attempts to use information gathered from the user to find an object that matches (making use of the rules base to find a match).

Knowledge base

- » The knowledge base is a repository of facts.
- » It stores all the knowledge about an area of expertise obtained from a number of expert resources.
- » It is basically a collection of objects and their attributes (see the example in Table 6.5).

▼ **Table 6.5** Sample knowledge base showing objects and attributes

Object	Attribute 1	Attribute 2	Attribute 3	Attribute 4	Attribute 5
Dog	mammal	lives on land	makes bark sounds	body is covered in fur	walks on four legs
Whale	mammal	lives in water	makes sonic sound	body covered in skin	swims; no legs
Duck	bird	lives in water	makes quack sounds	body covered in feathers	swims; has two legs

» So, if we had the following series of questions and answers:
  - Is it a mammal?   YES
  - Does it live in water?   YES
  - Does it make sonic sounds?   YES
  - Is its body covered in skin? YES
  - Does it have any legs?   NO

  the conclusion would be: it is a WHALE.

Rules base

» The rules base is a set of **inference rules**.
» Inference rules are used by the inference engine to draw conclusions (the methods used closely follow human reasoning).
» They follow logical thinking like the example above; usually involving a series of 'IF' statements, for example:
  IF continent = 'South America' AND language = 'Portuguese' THEN country = 'Brazil'.

Now that we know how an expert system works, it is important to find out how to set one up.

Setting up an expert system

» Information needs to be gathered from human experts or from written sources such as textbooks, research papers or the internet.
» Information gathered is used to populate the knowledge base, which needs to be first created.
» A rules base needs to be created; this is made up of a series of inference rules so that the inference engine can draw conclusions.
» The inference engine itself needs to be set up; it is a complex system since it is the main processing element, making reasoned conclusions from data in the knowledge base.
» The user interface needs to be developed to allow the user and the expert system to communicate.
» Once the system is set up, it needs to be fully tested; this is done by running the system with known outcomes so that results can be compared and any changes to the expert system made.

We will now consider three examples which make use of expert systems.

Example 1: medical diagnosis

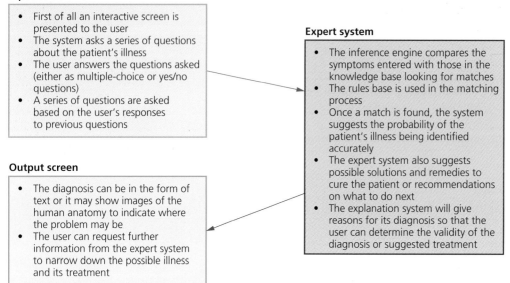

Input screen

- First of all an interactive screen is presented to the user
- The system asks a series of questions about the patient's illness
- The user answers the questions asked (either as multiple-choice or yes/no questions)
- A series of questions are asked based on the user's responses to previous questions

Expert system

- The inference engine compares the symptoms entered with those in the knowledge base looking for matches
- The rules base is used in the matching process
- Once a match is found, the system suggests the probability of the patient's illness being identified accurately
- The expert system also suggests possible solutions and remedies to cure the patient or recommendations on what to do next
- The explanation system will give reasons for its diagnosis so that the user can determine the validity of the diagnosis or suggested treatment

Output screen

- The diagnosis can be in the form of text or it may show images of the human anatomy to indicate where the problem may be
- The user can request further information from the expert system to narrow down the possible illness and its treatment

▲ **Figure 6.28** Medical diagnosis (example of use of an expert system)

Example 2: oil prospecting

» An interactive user screen appears (this is often made up of multiple-choice questions or yes/no responses).
» Questions are asked about geological profiles.
» Answers to questions/geological profiles are typed in by the operator.
» The next questions asked are based on the previous response(s) input by the operator.
» The **inference engine** searches the **knowledge base** using the **rules base**.
» The system suggests the probability of finding oil as an output.
» It also indicates the probable depth of deposits (usually as a % probability).
» The explanation system will also explain how the expert system arrived at its conclusions.
» It makes predictions about geological deposits above the soil.
» It produces contour maps showing concentration of minerals, rocks, oil, etc.

Example 3: route scheduling for delivery vehicles

An expert system could be employed to find the most efficient route for a parcel delivery van. The software will determine the fastest and least expensive route, as well as suggest the number of vehicles and drivers that should be used. The example in Figure 6.29

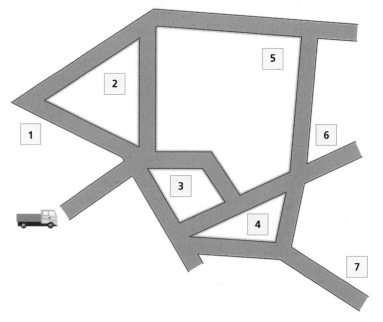

▲ **Figure 6.29** Most efficient route map

is fairly simple, but some national and international routes can be very complex. The inputs needed for the delivery system are:

» the number of drop-off points and their location
» the distance between the drop-off points
» the type of vehicle used
» delivery times expected at each drop-off point
» layout of the road network.

► Exercise 6h

1 Write down three advantages of using an expert system in route scheduling.
2 Write down three disadvantages of using an expert system in route scheduling.

► Exercise 6i

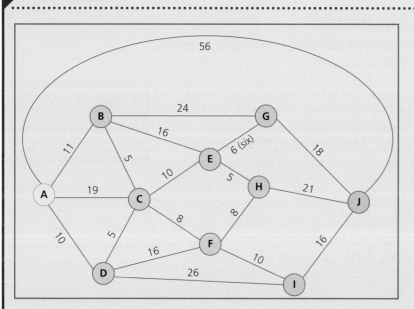

The map above shows the distances between ten towns, in kilometres.

A delivery company has to deliver a parcel from town 'A' to town 'J'.

Work out the shortest possible route the delivery van can take.

► Exercise 6j

1 Write a sequence of instructions to show how the following expert systems would be set up:
   a identification of a chemical found at, for example, a crime scene
   b a strategy game, such as chess
   c engine diagnostics for a racing car.
2 Write a sequence of instructions to show how the following expert systems would be used to:
   a diagnose circuit board faults in television sets
   b identify an 'unknown' chemical compound
   c identify a new species of flower
   d produce the best route for a delivery vehicle.

> ### Exercise 6k
>
> Which expert system terms are being described below?
> 1   A repository of facts made up of a collection of objects and their attributes.
> 2   It informs the user of the reasoning behind the expert system's conclusions and recommended actions.
> 3   It is made up of a user interface, explanation system and inference engine.
> 4   It contains a set of inference rules.

6.9 Computers in the retail industry

6.9.1 Computers in the retail industry

Computers are used in the retail industry at point-of-sale (POS) terminals, where they are also used in the automatic stock control systems.

Point-of-sale (POS) terminals

Barcodes now appear on most products sold in shops. They allow quick identification of product details once the barcode has been scanned by a **barcode reader**. Supermarkets, in particular, use **point-of-sale (POS) terminals** which incorporate a barcode reader to scan the barcode and retrieve the price of the article. It also relays information back to the computer system allowing it to update its files (more of this later).

Barcodes are made up of alternating dark and light lines of varying thickness. A number underneath the barcode usually consists of four parts: a country code, manufacturer's code, product code and a **check digit**. The check digit is a form of **validation** which is used to make sure no errors occurred during the reading of the barcode.

> ### Link
> Refer to Chapter 2 for more on barcodes.

ISBN 978-1-471-80721-3

9 781471 807213

▲ **Figure 6.30** Barcode sample

Barcodes are used in the automatic control of stock levels in a supermarket. The following sequence shows how barcodes and POS terminals are used in the automatic stock control system:

» Barcodes are attached to all items sold by the supermarket.
» Each barcode is associated with a stock file which contains details such as price, stock levels, product description – the barcode will act as the primary key in the file.
» A customer takes their trolley/basket to the POS terminal once they have completed their shopping.
» The barcode on each item is scanned at the POS – if the barcode cannot be read, then the EPOS operator has to key in the number manually.
» The barcode is searched for on the stock file until a match is found.

» Once the barcode has been found, the appropriate record is accessed.
» The price of the item is then found and sent back to the POS together with a product description.
» The stock level for the item is found in the record and is reduced by one and the new stock level is written back to the file.
  – If the number in stock of the item is less than or equal to the re-order/minimum number in stock, then the computer automatically orders a batch of items from the suppliers (supplier information would be found on another file called the order file or supplier file – the barcode would be the link between the two files).
  – Once goods have been ordered, the item is flagged on the file to indicate an order has been placed; this now prevents re-order action being triggered every time this item is scanned until the new stock arrives.
  – When new goods arrive, the barcodes on the cartons will be used to update the stock files; also any flags associated with these goods will be removed so that the stock checks can start to be made again.
» The above procedure is repeated until all the items in the customer's basket/trolley have been scanned.
» When all the items have been scanned, the customer is given an **itemised bill** showing a list (with prices) of everything they have bought.
» The computer also updates the files containing the daily takings.
» If the customer has a loyalty card, the system will also automatically update their points total.

Most supermarkets now allow customers to scan their own items at special checkouts; these basically work the same way as the normal POS terminals.

Electronic funds transfer at point-of-sale (EFTPOS)

When payment is made by card or electronic device (such as a mobile phone) at the POS terminal, it is known as electronic funds transfer at the point-of-sale (EFTPOS).

The process of checking credit and debit cards at a supermarket EFTPOS is much the same as was described for paying a restaurant bill in Section 6.6. The communication between the supermarket EFTPOS terminals and the bank take place through a secure connection over the internet.

We will consider payment by the following methods:

» chip and PIN
» contactless cards
» near field communication (NFC) devices.

Chip and PIN

The use of **chip and PIN** was discussed in Section 6.6. In the case of payment at a supermarket, this is usually done by inserting the card into a reader and then the procedure is identical to that described in Section 6.6. The reader makes a connection with the chip embedded in the card. By entering the PIN, a customer is carrying out a security check. The PIN and encrypted data from the chip is now sent to the customer's bank. If all security checks are OK (for example, a check whether the card has been stolen and a check whether the expiry date has been exceeded) and the customer has sufficient funds, then an authorisation code is sent back to the terminal and the funds are transferred to the supermarket's bank.

> **Link**
> ....
> For more on chip and PIN and contactless cards see Sections 6.6 and 2.2.

Advantages of chip and PIN cards

» They are more secure system than magnetic stripe cards (PIN typed in must match up with PIN stored on chip).
» It is a quicker system than magnetic stripe cards and allows for contactless payments to be made (with chip and PIN the card reader does not need to be actually connected to the internet/phone line to start the transaction process; with magnetic stripe cards, the card reader must first contact the customer's bank before any authorisation can take place).

Disadvantages of chip and PIN cards

» The risk of fraud when typing in the PIN – the customer needs to be careful to ensure the PIN is not being read by somebody else while typing it in.
» Some countries do not accept chip and PIN cards.

Contactless cards

The use of contactless card payments was discussed in Section 2.2, together with their advantages and disadvantages.

Near field communication (NFC) devices

Near field communication (NFC) technology is discussed in more detail in Section 6.10. When using NFC payment at a POS terminal the sequence of events taking place is:

» The electronic device (for example, mobile phone) is held close to the NFC reader (the terminal); this only works up to a distance of 5 cm, so the devices need to be very close together.
» When the NFC (contactless) payment is initiated, the NFC terminal and electronic device (smartphone) pass encrypted data back and forth to each other to enable the payment to be made.
» This is very secure because NFC communications are encrypted and are dynamic (which means encrypted data being shared changes every time a transaction takes place).
» Mobile phone manufacturers use **tokenisation** to improve security.

Use of tokenisation with mobile phones

Tokenisation is used when setting up a mobile wallet. The user takes a photograph of their credit card using the smartphone's camera. The details on the card (such as card number and name of bank) are securely sent by the smartphone manufacturer/mobile wallet company to the bank that issued the card. The bank replaces the details on the card with a series of randomly generated numbers (called **tokens**), which they send back to the mobile phone manufacturer, who then programs this random number into the user's smartphone. This random number is then the one used for transactions. This means that retailers or other third parties involved in mobile wallet transactions never have access to real credit card details – if their systems are hacked then the stored credit card details are not the real ones and therefore useless to the hackers.

Many smartphones are also protected by touch ID or face ID technology, which means that even if the smartphone is stolen, the thief still cannot use the smartphone to make payments.

6.9.2 Internet shopping

Internet banking and internet shopping

Using **internet banking** requires good online security. It allows the management of a bank account online, including the transfer of sums of money between accounts, payment of bills, ordering of statements, and so on. This is of particular benefit to people who are unable to visit banks during their normal opening hours or if travelling to the bank is difficult. There are many advantages of internet banking, but there are disadvantages too. As the amount of **online shopping** and banking increases, the positive and negative impacts on society become clearer.

Online shopping and banking means that more and more people are staying at home to buy goods and services, manage their bank accounts and book holidays, etc. This can all be done using a computer connected to the internet and some form of electronic payment (usually a credit or debit card). The following notes give a comprehensive list of the advantages and disadvantages of using the internet to carry out these tasks.

Because there is considerable overlap between the advantages and disadvantages of online banking and online shopping, these are both considered together here (refer also to Section 6.10 for more information on the retail sector).

Advantages of online shopping and banking

- » There is no longer a need to travel into town centres, thus reducing costs (money for fuel, bus fares, etc.) and time; it also helps to reduce town centre congestion and pollution.
- » Users now have access to a worldwide market and can thus look for products that are cheaper; this is obviously less expensive and less time consuming than having to shop around for goods or services in person and they will also have access to a much wider choice of goods.
- » Being able to access any shop or bank without the need to leave home may be of benefit to some people with disabilities and elderly people.
- » Because it is online, shopping and banking can be done at any time on any day of the week (i.e. 24/7) – this is particularly helpful to people who work during the day as the shops and banks can often be closed when they finish work.
- » People can spend more time doing other things, for example, going shopping to the supermarket probably took up a lot of time; by doing this online (and being able to set up repeat items) people are now free to do more leisure activities.
- » Similarly, paying bills in person or by posting cheques was time consuming – now this can be done simply and easily using online banking.
- » Many people find it less embarrassing to ask for a bank loan using the internet rather than enduring a face-to-face discussion with bank staff.
- » There are often long queues at the banks so internet banking saves time.
- » The shops and banks save money by not having as many staff working for them (reduced wage bill) or needing as many high-street premises (reduction in rental costs) – these savings may be passed on to the customer in the form of lower interest rates, cheaper goods or higher rates of interest for savers.

Disadvantages of online shopping and banking

- » There is the possibility of isolation and lack of socialisation if people stay at home to do all their shopping and banking.

151

» There are possible health risks associated with online shopping or banking because of lack of exercise; if people physically go shopping then they are getting some exercise.

» Security issues are a major concern (for example, hacking, stealing credit card details, etc.) as are viruses and other malware (for example, phishing, pharming, and so on).

» Accidentally using fraudulent bank or shopping websites is always a risk and this is linked to security issues.

» It is necessary to have a computer and to pay for the internet to take part in online shopping and banking.

» Unlike high-street shopping, it is only possible to see a picture of the goods, (which might not portray the exact colour of an item of clothing, for example) and nor can you try something on to see if it fits before buying them; you also have to wait several days for the goods to arrive and returning goods may be expensive and time consuming.

» Next-day delivery of individual items leads to more delivery traffic and pollution.

» High-street shops and banks are closing because of the increase in online shopping and banking and this is leading to deserted high streets.

» Local independent retailers may lose out to huge multinational retail companies.

» It is easier to make errors with online banking and transfer money incorrectly to different accounts.

Effects on companies due to the spread of online shopping and banking

Companies and other organisations have also been affected by the growth of ICT and online shopping and banking. Some of the effects are listed below:

» Companies can save costs because fewer staff need to be paid and it is not necessary to have as many shops and banks in high streets to deal with potential customers.

» Because the internet is global, the potential customer base is increased.

» There will be some increased costs, however, because of the need to retrain staff and the need to employ more staff in despatch departments.

» There are also costs due to the setting up and maintaining of websites to enable online shopping and banking.

» Because there is very little or no customer–employee interaction, this could lead to a drop in customer loyalty, which could lead to loss of customers (this could also be brought about by the lack of personal service associated with online shopping and banking).

» Robberies are less likely due to the decrease in the number of high-street banks.

» Banks also need to employ fewer security staff, which has a cost benefit.

> ### Exercise 6l
>
> 1 Revisit the earlier sections of this chapter and other parts of the book. Gather together your information and then write an article on the advantages and disadvantages of shopping on the internet compared to shopping on the high street.
>   Consider aspects such as convenience, costs and security.
> 2 Find out as many areas as you can in the retail industry that use barcodes (including QR codes) and explain why barcodes are used. What other methods exist which could replace barcodes? Why have these other methods not been adopted?

6.10 Recognition systems

6.10.1 Recognition systems

Recognition systems include OMR, barcode readers, QR code readers, OCR, RFID and biometric recognition systems. Many of these were discussed in Chapter 2 and earlier on in this chapter

This section will consider a number of applications which make use of these data recognition systems.

> **Link**
> ....
> See Section 2.2 for more on OMR, OCR, QR codes and RFID. Further discussion of biometric security is made in Section 8.3.

Optical mark recognition (OMR)

Use of OMR to read school registers

Other digital methods of registering students were mentioned earlier on in this chapter (i.e. use of magnetic stripe cards and biometrics). However, paper-based systems are still used in many schools. The paper-based registers are often scanned in to a computer using OMR. The attendance records are then stored on a central database.

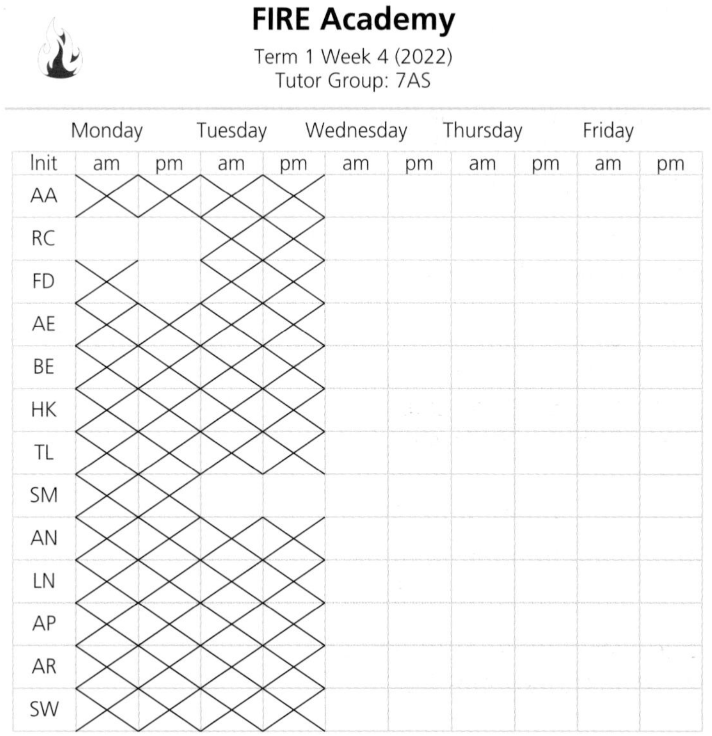

▲ **Figure 6.31** Sample register which can be read by OMR

The database can be searched or sorted to find data about the attendance of any student.

Use of OMR to read multiple-choice question (MCQ) papers

Completed multiple-choice forms can be scanned in using OMR. The forms have timing marks down one side – these timing marks pass under the first column sensor of the scanner. These marks indicate the position of each question on the paper. Using OMR software, a template is created to map out the X-Y coordinates of each lozenge (area which is filled in by pencil/ink or left blank) – a value is then assigned to each lozenge. As each question is scanned, a light passes through the scanner which picks up the position of any lozenge which has been filled in by pencil/ink. The position of the filled in lozenges is compared to the corresponding coordinates on the 'answer sheet template'. If the position matches to the X-Y coordinates, then the answer is recorded as being correct. The scanned results are exported to a database or spreadsheet.

If more than one lozenge is filled in for each question, then the OMR software simply discards that result. Marking MCQ sheets using OMR is much quicker and more accurate than doing the task manually. Because the results are automatically exported to a database or spreadsheet, it is much easier to analyse the results.

Advantages of OMR devices

» It is a very fast way of inputting the results of a survey, etc. – the documents are fed in automatically and there is no user input.
» Because there is no typing, they are more accurate than keying in the data.
» They are more accurate than OCR methods.

Disadvantages of OMR devices

» The forms need to be carefully designed to make sure the marks/shading are correctly positioned to gather accurate information.
» There can be problems if they have not been filled in correctly, and sometimes have to be manually checked before being read – this is both time consuming and expensive.
» They often only work with black pen or pencil.
» They are limited to the questions on the paper; it is not possible to get expansion to answers in a questionnaire, for example.

Link

A comparison between OCR and OMR devices was covered in Section 2.2.4.

Barcode readers

Please refer to Chapter 2 (Section 2.2.5) for information about barcode readers, including their advantages and disadvantages.

QR code readers

Please refer to Chapter 2 (Section 2.2.6) for information about QR code readers, including their advantages and disadvantages.

Optical character recognition (OCR)

The uses, advantages and disadvantages of optical character recognition (OCR) were discussed in Chapter 2 (Section 2.2.4). One important use of OCR was in the clearing of bank cheques, as discussed in Section 6.6. However, there is one additional, important application of OCR that should be mentioned here.

Automated number plate recognition (ANPR) systems

Automatic number plate recognition (ANPR) systems are used to read the number plates on cars in a number of applications.

▲ **Figure 6.32** Sample vehicle with number plate

In the example that follows, we will describe how ANPR is used in a car park to enable entry and exit to be automatically controlled by a computer system.

Step 1

A sensor detects a vehicle and sends a signal to instruct a camera to capture an image of the front of the vehicle (often an infrared camera is used to give a clearer image and for use at night).

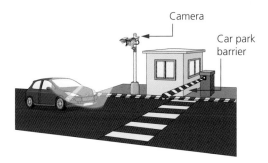

▲ **Figure 6.33** ANPR system

Step 2

i An algorithm is used to locate and isolate the number plate from the image taken by the camera. This algorithm also takes into account the size of the number plate and any damage or orientation. ──────────────▶ `1 A B C 2 3 4`

ii The brightness and contrast of the number plate is first adjusted (this ensures that the characters can be clearly read). ──────────▶ `1 A B C 2 3 4`
Each character on the number plate is then segmented. ─────────┐

iii Each character is then recognised using OCR software. The characters are ──▶ `1 A B C 2 3 4` converted into a string of editable text by the software.

iv This text string is then stored on a database.

Step 3

Once all of this has happened, the car park barrier is raised and the motorist is issued with a ticket. The ticket shows the date and time of entering the car park.

Step 4

When the motorist returns to the car park, they insert their ticket into a machine which calculates the car park charges. The payment is registered on the database.

The motorist then drives to the exit barrier and the ANPR system again reads the number plate and checks its database. If the number plate is recognised (and payment made), the exit barrier is raised.

Advantages of ANPR

» It can be used to automatically monitor average speed of vehicles over a stretch of road; this can be used in smart traffic management systems (see also Section 6.2).
» There is no need to employ car park security guards, which saves money.
» It is a much faster system than having to check a ticket at the exit; car parks can issue tickets on entry, but this ticket is simply used for payment purposes by the motorist before leaving the car park and is not used at the exit since payment will now be linked to the number plate on the car.
» It can be used to automatically control the entry and exit to a car park or private roads.

» It can be used as a security system; preventing illegal parking and preventing unauthorised access to private car parks.
» It can be used to analyse driver behaviour (that is, route choice and destinations) to help in transport planning.
» It can be used in inner-city congestion charging systems; it is possible to automatically charge a motorist if they enter a congestion zone, but also allows in permitted vehicles without charge (for example, emergency vehicles, buses and electric zero-emission vehicles).

Disadvantages of ANPR

» There is a lack of manned security car park surveillance which could lead to vandalism (and other crimes) because nobody is checking on a regular basis; CCTV is often used, but this is often just used 'after the event'.
» There could be invasion of privacy issues due to the recording of drivers' number plates.
» Damaged or very dirty number plates will not be recognised by the system.
» Number plate cloning; the ANPR system only recognises the number plate and not the car, so it is possible for a car to be fitted with a cloned number plate thus by-passing car park security, for example.

► Exercise 6m

Describe how automated number plate recognition (ANPR) systems can be used in smart traffic management systems. Your description should include how ANPR is used and how the data gathered by ANPR would be used in traffic management control and monitoring.

Radio frequency identification devices (RFID)

Radio frequency identification devices (RFID) were covered in Chapter 2 (Section 2.2). This section will look specifically at four uses of RFIDs:

» tracking of stock
» passports
» automobiles
» contactless payments.

First of all, we will consider the advantages and disadvantages of using RFID.

Advantages of RFID

» No line-of-sight contact is necessary; the tags can be read from a distance.
» It is a very robust and reliable technology.
» Tags are much more difficult to forge than barcodes; barcodes can be altered or even damaged, but RFID tags are more robust and difficult to alter.
» RFID tags can reduce the number of staff needed in, for example, a warehouse because tracking of items is automatic (thus reducing costs).
» It provides a very fast read rate (typically < 100 milliseconds to respond).
» It allows bi-directional data transfer (that is, it allows read and write operations to take place).
» Bulk detection is possible (that is, detect several RFID tags at the same time).

Disadvantages of RFID

» Tag collision – this is when the signals from two or more tags overlap, interfering with each other.
» Because RFID uses radio waves, they are relatively easy to jam or interrupt.
» It is relatively easy to hack into the data/signal transmitted by the tag.
» Although there is a potential saving in staff wages, the initial cost of an RFID system is more expensive than a comparable barcode system

Tracking of stock

As mentioned in Chapter 2, RFID readers use radio waves to read and capture information stored on a tag. Depending on the power of the radio waves used, the tag can be read from several metres (for example, in livestock tracking) to only a few millimetres (for example, in contactless card payments). The RFID tag is made up of two components:

» a microchip that stores and processes information
» an antenna which is used to receive and transmit data/information.

The tags can be passive or active. Passive tags use the reader's radio wave energy to relay back the information, whereas active tags use a small embedded battery to power the RFID. Passive tags are the most widely used because they are smaller and cheaper to implement than active tags. Because active tags have their own power supply, they can be read from up to 50 metres away.

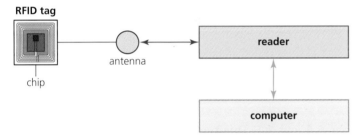

▲ **Figure 6.34** RFID tag showing antenna and chip

Tracking of stock using RFID involves either tracking of livestock (on a farm) or goods in a shop, supermarket or distribution centre.

» Livestock tracking is used to:
  – keep track of the whereabouts of every animal on a farm using active tags
  – allow farmers to identify who owns an animal; particularly important where animals graze freely on farms where it is possible for animals to stray into neighbouring fields
  – keep data about the animals on the tag (for example, medical history, date of birth, identification (passport) number, and so on).
» Retail make use of RFID tags in the following ways:
  – similar to barcodes, but can contain much more information and do not require any manual scanning; details, such as price, description, and so on, can all be stored on the tag and then automatically read at a checkout – a big advantage is that several tags can be read at the same time, thus speeding up the checkout process

- can be used in distribution centres; an item can easily be located because the tag can store its exact location in the warehouse
- allow automatic tracking of an item from warehouse to customer; the customer can be informed at all stages where the item is.

Passports

Tiny RFID chips and antenna (i.e. tags) are now embedded into passports. The RFID tags in passports have no power supply, so they are examples of passive tags. When the passport is presented to an RFID scanner, the scanning device provides enough energy so that the chip can broadcast its stored information. This information is then sent to a computer. The tiny chips can contain security data, which makes it almost impossible for a person to falsify their identity. For example, photographs and fingerprints can be encoded into these chips. The data sent to the computer is encrypted, increasing the security of the system. The RFID in a passport can be read from six metres which, of course, does pose a security risk; but this risk is mitigated against by encrypting the data.

▲ **Figure 6.35** RFID tag and antenna in a passport

Use of RFID in vehicles

RFID tags can be used in vehicles. The main reasons for doing this include:

» The tags allow or deny access to parking in a secure, private car park.
» RFID tags in lorries and delivery vans can be used at weigh-stations to ensure the vehicle is not carrying too much weight.
» Tags can be used on toll roads; the driver registers their vehicle and attaches a tag to the windscreen; as the vehicle approaches the barrier, a device near the barrier (a transponder) reads the tag and checks the stored reference number, and if it is valid the barrier will open without them having to stop.
» RFID tags can be used on a car production line to track its progress through the assembly process.

Contactless credit/debit cards

Contactless credit/debit cards were discussed in Sections 6.6 and 2.1. This type of card uses an embedded passive RFID tag:

» The chip in the RFID tag is passive and emits a low-powered radio wave when it comes into contact with an RFID reader.
» An antenna is built into the card to allow a connection with the contactless reader.
» The RFID reader picks up a signal from the chip and this initiates the payment process (see Chapter 2 for more details).

Near field communication (NFC)

As mentioned in Section 6.9, near field communication (NFC) can be used by smartphones when making payments. NFC is a subset of RFID technology, operating at a particular frequency, and is another standard for wireless data transmissions. In contrast to general RFID, the frequency at which NFC operates requires the sender and receiver to be in very close proximity, which makes communication more secure. In addition, and again in contrast to general RFID, NFC devices can act as a receiver (passive) or a reader (active). These features are what separates NFC from general RFID technology.

How smartphones use NFC to make payments was discussed in Section 6.9; the following notes give some further information about how NFC works. There are three distinct modes of operation with NFC:

» Peer-to-peer mode (used by smartphones):
  - This allows two NFC-enabled devices to exchange information with each other (for example, two smartphones sharing links, contacts and photographs with each other by tapping them together).
  - Both devices switch between being active (when **sending** data) and being passive (when **receiving** data).
» Read/write mode:
  - This is a one-way transmission of data.
  - The passive device (for example, a tablet) links up with another device and reads data from it.
  - This is used, for example, when an active tag is sending out advertising data to other devices.
» Card emulation mode:
  - In this mode, an NFC device can function as a smart or contactless card.
  - This allows the card to make payments (already discussed in Chapter 2).
  - It is often used as way of entering public transport systems, where the card is placed on an NFC reader to allow access to, for example, a metro system.

NFC has a range up to 5 cm and has a transmission rate of about 420 kilobits per second, which is much smaller than Wi-Fi or Bluetooth. However, NFC has very fast connectivity since, unlike Bluetooth, there is no need to **pair** the two devices connecting.

Biometric recognition systems

Biometric recognitions systems include:

» face recognition
» iris and retina recognition
» finger and thumb recognition
» hand recognition
» voice recognition.

Face recognition, and finger and thumb recognition systems are covered in depth in Chapter 8. Hand recognition (gesture control) and voice recognition systems are covered Chapter 1.

The advantages and disadvantages of different biometric recognition systems are covered in Table 8.3. For completeness, we will consider two additional examples here: retina recognition and iris recognition.

Retina recognition

» The retina is the light-sensitive area at the back of the eye that has a unique pattern of blood vessels.
» The retina cannot be seen without specialised equipment – this means it is a secure technology, but more expensive to implement.
» The special equipment is used to take an infrared photograph of the retina.
» It is quite invasive – the subject has to sit very still and stare directly into the light source.
» It is slower to scan and verify.
» It is only used in very specialised high-security settings.

Iris recognition

» The iris is the coloured part of the eye, surrounding the pupil.
» A digital camera is utilised which uses both visible and near infrared light to take a sharp photograph of a person's iris.
» The method produces a unique pattern of a person's iris by locating and taking an image of:
  – the centre of the pupil
  – the edge of the pupil
  – the edge of the iris
  – the eyelids and eye lashes.

The system works with contact lenses and glasses, and for blind people. It is used as a method for uniquely identifying a person and, because of the speed of verification (less than 5 seconds), is used a security system in the following areas:

» immigration control (in some countries)
» some banks have introduced this in some branches as a security feature.

> **Link**
> ....
> See Section 8.3 for more on biometric recognition systems, and Section 1.3 for voice and gesture recognition.

6.11 Satellite systems

6.11.1 Satellites

In this final section, we will be considering:

» global positioning systems and satellite navigation
» geographic information systems (GIS)
» media communication systems (satellite television and satellite phones).

Global positioning systems and satellite navigation

▲ **Figure 6.36** GPS and satellite navigation systems

Global positioning systems (GPS) are used to determine the exact location of a number of modes of transport (for example, aeroplanes, cars, ships, etc.). Cars usually refer to GPS as **satellite navigation systems** (i.e. 'satnav').

> **Advice**
>
> While the term GPS is often used generically, it actually refers to a specific global navigation satellite system (GNSS) owned and run by the USA. There are other GNSS that perform the same function, including the Russian GLONASS and the EU's Galileo.

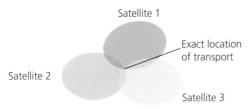

▲ **Figure 6.37** Three satellite system

Satellites surrounding the Earth transmit signals to the surface. Computers installed in the mode of transport receive and interpret these signals. Each satellite transmits data indicating its position and time. Satellites need very accurate timing in order to know their position relative to the Earth. They use atomic clocks, which are accurate to a billionth of a second per day. The computer on board the mode of transport calculates its exact position based on the information from at least three satellites.

In cars, the onboard satellite navigation system contains stored road maps. When combined with satellite positioning data, the car's exact location can be shown on the map and the driver can also be given verbal instructions such as: 'After 100 metres, take the next left turn onto the A1234'. A screen on the satnav device will also show the car's position in relation to the road network.

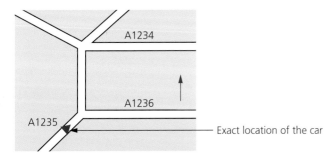

▲ **Figure 6.38** Satellite navigation system

Advantages of GPS and satnav

» The driver does not have to consult paper maps, so it is far safer.
» It removes errors (can warn drivers about one-way streets, street closures, etc.).
» The system can estimate the time of arrival.
» It is also possible to program in the fastest route, route to avoid towns, etc.
» The system can also give useful information such as location of petrol stations.

Disadvantages of GPS and satnav

» If the maps are not kept up to date, they can give incorrect instructions.
» Unless the system is sophisticated, road closures due to accidents or roadworks, can cause problems.
» Loss of satellite signals can cause problems.
» If an incorrect start-point or end-point is keyed in the system will give incorrect information.

Geographic information systems (GIS)

Geographic information system (GIS) is a computer system that allows us to map, model, query and analyse large amounts of data according to their location.

GIS allows users to create interactive queries, edit map data or analyse spatial information. (Spatial information refers to how objects fit together in space.) The technology combines maps with computer graphics and databases.

Essentially GIS enables the following:

» amalgamation of information into easily understood maps
» performance of complex analytical calculations and then presentation of the results in the form of maps, tables or graphics (or a combination of all three)
» geographers, scientists and engineers are able to see the data in several different ways in order to see patterns and relationships
» anything that can be placed on a map is a candidate for GIS.

The following example shows how these layering techniques are used to produce a visually effective answer to a query made in the GIS system:

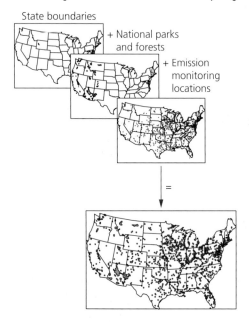

▲ **Figure 6.39** Layering of state boundaries using GIS

Carrying out queries on GIS systems (in a method similar to internet searches) will find data that matches the query. The data will be displayed in the form of a diagram, map or set of tables. By zooming into the map, it is possible to find finer details about the layering data used.

Examples of the use of GIS

» Emergency services use GIS to send the closest emergency personnel to a location.
» Biologists and environmentalists use GIS to protect animal life and plants in certain vulnerable areas (which meet a certain criteria after carrying out a search on the database).
» Teachers can use GIS in their geography, science or engineering lessons.

» It can be used for crime mapping in a region or in a country.
» It can be used for route monitoring (used in conjunction with route scheduling software).
» It can be used for management of agricultural crop data.
» It can address public health issues – it was used in 2020 and 2021 during the Covid-19 pandemic to show how the virus spread in different parts of the world and allowed data to be combined (such as, age groups, ethnic group, population density, and so on) to create a unique insight into how it spread.
» It can map of wildfire risks (it was used in Australia in 2019 during the wildfire outbreaks; it was possible to map out where and how the fire was spreading).

Advantages of GIS

» It allows geographical and thematic data of any kind to be combined in a way which shows how they are connected to each other.
» It allows the handling and exploration of huge amounts of data (massive number crunching).
» It allows data to be integrated from a wide range of very different sources (which appear at first to be totally unconnected).

Disadvantages of GIS

» The learning curve on GIS software can be very long.
» GIS software is very expensive.
» GIS requires enormous amounts of data to be input (thus increasing the chances of errors).
» It is difficult to make GIS programs which are both fast and user-friendly; GIS requires very complex command language interfaces to work properly.

Media communication systems

Communication media refers to a method of delivering and receiving data/information using telecommunications.

There are many types of media used to send and receive information (for example, fibre optics, copper cable and Wi-Fi); we will concentrate on the global communication method which makes use of satellites.

Satellites contain antennas, transponders (to allow receiving and sending of data), solar panels (for power from the Sun) and propulsion (to ensure the satellite is in the correct orbit at all times).

▲ **Figure 6.40** Satellite systems

Signals are converted to analogue (if necessary) and then beamed to the satellite from a satellite dish on the Earth. The signals are delivered by carrier waves which consist of radio waves. Each signal has its own frequency and bandwidth (the larger the bandwidth the more data can be transmitted).

Once the data reaches the satellite, it is then re-sent to Earth. The satellite usually 'boosts' the signal before sending it back. Often the frequency of the signal is changed to prevent the signal received being confused with the signal sent.

Satellite systems are used to transmit data from one part of the planet to another. Due to the great distances involved, cables would be too costly and there is also the problem of signal deterioration in cables over long distances.

Satellites systems are used to transmit television, telephone and internet data around the world.

Advantages of media communication systems

» They have good global coverage (covers the majority of the Earth's surface).
» They are cheaper, faster and safer than laying cables in difficult or treacherous terrain.
» They have a very high bandwidth.
» It is relatively easy to expand the network (there are numerous companies now manufacturing satellites for various uses).
» Security in satellite transmission is very good due to the fact that data is coded and the receiver requires decoding equipment to read the data.
» During emergency situations it is relatively easy to move stations on the ground from one place to another; satellites can also change their orbits if necessary, using built-in boosters.
» They are well-suited for broadcasting, that is, one satellite signal being picked up by many different receivers on the ground.
» Satellite receivers on the ground can be portable, enabling mobile communication in very remote locations.

Disadvantages of media communication systems

» There is a time delay in receipt of the signals (this can be a problem in voice communications, where even 0.5 seconds delay can be noticeable as the sound and video appear out of synchronisation) or there may appear to be an 'echo' on the sound (note that there would also be a time delay for long-distance fibre-optic communications too).
» The signals received can be affected by bad weather (for example, heavy rain or hailstones), obstructions (such as tree branches) and whether the satellite dish has been correctly orientated.
» Sunspot activity can affect the performance of a satellite.
» If they are not in a fixed position relative to the Earth then they need to be monitored and controlled on a regular basis to ensure they remain in the correct orbit.

Exam-style questions

1 The managers of a company are concerned about illegal parking in their car park. Drivers are parking their cars in the private car park and then walking to the local football match. There have been a few instances of damage to employees' cars. A decision has been made to install a number plate recognition system and barrier so they can control cars entering and leaving the car park. Anyone visiting the company will need to register their car's number plate with the receptionist prior to their visit.

   a Explain how this system could check that a car approaching the barrier had been registered with the receptionist beforehand. [4]

   b After a visitor parks their car, they have to report to the receptionist. They are then given a badge which contains an RFID tag. The chip in this tag is read to allow the visitor access to certain floors in the building. Prior to this electronic system, badges contained a barcode. Discuss the advantages and disadvantages of using RFID chips rather than barcodes on visitor's badges. [6]

   c The company would like to offer visitors access to their facilities, such as the restaurant, coffee shop and gift shop. Before arriving at the company, visitors are sent a QR code which they can download to their smartphone.
Describe how the visitor could use a QR code to find out more about the company. [3]

   d Payment at the restaurant is made using an NFC-enabled smartphone. Explain:
    i what is meant by NFC [2]
    ii how the smartphone can be used to make payments. [3]

2 You have been asked by your teacher to use a word processor to create a brochure for a new intake of pupils. The brochure will consist of:
  » Images of the school taken from a digital camera.
  » Printed archive photographs.
  » Information about the school already stored in text files.
  » Information to be typed directly into the brochure.

   a Describe the steps which you will need to take to create the brochure. [6]

   b When the brochure is being created, the word processing software automatically checks the spelling of the text as it is typed in and may suggest alternative words.
Explain why the suggestions may not always be appropriate. [3]

Cambridge IGCSE Information and Communication Technology (0417) Paper 11 Q7 a & b,
October/November 2019

3 Robots are being used in the oil industry to find new deposits under the Earth's surface.
   a Give **three** advantages of using robots rather than humans when searching for new oil deposits. [3]
   b Give **two** disadvantages of using robots rather than humans. [2]

4 An automatic washing machine contains a device to read RFID chips sewn into clothing. When an item of clothing is placed in the washing machine it is scanned.
   a Describe how the data is read from the RFID chip. [2]
   b Explain the benefits of using RFID technology in a washing machine. [2]

Cambridge IGCSE Information and Communication Technology (0417) Paper 11 Q9, May/June 2017

5 The city of Venice is in danger of being damaged due to rising sea levels. A new computer controlled flood defence system is being planned. The developers of the system are using a spreadsheet to model the plan.
   a Give **three** reasons why computer models are used to simulate the flood defence system. [3]
   b The city uses a manual system for detecting flood waters. This relies on people watching for the rising levels of water. Explain why creating a computerised system is better than using the manual system. [4]
   c The developers have used the results from the model to choose a computer controlled flood defence system. It will have a barrier which can open or close. Describe the role of the microprocessor in such a system. [5]

Cambridge IGCSE Information and Communication Technology (0417) Paper 11 Q10, May/June 2017

6 A theatre manager holds a number of music concerts through the summer months. She has decided to introduce an online booking system to replace her current paper-based booking system. Give **four** advantages of using an online booking system. [4]

7 The banking industry has rapidly changed over the last few years as modern technology has developed. Discuss the advantages and disadvantages of using online banking rather than other banking methods to the customer. [8]

Cambridge IGCSE Information and Communication Technology (0417) Paper 12 Q16, October/November 2017

8 Discuss the advantages and disadvantages of using internet shopping to both the customers and to the retail companies. [8]

9 Seven statements are shown on the left and seven computer terms are shown on the right.
By drawing arrows, connect each description to the correct computer term. [6]

Users watch movies or sound files on a device connected to the internet; there is no need to download the files first	Biomimetics
Simulation of a real system in order to study its behaviour; it is computer-generated and is based on mathematical calculations	Computer-aided learning
Type of vehicle which is effectively a robot capable of driving on the roads without a human driver	Media streaming
Temporary memory that compensates for the different download speeds and playback speeds of a device	Buffering
Use of a computer-based system to assist in the education of a student	Computer model
Automated transfer of money from one bank account to another; no physical money is actually transferred	Electronic funds transfer
Imitation of the elements of human nature to solve human anatomical problems	Autonomous

10 a Complete the diagram below, which shows the structure of an expert system, using the terms below. [4]

Explanation system   Inference engine   Knowledge base

Rules base   User interface

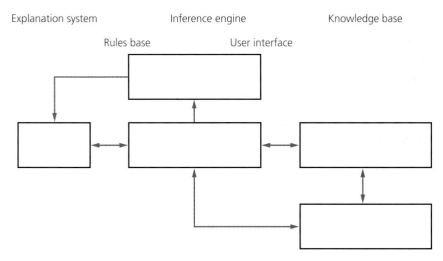

b Explain the function of the following expert system components: [10]
  i explanation system
  ii inference engine
  iii knowledge base
  iv rules base
  v user interface.

c Describe how an expert system could be used to diagnose a fault in a computer system. [5]

11 Each of the following ten statements are True or False.
Tick (✓) the appropriate box to indicate which statements are true and which statements are false. [10]

Statement	True (✓)	False (✓)
NFC can work up to 50 metres away.		
The RFID chip consists of a tag and an antenna.		
GIS systems require complex command language interfaces.		
Satellite signals are unaffected by bad weather and physical obstructions, such as tree branches.		
Building a computer model is often much cheaper than building the real thing.		
One advantage of CAL is the ability of the student to stop at any point and resume from where they left off at a later date.		
The first step in processing a cheque by taking an electronic image is called 'out clearing'.		
Electronic funds transfer is a very insecure payment method.		
3D printing uses five different coloured bio-ink cartridges (black, bio-grade black, cyan, yellow and magenta).		
Strategic games, such as chess, can be run on an expert system.		

7 The systems life cycle

In this chapter we will consider the stages and processes involved when replacing computer systems, from analysis of an existing system right through to evaluation of the new system.

Suppose a company has been using an existing computer system for a number of years. They have decided to replace the current system with a new one. After a number of years of successful operation, what would initiate this need to upgrade?

» The existing computer equipment is now obsolete (it cannot be repaired anymore).
» Changes to laws or taxes requiring radical overhaul of software.
» More suitable hardware is now available to improve efficiency and reliability.
» There is a need to expand the company.

There could be many more reasons.

The changes will involve an ICT solution, which means a **systems analyst** needs to be brought in to oversee the whole upgrade process. Their first task will be to analyse the existing (current) system, and then suggest a number of improvements that can be made. All these improvements need to be costed and their advantages over the current system need to be reported back to the company's management team.

Once a new system is agreed and it has been fully tested, it is then installed. It then needs to be fully evaluated and any changes made where necessary. Therefore, a cycle of events take place until a fully-working system is signed off and handed over to the management team. This whole process is called the **systems life cycle**.

There are many stages in the systems life cycle, which have been summarised in Figure 7.1.

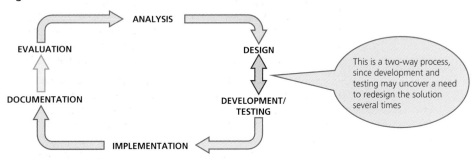

▲ **Figure 7.1** Systems life cycle

7.1 Analysis

The first stage in the process is the analysis of the current system. Figure 7.2 shows the stages in analysis.

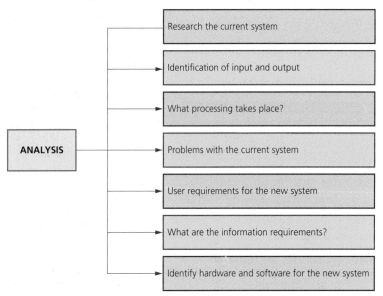

▲ **Figure 7.2** Analysis stage

7.1.1 Analyse the current system

There are four methods used to research the current system. The four methods used are:

» **observation**
» **questionnaires**
» **interviews**
» examination of existing documents.

▼ **Table 7.1** Methods of researching the current system

Name of research method	Description of research method	Advantages of research method	Disadvantages of research method
Observation	This method involves watching personnel using the existing system to find out exactly how it works.	» The analyst obtains reliable data » It is possible to get a better overall view of the system » Relatively inexpensive method because it only involves the analyst » All inputs and outputs of the current system are seen	» People are generally uncomfortable being watched and may work in a different way (known as the Hawthorne effect) » If workers perform tasks that contravene standard procedures, they may not do this while being watched
Interviews	This method involves a one-to-one question-and-answer session between the analyst and the user. It is a good method if the analyst wants to probe deeply into one specific aspect of the existing system.	» It gives the opportunity to motivate the interviewee into giving open and honest answers to the analyst's questions » The method allows the analyst to probe for more feedback from the interviewee (questions can be extended) » It is possible to modify questions as the interview proceeds and ask questions specific to the interviewee » Analyst can watch body language and facial expressions	» It can be a rather time-consuming exercise » It is relatively expensive (team of interviewers and analyst needed) » The interviewee cannot remain anonymous with this method, and may hide information or not be honest with their answers » Interviewee can give answers they think the interviewer wants to hear » Interviewees may not be available at times to suit the analyst
Questionnaires	This method involves distributing questionnaires to the workforce, clients or system users to find out their views of the existing system and to find out how some of the key tasks are carried out.	» The questions can be answered fairly quickly » It is a relatively inexpensive method (only need to produce questionnaires) » Individuals can remain anonymous if they want (therefore give more truthful answers) » Allows for a quick analysis of the data » Interviewees can fill in questionnaire in their own time » Allows a greater number of people to take part	» The number of returned questionnaires can be low; not always a popular method » The questions are rather rigid because they have to be generic; it is not possible to ask follow-up questions » No immediate way to clarify a vague answer to a question; it is not possible to expand their answers » Users tend to exaggerate their responses as they are anonymous » Because anonymous, the interviewees may not take it seriously
Looking at the existing documents	This method allows the analyst to see how existing files are kept, look at operating instructions and training manuals, check the accounts, etc. This allows the analyst to get some idea of the scale of the problem, memory size requirements, type of input/output devices needed, etc.	» This method allows information to be obtained which was not possible by any of the other methods » The analyst can see for themselves how the current system operates	» It can be a very time-consuming exercise » Because of the analyst's time needed, it is a relatively expensive method to use

7.1.2 Record and analyse information about the current system

Inputs, outputs, processing and current problems

The next stage in the process requires the analyst to find out:

» what input and output takes place
» what processing is done
» what problems exist with the current system
» user and information requirements for the new system.

One method the analyst can use is a **data flow diagram (DFD)**. Figure 7.3 shows an example of a DFD that follows the reservation system when booking a flight on an a aeroplane.

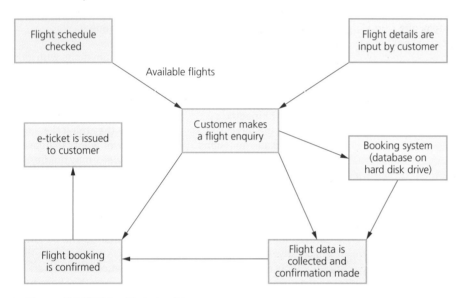

▲ **Figure 7.3** DFD for flight booking process

Advice

Producing a DFD is not required for this syllabus.

From the DFD, we can get the following information:

» what inputs take place during the customer enquiry (in this case, a customer keys in their flight details, such as names of passengers, passport numbers, dates of flight, and so on)
» what outputs are produced (in this case, on-screen and e-ticket (QR code) sent to customer's smartphone)
» what processing is done (check flights, process customer data, allocate flight reference number and access booking database; customer flight booking has to be added to database once all processing completed)
» what storage may be needed (a database is needed to store all the flight booking details).

As the analyst looks at each stage in the DFD process, they will then identify:

>> any problems that occur in the current system (this is done by looking at the data flows in each stage of the process and looking for bottlenecks and other potential areas where errors do or could occur)
>> user and information requirements (see below).

User requirements

The problem to solve is this: computer system developers do not really understand how a business works: business managers do not really know how computer systems could help them. The user requirements are designed to help with this problem:

>> User requirements are therefore written by the analyst for the business managers (who are the customers).
>> They are written in natural language with very few technical details or jargon.
>> Their purpose is to allow the customers to check that what the analyst proposes, following the investigations, is exactly what they originally specified; for example, if the company employs people with disabilities, does the new hardware take that into account?
>> The user requirements will also describe what the analyst thinks the customer does with their system.

Information requirements

>> This is the information needed to support the business.
>> The information requirements are made up of:
>> what? (that is, the data)
>> when? (that is, the timing).

A systems analyst turns the information and user requirements into a functional **requirements specification** (that is, how the new system will be developed and implemented, including timescales).

The requirements are typically defined as a list of, for example:

>> who the customers are and how they interface with the system
>> who the vendors are (the sellers of the products), and how they interface with the system
>> who the employees are and how they interface with the system.

7.1.3 System specification

The DFD and other information gathering processes allow the analysis team to identify what hardware and software is needed to run the new system.

Identify and justify hardware

>> Identification and justification of which input devices are needed might be, for example:
  - **barcode readers** (using barcode readers avoids the need to manually input data about goods, which is more efficient, less error-prone and less expensive in the long run)

- **scanners** (these could be used if it is necessary to convert any existing paper documents into an electronic format during the implementation stage)
- **touch screens** (this may be the best and most cost-effective way of gathering information from a business customer, for example, and to ensure an employee does not miss any important data during a customer conversation).
» Identification and justification of which output devices are needed; for example:
  - **3D printer** (if the company are manufacturing toys, for example, it is much more cost-effective to do a 'one off' using a 3D printer than making a toy in the conventional way)
  - **very large 60" (152 cm) monitors** (the company may be using CAD software and the need for very large, expensive monitors, may be justifiable)
  - **speakers** (the company may employ people with disabilities, so the need for verbal outputs from the computer may be a necessary requirement).

Identify and justify software

» Identification and justification of which software is required; for example:
  - **operating system** (which operating system is the most appropriate to meet the company needs)
  - **applications software:**
    - off-the-shelf software, which would save a lot of development time and costs, but may require compromises in how the company runs; off-the-shelf software (such as *Word* or *Excel*) also has a huge user-base in case of problems and a minimum of training will be required, because the software is well known
    - bespoke software (written specifically for the company) – this will require considerable time and money to develop, but will exactly meet the company's requirements; it will also require considerable training in using software unknown to the employees, and there will be no user-base to seek help (they will have to rely on the software development technical team, which could be expensive).
» Storage requirements also need to be considered; for example:
  - **size of storage** (how many bytes of storage are required for the systems to run now, and in the future)
  - **type of storage** (which storage type is the most suitable for the company: hard disk drives, solid-state drives or even magnetic tape drives) – the choice could depend on:
    - data access and data write speeds
    - number of read-write operations (there is still some doubt about the longevity of SSD if it has to endure large numbers of read-write operations)
    - type of access – can it be serial access to the data (all read in order) or does it need to be direct (no need to read all the data in order)
    - if huge amounts of storage are required and data access time is not that important, magnetic tape may still be the best option.

7.2 Design

7.2.1 Design

Once the analysis of the existing system has taken place, and the systems analyst has a better idea of the scale of the problem, then the next stage in the process is design. Figure 7.4 summarises the design stage.

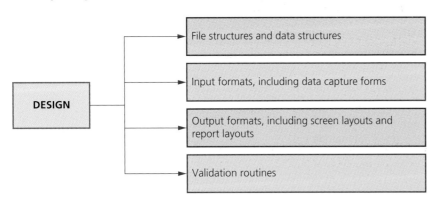

▲ **Figure 7.4** Design stage

File structures and data structures

In this section we will consider how the files containing data will be structured; it will also be necessary to consider the format of the data types being stored in the files. A file is made up of a number of **records**, and each record is broken up into **fields**. One of the fields must be unique and will act as the **primary key field** – this is to allow each record to be uniquely identified. An example of a record (in the file) is shown in Figure 7.5.

	Field 1 product_code	Field 2 year_of_manufacture	Field 3 product_description	Field 4 price_$	Field 5 department
Record 1	T4131618	2022	Digital camera	$405.00	T
Record 2	T5552200	2021	Memory card	$35.50	T
Record 3	A3110011	2020	Tripod for T4131618	$220.00	A
Record 4	A4567777	2021	Case for T4131618	$55.75	A
Record 5	B1110000	2022	Extra battery	$85.50	B

▲ **Figure 7.5** Typical file structure (showing records and fields)

Each field in the record now needs to be totally defined as follows:

» field name (for example, **product_code**)
» field length (what is the maximum number of characters that need to be stored)
» data type (see below)
» is any code being used (in this example, the codes T, A and B are being used – coding saves space in the file because only a single character is being used; this also speeds up entry and also reduces errors)
» the primary key field here will be **product_code** because it is unique.

Data types

We will now consider data types. The data types in Table 7.2 are the ones you are most likely to come across:

▼ **Table 7.2** Data types

Data type	Description	Examples
Alphanumeric	This type of data can store alpha characters (letters or text) and numeric data (numbers)	A345FF or 07432011122
Character	This is just a single letter (or text)	X or d
Text	This can be a string of letters or numbers or other symbols	example_of_text_string
Boolean	This data type stores data in a Yes/No or True/False format (logical options)	Y or N
Numeric	This data type is used to store numeric data which is used to perform calculations (this does not include telephone numbers, for example, because these have to be stored as alphanumeric data) There are several different types of numeric data:	
	Integer (whole numbers)	234 or –1245
	Decimal/real (non-integer values)	25.54 or –150.22
	Currency (allows inclusion of currency symbols)	$24.55 or €123.50
	Date/time (allows dates and time to be stored)	14/05/2020 or 12:45

It is now possible to complete the file structure for the example in Figure 7.5.

▼ **Table 7.3** Field lengths and data types

Field name	Field length	Data type
Product_code	30	Text
Year_of_manufacture	4	Numeric: integer
Product_description	40	Text
Price_$	6	Numeric: currency
Department	1	Character/text

Please note that the field lengths given in Table 7.3 are just 'possible' values. When assigning a field length, it is important to give a good estimate of what will be the smallest value needed to store the data items. If a field length of 50 is assigned to a field and the largest data item is only five characters, then this will be a large waste of memory space in a database because a field size of 50 would have been allocated for the whole file.

> **Exercise 7a**
> ....
> Which data types would you use for the following data items?
> | | | | | | |
> |---|---|---|---|---|---|
> | **i** | A21DD45678 | **v** | 01214444555 | **ix** | 22/10/2020 |
> | **ii** | Y | **vi** | 200 | **x** | 21:45 |
> | **iii** | Sample_data_items | **vii** | €55 | | |
> | **iv** | T or F (only) | **viii** | 24.12 | | |

7.2.2 Validation routines

When data is input into a computer system, there is a need to check that the data is acceptable. **Validation** is the process where data entered into a computer is checked to see if it satisfies certain criteria. It is an automatic check carried out by the computer as part of its programming.

For example, validation criteria could be that only positive numbers entered, or eight characters must be entered; any data failing these criteria should be rejected.

Validation is not a check on whether the data is correct or accurate; it is only a check to see if it is reasonable.

There are a number of validation routines that can be used. Some of the more common ones are described in Table 7.4.

▼ **Table 7.4** Validation checks (routines)

Validation check	Description	Examples
Range	This checks to see if the data input lies between an acceptable upper value and an acceptable lower value	Limiting a temperature range from 10 to 50 degrees Celsius
Type/character	This checks to see if the data entered is of the correct type (i.e. letter or number only)	A person's name should not contain numbers A person's height should not contain letters
Length	This checks to see if the data input contains only the required number of characters	If a password contains eight characters, then an input with seven characters or nine characters, for example, should produce an error message
Format	This checks to see if the data input is in the correct format	Ensures the date is entered in a format such as dd/mm/yyyy (e.g. 10/12/2023)
Presence	This checks that data has been entered into a field and it has not been left empty	For example, when using an online form, a person's telephone number may be a 'required field'; if no data is entered, this should give rise to an error message
Check digit	This is an extra digit added to a number which has been calculated from the other digits	Check digits can identify three types of error: 1 if two digits have been transposed during input; for example, 13597 instead of 13579 2 an incorrect digit has been entered; for example, 13559 instead of 13579 3 a digit has been missed out or extra digit added; for example, 1359 or 135799 instead of 13579 (in all three cases, the check digit (usually the last digit) would not be 9 if an error had been made)

> **Exercise 7b**
>
> 1 A password (which takes the form xxxxnnxx where x = a letter and n = a numerical digit) is being entered using an online form.
>   a Name three possible validation checks you could use.
>   b Give an example of an input that would pass each of your validation checks.
>   c Give an example of an input that would cause an error message for each of your validation checks.
> 2 The following data is being entered into a database:
>
> | Name: | |
> | --- | --- |
> | Date of birth: | (dd/mm/yyyy) |
> | Telephone number: | |
> | Order reference no. | (xxxxnnnn) |
> | Sex: | M ◯ or F ◯ |
>
> ▲ **Figure 7.6** Data capture form
>
> Give a suitable validation check for each of the five fields. A **different** validation check must be given for each field.
>
> Which field could be used as the primary (key) field?

7.2.3 Input formats (data capture forms)

Data capture forms are often used to input data into a computer. These forms ensure data is input into the computer in the correct format. They need to be designed very carefully to ensure that the format of the data matches, for example, the database where the data is being stored.

Data capture forms will be either paper-based or electronic-based depending on the application.

Paper-based forms need to:

» have a heading to make the purpose of the form clear
» make it clear to the person filling in the form where they must place their answers
» make use of text boxes which will limit the amount of information collected
» make use of character boxes for data such as surnames, telephone numbers, and so on (each box allows one character only)
» make use of printed text boxes to allow for easy input of items such as date of birth
» make use of tick boxes to make choices easier (such as sex – male or female)
» make sure there is sufficient space to write answers
» make use of clear fonts and clear text colours to ensure the form is easy to read.

Figure 7.7 shows a typical example, which allows data about a car for sale to be manually completed, for later input into a computer database.

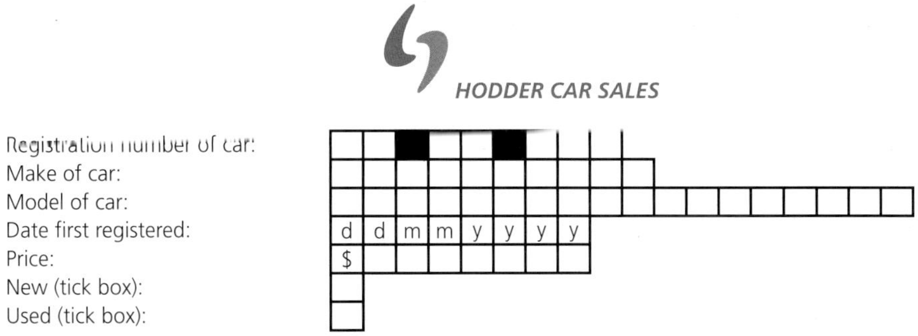

HODDER CAR SALES

Registration number of car:
Make of car:
Model of car:
Date first registered:
Price:
New (tick box):
Used (tick box):

▲ **Figure 7.7** Paper-based data capture form

A computer-based data capture form is slightly different. These often have the following features:

» use of text boxes to capture key data clearly
» use of on-screen help when completing the form
» use of drop-down/combo boxes where there are limited choices
» use of radio buttons and tick boxes requiring a single click of a mouse to select
» automatic validation of data as it is entered
» control buttons (such as next form, clear entry, save, etc.)
» double entry boxes (with verification rules) to check correctness of key data (for example, when keying in an email address).

In the car sales example shown in Figure 7.7, the following differences could be used with a computer-based data capture form:

» registration number: same as paper-based form
» make of car: make use of a drop-down box as there are a limited number of manufacturers
» model of car: same as paper-based form
» date first registered: use of drop-down boxes for day, month and year
» price: use boxes as shown but include a validation check
» new or used: use of tick box or radio button to indicate option
» other features: a back and forward button (to complete details of all cars), and a save button when the form is complete for each car.

> ## Exercise 7c
> ....
> Design a computer-based data capture form using the fields given above.
> Remember that it has to be completed online, so it should include radio buttons,
> drop-down boxes and so on. It should look a little different to the paper-based
> form shown in Figure 7.7.

7.2.4 Output formats – screen layouts and report layouts

The output from any system needs careful consideration because this is part of any user interface, and is the result of some form of processing. Screen outputs should be designed:

- » to make sure the size of all the output fields is correct
- » so that any instructions/descriptions are clear
- » so that the full screen is utilised (avoiding large areas of 'nothing')
- » so that colours and fonts (size and type) make the output clear.

If the output is on paper, then consideration must also be given to the type of output. Items such as headers and footers, fitting the page correctly, whether it should be in colour, and so on, all have to be carefully planned.

Reports (often the output from a database search) should clearly show all the fields that were included in the search criteria. The output is usually in the form of a table – the example in Figure 7.9 outputs a list of all sales managers over 40.

Details of employees

Employee No :	32110
First name :	Michael
Last name :	Pitt
Sex :	Male
Date of birth :	16/10/1979
Department :	Sales

Additional notes: Has the highest sales success for 2022 and should be considered to join the training department

[Print record]   [Next record]

▲ **Figure 7.8** Screen output example

Employees

Last Name	First Names	Job Title	Business Phone	Address
Pitt	Michael	Sales Manager	001 234 1235	2nd Avenue
Hawkin	Jason	Sales Manager	001 235 1245	4th Avenue
Amin	Manjit	Sales Manager	001 222 3456	9th Avenue
Clark	Katie	Sales Manager	001 234 1119	2nd Avenue
Fawkler	Jemima	Sales Manager	001 299 8745	11th Avenue

▲ **Figure 7.9** Report example

7.3 Development and testing

7.3.1 Testing

The need for testing

Once the design stage is completed, it is then necessary to create the system and fully test it. This section considers some of the development stages and testing strategies which are often adopted by systems analysts.

- » If the system contains files (for example, a database) then the file structure would need to be finalised at this stage (for example, what type of data is being stored in each field, length of each field, which field will be the key field, how will the data files be linked, etc.). Once the file structure has been determined it is then created and needs to be fully tested to make sure it is robust when the system actually goes live.

>> Because it is important that the correct data is stored in files (etc.) there are certain techniques that need to be adopted to make sure the data populating the files/database is at least of the right type and that it conforms to certain rules. Validation routines and verification methods are used to ensure this happens. Again, these routines have to be fully tested to ensure they do trap unwanted data, but also to make sure any data transferred from a paper-based system to an electronic system has been done accurately.

>> Obviously, any system being developed will have some form of user interface. The types of hardware have already been considered; how these are used to actually interface with the final system now needs to be identified. For example, how the screens (and any other input devices) will be used to collect the data and the way the output will be presented. If specialist hardware is needed (for example, for people with disabilities) then it will be necessary to finalise how these devices are used with the system when it is implemented. This will be followed by thorough testing to ensure the user screens are user-friendly and that the correct output is associated with the inputs to the system.

Test designs

Test designs cover how a system is to be tested. Table 7.5 shows the test designs that need to be considered, and how we can ensure the following aspects can be achieved:

>> testing the data structures
>> testing the file structures
>> testing the input methods
>> testing the output formats
>> testing the validation rules.

▼ **Table 7.5** Testing designs

Data structures	The test design should determine how we can test that all data is in a correct format or has been stored in the correct way (for example, whether tables hold data correctly)
File structures	The testing design should test that the file structures function correctly (i.e. data is stored in the correct format and can be correctly retrieved when required)
Input formats	The testing design should determine how we can test that all data can be entered into the system correctly (for example, if a date is to be entered does the input format permit this date to be entered correctly)
Output formats	The test design should determine how we can test that screen outputs and reports are all in the correct format (for example, are the output results clear, complete and correctly match the input data)
Validation routines	The test design should determine what data is needed to test to see if all the validation rules work (for example, does the system correctly reject unreasonable data being input)

Test strategies

>> Software is often developed in **modular** form. This method allows it to be broken down into smaller parts (known as modules). Each module is developed separately by a programmer (or team of programmers).

>> Each module needs to be tested separately to see if it functions correctly. Any problems resulting from the testing require the module to be modified and then tested again.

» Once the development of each module is completed, the whole system needs to be tested as a whole (with all modules functioning together). Even though each module may work satisfactorily, when they are all put together there may be data clashes or incompatibility, memory issues, etc.

» All of this may lead to a need to improve the input and output methods, file/database structures, validation and verification methods, etc. and then fully test everything again. It is a very time-consuming process, but has to be as perfect as possible before the system uses live data.

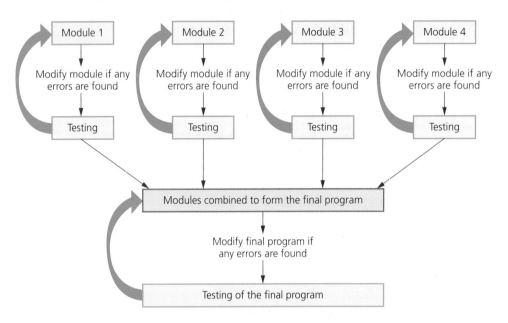

▲ **Figure 7.10** Module testing

Test plan, test data and live data

Once the testing designs and strategy have been determined, it then becomes necessary to formulate a test plan for each module. The test plan should include:

» a list of all the tests to be performed
» what data is to be used in the testing
» what type of testing the data is designed to check (i.e. normal, abnormal or extreme – see notes below)
» what live data should be used
» what the expected outcomes are from the testing
» do the actual outcomes match what is expected?

The list above included the types of data referred to as: normal, abnormal and extreme. Before looking at a sample test plan, we need to define these three types of data.

The example we will use is inputting a date into a database field. The entered data must take the format dd/mm/yyyy and all data must be numeric.

» **normal** – this is data which is acceptable/valid and has an expected (known) outcome; for example, the month can be **any** whole number in the range 1 to 12
» **extreme** – this is data at the **limits** of acceptability/validity; for example, the month can be either of the two end values i.e. 1 or 12

» **abnormal** – this is data **outside the limits** of acceptability/validity and should be rejected or cause an error message; for example, none of the following values are allowed as inputs for the month:
  - any value less than 1 (for example, 0, –1, –15, etc.)
  - any value greater than 12 (for example, 32, 45, etc.)
  - letters or other non-numeric data (for example, July, etc.)
  - non-integer values (for example, 3.5, 10.75, etc.).

Once a system has been fully tested, it is then tested with live data. This is data with known outcomes. Live data is entered into the new system and the results compared with those produced from the existing system. If the two outcomes do not match, then further modifications to the system may be needed. Table 7.6 shows an example of live data testing.

▼ **Table 7.6** Live data comparison table

Live data	Expected result	Actual result	Any actions?
January	An error message should be output	The data was accepted by system	Validation routines on month element need to be rewritten, then the system retested
0	The message 'a zero value is not a permitted input' should be output	The new system crashed when '0' was input	System needs an error trap, such as: IF INPUT = 0 THEN OUTPUT 'no zero values allowed'

Example of a test plan

The test plan shown in Figure 7.11 is designed to test a module where temperatures are input which must be in the correct range (21 °C to 50 °C). Any temperatures outside this range should be rejected. The input temperatures can be integer or real (decimal).

Data set	Data input	Type of data input	Expected outcome	Actual outcome
A	35	Normal	Data should be accepted	
B	45	Normal	Data should be accepted	
C	25.5	Normal	Data should be accepted	
D	21	Extreme	Data should be accepted	
E	50	Extreme	Data should be accepted	
F	fifty	Abnormal	Error message should be given	
G	20	Abnormal	Error message should be given	
H	51	Abnormal	Error message should be given	
I	-5	Abnormal	Error message should be given	
J	100.5	Abnormal	Error message should be given	

Data chosen should come from the test designs and strategy.

If the system worked correctly, then test results for this column should be the same as column 4; if there are any discrepancies, the module will need to be modified and the testing repeated.

▲ **Figure 7.11** Test plan example

> ## Exercise 7d

Use the example of a date in the format dd/mm/yyyy when answering the following three questions.

1 Consider the following 20 pieces of data and decide whether each data item is normal, abnormal or extreme (tick the appropriate box in the table).

Data item	Field	Normal	Abnormal	Extreme
15	month		✓	
12	month			✓
07	month	✓		
1.6	month		✓	
1	month			✓
0	month		✓	
13	month		✓	
March	month		✓	
1	day			✓
31	day			✓
18	day	✓		
Tuesday	day		✓	
45	day		✓	
0	day		✓	
30	day	✓		
0001	year			✓
2021	year	✓		
90.55	year		✓	
−25	year		✓	
1854	year	✓		

2 Describe what validation routines could be used to check the date if it was input on the screen as follows:

Day: ☐

Month: ☐

Year: ☐

Describe how it would be possible to avoid errors altogether when inputting the data in the form shown above.

3 Write test data for the following fields in a database (the data should try to cover all possible types of data). The database will store the following information:
- name of holiday resort
- average daily temperature (a whole number value is used)
- number of hours of sunshine per day (a whole number value is used).

Describe the validation routines that should be written into the database interface to check the above input values are reasonable.

7.4 Implementation

7.4.1 System implementation

Once the system is fully tested, the next stage is to fully implement it. Some of the stages in this process are shown in Figure 7.12.

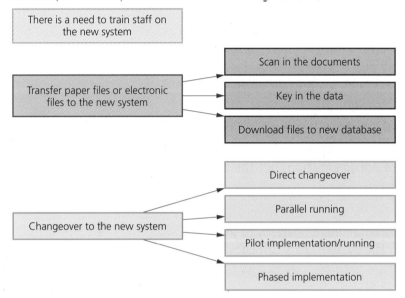

▲ **Figure 7.12** The implementation stage

▼ **Table 7.7** Methods used in changeover (part of implementation)

Implementation method	Design of implementation method	Advantages and disadvantages of the method
Direct	With this method the old system is stopped overnight and the new system introduced immediately	» This method can be disastrous if the new system fails because the old system is no longer available » The benefits are immediate » Costs are reduced (because only one system is used there is no need to pay for two sets of staff)
Parallel	With this method, the old and new systems are run side by side for a time before the new system takes over altogether	» If this new system fails, the old system is still available as a backup » It is possible to gradually train staff » It is more expensive than **direct** because extra staff are needed to run both systems together » It is also more time consuming than **direct** because data needs to be entered into two systems
Pilot	With this method, the new system is introduced into one branch or office of the company and its performance assessed before being introduced elsewhere in the company	» If the new system fails, only one part is affected; the remainder is unaffected » It is possible to train staff in one area only, which is much faster and less costly than **parallel** » The costs are also less than **parallel** because only one part of the system is being used in the pilot warehouse
Phased	With this method, only part of the new system is introduced and, only when it proves to work satisfactorily, is the next part introduced, and so on, until the old system is fully replaced	» If the latest part fails, it is only necessary to go back in the system to the point of failure; hence failure is not disastrous » More expensive than **direct** because it is necessary to evaluate each phase before moving to the next stage » Very time consuming because each part needs to be fully evaluated before making any further changes to the system » It is possible to ensure the system works properly before expanding

We will now consider **changeover** to the new system in more depth. As indicated in Figure 7.12, there are four common methods used for changing over from the old system to the new system. Each one has advantages and disadvantages which need to be weighed up before the most appropriate method is chosen for a particular application.

7.5 Documentation

7.5.1 Documentation

Once the new system is fully developed, a considerable amount of documentation also needs to be produced for:

1   people who may need to modify or develop the system further at some later stage
2   the end-user.

There is some overlap between the two types of documentation, but the basic requirements are shown below.

Technical documentation

Technical documentation is designed to help programmers/analysts to make improvements to the system or repair/maintain the system. This can consist of any of the following:

>> program listing/coding
>> programming language used
>> program flowcharts/algorithms
>> system flowcharts
>> purpose of the system/program/software
>> limitations of the system
>> input formats
>> hardware requirements
>> software requirements
>> minimum memory requirements
>> known 'bugs' in the system
>> list of variables used (and their meaning/description)
>> file structures
>> sample runs (with results and actual test data used)
>> output formats
>> validation rules
>> meaning of error messages.

User documentation

User documentation is designed to help users to learn how to use the software or system. This can consist of any of the following:

>> how to load/install/run the software
>> how to save files
>> how to do a search
>> how to sort data
>> how to print out
>> how to add, delete or amend records

>> the purpose of the system/program/software package
>> limitations of the system
>> screen layouts (input format)
>> print layouts (output format)
>> hardware requirements
>> software requirements
>> sample runs (with results and actual test data used)
>> error handling/meaning of errors
>> troubleshooting guide/help lines/FAQs (frequently asked questions)
>> how to log in/log out
>> tutorials
>> error messages/meaning of error messages
>> glossary of terms.

7.6 Evaluation

7.6.1 Evaluate a solution

Once a system is up and running it is necessary to do some **evaluation** and carry out any maintenance if necessary. The following is a list of some of the things to be considered when evaluating how well the new system has worked; this can ultimately lead to a redesign of part of the system if there is strong evidence to suggest that changes need be made (refer back to the Figure 7.1 in the introduction to this chapter).

>> Compare the final solution with the original task requirements.
>> Identify any limitations of the system.
>> Identify any necessary improvements that need to be made.
>> Evaluate the users' responses to using the new system.
>> Compare test results from the new system with results from the old system.
>> Compare performance of the new system with performance of the old system.
>> Observe users performing set tasks (compare old with new).
>> Measure the time taken to complete tasks (compare old with new).
>> Interview users to gather responses about how well the new system works.
>> Give out questionnaires to gather responses about the ease of use of the new system.
   Overall, is the new solution:
   - more efficient? (this might mean 'more efficient to use' or 'more efficient for the business')
   - easy to use?
   - appropriate for the task it was designed for?

Some results from the evaluation may lead to two things happening:

>> update of hardware because:
   - of feedback from end-users
   - new hardware comes on the market, necessitating change
   - changes within the company require new devices to be added or updated.
>> update of software because:
   - of feedback from end-users
   - changes to the company structure or how the company works that may require modifications to the software
   - changes in legislation that may require modifications to the software.

Exam-style questions

1 For each of these questions, choose the correct response from the five options given. [10]

a What validation type would make sure a post code, such as LA21 4NN, was entered in the correct layout?

a	Length check
b	Presence check
c	Range check
d	Format check
e	Type check

b What validation type would you use to make sure a number entered was > 0 but not > 100?

a	Length check
b	Presence check
c	Range check
d	Format check
e	Type check

c What validation type checks that a field in an online form is not left empty?

a	Length check
b	Presence check
c	Range check
d	Format check
e	Type check

d What validation type checks that the correct number of characters has been entered?

a	Length check
b	Presence check
c	Range check
d	Format check
e	Type check

e Data is to be entered in the format DDMMYY. Which of the following is NOT a valid date?

a	230421
b	010120
c	30th May 2024
d	050505
e	121221

f Which of the following statements is FALSE?

a	Validation can check that data entered is sensible
b	Validation can check a value lies between an upper and lower bound
c	Validation can check that a field in an online form is not left blank
d	Validation is an automatic check done by a computer
e	Validation can check that the data entered is correct

g Temperatures (which must be in the range 20 to 80 inclusive) are being input into a computer. Test data is being used to make sure the validation checks work. Which of the following are examples of extreme data?

a	0 and 100
b	19 and 81
c	20 and 80
d	21 and 81
e	−1 and 85

h What is the name given to data which is outside the limits of acceptability?

a	Normal
b	Live
c	Extreme
d	Abnormal
e	Erroneous

i Which of the following is NOT a valid method of implementing a new computer system?

a	Serial changeover
b	Direct changeover
c	Parallel running
d	Pilot implementation
e	Phased implementation

j Which of the following data-gathering methods suffers from the Hawthorne effect?

a	Examining existing documents
b	Interviewing customers who use the system
c	Interviewing staff who use the system
d	Observing workers doing the tasks
e	Filling in questionnaires

2 Carlos is designing a new computer system to replace an existing system.
   a Tick **four** items which will need to be designed. [4]

	Tick (✓)
Inputs to the current system.	
Data capture forms.	✓
Report layouts.	✓
Limitations of the system.	
Observation methods.	
Improvements to the system.	
User and information requirements.	
Validation routines.	✓
Problems with the current system.	
File structures.	✓

   b Before the system is implemented it needs to be tested. Different types of test data are used to test the system. An example of test data is live data.
   Describe what is meant by live data. [2]
   c Following the implementation of the system, technical documentation needs to be written.
   Identify **three** components of technical documentation which are not found in user documentation. [3]

Cambridge IGCSE Information and Communication Technology (0417) Paper 11 Q10, May/June 2018

3 A farmer has purchased a computerised milking system for her cows. She has asked a systems analyst to create a database to store details of the cows being milked. Examples of the details of the cows which will be stored are:

Breed_of_cow	Date_of_birth	Weight_of_cow	Average_milk_yield	Animal_passport_number
Holstein	25/02/2017	725.9	24.5	998/2017
Ayrshire	15/03/2016	715.0	20.1	972/2016
Jersey	25/02/2017	732.7	25.0	971/2016
Holstein	10/10/2016	715.0	25.0	765/2016

   a Complete the following table by entering the most appropriate data type for each field. For any numeric field, specify the type of number. [5]

Field name	Data type
Breed_of_cow	text
Date_of_birth	text
Weight_of_cow	text
Average_milk_yield	text
Animal_passport_number	text

b State which field would be the most appropriate for the primary key. [1]

c A validation check is used when entering the animal passport number into the database.
Name and describe the most appropriate validation check that could be applied to this field. [2]

*Cambridge IGCSE Information and Communication Technology (0417) Paper 11 Q9 a, b & c,
May/June 2018*

4 In the table below, by using a tick (✓) indicate whether each component is found in user documentation only, in technical documentation only or in both types of documentation. [5]

Description of component	Technical documentation (✓)	User documentation (✓)
How to sort the data		
Hardware requirements		
How to load and run the software		
Program flowcharts/algorithms		
Troubleshooting guide/FAQs		
Validation rules/routines		
Purpose of the system		
Program listing/coding		
Glossary of terms		
Meaning of error messages		

5 Put the following six stages of the systems life cycle into their correct order:
» Analysis
» Design
» Development and Testing
» Documentation
» Evaluation
» Implementation [3]

6 Which five computer terms are being described below? [5]

a A changeover method where the old system is stopped overnight and the new system is introduced straight away.

b A changeover method where the new system is introduced into one branch of a company and its performance assessed before being introduced in all the company's branches.

c Type of validation that checks whether or not the correct number of characters has been entered.

d Part of the system life cycle that considers data capture forms, file structures, validation and screen layouts.

e Software development technique where the program is broken down into smaller parts and each part is tested separately.

7 a Describe what is meant by the evaluation stage in the systems life cycle. [3]
b Give **two** reasons why hardware may need to be updated ten years after its initial introduction. [2]
c Give **two** reasons why software may need to be updated ten years after its initial introduction. [2]

8 A program is being written which only accepts numbers in the range 1 to 100 (inclusively) to be input. Validation routines are being used to check the input data.
a Name two validation routines which could be used to check the input data in this program. Give a reason for your choice in each case. [2]
b Test data can be normal, abnormal or extreme. Explain the differences in these three types of test data. Use examples to illustrate your answer. [3]
c For this program being written, indicate, by ticking the appropriate box, whether the following input data is normal, abnormal or extreme. [3]

	Normal (✓)	Abnormal (✓)	Extreme (✓)
52			
1			
104			
100			
twenty-five			
99			

d Explain what is meant by live data.
Describe how live data is used. [3]

9 An electric power company introduced computer monitoring and control systems in the year 2000. A project management team has brought in a systems analyst with a view to introducing a new system or upgrading their existing system.
The power company supplies the national grid with electricity and cannot go offline for more than a maximum of eight hours.
a Give **three** reasons why the project management team have decided to renew or upgrade their system. [3]
b Suggest **two** methods a systems analyst might use to research the current system. Justify your choice of methods. [4]
c Describe the best method of implementing a new system into the company. Justify your choice of method. [3]

10 Six descriptions are given on the left and ten computer terms are given on the right. By drawing arrows, connect each description to its correct term. [6]

Designed to help programmers/analysts to make improvements to the system or repair/maintain the system	User documentation
	Live data
This checks to see if the data entered is of the correct type (i.e. letter or number only)	Extreme data
	Direct changeover
Actual data used which has known outcomes	Type check
	Technical documentation
Part of a new system is introduced and, only when it proves to work satisfactorily, is the next part introduced, and so on, until the old system is fully replaced	Abnormal data
	Format check
This is data which is at the limits of acceptability or validity	Phased implementation
This is data which is outside the limits of acceptability or validity and should be rejected or cause an error message	Evaluation stage

Safety and security

This chapter covers safety and security issues when using computers in the office or at home. As the use of computers continues to expand, the health risks and security risks continue to increase. Many of these risks are associated with the internet which, by its very nature, poses a great risk to younger people unless they are vigilant at all times. But large businesses are also at risk from a number of threats, including hackers, pharming attacks and viruses. Many of the precautions people and business can take are common sense, but, equally, it also requires additional knowledge to know how to protect yourself from these external attacks, which can come from anywhere in the world.

8.1 Physical safety

8.1.1 Safety issues

Physical safety is a different issue to health risks (as discussed in Chapter 5.2). While health safety is how to stop people becoming ill, or being affected by daily contact with computers, physical safety is concerned with the dangers that could lead to serious injuries or even loss of life. Some of the more common risks, together with their major causes and possible prevention measures, are listed in Table 8.1.

▼ **Table 8.1** Physical safety hazards and prevention

Safety risk	Cause of safety risk	Prevention measures
Electrocution	» Spilling liquids/drinks on electric equipment » Exposed wires/damaged insulation » Unsafe electrical equipment » Unsafe electrics (for example, wall sockets) in the office	» Do not allow drinks to be taken into the computer room » Check all wires on a regular basis and renew wires if there is any sign of damaged insulation » Ensure all equipment is checked by a qualified electrician on a regular basis » Make use of an RCB (residual current breaker) to prevent electrocution

Safety risk	Cause of safety risk	Prevention measures
Fire hazard	» Overloaded wall sockets (several items plugged into one wall socket) » Overheating of computer equipment (due to poor heat dissipation) » Exposed wires causing a short circuit	» Increase the number of wall sockets and do not use too many extension blocks » Do not cover the cooling vents on computer equipment » Clean out dust accumulation in computers to prevent overheating » Make sure all equipment is fully tested on a regular basis » Ensure there is good room ventilation » Use low-voltage equipment wherever possible » Have a number of fully tested **carbon dioxide/dry powder fire extinguishers**
Tripping hazard	» Trailing wires on the floor » Damaged carpets and other flooring	» Use cable ducts to make the wires safe » Cover exposed wires and hide wires under desks away from general thoroughfare » Use wireless connectivity wherever possible, therefore eliminating the need for trailing cables
Personal injury	» Heavy equipment unstable or falling from desks » Desks collapsing under weight/desks not designed to take the weight	» Use desks strong enough to take the weight of the computer equipment » Use large desks and tables so that hardware is not too close to the edge where it could fall off

8.2 E-Safety

8.2.1 Data protection

Most countries have some form of **data protection act (DPA)**. This is legislation designed to protect individuals and to prevent incorrect or inaccurate data being stored.

Essentially, DPAs are set up to protect the rights of the individual about whom data is obtained, stored and processed – for example, collection, use, disclosure, destruction and holding of data. Any such act applies to both computerised and paper records.

Many data protection acts are based on eight principles, as outlined in Figure 8.1.

In many countries, failure to abide by these simple rules by anyone who holds data about individuals can lead to a heavy fine or even imprisonment.

1 Data must be fairly and lawfully processed.

2 Data can only be processed for the stated purpose.

3 Data must be adequate, relevant and not excessive.

4 Data must be accurate.

5 Data must not be kept longer than necessary.

6 Data must be processed in accordance with the data subject's rights.

7 Data must be kept secure.

8 Data must not be transferred to another country unless they also have adequate protection.

▲ **Figure 8.1** Main principles of data protection acts

There are general guidelines about how to stop data being obtained unlawfully:

» do not leave personal information lying around on a desk when not attended
» lock filing cabinets at the end of the day or when the room is unoccupied
» do not leave data on a computer monitor if it is unattended; log off from the computer if away from your desk for any length of time
» use passwords and user IDs, which should be kept secure; passwords should be difficult to guess/break and should be changed frequently (see earlier notes on passwords)
» make sure that anything sent in an email or fax (including attachments) is not of a sensitive nature.

All of the above are in addition to other security safeguards discussed elsewhere in this book.

8.2.2 Personal data

Personal data refers to any data concerning a living person who can be identified from the data itself or from the data in conjunction with other information. For example, 'Peter Smith has long purple hair and lives at 40 Green Street' would very clearly identify this individual!

Examples of personal data include:

» name
» address or email address (such as myname.lastname@mycompany.com)
» an ID card number/passport number
» an IP address
» cookie ID
» the advertising identifier on a mobile phone
» date of birth
» banking details
» photographs of the individual (for example, in full school uniform).

Some personal data is often referred to as sensitive (personal) data. Examples of sensitive data include:

» ethnicity or race
» political views
» membership of a political party
» membership of a trade union
» religion/philosophical beliefs
» sexual orientation/gender
» criminal record
» medical history
» genetic data/DNA
» biometric data.

Extra special care needs to be taken of sensitive personal data.

Whether data is personal or sensitive, it is imperative that all precautions are taken to keep it confidential, and prevent any inappropriate disclosure. This includes keeping data safe from hackers, for example, but it also means keeping data safe from accidental disclosure. One way to protect data if it is accidentally

> **Link**
> ....
> For more on passwords see Section 4.2.

disclosed is to encrypt it. You will read many ways of keeping data secure in this chapter and in other chapters throughout this textbook.

8.2.3 E-Safety

E-safety refers to the benefits, risks and responsibilities when using ICT. It is often defined to be the safe and responsible use of technology. However, e-safety is as much about user behaviour as it is about electronic security. In particular:

» when using the internet
» sending and receiving emails
» taking part in social media
» online gaming.

Using the internet

The following is a list of the precautions that can be taken to minimise the potential danger when using the internet:

» When using the internet make sure that the websites being used can be trusted (for example, look out for websites including **https** and/or the green padlock symbol).
» Only purchase items from websites that offer secure, encrypted connections (see Section 8.3).
» When using search engines, always make sure the device settings are set to 'safe search' and the highest possible level of security is used (also refer to Chapter 10).
» Only use websites recommended by teachers, parents or from trusted sources– refer to Chapter 10.
» Be careful what you download; is the material potentially harmful? Could it be malware? (We will be looking at malware later in this section.) It is essential that anti-virus or anti-malware software is always running in the background and is kept up to date.
» Always remember to log out of sites when you have finished using them; remember that **cookies** are used every time you log into a website (take particular care with websites that store key data such as bank account or credit/debit card details).

Sending and receiving emails

The following list highlights some of the dangers when sending and receiving **emails**. It is important to have an awareness of the risks when opening emails and how to deal with emails from unknown sources.

» Only open emails or attachments from known sources.
» Make sure your internet service provider (ISP) has an effective email filtering feature to ensure emails from unknown sources are put into your spam folder.
» Only reply to an email if you know the person who sent it (or the organisation, if you are 100 per cent certain it is genuine).
» Check that email addresses or website addresses pertaining to come from a genuine company always contain the real company's website address; for example, a web page with the address customer_accounts@gmail.com should

be treated with caution, whereas customer_accounts@amazon.com is more likely to be genuine.

» Think carefully before replying to an email and never include the name of your school/college, or any personal data that could identify you.

» Never send photos of yourself (particularly in school uniform, which could be used to identify your school).

» Beware of phishing and pharming scams (see Section 8.3).

» Protect your email account by using passwords which are difficult to guess, and change them on a regular basis (see Section 8.3).

» Take care when forwarding emails (see Chapter 10 for more details).

» Manually type in email addresses (do not copy and paste an email address from a recipient) because you may not spot typing errors or other clues that it is not genuine.

» Avoid clicking on hyperlinks within emails because it could be part of a phishing scam.

» Remember, the **unsubscribe** link at the bottom of an email could itself be fraudulent.

» Avoid using the Cc or To boxes when sending multiple emails; it is always a good idea to create emailing groups and put the name of the group into the Bcc box; in the To box, send the email to yourself – this will give you and your friends some protection because any unauthorised access will not get to see the email addresses of those in the emailing group (see Chapter 10 for more information).

> **Link**
> ....
> For more on email see Section 10.1.

Social media

When using social media sites, it is important to be careful and make sure you know how to block undesirable people. The following list shows some of the dangers and some of the ways to protect yourself:

» Do not publicly post or give out personal information to people you do not know, including email addresses or house addresses, because this could be used to find information about you or carry out identity theft.

» Do not send out photos of yourself to people you do not know; again this could lead to identity theft or somebody impersonating you (many of the photos on social media sites are false).

» Always make sure you use the privacy settings when posting photos of yourself on social media sites, so that only people you trust can see them.

» It is important that none of the photos you post can link you to a place or an address (for example, it is not a good idea to show the number plate on a car because it is possible to find your address from this information).

» Particular care should be taken not to post photos of yourself in some form of school uniform; again, this gives somebody information about where they can find you.

» Always maintain privacy settings to stop 'non-friends' from contacting you and also make sure you control who has access to your profile.

» Only make friends with people you know or are very well-known to other friends.

» Avoid using, or forwarding messages containing, inappropriate language.

» It is extremely important to be very vigilant when using social networking sites, instant messaging or chat rooms:
- Block or report anybody who acts suspiciously or uses inappropriate language.
- Be very careful with the language used in chat rooms:
  - Always use a nickname and NEVER your real name
  - Keep private and personal data secret.
- Do not enter private chat rooms – stay in public spaces (the danger signs are if someone wants to enter a private chat room, asks you to instant message or email, requests your telephone number or even suggests that you meet).
- Never arrange to meet anyone on your own, always tell an adult first and meet the person in a public place.
- Avoid the misuse of images, including forwarding on other images from other people.
- Always respect people's confidentiality.

> ## Exercise 8a
> Evaluate your own use of the internet, emails and social media/networking sites.
>
> Which of these e-safety strategies do you use every day?

Online gaming

Online gaming has increased over the last few years. There are many reasons for this, such as better internet connections, more sophisticated mobile devices (phones and tablets) and greater realism in recent games. It is important to be careful when using online gaming because is also carries risks. Many users think all the games players are like-minded and, therefore, there are no real risks associated with this type of communication. That is a dangerous assumption. Some of the known risks, associated with online gaming, reported over the years, include:

» predators (people who prey on others who they see as vulnerable)
» cyberbullying (the use of electronic communication to bully a person, typically by sending messages of an intimidating or threatening nature)
» use of webcams (the risks here are obvious!)
» voice-masking technology (to disguise a voice so you cannot tell their sex, age, or even their accent)
» it is often overlooked that online games are also a source of cyber attacks on a user's computer or mobile phone – viruses, phishing or spyware are well-reported examples of problems associated with certain online gaming
» violence in the game itself, which can lead to violent behaviour in reality.

As when using other platforms, you should not reveal any personal information about you or anyone else to anyone while gaming. This includes not using your real name.

> ## Exercise 8b
> Find out what safety measures should be taken when playing games on the internet.
>
> Write an article on these safety measures and include ways to minimise or remove these risks.

8.3 Security of data

8.3.1 Data threats

There are a number of security risks to data held on a computer/smartphone or data being transferred around networks. This section covers a large number of these risks:

»   hacking
»   **phishing**
»   vishing
»   smishing
»   **pharming**
»   viruses
»   malware
»   card fraud.

Each security risk together with its description, possible effects and risk mitigation will be set out as shown in Figure 8.2.

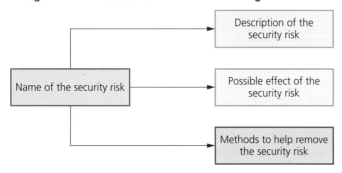

▲ **Figure 8.2** Security risks

Hacking

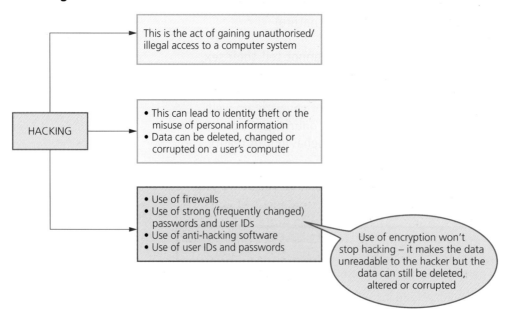

▲ **Figure 8.3** Risks of hacking

Phishing, smishing, vishing

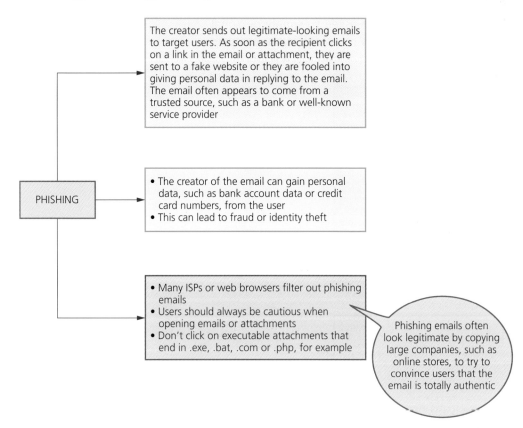

The creator sends out legitimate-looking emails to target users. As soon as the recipient clicks on a link in the email or attachment, they are sent to a fake website or they are fooled into giving personal data in replying to the email. The email often appears to come from a trusted source, such as a bank or well-known service provider

PHISHING

- The creator of the email can gain personal data, such as bank account data or credit card numbers, from the user
- This can lead to fraud or identity theft

- Many ISPs or web browsers filter out phishing emails
- Users should always be cautious when opening emails or attachments
- Don't click on executable attachments that end in .exe, .bat, .com or .php, for example

Phishing emails often look legitimate by copying large companies, such as online stores, to try to convince users that the email is totally authentic

▲ **Figure 8.4** Risks of phishing

Malicious use refers to, for example, data deletion, fraud, identity theft and selling on personal data. A good example of a phishing attack is when a user is sent an email saying they have ordered an item from an online store. They will be asked to click on a link to see the order details. The link takes the user to a web page that shows a product code that appears to come from a well-known company. A message, such as this will appear: 'if this order wasn't made by you, please fill out the following form to cancel your order in the next 24 hours'.

The form will ask for details such as credit card number, user's address, and so on. Some of the key clues are that links, such as 'how to contact us', do not work.

Smishing – this is short for 'SMS phishing'. It uses the SMS system of mobile phones to send out fake text messages. It is very similar to phishing. These scams often contain a URL or telephone number embedded in the text message. The recipient will be asked to log on to the website or make a telephone call. If they do, they will be asked to supply personal details such as credit/debit card numbers or passwords. As with phishing attacks, the text message will appear to come from a legitimate source and will make a claim, for example, that they have won a prize or that they need to contact their bank urgently. Most people believe that only computers are liable to security threats and that mobile phones are not at risk. This makes smishing a particularly dangerous security threat to many people.

Vishing (voicemail phishing) is another variation of phishing. This uses a voicemail message to trick the user into calling the telephone number contained in the message. As with all phishing attacks, the user will be asked to supply personal data thinking they are talking to somebody who works for a legitimate company.

Pharming

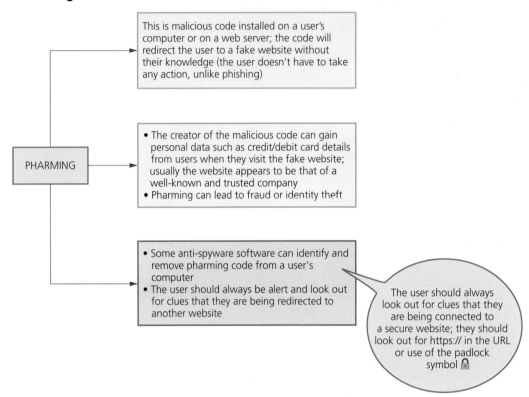

▲ **Figure 8.5** Risks of pharming

Viruses and malware

Malware is one of the biggest risks to the integrity and security of data on a computer system. Many software applications, such as anti-virus, are capable of identifying and removing most of the forms of malware. There are many forms of malware; this section details just a selection of those forms.

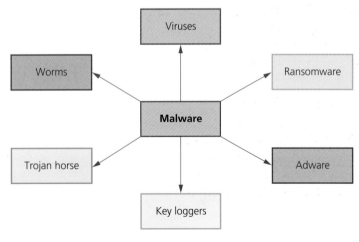

▲ **Figure 8.6** Malware types

Viruses are programs or program code that replicates (copies itself) with the intention of deleting or corrupting files and causing the computer to malfunction (for example, by deleting .exe files, filling up the hard drive with 'useless' data, and so on).

Viruses need an **active host** program on the target computer or an operating system that has already been infected, before they can actually run and cause harm (that is, they need to be executed by some trigger to start causing any damage).

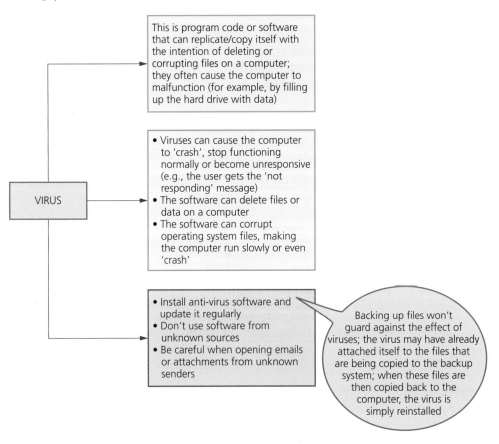

▲ Figure 8.7 Risks of viruses

Viruses are often sent as email attachments, and reside on infected websites or on infected software downloaded to the user's computer. Apart from all the usual safety actions (for example, do not open emails from unknown sources, do not install non-original software), always run an up-to-date virus scanner.

Worms

Worms are a type of stand-alone virus that can self-replicate. Their intention is to spread to other computers and corrupt whole networks; unlike viruses, they do not need an active host program to be opened in order to do any damage – they remain inside applications, which allows them to move throughout networks. In fact, worms replicate without targeting and infecting specific files on a computer; they rely on security failures within networks to permit them to spread unhindered.

Worms frequently arrive as message attachments and only one user opening a worm-infested email could end up infecting the whole network. As with viruses, the same safeguards should be employed, together with the running of an up-to-date anti-virus program. Worms tend to be problematic because of their ability to spread throughout a network without any action from an end-user; whereas viruses require each end-user to somehow initiate the virus.

Examples include the 'I love you' worm, which attacked nearly every email user in the world, overloaded phone systems and even brought down television networks. All of this makes them more dangerous than viruses.

Trojan horse

A **Trojan horse** is a malicious program which is often disguised as some legitimate software, but contains malicious instructions embedded within it. A Trojan horse replaces all or part of the legitimate software with the intent of carrying out some harm to the user's computer system.

They need to be executed by the end-user and therefore usually arrive as an email attachment or are downloaded from an infected website. For example, they could be transmitted via a fake anti-virus program that pops up on the user's screen claiming their computer is infected and action needs to be taken. The user will be invited to run fake anti-virus as part of a free trial. Once the user does this, the damage is done.

Once installed on the user's computer, the Trojan horse will give cyber criminals access to personal information on your computers, such as IP addresses, passwords and other personal data. **Spyware** (including key logging software) and ransomware are often installed on a user's computer via Trojan horse malware.

Because they rely on tricking end-users, firewalls and other security systems are often useless because the user can overrule them and initiate the running of the malware.

Key logging software

Key logging software (or **key loggers**) is a form of spyware. It gathers information by monitoring a user's keyboard activities carried out on their computer. The software stores keystrokes in a small file which is automatically emailed to the cybercriminal responsible for the software. It is primarily designed to monitor and capture web browsing and other activities and capture personal data (for example, bank account numbers, passwords and credit/debit card details). Key loggers can be detected and removed by anti-spyware software. Banks try and overcome this risk, by only asking for a different part of the password each time you log on (for example, 'please give the 3rd, 4th and 8th character in your password'). Sometimes drop-down boxes are also used because this involves on-screen selection using a mouse, which is difficult for the key logger to pick up. However, some key loggers work by capturing screen images at random intervals; these are known **screen recorders**.

> ### ▶ Exercise 8c
> Find out how banks overcome problems such as phishing, key logging software and hacking to ensure online banking is safe for their customers. When doing your research, also check out how risks at ATMs are mitigated by reading the section on card cloning and shoulder surfing (at the end of this section).

Adware

Adware is a type of malware. At its least dangerous, it will attempt to flood an end-user with unwanted advertising. For example, it could redirect a user's browser to a fake website that contains promotional advertising. They can be in the form of pop-ups, or appear in the browser's toolbar thus redirecting the search request.

Although not necessarily harmful, adware can:

» highlight weaknesses in a user's security defences
» be hard to remove – they defeat most anti-malware software because it can be difficult to determine whether or not they are harmful
» hijack a browser and create its own default search requests.

Ransomware

Essentially, **ransomware** are programs that encrypt data on a user's computer and 'hold the data hostage'. The cybercriminal just waits until the ransom money is paid and, sometimes, the decryption key is then sent to the user. It has caused considerable damage to some companies and individuals.

Imagine a situation where you log on to your computer, only to find the screen is locked and you cannot boot up your computer until the demands of the cybercriminal have been met. The malware restricts access to the computer and encrypts all the data until a ransom is paid. It may be installed on a user's computer by way of a Trojan horse or through social engineering.

When ransomware is executed, it either encrypts files straightaway or it waits for a while to determine how much of a ransom the victim can afford. The malware can be prevented by the usual methods (for example, by avoiding phishing emails); but once it is executed, it is almost impossible to reverse the damage caused. The best way to avoid a catastrophe is to ensure regular backups of key files are kept and therfore avoid having to pay a ransom.

Table 8.2 summaries the six types of malware described in this section.

▼ **Table 8.2** Summary of types of malware

Viruses	Programs or program code that can replicate/copy itself with the intention of deleting or corrupting files, or cause the computer to malfunction; they need an active host program on the target computer or an operating system that has already been infected before they can run
Worms	This is a type of stand-alone virus that can replicate itself with the intention of spreading to other computers; often uses networks to search out computers with weak security which are prone to such attacks
Trojan horses	These are malicious programs often disguised as legitimate software; they replace all or part of the legitimate software with the intent of carrying out some harm to the user's computer system
Spyware	Software that gathers information by monitoring, for example, all the activity on a user's computer; the gathered information is then sent back to the person who sent the software (sometimes they monitor key presses, which is referred to as key logging software)
Adware	Software that floods a user's computer with unwanted advertising; usually in the form of pop-ups, but can frequently appear in the browser address window redirecting the browser to a fake website which contains the promotional adverts
Ransomware	Programs that encrypt the data on a user's computer; a decryption key is sent back to the user once they pay a sum of money (a ransom); they are often sent via a Trojan horse or by social engineering

Card fraud

Card fraud is the illegal use of a credit or debit card. This can be due to:

» shoulder surfing when using the card on any device that requires keyboard entries (for example, an ATM or a handheld POS terminal)
» card cloning
» key logging software.

▲ **Figure 8.8** Automatic teller machine (ATM) and handheld point-of-sale (POS) terminal

Shoulder surfing

Shoulder surfing is a form of data theft where criminals steal personal information from a victim when they are using a cash dispensing machine (for example, an automatic teller machine – ATM), when paying for goods/services using a handheld point-of-sale (POS) device or even when paying using a smartphone. Examples of shoulder surfing includes:

» somebody watching you key in data, such as your PIN; this can be something simple like just looking over your shoulder or somebody watching from a distance using binoculars or using a video camera
» somebody listening in when you are giving credit or debit card details over the phone; by simply listening in, a criminal will gain very important data about your card
» some of the more sophisticated examples of shoulder surfing include the use of tiny digital cameras (placed near to the keyboard on the ATM or other device) which take high-quality images of the keys being pressed.

There are ways to overcome this security risk:

» When using ATMs shield the keyboard with your other hand so that no-one can see which keys you are pressing (many ATMs also have a small mirror built into them so you can see if somebody is standing right behind you).
» When using a mobile device (such as a smartphone, tablet or laptop) never key in data in a public place; nor should you speak card details into your smartphone in a public place.
» If you are using a public place, make sure you are nowhere near security cameras which could record passwords or other data about you; it is also a good idea to use biometrics (touch ID or face ID) on your smartphone or tablet, because these cannot be duplicated by simply watching you.

Card cloning

Card cloning is the copying of a credit or debit card which uses a magnetic stripe. Cloning of this type of card employs an electronic device known as a **skimmer.**

This is a data capture device that allows a criminal to record all of the data stored on the magnetic stripe on a card. Skimmers can be placed in ATM slots where they can read all the data from a card; this data is then copied to the magnetic stripe of a fake card. Even the security hologram can be copied. The skimmer is often a false front on the card slot on the ATM. To obtain the PIN to use with the newly cloned car, the criminal would also make use of shoulder surfing.

Smart cards, which contain a microchip, were introduced to combat card cloning and give considerably more security. Therefore, a different device, known as a **shimmer**, is now used to read these smart cards. This uses a paper-thin shim (that contains a chip and a flash drive) that can be put into a card reading slot. It is so thin that it is almost impossible to detect. When a customer puts their card into the reader slot, the shim reads all the data from the credit/debit card, allowing the criminal to create a fake replica credit/debit card. Although the chip itself cannot be cloned, all the data gathered from the cloned card is now stored on a magnetic stripe and a fake card is produced. The fake card can be used to make purchases where a magnetic stripe card is still acceptable; for example, when making purchases online.

Obviously, the best way to check on this type of fraud is to do regular checks of your spending and query any unusual activity.

Key logging
The use of key logging software has been discussed earlier. This is used to detect all key presses, such as when entering a credit or debit card:

» number
» security code (card verification value – CVV)
» PIN.

Because all this data can be obtained by key logging software, illegal use of a credit or debit card to buy things online is a continued risk.

8.3.2 Protection of data

Authentication is used to verify that data comes from a secure and trusted source. Along with **encryption** it strengthens internet security. We will be considering all of the following methods to protect the security of data:

» biometrics
» digital certificates
» secure sockets layer (SSL)
» encryption
» firewalls
» two-factor authentication
» user ID and password.

Biometric authentication

Biometrics relies on certain unique characteristics of human beings. Examples include:

» fingerprint scans
» signature recognition
» retina scans

» iris recognition
» face recognition
» voice recognition.

Biometrics is used in a number of applications as a security device. For example, some of the latest mobile phones require fingerprint matching before it can be operated; some pharmaceutical companies use face recognition or retina scans to allow entry to secure areas. We will now consider two of these biometric techniques in a little more detail.

Fingerprint scans

Images of fingerprints are compared against previously scanned fingerprints stored in a database; if they match then access is allowed. The system compares patterns of 'ridges' and 'valleys' which are unique.

An example of its use would be as a security method for entering a building. Fingerprint scanning techniques have the following advantages:

» Fingerprints are unique, therefore this technique would improve security because it would be difficult to replicate a person's fingerprints.
» Other security devices (such as magnetic cards) could be lost or even stolen, which makes them less effective.
» It would be impossible to 'sign in' for somebody else because the fingerprints would match up to one person only on the database.
» Fingerprints cannot be misplaced; a person always has them!

What are the disadvantages?

» It is relatively expensive to install and set up.
» If a person's fingers are damaged through an injury, this can have an effect on the scanning accuracy.
» Some people may regard it as an infringement of civil liberties.

▲ **Figure 8.9** Fingerprint pattern

Face recognition

Face recognition is used to identify somebody by their facial features. It is used by many modern smartphones as the method of identifying the owner of the phone, and for authorising purchases using the phone.

Figure 8.10 shows several of the positions used by the face-recognition software. The position of each facial feature is calculated by the software. These values are then compared to values already stored on a database. If the values match, then the face is recognised.

Data such as:

» distance between the eyes
» width of the nose
» shape of the cheek bones
» length of the jawline
» shape of the eyebrows

are all used to uniquely identify a given face.

Face recognition systems can be 'fooled' by wearing spectacles or by people changing their hair style and colour. However, the technology is improving.

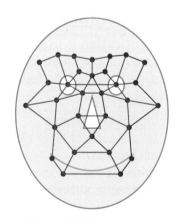

▲ **Figure 8.10** Face recognition

One drawback common to all biometric techniques is the need for the systems to store very personal data about users. Some people are uncomfortable with this idea. Table 8.3 shows a comparison of some of the other advantages and disadvantages of the six most common biometric techniques.

▼ **Table 8.3** Comparison of biometric types

Biometric technique	Advantages	Disadvantages
Fingerprint scans	» very high accuracy » one of the most developed biometric techniques » very easy to use » relatively small storage requirements for the biometric data created	» for some people it is very intrusive, because it is still related to criminal identification » it can make mistakes if the skin is dirty or damaged (for example, cuts to the finger)
Signature recognition	» non-intrusive » requires very little time to verify (about five seconds) » relatively low-cost technology	» if individuals do not sign their names in a consistent manner there may be problems with signature verification » high error rate of 1 in 50
Retina scans	» very high accuracy » there is no known way to replicate a person's retina pattern	» it is very intrusive » it can be relatively slow to verify retina scan with stored scans » very expensive to install and set up
Iris recognition	» very high accuracy » verification time is generally less than five seconds	» very intrusive » uses a lot of memory for the data to be stored » very expensive to install and set up
Face recognition	» non-intrusive method » relatively inexpensive technology	» it is affected by changes in lighting, the person's hair, their age, and if the person is wearing spectacles
Voice recognition	» non-intrusive method » verification takes less than five seconds » relatively inexpensive technology	» a person's voice can be easily recorded and used for unauthorised access » low accuracy » an illness, such as a cold, can change a person's voice, making absolute identification difficult or impossible

Digital certificates

A **digital certificate** is a pair of files stored on a user's computer – these are used to ensure the security of data sent over the internet. Each pair of files is divided into:

» a public key (which can be accessed by anyone)
» a private key (known to the computer user only).

For example, when sending an email, the message is made more secure by attaching a digital certificate. When the message is received, the recipient can verify that it comes from a known or trusted source by viewing the public key information (this is usually part of the email attachment). This is an added level of security to protect the recipient from harmful emails. The digital certificate is made up of six parts:

» the sender's email address
» the name of the digital certificate owner
» a serial number
» expiry date (the date range during which the certificate is valid)
» public key (which is used for encrypting the messages and for digital signatures)
» digital signature of certificate authority (CAs) – an example of this is *VeriSign*

Operating systems and web browsers maintain lists of trusted CAs
(Figure 8.11).

Secure sockets layer (SSL)

Secure sockets layer (SSL) is a type of protocol that allows data to be sent
and received securely over the internet.

When a user logs onto a website, SSL encrypts the data – only the user's
computer and the web server are able to make sense of what is being
transmitted. A user will know if SSL is being applied when they see http**s** (as
part of the website address) or the small padlock 🔒 in the status bar at the
top of the screen.

▲ **Figure 8.11** Digital IDs

The address window in the browser when https protocol is being applied, rather
than just http protocol, is quite different:

Using https: | 🔒 secure https://www.xxxx.org/documents |

Using http: | ⓘ http://www.yyyy.co.uk/documents |

SSL certificates are small data files that digitally bind an encryption key to an
organisation's details. When installed on a web server, it shows as the green
padlock and the https protocol ensures secure connections from a web server to a
web browser.

Figure 8.12 shows what happens when a user wants to access a secure website
and receive and send data to it:

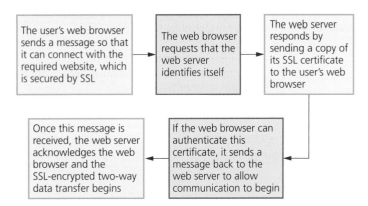

▲ **Figure 8.12** Communicating across a network using SSL

Examples of where SSL would be used:

» online banking and all online financial transactions
» online shopping/commerce
» when sending software out to a restricted list of users
» sending and receiving emails
» using cloud storage facilities
» intranets and extranets (as well as the internet)
» Voice over Internet Protocol (VoIP) when carrying out video chatting and/or
  audio chatting over the internet
» within instant messaging
» when making use of a social networking site.

Encryption

Encryption is used primarily to protect data in case it has been hacked or accessed illegally. While encryption will not prevent hacking, it makes the data meaningless unless the recipient has the necessary decryption tools (as described below).

Encryption uses a secret key that has the capability of altering the characters in a message. If this key is applied to a message, its content is changed, which makes it unreadable unless the recipient also has the same secret key. When this secret key is applied to the encrypted message, it decodes it, allowing it to be read.

The key used to encrypt (or encode) the message is known as the **encryption key**; the key used to decrypt (or decipher) the message is known as the **decryption key**. When a message undergoes encryption it is known as **cypher script**; the original message is known as **plain text**. Figure 8.13 shows how these two are linked together.

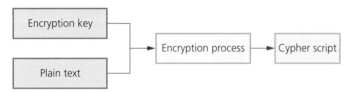

▲ **Figure 8.13** Encryption

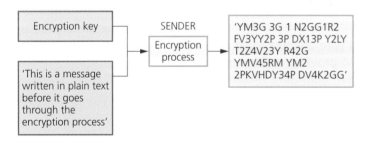

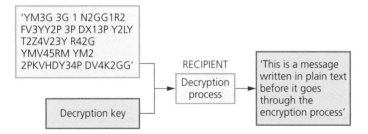

▲ **Figure 8.14** Example of encryption and decryption

Because the protection of data if it is intercepted or illegally accessed is of paramount importance, encryption has many applications:

» Due to the risks of pharming, hacking or spyware (and other forms of malware) it is important that data stored on HDDs or SSDs is encrypted; if data is then accessed illegally, it will be unreadable to the cybercriminal.
» Encryption of emails is also important (many of the safety aspects of sending and receiving emails was discussed in Section 8.2.3):

- Encryption of email contents protects sensitive information from being read by anyone other than the intended recipients; encrypted messages are meaningless to anyone without the decryption key.
- Hackers who gain unauthorised access to an email account can access attachments, content or even the whole email account.

▼ **Table 8.4** Which part of the email should be encrypted?

Encrypt the connection with your email provider:	Encrypt the actual email messages:	Encrypt stored or archived email messages:
» Encryption of the connection with your email supplier prevents unauthorised users from intercepting and capturing log in details as well as any email messages sent or received » As the emails leave your email supplier's server and travel to their destination server they are at risk; encryption will give the additional protection described above	» Encryption of emails themselves prevents a hacker making sense of any intercepted messages (keeping any sensitive or confidential information safe)	» Any backed-up messages stored on your email supplier's server also need to be encrypted » If a hacker acquires access to this server, they could then gain access to your stored or archived messages

Another important point about emails is that only encrypting sensitive or confidential messages is bad practice – this indicates to a hacker which emails they should target; encrypting all messages means the hacker has to try and decrypt every message to find the ones they want, which certainly will not make life easy for them.

Any data stored on the cloud should also be encrypted (see Chapter 4); it is good practice to encrypt data prior to uploading to the cloud provider – this means that even if the cloud supplier's servers are compromised, your data remains encrypted; here are two recent examples to indicate why encrypting your data on cloud storage is good practice:

» the celebrity photos cloud hacking scandal, in which more than 100 private photos and personal information of some celebrities were leaked; hackers had gained access to a number of cloud accounts, which enabled them to publish photos and other sensitive information on social networks and sell them to publishing companies

» the National Electoral Institute of Mexico suffered a cloud security breach in which 93 million voter registrations, stored on a central database, were compromised and became publicly available to everyone; to make matters worse, much of the information on this database also linked to a cloud server outside Mexico.

As mentioned earlier, https and SSL gives protection when transferring data across the internet.

Firewalls

A **firewall** can be software or hardware. It sits between the user's computer and an external network (for example, the internet). A firewall will help to keep potentially destructive forces away from a user's computer, by filtering incoming and outgoing network traffic. The criteria for allowing or denying access to a computer can be set by the user.

▲ **Figure 8.15** Firewall connection

The following list shows a number of the tasks carried out by a firewall:

» to examine the 'traffic' between user's computer (or internal network) and a public network (for example, the internet)
» checks whether incoming or outgoing data meets a given set of criteria
» if the data fails the criteria, the firewall will block the 'traffic' and give the user (or network manager) a warning that there may be a security issue
» the firewall can be used to log all incoming and outgoing 'traffic' to allow later interrogation by the user (or network manager)
» criteria can be set so that the firewall prevents access to certain undesirable sites; the firewall can keep a list of all undesirable IP addresses
» it is possible for firewalls to help prevent viruses or hackers entering the user's computer (or internal network)
» the user is warned if some software on their system is trying to access an external data source (for example, automatic software upgrade); the user is given the option of allowing it to go ahead or request that such access is denied.

The firewall can be a hardware interface which is located somewhere between the computer and the internet connection. It is often referred to in this case as a **gateway**. Alternatively, the firewall can be software installed on a computer; in some cases, this is part of the operating system.

Two-factor authentication

Authentication refers to the ability of a user to prove who they are. There are three common factors used in authentication:

» something you know (for example, a password or PIN code)
» something you have (for example, a mobile phone or tablet)
» something which is unique to you (for example, biometrics).

Two-factor authentication is a form of verification which requires two methods of authentication to verify who a user is. It is used predominantly when a user makes an online purchase, using a credit/debit card as payment method.

For example, suppose Kate wishes to buy a new camera from a website. She logs into the website using her computer. This requires her to enter a user name and a password, which is step one of the authentication process.

To improve security, an eight-digit PIN (called a one-time pass code) is sent back to her either in an email or as a text message to her mobile phone (the mobile phone has already been registered by Kate on the website as the second stage of the authentication process). Kate now enters this eight-digit PIN into her computer and she is now authorised to buy the camera.

▲ **Figure 8.16** Two-factor authentication using a mobile phone

Using the definitions of authentication at the start of this section, the mobile phone is something she has and the password/PIN code is something she knows.

User IDs and passwords

Passwords are used to restrict access to data or systems. They should be hard to break and changed frequently to retain any real level of security. In addition to protecting access levels to computer systems, passwords are frequently used when accessing the internet, for example:

» when accessing email accounts
» when carrying out online banking or shopping
» when accessing social networking sites.

It is important that passwords are protected; some ways of doing this are described below:

» Run anti-spyware software to make sure that your passwords are not being relayed back to anyone who put the spyware on your computer.
» Change passwords on a regular basis in case it has come into the possession of another user illegally or accidentally.
» Passwords should not be easy to break (for example, your favourite colour, name of a pet or favourite music artist); passwords are grouped as either strong (hard to break or guess) or weak (relatively easy to break or guess).
» It is possible to make a password strong but also be easy to remember; suppose we use the phrase: 'The 3rd planet is Earth: the 8th planet is Neptune' could give us an easy-to-remember password: T3piE:t8piN (which is certainly strong and difficult to break).
» Strong passwords should contain:
    – at least one capital letter
    – at least one numerical value
    – at least one other keyboard character (such as @, *, &. etc.)
    An example of a strong password would be: Sy12@#TT90kj=0
    An example of a weak password would be: GREEN

When the password is typed in, it often shows on the screen as ******** so nobody overlooking can see what the user has typed in. If the user's password does not match up with the user name then access will be denied. Many systems ask for the password to be typed in twice when being created, as a verification check (a check on input errors). To help protect the system, users are only allowed to type in their password a finite number of times – three times is usually the maximum number of attempts allowed before the system locks the user out. After that, the user will be unable to log on until they have re-set their password.

When using an online company, if a user forgets their password or they need to re-set it, they will be sent an email which contains a link to a web page where they can do so. This is done as an added precaution in case an unauthorised person has tried to change the user's password.

Passwords should be changed on a regular basis in case they become known to another user or even a hacker. In particular, it is important to prevent other people gaining access to your password by way of spyware or viruses – many methods to guard against this have been discussed earlier in this chapter.

As mentioned above, it is usually necessary to use a username as well as a password. This gives an additional security level because the username and password must match up to allow a user to gain access to, for example, a bank website.

▶ Exercise 8d

Which of the following are weak passwords and which are strong passwords?

Explain your decision in each case.
i   25-Apr-2005
ii   Password1
iii ChapTer@06
iv   rX!3&tp%
v   111111"

Exam-style questions

1 **a** Name **three** safety issues when using computer systems. [3]

  b For each named safety issue, describe **one** way to remove or militate against the risk. [3]

2 Internet banking can be used by bank customers to check their account balance.

  Many ways of logging into such a system involve the use of passwords.

  Describe **three** methods of minimising the possibility of passwords being misused or intercepted. [3]

Cambridge IGCSE Information and Communication Technology (0417) Paper 11 Q9 a, May/June 2016

3 There are a number of health and safety issues associated with the use of computers.

  Draw arrows from the terms **Health** or **Safety** to the matching issue. Use a maximum of four arrows. [4]

Health		Tripping over loose wires.
		Heavy equipment falling off tables and injuring people.
Safety		Clicking a mouse repetitively causing RSI.
		Overloading sockets causing a fire.

Cambridge IGCSE Information and Communication Technology (0471) Paper 11 Q5, May/June 2017

4 **a** Discuss the e-safety issues when using a social networking site. [7]

  b Data can be classified as personal or sensitive.

   Give **two** examples of each. [4]

5 Indicate, by ticking (✓) the appropriate box, which of the following are examples of a health risk and which are examples of a safety risk. [7]

Description of risk	Health (✓)	Safety (✓)
Tripping over a loose wire on the floor		
Headaches caused by the glare from a computer screen		
Risk of electrocution caused from damaged insulation on an electric cable		
Broken leg injury caused by falling equipment		
Irritation of the eyes caused by ozone gas coming from a laser printer		
Repetitive strain injury caused by repeated use of a keyboard		
Neck strain from sitting in a prolonged position in front of a computer monitor		

6 Seven ICT descriptions are shown on the left and seven ICT terms on the right.
By drawing arrows, connect each description to the correct term.　　[6]

Authentication method using, for example, fingerprint scans, retina scans or face recognition		Firewall
Result of putting a message through an encryption algorithm		Pharming
Electronic document that uses a public key and a private key which is used to secure data sent over the internet		Cypher text
Hardware or software that sits between a computer and an external network that filters traffic in and out		Virus
Protocol that allows data to be sent and received securely over the internet		Secure sockets layer (SSL)
Program code that copies itself with the intention of deleting or corrupting files on a computer; needs to be initiated by some event		Biometrics
Malicious code installed on a server or hard disk drive that redirects a web browser to a fake website without the user's knowledge		Digital certificates

7 Complete the following paragraph using words or phrases from the following list. Each word or phrase may be used once, more than once or not at all.

» authenticity	» link	» protocols
» biometrics	» password protected	» secure sockets layer
» digital certificate	» personal data	» sensitive data
» encrypted	» pharming	» smishing
» e-safety	» phishing	» user ID
» hacking	» privacy settings	» vishing

_____ refers to safety when using the internet.
Data, such as ethnic origin or political views, are examples of
_____ When using online social networks, it is important
to maintain _____ to control who has access to your
profile. Users have to be aware of _____, which is illegal
access to their computer, or to _____ which occurs
when legitimate-looking emails are received. In this security threat, as soon
as the _____ is clicked on, the user's browser is sent
to a fake website. This is similar to _____ where text
messages are sent out from a fake company. To prevent intercepted data being
understood by a hacker, it is _____. Protocols called
_____ are used on the internet to allow data to be sent
and received securely. They are often used with _____,
which are electronic documents which confirm the _____
of the sender of the data.　　[11]

8 a Explain what is meant by a firewall.　　[2]
　　b Describe **four** of the tasks carried out by a typical firewall.　　[4]

9 Explain each of the following terms and give an example of their use.
   a cloning of credit cards
   b fingerprint scanning
   c digital certificates
   d encryption
   e vishing   [10]
10 a Name **three** biometric authentication techniques.   [3]
   b For each named technique, describe the advantages and disadvantages
      of using it as a method of data security.   [6]
11 a Explain what is meant by the term authentication.   [2]
   b Explain what is meant by two-factor authentication.   [3]
12 a Explain why it is important to encrypt emails.   [3]
   b Explain why key logging software poses a security threat when
      purchasing items on the internet.   [3]

9 Audiences

9.1 Audience appreciation

When planning and creating ICT solutions, it is important to consider the audience who will either use or take part in the solution. We are going to use two different examples to show what could be meant by audience appreciation:

1 In the first example, we are going to consider using presentation software to make a presentation for an audience.
2 In the second example, we are going to consider the general audience requirements when developing a new website.

Both examples will follow very similar steps because the end results are very similar.

9.1.1 Giving a presentation to an audience

In this example, the ICT solution is a presentation aimed at a specific audience, using presentation software. When writing a presentation, you need to consider all of the following factors:

» The age of the target group (young children will have a different appreciation and response compared to a more mature group of adults, for example).
» The experiences of the audience (a board of company directors would expect a different approach compared to an audience composed of teenage school children).
» The expectation of the audience (for example, if you are advertising or giving a presentation on a new restaurant, an older audience might expect to see fine wines and good waiter service; whereas a group of students might be more interested in pizzas and fast counter service).
» Knowledge of the audience (for example, graduates in maths would be more comfortable seeing equations in a presentation than a group of history students).

How can you find out about the characteristics of your audience? The following are just some of the market research techniques you might employ to identify the characteristics of your target audience:

» interviewing a cross section of the target group to find out how to engage the audience (if this involves a major ICT solution, then this may have to involve many of the techniques that were described in Chapter 7)
» giving out questionnaires or online surveys to people in the target group to find out their background, interests, and so on, so that your solution can be tailored to meet the full expectation of the audience.

Once you have data from your audience, you can then carry out some analysis of it, to spot trends and draw some conclusions about them. The sophistication of data analysis would depend on how large the audience is likely to be.

Giving a sample presentation to an audience

Now consider a phone company who market a number of different mobile phones. The company has decided to produce two presentations, using an ICT solution, regarding the sales and features of the four different mobile phones they market and sell:

» one presentation is to be given to the mobile phone sales team who will receive different bonus payments depending on the phone sold
» a second presentation is to be given to a potential group of mobile phone customers.

How would these two presentations differ? The first group (the sales team), will have technical knowledge and will be interested in the profitability of each sale. The second group (end-users) will only be interested in the price and the features found on each phone.

Key factors when writing the presentations include:

» the language used
» the need for multimedia
» the length of the presentation
» the need for audience participation (an interactive approach)
» the examples used to illustrate certain points.

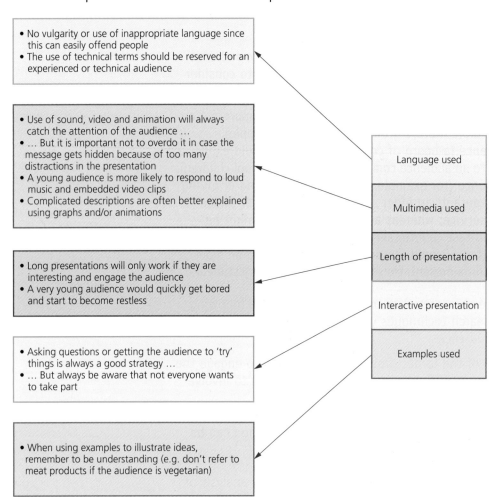

▲ **Figure 9.1** Key factors when making a presentation

> **Exercise 9a**

Using the mobile phone example described above, produce two different presentations to cover the two types of potential audience:
- the mobile phone sales team
- the potential mobile phone customers.

Explain why you have included certain features into each of your presentations.

9.1.2 Audience characteristics (when developing a new ICT solution)

In this example we are setting out to develop a new website. As with the example in Section 9.1.1, you need to consider certain factors regarding the audience:

» audience characteristics
» the needs of the audience
» why you need to consider the needs of your audience.

Audience characteristics

Who will be using the new website? First, consider the characteristics of your target audience when using the new website:

» age range
» income levels
» interests
» disabilities or impairments.

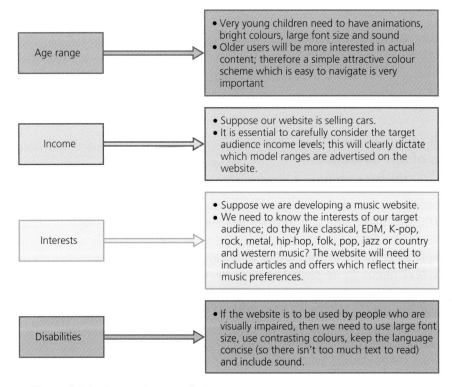

▲ **Figure 9.2** Audience characteristics

As in the previous example, you could determine the characteristics of the audience who are likely to use the new website by:

» interviewing a cross section of the target group
» giving out questionnaires or surveys to people in the target group to find out their background, interests, age range, and so on
» analysing this data and drawing conclusions about the audience.

Needs of the audience

Once you have established the characteristics of the audience that the website is aimed at, it is necessary to understand their specific needs in a bit more depth, to ensure the final product is fit for purpose. Figure 9.3 considers the needs of three different age groups who would use the new website.

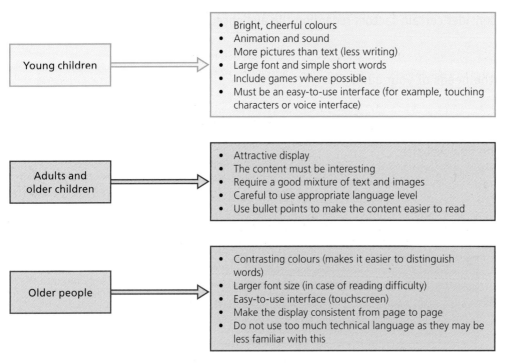

Young children
- Bright, cheerful colours
- Animation and sound
- More pictures than text (less writing)
- Large font and simple short words
- Include games where possible
- Must be an easy-to-use interface (for example, touching characters or voice interface)

Adults and older children
- Attractive display
- The content must be interesting
- Require a good mixture of text and images
- Careful to use appropriate language level
- Use bullet points to make the content easier to read

Older people
- Contrasting colours (makes it easier to distinguish words)
- Larger font size (in case of reading difficulty)
- Easy-to-use interface (touchscreen)
- Make the display consistent from page to page
- Do not use too much technical language as they may be less familiar with this

▲ **Figure 9.3** Audience needs

Why we need to consider the needs of our audience

Why is it important to respectfully consider these needs?

» If the audience is made up of older people, or people with disabilities, who have sight problems, then it is important to make sure the website has clear-to-read fonts.
» Complex language can be a real turn off to children or for people who have English as their second language; the text needs to be clear and easy to read for these reasons.
» It is necessary to hold the attention of the users, otherwise they will give up using the website.
» Good, attractive screen designs will attract users to the website.
» Keeping interfaces clear and easy to use keeps people engaged.
» Lots of typing can be very frustrating, as can badly designed websites where the user seems to go 'round in a big circle'.

If you know your audience and understand their needs before starting to develop the new ICT solution, then it is far more likely to be successful.

The ideas outlined in both examples above apply whenever you are developing a new ICT solution or product. As well as a presentation or website this could be a new computer game, a database or a new virtual reality system.

9.2 Copyright

9.2.1 Software copyright and piracy

Software is protected by **copyright** laws in much the same way as music CDs, movies, and articles from magazines and books are protected.

When software is supplied on CD, DVD or online there are certain rules that must be obeyed. It is illegal to:

» make a software copy and then sell it or give it away to a friend or colleague
» use software on a network or on multiple computers unless a licence has been acquired to allow this to happen
» use coding from the copyright software in your own software and then pass this software on or sell it as your own without the permission of the copyright holders
» rent out a software package without permission to do so from the publishers
» use the name of copyrighted software on other software without agreement to do so.

Software **piracy** is the illegal copying of software. It is a big issue among software companies. They take many steps to stop the illegal copying and to stop any illegal copies being used once they have been sold.

There are a number of ways software is protected – either by making the installer agree to certain conditions or by methods which require the original software to be present for it to work:

» When software is being installed, the user may be asked to key in a unique reference number or **product key** (a string of letters and numbers) which was supplied with the original copy of the software (for example: 4a3c 0efa 65ab a81e).
» The user will be asked to click 'OK'/'I AGREE' or put a cross in a box to agree to the licence agreement before the software continues to install.
» If supplied as a hard copy, the original software packaging often comes with a sticker informing the purchaser that it is illegal to make copies of the software; the label is often in the form of a **hologram** indicating that this is a genuine copy.
» Some software will only run if the CD, DVD or memory stick is actually in the drive; this stops illegal multiple use and network use of the software.
» Some software will only run if a **dongle** is plugged into one of the USB ports.

A dongle is a small device, usually plugged into one of the computer's USB ports. It is used to allow wireless communications with devices, such as a keyboard. It can also be used to protect software (for example, it may contain important files that mean the software will only run if the dongle is plugged into the computer).

The Federation Against Software Theft (FAST) was set up in the UK many years ago to protect the software industry against piracy. FAST prosecutes organisations and individuals who are involved in any copyright infringements. This is done by legal penalties for anyone found guilty of such infringement.

Similar organisations exist in many countries to globally protect software, and other intellectual property, from piracy. Examples include the International Intellectual Property Alliance (IIPA) in the USA and the Japan Intellectual Property Association (JIPA) in Japan.

The extract in Figure 9.4 is a typical example of how strict the anti-piracy laws are in many countries.

TRADERS FINED $100,000	
Two eBay traders (from the US) agreed this week to pay a total of $100,000 in damages after they were caught selling illegal copies of Norton security software.	The SIIA settled the case against the two traders who also agreed to stop selling illegal software and provided SIIA with records identifying their customers and suppliers.

▲ **Figure 9.4** Example of copyright infringement

> ## Exercise 9b
>
> The example given assumes that software is distributed on CD or DVD.
>
> However, software is often purchased using store apps, where it is downloaded to a device immediately after is paid for.
>
> How do you think software copyright infringements and software piracy are controlled when software is bought online in this way?

Exam-style questions

1 When giving a presentation to a large audience, the person giving the presentation has to consider a number of key factors:
 » the language that is used
 » what multimedia could be used
 » how long should the presentation last
 » if the presentation should be interactive
 » what would be suitable examples to use in the presentation.

Describe two aspects of each key factor that need to be considered by the presenter. [10]

2 A company has decided to develop a new online game which helps students revise their A Level Chemistry.
Describe what factors the company needs to consider when deciding who the audience will be for their new online game. Give examples to illustrate your answer. [8]

3 Tick (✓) which of the following are used to help maintain copyright and reduce piracy of software. [3]

	(✓)
Use of a product key	
Use of ethics in software	
Click on a check box agreeing to licence agreement	
Use of holographic images	
Make the software cheaper to develop	
Supply software on CD-ROM or DVD-ROM	

4 Explain each of the following terms: [6]
 a software piracy
 b product key
 c copyright infringement

5 An airport in southern Cyprus is designing a new information system. A number of automated information kiosks will be distributed throughout the airport. Customers can be any age from 18 upwards. It is also expected that Greek and English language will be used by all customers. The kiosks must also be user-friendly to people with a range of disabilities.
 a Describe the various audience characteristics that need to be considered when developing the new kiosk. [4]
 b Describe the needs of each age group and explain why it is important to consider these audience needs. [4]
 c Describe how the managers at the airport could determine the different characteristics of all the customers using the information kiosks. [4]

6 A programmer is developing a presentation of a new ICT solution for a conference and needs to consider the audience.
 a Using examples, explain why presentations and ICT solutions have to take into account the type of audience. [4]
 b The programmer is concerned that the software used for the presentation will be copied by the participants during the conference.
 Describe how the software could be protected from illegal copying. [4]

Cambridge IGCSE Information and Communication Technology (0417) Paper 12 Q16, February/March 2019

Communication

Communication

In this chapter you will learn about:
★ communication via emails, including:
  - uses and constraints
  - security
  - netiquette
  - making copies
  - language used
  - attachments
  - spam
★ effective use of the internet:
  - differences between the World Wide Web (WWW) and the internet
- intranets
- extranets
- blogs and wikis
- forums
- social networking
★ internet service providers (ISP)
★ search engines (including the evaluation of information found)
★ internet protocols
★ internet risks.

This chapter covers certain aspects of using the internet. We will consider rules and regulations when sending emails and look at several features of the internet. In particular, we will define and explain many of the internet terms used and how to search for information on the internet. Part of the chapter also considers the differences between the internet, the World Wide Web (WWW) and intranets.

10.1 Communication with other ICT users using email

10.1.1 Characteristics, uses and constraints

Emails are now one of the most common ways of communicating between people. However, there many rules we need to follow to ensure the security of the messages sent and also to prevent people writing anything which is regarded as unacceptable. This first part of the chapter considers these constraints.

Legislation

Many countries have laws to protect people against the misuse of emails. Figure 10.1 is a guideline on what these laws often require companies and individuals to do when sending out emails. The laws cover the use of emails and highlight a number of constraints; these will all be covered in this part of the chapter.

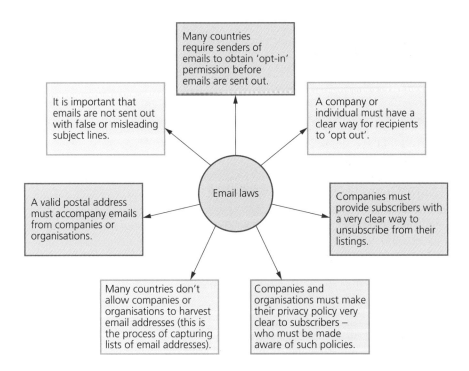

▲ **Figure 10.1** Email laws

Acceptable language

The language used by people when writing emails should follow an acceptable code of practice. The following is a list of unacceptable content to be used in emails, text messages and online forums:

- ›› obscene images
- ›› language that is regarded as abusive, profane, inflammatory, coercive, defamatory or blasphemous
- ›› racist, exploitative or violent messages
- ›› use of illegal materials or messages.

This list does not cover everything, but gives some idea of what is not acceptable when sending emails. It is not regarded as adequate that recipients can simply delete images or messages.

It is essential that anyone writing emails, or posting messages on bulletin boards, etc. is aware of the above constraints.

Guidelines set by an employer

It is imperative that any company (no matter how small or large) that employs people publishes guidelines regarding use of emails and other electronic communications. Guidelines must follow the laws in the particular country in which the company operates. Companies must indicate how they will ensure that all of their staff are following the rules. Figure 10.2 shows an example of the kind of things that might be included within a company's guidelines.

- All employees should only assume they can use a company's email system for business use; it is up to companies to decide if personal emails should be permitted on their systems

- Companies may specify which company devices are allowed to be used for sending and receiving emails

- The acceptable style and tone of emails should be made clear (see sections on acceptable language and netiquette); there needs to be a company standard style when sending emails

- It must be made clear what email content is not permitted

- Employees should be told to only use their own accounts when sending emails (and these accounts should be password protected)

- There must be clear rules regarding confidentiality of information and that all staff must be aware of their contractual obligations

- Staff need to be aware of the method and duration of storing emails

- Incoming emails should only be read by the recipient; they can only be read by another member of staff if so nominated

- The company policy on how to deal with and prevent viruses (and other security threats) must be clearly laid out (these could include use of anti-virus software, filtering of incoming and outgoing email traffic, use of auto-responders when staff are not in work, and so on)

- Monitoring of emails may be carried out and staff must be aware that the company has the right to read all emails

- Suitable ongoing training will take place to ensure staff follow company policy at all times and that the company policy on emails will be enforced at all times

▲ **Figure 10.2** Company email policy and guidelines

Copyright and security of emails

It is very important to realise that emails are subject to copyright laws. Just because it is relatively easy to forward an email does not mean it is always legal to do so. This is also true of any attachments sent with an email.

As with web pages, the copyright in an email is determined by its content.

Printing, copying or forwarding emails is generally not considered a breach of copyright unless the sender has indicated clearly that the message is confidential or the subject of copyright law. It is important that the recipient checks this out before forwarding it on to somebody else. Most companies or organisations will clearly set out their policies on sending emails and the material that they contain. This will be particularly true if the sender's email address is part of the company's name, for example, A.N.User@company_name.com. Emails and attachments from companies and organisations will usually contain some copyright statement, such as:

> *Any dissemination or copying of this email or attachment is strictly prohibited unless you are the intended recipient or are responsible for delivering the message to the intended recipient. If you have received this email in error, please let us know and then delete the original email and any attachments.*

It is common for the message to then make some statement that the views and opinions in the email may not represent those of the company, and that the contents may be subject to disclosure under any Freedom of Information legislation. Companies are clearly very concerned about any potential risk of copyright infringement.

Security and password protection

It is very important to consider the security of emails. Many security aspects have been covered elsewhere in this book but some of the factors to consider are repeated here for completeness.

Some methods of increasing the security of emails include:

» using strong passwords when logging on to your email account (for example, the name of your pet is a weak password; strong passwords contain a combination of letters, numbers and other symbols: Sy12@#TT90kj=0 would be regarded as a strong password)
» changing passwords on a regular basis
» using spam filters to remove certain suspicious emails to a 'junk folder' or even to block the email entirely
» running anti-virus and anti-spam software at all times on your computer, to protect against emails from unknown or malicious sources.

Emails are said to be vulnerable to both **passive** and **active attacks**. Passive attacks include the release of email material to other users without your consent. Active attacks involve the modification of your messages or even denial of service (that is, overloading your system by sending thousands of emails, which basically 'clogs up' your computer and makes internet access almost impossible). Active attacks can also involve viruses or phishing attacks (these are covered elsewhere in the book).

Link

See Section 8.3 for more on data security threats.

Netiquette

Netiquette is a shortened form of the phrase inter**NET** et**IQUETTE**, which refers to the need to respect other users' views and display common courtesy when posting views in online discussion groups or when sending out emails. It is very important to consider what you write always, because the reader cannot see your facial expressions or body language. What may have been intended to be humorous could offend somebody if they misunderstood your message, and they could draw the wrong conclusions. Always be aware of this when posting messages or sending emails.

There are a number of rules governing netiquette – one such source is *The Core Rules of Netiquette* by Virginia Shea (published in 1994); but Figure 10.3 gives you some idea of what constitutes netiquette.

1. Do not be abusive – do not threaten people or use personal violence.
2. Do not send spam – do not repeatedly send somebody the same information.
3. Be clear and succinct with your message – do not waffle.
4. Remember that posts are public in most cases and can be read by anyone.
5. Always check your spelling and grammar – give a good impression.
6. Respect people's privacy and do not discuss or publish information that might embarrass somebody.
7. Forgive people's mistakes – do not be compelled to respond to an error.
8. Do not use CAPITAL LETTERS to highlight comments – this is seen as 'shouting' in emails, text messages and online forums.
9. Do not plagiarise – always acknowledge quotes used in any messages you write.
10. Do not use too many emoticons as they might annoy your readers.

▲ **Figure 10.3** Rules of netiquette

Email groups

Email groups are used for a number of purposes:

»» It is easier for a user to send out multiple emails if the addresses are all grouped together under a single name; the user only needs to use that single name in the 'to' box.

»» Companies and organisations can group people together for marketing purposes, for example according to age, hobbies, favourite music and so on – this means that each email can target specific groups.

»» 'Spammers' can create email groups by buying addresses of people from certain companies or from software that 'raids' address books on computers or email companies – this means that several thousand people can be sent spam at one time.

»» Companies use email groups to set up meetings (for example, for a video conference) to ensure that everybody is always invited to attend – it would be easy to forget a person if the email addresses were all typed in individually; this way you can be sure all the correct recipients are sent messages.

Other email operations

Apart from the person you are sending the email to, there are other options available, such as:

» carbon copies (cc)
» blind carbon copy (bcc)
» forward
» attachments.

Carbon copies (Cc) and Blind carbon copies (Bcc)

The difference between carbon copies (Cc) and blind carbon copies (Bcc) is that the Bcc address details are invisible to everyone receiving the email, apart from the Bcc recipient. All recipients in a Cc list, however, can be seen by all other recipients.

The use of Cc is really just netiquette; those on the 'To' are the main recipients and those in the 'Cc' list are interested parties.

Bcc is often used as a security measure when using email groups. When sending an email to many recipients, the following is an added security to keep the addresses of everyone safe:

» Put your own email address in the 'To' field.
» Set up an email group containing all the recipients and give it a name; then store this.
» Put this named email group in the 'Bcc' field.
» This will provide some additional protection, because anyone seeing the email (authorised or unauthorised) will not be able to see the email addresses of the individual recipients.

> ## Exercise 10a
>
>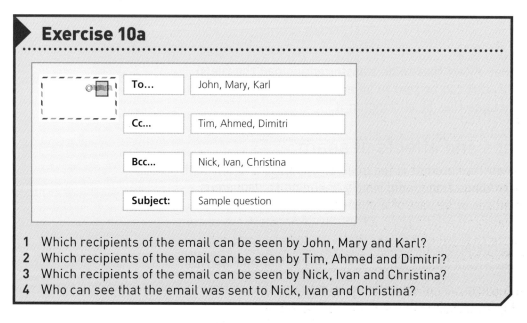
>
> 1 Which recipients of the email can be seen by John, Mary and Karl?
> 2 Which recipients of the email can be seen by Tim, Ahmed and Dimitri?
> 3 Which recipients of the email can be seen by Nick, Ivan and Christina?
> 4 Who can see that the email was sent to Nick, Ivan and Christina?

Forwarding of emails

Forwarding of emails should be treated with great care. Suppose your name is Dave and you work for a company with the domain hothouse-design.co.uk. You have been given a company email address box where all your emails are received: dave@hothouse-design.co.uk.

You have decided to forward all of your emails to dave2468@yahoo.com where you can read them at your leisure. This means that all your emails, including spam, will be sent to this yahoo address. Two problems exist here:

1 Some internet service providers (ISPs) do not recognise the true source of emails and regard all emails as actually coming from the hothouse-design.co.uk domain, **including** spam, because they will have been forwarded from that domain.
2 Some ISPs have spam filters in place based on email volumes from just one address.

Both outcomes are undesirable, because there will now be an increased risk that many of the emails sent to the Yahoo address will be spam. You could end up being blacklisted by your ISP. For this reason, many web hosts are now putting a ban on the email forward feature.

Attachments

Always treat attachments with great caution. Spam and phishing (see Chapter 8) emails can potentially contain malicious attachments. Your computer can become infected if the attachment contains an executable file. Examples of executable files are those ending in: .exe, .msi, .bat, .cmd, and so on.

It is also important to remember when sending attachments that the ISP will have a limit on the size of file that can be sent. Emails were never intended to include large files. It is probably better to look at alternatives when sending large files, such as:

» file compression (zip files)
» selecting a web service that allows files to be transferred: upload the file(s) and then create a link. This link can be sent in an email and the recipient can then easily download very large files by clicking on it.

10.1.2 Characteristics and effects of spam

Any unsolicited email sent over the internet is regarded as **spam**. It is often sent to multiple recipients and can range from being simply annoying to dangerous, because spam can contain viruses or be part of a phishing scam (see earlier chapters).

Spam can affect many online operations (for example, YouTube) where links (called 'spambots') are posted within videos which send users to another website.

While some regard spam as a cheap way of advertising to many people at the same time, most people consider it to be a big nuisance. The main disadvantages are:

» It uses up people's time.
» It generally annoys people.
» It uses up valuable bandwidth on the internet, slowing it down.

» It can have viruses attached or even be part of a phishing scam.
» It can clog up users' inboxes.

Spam is not just a problem for computer users – it can also affect mobile phones. In this case it is usually text messages being send to multiple phones. It is sometimes referred to as 'm-spam', 'mobile spamming' or 'spam SMS'). At the basic level it just annoys people, but with some mobile phone providers users are charged for each message they receive. It then becomes more than just an annoyance!

> **Link**
> ....
> Look back at Chapter 8 for ways to prevent spam.

10.2 Effective use of the internet

This section will consider the effective use of networks, such as the internet, intranets and extranets. This will include many of the features of each type of network.

10.2.1 Characteristics, uses, advantages and disadvantages of the internet

The differences between the internet and the World Wide Web (WWW)

The word **internet** comes from **INTER**connected **NET**work, because it is basically a worldwide collection of interconnected networks. The internet as a whole is actually a concept rather than something tangible (that is, something we can touch). However, it relies on a physical infrastructure that allows networks and individual devices to connect to other networks and devices.

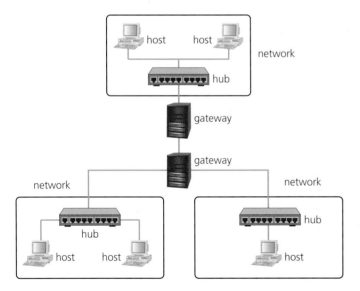

▲ **Figure 10.4** Diagram of the internet

In contrast, the **World Wide Web (WWW)** is only a **part** of the internet which users can access using web browser software. The World Wide Web consists of a massive collection of web pages, and has been based on the hypertext transfer protocol (http) since 1989. The World Wide Web is a way of accessing information **using** the internet; so, the internet and the World Wide Web are actually quite different. Table 10.1 summarises the differences.

▼ **Table 10.1** Summary of differences between the internet and the World Wide Web

Internet	World Wide Web (WWW)
» users can send and receive emails	» it is a collection of multimedia web pages and other information on websites
» allows online chatting (via text, audio and video)	» uses http(s) protocols to send hypertext markup language (HTML) documents
» makes use of transmission protocols (TCP) and internet protocols (IP)	» uniform resource locators (URLs) are used to specify the location of web pages
» it is a worldwide collection of interconnected networks and devices	» web resources are accessed by web browsers
	» WWW uses the internet to access information from web servers

Intranets and extranets

Many companies use an **intranet** as well as the internet. An intranet is defined as 'a computer network based on internet technology but designed to meet the internal needs for sharing information within a single organisation or company'. Access to an intranet is usually confined to a company or organisation and, unlike the internet, is not available to the general public.

Intranets reside behind a **firewall** and are only accessible:

» internally to members of the company, or
» to people given various levels of access who are external to the company (see later).

There are a number of reasons for adopting intranets rather than using the internet:

» Intranets are safer because there is less chance of external hacking or viruses.
» It is easier to prevent external links to, for example, certain websites.
» Companies can ensure that the information available is specific to their internal audience's needs.
» It is easier to send out sensitive messages in the knowledge that they will remain within the company.
» Intranets offer better bandwidth than the internet, therefore there are fewer connection limits than with the internet (that is, the number of bits per second that can be transmitted are usually higher within an intranet).

It is also possible to create **extranets** that allow intranets to be extended outside the organisation, but with the same advantages as an intranet; this allows, for example, trading partners to have controlled access to some information (commercially-sensitive information is password protected).

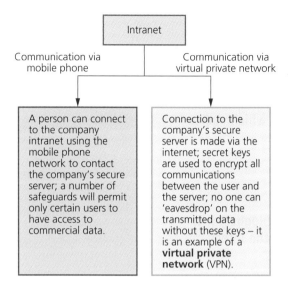

▲ **Figure 10.5** Connecting to an intranet though a mobile phone network or virtual private network

Figure 10.6 shows how intranets, extranets and the internet can all be connected together. Access to servers behind a firewall is limited for external users.

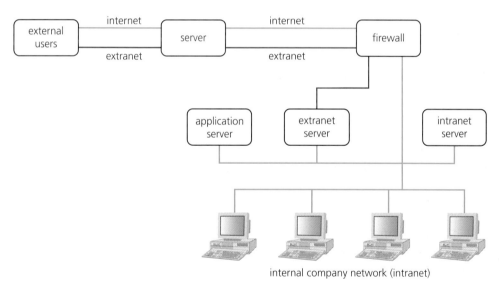

▲ **Figure 10.6** Connections between internet, intranet and extranet

What are the differences between the internet and an intranet?

» As discussed, the term internet comes from the phrase: INTERconnected NETwork.
» The term intranet comes from the phrase: INTernal Restricted Access NETwork.
» An intranet is used to give local information relevant to the company or organisation; whereas the internet covers everything.
» It is possible to block out certain websites using the intranet; while this is also possible with the internet, it is more difficult.

>> An intranet often requires a password and user ID, and can only be accessed from agreed points/computers; whereas the internet can be accessed by anyone from anywhere in the world, provided the user has an ISP account.

>> An intranet is behind a firewall, which gives some protection against hackers, viruses, and so on; there is much less protection against hackers and malware when accessing the internet.

>> Information used in intranets is usually stored on local servers, which makes it more secure from outside users for the same reasons as above.

Blogs, wikis, social networking sites and forums

Blogs

Web logs (**blogs**) are personal internet journals where the writer (blogger) will type in their observations on a topic (for example, a review about the latest movie release) and perhaps provide links to some relevant websites.

Blogs tend to range from minor projects (such as the performance of a rock star) through to important social issues. However, the comments made on blogs are NOT immune from the law; bloggers can still be prosecuted for writing offensive material.

Features of blogs:

>> updated on a regular basis by the author
>> usually organised in reverse chronological order (most recent to least recent entry)
>> normally public – anyone can read them
>> entries normally come from a single author
>> other internet users cannot change blogs – they can only read them.

Microblogs are similar to blogs, but are most often used on social networking sites to make short, frequent posts. The posts can be done using instant messaging, emails or use other social networking vehicles (such as tweets). Social networking sites use microblogs to allow members to update their personal profiles, for example.

Another version is a b-blog – short for business blog – which is used by businesses to promote themselves on the internet.

Wikis

Wikis are web applications or websites that allow any user to create and edit their web pages using any web browser. A wiki will support hyperlinks and uses a very simple syntax (known as wiki markup) to create pages. They have often been described as 'web pages with an <edit> button'.

Features of wikis:

>> anyone can edit, delete or modify the content
>> many authors can be involved in a wiki
>> it is possible to organise a page any way the author(s) wish(es)
>> shows/keeps track of all entries – that is, stores a document history
>> can be easily edited using a web browser
>> allows large documents to be seen by many people – it is easier than emailing several people.

Social networking sites

Social networking sites focus on building online communities of users who share the same interests and activities. They enable people to share photos, videos and music, hobbies, favourite eating places, and so on. The members do this by creating public profiles and thus form relationships with other users. The potential dangers of such sites were covered earlier in Chapter 8.

Features of social networking sites:

>> Each member is provided with free web space.
>> Each member can build their own private and public profiles.
>> It is possible to upload content such as text messages, photos and videos.
>> It is possible to 'write on each other's walls'.
>> Members are given free instant messaging and video chatting.
>> It is possible to email other members within the community.
>> Members can create pages where they can post photos, articles, and so on.
>> It is possible to invite people to become friends.
>> Members have control over who can access their private or personal data.

Forums

A **moderated forum** refers to an online discussion forum in which all the posts are checked by an administrator before they are allowed to be posted. Many users prefer this type of forum, compared to an unmoderated one, as the moderator can not only prevent spam, but can also filter out any posts that are inappropriate, rude or offensive, or even those that wander off the main topic.

The internet is essentially a huge **unmoderated forum**. No one 'owns' the internet, and it is essentially not policed. The only real safeguards are a voluntary cooperation between the users and the network operators. However, most social forums or networking groups on the internet have a set of rules or protocols that members are requested to follow or they will be deleted.

10.2.2 Functionality of the internet

This section will consider how it is possible to access the internet and use some of its features.

Internet service providers (ISP)

An **internet service provider (ISP)** is a company that provides users with access to the internet. It is normal to pay a monthly fee for this service. When a user registers with an ISP, an account is set up and they are given login details that include a user ID and password.

An ISP has the equipment and telecommunications lines required to access the internet – usually broadband connections which, in many cases, use fibre optic cables.

Web addresses, URLs, hyperlinks and web browsers

A **web browser** is software that allows a user to display a web page on their computer screen. They interpret or translate the HTML from websites and show the result of the translation. This can often be in the form of videos, images or sound.

> **Link**
> See Section 8.2 for more on e-Safety on social networking sites.

> **Link**
> For more on hypertext markup language (HTML), see Chapter 21.

Most web browsers share the following features:

» They have a home page.
» They have the ability to store a user's favourite websites/pages (known as bookmarks).
» They keep a history of the websites visited by the use (known as user history).
» They allow users to **navigate** backwards and forwards through websites.
» They have **hyperlinks** that allow users to navigate between web pages; these hyperlinks are shown as <u>blue underlined text</u> or use a small picture, such as a pointed finger 🖱, under a phrase or image; by clicking on these hyperlinks the user is sent to another website or web page.

Web browsers use **uniform resource locators (URLs)** to access websites, retrieve files, and so on. URLs are text addresses used to access websites. A URL is typed into a browser address bar using the following format:

protocol://**website address**/path/filename

where:

» protocol is usually either http or https
» **website address:**
    – domain host (www)
    – domain name (name of website)
    – domain type (.com, .org, .co, .net, .gov)
    – sometimes a country code (.uk, .us, .de, .in, .mu, .cn)
» path, which is a web page (if omitted then it is the root directory of website)
» filename is the item on the web page.

For example:

https://www.hoddereducation.co.uk/IGCSE/ICT

An error will occur if any part of the URL is incorrect. Most frequently, error page 'HTTP 404' will display on the computer screen.

10.2.3 Use of search engines

One of the most useful and powerful aspects of the internet is the ability to easily search through vast amounts of information on almost any given topic.

There are basically two ways of locating information from the internet. The first way is to type in the URL if you know the name of the website you wish to access. The second method is to use a **search engine** if you do not know where to find the information you are looking for.

Opening a website from a URL

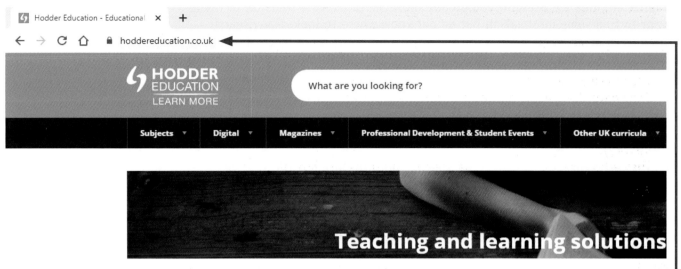

▲ **Figure 10.7** The home page for the website https://www.hoddereducation.co.uk/

As discussed, the URL contains the protocol, site address and file name. If you type in: https://www.hoddereducation.co.uk/ to a web browser as shown here, you will go to the home page for the website.

If you know the URL for a page within the website, you can type the full entry into the web browser to get a particular page. For example, if you want the IGCSE ICT page within the website, you could type in the full URL: https://www.hoddereducation.co.uk/cambridge-igcse-it to get the page shown in Figure 10.8.

If you want to use this page frequently, you can add it to your favourites which saves you having to type in the URL every time.

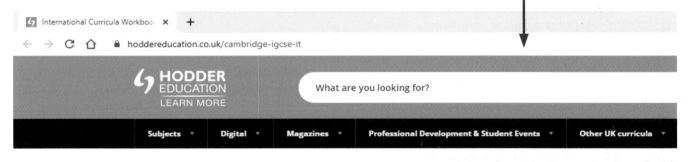

▲ **Figure 10.8** The IGCSE ICT page

It is also possible to search through the website using the navigation tools until you find the web page you are looking for.

Opening a website via a search engine

Search engines are useful if you do not know the URL of the website, or if you want to find some information but do not know where to look. Many search engines exist, and they search for websites using a variety of methods, but they all have one common underlying feature: they look up the words entered in the search box in their database of web pages to find out which of them match the search string or criteria. The more detailed or specific your search string, the more accurate the results (known as 'hits') will be.

▲ **Figure 10.9** A typical search engine

For example, if we type 'ICT text books' into a typical search engine, the options in Figure 10.10 will appear.

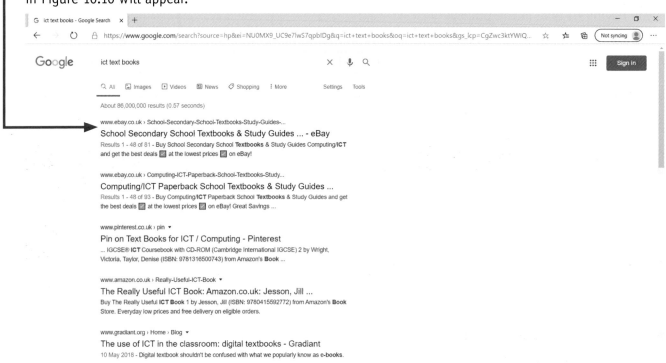

▲ **Figure 10.10** Initial search for 'ICT text books'

As you can see, about 86 million 'hits' or web pages have been found. This is a lot of information. We could narrow down the search by now typing in 'ICT text books+Hodder+IGCSE', and we now get a much-reduced selection (Figure 10.11).

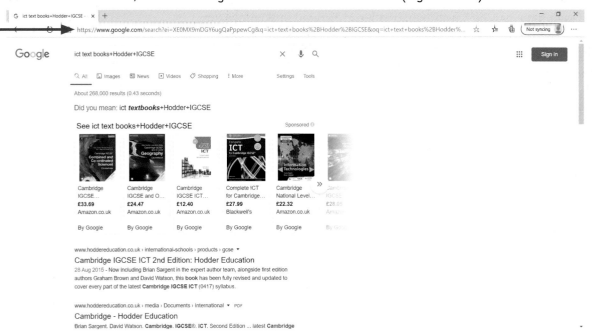

▲ **Figure 10.11** Reduced selection of search results

We now have reduced the number of web pages to 268 000, which is a vast reduction. However, the search can be further refined using the advanced search option, as shown in Figure 10.12.

▲ **Figure 10.12** Using the advanced search option

The result is now only about 300 hits.

Once the information is found it can then be saved or used as follows:

» saved as a favourite and accessed when required
» added as a hyperlink in a document
» an image of web page can be saved by using 'Print Screen' in Windows (or the equivalent – it varies between operating systems) and then pasted into a word-processor page
» information from the web page can be copied and pasted the into another document.

It is **very important** to acknowledge your sources of information when using information from a website in your own work, both to avoid plagiarism and because the information will be subject to copyright.

As we have already said, the internet is a vast and very useful source of information, but it is important to be aware of its disadvantages as well as its advantages.

Advantages of using the internet to find information

» Information on the internet tends to be up to date because it is quicker and easier to amend web pages than it is to, for example, reprint books.
» The internet has vast, almost limitless, amounts of information.
» Searching for information using a search engine is fast and easy.
» People can look for information in the comfort of their own home – there is no need to travel to a library to find required books.
» Information on the internet is essentially free of charge.
» Pages on the internet can have multimedia elements (for example, videos, animations, cartoons and music/voiceovers) that make learning more interesting and often makes it easier to understand the topics.

Disadvantages of using the internet to find information

» The internet is not regulated – anything can be posted on a web page and, consequently, information may be biased or totally incorrect (books, on the other hand, usually undergo some form of review before being published).
» There is always the risk of accessing inappropriate websites when using search engines; these can take many forms and can be very distressing to certain people.
» It is too easy to be distracted when searching on the internet – users can find computer games or enter social networking sites instead of doing their work.
» There is always the risk of 'information overload' if the user lacks the necessary experience or expertise when using search engines.
» Because it is very easy to copy material from the internet, there is a huge temptation to plagiarise material; this is more likely to occur than when using books.
» Some research skills are lost when using the internet as search engines do all the work for you.

Why internet searches are not always a fast way of finding information

When using search engines, there is always the danger of information overload. It is possible to find millions of websites that match the given criteria. Unless the user narrows down their search criteria, it can take a long time to find out exactly what they are looking for (see Figures 10.9 to 10.11). Also, if the user is uncertain of what needs to be asked, it can take a long time to obtain only relevant information.

Each search engine has to decide what they think is the most appropriate result for a search query. Exactly how each search engine decides on the rank of their search results is kept top secret. But search results may not always contain exactly what the user is looking for – more appropriate websites might be hidden deep within the search results. Search engines also rank the time it takes to load up pages from websites – the fastest are given priority when the results appear on the screen. All of this means that the user may not find exactly what they are looking for when using the search engine. It is common to assume that if the first page of search results does not contain what the user was looking for then it does not exist. This is not true. It might be that the search engine misunderstood what the user was looking for – or it might have listed the correct website on the eleventh page of search results.

The actual operation of search engines is very complex and is beyond the scope of this book.

10.2.4 How to evaluate information found on the internet

There are six criteria to consider when evaluating information found on the internet:

1 Is it possible to verify the legitimacy of who wrote the material posted on the website? Does the information come from a reliable source that can be verified?
2 Is there a way to check if the information is factually correct; can it be verified from another source; is it grammatically correct and free of spelling mistakes?
3 Is the article objective? Is there any evidence of bias (for example, does it contain links to organisations to support the 'bias' in the article and does it contain any advertising which reinforces the bias in the article)?
4 Is the information dated? When was it last reviewed and by whom?
5 Does the article cover all aspects and are all the arguments fully supported either by information supplied or references to external experts, or external links to well-respected organisations (such as universities)?
6 Does the website look legitimate? Do all the links in the website still work?

10.2.5 Internet protocols

Protocols are sets of rules agreed by the 'sender' and 'recipient' when data is being transferred between devices.

Hypertext transfer protocol (HTTP)

Hypertext transfer protocol (HTTP) is a set of rules that must be obeyed when transferring website data across the internet. When a web page is being accessed, entering http:// at the front of an address tells the web browser that 'http rules' for communication are to be obeyed.

If HTTP is omitted from the address, most web browsers now default to HTTP.

When some form of security (for example, SSL) certification or encryption is used (see below) then the protocol is changed to HTTP**S** (this is often seen along with the padlock symbol 🔒). The letter '**S**' in http**s** refers to secure(d).

File transfer protocol (FTP)

File transfer protocol (FTP) is a network protocol used when transferring files from one computer to another computer over the internet. It is similar to HTTP, but the protocol is specifically for the transfer of files.

Web browsers can be used to connect to an FTP address in much the same way as you would connect to an HTTP address, for example:
ftp://username@ftp.example.gov/

Secure sockets layer (SSL)

Secure Sockets Layer (SSL) is a protocol that allows data to be sent and received securely over the internet.

SSL is designed to work with communication protocols like HTTP and FTP. When used with HTTP, a user logs onto a website as normal, but SSL encrypts the data – only the user's computer and the web server are able to make sense of what is being transmitted. As mentioned earlier, a user will know if SSL is being applied when they see HTTP**S**, or the small padlock 🔒 in the status bar at the top of the screen.

The address window in the browser when HTTPS protocol is being applied, rather than just HTTP protocol, is quite different:

Using https:	🔒 secure	https://www.xxxx.org/documents

Using http:	ⓘ http://www.yyyy.co.uk/documents

You can refer back to Figure 8.12 (p. 210) to see what happens when a user wants to access a secure website and receive and send data to it.

Advice

The term **SSL certificate** was mentioned in Figure 8.12. An SSL certificate is a form of digital certificate which is used to authenticate a website. This means any communication or data exchange between browser and website is secure as long as this certificate can be authenticated.

Examples of where SSL would be used:

» online banking and all online financial transactions
» online shopping/commerce
» when sending software out to a restricted list of users
» sending and receiving emails
» using cloud storage facilities
» intranets and extranets (as well as the internet)

» Voice over Internet Protocol (VoIP) when carrying out video chatting and/or audio chatting over the internet
» used in instant messaging
» when making use of a social networking site.

10.2.7 Internet risks

Many of the risks associated with using the internet have been raised in this and earlier chapters. As long as users take all of the precautions covered in this book, they should find the internet a safe, enjoyable and very useful source of entertainment and material.

Unfortunately, the internet does contain inappropriate material, some of which is criminal in nature. Many users seem to think that because the internet is not policed, then they are unlikely to be prosecuted. This is of course untrue. To prevent inappropriate material finding its way on to the internet, should there be some form of control? Figures 10.13 and 10.14 detail some of the arguments.

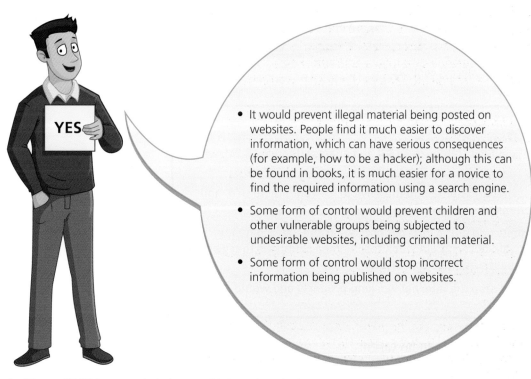

YES

- It would prevent illegal material being posted on websites. People find it much easier to discover information, which can have serious consequences (for example, how to be a hacker); although this can be found in books, it is much easier for a novice to find the required information using a search engine.

- Some form of control would prevent children and other vulnerable groups being subjected to undesirable websites, including criminal material.

- Some form of control would stop incorrect information being published on websites.

▲ **Figure 10.13** Arguments in favour of internet control

- Material published on websites is already available from other sources.

- It would be very expensive to 'police' all websites and users would have to pay for this somehow.

- It would be difficult to enforce rules and regulations on a global scale, as different countries have different laws.

- It can be argued that policing the internet would go against freedom of information/speech.

- Many topics and comments posted on websites are already illegal and laws already exist to deal with the offenders.

- Who is to decide what is illegal or offensive? Many things are only offensive to certain people (for example, religious comments) but not necessarily to the majority.

▲ **Figure 10.14** Arguments against internet controls

Exercise 10b

Looking at the arguments in favour (Figure 10.13) and against (Figure 10.14), what is your opinion?

Should we police the internet and tighten up the laws to prevent illegal use, and prevent the posting of offensive or harmful material?

Would increasing the monitoring of the internet prevent crime? Would it stop certain agencies hacking into government websites in other countries to try and alter the democratic processes in these countries?

Or do you believe this would stop the internet working properly and would it be an invasion of freedom of speech?

There are additional precautions that can be taken:

›› ISP companies give the 'bill payers' some control over what can be accessed. It is possible for concerned parents, for instance, to put filters onto the central router. This can prevent unnamed devices from accessing the internet through their router, or prevent named devices from gaining access to certain websites.

›› Similarly, mobile phone companies offer a similar service and can block access to certain websites. It is not fool-proof, but is an additional safety net.

›› Schools and textbooks can also play their part by educating users about the correct use of the internet – what to look out for and what precautions to take. Teachers are an excellent source of information; if a student wishes to access a new website, it is always worth checking with the teacher first to see if it is safe to go online and access the website.

Exam-style questions

1 Indicate which of the following statements are TRUE or FALSE by putting a tick (✓) in the appropriate box. [7]

Statement	TRUE (✓)	FALSE (✓)
The internet is part of the World Wide Web (WWW)		
All recipients of emails can see all the recipients in the Bcc and Cc lists		
Extranets allow intranets to be extended outside the normal organisation		
Forwarding of emails is always good practice to keep everyone in the organisation or family informed		
Using email groups increases the risk of identity theft		
Netiquette refers to the need to respect other users on the internet		
It is not always illegal to copy or forward email attachments		

2 Describe the features of the following:
 a Blog [2]
 b Wiki [2]

Cambridge IGCSE Information and Communication Technology (0417) Paper 11 Q16, May/June 2018

3 A company's employees can have access to the internet and the company intranet.
 Describe the differences between an intranet and the internet. [6]

Cambridge IGCSE Information and Communication Technology (0417) Paper 11 Q12, October/November 2019

4 Tick which of these statements apply to a Blog, a Microblog or a Wiki. [4]

	Blog (✓)	Microblog (✓)	Wiki (✓)
Very restricted on the size of the post			
Allows readers to edit posts			
Entries are **not** usually in chronological order			
Very difficult to customise			

Cambridge IGCSE Information and Communication Technology (0417) Paper 11 Q4, May/June 2015

5 Eight statements are given below. Indicate whether the statement is a feature of an intranet or the internet by putting a tick (✓) in the appropriate box.   [8]

	Intranet (✓)	Internet (✓)
Information on the network is specific to a particular company or organisation		
Requires a password and user ID to gain access to the network		
Allows public access to all information available		
The network is always behind a firewall, giving some hacking and virus protection		
It is possible to access the network from anywhere in the world using an ISP account		
The network is owned by a private company or organisation		
The network gives access to unlimited amounts of data on many topics		
There is an unlimited amount of traffic on this network		

6 Six descriptions are shown on the left and six computer terms on the right. Draw lines to connect each description to its correct term.   [6]

Description	Term
Discussion website consisting of discrete diary-style entries; displayed in reverse chronological order	Netiquette
Collection of articles that multiple users can add to or edit; users can use a web browser to edit or create the website	Extranet
Code of good practice that should be followed when using the internet or writing emails	Blog
Software application for accessing information on the World Wide Web; retrieves and translates HTML embedded in a webpage	Wiki
Type of intranet that can be partially accessed by authorised outside users	Search engine
Software that does a systematic trawl of websites to find websites based on given criteria	Web browser

7 For each of these questions, choose the correct response from the five options given.   [10]

   a Which of the following provides a user with internet access?

a	TCP
b	ISP
c	FTP
d	HTTP
e	HTTPS

b Which of the following is the meaning of the term URL?

a	Universal resource locator
b	Uniform radio looper
c	Uniform resource locator
d	Uniform radio locator
e	Universal resource looper

c In the term HTTPS, what does the 'S' stand for?

a	Simple
b	Standard
c	Server
d	Sockets
e	Secured

d Which of the following is the name of the protocol used when browsing a website?

a	TCP
b	HTTP
c	FTP
d	ISP
e	WWW

e Which of the following is a correct format of an email address?

a	name@website@info
b	www.nameofwebsite.com
c	name.website.com
d	@name.com
e	name@website.info

f When moving between websites, what is the correct name when doing this?

a	Downloading
b	Uploading
c	Surfing
d	Browsing
e	Attaching

g A file is transferred to a website using the following protocol?

a	HTTP
b	HTTPS
c	ASCII
d	FTP
e	ISP

h Which of the following is a function of a web browser?

a	Provides user with access to web pages
b	Allows a user to view web pages
c	Allows users to alter web pages
d	Acts as a search engine to locate web pages
e	Provides the protocol to allow access to web pages

i Which of the following is the name of the network that allows personal private networks to be extended outside organisations?

a	Intranet
b	Internet
c	Extranet
d	World wide net
e	Netiquette

j Unsolicited emails sent over the internet are called ...

a	Spam
b	SMS
c	Blogs
d	Domains
e	Hypertexts

SECTION 2

Practical

Chapters

11 File management

11.1 Manage files effectively

11.1.1 Manage files

Make sure that you are familiar with the file structure of your local system. If you are using stand-alone computer systems, files are likely to be stored on local hard disk drives (HDD) or solid-state drives (SSD). If you are using a networked system, files are likely to be stored on a network drive, usually in a secure area where only you have access. These can be managed, viewed and accessed using the program *File Explorer*. As each system is different, there are different ways of finding and opening this program. It may be shown as a folder icon on your taskbar like this.

If so, click on the icon to open the program.

If not, you can use the *Windows 10 Search* tool to find it.

Click in the box for the Search tool. The icon for *File Explorer* will appear in the Top Apps list here if you use it often, like this.

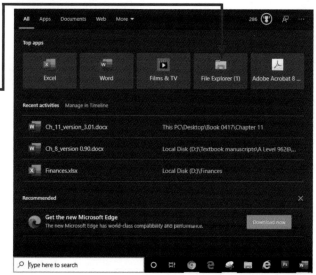

If it does not appear in the Top Apps list, type the text File Explorer into the Search tool so that the program appears in the Best match area like this.

Press the <Enter> key to open the program, which will look similar to this.

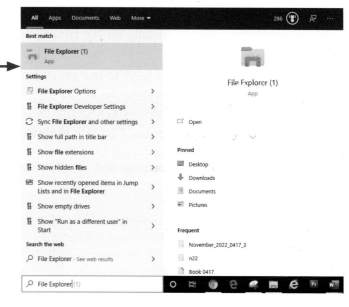

Another shortcut for opening *File Explorer* is to hold down the <Windows> key and press the <E> key.

On the left are a list of locations where files are stored. Because Quick access is selected, on the right, are a list of recently visited locations and files. Use the left pane to select the drive that you will use for your files. The local hard drive is often labelled as drive C. Network drives may be labelled with any letter, on the system shown here drive D is being used. When you select a drive, *File Explorer* changes to show the files on this drive.

Locate stored files

A drive contains folders, and each folder can contain files and/or sub-folders. The path to your current location is shown at the top of the window.

The left pane is used to locate the drive that you wish to use.

The right pane of the window shows the files and subfolders in this drive/folder. It can also give you other useful information such as the date the file was saved and the file type. Some of this information will be used later in this chapter.

To open a folder double click on the folder name in the right pane. When you double click on a folder notice that the path to your current location is updated.

Use these elements and the scroll bars to locate your stored files.

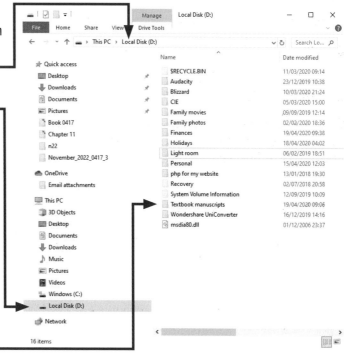

Open and import stored files

On most computers, double clicking on the file icon will open the file in the most suitable application.

There are times where you may wish to use other programs to open a file. For example, in the website authoring section you may wish to open a file in both a browser and in *Notepad*. In this case you can either:

» open the application, select the File tab, then Open
» drag the file into an open application
» right mouse click on the filename and use Open with...

Advice

In some schools, network managers may have disabled some of these methods of opening files. This is to help increase the network security and keep your work safe. If this is the case use one of the other methods to open files.

Link

Importing files will be covered in other chapters as different programs use different methods.

Save files in a planned hierarchical directory/folder structure

Work should always be saved using a planned folder structure. Here is an example of part of a folder from the development of this chapter of this book.

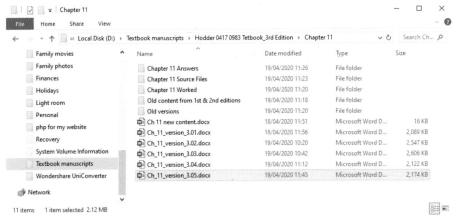

You can see that separate folders are used to hold each different section of the book. The answers are stored in a subfolder called 'Chapter 11 Answers', as are the source files. There is also a folder for old versions of the files, created during the chapter's development; this has been used so that the working folder does not get filled with lots of copies of the same file. The old versions of the file are dragged into the 'Old versions' folder at the end of each work period.

You can see that each file has been saved with a meaningful filename that includes a version number. This is called **version control**. This is really useful if you need to go back and look at your previous work. The folders can get very full, sometimes containing hundreds of versions of a file. When this happens, it can be a good idea to keep the last 20 versions of a file, plus every fifth file from the early editions (versions 5, 10 and so on), and then archive the other files before deleting them from the hard disk drive.

Task 11a

Create a new folder to store your work for this chapter in. Call this folder **Chapter 11**. Create two new sub-folders called **Source Files** and **Worked**. Open the file **remora.jpg** in a graphics package. Save the image **remora.jpg** in your Source Files folder.

Open the *File Explorer* window by pressing the <Windows> and <E> keys together. Click the left mouse button in the left pane to select the drive that you will use as your work area. Click in the right pane to move into the folder that you wish to use. The location of this will depend on the structure of the system you are using. Locate the required place in your folder structure.

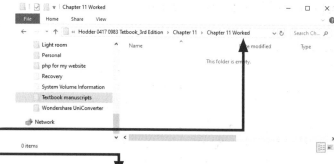

Click on the New folder icon.

Type Chapter 11 (the name for the new folder) then press <Enter>. Open this new Chapter 11 folder and use this method to create two new sub-folders called Source Files and Worked.

Locate and open the file remora.jpg in any graphics editing package. From the File tab, select Save as. You may also need to select the file type as JPEG in some packages. Select the Source Files folder that you have just created. Set the filename: to remora.jpg and click on Save.

Save files using appropriate file names

You should choose meaningful file names which give clues as to the contents of the file. This makes it easier for you to find the work in your user area when you look back at a later date. As mentioned earlier, use version numbers when saving files that are being developed. You can always check the date and time files were created or modified using their file details, but using meaningful filenames and version numbers allows you to see these details at a glance.

Display file details in a directory/folder

Task 11b

Edit the 'Source Files' folder created in Task 11a so that the date the file was created, and the image dimensions are displayed. Take a screenshot of this folder and save it in your 'Worked' folder.

You may need to display details of files that are not visible within *File Explorer*. Open File Explorer and locate the Source Files like this.

Click the right mouse button within the area indicated by the red rectangle.

This opens a drop-down menu similar to this. To add the date the file was originally created select the bottom option for **More...**

From the **Choose Details** window, scroll down the list until you locate **Date created**.
Click the left mouse button in the check box to select this option.

Scroll further down and select the option for **Dimensions** then click **OK**.

The source files folder will look similar to this.

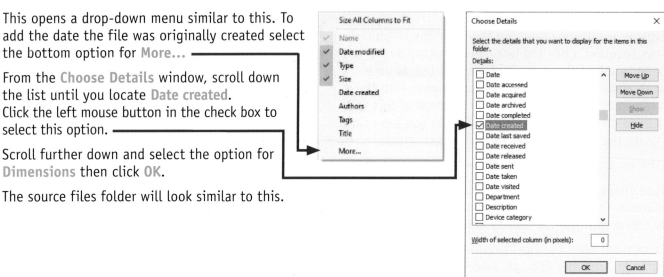

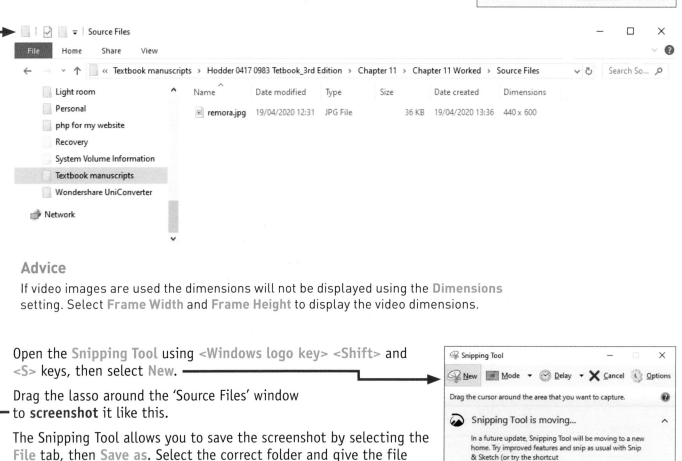

Advice

If video images are used the dimensions will not be displayed using the **Dimensions** setting. Select **Frame Width** and **Frame Height** to display the video dimensions.

Open the **Snipping Tool** using **<Windows logo key> <Shift>** and **<S>** keys, then select **New**.

Drag the lasso around the 'Source Files' window to **screenshot** it like this.

The Snipping Tool allows you to save the screenshot by selecting the **File** tab, then **Save as**. Select the correct folder and give the file an appropriate filename like **Screenshot of Source Files folder**, in JPEG format, then click **Save**.

Advice

An alternative to using the Snipping Tool is to use the **<ALT>** and **<Print Screen>** keys. This captures the current frame into the clipboard. The contents of the clipboard will need pasting into an application package for it be saved. If you need to paste into an Evidence Document, this method can save you time.

Save, export and print files in a variety of formats

Most of the specifics for this section of the syllabus are covered in following chapters. Although there are similarities in the methods of saving, exporting, and printing, these have been covered in detail for each application package used. Where evidence of how you answered a question is required, you can always screenshot the evidence and submit that. We have already introduced the Snipping tool, which is very useful. If you use screenshots, make sure that each screenshot shows all the information that is needed. Make sure that your screenshot is large enough so that all the information can be read by the examiner without the use of magnification devices. For example, your name, centre number and candidate number must be on all work, and if an item such as a 'browser view' is required, you must show the examiner that your web page is displayed in a browser, with the address of the web page visible, and not in an editing package.

From the **File** tab in most of the *Microsoft Office Suite* packages, you have the option to:

» **Save** – save the current file with the same filename
» **Save As** – save the current file with a new name, and/or new file type, and/or in a new location
» **Print** – print the current file
» **Export** – export, save a copy in **.pdf** format, or to change the file type in some packages.

11.1.2 File formats

The need for characteristics and uses of generic file formats

A generic file format can be opened in suitable software on most platforms (most types of computer). Questions will require you to open and edit data that is supplied to you; these files will always be in generic file formats.

Some file types used by *Microsoft Office*, such as *Excel* spreadsheets (.xlsx), *Word* documents (.docx), and *Access* databases (.accdb) are not generic. It is not always possible to open these packages on other platforms.

Generic file formats

Common generic text files include:

» **Comma separated values:** these files have a **.csv** file extension. This file type takes data in the form of tables (that could be used with a spreadsheet or database) and saves it in text format, separating data items with commas.
» **Text:** these files have a **.txt** file extension. A text file is not formatted and can be opened in any word processor.
» **Rich text format:** these files have a **.rtf** file extension. This is a text file type that saves some of the formatting within the text.

Common generic image files include:

» **Graphics interchange format:** these files have a **.gif** file extension. This format stores still or moving images and is an efficient method of storing images using a smaller file size, particularly where there are large areas of solid colour. It is widely used in web pages.

» **Joint photographic expert group**: these files have a **.jpg** (or sometimes a **.jpeg**) file extension. This format stores still images, but does not store moving images. It is an efficient method of storing images using a smaller file size and is widely used in web pages.

» **Portable document format**: these files have a **.pdf** file extension. This is a document which has been converted into an image format. It allows documents to be seen as an image so they can be read on most computers. The pages look just like they would when they are printed, but can contain clickable links and buttons, form fields, video, and audio. In PDF format you can protect a document to stop others from editing it.

» **Portable network graphics**: these files have a **.png** file extension. It is a file format that compresses graphics (image) files without any loss of image quality. It was created to replace graphics interchange format and is now the most used lossless image compression format on the internet.

Common generic video files include:

» **Moving pictures experts group layer 4**: these files have a **.mp4** file extension. It is not a single file format, but is a multimedia container which is used for storing video files, still images, audio files, subtitles, etc. This container is often used to transfer video files on the internet.

Common generic audio files include:

» **Moving pictures experts group layer 3**: these files have a **.mp3** file extension. It is a compressed file format used for storing audio files. This format cannot store still or moving images. The file sizes are relatively small, but with near-CD quality, which makes it suitable for use on the internet.

Common generic files used for website authoring include:

» **Cascading Style Sheets**: these files have a **.css** file extension. This is a style sheet which is saved in cascading style sheet format and is attached to one or more web pages (often written in HTML) to define the pages' colour scheme, fonts, etc.

» **Hypertext Markup Language**: these files have a **.htm** (or sometimes a **.html**) file extension. This is a text-based language used to create content that a web browser can display as a web page.

Common generic compressed files include:

» **Roshal archive**: these files have a **.rar** file extension. This is a container which can hold almost any file type in a compressed format. It is used to reduce the number of bytes needed to save a file, either to save storage space or to reduce transmission time. It was developed for *Windows* by a Russian software engineer Eugene Roshal and takes its acronym from **R**oshal **AR**chive.

» **Zip**: these files have a **.zip** file extension. This is a container which can hold almost any file type in a compressed format. It is used to reduce the number of bytes needed to save a file, either to save storage space or to reduce transmission time.

> **Link**
> ....
> See Section 11.2 for more on lossless compression.

11.2 Reduce file sizes for storage or transmission

11.2.1 File compression

The need to reduce file sizes for storage or transmission

All computer systems have a limited storage capacity, so the most efficient use of that storage space is important. The speed at which files are transmitted (sent) between one device and another is also dependent upon the amount of data being transmitted. This does not just affect transmission speeds on the internet, but also between the computers and devices like printers, network servers, and so on. This is also important when sending files as email attachments. The larger the file size, the more time it takes to transmit. Many email mailboxes have a limit as to the size of the files that can be sent/received.

Reducing file sizes for storage or transmission

Video files (because they contain thousands of still images) tend to be the largest files stored and transmitted. There are exceptions to this rule however – large database management systems like that used by the Driver and Vehicle Licencing Agency in the United Kingdom require immense amounts of storage. These systems continue to grow as organisations hold larger amounts of digital data within them.

Still images can vary in size. Lower resolution graphics, which are often used for web pages to speed up the loading time of the page, can be very small, but the higher the image resolution, the larger the file.

Where possible, image file sizes must be kept small, but not to the point where images become pixelated so that they are not clear.

This will mean resizing and/or resampling image files so that they require less storage space and less time to load. Resizing will change the physical dimensions (width and height) of the image and resampling changes the quality of the image. These elements will be studied in Chapter 12.

Using file compression

If a document contains lots of formatting or lots of images, its file size tends to be quite large. To reduce the file size for transmission (if the file is not to be edited) turn the file into portable document format, using the File tab, followed by Export. Select the Create PDF/XPS button.

Enter the new filename and click Publish to create the pdf which, as an image, should have a smaller file size, like this.

Export

Create PDF/XPS Document

Change File Type

Create a PDF/XPS Document
- Preserves layout, formatting, fonts, and images
- Content can't be easily changed
- Free viewers are available on the web

Create PDF/XPS

Ch_11_version_3.10.docx	19/04/2020 16:08	Microsoft Word Document	3,336 KB
Ch_11_version_3.11.docx	19/04/2020 16:12	Microsoft Word Document	3,320 KB
Ch_11_version_3.11.pdf	19/04/2020 16:12	Adobe Acrobat Document	698 KB

To send multiple files in the most efficient way it is more efficient to compress the files together as a single zip file. To do this you must open *File Explorer* with <Windows> and <E>. Hold down <Ctrl> and select the files to be zipped. With these files selected click the right mouse button to get the menu. Move the cursor down to the Send to option and the second menu appears. Click the left mouse button on Compressed (zipped) folder.

Edit the name of the folder, if appropriate.

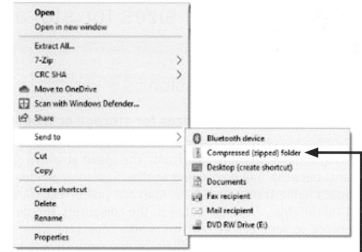

12 Images

12 Images

12 Images

In this chapter you will learn how to:
* ★ insert an image
* ★ resize an image to maintain or adjust the aspect ratio of an image
* ★ wrap text around an image
* ★ place an image with precision
* ★ place a border around an image
* ★ rotate an image
* ★ crop an image
* ★ reflect an image
* ★ adjust the brightness and contrast of an image
* ★ group and layer images.

In this chapter you will need the following source files:
* ★ dog.png
* ★ elephant.jpg
* ★ remora.jpg
* ★ robin.png
* ★ snow.rtf
* ★ snowangel.png
* ★ snowball.jpg
* ★ snowman.jpg
* ★ text1.png
* ★ text2.png
* ★ text3.png
* ★ trees.jpg
* ★ winter.pptx

12.1 Software tools

You will need to know how to place image files into different application packages. Where this is required in a web page please refer to Section 21.2.16. Images are unlikely to be included in the spreadsheets and databases elements of the course. However, images will be placed in both word-processed documents and presentations. First you must select images appropriate for the document's audience. Create a new folder called Chapter 12 and then create two new sub-folders called Source Files and Worked. Locate all the source files and copy them into your source files folder.

> **Link**
> ....
> See Section 21.2.16.

Task 12a

A short historical news article is to be given to young adults aged 15–25 to study.

Open the document **snow.rtf**. Insert the images **snowball.jpg**, **snowman.jpg** and **trees.jpg** at the end of the document.

This task requires a document rather than a presentation, although the methods shown are identical in both packages. Use the Search tool to find *Microsoft Word* and open this package.

From the File tab select Open and locate and open the file snow.rtf. Replace the text <Your Name> with your name, centre number and candidate number. Create a new folder called Task 12a. Select the File tab, then Save As to save your document, in this folder, as a Word document (.docx) with the filename task12a.

12.1.1 Insert images in a document or presentation

Move the cursor to the end of the document. Select the Insert tab, followed by Picture. This opens the Insert Picture window. Browse through the folders and files until you locate the file snowball.jpg.

Click the left mouse button on this file followed by Insert.

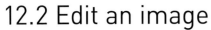

This will insert the image at the end of the document. Repeat this process for the files snowman.jpg and trees.jpg. Save the document as **task12a**.

You will notice that the images are inserted where the cursor was placed, at the end of the document. These will now need manipulating so that they become a part of the document, rather than just added to the end.

12.2 Edit an image

It is important that an image included in any document, presentation or publication in any form should be appropriate to the subject matter. If a document was about the snow, you may expect to see an image like this:

Making choices

Read the question and text carefully to try and understand which image would be the best and why. Does this image need editing? Is the image the correct shape to fit the position you wish to place it? If the image needed to be in landscape orientation you would need to crop it. Where do you crop it? If you crop the top off the image the watering can on the wall will be lost, which gives the viewer an idea of the depth of the snow, but so do the bricks in the wall. Do you crop the bottom from the image and remove lots of the white snow? The choices are yours depending upon what message you want the image to give. Is it the depth of the snow? Is it the dog playing in the snow?

If this image needs to be in landscape orientation and no alternative image is available, then you must crop the image rather than compressing or distorting it. Images should retain the correct proportions between width and height; this is called the aspect ratio.

Advice

Please note that you **must** ask for and be given permission to use an image in any publication. **Copyright** law in many countries will not allow you to use an image belonging to another person without their written consent.

Many copyright holders are happy for students to use their images for educational purposes without charging them, but you must obtain their permission to do so.

12.2.1 Resize an image

Task 12b

Open the file **task12a**.

Resize the image **snowball.jpg** to 8 cm high and maintain its aspect ratio. Place this at the top right of the first paragraph.

Resize the image of the snowman to 2.6 cm high and 2 cm wide. Save the document as task12b.

Resize an image in *Microsoft Word*
Find the image **snowball.jpg** in your document. Click the right mouse button on this image to get a drop-down menu. Select from this menu the Size and Position... option.

Advice

If the Size and Position... option does not appear, select Format Picture... followed by the Size tab.

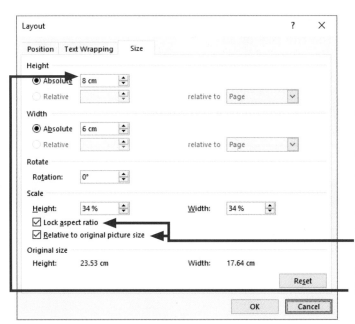

This opens the Layout window which should display the Size tab. If not select it.

The task instructs you to resize the image maintaining its aspect ratio. This means to keep the height and width in the same proportions as the original image, usually to ensure that you do not distort it. To do this, ensure that the two tick boxes related to the aspect ratio are both selected.

Change the Height of the image to 8 cm and click on OK.

Use a similar method to resize the clip-art image to 2.6 cm high by 2 cm wide. Select the snowman image and open the Layout window in the Size tab for that image. In this case different lengths and widths have been specified, but you have not been instructed to crop the image. This means that you will probably distort the image from its original proportions. To do this, first, make sure that both of the aspect ratio tick boxes have their ticks removed.

Use the Height box to change this setting to 2.6 cm and the Width box to 2 cm before clicking on ____OK____.

This will change the aspect ratio (proportions) of the image from this:

 to this:

Notice how the second image is slightly thinner but the same height. Save the document as **task12b**. You will continue working on this document in the next section in the next section.

Advice

If evidence of an image size or the aspect ratio is required, you can use screenshot evidence of this window.

Resize an image using a graphics package

Instead of editing in *Microsoft Word*, we can physically resize the image in a graphics package and then save the new image (usually with a new filename). This method has the advantage of being able to reduce the file size of an image, which is very useful in helping a web page to be downloaded and displayed more quickly. It has the disadvantage of using lower resolution images, which can appear pixelated, particularly if you wish to enlarge them. The graphics package we will use is called *GIMP*, which is an open source (free to use) raster graphics editor.

Task 12c

Open the file **remora.jpg**. Save a copy of this file in your 'Worked' folder. Resize this file to 80 pixels wide. Save this file as remora1.jpg. Reduce the resolution of the image further by downsampling and save the new image as remora2.jpg.

Open your 'Source Files' folder in the File Explorer window. Open the 'Worked' folder in a second copy of the File Explorer window. Click on the file in the 'Source Files' folder, hold down the left mouse button and drag the file remora.jpg from this folder into the 'Worked' folder.

From the 'Worked' folder, open the image remora.jpg in your graphics manipulation package. We have chosen *GIMP* for this task. Select the Rectangle Select Tool ————

and use this to lasso the image of the remora (fish). Before changing the image size check whether the Fixed drop-down menu is set to Aspect ratio. ————

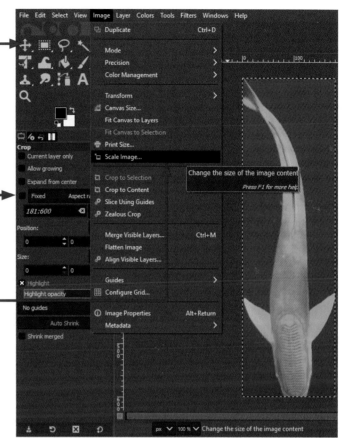

In *GIMP* (and many other packages, such as *Adobe Photoshop*) images are resized using the Image tab, followed by Scale Image.... ————

This opens the Scale Image window. To set the image width to 80 pixels, change the value in the Width: box ———— making sure that px is selected in the dropdown on the right. ————

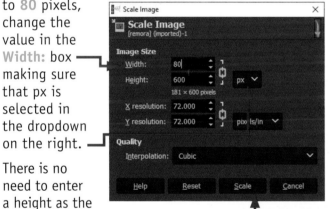

There is no need to enter a height as the image will maintain its aspect ratio as this had been fixed. To change the image size, click on the Scale ——— button.

This will alter the size of the image within the package like this. ————

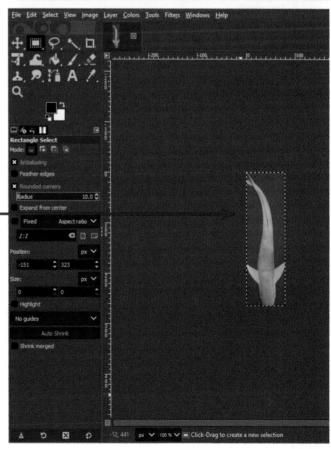

Advice

To intentionally distort an image you would fix the new width (or height) using the Fixed drop-down menu and enter a height as well as a width for the image.

To save the new image as a **JPEG** file, select File, then Export As... and enter the new filename **remora1.jpg** before clicking on ████. As this image will be saved in JPEG format, you are given options on the image quality that you require. These can be selected using the slide bar ────── or selecting from the drop-down menu. ──────

1 is the smallest file size that you can have, but also gives the poorest quality images. 100 is the highest quality, but results in large file sizes, which are much slower to download over the internet. Export the image with a quality of 60.

Resampling an image

This process of changing the image quality is called **resampling**. Images can be downsampled, meaning fewer pixels are used for the image, as you have just done by reducing the image quality. Images can also be upsampled by adding more pixels. Downsampling reduces the file size which helps web pages load more quickly. Export the same image again with the filename **remora2.jpg**, downsampling the image by lowering the resolution (quality) when saving. If you look at the files, you should see their sizes have decreased with each stage. ──────

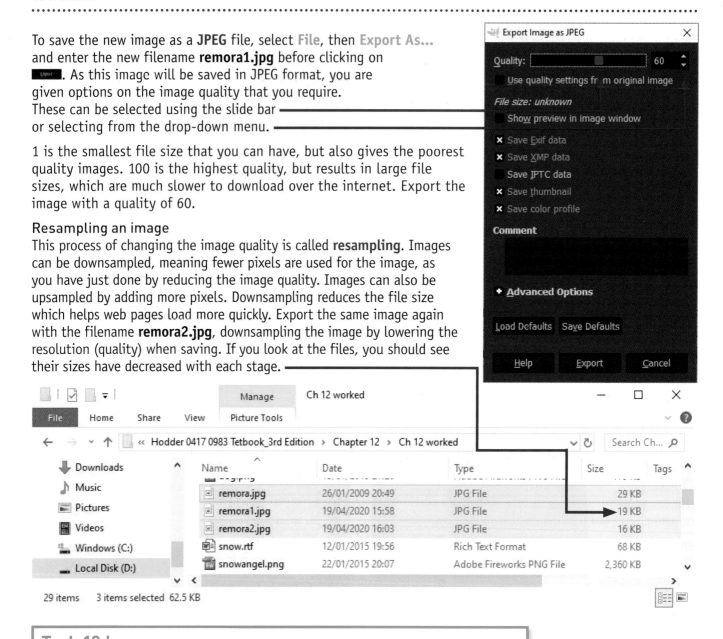

Task 12d

Open the file **task12b**.

Ensure that the text wraps around both of the images you placed in task 12b. Save the file as task12d.

12.2.2 Wrap text around an image

Task 12b required you to place the resized **snowball.jpg** image at the top right of the first paragraph. You are expected to align the image to the margins and to the top of the paragraph, but for this task there is a further instruction to wrap the text around the image. It is better to set the **text wrapping** first, then move the image into the correct position. Click the left mouse button on the image to select it. This opens the Picture Format tab. In the Arrange section, select the drop-down arrow next to the Wrap Text icon. ──────

Wrap Text ∨

You get a drop-down menu with layout options. Useful ones include:

» **In Line with Text** – this places the image as an in-line graphic which is treated as a text character within a line of text. It will move with the surrounding text if new text is inserted or deleted.
» **Square** – this places the image on the page and the text wraps (flows) around it. Use **More Layout Options...** to specify the type of wrapping that you require.
» **Tight** – this places the image on the page and the text wraps (flows) around it, similar to Square, but you cannot control the distance of the text from the image for the top and bottom settings, although you can to the left and right, using **More Layout Options...**.
» **Through** – this is very similar to tight and places the image on the page so the text wraps around the image with preset values.
» **Top and Bottom** – this places the image with the text above and below the image, but not wrapped to the side.
» **Behind Text** – this places the image behind the text. It can be used to set a background image in a document.
» **In Front of Text** – this places an image over the top of the text.
» **More Layout Options** – this can be used to give more options to the selected layout types above. For example, if a **Square** layout is selected you can specify where you wish to flow the text around the image and the distance of the text from the image on each side. This option also allows you to control the positioning of the image on the page.

For this task, set the text wrapping of the image to **Tight** using the drop-down menu.

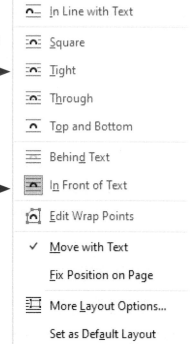

Advice

This menu can also be found by right clicking the mouse on an image and selecting **Wrap Text**.

Advice

Packages like Microsoft PowerPoint will not give text wrap options. Sometimes you have to layer objects on the slide or on the page in a document. To do this, click the right mouse button on the image and use the options like **Bring to Front** and **Send to Back**. This is also useful for placing overlapping images in a presentation or document.

12.2.3 Place an image with precision

You will be expected to place images precisely. To move and place this snowball image, click and hold the left mouse button on the image and drag it to the top right corner of the first paragraph. There are two methods of placing the image: the first is to drag it until the green guidelines appear at the top and right side of the image like this.

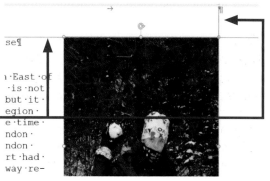

The second method is to roughly place the image and then right click on the image again. Select the Size and Position... option to open the Layout window. Select the Position tab.

Set the Horizontal alignment to Right aligned to the Margin.

Set the Vertical alignment to Top aligned to the top of the Line of text.

Click the OK button to place the image. Check that this has worked correctly. If not, this is usually due to the image being placed with too little precision when it was dragged and dropped. Try dragging and dropping the image again and repeat the process.

Repeat this process to place the resized image of the snowman at the top left of the second paragraph like this.

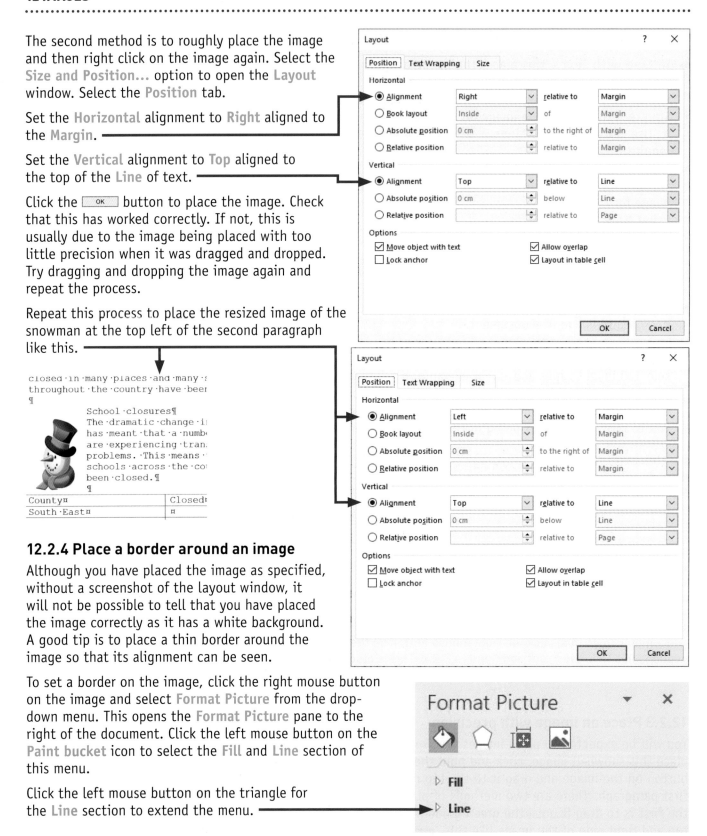

12.2.4 Place a border around an image

Although you have placed the image as specified, without a screenshot of the layout window, it will not be possible to tell that you have placed the image correctly as it has a white background. A good tip is to place a thin border around the image so that its alignment can be seen.

To set a border on the image, click the right mouse button on the image and select Format Picture from the drop-down menu. This opens the Format Picture pane to the right of the document. Click the left mouse button on the Paint bucket icon to select the Fill and Line section of this menu.

Click the left mouse button on the triangle for the Line section to extend the menu.

Left click on the **radio button** for Solid line, which again extends the options in the pane. Choose a (thin) line Width of 0.25pt.

The border now shows the precision placing of the image.

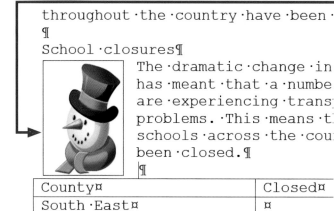

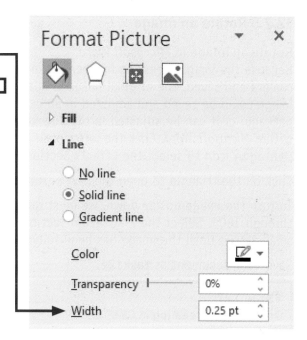

Save your document as **task12d**.

Task 12e

Open the file **task12d**.

The image **trees.jpg** has been taken on a digital camera. Place this image to the right of the table, aligned to the right margin. Resize this image if needed.

Place the image trees.jpg at the end of the document, as shown earlier in the chapter. Grab and drag the vertical borders in the table to narrow the column widths so that all text shows without wrapping, but no extra white space is shown. From this to this.

Using the ruler at the top, you can tell that the image will need to fit into a space from about 7 cm from the left of the page to 16 cm in. This means the image width should be about 9 cm wide (16 − 7 = 9). Use the methods learned earlier in this chapter, to resize the image to 9 cm wide while maintaining its aspect ratio. Set the text wrap so as to allow the image to sit to the right of the table. Drag the image into the correct position to the right of the table.

12.2.5 Rotate an image

Rotate an image in *Microsoft Word*

Because the image trees.jpg has been taken using a digital camera and saved, the original image is upside down. The image could be saved and adjusted in an external graphics package, or it can be adjusted in the Format Picture pane within *Microsoft Word*. Click the left mouse button on the Pentagon icon to select the Effects section of this menu.

Click on the triangle to open the 3-D Rotation options.

To turn the image upside down, we must rotate the image through 180°. Select the Z Rotation section and use the small arrows until the image has been fully rotated.

Save your document as **task12e**.

> ### Task 12f
> Open the file **trees.jpg** in *GIMP*.
>
> Rotate this image through 180° and save the new image as trees1.jpg.

Rotate an image in *GIMP*

Open the image **trees.jpg** in *GIMP*. Select the Image tab, then from the drop-down menu select Transform, then Rotate 180°. The image changes from this to this.

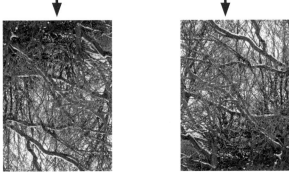

In *GIMP* you will need to save the file in the format of this application package, using the File tab, the Save As... then locate the correct folder. Set the filename as **trees2** and the extension will remain as **.xcf**. Saving it in the package's own file format will allow you to edit the image later if you need to (especially when we need to use layers later in the chapter). To complete the task, we need to save the new image as **trees1. jpg**. Select the File tab, then Export As... and set the filename to **trees1.jpg**. From the Export Image as JPEG window you can change the quality of the image using the slide bar.

As mentioned in Chapter 11, the higher the image quality, the larger the file size and therefore the file requires more storage capacity and transmission time. Move the slide bar to 60 then click on [Export].

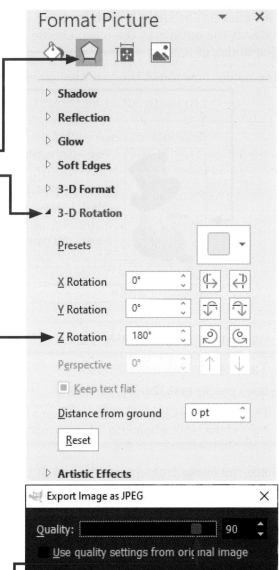

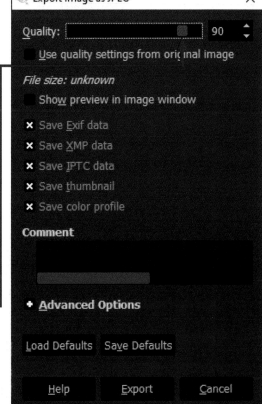

Task 12g

Open the file **task12e**.

Crop the image **trees.jpg** to remove the bottom 25% of it.

12.2.6 Crop an image

To **crop** an image is to cut off part of an image, which changes its aspect ratio but does not distort the image. Click the right mouse button on the **image trees.jpg** to get two menus and left click on Crop. ——

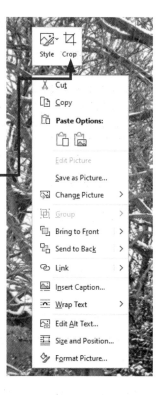

The drag handles for the image will change to crop handles. Drag the centre crop handle at the top of the image down so that about 25% (¼) of the image is selected (so that it becomes grey) like this. ——

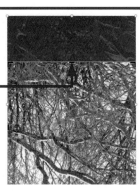

Look carefully at this image and you will see that with the crop tool selected, the image is upside down. This is because this image has already been rotated through 180° in Section 12.2.5, but cropping takes place on the original image. You will notice that you have dragged from the top of the image rather than the bottom of the image. Click the left mouse button on the text and the image will be cropped and appear the right way up, with the snow on the top of the branches, like this: ——

This image will need moving so that it aligns with the top of the table and right margin.

Save your document as **task12g**.

Task 12h

Open the file **task12g**.

Reflect the image **snowman.jpg** so that the snowman faces the other two images.

12.2.7 Reflect an image

Reflect an image in *Microsoft Word*
To reflect an image, left mouse click on the image, select the Format Picture pane, and then the Pentagon icon to select the Effects section of this menu. Do **not** select Reflection. Click on the triangle to open the 3-D Rotation options. ——

With the 3-D Rotation features, a reflection (flip) from left to right is an X rotation of 180 degrees and a (flip) reflection from top to bottom is a Y rotation of 180 degrees. Sometimes it is easier to perform these functions in a graphics package before placing the image.

For this task, set the X rotation of 180 degrees, like this. ——

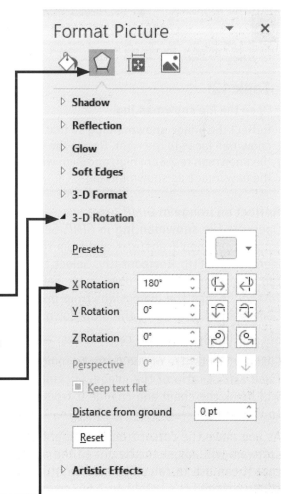

Save your document as **task12h**. The finished document should look like this.

Winter weather forces schools to close
By Graham Brown

On Monday February 2nd 2009 the South East of England was hit by snow. I know this is not unusual in many parts of the world, but it was interesting to watch the whole region grind to a virtual standstill. At the time of writing this article the major London airports of Heathrow, Gatwick and London City were all closed. Stansted airport had been closed but has just had one runway re-opened. Travel chaos has ensued, the M25 is closed in many places and many schools throughout the country have been closed.

School closures

The dramatic change in the weather has meant that a number of areas are experiencing transport problems. This means that many schools across the country have been closed.

County	Closed
South East	
Essex	250+
Hertfordshire	100+
Middlesex	80+
Sussex	50+
North	
Greater Manchester	100
Lancashire	70
Cumbria	34
Durham	70
Northumberland	33
Yorkshire	1

This table shows the number of schools reported closed. It is interesting to note that although the snow is no heavier in the South East of England, one of the eastern Counties has reported more than 250 of its schools are closed.

This gave the children lots time to play in the snow, snowballing, making snowmen and snow angels. The snow gave an added dimension, producing some very picturesque scenes, many captured on camera.

Task 12i

Open the file **snowman.jpg**.

Reflect the image **snowman.jpg** so that the snowman faces to the right. Resize the image of the snowman to 2.6 cm high and 2 cm wide. Save the new image as snowman1.jpg.

Reflect an image in *GIMP*

Open the file **snowman.jpg** in *GIMP*. Select the Image tab, then Transform and from the sub-menu select Flip Horizontally. Select the Image tab, then from the drop-down menu select Scale Image. Change the dimensions from pixels (px) to centimetres (cm) using the drop-down menu.

Set the height to 2.600 centimetres.

Click on the centre of the chain to remove the fixed aspect ratio of the image. Clicking on it will break the chain and change it from this to this.

As you move the cursor from the height box, the software will adjust the height to the nearest value that it can use to calculate the height. In this case it has changed the height to 2.593 cm.

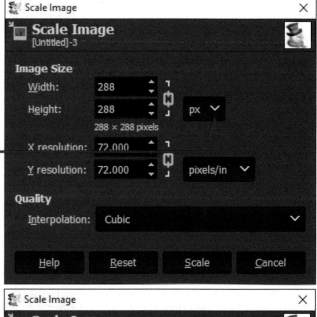

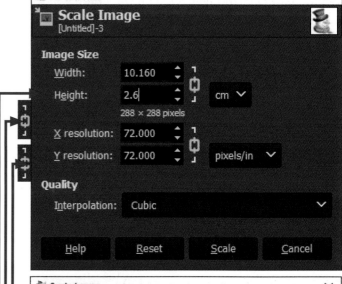

This is accurate enough for our purposes as it is 7/100 of a millimetre different. Set the width to 2.000 – as we can see the software has changed this to 2.005. Click on the on the 〖 Scale 〗 button to change the image.

Select the File tab, then Export As... and set the filename to **snowman1.jpg**

12.2.8 Adjust the brightness and contrast of an image

Open the file **trees1.png** in *GIMP*. Select the Colors tab and from the drop-down menu select Brightness-Contrast... which opens the Brightness-Contrast window. ————

Use the two sliders to edit both the Brightness and the Contrast until the image looks appropriate for the task. In this case set the brightness at +50 and the contrast at −40 like this. ————

Click on 〖 OK 〗. Use the methods described earlier to export the new image as **trees2.jpg**

Task 12j

Open the file **trees1. jpg**. Increase the brightness and decrease the contrast, so the image can be used as a background. Save the new image as trees2.jpg.

Advice

The brightness and contrast of an image can also be edited with the packages in Microsoft Office in a similar way, using the right-hand icon from the Format Picture pane, then selecting Picture Corrections and the sliders for Brightness and Contrast.

Task 12k

Create an image advertising a company called Winter Wonderland using the images **trees1.jpg**, **robin.jpg**, **text1.png** and **text 2.png**. Save the new image as card.jpg.

12.2.8 Layer images

Open the file **trees1.png** then drag the other images into *GIMP*. As you do so, these images are added to the original image but appear as separate layers. The layers can be seen in the bottom right corner of the window. ————

Three of these images have transparent backgrounds, as can be seen with the chequered patterns, but the trees.jpg layer must be the lowest layer, as this will be the background layer.

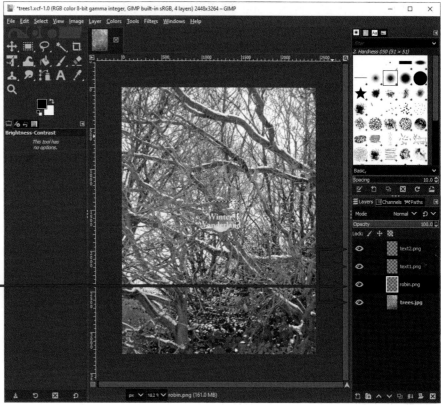

If it is not the lowest layer, then click on the layer and drag it down so it becomes the lowest of the four layers.

Advice

The layer at the top is the front layer and the bottom layer is the background layer. If a layer is higher in the list (nearer to the front) it may cover over the contents of a layer lower in the list.

Both the layers containing the text, although they are images of writing rather than editable text, need to be made much larger and grouped into a single layer. Select the layer text1.png then the Layer tab. From the drop-down menu select Scale Layer... then change the layer width to 2300 pixels, leaving the chain link fixed in place to maintain the aspect ratio of the layer.

Click on the [Scale] button. Repeat this process for the layer text2.png.

Select the move tool.

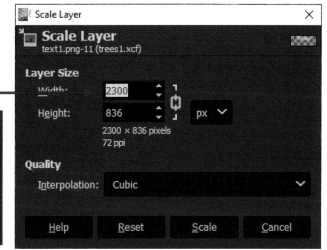

Select the image from the text1.png layer and place this at the top of the background. Repeat this process to place the text2.png layer just below the other text like this.

12.2.9 Group the layers

Now these layers are resized and placed together, we need to group the layers.

To group these layers we add the chain to both layers. Click the left mouse button to the right of the visibility eye for the chain to appear.

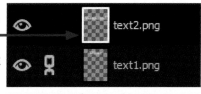

Move the robin, by selecting its layer and using the move tool so that it sits on a branch in the centre of the background image. The finished image looks like this.

From the File tab, select , Save As... to save the image as **card.xcf**. Use the File tab, then select Export As... to export the image as **card.jpg**.

If you open each of these files in a new version of *GIMP*, you can edit the layers, groups of layers and individual elements in the file **card.xcf**, but you cannot in the exported .jpg version. This is also the same if you export into .png format. The export has had the effect of flattening all the layers into one with all transparent areas from the individual layers being lost.

Activity 12a

Open the image **snowangel.png** in a suitable package. Rotate the image 90° clockwise. Save the image as snowangel1.png. Show evidence of the finished image, the filenames and file sizes.

Activity 12b

Open the presentation **winter.pptx** in a suitable package. Crop the bottom from the image **dog.png**, reduce its contrast and increase its brightness, placing it to fill the slide so that it becomes a background image.

Find a clipart image of a snowman. Resize it to 2 cm high. Place it 1 cm from the top of the slide and 1 cm from the left of the slide with no border. Save the file as Activity 12b.

Activity 12c

Open the file you saved in Activity 12b. Reflect (flip horizontally) the image of the snowman. Place a 1 pt red border around this image.

Activity 12d

Create an image advertising the Tawara Elephant Orphanage, using the images **elephant.jpg** and **text 3.png**. Place two copies of the elephant image like this. Group these two layers. Add the text so that the image looks like this.

Save the new image as Activity 12d.jpg.

13 Layout

Basic documents

This chapter will help you develop your document layout skills. The term 'document' does not just relate to a word-processed document, but can be a piece of written, printed, or electronic matter that provides information or evidence, or that serves as an official record. These can even include images such as photographs. Such documents will therefore include word-processed documents from *Microsoft Word*, reports from a database using *Microsoft Access*, spreadsheets, graphs and charts using *Microsoft Excel*, a presentation using *Microsoft PowerPoint* or a web page. Even though each of these packages requires different practical skills, they have many common elements which work in similar ways.

New documents need to be created with regard to the target audience for the document. The audience will often be a major factor in setting the styles that will be used within the document. One other very important element will be the accuracy of your data entry. Always check your documents for typing errors.

Plan it

Plan your document before starting it by making sure that you know:
- ★ What is the purpose of the document?
- ★ Who is the target audience?
- ★ How can it be made suitable for this audience?
- ★ What is the appropriate medium?
- ★ What is the appropriate package?

13.1 Create or edit a document

13.1.1 Create a new document

The method used to create a new document in most of these applications will depend on whether the package is already open in the computer.

Create a new document if the package is already open

To create a new document in most of these applications (databases, graphs, charts and web pages are different), open the application package and click on the **File** tab followed by New. It is worth saving your new document as soon as you have started it, and saving your work often, using the methods shown in Chapter 11.

Create a new document if the package is not open

This method does not apply to web pages. Open the application package. It may open a new document when the package is opened. In this case go to Section 13.2. If it does not automatically open a new document, then the Start screen for the package will open. Click on the icon at the top, towards the left side, for Blank document/workbook/database/presentation, depending upon the package selected. The different packages have different icons like this:

<table>
<tr><td>*Microsoft Word*</td><td>*Microsoft Excel*</td><td>*Microsoft Access*</td><td>*Microsoft PowerPoint*</td></tr>
<tr><td>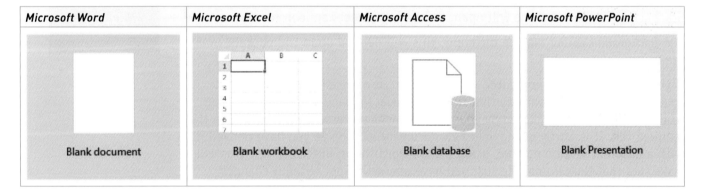</td><td></td><td></td><td></td></tr>
<tr><td>Blank document</td><td>Blank workbook</td><td>Blank database</td><td>Blank Presentation</td></tr>
</table>

13.1.2 Open an existing document

The method used to open an existing document in most of these applications will depend upon whether the package is already open in the computer.

Open a document if the software is already running

For most applications (databases, graphs, charts and web pages are different), click on the **File** tab followed by Open. Select Browse to help you find the document. ⟶

Other locations

This PC

Add a Place

Browse

Link

See Chapter 9 for more on target audience.

See Chapter 14 for more on document styles.

See Chapter 15 for more on checking typing errors.

Locate the folder that contains the document that you require. If the document can't be seen in the folder, then use the drop-down menu to change the file types so that it displays All Files (*.*) like this.

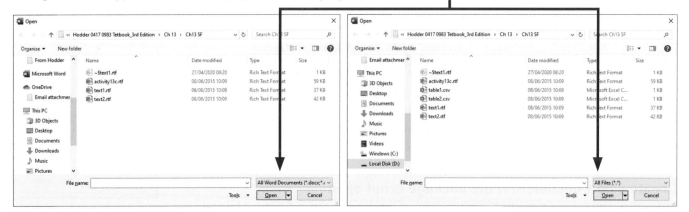

Click on the filename that you require from the list, then click Open. It is worth saving your new document as soon as you have opened it, with a different version number, using the methods shown in Chapter 11. This will make sure that the original file that you have opened is kept without changes.

Open a document if the software is not running

This method does not apply to web pages. Open the application package and the Start screen for the package will open. On the left select the icon for Open.

Open

The background colour may be different, this will depend upon the package you are using.

If you are using a home computer, you will see a list of recently used files that could be selected. It is unlikely that this will appear in many school systems due to the security settings placed by your network administrator. Locate and open the required file. It is worth saving your new document as soon as you have opened it, with a different version number, using the methods shown in Chapter 11. This will make sure that the original file that you have opened is kept without changes.

Advice

On a home computer, open *File Explorer* and double click the left mouse button on the filename or icon to open the file within the default software for that file type. This does not often work on many school systems, due to the security settings placed by the network administrator.

Task 13a

Create a new document. Open the file **text1.rtf**. Change the document heading to 'Winter weather forces schools to close'.

Save the document as task13a.

13.1.3 Enter and edit data

Data can include text and numbers. For the purposes of a document, both can be entered and edited in the same way through the keyboard.

Enter text or numbers in a document

Before starting this task, examine the file **text1.rtf**. As Task 13a makes no mention of the purpose of the task or its audience we cannot answer the first three document planning questions. After examining the file:

» the most appropriate medium would appear to be printed on paper (or if used electronically as a downloadable document)

» the most appropriate package would appear to be a word processor (although this may be converted into portable document format if used as a downloadable document).

Open the document text1.rtf in *Microsoft Word*.

Use the File tab and Save As... to save this document with the filename task13a as a *Word* document, rather than in rich text format.

To change the document heading, highlight the existing heading and overtype this with the new heading. Although this seems one of the easiest tasks, it is one where a significant number of students fail to check their data entry. You will need to be 100 per cent accurate with all data entry, including the use of capital and lower case letters. The top of the document should now look like this:

> Winter ·weather ·forces ·schools ·to ·close¶
> ¶
> On ·Monday ·February ·2ⁿᵈ ·2009 ·the ·South ·East ·of ·England ·was ·hit ·by ·snow. ·I · know ·this ·is ·not ·unusual ·in ·many ·parts ·of ·the ·world, ·but ·it ·was · interesting ·to ·watch ·the ·whole ·region ·grind ·to ·a ·virtual ·standstill. ·At · the ·time ·of ·writing ·this ·article ·the ·major ·London ·airports ·of ·Heathrow, · Gatwick ·and ·London ·City ·were ·all ·closed. ·Stansted ·airport ·had ·been ·closed · but ·has ·just ·had ·one ·runway ·reopened. ·¶

Save the changes to this document.

Task 13b

Open the file **task13a**.

Move the last sentence in the document so that it becomes the last sentence in the first paragraph.

Add a new subheading 'School closures' just before the second paragraph and add this short paragraph before the text <Place table here>:

The dramatic change in the weather has meant that a number of areas are experiencing transport problems. This means that many schools across the country have been closed.

In what is now the third paragraph change the word 'was' to 'is', and add the word 'has' between 'counties' and 'reported'.

Save the document as task13b.

Edit text or numbers in a document

There are a number of techniques that could be used to move the last sentence to the end of the first paragraph. These include cut and paste, copy and paste then delete the original, and drag and drop. It is recommended that you learn and practise all of these methods.

All three methods require you to highlight the correct section of text. A useful tip (especially if you are right-handed) is to highlight from the end of the text back to the beginning rather than the other way around. Highlight the text like this: ─────

```
England, ·one ·of ·the ·eastern ·counties ·reported ·more ·than ·250 ·of ·its ·
schools ·are ·closed.¶
¶
This ·gave ·the ·children ·lots ·time ·to ·play ·in ·the ·snow, ·snowballing, ·making ·
snowmen ·and ·snow ·angels. ·The ·snow ·gave ·an ·added ·dimension, ·producing ·some ·
very ·picturesque ·scenes, ·many ·captured ·on ·camera. ·Travel ·chaos ·has ·
ensued, ·the ·M25 ·is ·closed ·in ·many ·places ·and ·many ·schools ·throughout ·the ·
country ·have ·been ·closed.¶
```

Editing methods

You can now choose your method from the following.

Cut and paste
Click the right mouse button within the highlighted area to get the drop-down menu, then select **Cut**. This removes the sentence and places it in the windows **clipboard**. Move the **cursor** to the end of the first paragraph and right mouse click to obtain the drop-down menu again. This time select **Paste**.

Copy, paste and delete
Click the right mouse button within the highlighted area to get the drop-down menu, then select **Copy**. This copies the sentence to the clipboard but does not remove it. Move the cursor to the end of the first paragraph and right mouse click to obtain the drop-down menu and select **Paste**. Move back to the original sentence, highlight it and press the <Delete> key on the keyboard. Although this method takes longer than cut and paste, it does not remove the original sentence until the end of the process, so if you accidentally lose the sentence from the clipboard the original is still present.

> **Advice**
>
> Use <Ctrl><X> to **cut**, <Ctrl><C> to **copy** and <Ctrl><V> to **paste**.

Drag and drop
Click the left mouse button in the highlighted area and hold this down, moving the cursor to the end of the first paragraph. Release the left mouse button at that point and you will drop all of the highlighted text there.

> **Advice**
>
> Drag and drop is easy when both positions are on the screen at the same time, but harder when you need to scroll through the document before dropping.

Whichever method you use, make sure that the character spacing between the sentences and the line spacing between paragraphs matches the rest of the document. Check carefully for any inconsistencies.

To add the subheading, move the cursor to the end of the first paragraph and press the <Enter> key twice. (This will keep the same paragraph spacing as the rest of the document.) Now type the text 'School closures' followed by the <Enter> key. Type the new paragraph. Go back and check for data entry errors and the consistency of spacing. Correct any errors.

To change the word 'was' to 'is', locate the word and highlight it. Type in the word 'is' and it will replace the original. To insert the word 'has', place the cursor between the words 'counties' and 'reported'. Make sure that there is a single space on each side of the cursor before you type the word 'has'.

Save your document as **task13b**.

> ## Task 13c
>
> Open the file **task13b**. Insert the file **table1.csv** as a table within the document.
>
> Save the document as task13c.

13.1.4 Place objects

Place a table from a .csv file

Open *Microsoft Word*. Select the **File** tab, then **Open**, but you will not be able to see the file table1.csv as it is not in a format that *Microsoft Word* recognises. Click on **Browse**, then select **All Files (*.*)**.

Click on the file **table1.csv**, then click Open.

The file **table1.csv** looks like this when it has been opened in *Word*.

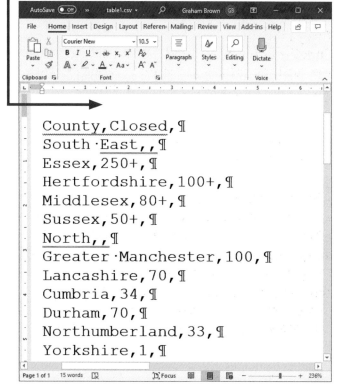

Now you need to edit it, to turn the 'comma separated values' into a table then copy it into the file that you recently saved. Highlight all the text (hold the <CTRL> key and tap the <A> key) and then select the **Insert** tab followed by the **Table** icon.

Click the left mouse button on **Convert Text to Table....**

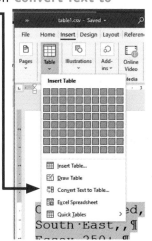

Because the text is highlighted it will be placed within the cells of a table. This opens the **Convert Text to Table** window. Click on OK to create the table. If *Word* does not offer you the correct values for rows and columns, because the .csv file contains both commas and carriage returns, then

County,Closed,¶
South·East,,¶
Essex,250+,¶
Hertfordshire,100+,¶
Middlesex,80+,¶
Sussex,50+,¶
North,,¶
Greater·Manchester,100,¶
Lancashire,70,¶
Cumbria,34,¶
Durham,70,¶
Northumberland,33,¶
Yorkshire,1,¶

the table may need editing by either removing blank rows and/ or columns. In this example, it has created an extra column to the right.

To remove this column, first click the left mouse button in a cell in the right-hand column. This removes the highlighting from the table. In the same cell, click the right mouse button to obtain a drop-down menu. From this menu select the Delete Cells... option. This opens the Delete Cells window.

Choose the radio button for Delete entire column followed by OK. Copy this table, open the document saved in Task 13b, then highlight the text <Place table here> and paste the table. Save the document as **task13c**.

The finished document should look like this.

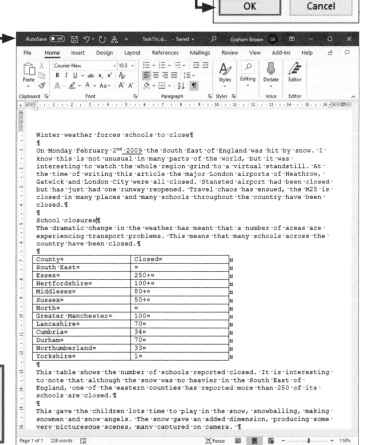

Advice

If you have to combine more than one file (sometimes with different file types), open each file as a new document, then copy and paste from one document to another. This method can reduce any problems that could occur with **embedded objects**.

Advice

An alternative method would be to open table1.csv in *Microsoft Excel* and copy and paste the table from there into a new document in *Microsoft Word*.

Place an image, graph, chart, spreadsheet or database extract in a document

Spreadsheet extracts, graphs and charts can be copied and pasted from *Excel* and edited as if they are an image within a document. If a database extract is to be included in another form of document, export this into rich text format (as shown in Chapter 18) before copying and pasting this into the document.

Link

Please refer to Chapter 12 for the placing and editing of images.

Place a screenshot in a document

To take a screenshot of the current screen use the <Print Screen> or <Prt Scr> key on your keyboard. This captures an image of the screen contents (the same as Copy) and places it in the clipboard. Paste this image into a document. To take a screenshot of a single window use <Alt> and <Prt Scr>. To take a screenshot of part of a window use the Snip tool (as shown in Chapter 11). Please note that if you want to show a drop-down menu that you are using in the screenshot, you must capture the whole screen and crop unused areas from the image.

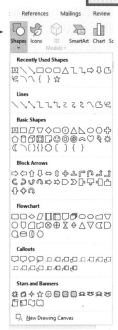

> **Link**
> ....
> See the section on cropping images in Chapter 12.

> ## Task 13d
>
> Open the file **task13c**. Place a red arrow from the end of the third paragraph so that it points at the figure 250+ in the table.
>
> Save the document as task13d.

Place a shape into a document

Open the file task13c. Click the left mouse button at the end of the third paragraph. Select the Insert tab, then select Shapes. Use the drop-down menu to select the type of shape required.

As you can see there are lots of different options available. You should choose one that would be appropriate for the task. Here are some options.

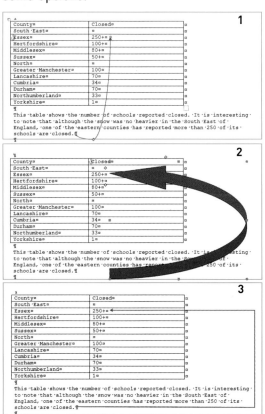

Many would select option 2, but notice that both of the first two options have arrows that cover part of the text. The second option does not start from the end of the text. This means that the third option is the only appropriate one from those shown.

Select the option for an Elbow Arrow.

Lines

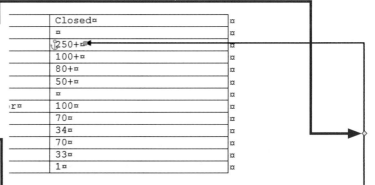

Click the left mouse button at the end of the word 'closed.' and attempt to drag the arrow so that it points at the end of '250+'. You will notice that you cannot get the elbow arrow to appear as it is shown in diagram 3 above. This has to be created using two different objects, one elbow arrow and one straight line. Drag the point of the arrow to the end of '250+' and the end without the arrow to the right end of the line with 'closed.' in it, like this.

County¤	Closed¤	¤
South ·East¤	¤	¤
Essex¤	⟨250+¤	¤
Hertfordshire¤	100+¤	¤
Middlesex¤	80+¤	¤
Sussex¤	50+¤	¤
North¤	¤	¤
Greater ·Manchester¤	100¤	¤
Lancashire¤	70¤	¤
Cumbria¤	34¤	¤
Durham¤	70¤	¤
Northumberland¤	33¤	¤
Yorkshire¤	1¤	¤

¶
This ·table ·shows ·the ·number ·of ·schools ·reported ·closed. ·It ·is ·interesting · to ·note ·that ·although ·the ·snow ·was ·no ·heavier ·in ·the ·South ·East ·of · England, ·one ·of ·the ·eastern ·counties ·has ·reported ·more ·than ·250 ·of ·its · schools ·are ·closed. ¶
¤

Drag the yellow handle to the right so that it is above the right-hand end like this.
Click the right mouse button on the elbow arrow. Select from the drop-down menu Format AutoShape/Picture to display the Format AutoShape window. Select the tab for Colors and Lines, then in the Line section use the drop-down palette to change the line colour to red.
If you wish to make the line more prominent, you can change the weight (thickness) of the line. Click on ⬚ OK .

Add a second straight line from the AutoShapes to join to the first line. Change the colour to red and make sure that the weight of the line matches than used for the elbow arrow. Hold down the <CTRL> key and click on the elbow arrow and then click the right mouse button on the line. Select Grouping from the drop-down menu, then select Group from the sub-menu. This groups the two objects together so that they behave like a single object. Save the document as **task13d**.

Closed¤	¤
¤	¤
⟨250+¤	¤
100+¤	¤
80+¤	¤
50+¤	¤
¤	¤
100¤	¤
70¤	¤
34¤	¤
70¤	¤
33¤	¤
1¤	¤

the ·number ·of ·schools ·reported ·closed. ·It ·is ·interesting · ough ·the ·snow ·was ·no ·heavier ·in ·the ·South ·East ·of · he ·eastern ·counties ·has ·reported ·more ·than ·250 ·of ·its · d. ¶

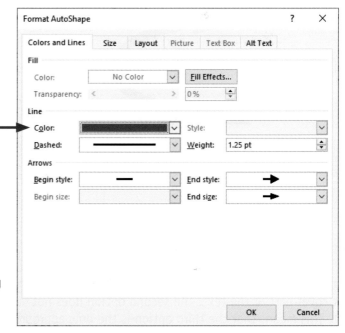

Advice

For screenshots in an evidence document, make sure that it is easy to read the contents of the screenshot but do **not** crop off the information that may be needed, for example: your name, Centre number and candidate number, the filename or the evidence that you are using a web browser rather than an editing package.

Activity 13a

Open the file **text2.rtf** and insert the file **table2.csv** as a table after the paragraph that ends 'This table shows the number of schools closed in some of the local authorities.'

Change the document heading to 'Snow brings disruption to Britain'.

Move the last paragraph in the document so that it becomes the first paragraph.

Add the following as a new paragraph immediately before the paragraph that starts 'Flights were suspended...':

Heavy snowfalls were reported to the north of London. London was also affected but not to the same extent as the disruption that had been caused the week before.

In the last paragraph change the word 'weird' to 'unusual' and add the word 'national' between 'many' and 'newspapers'.

Save and print this document.

13.1.5 Wrap text around a table, graph, chart or image

The methods learned in Chapter 12 also apply to text wrapping around graphs, charts and embedded objects, such as spreadsheet extracts and some tables.

13.2 Tables

13.2.1 Create a table

Tables of data may need to be inserted into your word-processed documents or presentations. You have already inserted a table from a .csv file in Task 13c.

Link

See Chapter 12 for text wrapping around images and Section 13.2.5 for text wrapping around tables.

Task 13e

Open the file **task13d**. Add the following text to the end of the document as a new paragraph:

Temperatures recorded at one weather station in Ross-on-Wye during the week read:

Below this text add a table like this:

Save the document as task13e.

Open the file **task13d** and add the text as a new paragraph to the end of the document.

To create a new table, you must first work out how many rows and columns the table contains. By counting them, you can work out that this table contains three columns and eight rows. Move the cursor to the correct place in the document, then select the **Insert** tab. In the **Tables** section click on the **Table** icon.

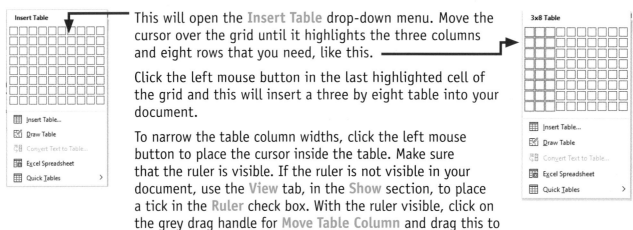

This will open the **Insert Table** drop-down menu. Move the cursor over the grid until it highlights the three columns and eight rows that you need, like this.

Click the left mouse button in the last highlighted cell of the grid and this will insert a three by eight table into your document.

To narrow the table column widths, click the left mouse button to place the cursor inside the table. Make sure that the ruler is visible. If the ruler is not visible in your document, use the **View** tab, in the **Show** section, to place a tick in the **Ruler** check box. With the ruler visible, click on the grey drag handle for **Move Table Column** and drag this to the left.

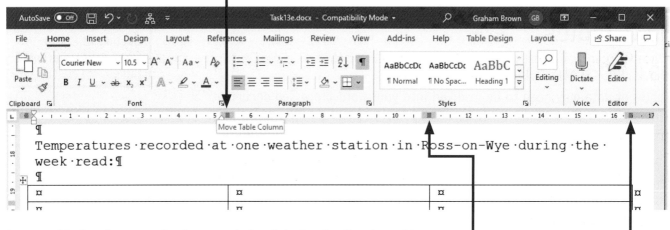

Repeat this for the second column and the right border for the table.

The table column widths will now be narrower like this.

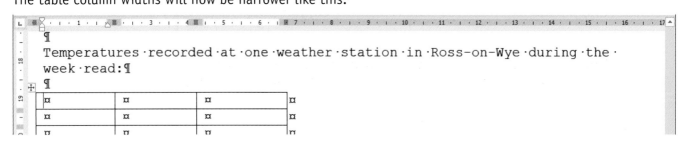

Save the document as task13e.

13.2.2 Place text or objects in a table

Task 13f

Open the file **task13e**. Add this text and the image **snowflake.jpg** to the table:

	Maximum	Minimum
2nd Feb	3	−1
3rd Feb	5	−3
4th Feb	5	−3
5th Feb	2	−1
6th Feb	2	−1
7th Feb	5	−3
8th Feb	4	−2

Save the document as task13f.

Place an object in a table

Place the cursor in the top left cell of the table. Use the Insert tab, in the Illustrations section, to select the icon for Pictures.

Select from the drop-down menu, This Device to open the Insert Picture window. Locate the image then click Insert.

The image will now appear in the table cell. You will notice it is much too large for the cell so you will need to use the corner drag handles to resize it to the required size while retaining the aspect ratio.

Insert Picture From

This Device...

Stock Images...

Online Pictures...

Place text in a table

To move from the first table cell to the second press the <Tab> key. Use the keyboard to type the text 'Maximum'. Repeat this process using the <Tab> key and typing to enter the rest of the text. Save the document as **task13f**.

Advice

If you need more rows than the eight available, move the cursor into the last cell of the table and press the <Tab> key to create a new row. If you need lots of new rows, hold down the <Tab> key.

Activity 13b

Create a new document with the title 'Skills to practise using tables'. Create this table, below the title.

Function	How	Feature		
Insert	Insert tab	Table		
	Right click	Rows		
	Right click	Columns		
Delete		Rows		
Format		Cells	Alignment	Left, right, centre, fully justified
				Top, centre, bottom
			Colour, shading	
	Rows		Breaks across page	
	Gridlines		Show	
			Hide	
Text wrapping		Cells		

Save this document.

13.2.3 Edit a table

Task 13g

Open the file **table.rtf**. Insert a new column to fit between the data for Bernice and David. Enter the following data into that column.

Student	**Charlie**
Mathematics	**27**
English	**59**
Physical Education	**98**
IT	**61**
Science	**33**

Enter a new row above Mathematics. Enter the following data into that row.

Student	**Alan**	**Zoe**	**Bernice**	**Charlie**	**David**
Subject					

Enter a new row above the top row.

Delete the row for Physical Education. Move the column containing Zoe to the right of the column containing David.

Merge all cells in the top row of the table and add the text 'Test scores for class X1' into this cell.

Save the document as task13g.

Insert a column

To insert a new column between those holding the data for Bernice and David, click the left mouse button within the table, anywhere in the column containing the data for Bernice. Select the Layout tab. In the Rows & Columns section these options are available. ————

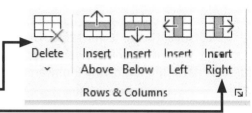

Select the option for Insert Right. ————

Move the cursor into the new column and enter the data given in the question into the new cells.

Insert a row

To insert a new row above Mathematics, click the left mouse button within the table, anywhere in the row containing Mathematics. Select the Layout tab, then from the Rows & Columns section, select Insert Above.

Move the cursor into the left cell of the new row and enter the text 'Subject'.

Use the same method to insert a new row above the top row.

Delete a row

To delete the row containing Physical Education, move the cursor into that row. From the Layout tab select the icon for Delete. ————

From the drop-down menu select the option for Delete Rows. ————

The best method to move the column containing Zoe to the right of the column containing David is to insert a new column to the right of the one containing David's data, to copy all the data for Zoe and paste this into the new column.

Delete a column

When the data is in this new column, move back to the third column and from the Layout tab select the icon for Delete, then Delete Columns.

Merge cells

To merge all cells in the top row of the table, highlight all these cells and from the Layout tab, in the Merge section, select Merge Cells. ————

Type the text 'Test scores for class X1' into this cell. Save the document as **task13g**. The finished table looks like this. ————

Editing a table

Test scores for class X1					
Student	Alan	Bernice	Charlie	David	Zoe
Subject					
Mathematics	45	54	27	16	32
English	22	89	59	65	57
IT	65	29	61	45	17
Science	16	57	33	35	28

Task 13h

Open the file that you saved in Task 13f. Sort the lower table into descending order of Minimum temperature. Save the document as task13h_min.

Sort the lower table into ascending order of Maximum temperature. Save the document as task13h_max.

Sort data

Open the file that you saved in Task 13f. Move the cursor into the lower table. As you do not want the column headings sorted within this data, highlight row 2 onwards, like this. ────────

	Maximum¤	Minimum¤
¤		
2nd ·Feb¤	3¤	−1¤
3rd ·Feb¤	5¤	−3¤
4th ·Feb¤	5¤	−3¤
5th ·Feb¤	2¤	−1¤
6th ·Feb¤	2¤	−1¤
7th ·Feb¤	5¤	−3¤
8th ·Feb¤	4¤	−2¤

Select the **Home** tab, then within the **Paragraph** section select the icon for **Sort**. ────

This opens the **Sort** window. The sort window suggests in the **Sort by:** box that we sort by the left column, as it displays '2nd Feb'. Use the drop-down menu to select **Column 3** from this list as the third column contains the minimum temperature values. As we change this column the **Type:** box changes from 'Text' to 'Number'. Click on the radio button for **Descending**, then on ⬛ OK . Save the document as **task13h_min**. The table changes to look like this. ────────

Paragraph

	Maximum¤	Minimum¤
¤		
2nd ·Feb¤	3¤	−1¤	¤
5th ·Feb¤	2¤	−1¤	¤
6th ·Feb¤	2¤	−1¤	¤
8th ·Feb¤	4¤	−2¤	¤
3rd ·Feb¤	5¤	−3¤	¤
4th ·Feb¤	5¤	−3¤	¤
7th ·Feb¤	5¤	−3¤	¤

Repeat this process. Change the **Sort by:** box to **Column 2** and select the radio button for **Ascending**. Save the document as **task13h_max**. The table now looks like this. ────

	Maximum¤	Minimum¤
¤		
5th ·Feb¤	2¤	−1¤	¤
6th ·Feb¤	2¤	−1¤	¤
2nd ·Feb¤	3¤	−1¤	¤
8th ·Feb¤	4¤	−2¤	¤
3rd ·Feb¤	5¤	−3¤	¤
4th ·Feb¤	5¤	−3¤	¤
7th ·Feb¤	5¤	−3¤	¤

13.2.4 Format a table

Tables can be formatted so that they can be aligned left, right or centrally between the margins. Text can be wrapped around the table or not as required. These features are found in the table properties: click the right mouse button in any cell of the table, then select Table Properties... and the Table tab within the Table Properties window. The table alignment can be selected in the Alignment section and text wrapping around the table can be switched on or off in the Text wrapping section.

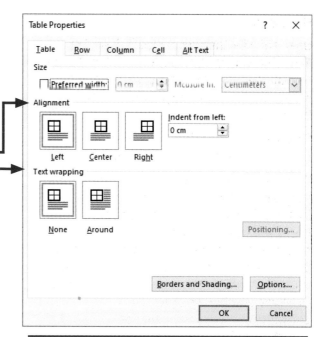

Task 13i

Open the file that you saved in Task 13f.

Narrow the columns in the top table so that there is a minimum of white space but no text wraps within a cell.

Set the text wrapping options for this table so that the body text of the document flows around the table.

Save the document as task13i.

Open the file that you saved in Task 13f. Move the cursor into the top table and double click the left mouse button on the vertical gridline.

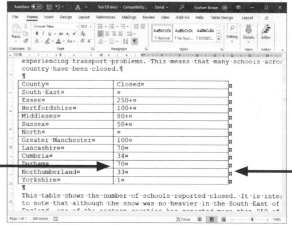

Repeat this with the right-hand gridline.

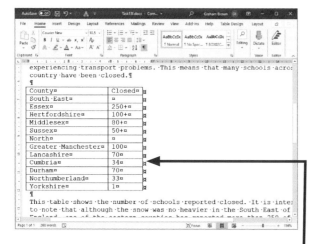

The table will look like this.

Save the document as **task13i**.

Wrap text around a table

Click the right mouse button in any cell of the table, then select Table Properties... and in the Table Properties window select the Table tab. Move the cursor into the Text wrapping section and select Around.

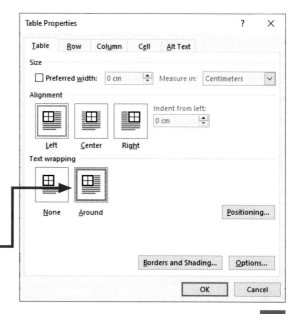

This will wrap the body text around the table. Click on ⬚ OK ⬚ to complete this. The table should look like this:

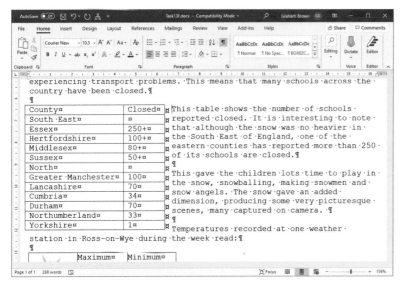

Save the document as **task13i**.

Task 13j

Open the file that you saved in Task 13i.

Right align all of the cells containing numbers in the second column of the top table. Centre align all of the cells in the top two rows and the row containing 'North'.

Make the top row of the table twice as high. Vertically align all data to the middle of each cell.

Merge the cells in rows 2 and 7 into single cells.

Save the document as task13j.

Horizontal cell alignment within a table

Move the cursor into the top table. To highlight all the cells containing numbers, click the left mouse button in the top of these cells and drag the mouse down. Select the Home tab. In the Paragraph section find the four icons for text alignment.

Click on the third icon to right align the contents of these cells.

Highlight all cells in the top two rows of the table as described above, hold down the <CTRL> key and drag over the contents of the cell containing 'North' so that all five cells are highlighted like this:

To centre align these cells select the Home tab, in the Paragraph section, find and click on the second icon.

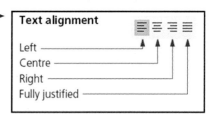

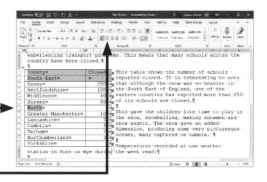

To make the top row of the table twice as high, grab the gridline below the top row and drag down so that it changes from this ⌐ to this. ⌐

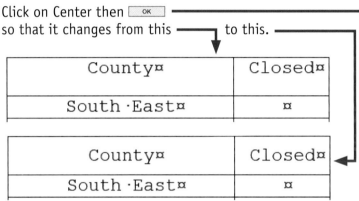

Vertical cell alignment within a table

You can see that the cell contents are aligned to the top of the cells in this row (and the rest of the table). You must vertically align all data to the middle of each cell. Highlight all the cells in the table and click the right mouse button in one of these cells. Select Table Properties... and the Cell tab.

Click on Center then [OK] so that it changes from this ⟶ to this. ⟶

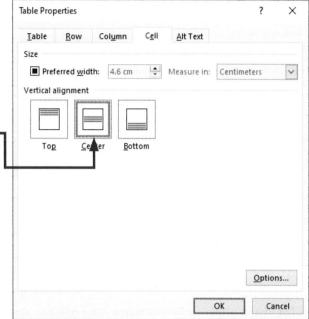

This method can also be used to set top or bottom aligned text within table cells. Merge the two cells in rows 2 and 7 of the table. You may have to re-format the contents of the merged cell in row 7 to be centre aligned as the merge may change the alignment to that of the final cell (which was right aligned). Save the document as **task13j**.

Task 13k

Open the file that you saved in Task 13j.

In the lower table, centre align the contents of row 1 both horizontally and vertically. Remove all gridlines from this table except those cells containing the maximum and minimum temperatures during this week.

In the top table, set the background colour of all cells in the top two rows and row 7 to yellow. In the lower table shade the background of the top row with pale blue coloured diagonal lines.

Save the document as task13k.

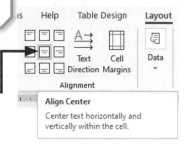

Highlight the top row of the lower table. Because this task requires you to set both vertical and horizontal alignment to these cells, select the Layout tab, in the alignment section select Align Center. ⟶

Show and hide table gridlines

To work on the whole of the lower table, click the right mouse button in this table. Select Table Properties... and the Table tab. Select the option for Borders and Shading.... ────────────────

This opens the Borders and Shading window. Make sure the Borders tab is selected and the Apply to: box is set to the whole Table. ────────────────

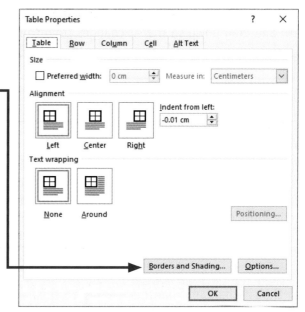

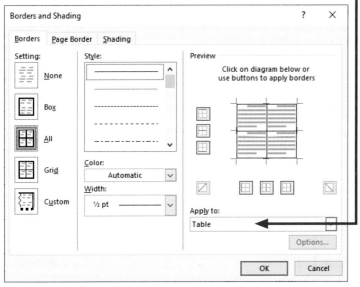

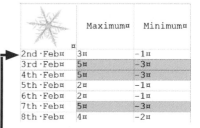

To remove all borders (the four lines around the outside) and gridlines (the lines within a table) click on

None, then click on ⌐OK twice. The borders and gridlines within the table will usually show as faint dashed lines (or very thin lines if you zoom in) that are visible on the screen but not when printed. Use the <Ctrl> key and cursor to highlight the cells containing the maximum and minimum temperatures for the week, like this. ────────────────

Click the right mouse button on one of these cells, select Table Properties... , the Table tab, then Borders and Shading....

As the Borders and Shading window opens, select the Borders tab. Make sure that the Apply to: box is set to Cell. ────────────────

To set all the borders and gridlines for only these cells, in the Setting: section, click on the icon for All. ────────────────

Advice

A quick method of editing the borders is to click on this diagram. ────────────────

Change the line widths, colours and turn lines on and off. Create a new table and play with the different options to see what they do.

The completed table will now look like this.

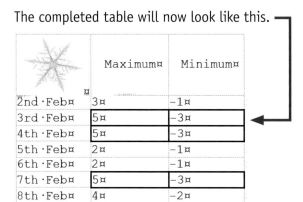

Set the background colour of table cells

In the top table, highlight all cells in rows 1, 2 and 7 together. Select the Home tab. In the Paragraph section click on the small triangle to the right of the Shading icon to get a drop-down menu/palette.

The palette gives you a range of greyscale shadings, the theme colours that are available, plus some of the standard colours. If the colour that you require is not present use the More Colors... option.

For Task 13k you need yellow so click on the yellow block in the palette.

Set the background shading of table cells

If a grey shading is required, the palette shown above can be used, but if different shading styles are required, as is the case for Task 13k, then using the table properties gives more options. Highlight the cells in the top row of the lower table. Click the right mouse button on one of these cells, select Table Properties..., the Table tab, then Borders and Shading.... As the Borders and Shading window opens, select the Shading tab.

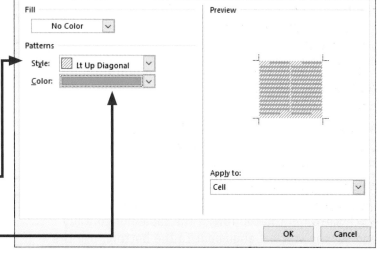

In the Patterns section, use the drop-down Style: menu to find a pattern that matches the task, for example Lt Up Diagonal.

Use the drop-down Color: palette (which is the same as used to set the yellow colour above) to choose a light blue colour.

Make sure that the Apply to: box is set to Cell, then click OK twice.

Save the document as **task13k**.

Advice

The Shading icon can also be found in a small menu like this by clicking the right mouse button when the text has been highlighted.

Activity 13c

Open the file **activity13c.rtf** in a suitable software package.

Merge all cells in the top row into a single cell. Centre align the text both horizontally and vertically. Shade this cell with a mid-grey background colour.

Merge cells 1 and 2, and merge cells 3 and 4 in row 2 of the table. Centre align all text in row 2 horizontally. Shade all three cells in this row with a light grey background colour.

Merge cell 1 in both rows 5 and 6. Merge cell 2 in both rows 5 and 6. Format each cell in rows 3 to 6 as it specifies in the table.

Replace the text <Your name> with your name.

Save the document.

Task 13l

Open the file **shipping.rtf**.

Edit the table to make the row height for the row containing Liverpool the same height as the other rows.

Edit the column widths and text wrapping so that the table looks like this.

Port¤	Number·of·million·tonnes· (rounded·to·the↵ nearest·million·tonnes)¤	Percentage·change· from·2017¤
Grimsby·and·Immingham¤	56¤	+3%¤
London¤	53¤	+7%¤
Southampton¤	35¤	0¤
Liverpool¤	33¤	0¤
Milford·Haven¤	31¤	-3%¤
Tees·and·Hartlepool¤	29¤	+1%¤
Felixstowe¤	28¤	-3%¤
Forth¤	27¤	-3%¤
Dover¤	25¤	-5%¤
Belfast¤	19¤	+4%¤

Save the document as task13l.

Link

Adjusting the row height, column width and text wrapping in *Excel* will be covered in Chapter 20.

Adjust row height

Open the file shipping.rtf and save this as task 13l.docx. Grab the horizontal line below row 5 and drag this line up to the text 'Liverpool'. You cannot drag it too high as *Word* will adjust the row height to fit the cell contents. The table changes from this to this.

Southampton¤	35¤	0¤
Liverpool¤	33¤	0¤
Milford·Haven¤	31¤	-3%¤

Southampton¤	35¤	0¤
Liverpool¤	33¤	0¤
Milford·Haven¤	31¤	-3%¤

To centre align the top row of the table horizontally and set the vertical alignment to the bottom, use the **Table** tab, in the **Alignment** section select **Align Bottom Center**.

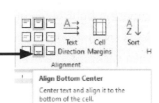

Align Bottom Center
Center text and align it to the bottom of the cell.

Adjust column width

Grab the vertical line to the right of the text 'Port' and drag it to the right so that the text 'Grimsby and Immingham' fit on a single line without the text wrapping. Do the same for the next two vertical lines until the top of the table looks like this.

Port¤	Number·of·million·tonnes· (rounded·to·the·nearest· million·tonnes)¤	Percentage·change· from·2017¤	
Grimsby·and·Immingham¤	56¤	+3%¤	
London¤	53¤	+7%¤	

Wrap text within a cell

In most packages like *Word* and *PowerPoint* text wrapping is done automatically by the package, although you can adjust where the text is wrapped, both by adjusting the column widths and by inserting soft returns using the <Shift> and <Return> keys. To adjust the middle cell in the top row to match the question a soft return needs to be entered to replace the space after the word 'the'. Highlight the space and press the <Shift> and <Return>

Port¤	Number·of·million·tonnes· (rounded·to·the↵ nearest·million·tonnes)¤	Percentage·change· from·2017¤
Grimsby·and·Immingham¤	56¤	+3%¤
London¤	53¤	+7%¤
Southampton¤	35¤	0¤
Liverpool¤	33¤	0¤
Milford·Haven¤	31¤	-3%¤
Tees·and·Hartlepool¤	29¤	+1%¤
Felixstowe¤	28¤	-3%¤
Forth¤	27¤	-3%¤
Dover¤	25¤	-5%¤
Belfast¤	19¤	+4%¤

keys. If you are working with the Show/Hide button on, you will notice that a small arrow ↵ has been shown rather than the usual symbol, called a Pilcrow ¶. The table should now look like this. Save the spreadsheet as **task13l**.

13.3 Headers and footers

13.3.1 What is a header and footer?

A **header** is the area of a document between the top of the page and the top margin. A **footer** is the area of a document between the bottom of the page and the bottom margin. You can insert text or graphics into headers and footers. This might include the author's name, the document's filename, page numbering, or even a company logo. Headers and footers can be found in many printed documents, including those that have been word-processed or desktop-published, and in presentations, reports from spreadsheets and databases and in **web pages**.

13.3.2 The purpose of headers and footers

Headers and footers are needed to make sure that each page (or pair of facing pages) have elements like the page number, book/document/chapter, logo, titles, filename, etc. placed consistently within them. If these are placed in the header or footer, they only have to be placed once but will repeat on every (or every other) page. This saves the author a great deal of time and effort, not having to duplicate their work on every page.

13.3.3 Create headers and footers

In all the packages within *Microsoft Office* the headers and footers have already been created and these can be opened, edited, resized, etc. rather than created. Most of these application packages use the **Insert** tab to access the header and footer. *Microsoft Access* uses the design view of a report and has not only page headers and footers but also report headers and footers. Headers and footers are not used in website authoring at this level. Each package then has a different method of entry.

> **Link**
>
> See Chapter 18 for further details of using *Microsoft Access*.

Open headers and footers in *Microsoft Word*

Open *Microsoft Word*, then from the Insert tab, find the Header & Footer section and select either the Header or Footer icon. —————

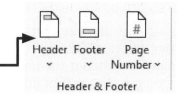

Some standard themed settings are available for you to choose from if you wish, but it is recommend that you select the option to Edit the Header/Footer.

Open headers and footers in *Microsoft Excel*

Open *Microsoft Excel*, then from the Insert tab, find the Text section and select the Header & Footer icon. —————

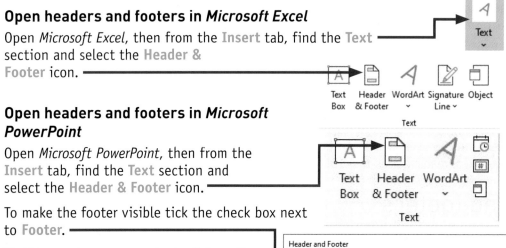

Open headers and footers in *Microsoft PowerPoint*

Open *Microsoft PowerPoint*, then from the Insert tab, find the Text section and select the Header & Footer icon. —————

To make the footer visible tick the check box next to Footer. —————

If slide numbers are required, click on the check box next to slide numbers and then click on Apply to All.

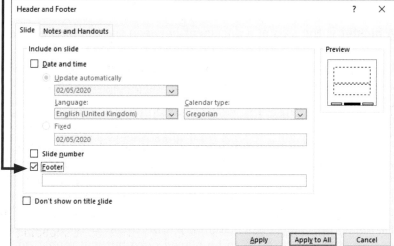

> ### Task 13m
>
> Open the file that you saved in Task 13k.
>
> Add your name on the left in the header, the text 'Historical Study' in the centre of the header and the text 'England 2009' on the right in the header.
>
> Save the document as task13m.

13.3.4 Align the contents of the header and footer

Use the ruler

Open **task13k** in *Microsoft Word*. Make sure that the ruler is visible at the top of the document. Open the header from the Insert tab, with Header, then Blank

> **Link**
> ....
> See Chapter 19 for more details.

header. Click the left mouse button on the text [Type here] in the header so that it looks like this.

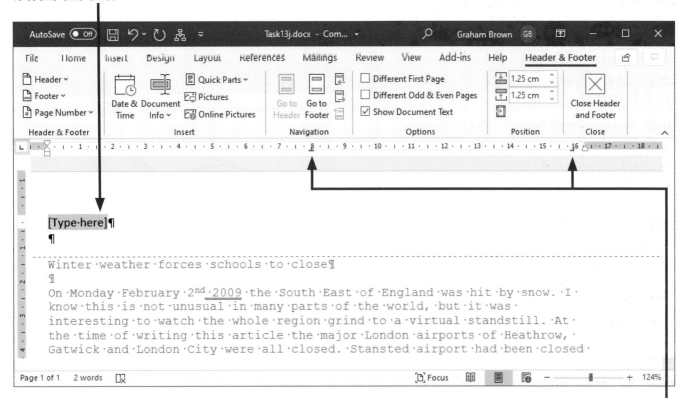

Check the alignment of the tab stops on the ruler before entering any text or object. In this case there are two tab stops placed on the ruler.

The left one of these is a centre-aligned tab and shows the centre of the page (although it is not precise in this example) and the right-hand tab stop shows the right-hand edge of the page, although we can clearly see that this does not match the full width (shown with the red arrow). These two **must** be placed together for the header to align to the edge of the body text. Grab the right-hand tab stop and drag this so that it sits over the right margin stop. Be careful not to drag the tab stop off the ruler or it will be removed. If this is difficult, hold down the <Alt> key while dragging it to stop it snapping to *Word*'s hidden gridlines.

Link

See Chapter 18 for further details of using *Microsoft Access*.

Advice

<Ctrl> <Z> undoes the last action and is a good tip if this tab stop has been accidentally removed.

The right tab stop should look like this.

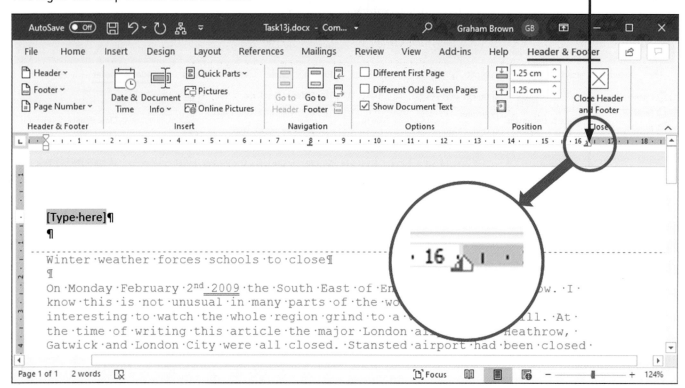

The right margin and tab stop have been placed at 16.3 centimetres from the left edge. The centre tab stop needs to be placed at 8.15 centimetres (half of this width). Use the left mouse button to drag the centre tab stop to this position.

Advice

You can always use the scale at the bottom right corner of the window to zoom in, if positioning the tab stop is difficult.

Click again on the text [Type here] and enter your name. Press the <Tab> key and enter the text 'Historical Study'. As you type this text you will see that it always stays exactly in the centre of the page. Press the <Tab> key again and enter the text 'England 2009'. As you enter it you should notice it always stays right aligned to the tab stops. The finished header looks like this.

Advice

Practise getting absolutely precise measurements for your tab stops.

Double click on **Close Header and Footer** to return to the page. You should be able to see the changes you have just made. Save your document as **task13m**.

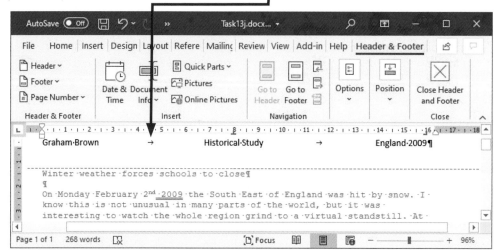

More on tab stops

There are four types of tab stop that you may need to use. These are:

Type of tab stop	Looks like	What does it do?
Left tab	All text and numbers	Aligns tabbed text, so that the left edge of the text is in a fixed position.
Centre tab	All text and numbers	Aligns tabbed text, so that the centre point of the text is in a fixed position.
Right tab	All text and numbers	Aligns tabbed text, so that the right edge of the text is in a fixed position.
Decimal tab	400000.53 4.3 2134	Aligns tabbed text, so that numeric data aligns with the decimal point in a fixed position.

For example:

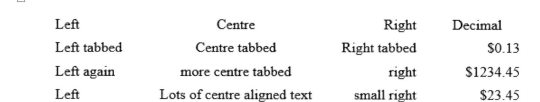

Left	Centre	Right	Decimal
Left tabbed	Centre tabbed	Right tabbed	$0.13
Left again	more centre tabbed	right	$1234.45
Left	Lots of centre aligned text	small right	$23.45

Tab stop positions can be added, edited or cleared from the Tabs window. To open this, select the **Home** tab, In the **Paragraph** section, double click to select the **Paragraph** group's dialog launcher in the bottom right corner.

Then from the paragraph window select the **Tabs...** button.

This can be used to create new tab stops. These are the tab stops for the example above.

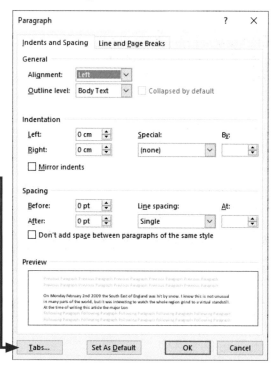

13.3.5 Place automated objects in headers and footers

Task 13n

Open the file that you saved in Task 13m.

Place in the footer the text 'Saved on' followed by the date, then the text 'at' and the time on the left, with the page number and total number of pages in the centre, and the automated filename and file path on the right.

Save the document as task13n.

Open **task13m** in *Microsoft Word*. Make sure that the ruler is visible at the top of the document. Select the **Insert** tab, in the **Header & Footer** section select the icon for **Footer**. Using the drop-down menu select **Blank (Three Columns)**. Change the positions of the centre-aligned and right-aligned tab stops so that they precisely match the page margins, like this (see Section 13.3.4).

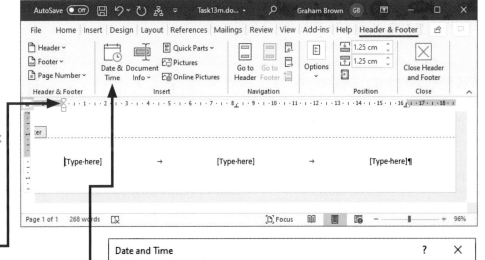

Automated date and time

Move the cursor over the left [Type here] and click the left mouse button to highlight it. Enter the text 'Saved on' followed by a space, then in the **Insert** section, click on the icon for **Date & Time**.

This will open the **Date & Time** window. Choose an appropriate date format, as the task does not tell you which one to use. This is a portrait page so a shorter version would be better. Here the top option is chosen from the menu followed by OK.

Type another space, the word 'at' followed by another space. Click on the icon for **Date & Time** and choose an appropriate time format followed by OK.

Automated page numbers

Move the cursor over the centre [Type here] and click the left mouse button to highlight it. Locate the **Header & Footer** section of the toolbar and click on the icon for **Page Number** to get the drop-down menu.

As you have moved to the correct position on the page already, click the left mouse button on **Current Position**.

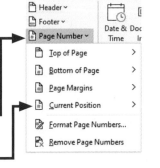

This opens another sub-menu from which you can choose the type of page numbering you require. Again, this is a portrait page so a shorter version would be better. If a simple page number was required, the top option Plain Number could be selected. As the task requires the page number and total number of pages to be displayed, scroll down the list and select from the Page X of Y section, the option for Bold Numbers.

Automated filename and file path

Move the cursor over the text [Type here] and click the left mouse button to highlight it. Select the icon for Document Info to get the drop-down menu.

To add the file name and file path to the footer click the left mouse button on File Path.

Sometimes if you have used long file and folder names, or there is a long file path, the header or footer may look crowded. Do not change the tabs as these will have been set to match the question, even if sometimes it looks unusual. You will notice that you did not have to use the option to add the file name as this is already included within the file path. The finished footer looks like this.

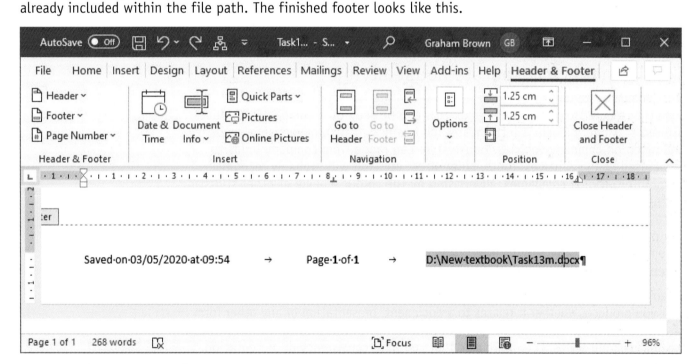

Save your document as **task13n**.

Activity 13d

Open the document that you saved in Activity 13c. Save it with the filename activity13d.

Place in the header: the text 'Created by' and your name on the left, and an automated filename on the right. Place in the footer: the text 'Page number' followed by an automated page number in the centre, and the text 'Last updated:' followed by the data and time on the right.

Save the document.

Styles

14.1 Corporate house styles

14.1.1 What is a corporate house style?

Most companies and organisations have a corporate house style. This is sometimes called 'corporate branding'. This can be seen on a company's products, printed stationery (such as letterheads and business cards), advertising, websites and often on company vehicles. House style can range from company logos to recognised colour schemes, fonts, point sizes, etc. You will probably recognise many international companies' advertising by the colour scheme or other stylistic features that they use, long before you can read the company name on the material. In ICT terms, you should always adopt a specific style for the work that you produce. Anything produced for a company will usually have a logo, colour scheme, font style, paragraph style, page layout (particularly if using headed notepaper), page formatting and defined styles for bullets and numbering.

When you produce work, it is important that you apply these styles to every element that you produce, whether it relates to a document, presentation or any other form of communication, especially when it is for customers or clients. The most important part of applying styles, is to make sure that you have consistency of presentation.

14.1.2 What is the purpose of a house style?

A house style is used to make sure that all documents and other materials from an organisation have consistency. It is used to save time in planning, setting up, creating and formatting documents and other materials. It is also designed to support brand recognition and reduces the risk of mistakes in documents, such as typing errors in an address or telephone number, or in missing an important element like a logo.

14.1.3 Match the specified house style

You must always make sure that all work produced matches the house styles given to you, which may look like these examples.

Example 1 House style for a website

Create and apply the following styles to all web pages:

Style	Definition
h1	Font – Arial Bold. If this is not available use Arial. If neither of these fonts are available, use the browser's default sans-serif font. 24 point font. Black. Italic.
p	Font – Times. If this is not available use Times New Roman. If neither of these fonts are available, use the browser's default serif font. 11 point font. Black.
table	Gridlines visible and 2 points thick. Light grey background colour. Foreground colour #100080.

Example 2 House style for a presentation

The master slide must have:

» a yellow background
» a 4-point thick dark blue horizontal line 4 cm from the top of the slide
» the logo logo.jpg placed in the bottom left corner of the screen
» the text **Corporate House Styles** in a navy blue, underlined, 36-point, serif font, above the dark blue horizontal line, with no text wrap, aligned to the right of the slide
» automatic slide numbers in the bottom right corner
» first level bullets formatted in a 24-point, blue (#0000FF) italic sans-serif font with a hollow disc bullet style.

Example 3 House style for a word-processed document

Create, store and apply the following paragraph styles:

	Font style	Font size	Alignment	Enhancement	Line spacing	Spacing before	Spacing after
Heading	sans-serif	24 point	right	bold, italic	Single	0	6 point
Subhead	sans-serif	16 point	centre	underlined	Single	0	6 point
Body text	serif	11 point	left		Single	0	11 point
Bulleted list	serif	10 point	left with 2 cm indent		Single	0	0
Header	serif	10 point	to page margins	bold			
Footer	serif	10 point	to page margins	bold			

Different techniques are required to apply these styles; each technique being package-specific. However, applying these styles will result in each document, web page or presentation slide having the same formatting, colour scheme and layout. In the case of the website, the styles would be applied in a Cascading Style Sheet. For the presentation, the master slide would be created, then a theme applied. For the document, styles are defined and then applied to the text and layout. As similar styles can be applied in a number of ways in different packages, we will start by looking at the common terms and concepts.

Link

For more on CSS see Chapter 21.

For more on Master Slides see Chapter 19.

14.1.4 Font styles and sizes

Serif and sans-serif

Text can be changed to have different font faces, colours and sizes and can have a number of enhancements added. These are useful for making text stand out. Font faces are grouped into two main types: **serif** fonts and **sans-serif** fonts. These are not the name of the font face, but are the generic types that describe the properties of the font.

A serif font looks like this: **This is a serif font** and a sans-serif font looks like this: **This is a sans-serif font**.

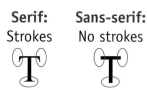

Serif: Strokes

Sans-serif: No strokes

The word 'serif' describes the short strokes at the end of individual letters. Sans-serif fonts do not have these short strokes. If you are asked to set text in a sans-serif font, you must find any font in your word processor that does not have these serif strokes. Serif fonts are often used in newspapers and books as they are usually easier to read than sans-serif fonts. It would be appropriate to use sans-serif fonts for emphasis or for titles or subtitles. It is not sensible to use more than two different font faces on any page. You can use other enhancements to make text stand out, such as bold, italics, underline and highlighting. Other elements, such as coloured text and backgrounds, can also be used to emphasise text.

Font size

Font sizes are measured in points. There are 72 points to an inch (around 28 points to a cm). If you are asked to produce text of an appropriate size, for most adults 10 point is appropriate as **body text**, but older readers may prefer 12 point. Anything above 14 point is generally unsuitable as body text for adults, but may be ideal for children. In stories for children learning to read (ages four to six) it may be appropriate to use a font size that is 20 or 24 points, to make it easier to make out the letter shapes. Larger font sizes would also be appropriate as body text for the partially sighted. Much depends upon the target audience.

Font face

The font face is the design of the typeface. Different fonts like Arial, Arial Narrow and **Arial Black** all have the same design for each letter but have different widths. Some fonts can be the same size but appear to be different heights. For example, all of these fonts are 11 points high:

ALGERIAN, *Brush Script Std*, *Edwardian Script ITC* and Arial.

The height of the font is measured using the measurement from the top of the letter with the tallest **ascender** (often the letter 'h'), to the bottom of the one with the longest **descender** (i.e. the bit that descends below the line, often the letter '*f*').

14.2 Create, modify, update and apply consistent styles

14.2.1 Create styles in a document

For this section we will focus on the application of styles within a word-processed document. A document contains layout and font styles. In *Microsoft Word*, the layout styles are stored in a document template which is usually hidden from you. As you create a new document, a set of default styles are applied to it. They include the page orientation, margin settings, settings for the header and footer as well as different font styles which Microsoft have called 'Themes'.

Task 14a

Open the document you saved as **task13n**. Create, store and use the following styles in this document.

	Font style	Font size	Alignment	Enhancement
Header	serif	10 point	to page margins	bold
Footer	serif	10 point	to page margins	bold

Save the document as task14a.

Open the file task13n in *Microsoft Word*. Save this as **task14a**. We will start in the header. Open the header of the document and highlight all the text in the header, like this.

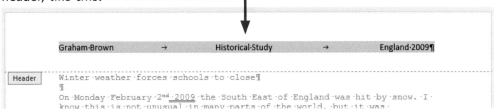

Select the Home tab. In the Font section find the dropdown menu for the font face.

Set the font face to Times New Roman, which is a serif font. Set the Font Size to 10 point using the drop-down menu next to the font size.

The text in the header does align to the page margins (you took great care getting that right in Chapter 13) so the last part of this style is to embolden (add the bold enhancement) to this text. With all the header text highlighted select the Home tab. In the Font section click on the icon for bold.

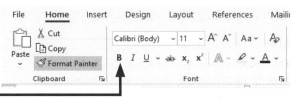

Advice

Another way of making text bold in *Microsoft Word* is by pressing <Ctrl> and <B> together.

The header will now look like this.

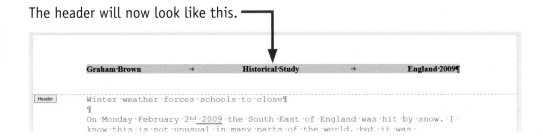

Make sure that the text in the header is highlighted and that you have the **Home** tab selected. Locate the **Styles** section and then click on the lower drop-down menu button for the **Styles** section.

AaBbCcDc	AaBbCcDc	AaBbC	AaBbCcl	AaB
¶ Normal	¶ No Spac…	Heading 1	Heading 2	Title

Styles

The list of defined styles will expand. Click on the option to **Create a Style**.

AaBbCcDc	AaBbCcDc	AaBbC	AaBbCcl	AaB
¶ Normal	¶ No Spac…	Heading 1	Heading 2	Title
AaBbCcD	*AaBbCcDc*	**AaBbCcDc**	AABBCCDC	
Subtitle	Emphasis	Strong	Subtle Ref…	

A₊ Create a *Style*
A₯ *Clear Formatting*
A₊ *Apply Styles…*

This opens the **Create New Style from Formatting** window. Enter a **Name:** for this style, for example: **14a_header** (to help us remember that is the style set for the header in Task 14a).

Create New Style from Formatting ? ✕

Name:
14a_header

Paragraph style preview:

Style1

OK Modify… Cancel

Create New Style from Formatting ? ✕

Properties

Name: 14a_header

Style type: Linked (paragraph and character)

Style based on: ¶ª Header

Style for following paragraph: ¶ 14a_header

Formatting

Times New Roman 10 **B** *I* U Automatic

Previous Paragraph Previous Paragraph Previous Paragraph Previous Paragraph Previous Paragraph Previous Paragraph Previous Paragraph Previous Paragraph Previous Paragraph Previous Paragraph

Graham Brown   **Historical Study**   **England 2009**
Following Paragraph Following Paragraph Following Paragraph Following Paragraph Following Paragraph
Following Paragraph Following Paragraph Following Paragraph Following Paragraph Following Paragraph
Following Paragraph Following Paragraph Following Paragraph Following Paragraph Following Paragraph
Following Paragraph Following Paragraph Following Paragraph Following Paragraph Following Paragraph
Following Paragraph Following Paragraph Following Paragraph Following Paragraph Following Paragraph
Following Paragraph Following Paragraph Following Paragraph Following Paragraph Following Paragraph
Following Paragraph Following Paragraph Following Paragraph Following Paragraph Following Paragraph

Font: Times New Roman, 10 pt, Bold, Style: Show in the Styles gallery
Based on: Header

To view or edit the details of the style you can use Modify… to open this window.

This shows the style name and all the details of the changes we made to the style.

Advice

Use this window if you need to display a style that you have created.

After you click OK this style appears in the list of styles in the toolbar.

☑ Add to the Styles gallery ☐ Automatically update
◉ Only in this document ○ New documents based on this template

Format ▾   OK Cancel

Move to the footer of the document. Before setting the styles, check the footer contents. The automated filename and path have not changed and still show the document as task 13n.

AaBbCcDd	AaBbCcDc	AaBbCcDc	AaBbC	AaBbCcl
14a_header	¶ Normal	¶ No Spac…	Heading 1	Heading 2

Styles

Footer

Saved on 03/05/2020 at 09:54   Page **1** of 1   D:\New textbook\Task13n.docx

Your file path will not be the same as the one shown here. To update the filename, click the right mouse button on the filename/path to get the drop-down menu. Click on Update Field. The filename will have changed to look similar to this. ─────────┐

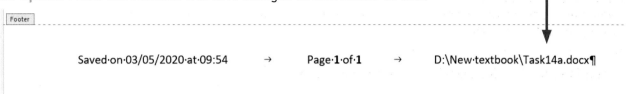

Footer

Saved·on·03/05/2020·at·09:54   →   Page·1·of·1   →   D:\New·textbook\Task14a.docx¶

To apply this new style to the footer, highlight all of the text in the footer, select the Home tab and in the Styles section, then click the left mouse button on the style you called 14a_header.

Save the document. The footer should now look similar to this. ─────────┐

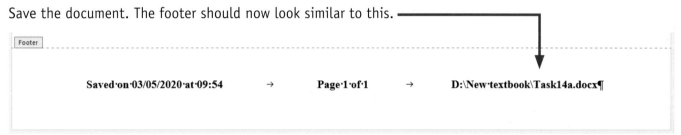

Footer

Saved·on·03/05/2020·at·09:54   →   **Page·1·of·1**   →   **D:\New·textbook\Task14a.docx¶**

Task 14b

Open the document you saved as **task14a**. Add the text 'Winter wonderland or woe?' as a new main heading at the start of the document. Add the text 'School closures' as a subheading before the second paragraph. Create, store and use the following styles in this document.

	Font face	Font size	Alignment	Enhancement	Line spacing	Spacing before	Spacing after
Heading	sans-serif	24 point	right	bold, italic	Single	0	6 point
Subheading	sans-serif	16 point	centre	underlined	Single	0	6 point
Body text	serif	11 point	left		Single	0	11 point

Save the document as task14b.

Open the document that you saved in Task 14a. Move to the top of the document and add the text 'Winter wonderland or woe?' as a main heading before the subheading 'Winter weather forces schools to close'. Remove all blank lines from the document using the cursor and <Delete> key.

When defining the font styles, always start with the body text. Many people start by highlighting all the text using <Ctrl> and <A>, but for this task, just highlight the first paragraph. This will let you practise applying this style to the other paragraphs later.

Select the Home tab. In the Font section, set the font face to Times New Roman. Set the Font Size to 11 point using the drop-down menu. In the Paragraph section, set the text alignment to left using this icon.

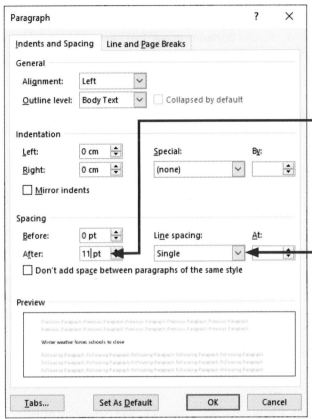

In the Paragraph section, select the Paragraph Settings arrow to open up the Paragraph window. Find the Spacing section and in the Line spacing: box, use the drop-down list to select Single.

Move to the After: box and type the value 11.

Often you can use the up and down arrows to select the value but '11 pt' is not in those listed.

Advice

Use the Show/Hide icon from the home tab to show all hidden characters such as returns and tabs.

Click on OK to format this paragraph. From the Home tab, click the lower drop-down menu button for the Styles section. Click on Create a Style to open the Create New Style from Formatting window.

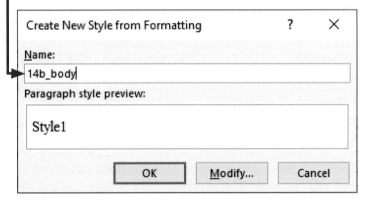

Enter a Name: for this style, for example: 14b_body (to help us remember that is the style set for the body text in Task 14b). To view or edit the details of the style you can use Modify..., but as the style looks correct, click on OK.

14.2.2 Apply styles consistently in a document

The style we have created for the first paragraph needs to be applied to each paragraph within the document. We do not to recreate the style each time, we just need to apply the style to each paragraph. To do this, click the cursor into each paragraph in turn, then click the left mouse button on the style you called 14b_ body.

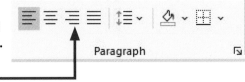

Create the heading style

Highlight the text for the main heading. In the Font section, set the font face to Arial, which is a sans-serif font (it does not have serifs). Set the Font Size to 24 point. In the Paragraph section, select the text alignment to the right using this icon.

Open up the Paragraph window (as described previously). In the Spacing section, leave the line spacing as Single (as no spacing has been specified), but change the spacing After: to 6 point. Click on ⟦ OK ⟧ to close this window. With the heading still highlighted, go to the Font section and click the left mouse button on the Bold icon to embolden the text. ————————————→

Click the left mouse button on the Italic icon to italicise the text. ——

From the Home tab, click the lower drop-down menu button for the Styles section. Click on Create a Style to open the Create New Style from Formatting window. Enter a Name: for this style, for example: 14b_heading, then click on ⟦ OK ⟧.

Create the subheading style

Use the same method to set the font style to the same sans-serif font (Arial) as the heading style. It is good practice to use as few fonts as possible within a document – two or three are acceptable. Set the size to 16 point and spacing as for the heading style. To centre align the text, move to the Paragraph section and use this icon. ————————————→

In the Font section select the underline icon. ————————————→

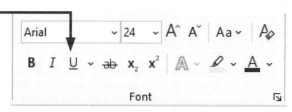

From the Home tab, click the lower drop-down menu button for the Styles section. Click on Create a Style and call this style 14b_subheading.

Apply the subheading style

Add the new subheading 'School closures' immediately before the second paragraph. Click on the subheading and click on this style. Save the document which should look similar to this. ——

Advice

If you are asked to enhance text (for example 'make this text bold'), do not use other enhancements as well (such as underline or italic).

Graham Brown   Historical Study   England 2009

Winter wonderland or woe?

Winter weather forces schools to close

On Monday February 2nd 2009 the South East of England was hit by snow. I know this is not unusual in many parts of the world, but it was interesting to watch the whole region grind to a virtual standstill. At the time of writing this article the major London airports of Heathrow, Gatwick and London City were all closed. Stansted airport had been closed but has just had one runway reopened. Travel chaos has ensued, the M25 is closed in many places and many schools throughout the country have been closed.

School closures

The dramatic change in the weather has meant that a number of areas are experiencing transport problems. This means that many schools across the country have been closed.

County	Closed
South East	
Essex	250+
Hertfordshire	100+
Middlesex	80+
Sussex	50+
North	
Greater Manchester	100
Lancashire	70
Cumbria	34
Durham	70
Northumberland	33
Yorkshire	1

This table shows the number of schools reported closed. It is interesting to note that although the snow was no heavier in the South East of England, one of the eastern counties has reported more than 250 of its schools are closed.

This gave the children lots time to play in the snow, snowballing, making snowmen and snow angels. The snow gave an added dimension, producing some very picturesque scenes, many captured on camera.

Temperatures recorded at one weather station in Ross-on-Wye during the week read:

	Maximum	Minimum
2nd Feb	3	-1
3rd Feb	5	-3
4th Feb	5	-3
5th Feb	2	-1
6th Feb	2	-1
7th Feb	5	-3
8th Feb	4	-2

Activity 14a

Open the file **activity14a.rtf**. This document has four headings, a table, a bulleted list and body text. Add your name to the left in the header. Add an automated date and time on the right in the footer. Create, store and apply the following styles in this document.

	Font style	Font size	Alignment	Enhancement	Line spacing	Spacing before	Spacing after
Heading	sans-serif	20 point	centre	bold, underlined	single	12 point	6 point
Body text	serif	12 point	fully justified		1.5	0	6 point
Header	sans-serif	12 point	to page margins	italic			
Footer	sans-serif	12 point	to page margins	italic			

Do not format the table or bulleted list. Save and print this document.

14.2.3 Modifying and editing the styles in a document

Task 14c

Open the document you saved as **task14b**. Change all the subheading styles to have a dark blue font with a yellow highlighted background. Save the document as task14c.

Open the document that you saved in Task 14b. Highlight the top subheading. Select the **Home** tab and in the **Font** section click the left mouse button on the small arrow to the right of the **Font Color** icon.

This opens a colour palette, which looks like this.

Select a dark blue font colour from the palette. If the exact colour you are looking for is not present you can use the **More Colors** option to see more. For this task, the dark blue in the standard colours section looks ideal so select that one.

The task asks for a yellow highlighted background (not filled), so with the subheading still highlighted, left click the mouse button on the small pentagon to the right of the **Text Highlight Color** tool.

This opens the text highlighter palette. Select the yellow highlighter colour which will highlight the selected text.

To change the style you created for the subheading, move the cursor to the **Styles** section and right mouse click on the style **14b_subhead** to open a drop-down menu. Use the left mouse button to select the option for **Update 14b_subhead to Match Selection**.

You will notice that the colour of the font has changed in the style – you have modified that part of the style, but the highlighting has not appeared.

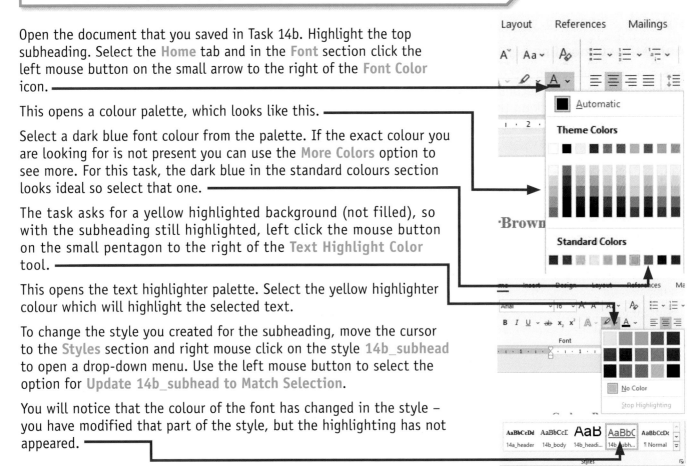

That is because not every feature of the word processor can be set into a document's saved styles. The new style has been applied to every subheading in the document, without the need for you to change the colour by hand.

As the highlighting does not save with the styles it will need to be applied for each subheading. In this case there is just the one subheading, but in a large document that could be time consuming. Highlight the subheading School closures in yellow. Save the document as **task14c**.

14.2.4 Use format painter

If you need to copy formatting (including the styles you have defined) from one part of a document and apply it to another, you can use the **format painter**. For example, if you have just set some text red and emboldened and want to copy that formatting onto another area of text, this method copies the formatting and the defined style.

Place the cursor within (or highlight) the text you wish to copy the formatting from and click the left mouse button. Select the Home tab. In the Clipboard section, click on the Format Painter icon.

Move the cursor to the text that you wish to format. If it is a single word, then click the left mouse button anywhere within that word. If the area is more than one word, highlight the new text and the formatting from the original text will be applied to this text. Format painter is also used to copy styles in spreadsheets and presentations as well as in word processing.

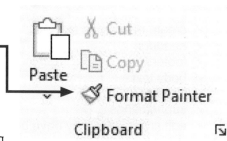

Advice

Use Format Painter with care – it copies paragraph formatting as well as font formatting. For example, if the area copied from is part of a bulleted list, when the format is applied, the new text also becomes a bulleted list in the same style.

14.2.5 Bulleted and numbered lists

There are two types of list that you need to know about: bulleted lists and numbered (or sometimes lettered) lists. Bulleted lists contain a bullet point (character) at the start of each line to show that it is a new item in a list of other similar items.

Task 14d

Open the file **lists.rtf** and place your name on the right in the header in a 14-point serif font. Place the filename in the centre of the footer.

Change the 11 items listed into a bulleted list. Use a bullet of your choice. Make sure that this bulleted list is indented by at least 3 cm.

Set items 2 to 6 inclusive as a sub-list with a different bullet of your choice, indented by at least 4 cm.

Save the file as task14d.

Open the file lists.rtf and create the header and footer as described in the task. To add bullet points to a list, highlight all of the text to be added, in this case all 11 items. Select the Home tab, the Paragraph section and click on the Bullets icon.

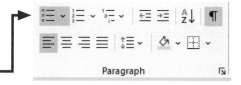

This will place bullet points next to each of the list items. To choose the type of bullets used, select the drop-down handle instead of the icon. ——————

Select the type of bullet point that you require from Bullet Library.

In this case, you can choose any symbol, such as the ✓. The bulleted list will look like this.

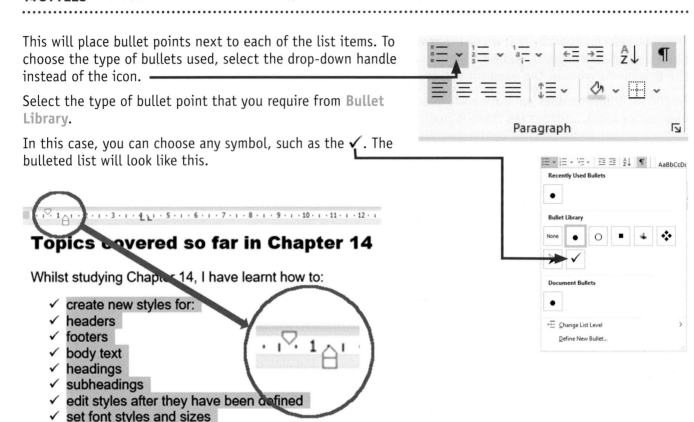

Topics covered so far in Chapter 14

Whilst studying Chapter 14, I have learnt how to:

- ✓ create new styles for:
- ✓ headers
- ✓ footers
- ✓ body text
- ✓ headings
- ✓ subheadings
- ✓ edit styles after they have been defined
- ✓ set font styles and sizes
- ✓ emphasise text
- ✓ use format painter
- ✓ use lists

Notice how the bulleted list has been indented automatically in from the left margin, although not by at least 3 cm. To indent it further, you need to change the paragraph setting on the ruler.

Advice

If the ruler cannot be seen at the top of the page, use the View tab, and tick the checkbox for Ruler.

Highlight all of the bulleted list. On the ruler, click the left mouse button on the rectangle (not the pentagon) and hold it down while dragging the handle to the right. Make sure that both handles are more than 3 cm to the right of the margin. The left end of the finished ruler should look like this. ——————

The bulleted list will now be indented like this. ——————

To create the sub-list, highlight only items 2 to 6 (headers to subheadings). Click the left mouse button on the Increase Indent icon. ——————

pics covered so far in Chapter 14

lst studying Chapter 14, I have learnt how to:

- ✓ create new styles for:
- ✓ headers
- ✓ footers
- ✓ body text
- ✓ headings
- ✓ subheadings
- ✓ edit styles after they have been defined
- ✓ set font styles and sizes
- ✓ emphasise text
- ✓ use format painter
- ✓ use lists

You may need to click this a few times to move the indented sub-list far enough to the right like this.

Select the type of bullet point that you require from Bullet Library for this sub-list. Save the document.

Task 14e

Open the file saved in **Task 14d**.

Change the first level bulleted list into a numbered list using Arabic numerals, and the second level list into a lettered list starting with a).

Save the file as task14e.

Open the file and highlight the entire bulleted list. Select the Home tab, the Paragraph section and click on the Numbering icon.

This will place numbers next to each of the list items. To choose the type of numbering used, select the drop-down handle instead of the icon.

Select the type of numbering that you require from Numbering Library. In this case you can choose the Arabic numerals, as that was specified in the task.

The extra indentation for the first level bullet points has been lost, so this will require you to reset the tab stop positions for these items.

Highlight the second level bullets and move the tab stop to the correct position. Again, use the Numbering Library from the drop-down list to choose the correct formatting for these items.

It should look like this.

Make sure that, if the bulleted list contains short items that would make up the end of a sentence, it has a colon before the list, each list item starts with a lower-case character and only the last item in the list has a full stop. Add the full stops to the appropriate places before you save the file.

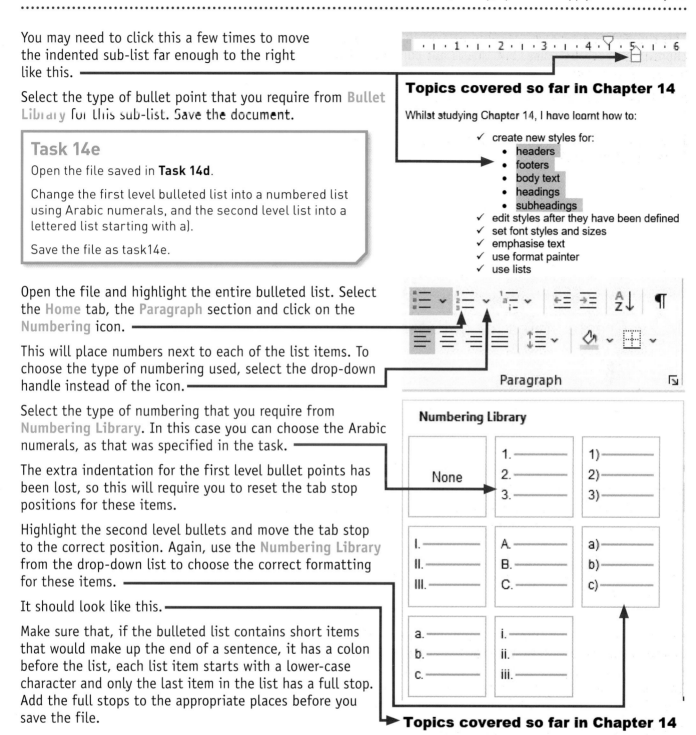

Topics covered so far in Chapter 14

Whilst studying Chapter 14, I have learnt how to:

- ✓ create new styles for:
  - headers
  - footers
  - body text
  - headings
  - subheadings
- ✓ edit styles after they have been defined
- ✓ set font styles and sizes
- ✓ emphasise text
- ✓ use format painter
- ✓ use lists

Paragraph

Numbering Library

None

1.	1)
2.	2)
3.	3)

I.	A.	a)
II.	B.	b)
III.	C.	c)

a.	i.
b.	ii.
c.	iii.

Topics covered so far in Chapter 14

Whilst studying Chapter 14, I have learnt how to:

1. create new styles for:
   a) headers
   b) footers
   c) body text
   d) headings
   e) subheadings
2. edit styles after they have been defined
3. set font styles and sizes
4. emphasise text
5. use format painter
6. use lists

The auto-correct function in *Word* will often try to place capitals on each list item, but this is not correct as each one is not a new sentence. You must adjust these to get a list looking like this.

► **Topics covered so far in Chapter 14**

Whilst studying Chapter 14, I have learnt how to:

1. create new styles for:
   a) headers
   b) footers
   c) body text
   d) headings
   e) subheadings.
2. edit styles after they have been defined
3. set font styles and sizes
4. emphasise text
5. use format painter
6. use lists.

Activity 14b

Open the file **activity14b.rtf** and place your name on the left, today's date in the centre and the filename on the right in the header. Make the blue text into a bulleted list, using a bullet of your choice. Make sure that this bulleted list is indented by at least 2 cm. Make the green text into a numbered list, using numbers followed by a bracket. Make the red text into a bulleted sub-list, indented from the numbered list using different bullet points. Change the colour of all the text to black.

Save the file with a new name.

14.2.6 Create styles for bulleted and numbered lists

Task 14f

Open the document you saved as **task14c**.

Add the contents of the file **advice.rtf** before the paragraph that starts 'Temperatures …'. Create, store and use the following styles in this document.

	Font face	Font size	Alignment	List type	Line spacing	Spacing before	Spacing after
List – level 1	serif	11 point	Left – indent 1 cm	Numbered list	Single	0	0
List – level 2	serif	11 point	Left – indent 2 cm	Bulleted list with arrow	Single	0	0

Save the document as task14f.

Open the files task14c and advice.rtf in your word processor. Copy and paste the contents of advice.rtf into the document before the paragraph that starts 'Temperatures …'. Click inside the paragraph that starts 'The United States government …' and set the style to 14b_body that you defined earlier. Start by setting up the first level bullet style on the single line that starts 'Before winter approaches …'. When you set this text to an 11-point serif font, you must use the same font as the body text. Use Format Painter to apply body text formatting to the single line, then to change the list type to a numbered list by selecting the numbered list icon.

Change the indent to exactly 1 cm using the ruler. Change the line spacing to single line with no spacing before and after. From the Styles section, use Create a Style. In the Create New Style from Formatting window, enter a Name: for this style, for example: List-L1, then click on ⬚ OK ⬚.

To set up a style for the second level list, apply the new style List-L1 to the single line that starts 'Rock salt or more …'. Click the left mouse button on the Increase Indent icon.

Then click on the drop-down handle next to the Bullets icon. Select the type of bullet point that you require from Bullet Library. In this case, choose an arrow to match the task. ————————

From the Styles section, use Create a Style. In the Create New Style from Formatting window, enter a Name: for this style, for example: List-L2, then click on ⌐ OK ⌐.

Highlight all the other level 2 bullets in the document and click on the List-L2 style. ————————

Highlight the other two level 1 lists in the document and click on the List-L1 style. ————————

Save the document as **task14f**. The completed list should look like this. ————————

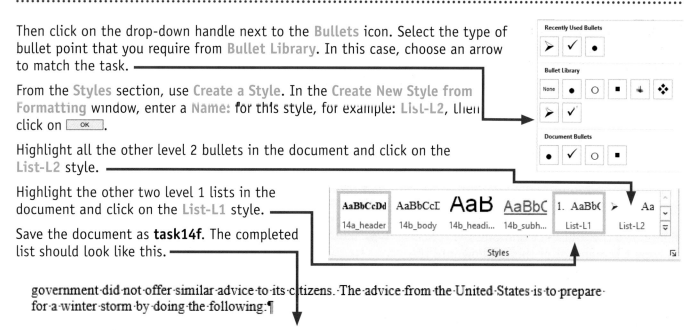

government did not offer similar advice to its citizens. The advice from the United States is to prepare for a winter storm by doing the following:¶

    1.→Before winter approaches, add the following supplies to your°emergency kit:¶
      ➤→Rock salt or more environmentally safe products to melt ice on walkways. ¶
      ➤→Sand to improve traction.¶
      ➤→Snow shovels and other snow removal equipment.¶
      ➤→Sufficient heating fuel. You may become isolated in your home and regular fuel sources may be cut off. Store a good supply of dry, seasoned wood for your fireplace or wood-burning stove.¶
      ➤→Adequate clothing and blankets to keep you warm.¶
    2.→Make a°Family Communications Plan. Minimize travel. If travel is necessary, keep a disaster supplies kit in your vehicle.¶
    3.→Bring pets/companion animals inside during winter weather. Move other animals or livestock to sheltered areas with non-frozen drinking water.¶
Temperatures recorded at one weather station in Ross-on-Wye during the week read:¶

Activity 14c

Open the file you saved in Activity 14a. Save this file as activity14c. Edit and update the contents of the footer.

Create, store and apply the following styles to the bulleted lists in this document.

	Font face	Font size	Alignment	List type	Line spacing	Spacing before	Spacing after
List – level 1	serif	12 point	Left – indent 1.5 cm	Bulleted list with arrow	Single	0	0
List – level 2	serif	12 point	Left – indent 3 cm	Bulleted list with square bullet	Single	0	0

Save the file with a new name.

14.2.7 Modify and evidence your styles

If you are required to produce evidence of the styles you have created or amended, select the Home tab. In the Styles section, click the right mouse button on the style that you have defined and want to evidence. ──────

Select Modify from the drop-down list to open the Modify Style window. ──────

The style can be edited from the Modify Style window. ──────

Hold down the <Alt> key and press <Prt Scr> to copy a screenshot of this window into the clipboard. This can then be pasted as evidence of your method.

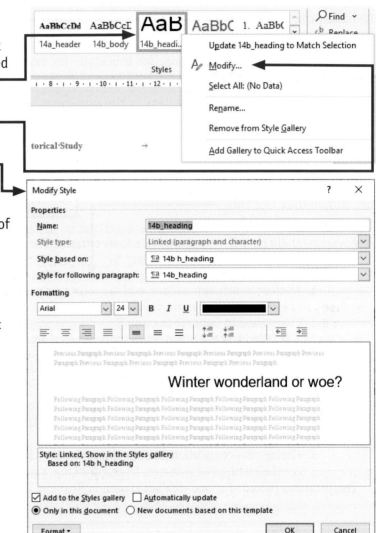

Advice

Do not create a screenshot with the mouse hovering over a style in the Styles window. While this shows much of the style definition it does not show the font face that you have selected.

15 Proofing

15.1 Software tools

The latest versions of *Microsoft Office* automatically check the document for spelling and grammar errors. Any words or phrases found in a document that are not in the dictionary will be flagged as an error. Do not worry about the differences in spelling that can occur with dictionaries from different regions, for example 'centre' and 'center', except when creating your web pages and stylesheets in Chapter 21. The software may flag some names as errors even if they are spelt correctly, so be careful not to change the spelling of names, especially of companies, people or places. Each time an error is flagged, read it carefully and decide whether to change or ignore the spelling, using the buttons in the pane.

15.1.1 Spell check

You need to make sure that your work is spelled correctly and contains no data entry errors or 'typos' (these are mistakes that you make when typing in the data). Errors may already exist in the documents you have to work on. Sometimes these are spelling errors which look like this.

This·speeling·is·incorrect.

Errors like this need to be corrected.

What is spell check?

Spell check is a test carried out by the software, often a word processor on the text. As you work, it checks each word and compares it to those held in its dictionary. If the words match, then the software moves on and checks the next word. If the word does not match one in the dictionary, then it uses a red wavy underline to highlight the word to suggest it may be an error.

Does the spell check always work?

If the word processor shows the red wavy underline, it may not be a spelling error. The red underline tells you that *Word* has compared this word to its dictionary and not found a match. Not all computers have the same dictionaries in them. The dictionaries will depend on the regional settings used when setting up your computer. Sometimes, as in the case above, it is a spelling error; at other times words like 'Tabara' are flagged as a spelling error because the dictionary does not contain the name of this (made-up) place. When a person's name is entered into a word processor, some names will be shown as an error and other names will not.

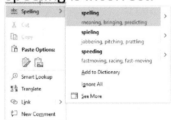

Suggested spellings

When *Word* shows you a suggested error, right mouse click on it and a drop-down menu of suggested words will appear, like this.

For the word 'Tabara' no change needs to be made, but in the case of a genuine error like this, a list of suggested words is shown. Choose the word which is the most appropriate. In this case it would be 'spelling'.

Other errors

Sometimes other errors may be flagged as spelling errors, like this.

This example shows a repeated word, 'not', which needs removing. Delete the extra word to correct this error.

15.1.2 Grammar check

What is a grammar check?

A grammar check will check the text against a number of grammatical rules that help you to improve the language structure of your work. You will not need to correct grammar errors shown in text provided for you in source files. A grammar error is shown with a blue wavy underline like this.

This is a sentence, This is another

In this case the error is a missing full stop (a comma has been used instead) at the end of the word 'sentence'. The word processor has recognised that there is an error although it suggests changing the underlined text to 'this' (with a lower case 't') rather than having two sentences.

Edit the text (by changing the comma to a full stop) to correct this error.

Activity 15a

Open the file **activity15a.rtf**. Remove all errors, save and print the document.

15.1.3 Validation routines

What is validation?

Validation is checking that data entered is reasonable. It is often a process where data is checked to see if it satisfies certain criteria when input into a computer – for example, to see if data falls within accepted boundaries.

Link

For further details of validation, including the types of validation, see Section 7.2.

Appropriate types of validation

You may be required to apply appropriate validation rules in a database or spreadsheet. When you are asked to do this, it is important that you review all the different validation types, and decide which would be most appropriate. For example, you would not use a type check on a book title as book titles can contain any type of character (in fact you would be unlikely to find a validation check of any kind to check this type of data). A length check would not pick up transposed digits in an ISBN, but could be used as well as a check digit for double checking. Another example is that a range check is unlikely to be appropriate on a bar code.

Task 15a

The data file **gym.csv** will be used both to create a database and a spreadsheet. Select the most appropriate validation type for the month field in this data.

Examine the data in the file **gym.csv**. Using the list of validation types in Section 7.2, compare each type of check to see if it could be applied to the data in the month field. Use a table similar to the one below to help you.

Validation check	Appropriate?	Selected?
Range check	Yes, select integer, >0 AND <13	Yes
Length check	Yes, restrict to two characters, but would not stop 13, 14, etc.	
Character check	No, database would restrict to numbers if numeric data selected	
	Yes, in spreadsheet – need to check numeric not text, but would not restrict to correct values	
Format check	No	
Limit check	No, would only restrict one end of the range	
Presence check	Yes, would be appropriate, but would only check something had been entered	
Consistency check	No, this is a single field with no other related field/s	
Check digit	No	

After working through each type of validation check, it is most appropriate to use a range check.

Task 15b

Create a database with the file **gym.csv**. Validate the month field.

Validation in Access

Using the methods shown in Chapter 18, examine the file **gym.csv** and use it to create a new database. Open the table in Design View and select the Month field. In the General tab, move the cursor into the Validation Rule box.

You decided above that the most appropriate validation rule to apply to this field was a range check with >0 AND <13. The field has already been set to a numeric field with Integer sub-type. Type the validation rule into this box.

In the Validation Text box add suitable text that tells the user that they have made a data entry error and gives them information as to what is acceptable data for this field. It may look like this.

Save the database.

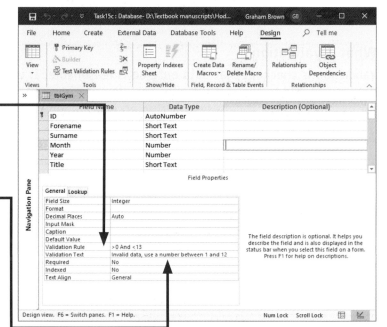

> ## Link
> See Chapter 18 for more on setting up a new database.

Task 15c
Open the database saved in Task 15b, add a new field called <Title>. Validate this field to make sure only Mr, Mrs, Miss, or Dr are allowed.

Open the database saved in Task 15b and, using the methods shown in Chapter 18, add a new field called Title to the Gym table with the data type Text. Set the Field Size to 4 characters, as 'Miss' is the longest entry and this has four letters. Set the Validation Rule for this field to restrict the data entry to only 'Mr', 'Mrs', 'Miss' or 'Dr'. Add an appropriate message as Validation Text. The finished field should look similar to this.

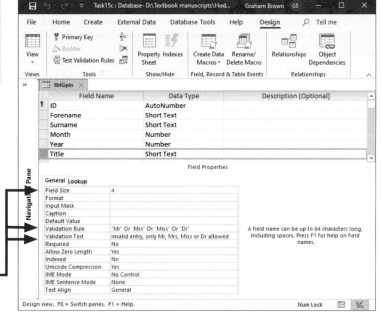

Open the table and add a new record to the database. Try entering this date: 14/14/1992, and this title: 'Ms'. What happens and why?

Save the database.

Task 15d
Create a spreadsheet with the file **gym.csv**. Validate the cells in rows 2–30 of the month column.

Validation in Excel

Link

See Chapter 20 for more on setting up a new spreadsheet.

Using the methods shown in Chapter 20, examine the file **gym.csv** and use it to create a new spreadsheet. You decided above that the most appropriate validation rule to apply to this field was a range check with >0 AND <13. Highlight cells C2 to C26. Select the Data tab, then in the Data Tools section, select the Data Validation icon.

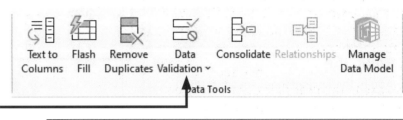

This opens the Data Validation window. Click to select the Settings tab, if it is not already selected, and move the cursor into the Allow: section. Select the drop-down list, then choose Whole number.

This will make sure that only integers can be entered into these cells. When this value has been selected, more options appear within this window.

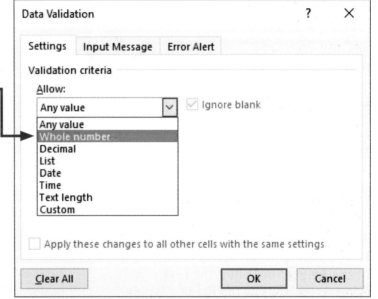

From the drop-down list in the Data: box, select between, if it is not already selected. Using 'between' in *Excel*, means that you have to give the smallest and largest acceptable values. In the Minimum: box enter 1, (which is extreme data as it is the smallest acceptable value) and in the Maximum: box enter 12.

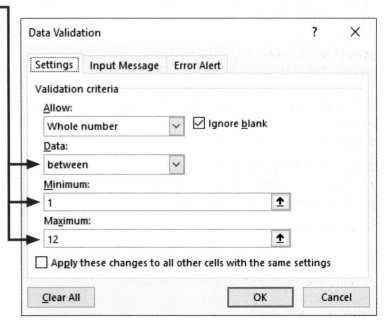

Select the Error Alert tab. Select an appropriate title for this error message and enter it in the Title: box. In the Error message: box, enter a similar message to the one entered in Task 15b. It may look like this.

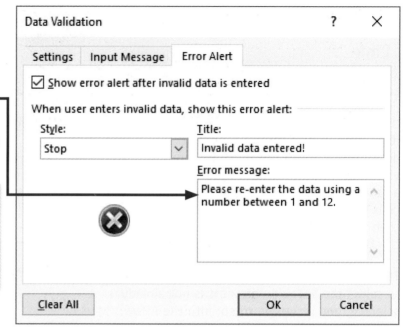

Click on OK. Test your validation routine with normal, abnormal and extreme data. Save the spreadsheet.

Task 15e

Add to the spreadsheet saved in Task 15d, a new column 1 with the label 'Title'. Validate the cells in rows 2–30 of this column to make sure only Mr, Mrs, Miss, or Dr are allowed.

Open the spreadsheet saved in Task 15d and, using the methods shown in Chapter 20, insert a new column before column 1. In cell A1 add the label Title. Highlight cells A2 to A26. Select the Data tab. In the Data Tools section, select the Data Validation icon to open the Data Validation window. Select the Settings tab, if it is not already selected, and move the cursor into the Allow: section. Select the drop-down list, then choose List.

In the Source: box enter the text Mr, Mrs, Miss, Dr as the list of possible acceptable entries, like this.

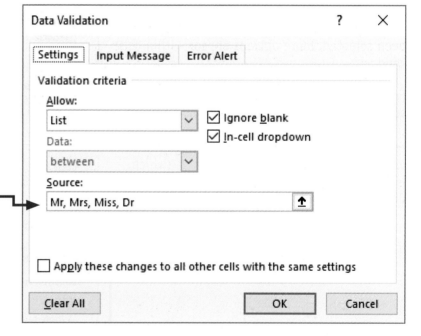

Select the Error Alert tab. Select an appropriate title for this error message and enter it in the Title: box. In the Error message: box enter a similar message to the one entered in Task 15c. Click on OK. Test your validation routine with all four pieces of normal data and with abnormal data. Try things like 'dR', 'dr', 'mr' or 'mR' as part of your abnormal data. There will be no extreme data as this is not a range of possible answers with a highest and lowest value. Save the spreadsheet.

15.2 Proofing techniques

Proofing techniques are not the validation checks that you have studied in
Section 15.1, but other ways of reducing the number of errors in your work.
The term 'proofing' in printing means to make sure that the work is accurate. It
should include checking not only spelling, punctuation and grammar, but also
page layout, including:

» the correct application of styles
» the correct margin settings
» images placed as specified
» text wraps as specified
» images not distorted
» objects fitting within the boundaries of a page/column/slide
» objects not overlapping (unless specified in a question)
» no lists (bulleted or numbered) split over two columns/pages/slides
» no tables (bulleted or numbered) split over two columns/pages/slides
» no blank columns, pages or slides
» no widows or orphans.

Part of the proofreading and error correction will be to check for widows and
orphans. A **widow** is the last line of a paragraph that appears alone at the top
of a new page or column. An **orphan** is the first line of a paragraph (or heading)
that appears alone at the bottom of a page or column. Even though *Microsoft
Word* often applies automatic widow and orphan control, it is always good
practice to check that widows and orphans have been removed. Make sure that
other objects, such as bulleted or numbered lists, tables, graphs and database
or spreadsheet extracts are not split over two columns or pages. Again, inserting
appropriate breaks should avoid these problems.

15.2.1 Accuracy of data entry

It is important that you read through all of the work and make sure that the text
or data that you have typed is 100 per cent accurate. Check that your documents
have consistency in all areas, not only fonts and styles, but also in line spacing
and paragraph spacing. It is very easy to follow the instructions, for example, to
remove a page break, only to find that you have accidentally inserted an extra
carriage return. If you have inserted section breaks or page breaks, make sure
that there are no blank pages.

The importance of accurate data entry

It is critically important that data entered into computer systems is accurate. For
example, if your school stores your doctor's telephone number on its system and
this number contains an error, in an emergency they may not be able to contact
the doctor. Another example is if a bank took $10 000 from a bank account,
rather than $10, then this would have serious consequences financially. Errors
in numeric data will cause problems if any calculations are performed. Imagine
the costs of a data entry error if a rocket was being sent into outer space and
one of its navigation systems was given some data with an error in it, or the
consequences of a data entry error in the control of a nuclear reactor.

Common data entry errors

The most common data entry errors include:

➤ spelling errors
➤ errors in the use of capital letters (such as Capital letters Placed in the middle of A sentence, or not used where instructed)
➤ transposed numbers (such as 21 instead of 12).

All of these errors can be removed by carefully checking every item of data entered when you have completed each step. Visually verify every character that you enter.

Other common errors are found in the spacing of characters in text entry: sometimes words have too many spaces between them and there are even times when spaces are missed. There are sometimes factual errors, even if someone else has proofread and corrected your work, although you would hope this was not the case. It is possible that you may get source files in different forms that contain errors for you to correct.

At the end of every piece of work, check it carefully for data entry errors and consistency of your presentation.

15.2.2 Verification

What is verification?

Verification is a way of preventing errors when data is copied from one medium to another (for example, from paper to disk/CD). Verification does not stop all errors, but helps to reduce the errors made when data is entered into the computer, by checking the accuracy of data entry. There are two common ways that verification checks are carried out. These are called 'visual verification' and 'double data entry'.

> ### Advice
> If the word 'verification' is used in a question, call this method 'visual checking'. If the word is not used in the question call it 'visual verification'.

Visual verification

Visual verification can also be called a visual check. Visual verification is checking for data entry errors by comparing the original paper documents with the data entered into the computer. This does not make sure the data is correct. For example, if the original document contained an error (for example, the telephone number 842211 was recorded as 841122) then this error would be copied onto the computer. This is not the same as proofreading.

Double data entry

Data is entered into a system twice (often by two different people). The two sets of data are then compared by the computer and if there is a difference in the data it is flagged as an error. It can then be corrected by the user. A simple example of this is when you are asked on a website to create a new password, you must enter the password twice. The computer checks the two passwords are the same before allowing you to continue. This does not check that the passwords are correct – for example, if you make the same spelling error in both passwords the data will verify but would still contain an error. In the case of these passwords the computer will check they are the same when the second password is entered. In the case of documents, two people would enter the data and the computer would verify they are the same after all the data has been entered.

Why are validation and verification needed?

Validation and verification, when used together, will help to reduce the number of errors in data entry. Even together they do not stop all data errors occurring. For example, imagine a school has a telephone number of 842211, but this is recorded in the original documents as 841122. This error would not be found or corrected through visual verification or double data entry. If the most appropriate validation is applied (to either a database or spreadsheet), for example to make sure that all telephone numbers are six digits long and start with a 5, 8 or 9, then again 841122 would pass the validation tests but if someone then tried to telephone the school it would not work.

A company supplying electricity sends bills to its customers that are between $100 and $500 would need both validation and verification because:

» data might be sensible but has not been transcribed/transferred accurately – for example, an electricity bill for $329 may have been copied as $320 – it is still sensible but has not been copied accurately
» data might have been transcribed/transferred accurately but may not be sensible – for example, an electricity bill of $3000.

Using validation in addition to verification would trap both errors, verification for the first example and validation for the second.

15.2.3 Proofreading

Although detailed knowledge of proofreading is not part of the syllabus, it is a term often used (incorrectly) by students. Proofreading is part of the proofing process. Proofreading is not a form of verification. It is the careful reading and re-reading of a document (before it is finally printed) to detect any errors in spelling, grammar, punctuation or layout, whether or not they were in the original document. This process is more than just verification; verification simply checks the transcription of data from one medium to another. If the original data contains errors, then the verified data will contain the same errors. Proofreading should help to remove many of these errors by checking that the data is correct, not just accurately transcribed.

16 Graphs and charts

16.1 Chart types

You may be asked to select an appropriate chart for a purpose. It is often very difficult to work out which chart is the most appropriate. The choice will be between a pie chart, a bar chart and a line graph.

16.1.1 Pie charts

If you are asked to compare percentage values, a pie chart is often the most appropriate type because pie charts **compare parts of a whole** or fractions of a whole. An example would be comparing the percentage of children who preferred ice cream, jelly or trifle.

16.1.2 Bar charts

Bar charts **show the difference** between different things. A bar chart is traditionally a graph with vertical bars, but it is called a column graph in *Excel*. This is a little confusing, but to create a vertical bar chart you would need to use the 'column chart' and for a horizontal bar chart (with the bars going across the page) you would need to use the 'bar chart'. An example would be showing the number of items sold by five people in the same month.

> **Advice**
>
> Do not use stacked column charts or stacked bar charts.

16.1.3 Line graphs

Line graphs are used to plot **trends** between two variables. An example would be plotting the temperature of water as it was heated against time. You could then find any point in time on the graph and be able to read the corresponding temperature, even if the temperature had not been taken at that time.

16.2 Create a chart

To create a chart, you have to highlight the data that you wish to use. This is highlighted in the same way as other data in a **spreadsheet**. Sometimes you need to create a graph or chart using **contiguous** data (the data you use for this is in rows/columns which are next to each other, such as columns B and C). Other times you need to create a graph or chart using **non-contiguous** data (the data you use for this is in rows/columns which are not next to each other, such as columns B and F). To select non-contiguous data, hold down the <Ctrl> key while making your selections.

> ## Task 16a
>
> Open the file **employees.csv**. This shows the job types, the number of employees with that job type and the percentage of employees with that job type.
>
> Create an appropriate graph or chart to show the number of employees with that job type.

	A	B	C
1	JobTitle	Number of staff	Percentage
2	Director	3	0.048387097
3	Engineer	12	0.193548387
4	Analyst	4	0.064516129
5	Sales	16	0.258064516
6	Programmer	9	0.14516129
7	Tester	5	0.080645161
8	Clerical	13	0.209677419
9		62	

Open the file employees.csv and highlight only cells A1 to B8 (which is an example of contiguous data). The highlighted data should look like this. ——

This highlighted area will be the cells used to produce the graph. Notice that the cells containing the column headings (A1 and B1) have been included in this selection as they will be used as the labels in the chart (they can be changed later if the question asks for different labels).

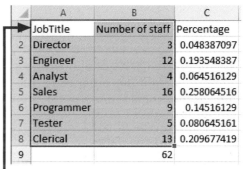

Decide what type of chart you will need for this task. Look at the data and decide if it compares parts of a whole, shows trends between two variables or shows the difference. In this task the data shows the different numbers of employees in each job type, so a bar chart is the most appropriate chart type, and in this case, you can use a vertical bar chart. ——

Select the Insert tab and find the Charts section. Select a vertical bar chart (labelled Column in *Excel*); this can be selected using the small icon of a Bar chart.

Note that we have not used *Excel*'s 'Recommended Charts' as this feature does not always select the most appropriate type chart for a given task. Click on the bar chart icon and this drop-down list of chart types appears. Select the first 2-D Column chart from the list. ——

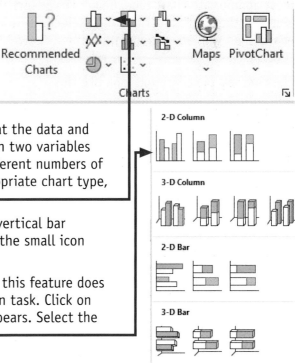

This is a vertical bar chart, although it is called a column chart in *Excel*, and it will be created automatically for you. The chart will look similar to this.

Save this in spreadsheet format as **task16a**.

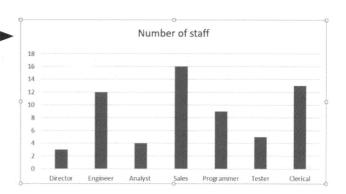

Advice

Keep your charts simple – do not use 3-D charts or add features that are not a necessary part of a task. A simple chart is often more effective.

Task 16b

Open the file **employees.csv**. Create an appropriate graph or chart to show the percentage of employees with that job type.

Open the file and, using the <Ctrl> key and the mouse, highlight cells A1 to A8 and C1 to C8 (which is an example of non-contiguous data). Do not highlight any other cells. The highlighted spreadsheet should look like this.

	A	B	C
1	JobTitle	Number of staff	Percentage
2	Director	3	0.048387097
3	Engineer	12	0.193548387
4	Analyst	4	0.064516129
5	Sales	16	0.258064516
6	Programmer	9	0.14516129
7	Tester	5	0.080645161
8	Clerical	13	0.209677419
9		62	

Decide what type of chart you will need for this task. Again, look at the data and decide if it compares parts of a whole, shows trends between two variables or shows the difference. In this task the data compares parts of the whole, so a pie chart is the most appropriate chart type. Select the Insert tab and find the Charts section. Then select a Pie chart, then the left option within the 2-D Pie section.

The finished pie chart will look like this.

Save this chart in spreadsheet format as **task16b** for later use.

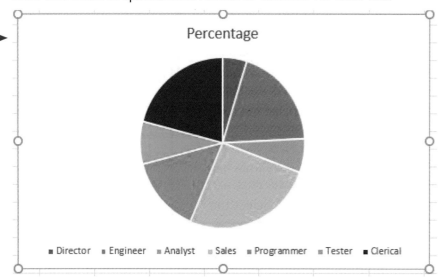

Task 16c

Open the file **rainfall.csv**. Create an appropriate graph or chart to show a comparison of the monthly data for towns A and B.

Open the file and highlight cells A1 to C15. Decide what type of chart you will need for this task. Again, look at the data and decide if it compares parts of a whole, shows trends between two variables or shows the difference. This task mentions periods of time, which suggests a trend. In this task, it is seeing how the total amount of rainfall changes/varies over a period of 12 months. Because specific dates are used and the rainfall is cumulative, a line graph is the most appropriate chart type. As there are two towns shown in the data, you will make a comparative line graph using both data sets. Select the Insert tab and, in the Charts section, select a Line graph and then the top left icon from the 2-D Line section.

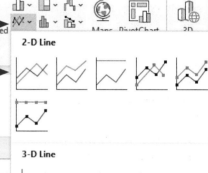

The finished line graph will look like this.

Save this chart in spreadsheet format as **task16c** for later use.

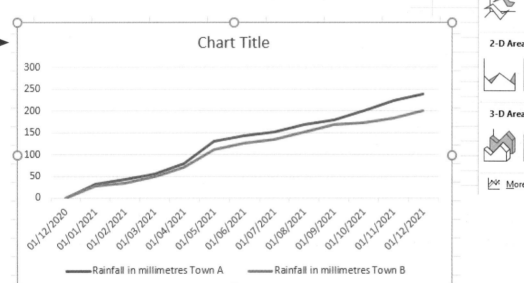

331

16.3 Label a chart

Charts have different types of labelling, as shown in this example.

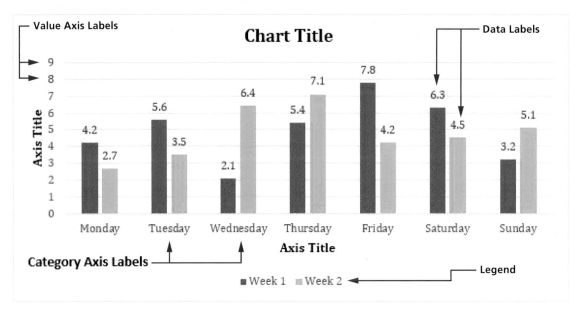

Task 16d

Open the file saved in task 16a and add appropriate chart labels.

Open the chart saved in Task 16a. Although *Excel* attempts to complete the chart – it has added a chart title and axis labels – it is still incomplete. All charts need to be fully labelled. Click the left mouse button on the chart to select it and select the Chart Elements icon.

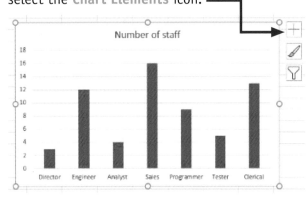

Tick the check box for **Axis Titles**.

Select the right arrow and tick the check boxes for **Primary Horizontal** and **Primary Vertical** axes.

Move the cursor into each label box and type each label.

If you are given the chart title, enter it very carefully and exactly as shown in the question; if not, change the text in the question into a chart title so that it gives as much information as possible to the reader. Include your name, centre number and candidate number in the chart labelling. As there is only one set of values (data series) in this chart, a legend (or key) is not needed.

Save this chart in spreadsheet format as **task16d**.

The finished chart may look like this.

Advice

The category axis in a vertical bar chart is the *x*-axis and displays the names of the different categories; the value axis is the *y*-axis and displays the number values.

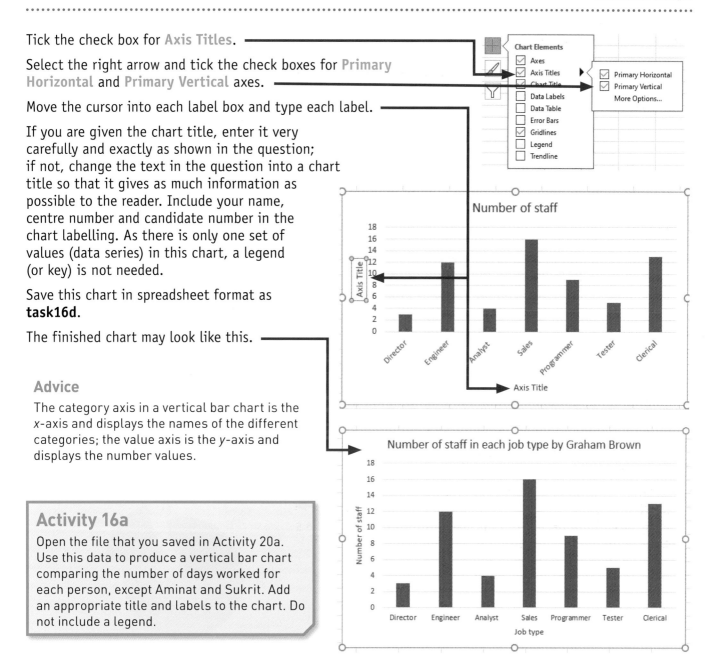

Activity 16a

Open the file that you saved in Activity 20a. Use this data to produce a vertical bar chart comparing the number of days worked for each person, except Aminat and Sukrit. Add an appropriate title and labels to the chart. Do not include a legend.

Activity 16b

Open the file **webhits.csv**. This contains data about the number of members of an online book club and the average number of website hits each week over a nine-year period. Create and label an appropriate graph or chart to show a comparison of these two sets of data.

Task 16e

Open the chart saved in Task 16b. Display all sector labels and percentage values on the chart. Do not display a legend. Extract the sector for engineers. Make this sector red.

Open the chart saved in Task 16b. Click on the chart with the left mouse button and select the Style icon.

This displays a list of styles to choose from. You can scroll through the list and choose the style you want.

Careful selection here can save you a lot of work. Sometimes the best choice can also contain a legend, but this is easy to remove. Select the Chart Elements icon and remove the tick from the legend box.

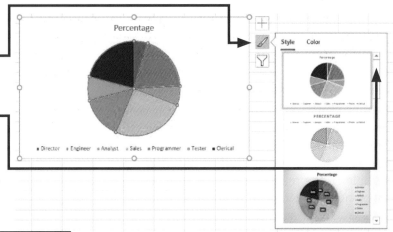

For this task this layout has been chosen.

To extract the sector for Engineer, click the left mouse button on the sector so that only that sector is selected like this.

Click again and hold down the left mouse button on this sector and slowly drag the sector out in the direction shown by the purple arrow.

The chart should now look like this.

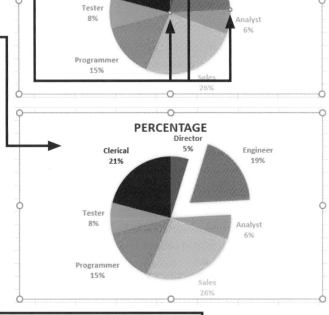

Select only this sector again. To make this sector red, right mouse click on the sector for engineers and select the Fill tool.

The drop-down palette of theme colours appears. For this task, select the red colour for the sector.

Click the left mouse button to select only the sector label for Engineer. Right mouse click on it, then select Font from the drop-down menu. In the Font window change the Font Color to red using the drop-down palette.

You can always use this method to change sector colours so that text (if it is within the sector) can be easily read.

The chart should now look like this.

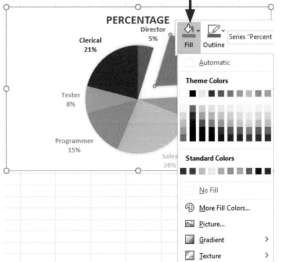

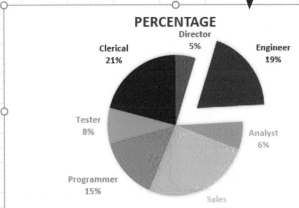

The Fill tool is very useful in many types of chart, including bar charts, for changing the colours of different sectors or bars. If a chart (or a document including a chart) has to be printed in black and white, it would be difficult to tell which sector or bar is which. So that charts displayed or printed in black and white are easy to read, use the range of texture, pattern and gradient fills to make each bar or sector look different.

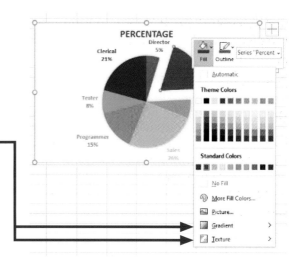

Save the chart in spreadsheet format as **task16e**.

Advice

It is worth spending time browsing through each of these chart layouts to see what is available.

Activity 16c

Open the file that you saved in Activity 20m.
- » Create a pie chart showing the name of each house (the colours) and the percentage of the class in that house.
- » Add the title 'Percentage of students in each house'.
- » Change the colour of each sector to match the name of the house.
- » Extract the sector for the Yellow house.

Activity 16d

Open the file **project.csv**.

Create a pie chart to compare the number of hours worked by the people with each type of job. Make sure that each type of job can be clearly identified when printed in black and white.

16.4 Use secondary axes

Task 16f

Open the file **rainfall.csv**. Create an appropriate graph or chart to show a comparison of the rainfall and average temperatures for each month in only Town A. Add a second value axis to the chart for the temperature series and label and scale these axes appropriately.

Open the file rainfall.csv and highlight the dates and data for Town A; this is in cells A1 to B15 and D1 to D15. Select the Insert tab then, in the Charts section, select the Insert Combo Chart icon.

Select the bottom option to Create Custom Combo Chart....

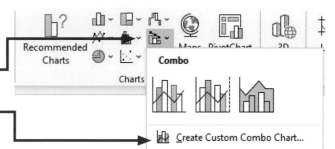

This allows you to compare two values using bar charts and/or line graphs and opens the Insert Chart window set to Combo charts.

Both of the data series chosen show trends between two variables (rainfall will be plotted against the date, and average temperature will be plotted against the date) so using line graphs for both series would be the most appropriate chart type. To make this happen choose the Chart Type as Line for both series, like this. ─

It is difficult to read the values for the temperature as the scale on the value axis is too large to show the temperature data in a useful form.

Adding and scaling a second value axis will make it easier to read the graph. Click the left mouse button in the tick box for Secondary Axis for the temperature data series (the one shown in orange).

Your graph will now look similar to this. ─

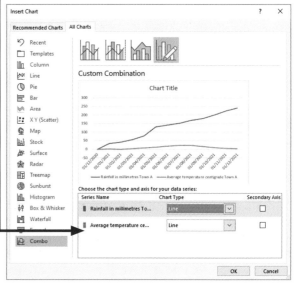

Click the ⬚ OK ⬚ button to create the chart. *Excel* has attempted to scale these axes but you are now going to adjust them further.

You will change the primary axis so that it is set between 0 and 250 and the secondary axis so that it is set between −2 and 24. These values have been extracted from the original data: the total cumulative rainfall is 240 mm, so we will choose 250, so that the scale can go up in increments (steps) of 50; the temperature changes between −1 and 23 degrees, so we will use −2 and 24 so the scale can go up in steps of 2. For this axis it would be acceptable to use the values −5 to 25 suggested by *Excel*.

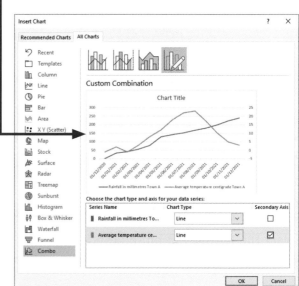

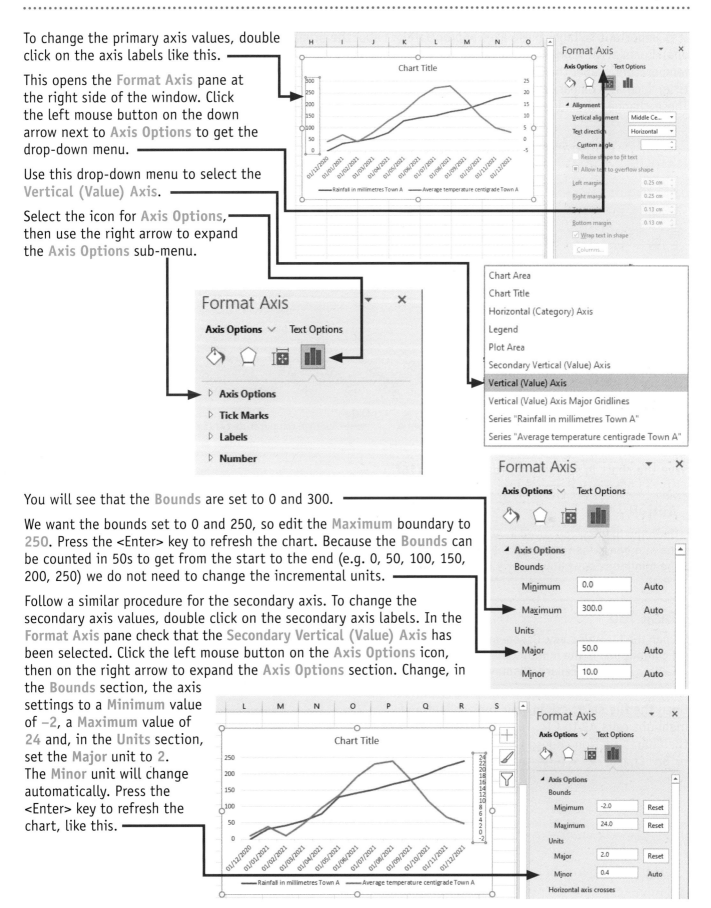

To change the primary axis values, double click on the axis labels like this.

This opens the Format Axis pane at the right side of the window. Click the left mouse button on the down arrow next to Axis Options to get the drop-down menu.

Use this drop-down menu to select the Vertical (Value) Axis.

Select the icon for Axis Options, then use the right arrow to expand the Axis Options sub-menu.

You will see that the Bounds are set to 0 and 300.

We want the bounds set to 0 and 250, so edit the Maximum boundary to 250. Press the <Enter> key to refresh the chart. Because the Bounds can be counted in 50s to get from the start to the end (e.g. 0, 50, 100, 150, 200, 250) we do not need to change the incremental units.

Follow a similar procedure for the secondary axis. To change the secondary axis values, double click on the secondary axis labels. In the Format Axis pane check that the Secondary Vertical (Value) Axis has been selected. Click the left mouse button on the Axis Options icon, then on the right arrow to expand the Axis Options section. Change, in the Bounds section, the axis settings to a Minimum value of −2, a Maximum value of 24 and, in the Units section, set the Major unit to 2. The Minor unit will change automatically. Press the <Enter> key to refresh the chart, like this.

It is important to label these axes appropriately. Label the primary axis (the left one) 'Cumulative rainfall in millimetres' and the secondary axis 'Average daily temperature'. Label the category axis 'Date'. Label the chart with a meaningful title, such as 'Comparison of rainfall and temperature in Town A by <your name>'. These changes should leave the chart looking like this.

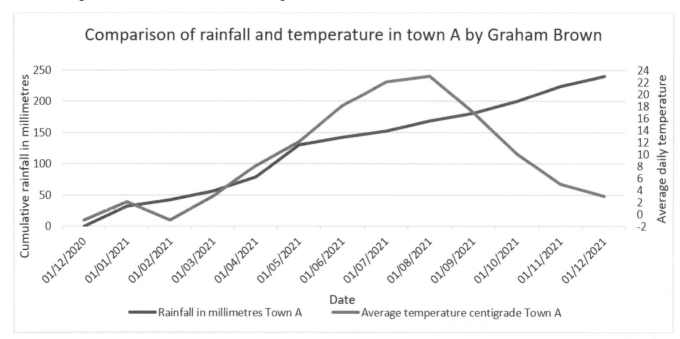

Save the chart in spreadsheet format as **task16f**.

Activity 16e

Open the file that you saved in Activity 16b. Add a second value axis to the chart for the number of members and set the maximum value for this axis to 3200 and keep the minimum value at 0.

Task 16g

Open the file **sales.csv**. Create and appropriately label a graph or chart to show a comparison of the monthly sales income from two branches of a company in Tawara and Port Pepard. Display the value axis labels to two decimal places.

Open the file sales.csv in your spreadsheet and highlight cells A2 to C14. From the Insert tab, in the Charts section choose the icon for Insert Column or Bar Chart.

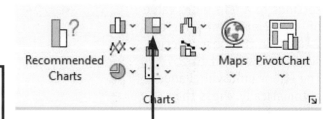

Select the top left option for a Clustered Column chart. Add appropriate labels to the chart like this.

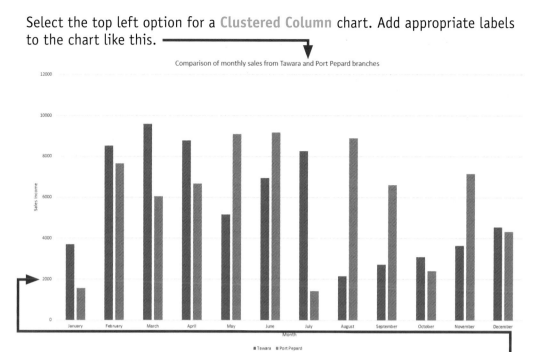

You will notice that the chart does not display the value axis labels to two decimal places.

Format numerical values to a specified number of decimal places

Click the left mouse button on the value axis labels, then from the Format Axis pane, select the option for Number.

In the Category box, select from the drop-down list the option for Number. Make sure that the Decimal Places box contains the number 2. The value axis labels now appear in the correct format for this task.

Save this as **task16g**.

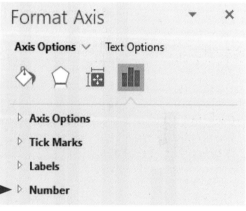

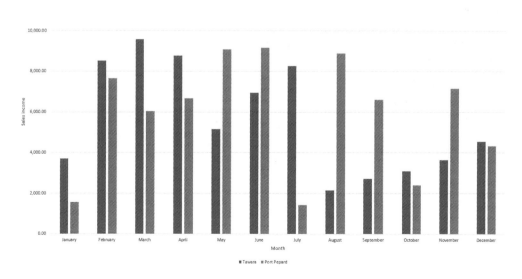

Task 16h

Open the file you saved in Task 16g. Edit the value axis labels so that they display as currency in dollars set to two decimal places.

Format numerical values to display currency symbols

Open the chart and select the value axis labels using the left mouse button. In the Format Axis pane, open the Number section. In the Category box, select from the drop-down list the option for Currency. Make sure that the Decimal Places box contains the number 2. In the Symbol box, select from the drop-down list one of the currency symbols for dollars ($).The value axis labels now appear in the correct format for this task.

Save this as **task16h**.

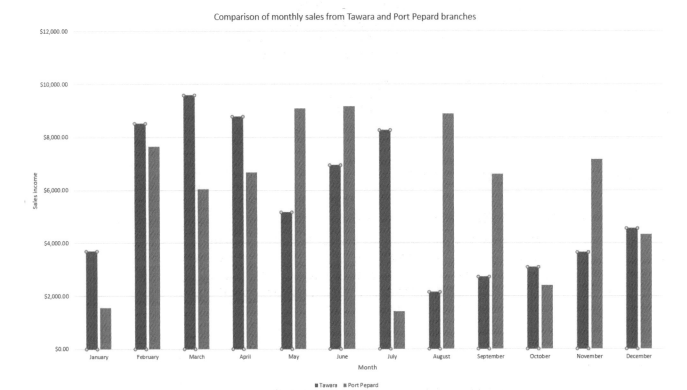

Comparison of monthly sales from Tawara and Port Pepard branches

17 Document production

17.1 Organise page layout

17.1.1 Set the page size and orientation

You may be presented with documents with different page layouts and given instructions to reformat them. Do not assume that a document is already set as specified. If it is in text (.txt) format, it will use the default settings of your word processor. If it is opened in rich text format (.rtf) or was saved as a *Word* document, it will keep the settings used to save the file.

> **Task 17a**
>
> Open the file saved in Task 14f.
>
> Change the page size to A5 and the orientation to landscape. Set the top and bottom margins to 3 cm and the left and right margins to 3.5 cm. The document is going to be bound along the top edge. Add a 2 cm gutter to the document.
>
> Save the document as task17a and print the document.

Open the file saved in Task 14f and save the document as **task17a**. Move into the footer and right mouse click on the date to get the drop-down menu. Select Update Field. Repeat this for the time and for the filename. Double click on the body text to leave the footer.

Set the page size

Select the Layout tab and in the Page Setup section click the left mouse button on the icon at the bottom right corner of the box, to open the Page Setup window.

This window can be used to change the page size, orientation (to make the page tall or wide) and the page margins. To change the paper size, click on the Paper tab.

Find the Paper size: section and select A5 from the drop-down list.

Set the page orientation

To change the page orientation, remain in the Page Setup window and select the Margins tab.

Find the Orientation section of the window. Click the left mouse button on the Landscape icon to change from portrait to landscape.

17.1.2 Set the page margins

Remain in the Page Setup window and in the Margins tab. To set the top and bottom margins to 3 cm, select the Margins section.

Either highlight the text within the Top: and Bottom: boxes and type in the new values or use the scroll handles to change the values in each of the boxes. Change the left and right margins to 3.5 cm using a similar method in the Left: and Right: boxes. Click on OK.

17.1.3 The purpose of setting gutter margins

If the document is to be part of a bound book or booklet, a **gutter** will be needed. This is an area outside the margins that is used to bind (glue or fasten) the book together. The gutter can be placed to the left or top of the page, depending upon the type of binding to be used.

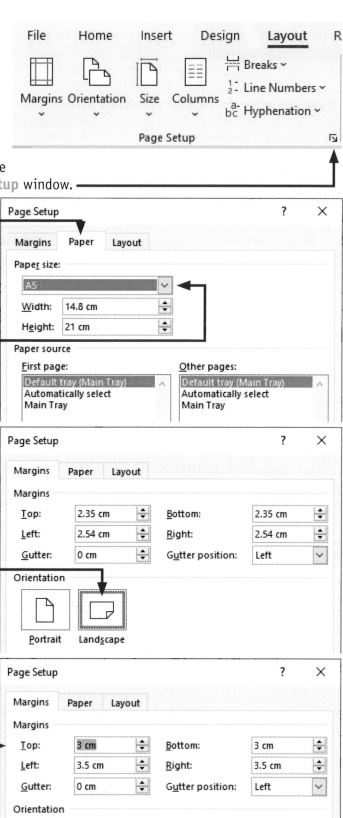

Set the gutter

Remain in the Page Setup window and in the Margins tab. The gutter is set in the same way, in the Margins section of the window. In this case change the Gutter: size to 2 cm and the Gutter Position: to Top.

This is where the printed publication will be bound.

Edit headers and footers

Check the alignment of your headers and footers to the new page margins. You will notice that changing the margins does not change the header and footer positions.

The left margins are still aligned as we would expect, but the centre tab stops and right tab stops are now in the wrong position.

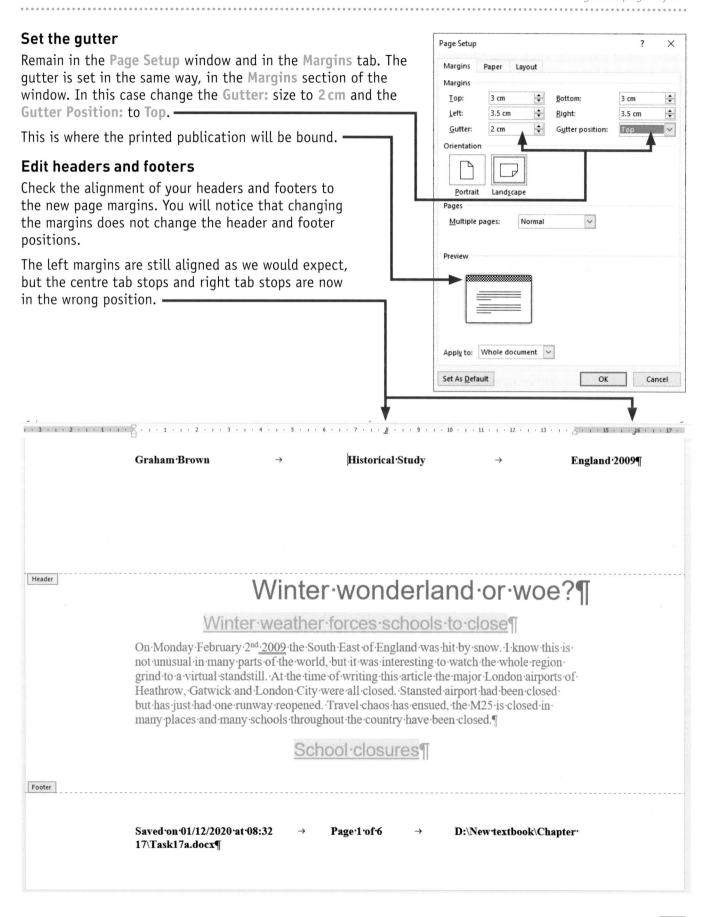

Because the width within the margins is now 14 cm, move the centre tab in the header to 7 cm and the right tab stop to 14 cm. Use the methods learned in Section 13.3 to change the tab stops in both the header and footer so that all text aligns to the page margins.

After doing this you can see a problem with the header and one with the footer. The header text is in the gutter (where the pages would be glued or bound). To change the vertical alignment of this header text, use the methods described above to open the Page Setup window and select the Layout tab. In the From edge: section, *Word* has set the distance from the Header text to the top of the page at 1.25 cm.

This is the default value on my computer, but the value shown on yours may differ. Take this value and add the 2 cm depth of the gutter to it, so on my computer it will become 1.25 + 2 = 3.25. Enter the new value, either by typing it or using the small arrows at the side. The window will change to look like this.

Click on OK. You will see the text in the header move down, out of the gutter area.

The text on the right in the footer is too long to fit into the space provided by the word processor, so it has wrapped onto the next line. This is because a file name and file path are both required and now that the page is A5 (which is half the size of A4) it does not fit.

There are two ways to solve this problem.

Page Setup

Margins | Paper | Layout

Section start: New page
Suppress endnotes

Headers and footers
Different odd and even
Different first page
From edge: Header: 1.25 cm Footer: 1.25 cm

Page Setup

Margins | Paper | Layout

Section start: New page
Suppress endnotes

Headers and footers
Different odd and even
Different first page
From edge: Header: 3.25 cm Footer: 1.25 cm

Page
Vertical alignment: Top

Preview

Apply to: Whole document | Line Numbers... | Borders...

Set As Default | OK | Cancel

many·places·and·many·schools·throughout·the·country·have·been·closed.¶

School·closures¶

Footer

Saved·on·01/12/2020·at·08:32 → **Page·1·of·6** → **D:\New·textbook\Chapter·17\Task17a.docx**¶

Change the font style

You can choose a narrower font face like Arial Narrow rather than Arial for sans-serif, or Bodini MT Poster Compressed rather than Times New Roman for serif. Make this change to all the serif or sans-serif style definitions so that it happens automatically. Although this may help, it may also make the text very difficult to read, especially in a serif font.

Change the file name or path

Word has already attempted to split this onto a second line. It will only split filenames and paths that contain spaces. Remove all the spaces from the filename and path to change it from this to this. Changing the file name or path to make them shorter (but still meaningful) is the best solution. Save the document. The finished footer may look like this.

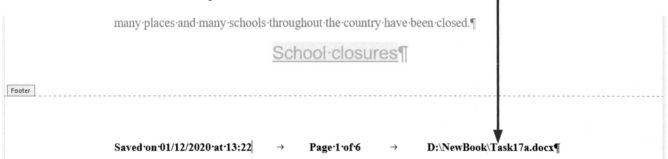

17.1.4 The purpose of setting page, section and column breaks

As you have already studied widows and orphans in Chapter 15, they should always be avoided when producing a document. Although (depending upon your word processor's setup) automatic widow and orphan control is often running in your word processor, there are times when they need to be manually removed. They can be manually removed by inserting a page break, section break or column break.

Link

See Chapter 11 for more on using appropriate file names.

17.1.5 Use page, section and column breaks

Breaks can be used within a document to force text onto a new page or into the next column (if columns are being used), or to define areas with different layouts, for example, where part of a document is formatted in landscape orientation and part is in portrait.

Page break

This forces the text onto the start of a new page, leaving **white space** at the end of the previous page. It is particularly useful for removing widows and orphans from your document, although *Word* will often do this for you.

Column break

A column break is used to force the text into the top of the next available column, which may be on the same page or may be on the next page. This is also useful for removing widows and orphans.

Section break

A section break is used to split areas of a document with different layouts. There are two types of section break: one forces a page break as well as the change in layout and the other is a continuous break, which allows different layouts on the same page.

> ### Task 17b
>
> Open the file saved in Task 17a.
>
> Remove the gutter margin from the document.
>
> Keep only the two titles on the first page of the document. Set the orientation of the first page to portrait and the rest of the document to landscape. Set all of the body text except the tables into two columns, with a 12 mm spacing and vertical line between the columns.
>
> Save the document as task17b.

Open the file saved in Task 17a.

Remove the gutter margin by opening the Page Setup window, in the Margins tab set the Gutter position: to 0. Use the Layout tab to change the header back to 1.25 cm from the page edge. Save the document as **task17b**.

Move the cursor to the place where the first break needs to be inserted. This will be just before the text 'On Monday …'. Because this break will be the separator between two different types of layout (page 1 being portrait and page 2 onwards being landscape), you need to insert a section break for a new page rather than just a page break. To do this, select the Layout tab and click on the small down arrow next to the Breaks icon.

This drop-down list will appear. In Section Breaks, click the left mouse button on Next Page.

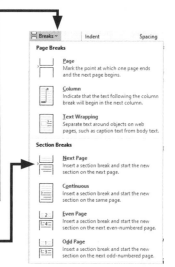

Advice

If you select the Home tab on the Toolbar and click on the Show/Hide icon, the section break will be visible like this:

·forces·schools·to·close :::· Section Break (Next Page) :::·

As the document is currently in landscape orientation, move the cursor to page 1, the section that needs to be changed to portrait orientation. Then select the Layout tab again, followed by the Orientation icon, then use the drop-down menu to click on Portrait. You will notice that the word processor has only changed the orientation of this page (because you inserted the section break).

The header and footer settings have not been automatically amended for the new layout of this page, so we need to edit them. Double click the left mouse button into the header on **page 2**. Look in the Design tab of the Header & Footer Tools.

You can see that this shows that the header in section 2 is linked to the header in section 1.

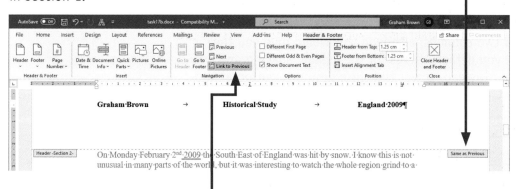

Click on the icon for **Link to Previous** so that the highlighting on this icon and the **Same as Previous** box are not seen. Now move the cursor into the header for page 1 and edit the tab stops for this section only, like this.

Repeat this for the footer. The text does not fit across the page so press the <Return> key after each item to move the next onto a new line like this.

Save your work. This task is continued in the next section.

17.1.6 Use columns

Columns can be used to give a layout similar to that found in a newspaper. You may be required to format a document, or part of a document into a number of columns. If you are going to have different column settings for different parts of the document, you must decide where you are going to split the document into the different sections. However, this information is often given to you in the question.

For Task 17b you need to add three more section breaks to the document, so that the body text and the tables can have different layouts. Where the table is split over two pages, you will use a section break for the next page.

Click the left mouse button to place the cursor where you want each break inserted (that is, just before the first table), then in the **Layout** tab click on the **Breaks** icon, followed by the **Section Breaks** option for **Next Page**. This is needed so that the table is not split over two pages. Move the cursor to the end of the first table, just before the text 'This table shows...'and place a **Continuous** section break. Move to the start of the second table and place a **Continuous** section break.

Set the number of columns, their width and the spacing between them

Click the left mouse button to place the cursor within the text of the first paragraph. From the **Layout** tab click on the **Columns** icon.

Do **not** select the option for two columns; although this would give you the correct columns, it will give you default values for the column spacing and would not give you the vertical line. Instead, select the **More Columns** option at the bottom of the drop-down list.

This opens the **Columns** window. Change the **Presets** from **One** column to **Two**.

Place a tick in the **Line between** box to place the vertical line.

Change the **Spacing:** from its default value to **1.2 cm** (12 mm).

Make sure that the **Apply to:** box contains a reference to **This section**.

Change the columns by clicking the left mouse button on OK.

Move the cursor into the first paragraph after the table and repeat this process for the final section of the document.

Advice

If you have just formatted the first section like this, moving the cursor into the final paragraph and pressing <Ctrl> and <Y> will repeat your last action. This is much quicker than repeating this process.

Sometimes when you have followed all the necessary steps, a page does not look as it should. In this case, page 2 has a heading which has become an orphan.

To solve this problem, place the cursor just before the heading. From the **Layout** tab select the **Breaks** icon then from the **Page Breaks** section select **Column**.

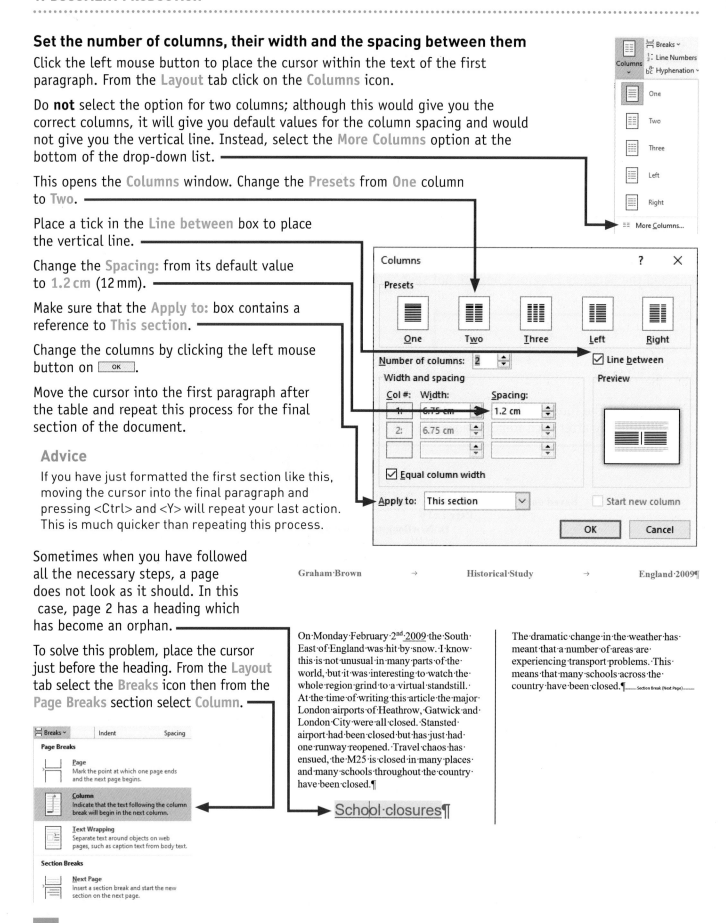

Graham·Brown → Historical·Study → England·2009¶

On·Monday·February·2nd·2009·the·South·East·of·England·was·hit·by·snow.·I·know·this·is·not·unusual·in·many·parts·of·the·world,·but·it·was·interesting·to·watch·the·whole·region·grind·to·a·virtual·standstill.·At·the·time·of·writing·this·article·the·major·London·airports·of·Heathrow,·Gatwick·and·London·City·were·all·closed.·Stansted·airport·had·been·closed·but·has·just·had·one·runway·reopened.·Travel·chaos·has·ensued,·the·M25·is·closed·in·many·places·and·many·schools·throughout·the·country·have·been·closed.¶

School·closures¶

The·dramatic·change·in·the·weather·has·meant·that·a·number·of·areas·are·experiencing·transport·problems.·This·means·that·many·schools·across·the·country·have·been·closed.¶ Section Break (Next Page)

Place the cursor at the end of the text '...during the week read:' on page 5. Use a similar method to insert a page break so that the second table moves onto page 6. Save the document as **task17b**.

Task 17c

Open the file saved in Task 17b.

Set the first level bullets to be indented by 3 mm and the second level bullets to be indented by 6 mm from the margin. Save the document as task17c.

Open the document saved in Task 17b. Select the Home tab and modify the Styles List-L1 and List-L2 so that List-L1 has a 0.3 cm indent, with the text indented to 0.8 cm and List-L2 has a 0.6 cm indent, with the text indented to 1.1 cm.

Activity 17a

Open the file **activity17a.rtf**.

Change the page size to A4 and the orientation to portrait. Set all the margins to 4 cm and remove the gutter. Place the date on the left, the filename in the centre and the time on the right in the header.

Place your name on the left and an automated page number on the right in the footer. Ensure that the header and footer are 2 cm from the top and bottom of the page respectively. Print the document. Save the file with a new filename.

Activity 17b

Open the file you saved in Activity 17a.

Change the body text of only the first page so that it is set in two columns with a 1 cm spacing and a vertical line between the columns. Save the file with a new filename.

Activity 17c

Open the file saved in Activity 17b.

Change the page margins to 2 cm and the alignment of the header and footer to fit the margins. Ensure that the header and footer are 1 cm from the top and bottom of each page. Add a new title 'Arctic blast grips the United Kingdom' at the start of the document. Place the two titles on a single portrait page with a single column. All other text should be on landscape pages, in three columns with 1.5 cm column spacing.

Save the file with a new filename.

17.2 Format text

17.2.1 Set text alignment

Text can be aligned in four basic ways. It can be aligned:

>> to the left margin with a ragged right margin which is called 'left aligned'
>> to the centre of the page, which is called 'centre aligned'
>> to the right margin, which is called 'right aligned'
>> to both margins which is called 'fully justified'.

As you saw in Section 14.2, the text is aligned by selecting the text and then using the alignment icons. These icons are found in the Home tab, in the Paragraph section.

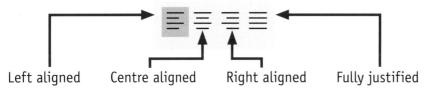

Left aligned   Centre aligned   Right aligned   Fully justified

---

Activity 17d

Open the file **activity17d.rtf** and place your name in the centre of the header. Make only the title a 36-point sans-serif font that is centre aligned and fits in a single, full width column.

Move the third paragraph so that it becomes the last paragraph. Fully justify the body text. Centre align the second paragraph. Left align the third paragraph. Right align the fourth paragraph. Make the first word 'grew' in the story 16 point, the second 'grew' 20 point and the third 'grew' 24 point.

Save the file with a new filename.

17.2.2 Set line spacing

Line spacing is usually set as part of a defined style. More details of setting the line spacing as part of a style can be found in Section 14.2. Different line spacing can be used to present different page layouts. The most commonly used layouts are single line spacing, 1.5 line spacing and double line spacing. To change the line spacing in a paragraph, select the Home tab, and look in the Paragraph section to find the Line Spacing icon. Select this icon to open this drop-down menu.

Although you can change the line spacing of a paragraph from here, select Line Spacing Options... to open the Paragraph window, which gives you more options.

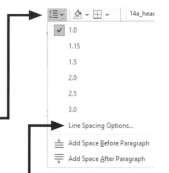

To change the line spacing, select the Line Spacing: drop-down menu. This will allow you to define an exact number of lines, which is very useful for title pages, where lines may be spaced out, perhaps needing to be five or six lines apart.

Ensuring that line spacing on a page is consistent is just as important as setting the line spacing. It is often wise to select all text and adjust the line spacing together. If you move, copy, insert or delete text from your document, always check that the line spacing is correct after you have made any change. Each paragraph and heading can have the spacing before and after it set using the same Paragraph window. This is set in the Spacing section, where the space before and after any paragraph (a title is counted as a paragraph) can be edited.

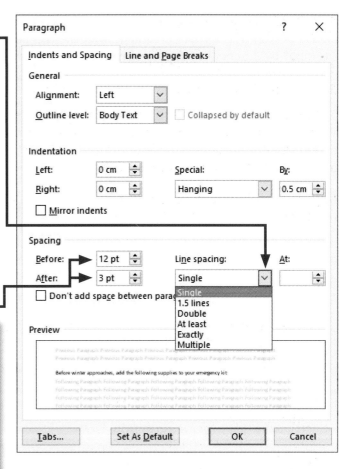

Activity 17e

Open the file that you saved in Activity 17d. Make the first paragraph single line spacing, the second paragraph 1.5 line spacing and the third paragraph double line spacing. Do not change the line spacing in the rest of the document.

Set the heading spacing to 12 points before and 24 points after the paragraph.

Save the file with a new filename.

17.2.3 Set tabulation settings

Paragraphs can be formatted with different settings for the first line of a paragraph and the other lines in a paragraph. These settings are all changed on the ruler, which looks like this.

On the left side of the ruler are two settings for the left margin. The top pentagon adjusts the first line of the paragraph, the bottom pentagon aligns the rest of the paragraph, and the rectangle below moves the whole paragraph.

Task 17d

Open the file **tabulation.rtf** and place your name on the left in the header.

Set the first line of the first paragraph as indented text, indented by 2.5 cm. Indent the whole of the second paragraph by 2.5 cm. Set the fourth and fifth paragraphs as hanging paragraphs with a 2.5 cm tab. In the fifth paragraph make the text 'Good Use' a subheading. Save the file with a new filename.

Open the file and place your name in the header. Click the left mouse button in the first paragraph. Drag the top pentagon to the right by 2.5 cm like this. ──────

This paragraph contains indented text. This means that the left margin on the first line is indented from the rest of the paragraph. The top margin setting on the ruler is indented to the right of the lower margin setting. ¶

To indent the whole of the second paragraph, click in that paragraph and then drag the small rectangle across to the right by 2.5 cm like this. ──────

The whole of this paragraph has been indented from the left margin and is called an indented paragraph. This is sometimes used to show sub-text within a document, or for showing a quotation from another author. ¶

Highlight both the fourth and fifth paragraphs and drag the bottom pentagon to the right by 2.5 cm like this. ──

This paragraph is a normal paragraph with no indents and no hanging first line. The margin settings on the ruler are directly above each other. ¶

To make the text 'Good Use' a subheading, remove the full stop and space at the end of it and replace it with the <Tab> key. The finished document looks like this. ──────

This paragraph is called a hanging paragraph. This means that the first line of the paragraph is aligned to the margin and all other lines are left hanging. The bottom margin setting on the ruler is indented to the right of the top margin setting. ¶

Good use → One really good use of a hanging paragraph is for short titles like this one to be followed by the relevant text. By setting a tab stop on the first line, the short title can be used as a heading. This layout can give each heading a powerful effect on the page, without any other text enhancement like enlarging or emboldening the text. ¶

Activity 17f

Open the file that you saved in Activity 17c.

Add the text 'History item 1' as a new line to the start of the document. Format this text in the same style as the rest of the page. Change the title 'Weather update' to 'February 2009'.

Set all of the text on the first page to be spaced five lines apart and all other text in the document to be single line spacing with no spacing before each paragraph and 24 point spacing after each paragraph. Indent all the paragraphs on the second page by 5 mm.

Save the file with a new filename.

As we saw in Chapter 14, we can add tab stops to the ruler. This is sometimes used for organising tabular data that will not be stored in tables. It allows us to align text to the tab stop position using either by left, centre, right or decimal alignment. Each of these tab stops have a different symbol on the ruler and look like this.

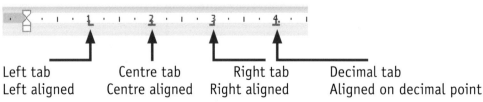

Left tab	Centre tab	Right tab	Decimal tab
Left aligned	Centre aligned	Right aligned	Aligned on decimal point

Task 17e

Open the file **buildingsupplies.txt** in your word processor and place your name on the left in the header.

Format the text so that it looks like this:

```
Data showing costs of building items

Number  Forename Surname Item         Type            Number      Cost
1004        John Smith   Bricks       LBC Heather       3900  £3712.41
1005        John Smith   Blocks       Celcon Thermalite  420   £451.25
1006        John Smith   Wall Starter Steel                6    £65.65
1007        John Smith   Sand         Soft building        3   £149.97
1008       James Lee     Bricks       LBC Flettens      1000   £754.21
1009    Jennifer Tang    Bricks       LBC Heather       1000  £1050.20
1010    Jennifer Tang    Blocks       Celcon Thermalite  160   £170.00
```

Save the file as a word-processed document with the filename task17e.

Open *Microsoft Word*, then open and examine the file buildingsupplies.txt. Save this as a word-processed document with the filename **task17e**. Place your name on the left in the header. When you examine the file with show/hide visible you will notice that it contains a number of tabs which look like this.

The text looks disorganised because each time the word processor finds a tab (arrow) it jumps the text to the next tab stop on the ruler, but as none have been defined it is using its default settings.

Highlight all the text in lines 3 to 10 like this.

Select the Home tab, then in the Paragraph section select Paragraph Settings.

In the bottom left corner of the Paragraph window, click on the ⟨Tabs...⟩ button. This opens the Tabs window.

At the moment this shows that there are no tab stops set within the highlighted area of the document. Move the cursor into the Tab stop position: box and type in 3.5 cm. Select the radio button for Right, then click on the ⟨Set⟩ button. This tab stop should appear like this.

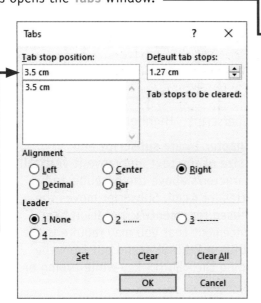

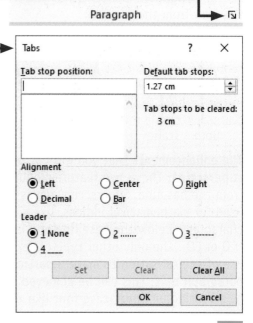

This will right align the customer's forenames.

Repeat this process and set a tab stop at 3.75 cm with the radio button in the Alignment section set to Left.

Place two more tab stops at 5.5 cm and 8.5 cm with the Alignment set to Left.

The next two columns contain numeric data which should be aligned with their decimal points. Set the last two tab stops at 13.75 cm and 16 cm, both with the Alignment radio buttons set to Decimal. The finished Tabs window will look like this. ————

Save this document. The ruler with the tab stops visible and alignment of the tabulated text will look like this. ————

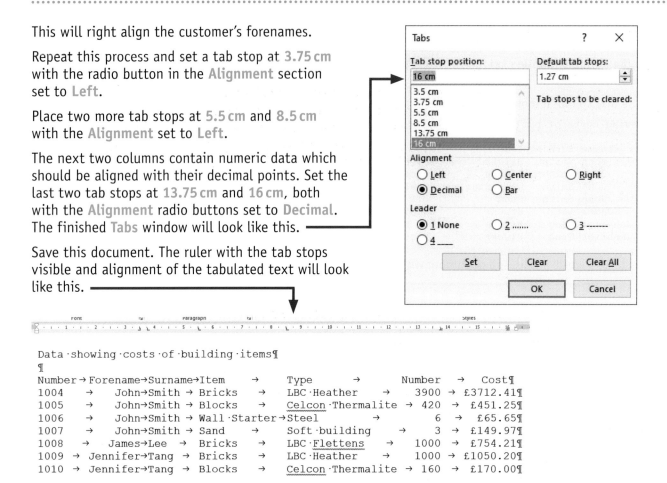

```
Data·showing·costs·of·building·items¶
¶
Number→Forename→Surname→Item        →        Type        →        Number    →    Cost¶
1004    →    John→Smith → Bricks    →    LBC·Heather    →    3900 → £3712.41¶
1005    →    John→Smith → Blocks    →    Celcon·Thermalite → 420 →  £451.25¶
1006    →    John→Smith → Wall·Starter→Steel        →        6 →   £65.65¶
1007    →    John→Smith → Sand      →    Soft·building    →    3 →  £149.97¶
1008    →    James→Lee  → Bricks    →    LBC·Flettens    →    1000 →  £754.21¶
1009  → Jennifer→Tang  → Bricks    →    LBC·Heather    →    1000 → £1050.20¶
1010  → Jennifer→Tang  → Blocks    →    Celcon·Thermalite → 160 →  £170.00¶
```

17.2.4 Set text enhancement

We have already looked at some elements of text enhancement in Section 14.1.4. Enhancements, such as bold, italics, underline and highlighting, which are used to make text stand out. These can be found from the Home tab in the Font section. Highlight the text that you wish to apply the enhancement to and select the icon from those shown.

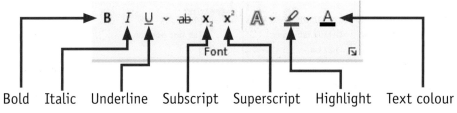

Bold   Italic   Underline   Subscript   Superscript   Highlight   Text colour

The enhancements that you did not use in Chapter 14 are **subscript** and **superscript**. These two features reduce the size of the text and move it vertically from the baseline. Superscript moves the character/s above the baseline and is used for mathematical indices, like x^2, 3 metres^2 or 4 cm^3. Subscript moves the character/s below the base line and is often used for scientific notation like H_2O or CO_2. The only other type of text enhancement that you may require is the use of capitalisation to make a particular WORD or PHRASE stand out from the paragraph text. This can be achieved by holding the <Shift> key while typing or by selecting an upper-case font like ALGERIAN.

17.2.5 Create or edit lists

Format bulleted or numbered lists

Although individual styles can be set for small portions of text, it is better to set these as defined styles and apply the styles to parts of the document, in this case lists. These elements have already been covered in detail in Section 14.2.5. For one-off lists where styles are not specified you can use the same techniques to apply a bulleted or numbered list to the specified text without saving it as a style. The same techniques used in Chapter 14 can also be used to edit bulleted or numbered lists.

Link
....
For more on lists see Chapter 14.

17.2.6 Find and replace text

Task 17f

Open the file saved in Task 17e.

The company LBC has been taken over and is now known as TBC. The company do not stock 'Celcon Thermalite' blocks but supply 'Thermacool' blocks. Change these products and save this document with the filename task17f.

Open the file and save it as **task17f**. Select the Home tab and find the Editing section of the toolbar (on the right), then click on the Replace icon. This opens the Find and Replace window in the Replace tab. Enter in the Find what: box the text LBC and in the Replace with: box enter TBC like this.

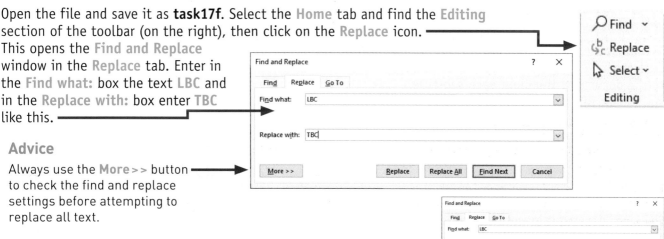

Advice

Always use the More >> button to check the find and replace settings before attempting to replace all text.

Select the More >> button to expand the window like this. It is sensible to match the case of the text you are searching for, just in case the letters lbc could appear in any other part of the document (perhaps as part of another word). To do this tick the check box for Match case. It is also sensible to replace only whole words by ticking the check box for Find whole words only, this also helps reduce errors. When both of these have been ticked, click on the button to Replace All. This replaces all three instances of this text in the document.

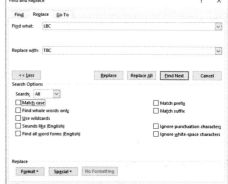

Advice

There is also an option to replace each instance in turn, which allows you to check that each replacement is correct.

Repeat this process to replace 'Celcon Thermalite' with 'Thermacool'. You will notice that you cannot use the 'Find whole words only' box as you are replacing more than a single word.

17.2.7 Add and delete bookmarks

Add a bookmark

Task 17g

Open the file **hardware.rtf**.

Add bookmarks to the title and each sub-title within the document.

Save this as a word document with the filename task17g.

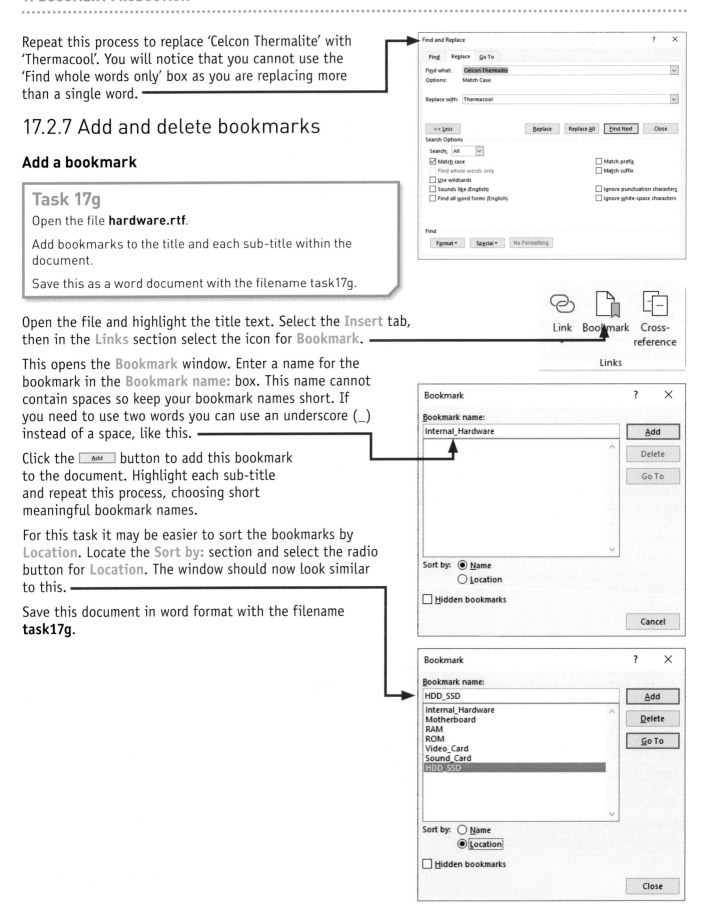

Open the file and highlight the title text. Select the Insert tab, then in the Links section select the icon for Bookmark.

This opens the Bookmark window. Enter a name for the bookmark in the Bookmark name: box. This name cannot contain spaces so keep your bookmark names short. If you need to use two words you can use an underscore (_) instead of a space, like this.

Click the Add button to add this bookmark to the document. Highlight each sub-title and repeat this process, choosing short meaningful bookmark names.

For this task it may be easier to sort the bookmarks by Location. Locate the Sort by: section and select the radio button for Location. The window should now look similar to this.

Save this document in word format with the filename **task17g**.

Delete a bookmark

Task 17h

Open the file saved in Task 17g.

Remove the bookmark 'Internal_Hardware'. Use the bookmarks to navigate to the bookmarks for 'Video_card', then for 'Motherboard'. Save this document with the filename task17h.

Open the file, select the Insert tab, then Bookmark to open the Bookmark window. Click on the bookmark name for Internal_Hardware, then click on the ⬚ Go To button. Once you have moved to this bookmark, select the ⬚ Delete button. This bookmark has now been removed from the document.

To navigate around a document, especially if the document is a large one, you can use the bookmarks. For this task you must navigate to the bookmark for Video_card, select the Insert tab, then Bookmark, and from the Bookmark window click on the bookmark for Video_Card from the list.

Select the ⬚ Go To button to navigate to the correct place in the document. Use this method to navigate to the Motherboard section of the document. To close the Bookmark window click on the ⬚ Close button. Save this document with the filename **task17h**.

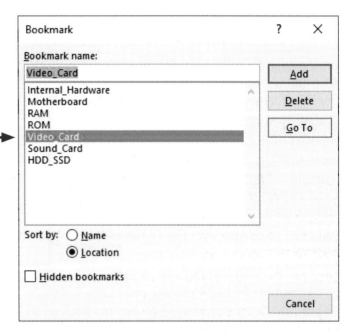

17.2.8 Add and delete hyperlinks

Add a hyperlink

Task 17i

Open the file saved in Task 17h.

At the start of the document, between the title and sub-title add a contents page, hyperlinking the contents items to the bookmarks set in Task 17g.

Save this document with the filename task17i.

Open the file saved in Task 17h. Copy each of the sub-titles and paste them to create a contents list on the first page. Add a page break so that only the title and contents are on the first page like this.

On this page, highlight the text Motherboard. Select the Insert tab, then in the Links section, click on the icon for Link.

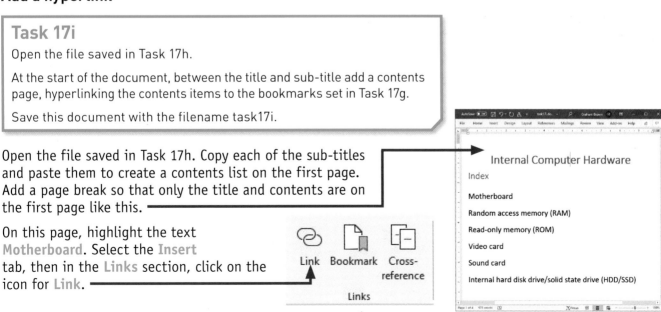

This opens the Insert Hyperlink window. This can be used to link to external documents, web pages or even to email addresses, but for this task we will create the hyperlink to a place within this document. Find the Link to: section and click on Place in This Document.

In the Select a place in this document box: are a list of all headings and bookmarks within the document. Select in the Bookmarks list, the bookmark for Motherboard, then click the OK button.

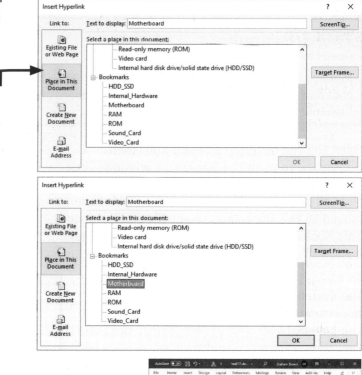

On the first page the text changes to be blue and underlined to show that it has become a hyperlink.

Use this method to create hyperlinks from the text in the contents to each bookmark created in the document. When all the hyperlinks have been created you can use them to navigate from the contents to the correct place in the document.

Save this document with the filename **task17i**.

Advice

A shortcut to create a link (which may not work on all systems) is to highlight the text to be linked, right mouse click on this text and select the Link option.

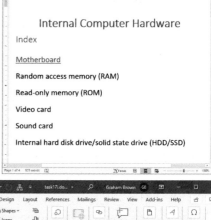

Edit a hyperlink

To edit a hyperlink, click the right mouse button on the hyperlinked text to get the drop-down menu like this.

Select the option for Edit Hyperlink. This opens the Edit Hyperlink window, which is the same as the Insert Hyperlink window.

Remove a hyperlink

To remove a hyperlink, click the right mouse button on the hyperlinked text and select the option for Remove Hyperlink. This removes the hyperlink and the text changes back to its original text colour.

18 Databases

18.1 Create a database structure

18.1.1 What is a database?

A **database** is an organised collection of data. A database program is software which stores and retrieves data in a structured way. This includes the data that is stored and the links between the data items. All databases store data using a system of files, records and fields:

» A **field** is a single item of data, such as a forename or date of birth. Each field has a field name that is used to identify it within the database. Each field contains one type of data, for example numbers, text or a date.
» A **record** is a collection of fields, for example, all the information about one person or one item. These may contain different data types.
» A **file** (in database terms) is an organised collection of records, usually where all the records are organised so that they can be stored together. A file can have one or more tables within it.

Although all databases have these three elements in common, there are two types: **flat-file databases** and **relational databases**.

18.1.2 Flat-file databases

A flat-file database stores its data in one **table**, which is organised by rows and columns. For example, in the following database about teachers, each record (row) in the table contains data about one person. Each column in the table contains a field, which has been given a field name, and each cell in that column has the same, predefined data type.

Field name	Teacher_ID	Forename	Surname	Subject	Room
	AVA	Anthony	Varela	Maths	51
	GBA	Graham	Barney	Science	14
Records	JKW	Jennie	Kwong	English	42
	PTY	Paul	Tyrell	Science	8
	SJR	Sarah	Jordan	English	39

Fields

18.1.3 Relational databases

A relational database stores data in more than one linked table, stored in a file. Relational databases are designed so that the same data is not stored many times. The tables within a relational database are linked with relationships (hence the name).

Key fields

Each table within a relational database will have a key field. The relationships linking the tables use these key fields.

Primary and foreign key fields

Most tables will have a **primary key** field that holds unique data (no two records are the same in this field) and is the field used to identify that record. Some tables will have one or more **foreign key** fields. A foreign key field in one data table stores values from a primary key field in another table.

Using the earlier example, if we wanted to add to the table the names of each student taught by each teacher using a flat-file database, the table would look like this:

Teacher_ID	Forename	Surname	Subject	Room	Student_ID	Student_FName	Student_SName
AVA	Anthony	Varela	Maths	51	G12345	Jasmine	Hall
AVA	Anthony	Varela	Maths	51	G12346	James	Ling
AVA	Anthony	Varela	Maths	51	G12348	Addy	Paredes
AVA	Anthony	Varela	Maths	51	G12349	Hayley	Lemon
AVA	Anthony	Varela	Maths	51	G12351	Jennie	Campbell
GBA	Graham	Barney	Science	14	G12345	Jasmine	Hall
GBA	Graham	Barney	Science	14	G12348	Addy	Paredes
GBA	Graham	Barney	Science	14	G12349	Hayley	Lemon
JKW	Jennie	Kwong	English	42	G12345	Jasmine	Hall
JKW	Jennie	Kwong	English	42	G12349	Hayley	Lemon
JKW	Jennie	Kwong	English	42	G12351	Jennie	Campbell
PTY	Paul	Tyrell	Science	8	G12346	James	Ling
PTY	Paul	Tyrell	Science	8	G12351	Jennie	Campbell
SJR	Sarah	Jordan	English	39	G12346	James	Ling
SJR	Sarah	Jordan	English	39	G12348	Addy	Paredes

If the data is split into two tables – one for the teachers and one for the students – that are linked together, it can be stored and retrieved more efficiently, like this:

Teachers table:

Teacher_ID	Forename	Surname	Subject	Room
AVA	Anthony	Varela	Maths	51
GBA	Graham	Barney	Science	14
JKW	Jennie	Kwong	English	42
PTY	Paul	Tyrell	Science	8
SJR	Sarah	Jordan	English	39

Students' table:

Student_ID	Student_FName	Student_SName	English	Maths	Science
G12345	Jasmine	Hall	JKW	AVA	GBA
G12346	James	Ling	SJR	AVA	PTY
G12348	Addy	Paredes	SJR	AVA	GBA
G12349	Hayley	Lemon	JKW	AVA	GBA
G12351	Jennie	Campbell	JKW	AVA	PTY

These two tables are linked with a 'one-to-many' relationship, because one teacher's record is linked to many students' records. The primary key fields (which **must** contain unique data) are the Student_ID and Teacher_ID.

18.1.4 Advantages and disadvantages of using flat-file and relational databases

From the example above you can see how much internal memory and external storage space is saved by not storing data more than once. Imagine the space saved for a school with over a hundred teachers and over a thousand students, or in a national database with data on every driver and every vehicle registered in a country.

There are three common types of changes which can be made to the data contained in a database. Records/data can be added, edited or deleted. Because data is not repeated in a relational database, each change to an item of data or to a record has to be made only once. It is also much easier for users to produce reports from a relational database, where data is held in two or more tables, than from two or more flat-file databases.

Although people often think that it is quicker to search using relational rather than flat-file databases, it is not always the case. In some cases, where indexed values are used, it can be true. It depends on the structure of both databases and the quantity of the data being searched.

You will need to create both flat-file and relational databases, but the data for these will be provided. You will be using *Microsoft Access*, which is part of the *Microsoft Office* suite. When used with a single table *Access* is a flat-file database, but it can also be a relational database when used with more than one linked table.

18.1.5 Data types and sub-types

When you create a new database you will set a data type for each field. The data type tells *Access* how to store and manipulate the data for each field. You will usually decide what data type should be used for each field. There are a number of data types that you can use and different packages may have different names for them. The list below shows the generic names for these data types but, depending on the package used, you may have different names. For example, in *Access* an **alphanumeric** field is called a text field. The three main types of field are **alphanumeric**, **numeric** and **Boolean**.

Advice

While it is listed in the syllabus, in *Access* 'percentage' is not a numeric data sub-type, it is just a formatting option.

» **Alphanumeric** data can store alpha characters (text) or numeric data (numbers) that will not be used for calculations. In *Access* this is called a text field.
» A **numeric** data type (as the name suggests) is used to store numeric values that may be used for calculations. This does not include numeric data such as telephone numbers, which should be stored in an alphanumeric data type.
    In *Access* this is called a number field. There are different types of numeric field including:
  – **integer** sub-type, which stores whole numbers. In *Access* you can select an integer field or a long integer field. It is wise to use a long integer field if it is going to contain three or more digits
  – **decimal** sub-type, which will allow a large number of decimal places, or a specified restricted number if this is set in the field properties when the database is created
  – **currency** sub-type, which will allow currency formatting to be added to the display. This includes currency symbols and regional symbols. The database does not store these symbols as this would use up valuable storage space
  – **date and time** sub-type, which stores a date and/or time as a number.
» A **Boolean** (or logical) data type stores data as 0/-1 but can display it as Yes/No (or True/False, 0/1).

There are other data types, such as autonumber (which generates unique numbers), but as they are not available in all packages you do not need to worry about them. Some packages, such as *Access*, have long and short versions of their data types (for example, long text and short text) but these are still versions of alphanumeric data types.

Other data types that are not studied in depth here can often be found in commercial databases – for example, placeholders for media such as images, soundbites and video clips. These are often used in web applications where a **back-end database** holds the media to be displayed in another application, such as a web page. As stated above, you will be using *Access*. *Microsoft Excel* is **not** suitable for database tasks as you cannot define data types.

Advice

The data types that you select when creating your database will restrict what data can be stored in your database. If you set a numeric field to be an integer (with 0 decimal places), then import data with 2 decimal places, like 45.87, *Access* will only store 45. The rest of the data will be lost and cannot be recovered. It is important that you chose your data types very carefully.

Task 18a

You work for a small garage called 'Dodgy Dave's Motors'. This garage sells used cars. Using a suitable database package, import the file **cars.csv**. Assign the following data types to the fields.

Field name	Data type
Who manufactured the car?	Text
Model	Text
Colour	Text
Price that we bought the car for	Numeric/Currency/2 decimal places
Price that we will sell the car for	Numeric/Currency/2 decimal places
Year	Numeric/Integer
Extras	Text
Does the car need cleaning?	Boolean/Logical

Some field names are inappropriate. Create appropriate and meaningful field names for those fields. You may add another field as a primary key field if your software requires this.

Save the database.

It is important to make sure that you use the field names exactly as given in a question, unless you are asked to provide appropriate and meaningful field names. In this task you are asked for appropriate and meaningful field names, so start by looking at the detailed descriptions given instead of the field names, or even examine the data to work out what information each field contains.

For this task, the descriptions help you to work out meaningful field names. These should always be short enough to allow printouts to fit easily on to as few pages as possible. The first example is Who manufactured the car?; this could be shortened to Manufacturer or even Make. Make is short, meaningful and appropriate, so use that. Price that we bought the car for could be changed to Purchase Price, Purchase, P Price, P_Price or just PPrice. Although *Access* will allow any of these, do not use field names with spaces in them, as they may cause problems if you try to do more complex operations with the database. You could use any of the other three options, as all would be acceptable. For this task, use PPrice. Similarly, the next field can be called SPrice. Consider the final field, Does the car need cleaning?. Simply using the fieldname Clean could give the wrong idea, as it could mean 'Does the car need cleaning?' or 'Is the car clean?'. It is sensible to plan this and make the changes in the .csv file before importing the data into *Access*.

Open the cars.csv file in *Excel*. Move into the relevant cells and type in the new field names. Check the spelling carefully before resaving the data file. Save it with the filename **cars1.csv** so that you do not lose the original data file. Task 18a is continued in the next section.

18.1.6 Create a flat-file database from an existing file

Advice

Check that the data files are in the correct format for your regional settings before attempting this section (see Introduction, page 12).

Open *Access* and select the Blank desktop database icon. ──────

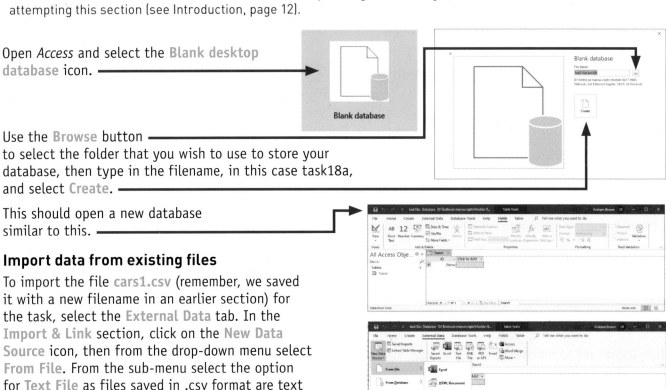

Use the Browse button ────── to select the folder that you wish to use to store your database, then type in the filename, in this case task18a, and select Create. ──────

This should open a new database similar to this. ──────

Import data from existing files

To import the file cars1.csv (remember, we saved it with a new filename in an earlier section) for the task, select the External Data tab. In the Import & Link section, click on the New Data Source icon, then from the drop-down menu select From File. From the sub-menu select the option for Text File as files saved in .csv format are text files with each data item separated from the next by a comma.

This icon opens the Get External Data – Text File window, like this. ──────

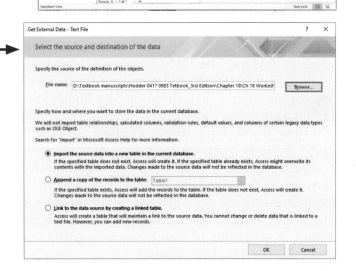

Use the Browse... button to find the file cars1.csv then click on the Open button.

Make sure that the top radio button is selected. This will make sure that the data is saved in a new data table. Click on OK.

Advice

A common error is selecting the bottom option to link the database to data held in a spreadsheet, so be careful to avoid this.

The Import Text Wizard window will open. As comma separated value (.csv) files are delimited files (the comma is the delimiter), select the Delimited radio button and click on [Next >].

For the next part of the wizard, make sure that Comma is selected using the radio buttons (unless you have changed the .csv file so that it uses semicolons as delimiters). Examine the first row of the data and decide whether this row contains the field names that you need or if it contains the first row of data. If the first row contains the field names click on the First Row Contains Field Names tick box.

As you tick this box, the first row changes from this to this.

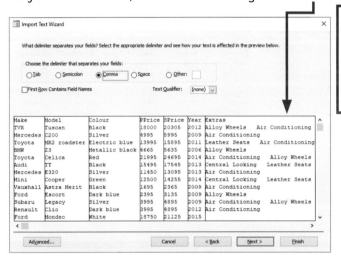

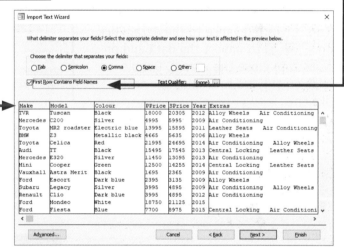

Click on the [Advanced...] button to open the Import Specification window.

18.1.7 Set appropriate data types

Check that all the field names and data types match those specified in the task. In this case the PPrice, SPrice and Valet fields do not have correct data types. The PPrice and SPrice fields need to be changed to numeric (currency) fields and the Valet field needs to be changed to a Boolean (Yes/No) field.

Advice

.txt and .rtf files may have different characters to separate each data item. If either of these file types is to be used, open the file in *Notepad* and examine the data. Work out which character is the separator and select this instead of a comma or semicolon.

To change the PPrice field into a numeric field with a currency sub-type, click on the Data Type cell for this field and use the drop-down list to select the Currency data type.

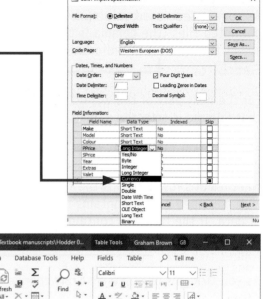

Repeat this process for the SPrice field. For the Valet field, use the drop-down list to change the Text data type into a Yes/No data type. When all of these changes have been made, click on OK . Select Next > twice.

In the next screen, ensure that the radio button for Let Access add primary key is selected – this adds a new field called ID to the table; *Access* will use this as the primary key field. Click on Next > and in the Import to Table: box, enter tblCars. This is a meaningful table name as 'tbl' shows you that it is a table and 'Cars' gives relevance to the data. Click on Finish to import the data and on Close to close the wizard. Double click on tblCars to display the table like this.

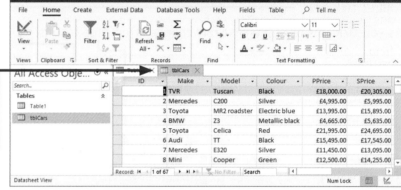

Advice

The icon in the Views section of the Home tab will let you change between Datasheet and Design View.

Edit data types

Changes to the data types, or other properties, can be made from the Home tab. In the Views section click on the Design View icon.

Set the number of decimal places

The task instructed you to set the PPrice field to two decimal places. You can check this by clicking the left mouse button in the PPrice field and viewing the number of Decimal Places in the General tab at the bottom of the window.

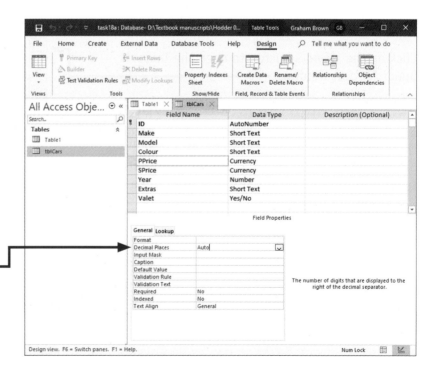

This is set to automatic. Click on the cell containing Auto and use the drop-down list to set this to two decimal places.

Repeat this process for the SPrice field.

Set the display format of Boolean fields

To change the Boolean field so that it displays Yes or No (note, it does not store the data like this), click in the Valet field. In the General tab, select the Format cell. Use the drop-down list to select the Yes/No option.

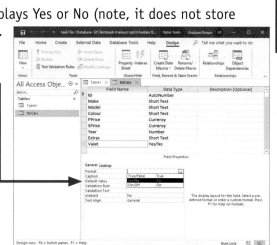

Save the database as **task18a**.

> **Advice**
>
> If you need percentage values, set an integer or long integer data type and select Percentage from the Format drop-down menu for this field.

Activity 18a

You work for a shop selling office supplies called 'Easy as ABC'. Using a suitable database package, import the file **stationery.csv**. Use these data types for each field.

Field name	Data type
Code	Numeric/Integer
Type of product to be sold	Text
Description of the product to be sold	Text
Quantity of items in each pack	Numeric/Integer
Colour	Text
Sales price	Numeric/Currency/2 decimal places
Purchase price	Numeric/Currency/2 decimal places
Discount	Boolean/Logical

Some field names are inappropriate. Create appropriate and meaningful field names for those fields. Use the Code field as your primary key. Save the database.

18.1.8 Enter data using a table

Data is normally entered into a database using a form but, if a form is not asked for, it may be quicker to use the table to enter new data.

Task 18b

Open the database that you saved in Task 18a. Add this new car to the database.

Make	Model	Colour	PPrice	SPrice	Year	Extras	Valet
Ford	Focus	Silver	1350	2285	2008	Alarm Central Locking Alloy Wheels	Yes

Save the database as Task 18b.

Open the database saved in Task 18a. First click on the [Enable Content] button. ——

To open the table in Datasheet View, double click the left mouse button on the table name. ——

To make sure that all the columns are fully visible, click the left mouse button on the grey square to the left of the ID field name to highlight the entire datasheet. ——

Move the cursor between two field names until it looks like this —— and then double click.

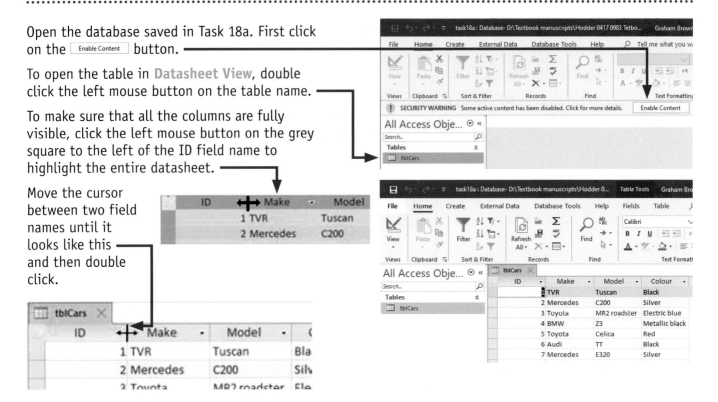

This will adjust the display widths of the columns. Scroll down the list of cars until you reach the entry with a star next to it, which will allow you to add a New car at the bottom.

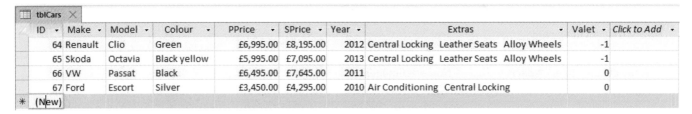

Click the cursor in the Make cell for the new car and add 'Ford'. The new ID number will automatically appear in the ID field, as you set this field as an AutoNumber data type. Move the cursor and enter the Model, Colour, Year and Extras data from the task in the same way. You can always use copy and paste for some data. For example, if you need to make sure the spelling of 'Focus' is correct, copy and paste it from record 47 above. For the PPrice and SPrice fields, enter only the numbers (and decimal point if this is required). Do not attempt to enter any other characters, such as the currency symbol. As you press the <Enter> key after adding the prices *Access* will set the data into currency format. Each time you press the <Enter> key, *Access* automatically saves the changes you made to the data. The Valet field will automatically default to 'No'. Move into this field and enter 'Yes' in this cell. *Access* will automatically save each item of data as you enter it.

Check your data entry carefully using **visual verification**. This is when you compare the original data on paper (in this case, in the Task 18b brief) with the data that you have entered into the computer. Data entry errors in a database may cause problems when you try to use the database to search or sort. Save the database as **task18b**.

18.1.9 Add a field to an existing table

Task 18c

Open the database that you saved in Task 18b.

Add a new field to the database called **PDate**. Add the purchase date of 20 December 2020 for the last car added to the database. Save the database as Task 18c.

Open the database and open the table tblCars in Design View. Move to the empty row below the Valet field and enter the Field Name PDate.

In the Data Type box use the drop-down list to select the Date/Time type.

Choose the most appropriate Format for the task. In this case, the task asks for a Long Date format.

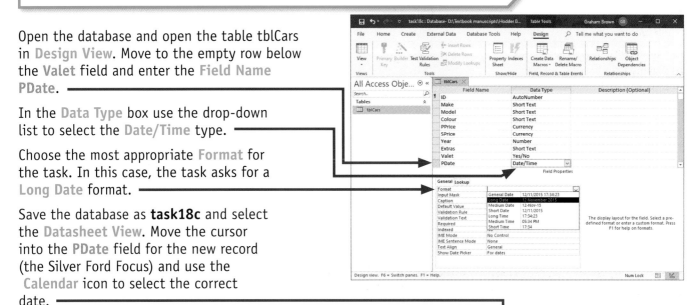

Save the database as **task18c** and select the Datasheet View. Move the cursor into the PDate field for the new record (the Silver Ford Focus) and use the Calendar icon to select the correct date.

You may need to double click to the right of the PDate column to widen the column. Save the database as **task18c**.

Activity 18b

Open the file saved in Activity 18a.

Add these three items of stationery to the database.

Code	Type	Description	Quantity	Colour	SPrice	PPrice	Discount
44282	Lever Arch File	Laminated Lever Arch Files	1	Red	57.22	28.96	No
44283	Lever Arch File	Laminated Lever Arch Files	1	Yellow	57.22	28.96	No
47478	Spine Label	Eastlight Spine Labels	100		30	13.86	Yes

Some field names are inappropriate. Create appropriate and meaningful field names for those fields. Use the Code field as your primary key. Save the database.

18.1.10 Create a relational database

Task 18d

You work for Tawara High School. You will edit some data about the Mathematics Faculty. Using a suitable database package, import the file **teachers.csv**. Use these field names and data types:

Field name	Data type
SCode	Text
FName	Text
SName	Text
Subject	Text
Room	Numeric/Integer

Set the SCode field as a key field. Import the file **students.csv** as a new table in your database. Set the Student_ID field as a key field. Create a one-to-many relationship as a link between the SCode field in the Teachers' table and the Maths field in the Students' table.

Use the techniques you practised in Task 18a to import the two tables into the database so that each table looks like this.

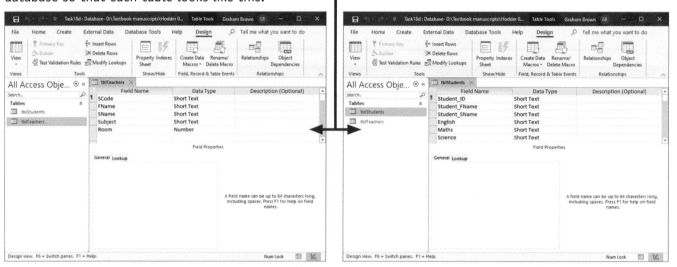

Select the Database Tools tab, locate the Relationships section, then click on the Relationships icon.

Double click on the icon for Add Tables to open the Add Tables Pane on the right. Hold down the <Shift> key and select each table in turn so that both are highlighted at the same time, then click on the [Add Selected Tables] button. Close the Add Tables pane. After both tables have been added, the Relationships tab should look like this.

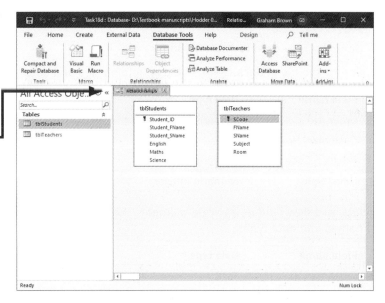

Move the cursor to sit over the bottom right corner of the Students' table so that it changes to a drag arrow; expand it slightly so that all the field names are fully visible.

To create the one-to-many relationship between the SCode field in the Teachers' table and the Maths field in the Students' table; move the cursor to the tblTeachers table and click the left mouse button on the SCode field. Hold down this button, drag the cursor to the tblStudents table and drop it on the Maths field. The Edit Relationships window will appear.

This window shows the link between the fields in both of the tables. The bottom of the window displays the type of relationship that you have created.

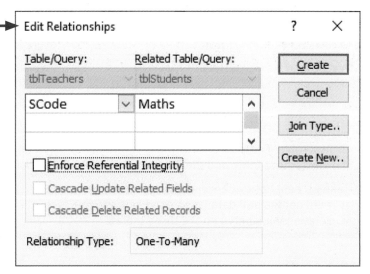

You cannot change it here: if the relationship is not the correct type, you have probably missed setting one of the key fields.

To correct this, click the [Cancel] button, add the key field and redo this task. You will be expected to show how you created the relationship. A screen shot of this window taken with the <Alt> and <Prt Scr> keys will copy this into the clipboard. Paste this into the document that you will present as evidence of your method. When you click [Create] the window will disappear and the Relationships tab will look like this.

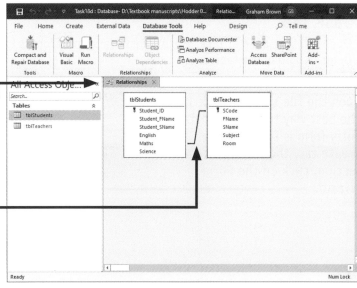

In this relationship SCode is the primary key field in tblTeachers and Maths is the foreign key field in tblStudents. If you wish to view or edit the relationship again, you can double click the mouse on the relationship line that joins the two tables.

Save the database as **Task18d**.

Activity 18c

Open the file saved in Activity 18b.

Import the file **orders.csv**. Use these field names and data types:

Field name	Data type
Order_No	Numeric/Integer
Customer_No	Text
Product_Code	Numeric/Integer
Units_Sold	Numeric/Integer

Assign a new field as a key field. Import the file **customers.csv**. Use these field names and data types:

Field name	Data type
Customer_ID	Text
Name	Text
Address_1	Text
Address_2	Text
Address_3	Text
Zip_Code	Text
Discount_%	Numeric/2 decimal places

Set the Customer_ID field as a key field. Create a one-to-many relationship between the Code field in the Stationery table and the Product_Code field in the Orders table. Create a one-to-many relationship between the Customer_ID field in the Customers table and the Customer_No field in the Orders table.

Take screenshot evidence showing the:
» field names and data types used in these two tables
» relationships between the three tables.

18.1.11 Create a data entry form

Task 18e

Open the file saved in Task 18d. Add new data entry forms to collect data for all fields in both of the tables.

Open the file saved in Task 18d. The best way to create a data entry form is to select the Create tab, then in the Forms section, click on the Form Wizard.

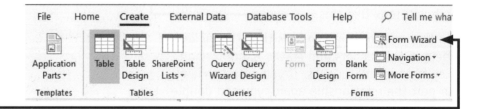

The **Form Wizard** window opens. Select the table that holds the fields that you will include in the form. If the form needs fields from more than one table, then select a query (you will use these later in the chapter). We will create the first form by selecting **tblStudents**, so leave that selected in the top selection box.

You can move each field across into the form using the single arrow key, but, as you want all the data from this table on the form, use the double arrow key.

All of the fields move into the selected fields box. Click on **Next >**. Choose the layout of the screen that you require (**Columnar** has been chosen for this task) before clicking on **Next >** again. Change the title of the form to **frmStudents** so that you can easily tell that it is a form. Click on **Finish** to open the form.

The bottom of the form has a navigation bar which can be used to move from record to record like this.

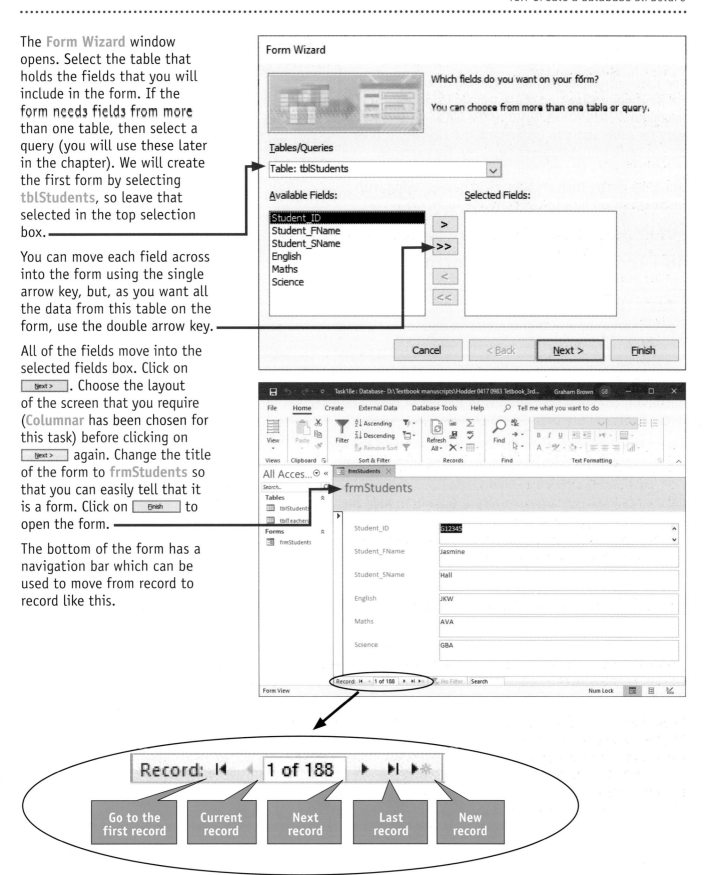

Repeat this process for **tblTeachers** to create the second data entry form, which should look like this.

The data entry form may need editing to make it easier for a different target audience to use. Using short and meaningful field names to store the data may not be easy for other users to understand, particularly if they do not work with databases regularly. For example, if children were to add their data, simple questions would be better than encoded field names, along with instructions on how to complete the form.

Save the database as **task18e**.

18.1.12 Edit a data entry form

> ### Task 18f
>
> Open the file saved in Task 18e. Edit the data entry form for student data to make it easier for students to enter their own data.

Open the database saved in Task 18e. Double click the left mouse button on **frmStudents**, which is in the list of database objects under forms, on the left.

Select the **Home** tab, then the drop-down arrow in the **Views** section to get the drop-down menu for the different ways of viewing the form. Select **Design View**.

Click on the **Shutter Bar Open/Close Button** to hide the 'Navigation pane', giving you more room to work.

The tab will change automatically to **Design**. From the **Tools** section of this tab, select the **Property Sheet** icon.

This will open the **Property Sheet** pane for the current object. Move the cursor into the **Form Header** and click on the outline of the text box so that it changes to orange.

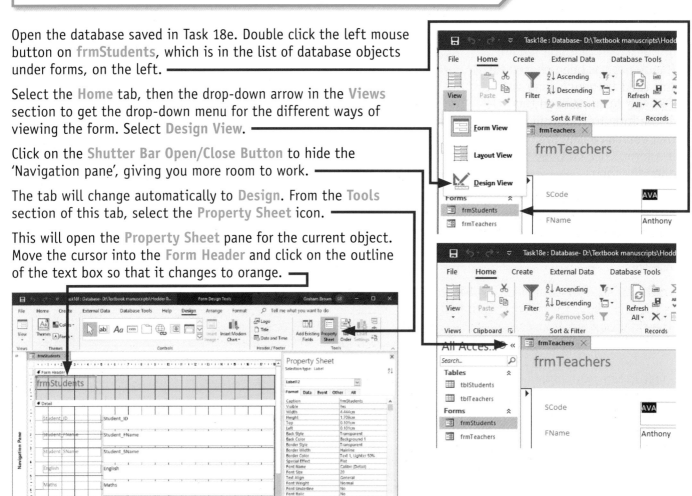

Highlight the text in this label box and change it to a more suitable heading. If the text does not fit in the label box, grab the drag handles and make it larger. You may not be able to see the lower drag handles; if you need to use them, drag the **Detail** bar down slightly, but remember to move it back up again later. If you wish to change the font, colours or formatting of the text (or any other form element) this can be done in the **Property Sheet**. In this example, **Text Align** has been changed to **Center**. ──────

The **Fore Color** and **Back Color** have also been changed by clicking on them, then the `Insert ▾` button to their right, then by choosing colours from the palette.

As students would be expected to enter their own data, it is important to tell them what to do. From the **Controls** section of the toolbar, select the **Label** icon. ──────

Drag a new label box into the header and enter some instructions to help the students to understand what to enter, like this. ──────

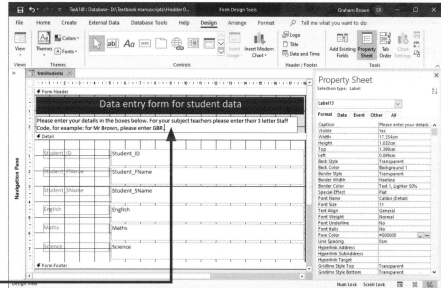

In the **Detail** row each field has two boxes. The left one is the label box. This is what is displayed to the user. The right box is a text box and this is joined to the data table. This box is where, when the form is displayed in **Form View**, the user will enter the data. Select each label in turn and edit the text so it is more meaningful for the students. You may need to resize some of the label boxes so that all the text fits. Each box has a large drag handle in the top left corner that will allow you to drag the box around the form to rearrange the form without resizing the box. This is useful if you are creating your form to a particular design. From the **Views** section of the toolbar, use the drop-down arrow under the **View** icon to select **Form View** like this. ──────

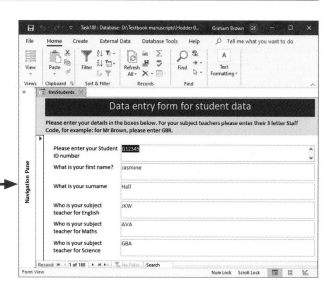

Save the database as **task18f**.

18.1.13 Add a new field to an existing form

Task 18g

Open the file saved in Task 18f.

Two new fields are to be added to the students' data. Use these field names, data types and field descriptions:

Field name	Data type	Description
Year_Group	Numeric/Integer	The school year between 7 and 11 inclusive
Tutor	Text	The name of the student's tutor

Open the database. Remember you hid the Navigation Pane. Restore it using the Shutter Bar Open/Close Button arrow. ⟶ 〉〉

Open tblStudents in Design View. In the blank row below the 'Science' field, enter the Field Name, Year_Group (you cannot shorten it to Year as this is a reserved word in *Access* – try it and see ...). The Data Type always starts in Short Text format; click on that cell and use the drop-down menu to select Number.

Type the field description into the Description box (copy the text from the table in the task). This helps to document the database. In the blank row below this, add the new Field Name, Tutor. Leave the Data Type as Short Text. Type the Description, again using the text from the task. To help improve the form and to save lots of storage space, we know that the tutors' initials are three characters in length. In the General tab at the bottom, set the Field Size to 3.

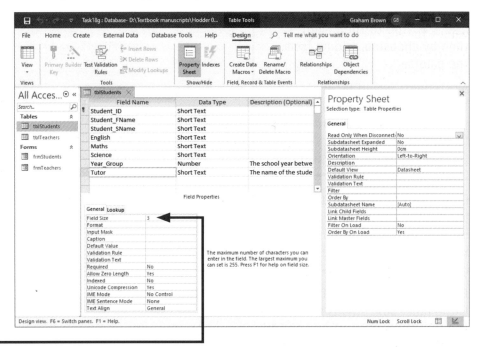

Save the changes to the table, then close it.

Open frmStudents in Design View. Pick up the top of the Form Footer and drag it down to give enough room to add the two new fields.

The Year_Group field could appear on the form as a text box but, as this data can only hold five possible values (because Tawara High School only has years 7, 8, 9, 10 and 11) it would be a suitable field for radio buttons (*Access* calls these Option Buttons) within an option group. From the Design tab, in the Controls section, select the Option Group icon. You may need to use the drop-down menu to find it.

Controls

18.1.14 Edit a data entry form

Use radio buttons

Drag the frame for the Option Group into the Detail section of the form, clicking the left mouse button once; this action will open the Option Group Wizard window. Enter six Label Names, one item on each row – in this case Year 7, Year 8, Year 9, Year 10, Year 11 and an additional option for 'No year group selected' – before clicking on Next > .

In the next window choose the top radio button option for Yes, the default choice is: and select the option you typed in for No year group selected.

Click Next > . Each label has a value assigned to it. *Access* has tried to assign values for you, but you need to change all the settings in this example. For Year 7 set the value to 7, Year 8 set to 8, and so on. For No year group selected set the value to 0.

When you have changed all of the values click Next > . In the next window, change the radio button from the top option to Store the value in this field:. Using the drop-down menu to the right, select the Year_Group field.

This will make sure that, when a radio button is selected, the value for that radio button is stored in the correct field, Year_Group, within the table. Click Next > to choose the style of options selected (radio buttons (which the software calls option buttons), tick/check boxes, or toggle buttons) and to choose how the Option box will appear on the form. Make your choices, then click Next > .

Give the frame a meaningful caption such as Which year group are you in? before selecting Finish .

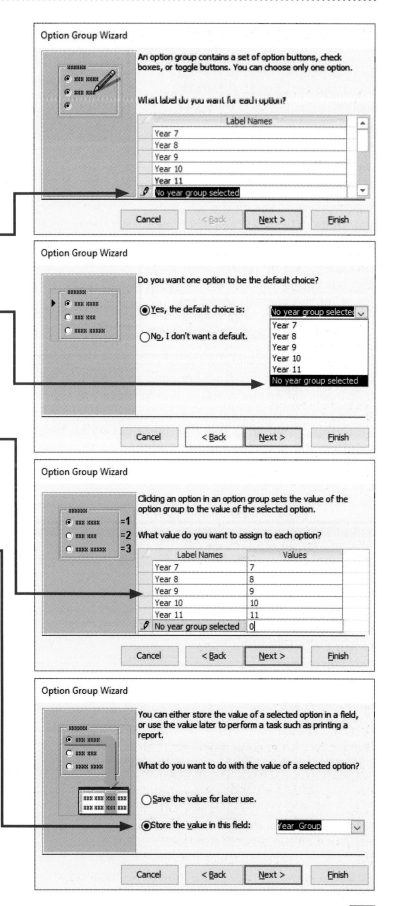

377

The option block will look similar to this in Design View.

To add the Tutor field to the form, select the Text Box icon from the toolbar.

Drag the text box for the Tutor field on to the form; you do not need much space as this field only needs to hold three characters.

Resize the label box on the left and add the text Tutor as the label. The text box label looks like this.

Click the cursor on the Unbound text box and, within the Property Sheet for this control, select the Data tab. In the Control Source box, use the drop-down menu to select the Tutor field.

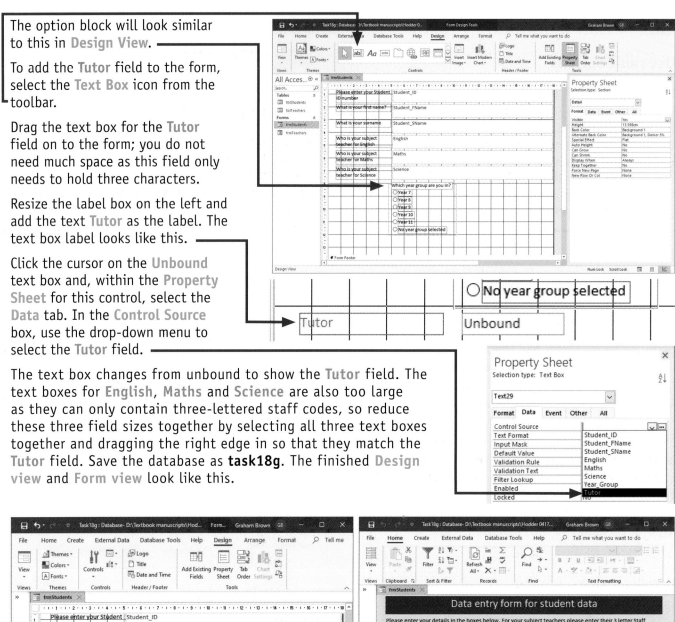

The text box changes from unbound to show the Tutor field. The text boxes for English, Maths and Science are also too large as they can only contain three-lettered staff codes, so reduce these three field sizes together by selecting all three text boxes together and dragging the right edge in so that they match the Tutor field. Save the database as **task18g**. The finished Design view and Form view look like this.

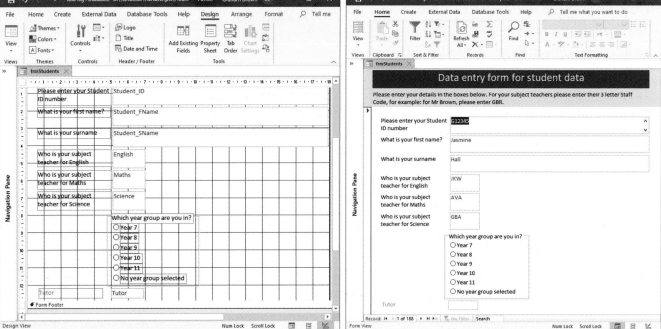

Advice

If this was a task you were completing, you would need to remember to add all your required personal information in a new label box.

18.1.15 What does a well-designed form look like?

The most important feature of form design is to keep the form simple, with clear questions, using **closed questions** where possible. This will limit the different answers to be stored in the database and will make it easier to search the database. A well-designed form has similar fields grouped, but not crowded, together, with white space between each data entry box.

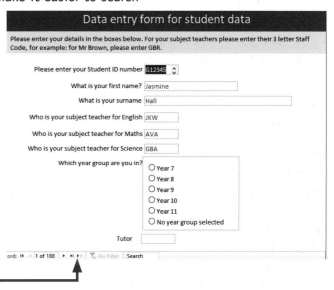

This form has many features of a well-designed data entry form. The form has a title that states what data is being collected. There are instructions on filling in the form. The questions are not just the field names but written questions. Each field has appropriate space for the data that will be added, and there is space between each field. The form has been appropriately filled by the text boxes but there is enough white space to keep it from being overcrowded. Radio buttons (or drop-down menus) are used where possible. There are navigation buttons on the form (already added by *Access*) to allow a user to add new records and move between records. In this form all of the data is important; in some forms key fields can be highlighted to show that this data must be completed before the record can be saved.

In Design View of the form, move and resize the controls so that your form looks like the diagram above. Change the text to be right aligned text in each of the label boxes. Re-save the database.

Use drop-down menus

It is often easier for the user of a database to use a drop-down menu to select data rather than typing each data item every time. These can only be used when there are a limited number of possible entries for a field, so fields containing data such as names could never use drop-down menus – unless they contained every name in the world, which would not be practical.

> **Task 18h**
>
> Open the file saved in Task 18g.
>
> Change the **Tutor** field so that the user can select their tutor from the list of staff codes in tblTeachers.

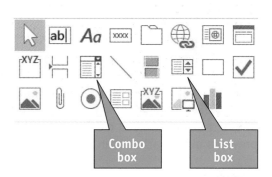

Open the file saved in Task 18g and open frmStudents in Design View. Delete the controls for the **Tutor** field (both the label and text box). You will replace the text box with another type of control. From the Design tab, in the Controls section there are two suitable options, a combo box or a list box. If you wish to allow the user to type new items into the drop-down list then a combo box would be suitable, but for this task, where you do not want the user to be able to add to the list items, select a List box.

Drag the control onto the form. The List Box Wizard window opens. Select the

radio button for I want the list box to get the values from another table or query, as the data is held in the teachers table. Click on [Next >]. In the next window select Table: tblTeachers then click on [Next >]. Double click the left mouse button on the SCode field to move it from the 'Available fields:' to the 'Selected fields:', then click [Next >]. Select the SCode field in box 1 and make sure that the 'Ascending' button is visible, to show the list in alphabetical order. Click [Next >]. Adjust the SCode column width using the drag handle, then click [Next >]. The value that you select will need to be stored in the Tutor field so select from the Store that value in this field: drop down menu the option for Tutor.

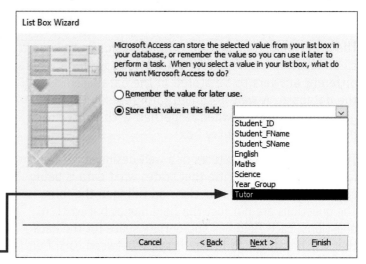

Click on [Next >] Tutor, then change the label for the list box name from the suggested name to Tutor, then click on [Finish]. Resize/move the controls and change the alignment of the text in the label to right aligned so that it matches the other labels. Save the database as **task18h**.

18.2 Manipulate data

18.2.1 Perform searches

You can search for data in *Access* using a query. This allows you to select a subset of the data stored in your table. Each query is created, saved and can be used again later. If new data is added to the table, when you open a query again it will select the subset from all the data, including the new data.

Task 18i

Open the file that you saved at the end of Task 18c.

A customer would like a car made by Ford. Find the customer a list of all the cars in the garage made by Ford.

Open the database that you saved at the end of Task 18c. You do not need to open the table that you created earlier. Select the Create tab and find the Queries section. Click on the Query Wizard icon.

This is the easiest way of performing a search and opens the New Query window. Select the Simple Query Wizard and click on [OK]. In the Simple Query Wizard window, make sure that the correct table name has been selected in the Tables/Queries box. As this is your first query this is the only option in this box, but each time you create a new query it will be shown here. If you select a previous query rather than the table, you are likely to get incorrect results.

For this task it would be appropriate to show the customer all the fields except the ID field, the price that the garage bought the car for (the PPrice field) and the date the garage purchased the car (the PDate field).

Move all of the fields into the query using the double arrow key.

Select the ID field, the PPrice field and the PDate field in turn and click on the single arrow to remove them from the selection.

When you have got only the required fields, click on ☐ Next > ☐. Select ☐ Next > ☐ again.

You need to enter a name for the query. This query may be turned into a report at some point and the name you give the query may become the title for the report. You may therefore wish to add your name to the query name, like this.

Select the radio button for Modify the query design, then click on ☐ Finish ☐.

This opens the query in Design View. Datasheet View can be seen at any time by selecting the drop-down list under the View icon. However, at the moment the query will still contain all of the records as you have not yet performed the search, so make sure you are in Design View.

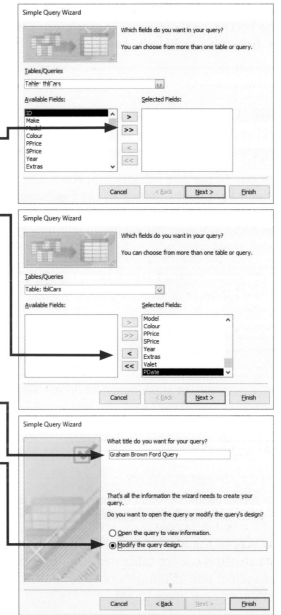

To perform the query, move the cursor into the Criteria: row of the Make field and type in Ford.

You do not need to use speech marks as *Access* will put these in for you. This will extract only the cars made by Ford.

Now select the Datasheet View to see the results of the query. The number of records can be seen at the bottom of the window in this view. There should be 25 Ford cars in the query. Save the database as **task18i.**

Task 18j

Open the file that you saved at the end of Task 18i.

The manager would like to see all the details of all the Fords that need valeting.

Create a query in a similar way to the one for Task 18i. Make sure you have tblCars selected and not your Ford query. Select all the fields and, when in Design View, enter Ford in the Criteria: row of the Make column and Yes in the same Criteria: row for the Valet column. The selection will look like this and only two cars will be found using this search.

Advice

This is called an AND Query, because the Make has to be Ford AND the Valet field has to be Yes.

Task 18k

Open the file that you saved at the end of Task 18j.

The manager would like to see all the details of all the cars made by Ford or Vauxhall.

Create a query in a similar way to the one for Task 18j. In the Simple Query Wizard window, make sure that the correct table name has been selected in the Tables/Queries box. If you select one of the previous queries rather than the table, you are likely to get incorrect results.

Select all the fields and, when in Design View, enter Ford or Vauxhall in the Criteria: row of the Make column. The selection will look like this. ———

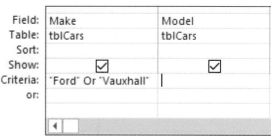

37 cars will be found using this search.

Save this as **task18k.**

Advice

Another way of doing this is to type Ford in the Criteria: row and Vauxhall in the or: row.

Task 18l

Open the file that you saved at the end of Task 18k.

The sales manager would like to see details of all the cars in stock not made by Ford.

Create a query in a similar way to the one for Task 18k. Select all the fields and, when in **Design View**, enter **Not Ford** in the **Criteria:** row of the **Make** column. The selection will look like this. ━━━━━━━━━━━━━━━━━➤

43 cars will be found using this search. Save this as **task18l.**

Field:	Make	Model	
Table:	tblCars	tblCars	t
Sort:			
Show:	☑	☑	
Criteria:	Not "Ford"		
or:			

Task 18m

Open the file that you saved at the end of Task 18l.

The manager would like to see all the details of all the cars that have alloy wheels.

By examining the data in the database, you can see that the text 'Alloy Wheels' could appear in the **Extras** field. It may not be the only extra that a car has – there could be other extras listed before it or after it within the field.

To find all the cars with this extra you must create a query in a similar way as for Task18k. Select all the fields and, when in **Design View**, in the **Criteria:** row of the **Extras** column, enter the text *Alloy Wheels*. The stars tell *Access* that you are performing a **wildcard search**. This is a search which looks for the words 'Alloy Wheels' (including the space) anywhere in the **Extras** fields' contents. The selection will look like this. ━━━━━

35 cars will be found using this search. Save this as **task18m.**

Field:	Extras	Valet
Table:	tblCars	tblCars
Sort:		
Show:	☑	☑
Criteria:	Like "*Alloy Wheels*"	
or:		

Advice

To search for something that is at the start of the data, use Text*; for example, **Bl*** in the **Colour** field will find all the cars with the first colour Blue or Black, but would not find colours such as Light Blue. Placing the star at the start of a search string will only find those things ending with the search string.

Task 18n

Open the file that you saved at the end of Task 18m.

The sales manager would like to see details of all the cars in stock for sale for less than or equal to £4125.

Create a query in a similar way as for Task 18m. Be careful not to use symbols such as < or £ in the query name. Select all the fields and, when in **Design View**, enter <=4125 in the **Criteria:** row of the **SPrice** column. The selection will look like this. ━━━━━━━

Field:	SPrice	Year	E
Table:	tblCars	tblCars	t
Sort:			
Show:	☑	☑	
Criteria:	<=4125		
or:			

19 cars will be found using this search.

Similar mathematical formulae can be used, with < for less than, > for greater than, >= for greater than or equal to, and = for equals. These mathematical formulae cannot be used for queries involving text fields but can be used for any numeric, date or time fields.

Task 18o

Open the file that you saved at the end of Task 18h.

Find Mr Varela a list of all the students that he teaches for Maths; include in this extract his full name and teaching room.

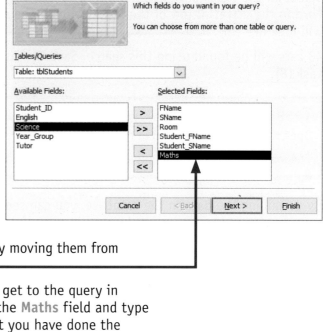

Open the database that you saved at the end of Task 18h. Create a new query using the Query Wizard. This is the easiest way of performing a search and opens the New Query window. Select the Simple Query Wizard then, in the Tables/Queries box, select the table tblTeachers. Move across to the right to the FName, SName and Room fields. Move back into the Tables/Queries box and select the table tblStudents. Select the Student_Fname, Student_SName and Maths fields by moving them from Available Fields: to Selected Fields:, like this.

Click on Next >. Continue through the wizard until you get to the query in Design View. Move the cursor into the Criteria: row of the Maths field and type in AVA. Open the query in Datasheet View to check that you have done the query as specified.

The Maths field does not need to be shown; to hide it (do not delete it or the selection of the data will also be lost) move back into Design View. Move the cursor into the Show: row of the Maths field and remove the tick from the check box.

This field is present in the query but will not be shown. This query should return 31 records. Save the database as **task18o**.

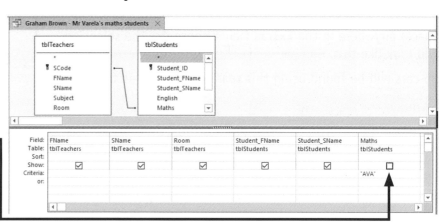

Activity 18d

Open the file saved in Activity 18c.

Search the database to find the following information for your manager. For each search, show how you performed the search and the results of the search; the results must show all the fields in the stationery table.
1 Find all of the blue stationery items.
2 Find all of the blue or black stationery items.
3 Find all of the items where the colour is not blue.
4 Find all of the red items where the discount is 'yes'.
5 Find all of the items where the type contains the word 'file'.
6 Find all of the items where the description contains the word 'file'.
7 Find all of the items with a quantity of less than or equal to 10.
8 Find all of the items where the quantity is 10.
9 Find all of the items with a quantity of greater than 1.
10 Find all of the items with a quantity of greater than or equal to 10.
11 Find all of the items where the sale price is less than £10.

18.2.2 Perform calculations

Use formulae in queries

You are sometimes asked to perform calculations at run time. This could be done in one of two ways. The first method is by creating a calculated field, so that each record has a calculation performed on it and the results are stored in a query. The other method is to calculate on all (or a selection of) the records, for example to add (sum) the data from a number of records.

> ## Task 18p
>
> Open the file saved in Task 18n.
>
> Produce a new extract from all the data that:
> » contains a new field called **Profit** which is calculated at run time – this field will subtract the purchase price from the sale price
> » contains a new field called **Percent** to calculate the percentage profit for each car at run time. This field will divide the profit by the sale price.

To create a field that is calculated at run time, you must first open a query. For this task the query will not be used to search for data but to perform the

calculation. Select the **Create** tab, then click in the **New Queries** section on the **Query Wizard** icon; select the **Simple Query Wizard**. Then click on [Next >]. In the **Tables/Queries** box select the table **tblCars** as the source of the data. Select all fields using the double arrow key. Click on [Next >] twice, name the query **Profit calculation**, select the radio button for **Modify the query design**, then click on [Finish].

In the **Design View** of the query, use the bottom scroll bar to scroll to the right and find the first blank field like this. ——————

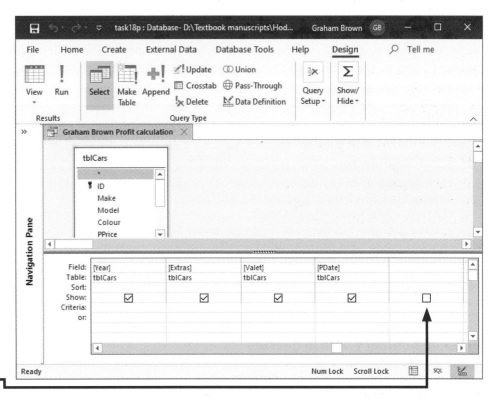

Move the cursor into the **Field** row for the first blank field. Enter the name **Profit** that you wish to give this calculated field followed by a colon. The colon tells *Access* that the next section is a calculation. Within the calculation, you must place square brackets around each field name so that *Access* looks up the data from the relevant field.

For this task, you need to subtract the purchase price from the sale price. The finished calculation will appear like this. ————————————————→

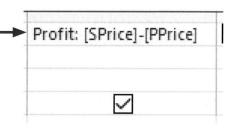

Profit: [SPrice]-[PPrice]

In the Views section, select the Datasheet View. Calculate the profit for three or four cars by hand or using a calculator and compare with the results in the query to check that you have entered the formula correctly.

Advice

Use + for addition, - for subtraction, * for multiply and / for divide.

Do not worry about the formatting of the calculated field. This will be done at a later stage.

The task requires you to create a second calculated field, so it would be sensible to include the new field now and complete the formatting later. To create a new field called Percent, follow the same procedure, this time adding a formula to divide the profit by the purchase price. ————————————————→

Profit: [SPrice]-[PPrice]	Percent: [Profit]/[PPrice]
☑	☑

Again, check the calculations with a calculator to ensure that you have not made an error when entering the formula. When you have calculated this field and view the query in Datasheet View, you may see the values displayed as #####. This means the column is too narrow to see all the data. Drag the right column handle to the right so that the data is fully visible. Save the database and close the query.

Activity 18e

Open the file saved in Activity 18d.

Produce a new extract from all the data in the stationery table that:
» contains a new field called Profit which is calculated at run time – this field will subtract the purchase price from the sale price
» contains a new field called Percent to calculate the percentage profit for each car at run time – this field will divide the profit by the sale price
» contains a new field called UnitProfit – this field will divide the profit by the quantity.

For each calculated field, show how you performed the calculation and the results of the calculation.

Present summary data in queries

Task 18q

Open the file saved in Task 18p.

Select only the cars made by Audi, BMW or Mercedes. Produce a new extract from all the data which, for the each of these makes of car, calculates:
» the sum of the sale price
» the average sale price
» the number of ctars in stock.

Sort this data into descending order of average sale price.

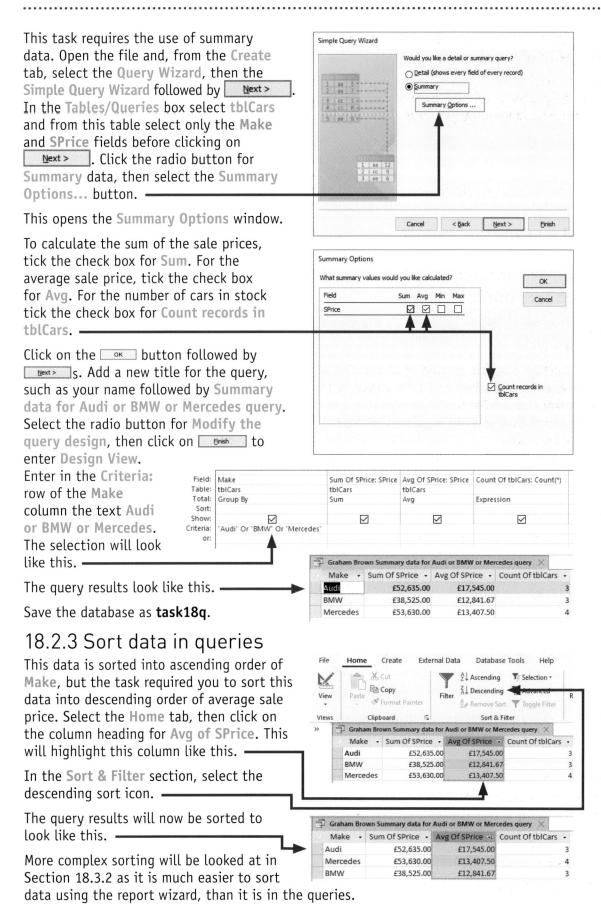

This task requires the use of summary data. Open the file and, from the Create tab, select the Query Wizard, then the Simple Query Wizard followed by Next >. In the Tables/Queries box select tblCars and from this table select only the Make and SPrice fields before clicking on Next >. Click the radio button for Summary data, then select the Summary Options... button.

This opens the Summary Options window.

To calculate the sum of the sale prices, tick the check box for Sum. For the average sale price, tick the check box for Avg. For the number of cars in stock tick the check box for Count records in tblCars.

Click on the OK button followed by Next >s. Add a new title for the query, such as your name followed by Summary data for Audi or BMW or Mercedes query. Select the radio button for Modify the query design, then click on Finish to enter Design View.

Enter in the Criteria: row of the Make column the text Audi or BMW or Mercedes. The selection will look like this.

The query results look like this.

Save the database as **task18q**.

18.2.3 Sort data in queries

This data is sorted into ascending order of Make, but the task required you to sort this data into descending order of average sale price. Select the Home tab, then click on the column heading for Avg of SPrice. This will highlight this column like this.

In the Sort & Filter section, select the descending sort icon.

The query results will now be sorted to look like this.

More complex sorting will be looked at in Section 18.3.2 as it is much easier to sort data using the report wizard, than it is in the queries.

Open the file saved in Activity 18e.

Select all types of items, except for any binder. Produce a new extract from all of the stationery data which, for each type of item, calculates:
» the average purchase price
» the average sale price
» the number of items in stock.

Sort this data into descending order of average purchase price.

Show how you performed the summary query and the results of the calculations.

18.3 Present data

18.3.1 Produce a report

The word 'report' can be quite confusing. A dictionary definition is 'a document that gives information about an investigation or a piece of research'. For our purposes, a report has this generic meaning: 'a document that gives information'. This is often confused with a report created in *Access*. The report created in *Access* will often be the most suitable report for a task, but sometimes it may be better to produce a report in a word processor, copying and pasting information into a document. For each task you will need to decide which method is the most suitable.

Task 18r

Open the file saved in Task 18q.

Produce a report that:
» shows all of the cars made by Ford
» displays only the **Make**, **Model**, **Colour**, **SPrice**, **Extras** and **Valet** fields within the width of a landscape page
» has the text 'Report by' and your name on the left in the header of each page
» has a title 'All Ford cars in stock' centre aligned at the top of the first page
» has a subtitle 'request for Mr David Watson' right aligned, in red, at the top of the first page.

Open the database saved in Task 18q. Select the **Create** tab and find the **Reports** section. Click on the **Report Wizard** icon to open the **Report Wizard** window.

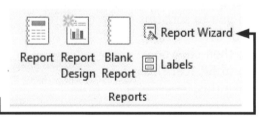

Advice

You **must** create the query first and then base the report on the query.

In the Tables/Queries box you need to select the correct query. For this task the report will be based on the query to select only the Fords (you created this query in Task 18i). Use the arrow buttons to move the fields required by the question from Available Fields: into the Selected Fields: box like this. ──────

Advice

If a question asks for specified fields (as this task asks for 'displays only the Make, Model, Colour, SPrice, Extras and Valet fields') make sure you do not add extra fields. Make sure that you also place the fields in the order specified in the question.

Click on [Next >]. Grouping is not needed at this level, so click on [Next >] again. You have not been asked to sort the report for this task (this is covered later in the chapter), so click on [Next >] again to get this Report Wizard window. ──────

Use the Layout section to choose how the page will be laid out; in this case a Tabular format has been selected. ──────

The task asked you to select a single landscape page. The page orientation is chosen using the Orientation radio buttons. Select Landscape then click on [Next >].

Change the report name so that it reads 'All Ford cars in stock' (which is the title from the task). As you still need to add the subtitle and ensure that the layout is correct, select the Modify the report's design radio button and click on [Finish]. The Design View of the report will look similar to this. ──────

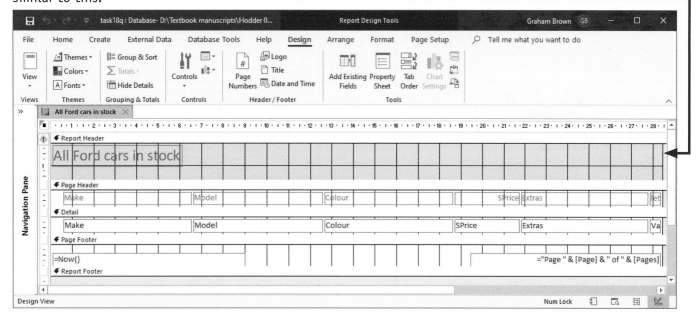

The first page of the finished report will look similar to this.

All Ford cars in stock

request for Mr David Watson

Report by Graham Brown

Make	Model	Colour	SPrice	Extras	Valet
Ford	Escort	Dark blue	£3,135.00	Alloy Wheels	No
Ford	Mondeo	White	£21,125.00		No
Ford	Fiesta	Blue	£8,975.00	Central Locking Air Conditioning	Yes
Ford	Mondeo	Silver	£3,795.00	Air Conditioning Alloy Wheels	No
Ford	Galaxy	Dark blue	£6,875.00	Air Conditioning	No
Ford	Mondeo	Black	£5,995.00	Central Locking Leather Seats Alloy Wheels	No
Ford	Mondeo	Silver	£8,425.00	Alarm Central Locking	No
Ford	Ka	Dark blue	£4,075.00	Air Conditioning	No
Ford	Ka	Green	£4,115.00	Central Locking	No
Ford	Ka	Black	£7,925.00	Alarm Central Locking	No
Ford	Ka	Silver	£4,125.00	Central Locking	No
Ford	Focus RS	Electric blue	£24,705.00	Alloy Wheels Alarm	No
Ford	Focus	Orange	£7,375.00	Alarm Central Locking	No
Ford	Escort RS turbo	Silver	£3,245.00	Alarm Central Locking Alloy Wheels	No
Ford	Escort RS turbo	Black	£4,465.00	Air Conditioning	No
Ford	Escort RS turbo	Saphire Blue	£3,795.00	Air Conditioning	No
Ford	Mondeo	Brown	£3,795.00	Alloy Wheels Alarm	No
Ford	Mondeo	Lime green	£4,355.00	Central Locking Leather Seats Alloy Wheels	No
Ford	Mondeo	Blue	£3,245.00	Alloy Wheels Alarm	No
Ford	Escort	Silver	£3,355.00		No
Ford	Escort	Black	£3,035.00	Central Locking Air Conditioning	No

25 June 2020

Page 1 of 2

If you had selected different layout options such as justified, or columnar, the first page of each report would look similar to this.

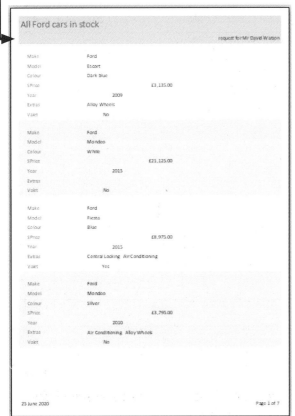

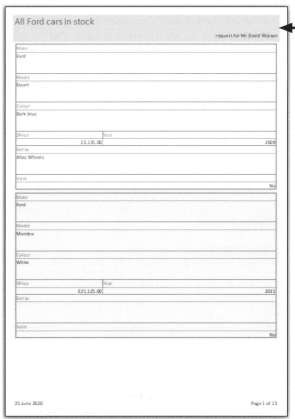

Each section of the report is shown with a light grey bar. The top section is the Report Header. Anything that you place in this section appears only once at the start of the document. Anything that you place in the Page Header is shown at the top of each page, in this case the field names. Similarly, information in the Page Footer is shown at the bottom of each page. The Report Footer appears at the very end of a report, although in this example the Report Footer is empty (it is not shown in white) and therefore will not be shown in this document. The Detail section is the most important, as this single row is where the data is shown for each car. This single row will appear as many rows (as many as there are Ford cars in the database) and display the details of each record.

The task asks you to place your name on the left in the header of each page. Move the cursor to the top of the light grey bar showing the Detail row; click on this so that the cursor changes into an arrow like this.

Hold the left mouse button down and drag the top of the Detail row down about 8 mm. Select all of the controls (objects) in the Page Header by dragging (and holding) the left mouse button. Move all of these controls down the page about 8 mm, so that they look like this.

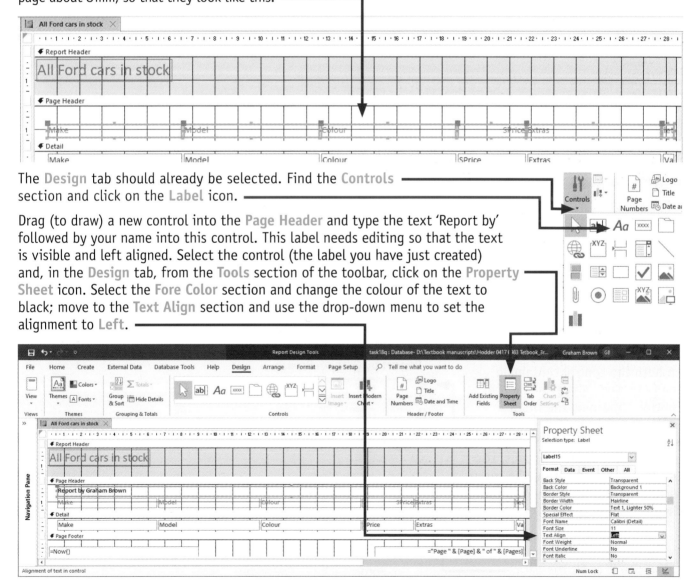

The Design tab should already be selected. Find the Controls section and click on the Label icon.

Drag (to draw) a new control into the Page Header and type the text 'Report by' followed by your name into this control. This label needs editing so that the text is visible and left aligned. Select the control (the label you have just created) and, in the Design tab, from the Tools section of the toolbar, click on the Property Sheet icon. Select the Fore Color section and change the colour of the text to black; move to the Text Align section and use the drop-down menu to set the alignment to Left.

To see what the report will look like at any time, find the Views section of the Design tab and select the Report View. Use this section to change back to the Design View at any time.

The title 'All Ford cars in stock' needs to be centre aligned. Click on the control containing this label and use the drag handle to stretch the control to 26.5 cm (almost the edge of the page). You may need to close the Property Sheet to see this. If you stretch the control further to the right it will add another page width to the final printout, wasting paper when it is printed and will no longer fit to a single page width. Once the control fits the page width, move to the Property Sheet and use the Text Align section to centre align the label.

To add the subtitle, drag the light grey bar for the Page Header down about 8 mm. Add a new label, the full width of the page, in the Report Header just below the title. Type the text 'request for Mr David Watson' into this control. Set the Fore Color to red as before and right align this subtitle in the Property Sheet by changing the Text Align to Right. The Design View of the report looks like this.

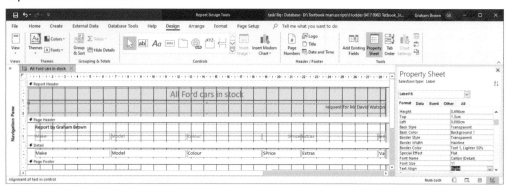

Move to the Home tab and, in the Views section, select Layout View. You can see that not all of the data within the report is fully visible.

Hold down the <Ctrl> key and click on both the control containing the field name Make and on the control containing the first car in the Detail row. Click the left mouse button again on the right edge of one of these controls. Use the drag arrow to narrow the space for these controls, making sure all the names are visible, like this.

Repeat this process to move the Model field closer to the Make field and resize it to fit the data.

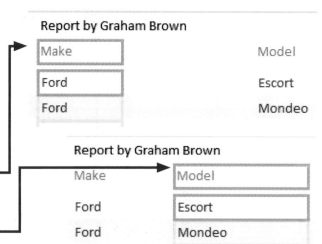

Repeat this process for each field. Save the database as **task18r**. The report should look like this.

All Ford cars in stock					
					request for Mr David Watson

Report by Graham Brown

Make	Model	Colour	SPrice	Extras	Valet
Ford	Escort	Dark blue	£3,135.00	Alloy Wheels	No
Ford	Mondeo	White	£21,125.00		No
Ford	Fiesta	Blue	£8,975.00	Central Locking Air Conditioning	Yes
Ford	Mondeo	Silver	£3,795.00	Air Conditioning Alloy Wheels	No
Ford	Galaxy	Dark blue	£6,875.00	Air Conditioning	No

Activity 18g

Open the database that you saved in Activity 18f.

Produce a report that:
» displays all the data in the stationery table within the width of a landscape page
» has your name on the right in the header of each page
» has a title 'All stationery in stock' centre aligned at the top of the first page
» has a subtitle 'request for the manager' right aligned at the top of the first page.

Task 18s

Open the database that you saved at the end of Task 18r.

Produce a report that:
» displays all the data for the **Make**, **Model**, **Colour**, **SPrice**, **Year** and **Extras** fields for all the cars with alloy wheels from Task 18l, within the width of a portrait page
» has your name in the report header followed by 'Cars with alloy wheels'.

Open the file task18t. Select the Create tab and, in the Reports section, click on the Report Wizard icon. In the Report Wizard window, in the Tables/Queries box, select the query for alloy wheels (that you created in Task 18m). As the task says 'display all the data', and specifies the fields, use the arrow buttons to move only these fields from Available Fields: to the Selected Fields: box. Go through the wizard as you did for the previous task, making sure that you set the page Orientation to Portrait. When the wizard has finished, the report is created and looks similar to this.

Graham Brown Alloy wheels					

Make	Model	Colour	SPrice	Year	Extras
TVR	Tuscan	Black	£20,305.00	2012	Alloy Wheels Air Con
BMW	Z3	Metallic black	£5,635.00	2006	Alloy Wheels
Toyota	Celica	Red	£24,695.00	2014	Air Conditioning Allo
Audi	TT	Black	£17,545.00	2013	Central Locking Leat

You can see that *Access* has attempted to make all the fields fit across the page, but this has not been successful as not all of the data is fully visible.

You must show all of the required data in full. Use the methods you used in Task 18m to reduce the widths of the **Make**, **Model** and **Colour** fields (and their labels) and try to enlarge the Extras field so that all its data can be seen. Using both the Design View and Layout View will make this easier.

Graham Brown Alloy wheels					
Make	Model	Colour	SPrice	Year	Extras
TVR	Tuscan	Black	£20,305.00	2012	Alloy Wheels Air Conditioning
BMW	Z3	Metallic black	£5,635.00	2006	Alloy Wheels
Toyota	Celica	Red	£24,695.00	2014	Air Conditioning Alloy Wheels
Audi	TT	Black	£17,545.00	2013	Central Locking Leather Seats Alloy W

Change to Report View and check that all the data and labels fit within the width of a single page. Other than the Extras field (which holds the most data), all fields are now fully visible. Even after narrowing the field widths, not all the data in the Extras field fits into the available space.

We can enlarge the Extras field by making the control for that field twice as deep. Change to Design View and click the cursor on the top edge of the Page Footer. Drag this down about 8 mm. In the Detail row, click the cursor on the lower edge of the Extras control. Drag this down to double the height of this control.

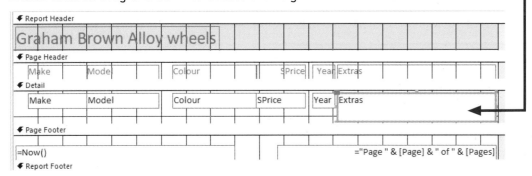

Change to Report View and check that all the data and labels fit within the width of a single page. Save the database as **task18s**. The report should look similar to this.

Graham Brown Alloy wheels					
Make	Model	Colour	SPrice	Year	Extras
TVR	Tuscan	Black	£20,305.00	2012	Alloy Wheels Air Conditioning
BMW	Z3	Metallic black	£5,635.00	2006	Alloy Wheels
Toyota	Celica	Red	£24,695.00	2014	Air Conditioning Alloy Wheels
Audi	TT	Black	£17,545.00	2013	Central Locking Leather Seats Alloy Wheels
Ford	Escort	Dark blue	£3,135.00	2009	Alloy Wheels

Activity 18h

Open the database that you saved in Activity 18g.

Produce a report that:
» displays the data for all the items where the quantity is greater than or equal to 10, selected in Activity 18d, within the width of a portrait page
» has your name in the header of each page
» has a title 'Quantity > = 10' centre aligned at the top of the first page.

Advice

The Discount field can appear as Yes/No, True/False or as a tick box. All of these would be correct for this activity.

Export data

Sometimes whole reports, queries or the data within them need to be exported into other packages to be manipulated as part of a report for someone, or to create a graph or chart.

> ### Task 18t
>
> Export the report saved in Task 18s into rich text format so it can be included in a word-processed document.

In the Navigation pane (on the left side of the window), find the report that you saved in Task 18s and right click the mouse button on the report name to get the drop-down menu.

Select the option to Export. This will open another drop-down menu. You need to export into .rtf format, so select Word RTF File.

This opens the Export – RTF File window. Click on the Browse... button to select a folder to save the document into. You will need to use this file for another task, so select the tick box for Open the destination file after the export operation is complete, then click on OK. The exported file will appear in *Microsoft Word*. Close the Export – RTF File window.

Advice

If you need to export a report without any formatting, select the Text File option.

Advice

If you need to export the data into .csv format (comma separated values), export it first into *Excel*, then save it in .csv format from *Excel*.

> ### Activity 18i
>
> Export the report saved in Activity 18h into:
> - » rich text format
> - » a format that can be used to produce a graph
> - » comma separated value format.

Hide data in a report

There are times when information in a report needs to be hidden in some way. In real applications a single report would be created for more than one task and some data would be hidden. This process is often done automatically using a created report and a programming language. Although that is beyond the scope of this book, the ability to hide fields within a report is useful. An example of this is when an invoice is produced for a customer and the same document is used as a delivery note, so that it shows the details of the items ordered but the costs are hidden. In *Access* this can be done in one of two ways: the first is to make a control invisible; the second is to use a background colour that matches the text colour.

Task 18u

Create a new report showing all the data for all the cars in stock made by Audi, BMW or Mercedes.

Hide all the labels and data for the **ID**, **Valet** and **PDate** fields from the report. Hide the **PPrice** data (but not the title) by setting a black background.

Using the methods used so far in this chapter, create a new query from **tblCars** to select the three makes of car. Create a new report set in landscape format to display all fields for these cars, like this.

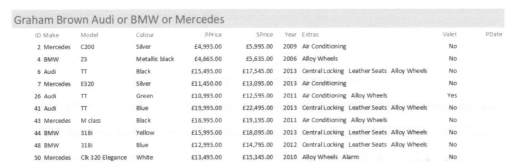

Go into the **Design View** of the report; holding down the <Ctrl> key select all the controls for the **ID**, **Valet** and **PDate** fields. Open the **Property Sheet** and, in the **Visible** section, change the setting from **Yes** to **No**, which will hide these controls. ──────────

To set a black background for the **PPrice** data, in the **Detail** row of the report select the control for **PPrice**. Move the cursor into the **Property Sheet**, selecting the **Format** tab. Find the **Back Color** section and use the [Insert ▾] icon to select the colour palette. ──────────

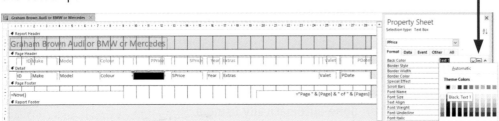

Select the black colour rather than the white background. Set the Fore Color to black in the same way. Change from Design View into Report View to see the changes.

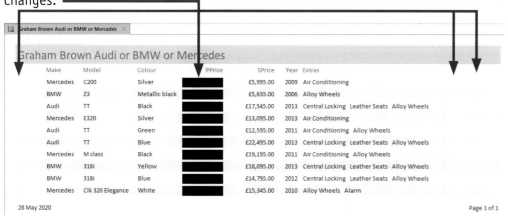

Save the changes to the report and close it.

Advice

Open the file you saved in Activity 18h. Move to **All Access Objects** and **Reports**. Use copy and paste to make a copy of the report for the quantity is greater than or equal to 10, before starting Activity 18j.

Activity 18j

Open the report created in Activity 18h.

Hide the label and data for the **Discount** field in the report and hide only the data in the **PPrice** field by setting a black background.

Advice

If you wish to change the display formats of any field, this can also be done in the **Property Sheet** pane using the **Format** tab. However, it is better to set the formatting for the fields in the **Design View** of the table as changing the display properties will not change the way that the data is stored, and this could lead to errors if fields are used for calculations.

Produce labels

You may be required to produce other forms of output from your database, for example, producing labels to advertise a product or address labels for mailing letters to customers.

Task 18v

Open the file that you saved at the end of Task 18t.

Find all the cars with a sale price of less than £4000 and, for these cars, produce labels that:
» have a page orientation of portrait
» fit two side by side on the page
» have a 16-point, centre aligned heading 'Special Offer' at the top of each label
» show only the fields **Make**, **Model**, **Colour**, **SPrice**, **Year** and **Extras**, sorted into make and model order
» have your name at the bottom right of each label.

Design a new query to extract only the cars with a sale price of less than £4000, selecting only the Make, Model, Colour, SPrice, Year and Extras fields from the table as you step through the Simple Query Wizard. When you have selected these cars, close the query and click the left mouse button on the query so that it is highlighted like this.

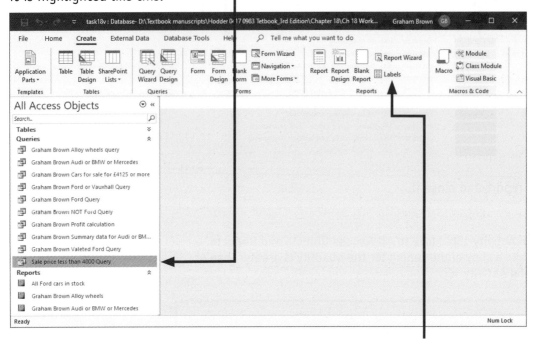

From the Create tab, find the Reports section and click on the Labels icon.

This opens the Label Wizard. Select any label format that contains two labels across the page; in this case, use the Avery J8166 labels as they are slightly larger than some of the other labels (and it is therefore easier to fit all the data and labels on to each label). Click on Next >.

The next screen asks for the font size and colour of the text on the label. Leave this set to a small size (it is easier to enlarge this later, if needed, rather than to reduce it), such as 8 points high. Click on Next >.

Type the text 'Special Offer' in the grey area as the top row of the label. Press <Enter> to move down to the second row.

In Available fields: double click on the Make field. Press <Enter> to move to the next line. Add each field in the same way, entering the new line then

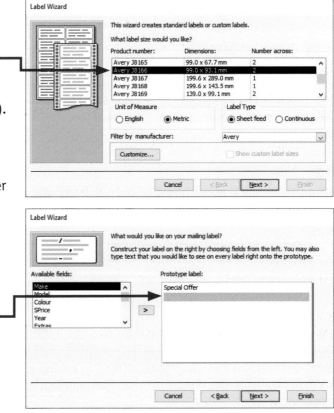

the field. When all of the fields have been moved across, add a final row with your name, then click on

Next > .

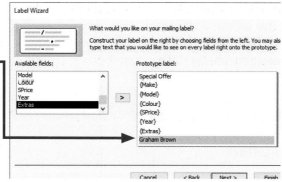

Move the Make, then Model fields across into the right to sort the labels by make and model as specified in the task, then click on Insert ▾.

Give the labels an appropriate name and select the radio button for Modify the label design. Click on Finish .

The Design View looks like this.

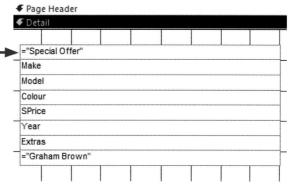

Select all the controls except the one containing the text 'Special Offer'. Drag these down about 8 mm. Move the lower control down the label about 8 mm. Select the middle six controls and move the left edge to the right about 25 mm.

Select the control containing the text 'Special Offer' and stretch it down to give it more space. Open the Property Sheet and set the Font Size to 16 and the Text Align to Center. Stretch the Extras field down to give it more space, so that all the data should be visible. This will need to be checked when the labels are produced and edited again if necessary. Your name at the bottom of the label should also be right aligned by setting the Text Align to Right. Check the labels' layout from the Home tab, using Print Preview to see all the labels set out on the sheet or Report View to see a single label. Save the labels, which should look like this.

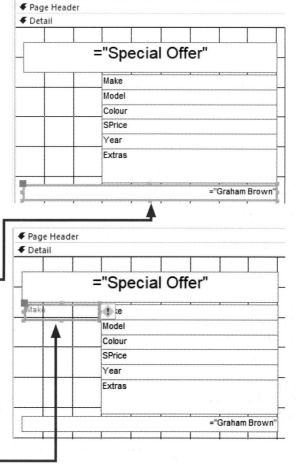

The six middle controls (those containing the fields) need labels. Click on the Design tab and select the label box. Drag the label box out to the left of the Make field, enter the text 'Make' and, in the Property Sheet, set the Font Size to 8. Set the Height of this control to the same as the Make field control. It should now look like this.

Copy this control, paste it five times and move the new labels to the left of each field. Edit the text so that each label box shows what the field is. The label has changed to look like this. ──────

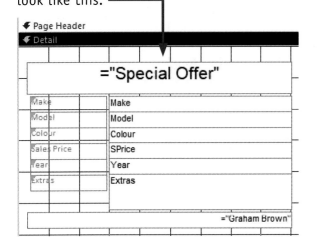

Check the labels' layout from the Home tab using Print Preview to see all the labels set out on the sheet. ─────────────

If need be, make any adjustments to the controls. Save the labels.

Activity 18k

Open the database that you saved at the end of Activity 18j. Find all the stationery items where the discount is 'Yes' and the sale price more than £30.

For these items produce labels that:
» have a page orientation of portrait and fit two side by side on the page
» have a 20-point, right-aligned heading 'Discount Offers' at the top of each label
» show only the fields Type, Description, Colour and SPrice, sorted into colour order
» have your name centre aligned at the bottom of each label.

Format reports

Task 18w

Open the file saved in Task 18v. Using the extract that contains the calculated fields Profit and Percent, produce a new report from all the data that:
» has the PPrice, SPrice and Profit fields formatted as Euro with two decimal places
» has the Percent field formatted as a percentage value with no decimal places.

Open the file saved in Task 18v. Create a new report from all the data in the extract using the Report Wizard. In the Tables/Queries box select the profit calculation query as the source of the data. Select all fields using the double arrow key. Click on [Next >] three times. Set the page Orientation to Landscape then click on [Next >]. Use Profit calculation as the report title. Select the radio button for Modify the report's design, then click on [Finish]. Adjust all the field widths so that all the data fits on the page.

Move to the Detail row of the report. Hold down the <Ctrl> key and select the PPrice, SPrice and Profit field controls. In the Property Sheet select the Format tab and use the drop-down menu in the Format section to select Euro.

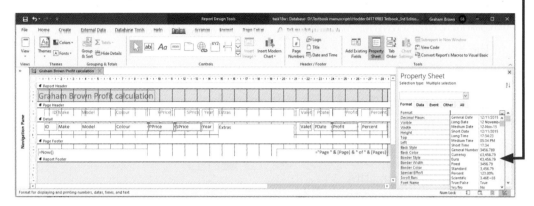

Move to the Decimal Places section and select 2. Click on the View icon to go into Report View and check that the formatting for these fields is in Euro and contains two decimal places.

Repeat this process for the Percent field. Click the left mouse button on the control for Percent in the Detail row of the report. Select the Format tab and use the drop-down menu in the Format section to select Percent from the drop-down list. Move to the Decimal Places section and select 0. Go into Report View to check that the formatting for this field is now correct and contains no decimal places. This is fine, but some field widths may need readjusting so that all data and labels are fully visible. Adjust these before saving the completed report.

Advice

If a question asks for a currency not held in this drop-down menu, select your local Currency format.

Activity 18l

Open the file saved in Activity 18k.

Using the extract that contains the calculated fields Profit, Percent and UnitProfit, produce a new report. Apply appropriate formatting to this report. All currency values must be in Euros with two decimal places. All percentage values must be set to one decimal place.

Formulae in reports

Other calculations may be needed on the data selected. These include calculating the sum (total), average, maximum or minimum values of selected data, or counting the number of items present in the selected data. All of these functions can be produced within a report in *Access*.

Task 18x

Open the file saved in Task 18w. Produce a new report from all the data that:
» displays at the bottom of the report the total profit if all the cars were sold
» displays at the bottom of the report the maximum, minimum and average profit values
» displays the number of cars in this report.

You can use the Profit calculation report from Task 18v to help you with this task. Close this report (if it is open) and right mouse click on it once in the Navigation pane so that you get the drop-down menu. Select Copy, then Paste a new version into the pane with a name that relates it to Task 18x. Open this report in Design View.

Click the left mouse button on the bottom edge of the Report Footer and drag this down about 2 cm, so that this footer is now visible. Select the Design tab, move to the Controls section and select the Text Box icon. ——————

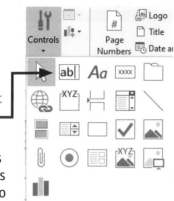

Move down into the Report Footer, click the left mouse button and drag to place a new control, in this case a text box, directly below the Profit column. This positioning is important as this control will be used to calculate the total profit for the data in this report. ——

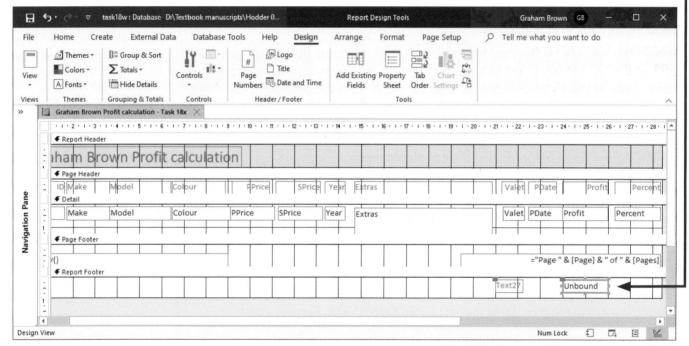

If the Properties pane is not showing, right click the mouse button on the text box that you have just created then select Properties from the drop-down menu. In the Property Sheet select the All tab, find the Control Source section and type the formula =SUM([Profit]) into this row. The Property Sheet will change to this. ——

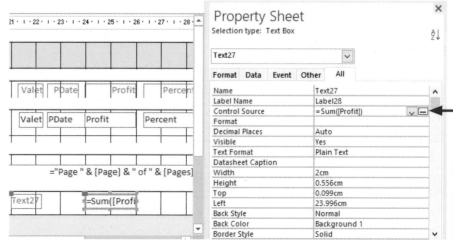

The round brackets are part of the SUM function; the square brackets tell *Access* that this is a field (in this case the **Profit** field calculated at run time). Format this control as **Euro** and set the **Decimal Places** to **2**.

Move the cursor into the label for this text box and type in the **Caption** 'Total Profit'. This can be entered in the label or in the **Property Sheet** pane using the **Caption** row like this.

Change to **Report View** and make sure that the control is in the correct place and appears to give the right answer (it is not too large or too small).

Rather than repeating this process four more times, it will be quicker to copy and paste these controls and edit each one to give the required results. Use the **lasso tool** to highlight both the **Text Box** and its **Label**. Use <Ctrl> and <C> to copy, then use <Ctrl> and <V> to paste the copies of these controls. Using <Ctrl> and <V> pastes the new controls directly under the existing ones and you do not need to reorganise the controls. It also extends the bottom of the **Report Footer** as needed. If you right mouse click and use **Paste** from the drop-down menu, this pastes the controls in the top left-hand corner of the **Report Footer** and you then have to drag and position each set of controls. Repeat <Ctrl> and <V> until you have five sets of controls like this.

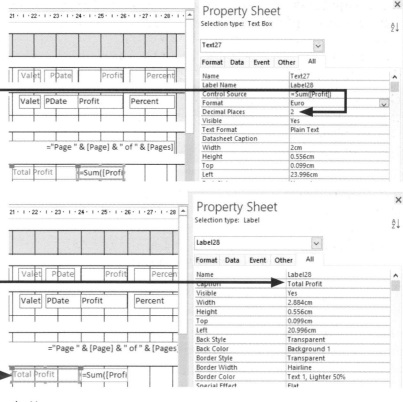

Advice

The lasso tool can be accessed by dragging with the left mouse button clicked down.

In the last four controls containing labels, change the **Captions** to 'Maximum profit', 'Minimum profit', 'Average profit' and 'Number of cars'. Select the second **Text Box** (for the maximum profit) and change the formula so that it becomes **=MAX([Profit])**. Change the formulae for the minimum profit so that it becomes **=MIN([Profit])** and for the average profit so that it becomes **=AVG([Profit])**. In the final control to count the number of cars, change the formula so that it becomes **=COUNT([Profit])**. The controls should now look like this.

In the **Property Sheet** pane for the final **Text Box**, change the **Format** back from Currency to **General Number**. Set the **Decimal Places** for this control to **0**. Check the layout and calculations in **Report View**. The completed calculations look like this.

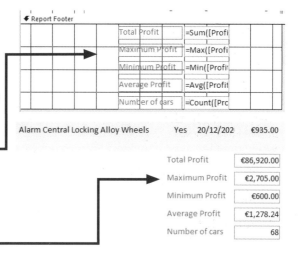

Save the report. If you need to show evidence of the formulae that you used, use screenshot evidence of the calculated controls.

Advice

If you are using screenshot evidence of calculated controls, make sure that each control is wide enough to show all of the formulae in full.

Activity 18m

Open the file saved in Activity 18l. Copy and edit the report which contains the calculated fields to produce one that:
» displays at the bottom of the report the maximum and minimum percentage profit for all the stationery items in stock
» displays at the bottom of the report the average profit per item
» displays the number of items in stock
» uses appropriate formatting for all data.

18.3.2 Sort data in a report

Although *Access* has the ability to sort data in both tables and queries, it is easier to save the sorting until the data is produced in an *Access* report.

Task 18y

Open the file saved in Task 18x. Produce a report that:
» displays all the data for the cars made by Ford or Vauxhall
» fits within the width of a single page
» is sorted into ascending order of make and model, then into descending order of sale price
» has your name in the report header followed by 'Ford or Vauxhall'.

You created the query in Task 18k. To produce this report, select the Create tab and click on the Report Wizard icon. In the Tables/Queries box select the Ford or Vauxhall query. Select all fields using the double arrow key and then click on [Next >] twice to open the Sorting window. Use the drop-down lists to select the Make field, then the Model field and, finally, the SPrice field. For the SPrice field, click on [Ascending] to the right of this field and it will toggle (change) to [Descending] like this. ——————

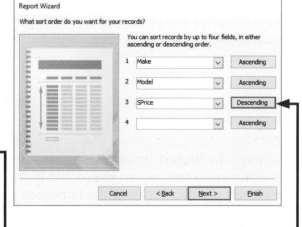

When the fields have been set as shown, click on [Next >]. Set the Orientation to Landscape and run through the final stages of the wizard, giving this report a suitable name. This process is the same for other data types such as dates.

Activity 18n

Open the file saved in Activity 18m. Produce a new report from all the data that:
» displays all the blue or black stationery items
» fits within the width of a single page
» is sorted into ascending order of colour and type, and then into descending order of description
» has your name in the report header followed by 'Blue or black stationery items'.

---

19 Presentations

In this chapter you will learn how to:
★ understand what a presentation is
★ create a presentation using a text file
★ use a master slide to place objects
★ apply slide layout
★ insert a new slide
★ move a slide
★ delete a new slide
★ insert and edit objects on a slide
★ create audience and presenter notes
★ insert and edit a hyperlink on a slide
★ insert an action button on a slide
★ add alternative text/ScreenTip to an object
★ apply transitions between slides
★ apply animation effects
★ hide a slide within a presentation
★ display a presentation
★ print a presentation.

For this chapter you will need these source:
★ computer.png
★ email.png
★ html.rtf
★ powerpoint.rtf
★ pressound.mp3
★ presvideo.avi
★ slogan.jpg
★ webpage.rtf
★ website.jpg

19.1 Create a presentation

19.1.1 What is a presentation?

A presentation is a series of slides used to give information to an audience. A presentation can be used in many different ways: to teach or inform as a visual aid in a lecture, or as a constant on-screen carousel giving information or advertising, for example, in a shopping centre or mall.

The media for delivery and type of presentation developed will depend on the purpose of the presentation and the target audience. For example, you would design a presentation on road safety to a class of five-year-old children to be:

» short (for a short attention span)
» have only a few simple words (as they cannot read fluently)
» contain bright, colourful, moving images (to keep their attention).

The media for the delivery of this presentation would be a multimedia projector and large screen. It is important to understand all of this information before starting to design and develop a presentation, as different media will require different screen/page sizes. Most presentations will require a consistent colour scheme and consistently applied styles to all slides. You will be given details of these colour schemes and styles in any questions. Consistency is really important in the development of your presentations; simple themes and colour schemes using one or two fonts save presentations from being messy and disorganised. A well-structured and organised presentation usually says to the audience, 'I am a well-organised and reliable person'. One way of doing this is to use a master slide.

19.1.2 Create a presentation using a text file

If you are given a source file that contains the slide contents, in older versions of *PowerPoint* the slide master/s will need to be created first and the slide contents imported. In more recent versions, the slide contents will need to be opened and the master slide created after the contents. If new slides or slide contents are to be added by hand, then setting up the master slide would be a good starting point.

Task 19a

Open the file **powerpoint.rtf**, which will be used to create a short presentation for IGCSE students telling them how to use *PowerPoint*. The medium for delivery will be a multimedia projector with a 4:3 aspect ratio.

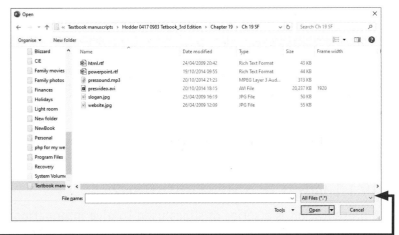

Open *PowerPoint* and double click the left mouse button on **Blank Presentation**. Select the **File** tab followed by **Open**. Find the source file using the **Browse** option, which opens the **Open** window. Select the correct directory and change the file type box from **All PowerPoint Presentations** to **All Files**.

The source files will be supplied as either text files (in .txt format) or rich text files (in .rtf format). The difference between the two is that .rtf files hold some formatting and styles (such as text size and fonts) while .txt files only contain the characters and no formatting or styles.

Double click the left mouse button on the file powerpoint.rtf. The file opens like this.

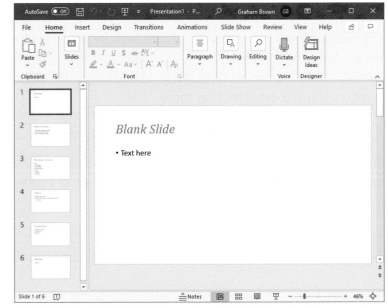

Change the slide size

The layout of a presentation will depend on the medium for its delivery. In this task you are told that the medium for delivery will be a multimedia projector with a 4:3 **aspect ratio**. If you are not told the aspect ratio in the question, assume that it is 4:3 for multimedia projectors and 16:9 for presentations using a monitor. To change the slide size, go to the size section of the toolbar, click on the Design tab, then in the Customize section, click on the Slide Size icon. This drop-down menu appears.

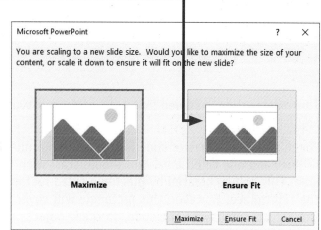

Select the correct aspect ratio for the task, in this case Standard (4:3). Because the slide contents have been opened and the default setting for *PowerPoint* on this computer is an aspect ratio of 16:9, we get this pop-up window. If you get this message, select the Ensure Fit button.

Save this as a presentation with the filename **task19a**.

Before changing any of the slides, you will now create and edit the master slide.

19.2 Use a master slide

A master slide allows you to design the layout of all your slides before you start adding objects (such as text or images) to individual slides. It holds information on colours, fonts, effects and the positioning of objects on the slides.

19.2.1 Use a master slide to place objects

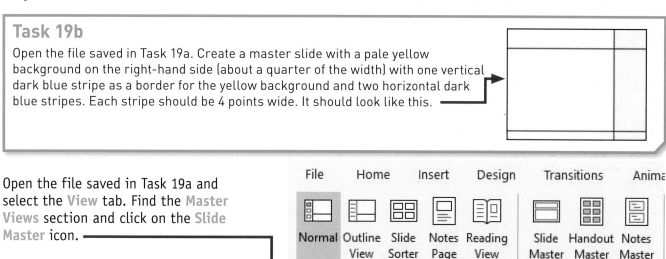

Task 19b

Open the file saved in Task 19a. Create a master slide with a pale yellow background on the right-hand side (about a quarter of the width) with one vertical dark blue stripe as a border for the yellow background and two horizontal dark blue stripes. Each stripe should be 4 points wide. It should look like this.

Open the file saved in Task 19a and select the View tab. Find the Master Views section and click on the Slide Master icon.

The display will change to this.

Use the scroll bar on the left of the window to scroll to the top and select the Primary Master Slide (the top one).

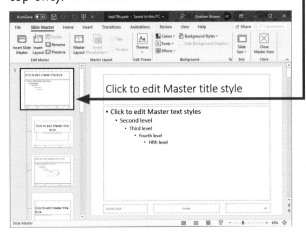

This master slide is copied by all the other sub-types that are listed below it.

For this task, the master slide has to contain a number of lines and one filled area. You should start with the filled area. This will be created by placing a filled rectangle in the right place. However, this rectangle will cover some of the objects already on the slide, so these objects must be resized or moved out of the way first. Select the title text placeholder and use the drag handle to resize this text box.

Repeat this for the body text placeholder on the master slide. This box has also been made less deep using the lower drag handle to create space to move the slide numbering.

The text box containing the slide numbering is too small to resize, so this will need to be moved from the right-hand side. Drag the entire text box into the space created below the body text box. The page layout should now look like this.

Select the Insert tab and find the Illustrations section. Click on the Shapes icon and select the Rectangle option from the drop-down menu.

Use the drag tool to drag a new rectangle that fills about a quarter of the right-hand side of the slide. Make sure that this rectangle fits to the top, bottom and right edges of the slide and leaves no white space.

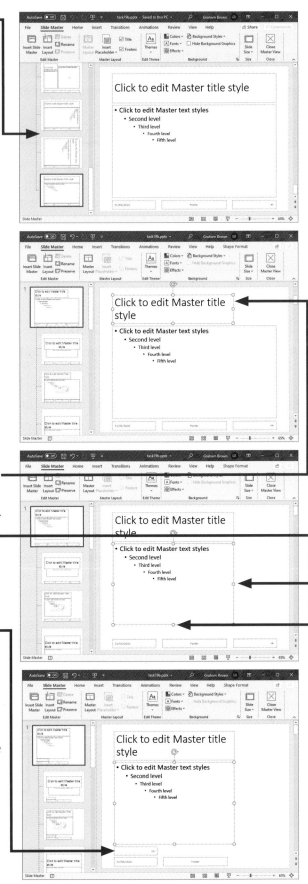

Advice

Many shapes, such as the rectangle, can also be found in the Drawing section of the Home tab.

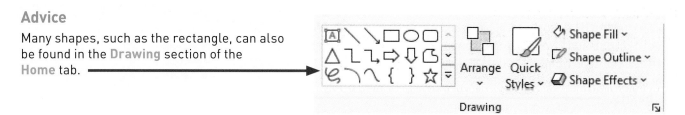

You now need to edit the appearance of the rectangle. Select the Home tab and find the Drawing section. Use the Shape Fill icon to select the fill colour and click on the Shape Outline icon, followed by No Outline from the sub-menu.

This removes the border from the rectangle. The master slide should look like this.

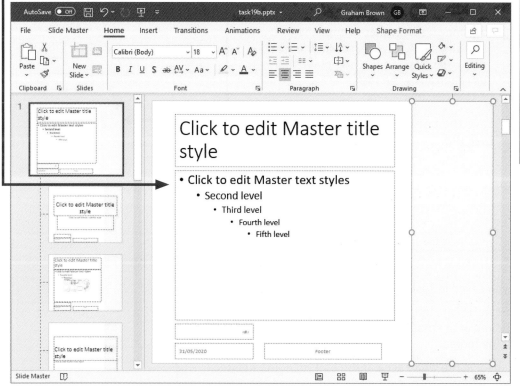

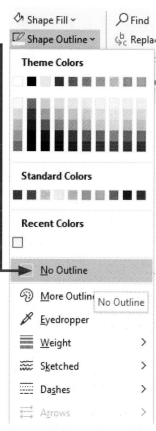

You will notice that all the other master slides (down the left-hand side of the window) now show the yellow background.

Next you need to add the three blue lines to the slide. Select the Home tab then, in the Drawing section, select the Shapes icon and click on the Line option from the drop-down menu. Use the drag tool to draw a vertical line on the border between the yellow and white areas.

Advice

Holding down the <Shift> key while placing the line forces it to be either vertical, horizontal or at 45 degrees.

Use the Shape Outline icon to change the line colour to dark blue. The Shape Outline icon can also be used to change the line thickness. Select Weight and, from the sub-menu, select the line weight. For this task the line weight should be 4 points. This option is not available from this menu so select the nearest weight available, in this case 4½ points.

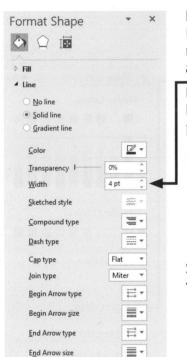

Right mouse click on the line and select Format Shape... from the drop-down menu. From the Format Shape pane adjust the line Width: to 4 points.

Repeat this process to add the two horizontal lines to the master slide in the positions shown in the task.

Advice

You may find it easier to copy the first line and paste it twice; rotate the two new copies and resize and place them as required by the task.

Save the presentation with the filename **task19b**.

Task 19c

Open the presentation that you saved in Task 19b.

Include the heading 'Using PowerPoint', left aligned in a dark blue, 60-point serif font above the blue line at the top of the master slide. Include an automated slide number in the bottom left of the footer.

Enter your name, centre aligned, in the white area at the bottom of the master slide. Use a black, 14 point, serif font.

Place the image **computer.png** in the right-hand area. Crop and/or resize the image so that it fits within the yellow area and will not overlay the dark blue lines. Do not distort the image. Make sure that the image fills more than 50 per cent of the available space. Save your presentation.

To include the heading, add a new text box in the top left section of the slide. This text box will replace the title text box, so move the title text box down the slide to below the blue line. Go to the Insert tab and in the Text section click on the Text Box icon. Drag out a new text box then select the Home tab and find the Font section. Set the font size to 60 point and select a serif font, for example Times New Roman. Enter the text 'Using PowerPoint' into this text box. You may need to move/resize the master text styles box. The window should now look like this.

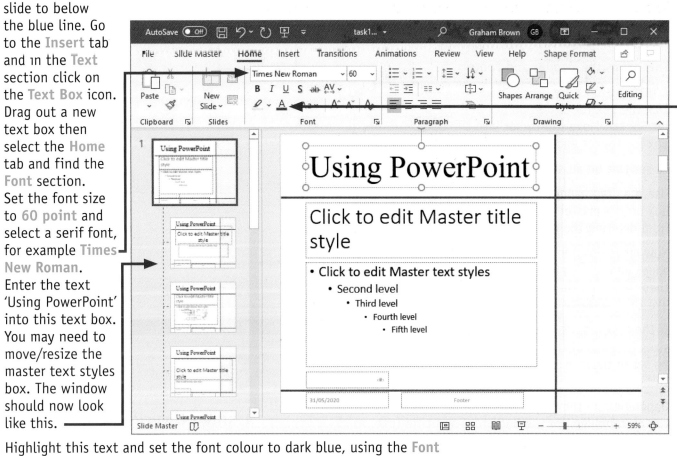

Highlight this text and set the font colour to dark blue, using the Font Color icon.

As the text is already left aligned, do not adjust the alignment. Notice how the text box has been aligned with the other objects on the slide so it can be checked that the text is left aligned.

The automated slide number is in the object moved from the right side of the footer. The task asks for this to be placed on the left in the footer. Resize this object (as shown previously) and change its alignment to left aligned by clicking on the Align Text Left icon in the Paragraph section under the Home tab. Drag the box into the bottom left corner. As the date is not required on all pages, this object can be deleted before moving the automated slide number.

Enlarge the automated footer so that it fills the width of the white space, as shown. Make sure that you enlarge the footer so that it is the same width as the main text box and overlaps the slide number, which will ensure that it can be seen that the object is centre aligned within the text area. Change the text and the slide number to a black, 14-point, serif font as described in the task. The finished footer area should look like this.

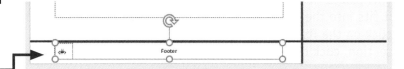

Although you have set the footer area on the master slide, you have not yet added your name to the footer, nor told *PowerPoint* to display the page numbers. To do this, select the Insert tab then, in the Text section, click on the Header & Footer icon. ─────────────

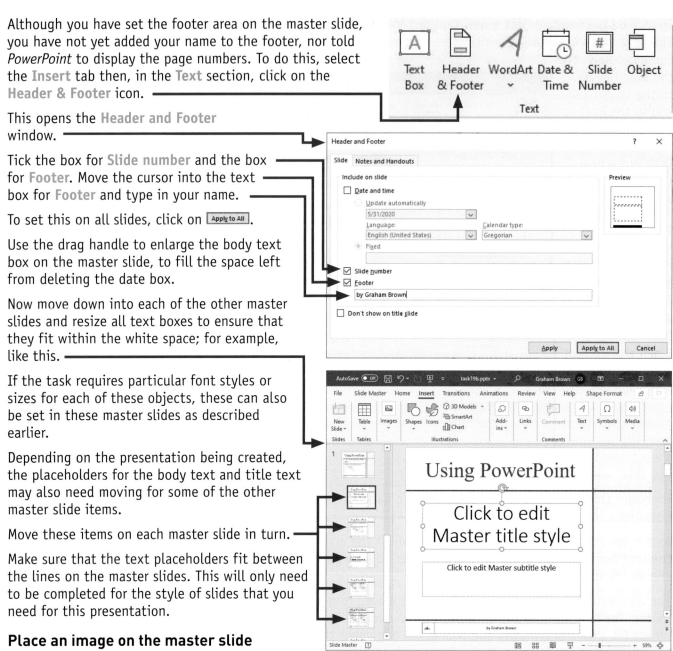

This opens the Header and Footer window. ─────────────

Tick the box for Slide number and the box for Footer. Move the cursor into the text box for Footer and type in your name.

To set this on all slides, click on Apply to All.

Use the drag handle to enlarge the body text box on the master slide, to fill the space left from deleting the date box.

Now move down into each of the other master slides and resize all text boxes to ensure that they fit within the white space; for example, like this. ─────────────

If the task requires particular font styles or sizes for each of these objects, these can also be set in these master slides as described earlier.

Depending on the presentation being created, the placeholders for the body text and title text may also need moving for some of the other master slide items.

Move these items on each master slide in turn. ───────

Make sure that the text placeholders fit between the lines on the master slides. This will only need to be completed for the style of slides that you need for this presentation.

Place an image on the master slide

To insert an image, return to the top Slide Master and select the Insert tab. In the Images section click on the Pictures icon to open the drop-down menu. Select the Insert Picture From option for This Device…. This opens the Insert Picture window. Locate the file computer.png and click on Open

This places this image on to the master slide. Move and resize it so that it fits into the correct area. To crop the image, select the image and click on the Picture Format tab if it is not already selected. In the Size section, click on the Crop icon. ─────────────

With the crop tool selected, use the drag handles of the image to crop the edges so that it changes from this to this.

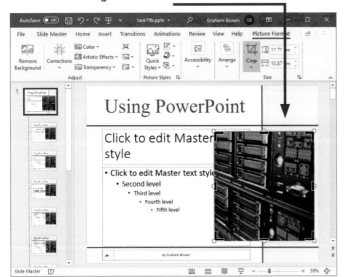 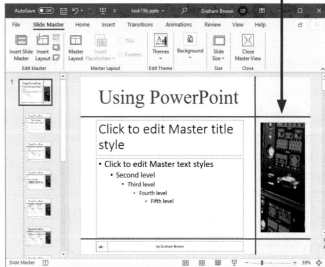

When the master slide is complete, select the View tab and, in the Presentation Views section, click on the icon for Normal page layout. Save your presentation as **task19c**.

Create styles for slide layout

Task 19d

Open the presentation that you saved in Task 19c. Create the following styles of text throughout the entire presentation:

» heading: dark blue, serif, left aligned, 40 point

» subheading: blue, sans-serif, centre aligned, 30 point

» bulleted list: black, sans-serif, left aligned, 24 point.

Save the presentation.

Select the View tab followed by Slide Master and select the Primary Master Slide (the top master slide). Highlight all the text in the heading (title) style placeholder and click the right mouse button to obtain a drop-down menu and miniature toolbar to allow you to edit the text style.

The heading style needs to be a dark blue, left aligned, serif font. Select a serif font, such as Times New Roman, using the font list. Use the Text Color icon to select a dark blue colour and (if need be) use the Align Text Left icon to change the text alignment. Use the drop-down list for the Font Size to change it to 40 point. The text box should now look like this.

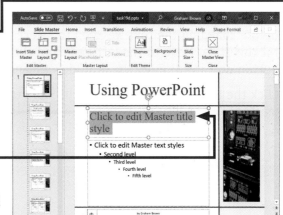

Use a similar method to set the first level of the bulleted list to a black, sans-serif, left-aligned font (no changes are needed for these parts), 24 point high. Adjust the font sizes for the other levels of bullet points so that they are smaller relative to this one.

The subheading style is not visible in this master slide, so you need to move into the master slide for the Title Slide Layout (the first master slide down). Highlight the text for the Master subtitle style and set this to a blue, sans-serif, centre aligned, 30 point font. Use the same method as you did for the Master title style. Move through each slide master in turn and edit any of the styles on other page layouts that need to be set.

Select the View tab and the Normal icon. Check each slide carefully to make sure that the styles that you have changed have been applied to each slide of the presentation.

It is very important to make sure that all slides are consistent. Do not assume that the software itself will format the slides correctly and do check each slide carefully. Save your presentation as **task19d**.

19.3 Edit a presentation

19.3.1 Apply slide layout

The styles created on the master slide in task 19d should have been applied to all the text on the slides in the presentation, but it is always worth checking each slide carefully to make sure that the styles on the slides match those required by the task. Should there be any text not formatted as required by the task, it can be amended on each slide. This sometimes occurs when *PowerPoint* resizes text to make it fill the available space on a slide. Save the presentation again as **task19d**.

Task 19e

Open the presentation that you saved in Task 19d. Change the layout of slide 1 to be a title slide.

Add a new slide between slides 4 and 5. This slide will contain a heading, a chart and a bulleted list. Save the presentation.

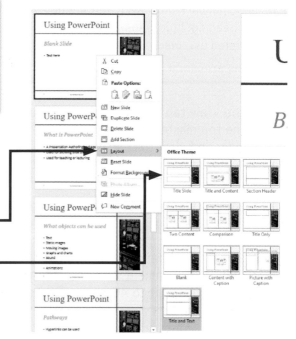

Open the presentation saved in Task 19d. Select slide 1. Slide 1 is not formatted as a Title Slide with a title and subtitle, so before changing the text we need to select the correct layout for this slide. Move to the left pane and click the right mouse button on Page 1. From the drop-down menu select Layout.

Click the left mouse button on Title Slide to apply this slide master to this slide.

We will add the text to this slide later in the chapter.

19.3.2 Insert a new slide

Move back into the left pane. To select where to place the new slide, click the cursor between slides 4 and 5 so that it shows a red horizontal line like this.

Select the Insert tab and, in the Slides section, select the drop-down menu for New Slide. Look at the different slide layouts available from this menu.

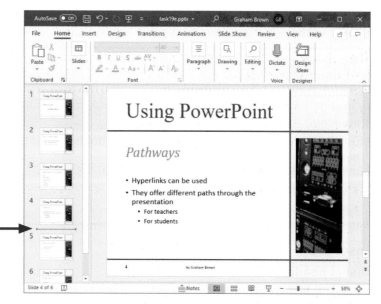

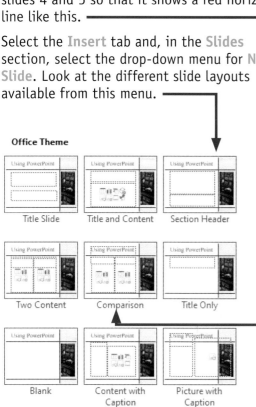

Select the layout that matches the slide you are going to produce. This slide needs a small bulleted list and a chart, so the most appropriate slide type will be Comparison. Although the options for 'Content with Caption' and 'Two Content' both look correct, it is more difficult to manipulate the contents of both of these boxes than it is using the 'Comparison' boxes. The 'Comparison' boxes both have bulleted lists available. Click once on this icon to get the new slide.

Save the presentation as **task19e**.

19.3.3 Move a slide

Task 19f

Open the presentation that you saved in Task 19e. Move slide 4 so that it is after the current slide 5. Delete slide 7. Save the presentation.

Open the presentation saved in Task 19e. In the left pane. select slide 4 and hold down the left mouse button on this slide. Drag it down to below slide 5 like this.

Slides 4 and 5 have now changed places and been renumbered like this.

19.3.4 Delete a slide

The task requires you to delete slide 7 from the presentation. In the left pane, click on slide 7 to select it, like this.

Click the right mouse button on this slide to get the drop-down menu and select the option for Delete Slide. Save the presentation as **task19f**.

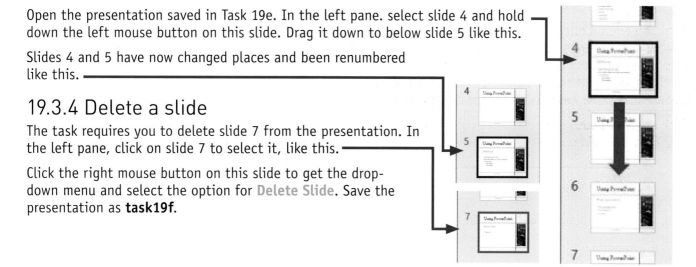

19.3.5 Insert and edit objects on a slide

> ### Task 19g
> Open the presentation that you saved in Task 19f.
>
> On slide 1 add the heading 'Hints and tips', and add the subheading 'for IGCSE students'.
>
> On slide 4 add the heading 'Ease of use' and on the left of the slide add this bulleted list:
> - 86% of students found it easy to use
> - 120 students in the sample.
>
> Save the presentation.

Insert text

Insert heading
Open the presentation saved in Task 19f. Select slide 1. Replace the text 'Blank Slide' with the heading Hints and tips.

Insert subheading
In the lower placeholder, for the subheading, replace the text 'Text here' with for IGCSE students, so that slide 1 looks like this.

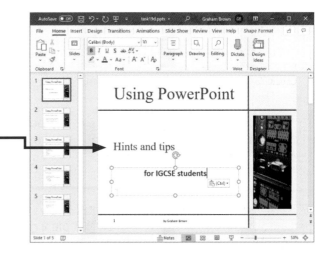

Click the left mouse button on slide 4 to select it. Delete both of the top text boxes that say 'Click to add text'. These are not needed in this slide. To do this click on the line for the text box and press the <Backspace> or <Delete> key. Use the drag handles to edit the two larger placeholders below them to make them fit the available space. The slide will change from this to this.

Click in the title placeholder and add the heading 'Ease of use'.

Insert a bulleted list

Select the left placeholder object below the title. Click on the bulleted text 'Click to add text'. This will change this object into a text box. Type in the text '86% of students found it easy to use', ‹Return›, '120 students in the sample', so that it looks similar to this. Save the presentation as **task19g**.

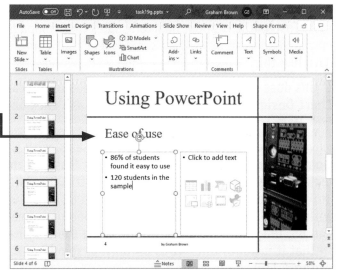

Create a chart in *PowerPoint*

> ## Task 19h
>
> Open the presentation that you saved in Task 19g.
>
> On slide 4 add a chart created from this data: Easy – 103, Difficult – 12, No response – 5. Show the percentage of students in each category.
>
> Save the presentation.

Open the presentation saved in Task 19g. Select slide 4. Click on the chart icon in the right object on this slide. This opens the Insert Chart window.

You must decide which type of chart is the most appropriate for the task. In this case, you are told to show the percentage of students in each category. There is a clue to the need for percentage values in the bullet points on the left of the slide. Because the chart needs to show percentage values (parts of a whole), a pie chart is the most appropriate type of chart.

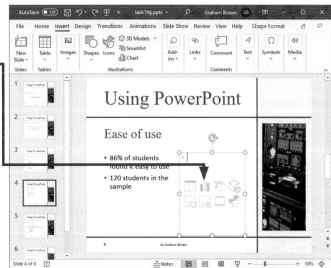

Select, from the All Charts list, a Pie chart, then choose a simple layout (the left option) from the vailable chart types and click on ⬚ OK ⬚. This opens a default pie chart, but does not use the correct data. The slide should now look like this.

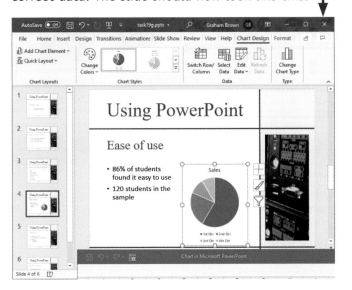

As you can see, the chart does not relate to the data for this task. Instead, it is about quarterly sales in a company. It may also open an *Excel* style spreadsheet that contains the data like this.

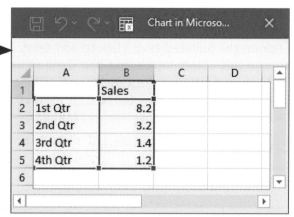

If this does not appear, with the chart selected, locate the Chart Design tab, find the Data section and click on the Edit Data icon.

Move into cell B1 and replace the label 'Sales' with the word 'Students'. In cell A2, enter the text 'Easy' so that it replaces the existing text, in A3 type 'Difficult' and, in A4, 'No response'. Replace the sales figures in B2 with 103, in B3 with 12 and, in B4, with 5. Delete the contents of cells A5 and B5. Drag the blue range marker using the drag handle so that it includes cells A1 to B4 only. It should now look like this.

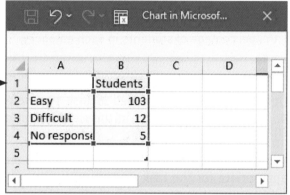

The slide now contains the chart. Close the spreadsheet containing the data. Save the presentation as **task19h**.

Advice

Charts may be created from **contiguous** or **non-contiguous** data and can have features such as titles, legends and labels for axes and sectors. All the features that you studied in Chapter 16 can be applied to a graph or chart before it is cut and pasted into the slide.

Insert a chart imported from a spreadsheet

The latest versions of *Microsoft Office* have made the process of creating a chart in *Excel* almost identical to the creation of a chart within *PowerPoint*. In *Excel* select the Insert tab and, in the Charts section, click on Pie Chart. For more detail of the production of the chart please refer to Chapter 16. When the chart has been created and fully labelled, copy the chart in *Excel* and paste it on to a slide in *PowerPoint*. Resize the chart to fit the available space.

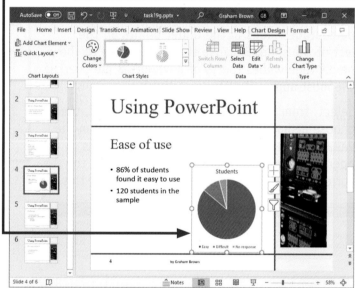

Insert a still image on a slide

Task 19i

Open the presentation that you saved in Task 19h.

Add the image **slogan.jpg** to the bottom of the final slide, above the blue line. Crop the image so that the red line and all contents below the slogan are removed. Resize the image so that it fits about 5 mm from the left edge of the slide, 2 mm above the lower blue line and 5 mm to the left of the vertical blue line, maintaining its aspect ratio. Adjust the brightness and contrast of the image so that the background colour (pale yellow) is not visible. Save the presentation.

In Task 19c you inserted a new image into the master slide. For this task you are going to insert an image into a normal slide.

Advice

It is easier to manipulate these objects if the ruler is showing. To select the ruler, use the **View** tab, find the **Show/Hide** section and click on the tick box for **Ruler**.

Open the presentation saved in Task 19h and use the **Slides** tab to open slide 7. Select the **Insert** tab, locate the **Images** section, then click on the **Pictures** icon and from the drop-down menu select **This Device**. This opens the **Insert Picture** window. Search through the files until you locate **slogan.jpg**, select the file and click on [Insert ▾] to insert the image into the slide. Click the left mouse button on the image and from the **Picture Format** tab click on the **Crop** tool icon.

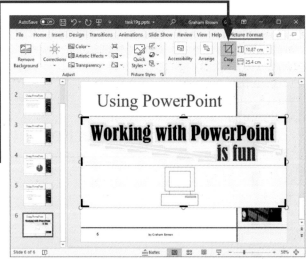

Drag the lower crop handle up the screen above the red line, but below the red text, to crop the image. Click the left mouse button off the image then back on it and drag the image down so that the left and bottom edges are in the correct place on the slide.

Grab the top right drag handle and drag this to resize the image to the correct position to the left of the vertical blue line. The image should now look like this.

To remove the pale yellow background colour from this image, you need to adjust the image brightness and contrast. Click the right mouse button on the image and select **Format Picture...** from the drop-down menu. This opens the **Format Picture** pane to the right of the slide. Select the **Picture** option from the right. Click on the **Picture Corrections** option to open this menu.

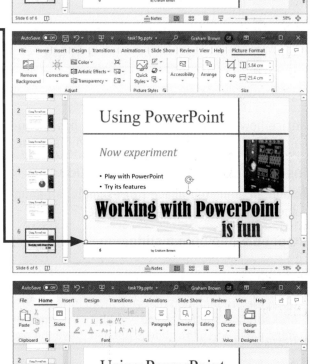

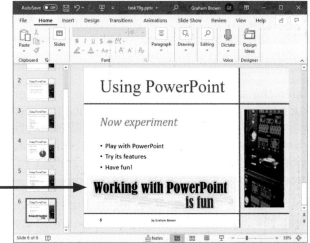

Move the sliders for the Brightness and Contrast, so that the pale-yellow background disappears but the other colours remain unaffected. These figures are found using trial and error: both settings change from 0% to a brightness of around 35% and a contrast of around 75%.

When you have completed this, close the Format Picture pane. The slide should now look like this.

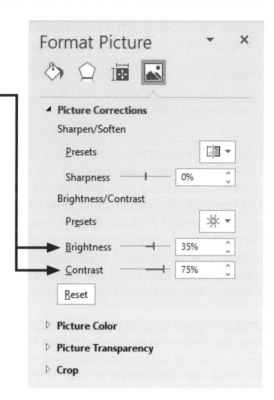

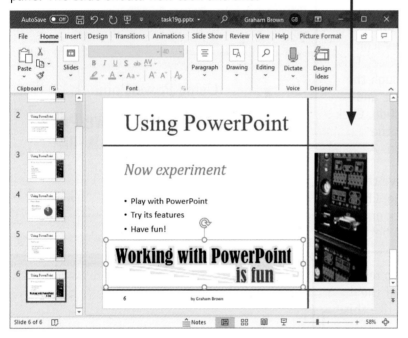

Notice how the red colour in the text has changed from its original dark red colour (see above) to this shade of red. Save the presentation as **task19i**.

Insert an animated image on a slide

To add an animated image (for example, an animated gif file) to a slide, use the same method as adding a still image.

Insert a video onto a slide

Task 19j

Open the presentation that you saved in Task 19i. Add a new slide at the end of the presentation into which you will place the video **presvideo.avi**. Make sure that this video plays when the slide is opened. Save the presentation.

Open the presentation and scroll down in the left pane to the end of the last slide. Click just below this slide to place the orange line at the bottom like this. From the Home tab select, from the Slides section, the New Slide icon and then click on the Title and Content option. Add an appropriate title, such as 'Sample video', in the title placeholder. Look carefully in the centre of the content placeholder and choose the Insert Video icon.

In the Insert Video window, locate the file presvideo.avi then click [Insert ▾]. Drag the video so that it sits centrally in the area, ignoring the controls at the bottom.

Click on the **Playback** tab and find the **Video Options** section. Set the **Start:** setting to **Automatically** using the drop-down menu.

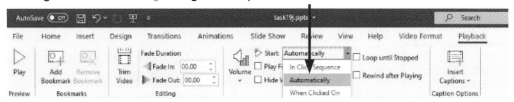

The video will now play when the slide is opened. Save the presentation as **task19j**.

Insert an audio clip into a slide

Task 19k

Open the presentation that you saved in Task 19j. Add the audio clip **pressound.mp3** to slide 1. Play this sound track only once when the presentation is run. Save the presentation.

Open the presentation in slide 1. Select the **Insert** tab, locate the **Media** section, click on the **Audio** icon, then from the drop-down menu click on **Audio on My PC....**

From the **Insert Audio** window, locate and choose the file **pressound.mp3** and click on [Insert ▼]. The audio file (sometimes called a sound clip) is now on this slide. The toolbar changes to the **Playback** tab. Move the cursor to the **Audio Styles** section and double click the left mouse button to select **Play in Background**.

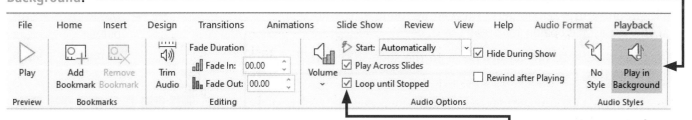

This will automatically change some of the other settings, for example, the **Start** option changes from 'On Click' to 'Automatically' and the 'Play Across Slides' and 'Loop until Stopped' check boxes have been ticked.

As the question asks for the audio track to be played only once, remove the tick from the **Loop until Stopped** check box. Test the presentation to check that it works. Save the presentation as **task19k**.

Insert a table on a slide

Task 19l

Open the presentation that you saved in Task 19k. Add, below the bulleted list on slide 4, a table like this:

Number of students	
Easy to use	103
Difficult	12
No response	5

Save the presentation.

Open the presentation and move to slide 4. Select the **Insert** tab, then from the **Tables** section select **Table**. When the drop-down table selector appears, drag the cursor over this to get a **2 × 4 Table**. ——————

Click the left mouse button when the 2 × 4 is selected and the table appears like this. ——————

Highlight the two cells in the top row together and click the right mouse button to get the drop-down menu. Select **Merge Cells** from this menu. Enter the text from the task into the table so that it looks like this. ——————

The table needs to be formatted to match the task. Use the methods learned in Section 13.2 Tables, to perform the following actions. Resize the columns so that there is no excessive white space. Centre align the contents of row 1. Right align all numeric values. The table should look like this. ——————

Make sure that the table is selected, then from the **Table Design** tab, in the **Table Styles** section, use the drop-down menu to select a style with a white background and black borders. This can be found at the bottom of the list as the option for **Clear Table**. ——————

Drag the table into the correct place on the slide so that it looks like this. ——————

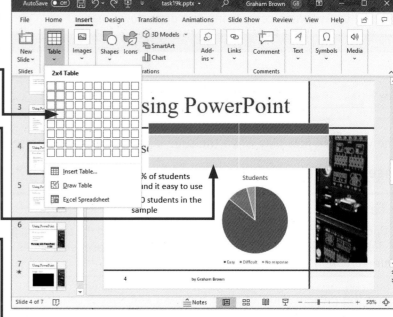

Number of students	
Easy to use	103
Difficult	12
No response	5

Number of students	
Easy to use	103
Difficult	12
No response	5

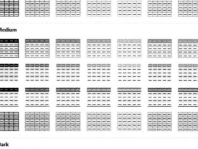

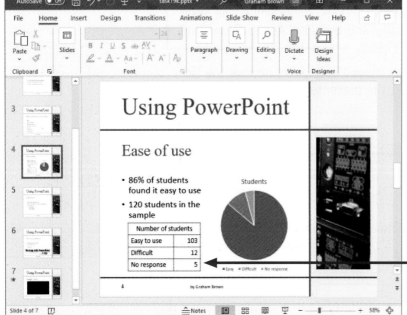

Save the presentation as **task19l**.

Insert other symbols and shapes on a slide

Task 19m

Open the presentation that you saved in Task 19l. Add:

» an arrow on slide 4 pointing from the first bullet point to the largest segment of the pie chart

» a callout box on slide 5 telling the reader that the image has been placed on the master slide

» the text '© Microsoft' at the end of the first bullet point on slide 6 in a black, 12-point, sans-serif font

» a 6-point, horizontal, red line on slide 6, above the image you inserted in Task 19i.

Open the presentation and select slide 4 using the left pane. Select the Insert tab, locate the Illustrations section, then click on the Shapes icon. A drop-down menu of available shapes will appear.

Select an arrow to be included on the slide.

Click the left mouse button where you want the arrow to start and drag the point of the arrow to the position that you want it to finish. This selects the Shape Format tab. You can adjust the colour and weight of the arrow using the Shape Styles section if required. The finished slide should look like this.

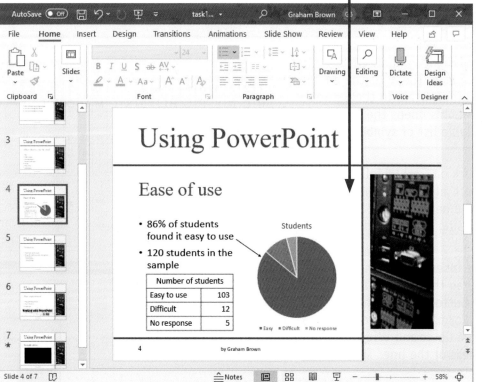

To place the callout box on slide 5, select slide 5 and again select the Insert tab, locate the Illustrations section, then click on the Shapes icon. This time select a callout box from the Callouts section of the drop-down menu.

Click on the slide and drag the callout box to draw it. It is easier if you make the box too large and reduce the size later.

When you have placed the box, grab and drag the yellow handle to move the point of the callout box so that it points to the image.

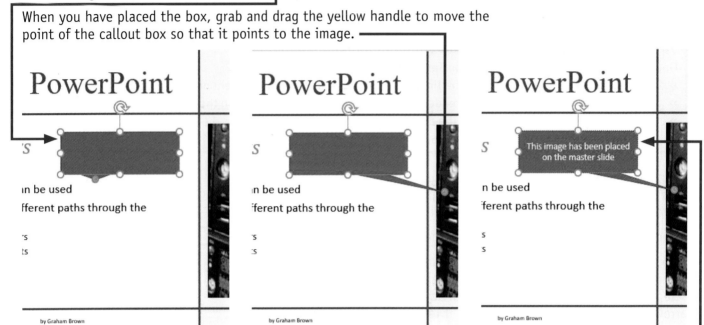

Type the text that you require into the callout box (you cannot see the cursor as you can with a text box) and then resize the callout box using the drag handles. It may look similar to this.

Move to slide 6. To insert the copyright symbol, click the left mouse button to place the cursor after the 't' at the end of the first bullet point. Select the Insert tab, in the Symbols section click on the Symbol icon. This opens the Symbol window. Scroll through the available list of symbols until you find the '©' symbol.

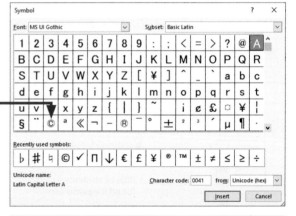

Click on this symbol and then click on Insert followed by Close. Add the text 'Microsoft' after the symbol and highlight both the symbol and the new text. Set this to a black, 12-point, sans-serif font using the methods learned earlier in the chapter.

To insert the red line, select the Insert tab, then click on the Shapes icon and select a line. Drag the line horizontally across the page. Click the right mouse button on the line and use the drop-down menu, selecting Format Shape, to open the Format Shape pane. Use the Line Color and Width sections to change the colour and thickness of the line. The completed slide should look similar to this.

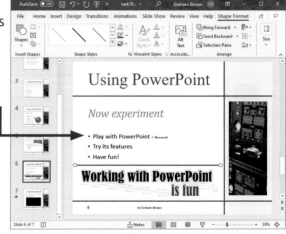

Save the presentation as **task19m**.

Activity 19a

You are going to create a short presentation for IGCSE students giving them advice on website authoring. The medium for delivery will be a multimedia projector.

Create a master slide with a green background at the top (about $\frac{1}{8}$ of the height) and at the bottom of each slide (about $\frac{1}{16}$ of the height) with a dark green horizontal line as a border between the white and green backgrounds. Add two vertical dark green lines to the left of the slide. Each line should be 6 points wide. It should look like this.

Include the heading 'HTML', right aligned, in a black, 40-point, sans-serif font at the top of the master slide (as shown above). Include an automated slide number in the footer, in the green area to the left of the two vertical lines. Make this a 14-point, black, sans-serif font. Include your name right aligned in the footer in the same style as the page numbering.

Set the following styles of text throughout the entire presentation:
- » heading: black, sans-serif, left aligned, 40 point, within the green 'header' section
- » subheading: red, serif, centre aligned, 40 point
- » bulleted list: dark green, serif, left aligned, 32 point
- » level 2 bulleted list: dark green, serif, left aligned, 24 point.

Place a very small image of a computer or peripheral in the bottom right corner of the white space. Crop and/or resize the image so that it fits. Do not distort the image. Import the file **html.rtf**, placing the text as slides in your presentation software. On slide 1 add the heading 'Hints and tips' and the subheading 'for IGCSE and Level 2 students'. Use this data to create a chart: Text editor – 42, FrontPage – 37, Dreamweaver – 31. Show the percentage of students in each category. Insert this chart into slide 5 with the heading 'Percentage of users from the survey'.

19.3.6 Audience and presenter notes

The delivery of a presentation with a multimedia projector may include the use of **audience notes** and/or **presenter notes**.

Audience notes

Audience notes are paper copies of the slides of a presentation that are given to the audience so that they can take them away and refer to them after the presentation. Sometimes people will want to write their own notes on their audience note printouts during a presentation. These can be printed in different formats, with several slides on a page, or just one slide with space for the person to add their own notes.

Presenter notes

Presenter notes are a single copy of the slides from a presentation, with prompts and/or key facts that need to be told to the audience by the person delivering the presentation. These notes are sometimes printed and not usually given to the audience.

Add presenter notes

Task 19n

Open the presentation that you saved in Task 19m. Add the following presenter notes to the slides:

» **Slide 1**: Welcome to this presentation giving you useful hints and tips on using *Microsoft PowerPoint* for your IGCSE practical examinations.

» **Slide 2**: The presentation that you are watching has been made using *PowerPoint*.

» **Slide 4**: Graphs and charts can be added to enhance a presentation.

» **Slide 5**: Hyperlinks can be used to give different paths or to open external websites or documents.

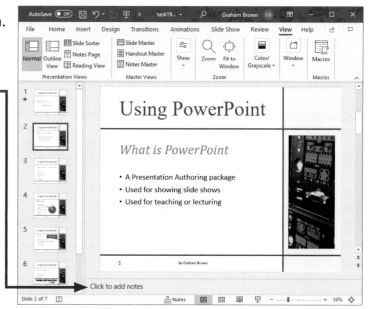

Open the presentation that you saved in Task 19m. From the View tab select Normal view. Locate the Show section and make sure that Notes is selected. When selected this will show the presenter notes area of the page.

Move the cursor to the Notes area of the screen. Click the cursor into this box and type the presenter notes for slide 1. Use the left pane to select the next slide and continue with this process until all of the presenter notes have been entered. Not all of the slides have presenter notes. These notes will not appear on the slides when the presentation is run. You will learn how to print these so that the presenter can read from them later in the chapter.

Save the presentation as **task19n**.

Advice

Take great care when entering data in presenter notes. Check carefully the use of capital letters and punctuation.

Task 19o

Open the file **webpage.rtf** which will be used to create a short interactive presentation in 4:3 format.

Add your name to slide 1. Add the following links to the slides:

» Slide 2: The text for the three layers will become buttons to access the relevant slides.

» Slides 2–5: The text 'Extra help' will link to slide 6.

» Slides 3–6: An action button placed in the bottom right corner of the slides to return to slide 2.

» Slide 6: The text 'Document on HTML' will link to the document html.rtf.

» Slide 6: The text 'Hodder website' will link to https://www.hodder.co.uk/

» Slide 6: The text 'Email the author' and the image email.png will both prepare an email message to graham.a.brown@hotmail.co.uk

Using the methods learned earlier in the chapter open the file webpage.rtf, set the aspect ratio to 4:3, add your name to slide 1 and save the presentation as **task19o**.

19.3.7 Insert and edit a hyperlink on a slide

Insert a hyperlink from text

Move to slide 2. Highlight the text 'Extra help' and select the Insert tab. In the Links section select the Link icon.

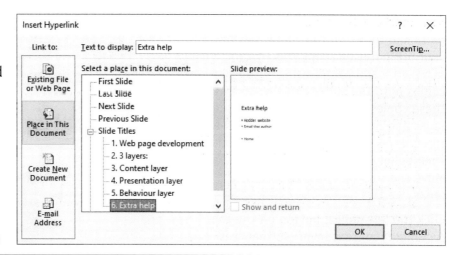

From the drop-down menu select Insert Link... to open the Insert Hyperlink window. This needs to link to slide 6 so in the Link to: section select Place in This Document. In the Select a place in this document: box select the option for 6. Extra help like this.

Click [OK] to create the hyperlink and repeat this process for slides 3 to 5.

> **Advice**
>
> You can copy and paste this hyperlinked text onto the other slides to save time.

Insert a hyperlink from an object

Move to slide 2. From the Insert tab, in the Illustrations section, select the Shapes icon, using the drop-down menu select, from the Rectangles section, the left icon like this.

Drag the cursor over part of the slide so that the rectangle appears as a button. Click within the rectangle and enter the text Content layer.

> **Advice**
>
> You can copy and paste this text from the bulleted list to save time.

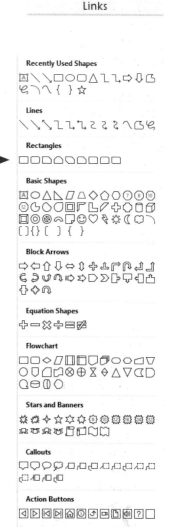

You can resize the text and format this rectangle to match the colour scheme of your presentation. Copy this rectangle using <Ctrl> <C> and paste, using <Ctrl> <V>, two copies onto the slide. Edit the text within these copies so that they show Presentation layer and Behaviour layer. Delete the first three items of the bulleted list and move the final bullet for extra help down the slide. Move the three rectangles so that the slide looks like this.

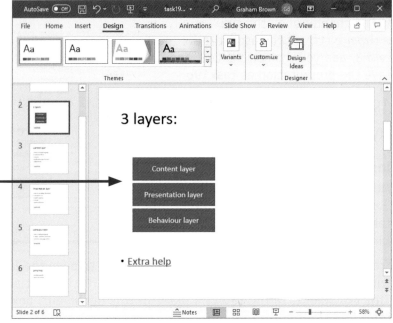

Click the left mouse button on the top rectangle (Content layer) so that it is selected. Make sure it is the object selected and not the text within it. Select the Insert tab, then in the Links section, select the Link icon.

From the drop-down menu select Insert Link... to open the Insert Hyperlink window. This needs to link to slide 3 so in the Link to: section select Place in This Document. In the Select a place in this document: box select the option for 3. Content layer like this.

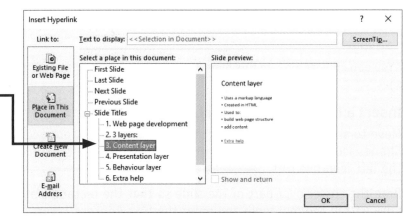

Click ⬛ OK ⬛ to create the hyperlink and repeat this process for the rectangles (which will now become buttons) to slides 4 and 5.

Edit a hyperlink on a slide

The easiest way to edit a hyperlink, is to click the right mouse button on the hyperlinked object/text/image, then select from the drop-down menu the option for Edit Link.

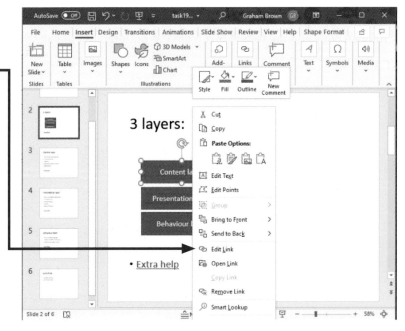

This will open the Edit Hyperlink window which is almost the same as the 'Insert Hyperlink' window. You can change or remove the hyperlink from here.

Insert a hyperlink to an external file

Move to slide 6. Highlight the text 'Document on HTML', select the Insert tab, then in the Links section, select the Link icon, then Insert Link... to open the Insert Hyperlink window. This needs to link to an existing document so in the Link to: section select Existing File or Web Page. Find and select the required file, in this case html.rtf then click ⬚ OK ⬚.

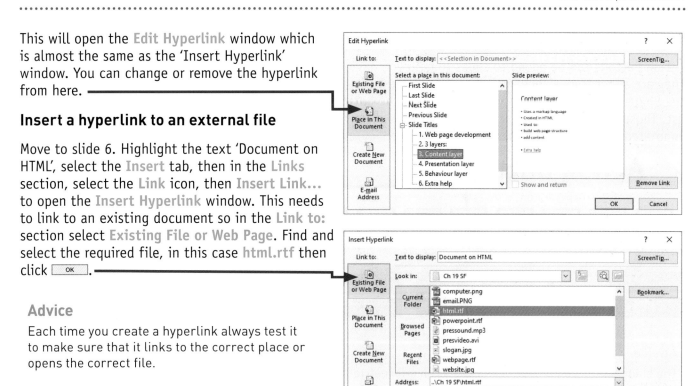

Advice

Each time you create a hyperlink always test it to make sure that it links to the correct place or opens the correct file.

Insert a hyperlink to a website

While not a required skill, this is a useful skill to be able to do. Even without the internet available, you can link to your local web pages as you work through Chapter 21. On slide 6 highlight the text 'Hodder website', open the Insert Hyperlink window using the methods learned earlier in the chapter. This needs to link to a web page so in the Link to: section select Existing File or Web Page. Place the cursor in the Address: box and type the web address which is https://www.hodder.co.uk/ then click ⬚ OK ⬚.

Insert a hyperlink to send an email

On slide 6 highlight the text 'Email the author', open the Insert Hyperlink window using the methods learned earlier in the chapter. This needs to link to an email address so in the Link to: section select E-mail Address. Place the cursor in the E-mail address: box and type the email address, which is graham.a.brown@hotmail.co.uk If you wish to add a subject line to the message do so in the Subject: box, then click ⬚ OK ⬚.

Place the image email.png on slide 6 using the methods learned earlier in the chapter. Highlight this image and open the Insert Hyperlink window. Create the same link to this email address as you did from the text, like this.

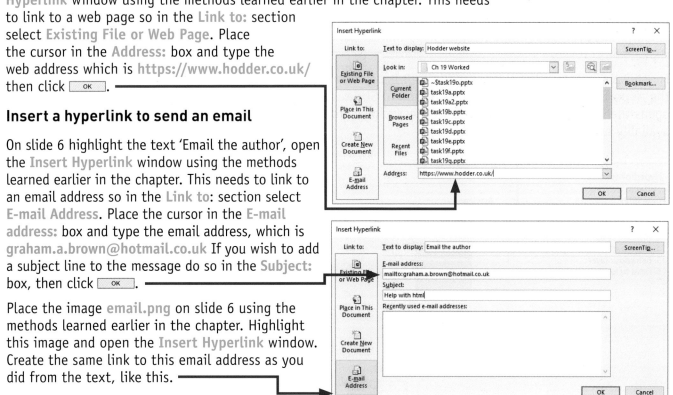

19.3.8 Insert an action button on a slide

Action buttons can be added to slides to help you navigate between the slides. They are all located within the **Insert** tab, in the **Illustrations** section, using the **Shapes** icon. The action buttons appear at the bottom of the drop-down list. Those action buttons that you may find useful for this course have been annotated with callout boxes.

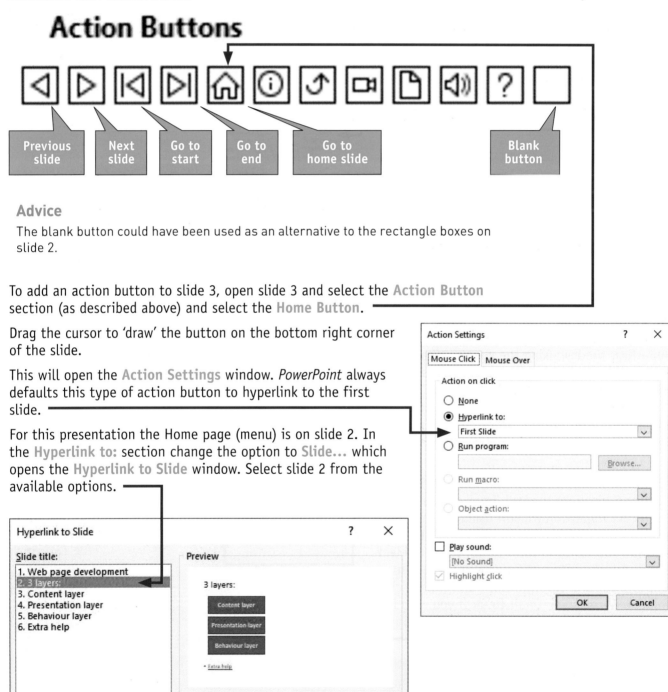

Advice

The blank button could have been used as an alternative to the rectangle boxes on slide 2.

To add an action button to slide 3, open slide 3 and select the **Action Button** section (as described above) and select the **Home Button**.

Drag the cursor to 'draw' the button on the bottom right corner of the slide.

This will open the **Action Settings** window. *PowerPoint* always defaults this type of action button to hyperlink to the first slide.

For this presentation the Home page (menu) is on slide 2. In the **Hyperlink to:** section change the option to **Slide...** which opens the **Hyperlink to Slide** window. Select slide 2 from the available options.

Click on ⟦ OK ⟧ to return to the Action Settings window. You will notice that the Hyperlink to: box has changed to the title text of slide 2.

Click on ⟦ OK ⟧, then copy and paste this action button into slides 4, 5 and 6. Test all the hyperlinks that you have created. Save the presentation.

19.3.9 Add alternative text/ScreenTip to an object

Add a ScreenTip to an object

A ScreenTip can be used to describe the function of an object and is visible when the mouse hovers over an object.

> **Task 19p**
>
> Open the presentation saved in task 19o. Add to the content layer button on slide 2:
> » a ScreenTip 'Button to take you to the content layer slide'
> » alternative text 'Select the content layer button to open the content layer slide'.

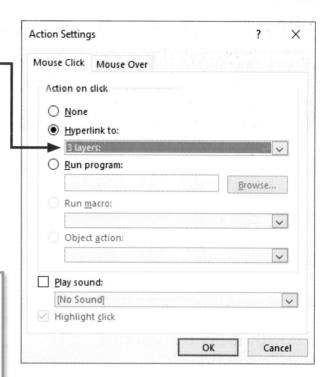

Open the presentation saved in task 19o. Open slide 3 and highlight the rectangle containing the text 'Content layer'. Click the right mouse button on this rectangle and from the drop-down menu, select Edit Link. This opens the Edit Hyperlink window. Click on the ScreenTip button.

This opens the Set Hyperlink ScreenTip window. In the ScreenTip text: box enter the text Button to take you to the content layer slide, like this.

Click on ⟦ OK ⟧ twice. Now as you hover the mouse over the rectangle/button the ScreenTip will appear.

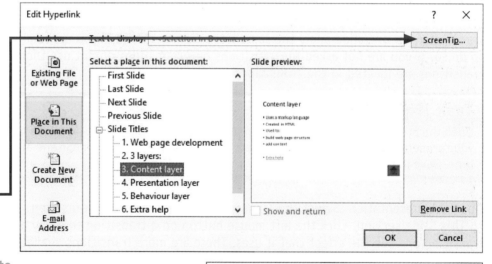

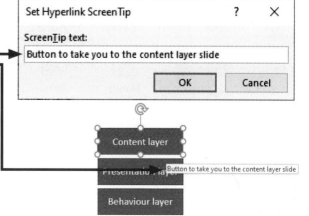

Add alternative text to an object

Alternative text is used to describe the object to those users with visual impairments. The content of the alternative (often shortened to 'alt') text is read by a screen reader and read aloud to the user.

Highlight the rectangle containing the text 'Content layer'. Click the right mouse button on this rectangle and from the drop-down menu, select Edit Alt Text. This opens the Alt Text pane. Add to the Alt Text box the text Select the content layer button to open the content layer slide. The window will look similar to this.

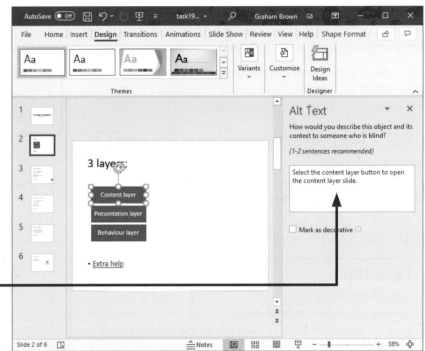

19.3.10 Apply transitions between slides

Transitions between slides are the methods used to introduce a new slide. This can be simply replacing the existing slide with a new slide or using a number of different features to change from one to another. It is important that all transitions between slides are consistent. When you have selected the transaction for one slide apply the same transition to others if you are required to do so. If you are not asked for transitions between slides do not use them. All transitions are located in the Transitions tab.

> ## Task 19q
> Open the presentation saved in task 19n. Apply transitions between all slides in your presentation. Animate all the bullets on slide 3 so that they appear one at a time. Save the presentation.

Open the presentation. Select the Transitions tab and find the Transition to This Slide section. Click the left mouse button on a transition to apply a transition and see the effect that it uses. There are more transitions available; you can use the scroll bar to see them.

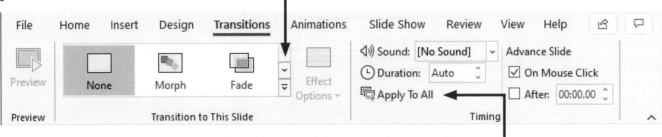

Click on the icon to select the transition that you wish to use, for example: Fade and then click on the Apply To All icon to apply the same transition to all slides.

Advice

Always use the same transition effect between slides and the same animation effect throughout the whole presentation. Consistency in these areas is just as important as using consistent styles and colour schemes.

19.3.11 Apply animation effects

To animate any object in *PowerPoint*, whether it is text, images, shapes or any other object the process is the same and always starts with highlighting the object/s to be animated. Rather than repeat the instructions a number of times we will use the example of animating a bulleted list. All animations are located in the Animations tab.

Select slide 3 and highlight only the first item in the bulleted list. Select the Animations tab and find the Animation section. All the animation styles can be found using the Add Animation drop-down menu – the green ones are 'Entrance' animations, the yellow ones are effects used for 'Emphasis' and the red are 'Exit' animations. Select one of the animations from the Entrance section – here, Float In has been chosen. Click the left mouse button to apply an animation and its effect. There are more animations available; you can use the scroll bar to see them.

Click on the icon to select the animation that you wish to use. To set each bullet to be individually animated, select them one at a time to apply the animation to each individually. To change when the bullets appear, use the Start and Delay options.

Opening the Animation Pane allows you to see the timings and to edit these by right mouse clicking on each item and selecting Start After Previous so it looks like this.

The task instructed you to 'animate all the bullets so that they appear one at a time', so here, Float In has been selected (to be consistent with the first one) for each bullet point. This sets the animation. The timings are set as shown above, so there is a small delay between each bullet; in this case the chosen delay was one second, but this has only been applied to the first bullet, the other bullets copied this value from the previous one/s.

It is a good idea to keep the Animation Pane open so that,

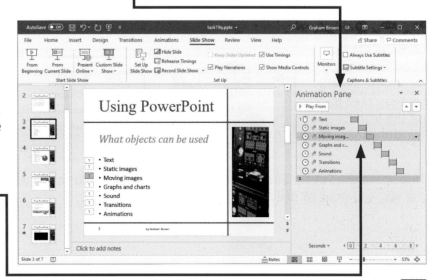

when you need to show evidence of your animation effects, these can be seen.

To test the animations, highlight those you wish to test (hold down <Ctrl> and select each row in the Animation Pane and click on ▷ Play Selected). Save the presentation as **task19q**.

19.3.12 Hide a slide within a presentation

> **Task 19r**
> Open the presentation saved in task 19q. Hide slide 7.
> Save the presentation.

Open the presentation and display it so that slide 7 is visible in the left pane. Click the right mouse button on this image of slide 7 to get the drop-down menu. Select Hide Slide from this menu.

The slide number now shows as crossed through to show that the slide is not visible.

19.4 Output a presentation

19.4.1 Display a presentation

The easiest way to display a presentation is to press the <F5> key, which runs the presentation from the start. An alternative is to select the Slide Show tab and choose from the options to start: From Beginning, From Current Slide, or Present Online and allow others to download and run your presentation.

To stop a presentation that is running press the <Escape> key.

Set up the slide show

To set up the slide show, select the Slide Show tab, locate the Set Up section, then click on the icon for Set Up Slide Show.

This opens the Set Up Show window, which will allow you to set the show up in the way you want to deliver it.

Set up the slide show for a looped on-screen carousel

If the show is to be used as an on-screen carousel, perhaps to show messages around a building or to visitors in a foyer, it is usual to loop the show continuously. This is selected by ticking this box.

As well as placing a tick in this check box and clicking on [OK] you will also need to set each slide to be timed. The easiest way is to click on the button for Record Slide Show.

From the drop-down menu Record from Beginning, use the red record button in the top left corner to start the recording of your timings. These timings will then be set within your presentation so that it can run without a presenter. You will also need to set the audio file to play automatically using the methods learned earlier in the chapter.

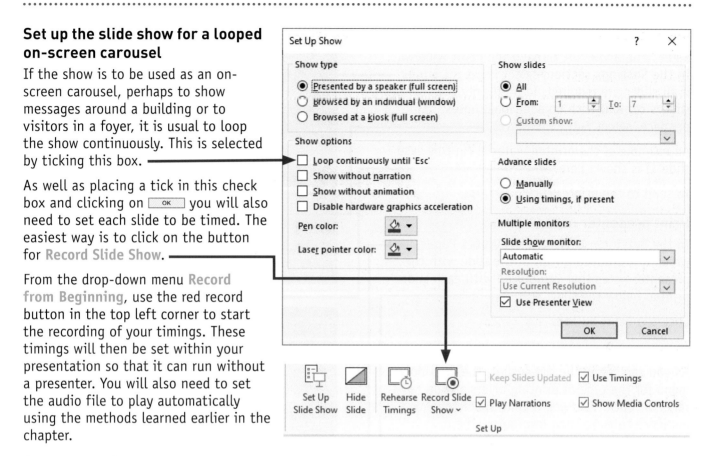

Set up the slide show to be presenter controlled

From the Set Up Show window, select a Show Type of Presented by a speaker (full screen) which will automatically remove the tick from the check box for 'Loop continuously until Esc'. Your presentation will already be set up to be presenter controlled, requiring mouse clicks to move from slide to slide and sometimes from bullet point to bullet point.

Other options for showing the presentation manually, with or without the animations running, can also be selected from this window. When you have made your choices select the [OK] button.

19.4.2 Print the presentation

To print evidence of your work, you must identify what types of printouts are required. Sometimes you will be expected to print only the slides, but more often you will need to print audience or presenter notes; for these printouts you will need to select File and Print. Screenshots are the best way to show evidence of transitions and animations.

> ## Task 19s
>
> Open the presentation saved in task 19r. Print your presentation showing:
> » full page slides
> » presenter notes
> » audience notes with three slides per page and space for the audience to make notes
> » evidence of the transitions between slides
> » evidence of the animations used on slide 3.

Print full page slides

Select **File** and **Print** to open the **Print** window. In the **Settings** section, select **Print All Slides** if all slides are required. To print only the slide/s content with no additional notes or space, select **Full Page Slides**.

An example of the printed material (in this case slide 1) is shown here.

To send to the printer click on **Print**.

Print presenter notes

In the **Settings** section, select **Notes Pages**, which will produce a view of the slide with the presenter notes that you placed with each slide printed below the slide.

Click the **Print** button.

Print audience notes (handouts)

As you can see in the screenshot, the drop-down menu for the type of printing offers a wide range of options. If you require space for the audience to make their own notes, then **3 Slides** per page is the best option.

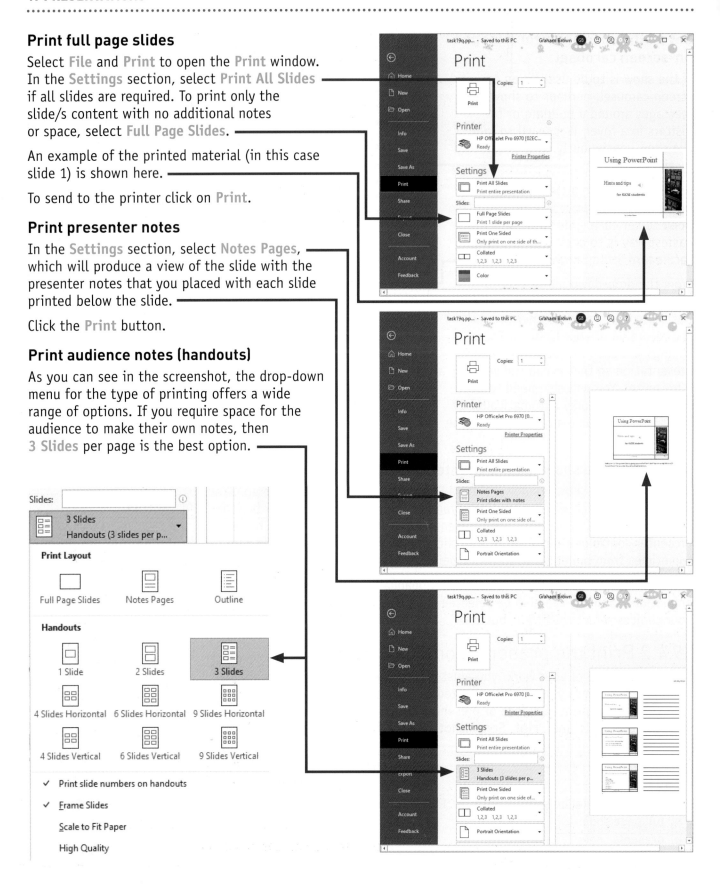

Print evidence of slide transitions

Select the View tab, locate the Presentation Views section, then click on the icon for Slide Sorter view.

Use the <Print Screen> key on your keyboard to copy this into the clipboard and paste the image into a word-processed document so that you can add your name and other details before sending it to the printer.

You can see from the Slide Sorter view the evidence that transitions have been added to each slide.

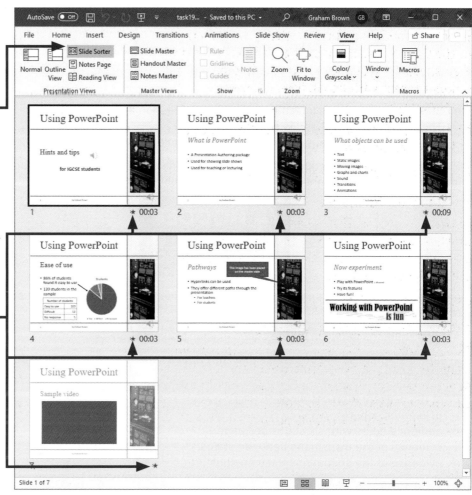

Print evidence of animations

Select the View tab and click on the Normal icon to return to the Normal view of the slides. Select slide 3. Make sure that the Animation Pane is visible to the right of the slide. Use the <Print Screen> key on your keyboard to copy this into the clipboard. Paste the image into a word-processed document so that you can add your name and other details before sending it to the printer.

The numbering next to each bullet point shows that each

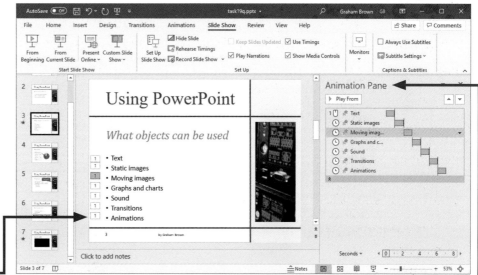

bullet is animated separately from the others. Further detail about the animation of the bullets can be seen in the Animation Pane.

Activity 19b

Open the presentation that you saved in Activity 19a. Add the following presenter notes to the slides:

» Slide 1: Welcome to my presentation giving tips about website authoring using HTML.
» Slide 4: An intranet is internal within an organisation and is managed. The internet is global and is not managed.
» Slide 6: There are many other websites that can offer you help.

Place the image **website.jpg** on the left side of slide 6 below the bullets. Crop this image so that only the light blue part of logo is visible as shown below.

Add a red arrow, 3 points wide, from the text 'Hodder Education website' to point to this image.

Apply transitions between all the slides in your presentation.

In slide 3 animate all the bullets so that they appear one at a time, in the order that they are in the list.

Print the presentation showing:

» presenter notes
» audience notes with six slides per page
» evidence of the transitions between slides
» evidence of the animations used on slide 3.

Spreadsheets

In this chapter you will learn how to:
- ★ create and edit a spreadsheet model
- ★ create formulae using cell references
- ★ understand the order of mathematical operations
- ★ understand absolute and relative cell referencing
- ★ replicate formulae using absolute and relative cell references
- ★ ensure the accuracy of data entry
- ★ merge cells
- ★ use formulae
- ★ understand the difference between a formula and a function
- ★ use functions
- ★ use nested functions
- ★ use external data sources within functions
- ★ search and select data
- ★ sort data
- ★ display either formulae or values
- ★ adjust rows and columns
- ★ wrap text within a cell
- ★ enhance a spreadsheet
- ★ format numeric data
- ★ use conditional formatting
- ★ adjust the page orientation
- ★ control the page layout for printing.

For this chapter you will need these source files:
- ★ classlist.csv
- ★ client.csv
- ★ client1.csv
- ★ clothing.csv
- ★ clubs.csv
- ★ costs.csv
- ★ items.csv
- ★ jobs.csv
- ★ operators.csv
- ★ project.csv
- ★ rooms.csv
- ★ salary.csv
- ★ sales.csv
- ★ staff.csv
- ★ tasks.csv
- ★ teachers.csv
- ★ tuckshop.csv
- ★ tutors.csv

20.1 Create a data model

What is a data model?

A **spreadsheet model** is used to explore different possible answers. These models are often financial, mathematical or scientific. It is sometimes called a 'what if' scenario or 'what if' modelling. It lets you change data in the spreadsheet to see what will happen to the results. It is useful to know how to build a simple spreadsheet model and edit (change) the data within the model, or even change the model itself, to produce different results.

20.1.1 Create and edit a spreadsheet model

Spreadsheet basics

You will use *Microsoft Excel* to create your data model. Select the *Excel* icon from the desktop. From the next screen select 'Blank workbook'.

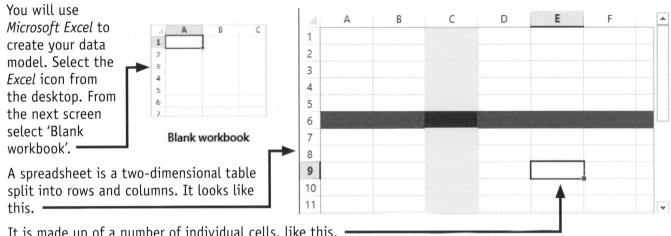

Blank workbook

A spreadsheet is a two-dimensional table split into rows and columns. It looks like this.

It is made up of a number of individual cells, like this.

This cell (with the darker outline) is the cell that has the cursor within it. To help us to use individual cells in a spreadsheet, each cell has an address. In this example the cell with the cursor in it is called cell E9 and the cell that has been coloured red is called cell C6. The red cell and all of the yellow cells are in column C, and the red cell and all of the blue cells are in row 6. A spreadsheet is sometimes called a sheet or even a worksheet. Many sheets can be held within a single workbook in *Excel*.

Insert cells, rows and columns

To insert a cell into a spreadsheet, click the **right** mouse button on the spreadsheet where you wish to insert the cell. From the drop-down menu select Insert... which opens the Insert window.

This will allow you to insert a cell (by selecting one of the top two options, which creates the space for the cell by moving all other cells to the right or down, depending on your choice) or allow you to insert a row or a column.

Delete cells, rows and columns

To delete a cell from a spreadsheet, click the **right** mouse button on the cell you wish to delete. From the drop-down menu select Delete... which opens the Delete window.

This will allow you to delete a cell (by selecting one of the top two options, which removes the cell by moving all other cells to the left or up) or allow you to delete a row or a column.

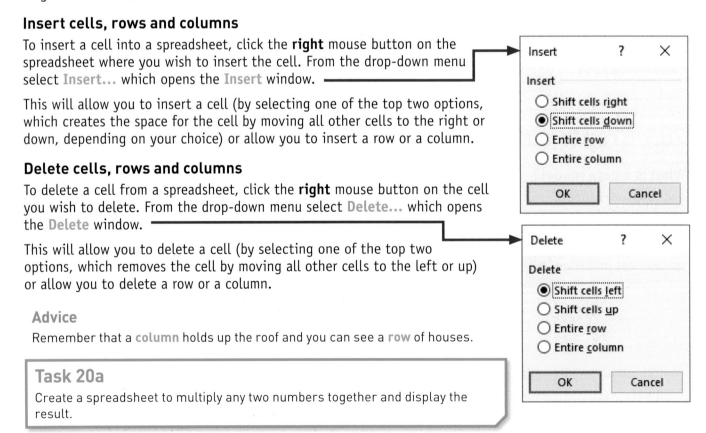

> **Advice**
>
> Remember that a **column** holds up the roof and you can see a **row** of houses.

> **Task 20a**
>
> Create a spreadsheet to multiply any two numbers together and display the result.

The contents of a spreadsheet cell can be:

» a **number**
» text, which is called a **label**
» a **formula**, which always starts with an = sign.

20.1.2 Create formulae using cell references

Move the cursor into cell A1 and click the left mouse button. Type in the label 'Multiplying two numbers'. Move the cursor down into cell A2 and enter a number. Repeat this for cell A3. In cell A4, enter the formula =A2*A3 so that the spreadsheet looks like this.

You will see that the formula is not visible in the sheet and that the cell A4 only contains the answer to the calculation within this cell. The formula for the cell containing the cursor can be seen in the formula bar.

If you have created the spreadsheet as shown, you should be able to change the contents of cells A2 and A3 to multiply any two numbers together. The changing of cells to see the results is called **modelling**.

If you enter large numbers into cells A2 and A3, the result in cell A4 may not appear as you expect it to. It may look like this.

This tells you that the number is too large to fit into the column. To expand the width of the column, move the cursor to the end of the column heading for column A like this.

Double click the left mouse button to expand the column width to fit the longest item stored in this column. The spreadsheet now looks like this. You can see how the label and all of the data are fully visible.

Save your work in your Task20a folder.

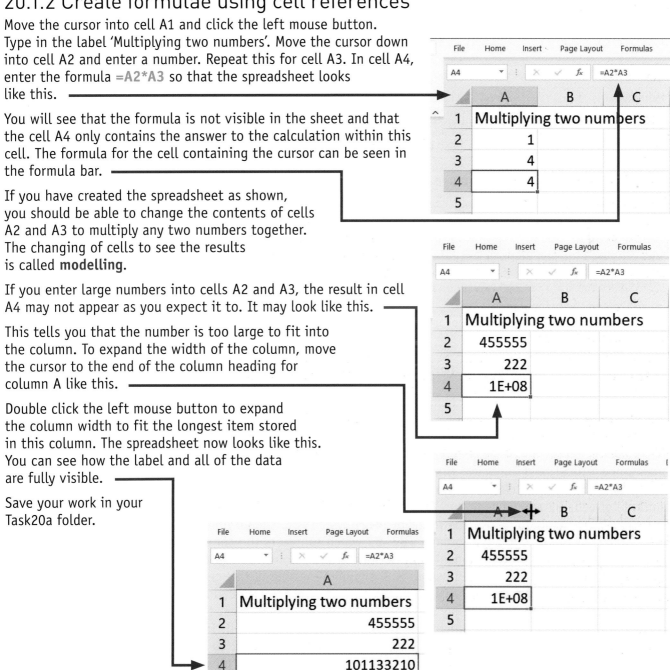

Advice

You **must** show the contents of all cells fully in your spreadsheet printouts so that your method and results can be seen.

Using arithmetic operators in formulae

Arithmetic operators are placed in a formula and can be used to add, subtract, multiply, divide and calculate indices (powers) of a number. Each of these operators has a symbol used within the spreadsheet, some of which are shown in Table 20.1.

▼ **Table 20.1** Arithmetic operators

Operation	Operator	Example	What does this do?
Add	+	=A4+B4	Takes contents of cell A4 and adds contents of B4
Subtract	–	=A4–B4	Takes contents of cell A4 and subtracts from it contents of B4
Multiply	*	=A4*B4	Takes contents of cell A4 and multiplies by contents of B4
Divide	/	=A4/B4	Takes contents of cell A4 and divides by contents of B4
Indices (powers)	^	=A4^2	Takes the contents of cell A4 squared (multiplies A4 by itself) – for example if A4 contained the number 3 then this would be 3^2 which is 3*3 which is 9

Task 20b

Create a spreadsheet that looks like this:

Place a formula in cell:

» B5 to add the two numbers
» B6 to subtract the second number from the first number
» B7 to multiply the two numbers
» B8 to divide the first number by the second number
» B9 to calculate the first number to the power of the second number – for example, first number$^{(second\ number)}$.

◢	A	B
1	Numbers	
2	First number	4
3	Second number	2
4		
5	Add	
6	Subtract	
7	Multiply	
8	Divide	
9	Indices	

Open a new spreadsheet and enter the data as shown. Resize column A so that all the text is visible. In cell B5, enter the formula =B2+B3 which adds the contents of cells B2 and B3 together. At the moment they contain 4 and 2 so, when you press the <Enter> key, the result of (4+2), which is 6, should be visible in this cell. In cell B6, enter the formula =B2–B3 which subtracts the contents of cell B3 from cell B2. At the moment they contain 4 and 2 so, when you press the <Enter> key, the result of (4–2), which is 2, should be visible in this cell. In cell B7, enter the formula =B2*B3 which will multiply the contents of cells B2 and B3 together. At the moment they contain 4 and 2 so, when you press the <Enter> key, the result of (4*2), which is 8, should be visible in this cell. In cell B8, enter the formula =B2/B3 which will divide the contents of cell B2 by the contents of cell B3. At the moment they contain 4 and 2 so, when you press the <Enter> key, the result of (4/2), which is 2, should be visible in this cell. In cell B9, enter the formula =B2^B3 which will take the contents of cell B2 and index it to (set to the power of) B3, at the moment they contain 4 and 2 so, when you press the <Enter> key, the result of (4² or 4*4), which is 16, should be visible in this cell so that the spreadsheet looks like this.

	A	B
1	Numbers	
2	First number	4
3	Second number	2
4		
5	Add	6
6	Subtract	2
7	Multiply	8
8	Divide	2
9	Indices	16

Save the spreadsheet as **task20b**. Change the number/s in B2 and/or B3 to see what happens to the other cells.

Advice

While functions like SUM, PRODUCT or POWER could also be used to perform these tasks, using arithmetic operators provides the most efficient method.

This works well because only a single operator is used in each formula, but becomes more complicated when multiple operators are used in a formula. To understand how the computer processes multiple operators you need to understand the order of mathematical operations.

20.1.3 Order of mathematical operations

When you are given multiple calculations like this you need to decide which calculations to perform first: **7 + (6 × 5² + 3)**

On paper (do not use a calculator or computer) try to calculate the answer.

The order in which we perform these calculations can lead to different answers. Computers and most calculators perform the calculations according to a given set of rules, known as the order of operations. These rules, in order, are:

» do things in **B**rackets first
» All **I**ndices (powers and roots, sometimes called exponents) second
» **D**ivide and **M**ultiply third
» **A**dd and **S**ubtract fourth
» otherwise just go left to right.

Try the calculation again using these rules. You should do the part in the brackets first, so (6 × 5² + 3), starting with the indices, so 5² is 5*5 which is 25, leaving the bracket as (6 × 25 + 3). Next within the bracket we multiply, so 6 × 25 = 150, leaving the brackets as (150 + 3). Add these together to get 153. Now back to the calculation, 7 + (6 × 5² + 3), we know that the brackets work out to 153 so 7 + 153 = 160. Is that the same answer that you first calculated?

How do I remember this? BIDMAS

B	**B**rackets first
I	**I**ndices (i.e. powers and square roots, etc.)
DM	**D**ivision and **M**ultiplication (left to right)
AS	**A**ddition and **S**ubtraction (left to right)

Divide and Multiply rank equally (and go left to right). Add and Subtract rank equally (and go left to right). After you have done **B** and **I**, just go from left to right doing any **D** or **M** as you find them. Then go from left to right doing any **A** or **S** as you find them.

20.1.4 Cell referencing

Relative referencing

In Task 20a and Task 20b we entered formulae into a cell which contained a reference to another cell, for example, in Task 20b, in cell B5 we entered =B2+B3. This formula refers to two different cells B2 and B3. If we were to try and use *Excel*'s tools to replicate (copy) this formula into other cells, these cell references would change and no longer point to these cells. For example, if we replicated the formula down, the cell below (B6) would contain =B3+B4. The cells B2 and B3 use what is called **relative cell referencing**, meaning that the values change when they are replicated.

Absolute referencing

If we wished these cell references to stay the same (and still point to cells B2 and B3 when replicated) we have to change them into formulae with **absolute cell referencing**. To fix these cells we add a dollar ($) sign between the part of the reference that is to be fixed. For example: if we change cell B5 to =$B$2+$B$3, then replicate this cell down, the cell below would also contain =$B$2+$B$3, as the references are fixed and therefore do not change.

If we chose to change cell B5 to =$B$2+B3, then replicate this cell down, the cell below would now contain =$B$2+B4, as the absolute reference has been fixed yet the relative reference changes with each row/column.

Create a data model

> **Task 20c**
> Create a spreadsheet to display the times table for any number you choose to enter. Print your spreadsheet, showing values and formulae.

For this task, you need to design and create the data model to calculate and display the times table for any number that you choose. You must therefore have a single cell that contains the number to use for all the calculations. In this model you can place a simple number, such as 2, in cell A1, so that you can easily tell if you have made a mistake with your formulae later on. Type the label 'Times Table' in cell A2.

You are going to create the times table in cells A3 to B12. The cells in column A hold the number to multiply by and the cells in column B hold formulae to calculate the answer. Move the cursor into cell A3 and enter the number 1, then move into cell A4 and enter the number 2. Rather than repeating this process another eight times for the numbers 3 to 10, highlight cells A3 and A4, as shown here. Move the cursor to the drag handle in the bottom right corner of these cells. ────────────────

Click and hold the left mouse button on the drag handle, dragging it down to the bottom right corner of cell A12. This replicates (copies) the cell contents. *Excel* realises that the numbers in cells A3 and A4 increase by one, so uses this pattern as it replicates the cells down.

20.1.5 Replicate formulae using absolute and relative cell references

Move the cursor into cell B3 and enter the formula =A3*$A$1. This formula uses both absolute ($A$1) and relative (A3) cell referencing. The $ symbols in the reference to cell A1 will be used by *Excel* to keep that cell reference the same when this cell is replicated into cells B4 to B12. Use the drag handle in cell B3 to replicate this formula into the cells down to B12. The results should look like this.

Display and print spreadsheet values

Without checking the formulae, you can see that this has produced the correct results for the two times table. Change cell A1 to another number to check that the formula works correctly. Add your name to the Spreadsheet, then print this 'values' view of the spreadsheet using the File tab, followed by Print and then the Print button.

Print

Display and print spreadsheet formulae

To display (and then print) the formulae used in the spreadsheet, select the Formulas tab and find the Formula Auditing section. Click on the Show Formulas icon. The spreadsheet now looks like this.

Each of these formulae contains both absolute and relative referencing. In cell B3, the reference to cell A1 (with the $ symbols) is an absolute reference and the reference to cell A3 is a relative reference. You can see from this view that the reference in cell B3 to cell A3 has been changed as the cell has been replicated as it uses relative referencing, but the reference to cell A1 has not been changed during the replication, because absolute referencing has been used.

To return to the view of the spreadsheet that shows the values, click on the Show Formulas icon again.

More editing tools

Other standard *Windows* editing tools can be used in *Excel*, such as cut, copy and paste. These can be used to copy the contents of one cell into another cell. An alternative method of replicating cell B3 into cells B4 to B12 is to enter the formula in cell B3, click the right mouse button on this cell and select Copy from the drop-down menu. Highlight cells B4 to B12 and right mouse click, selecting Paste from the drop-down menu. This will paste the formulae, adjusting the cell references for A3 as this is a relative reference but keeping the absolute reference for A1. The results are identical.

	A	B
1	2	Times Table
2		
3	1	
4	2	
5	3	
6	4	
7	5	
8	6	
9	7	
10	8	
11	9	
12	10	

	A	B
1	2	Times Table
2		
3	1	2
4	2	4
5	3	6
6	4	8
7	5	10
8	6	12
9	7	14
10	8	16
11	9	18
12	10	20

	A	B
1	2	Times Table
2		
3	1	=A3*$A$1
4	2	=A4*$A$1
5	3	=A5*$A$1
6	4	=A6*$A$1
7	5	=A7*$A$1
8	6	=A8*$A$1
9	7	=A9*$A$1
10	8	=A10*$A$1
11	9	=A11*$A$1
12	10	=A12*$A$1

20.1.6 Ensure the accuracy of data entry

When you are asked to 'create a data model that looks like this', make sure that you copy the model in the question exactly as shown. Do not try to make improvements or use other features (such as colour and formatting) unless asked to do so. This is very important. Do not insert rows or columns, or remove rows or columns containing blank spaces, unless instructed to do so.

When you type data into a spreadsheet (or any other form of document) you must make sure that the data that you have entered is identical to the original source document or question. Do not rush the data entry and check carefully that it has been entered with 100 per cent accuracy. This is even more important when working in a spreadsheet because one error, for example a mistyped number or decimal point in the wrong place, could cause all of the data in the spreadsheet to be incorrect. Care must also be taken when entering a formula, as one small error is likely to stop the spreadsheet working as it is expected to.

20.1.7 Merge cells

> ### Task 20d
>
> Open the spreadsheet saved in Task 20b. Change the text in cell A1 to **Please enter two numbers in cells B2 and B3**.
>
> Merge cells A1 and B1 and wrap the text in this merged cell. Save your spreadsheet.

Open the spreadsheet and add the text to cell A1 like this.

The text in cell A1 is too long to fit within the space so you have been instructed to merge cells A1 and B1. Highlight both cells together like this.

Select the Home tab, then in the Alignment section select the icon for Merge & Center.

The two cells have been merged but all the text is still not visible. Increase the height of the cell by dragging the arrow down like this.

Select, again from the Alignment section, the icon for Wrap text.

The text in the cell will now wrap onto two lines within the merged cell and appear like this.

Save the spreadsheet as **task20d**.

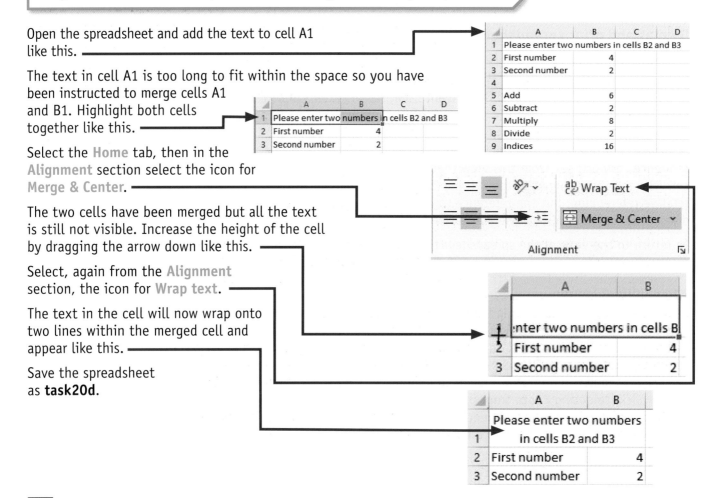

20.1.8 Use formulae

You have already met simple mathematical operators, but to refresh:

» For addition use the + symbol.
» For subtraction use the – symbol.
» For multiplication use the * symbol.
» For division use the / symbol.
» For indices use the ^ symbol.

We will use these operators to edit another spreadsheet where the task uses different mathematical terms.

Task 20e

Open the file **operators.csv**.

Choose two numbers. Place these in cells B1 and B2. Calculate in cell:
» B4, the sum of the two numbers
» B5, the difference between the two numbers
» B6, the product of the two numbers
» B7, the contents of cell B1 divided by the contents of cell B2
» B8, the contents of cell B1 to the power of the contents of cell B2.

Check that the formulae have worked before printing your spreadsheet showing the values and again showing the formulae used.

Open the file operators.csv in *Excel*. Extend the width of column A so that all the labels are fully visible. Move the cursor into cell B1 and enter the number 4, then into cell B2 and enter the number 2. These numbers have been chosen so that you can easily check your calculations. It is wise to perform all calculations by hand before entering the formulae. This will make sure that you understand the formulae that you are using, and you will be able to see the results of the calculation before the computer has shown you its results. These calculations may look like this.

Number X	4
Number Y	2

X+Y	4+2=6
X-Y	4-2=2
X*Y	4*2=8
X/Y	4/2=2
X^Y	4^2=16

» **Addition:** move the cursor into cell B4. The sum of the two numbers is needed in this cell, which means to add the contents of the two cells together. There are two ways of doing this: one method uses the + operator and the second uses a function. You will be shown how to use the SUM function later in this chapter, but the formula to enter in this cell for the + operator is =B1+B2. This can be typed in followed by the <Enter> key, or you can type the = sign, click the cursor into cell B1, type + and click in cell B2 before pressing the <Enter> key.

» **Subtraction:** move the cursor into cell B5. The difference between two numbers is needed in this cell. Enter (using either of the methods described in the addition section above) the formula =B1–B2, followed by the <Enter> key.

» **Multiplication:** move the cursor into cell B6. The product of two numbers means to multiply the two numbers together; you need to enter the formula =B1*B2, followed by the <Enter> key.

» **Division:** move the cursor into cell B7. This cell needs a calculation to divide the contents of cell B1 by the contents of cell B2 using the formula =B1/B2, followed by the <Enter> key.

>> **Indices:** Move the cursor into cell B8. This cell needs to calculate the contents of cell B1 to the power of the contents of cell B2 using the formula **=B1^B2**, followed by the <Enter> key.

Advice

The ^ symbol is often found using <Shift> and <6>.

To check that the formulae are correct, compare your original paper-based calculations with the values in the spreadsheet.

	A	B
1	First number - X	4
2	Second number - Y	2
3		
4	Sum of X and Y	6
5	Difference between X and Y	2
6	Product of X and Y	8
7	X divided by Y	2
8	X to the power Y	16

You will notice that the values chosen earlier in this task were carefully selected to make the maths easy. The more difficult calculations are likely to be the division and indices. These numbers were selected so that the 4 divided by 2 gives an easy result; 4 to the power of 2 is also reasonably easy (4×4).

Print the values, making sure that your name is fully visible on the printout. Select the Formulas tab, then click on the Show Formulas icon to change the display to show the formulae, which should appear like this.

Save and print the spreadsheet.

20.1.9 Named cells and ranges

When an individual cell or an area of a spreadsheet is going to be used a number of times within the formulae of a spreadsheet, it is often a good idea to give it a name. This name should be short and meaningful. In the case of a large spreadsheet, it is easier to remember the name of a cell, for example VAT or AveMiles, rather than trying to remember the cell reference, for example AC456 or

	A	B
1	First number - X	4
2	Second number - Y	2
3		
4	Sum of X and Y	=B1+B2
5	Difference between X and Y	=B1-B2
6	Product of X and Y	=B1*B2
7	X divided by Y	=B1/B2
8	X to the power Y	=B1^B2

X232. Once a cell or a range of cells has been named, you can use this name in all your formulae.

Task 20f

Open the file **sales.csv**. This spreadsheet will be used to calculate bonus payments to sales staff for a small company.

Name cell B1 'Unit'. Name cells A5 to C7 'Rate'. Name cells B11 to G18 'Sold'.

Create a named cell

Open the file. Save this spreadsheet with the filename task20f as an *Excel* workbook, **not** in .csv format. Find cell B1. You will name this cell 'Unit'. Right click on the mouse in this cell to get the drop-down menu. Select the option to Define Name... which will open the New Name window. In the Name: box, *Excel* will suggest a name for the range. It uses the layout of your spreadsheet to do this. When answering questions, ignore this suggestion (in this case the name that it suggests is too long to be used) and overtype it with the word as instructed in the question, in this case **Unit**. Add suitable text in the **Comment** box so that the window looks like this. ──────

To name the cell click on ⬚ OK ⬚.

When you move the cursor into cell B1, you will see in the **Name** box that it is now called **Unit**. ──────

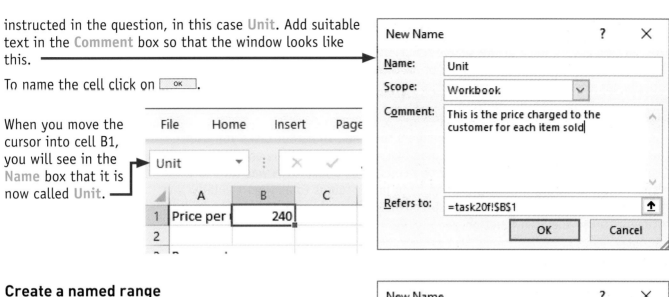

Create a named range

To create the named range for the rate, you must highlight the cells between A5 and C7. Do this by clicking on cell A5 and, while holding down the left mouse button, dragging the cursor to cell C7. Click the right mouse button within the highlighted range to get the drop-down menu. Change the contents of the **Name:** box to **Rate**. Check that the **New Name** window looks like this before clicking on ⬚ OK ⬚. The name of the range is only visible in the **Name** box when just the cells in the range are highlighted. ──────

The final named range can be created in a similar way. Highlight cells B11 to G18, then name this range **Sold**. ──────

Save the spreadsheet. Each of these named cells and ranges will be used in other tasks.

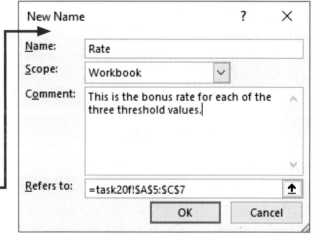

20.1.10 What are formulae and functions?

A formula in *Excel* starts with an = sign. It could be a simple formula using mathematical operators, such as =B1+B2, a complex formula using nested statements (this will be explained later in this chapter) or a formula including functions. A function has a predefined name such as **SUM** or **AVERAGE**, to perform a particular calculation. It is an operation built into the spreadsheet. There are many of these functions in *Excel*, many of which are beyond the scope of this book, but each has a reserved function name. If a question asks you to choose your own name for a cell or range, you cannot use these function names. (Note that the plural of 'formula' can be 'formulae'.)

20.1.11 Use functions

This section covers some of the simple functions available in *Excel*, but does not describe all of the functions available or all those that you may need to use. A formula can contain one or more functions.

SUM

The **SUM** function adds two or more numbers together. In earlier tasks you used the mathematical operator + and formulae like =B1+B2 to add the contents of two cells together. As there were only two cells to be added, this was the most efficient way of doing this. If there had been more figures to add, particularly if they were grouped together in the spreadsheet, it would have been more efficient to use the **SUM** function.

Task 20g		A	B
	1	**Rate of pay**	£12.80
Copy this spreadsheet model and calculate:	2		
» the total number of hours worked by all of these five people	3	**Name**	**Hours**
	4	David Watson	26
» the average number of hours worked per person	5	Graham Brown	20
» the maximum number of hours worked by any of these five people	6	John Reeves	17
	7	Brian Sargent	4
	8	Dan Bray	13
» the minimum number of hours worked by any of these five people.	9	**Total**	
	10	**Average**	
	11	**Maximum**	
	12	**Minimum**	

Open a new sheet and copy the labels and values exactly as shown in the table. Select the Home tab and use the **B** (bold) icon to embolden the cells shown. To find the total number of hours worked you will need to click the cursor into cell B9 and use **SUM** to add up the list of numbers. Enter the formula =SUM(B4:B8). This should give the value 80.

An alternative way to use this function without typing it into cell B9 is for you to use **AutoSum.** Move the cursor into cell B9, select the Home tab and find the Editing section. Click on the AutoSum icon. ──────

This will place the SUM function into cell B9 and attempt to work out which cells you wish to add up (by looking at the layout of your spreadsheet). It does not always get this range correct, so check carefully. If the range is correct (as it is in this case) press the <Enter> key to accept the **AutoSum.** If it is not correct, you can highlight the cells to be added before pressing the <Enter> key.

Advice

An alternative method is to enter =SUM(then drag the cursor to highlight cells B4 to B8, then type) and press the <Enter> key.

There are many ways of using the SUM function, some of which are shown in Table 20.2.

▼ **Table 20.2** Ways of using the SUM function

Function	Equivalent formula	What it does
=SUM(B4:B8)	=B4+B5+B6+B7+B8	Adds up the contents of all the cells in the range B4 to B8
=SUM(D3,D8,D12)	=D3+D8+D12	Adds up the contents of cells D3, D8 and D12
=SUM(D5:D8,F2)	=D5+D6+D7+D8+F2	Adds up the contents of the cells in the range D5 to D8 and the contents of cell F2
=SUM(MyRange)	None	Adds up the contents of all the cells within a named range called MyRange; this can be used with any named range

As you can see, the range of cells selected within these functions can include a number of individual cells, ranges of cells, named ranges, named cells or a combination of these. The AVERAGE, MAX (maximum), MIN (minimum), and COUNT functions also work like this.

AVERAGE

To find the average (mean) number of hours worked, click the cursor into cell B10 and use **AVERAGE** to calculate the mean (average) of a list of numbers. Enter the formula **=AVERAGE(B4:B8)**. This should give the value 16. There are many ways of using the AVERAGE function, some of which are shown in Table 20.3.

▼ **Table 20.3** Ways of using the AVERAGE function

Function	Equivalent formula	What it does
=AVERAGE(B4:B8)	=(B4+B5+B6+B7+B8)/5	Calculates the mean of the cells in the range B4 to B8
=AVERAGE(D3,D8,D12)	=(D3+D8+D12)/3	Calculates the mean of the cells D3, D8 and D12
=AVERAGE(D5:D8,F2)	=(D5+D6+D7+D8+F2)/5	Calculates the mean of the cells in the range D5 to D8 and cell F2
=AVERAGE(MyRange)	None	Calculates the mean of the cells in a named range called MyRange

MAX

To find the person who worked the most hours, click the cursor into cell B11 and use **MAX** to select the largest (maximum) figure within the list of numbers. Enter the formula **=MAX(B4:B8)**. This should give the value 26.

MIN

To find the person who worked the least number of hours, click the cursor into cell B12 and use **MIN** to select the smallest (minimum) figure from the list. Enter the formula **=MIN(B4:B8)**. This should give the value 4. Save this spreadsheet as **task20g**.

The finished spreadsheet should look like this.

	A	B
1	Rate of pay	12.8
2		
3	**Name**	**Hours**
4	David Watson	26
5	Graham Brown	20
6	John Reeves	17
7	Brian Sargent	4
8	Dan Bray	13
9	**Total**	**80**
10	**Average**	**16**
11	**Maximum**	**26**
12	**Minimum**	**4**

Activity 20a

Open the file **tuckshop.csv**.

In cells B14 to B17, calculate the total number of days that all the students worked in the school shop, the average number of days worked, and the maximum and minimum values.

Place your name on the spreadsheet. Print your spreadsheet showing the values, then print your spreadsheet showing the formulae used.

Task 20h

John Reeves did an extra four hours work. Change the spreadsheet that you created in Task 20g to show the new figures. The manager wants to see the average number of hours worked displayed as:

» an integer value
» rounded to the nearest whole hour.

Print two copies of the spreadsheet showing these values.

Open the file **task20g**. Change the contents of cell B6 to 21 to add the four extra hours that he worked. This gives an average value of 16.8 hours. Move the cursor into cell C9 and enter the text 'Integer', then move into cell D9 and enter the text 'Rounding'. To get the first value requested by the manager, we have to set cell C10 to hold an integer value.

INT

In mathematics, an integer is the word used to describe a whole number (with no decimals or fractions). In *Excel*, the **INT** function takes the whole number part of a number and ignores all digits after the decimal point. Move the cursor into cell C10 and enter the formula =INT(B10). This should give the value 16.

Advice

Setting a cell as an integer value will remove the decimal/fraction part of the number. This is not the same as formatting a cell to 0 decimal places, which stops the decimal/fraction part from being displayed but will still be used in a calculation.

ROUND

Move the cursor into cell D10 and enter the formula =ROUND(B10,0). This uses the **ROUND** function, which takes the content of cell B10 and rounds the number to 0 decimal places: if the first digit after the decimal point is five or more the number in cell D10 will be increased by one. For example, in cell B10 the value is 16.8, so the content of D10 is 17, as it has rounded the value to the nearest whole number. The spreadsheet should look like this.

	A	B	C	D
1	**Rate of pay**	12.8		
2				
3	**Name**	**Hours**		
4	David Watson	26		
5	Graham Brown	20		
6	John Reeves	21		
7	Brian Sargent	4		
8	Dan Bray	13		
9	**Total**	84	Integer	Round
10	**Average**	16.8	16	17
11	**Maximum**	26		
12	**Minimum**	4		

Rounding can be used with any number of decimal places, for example using rounding for currencies with two decimal places can avoid calculation errors.

Table 20.3 shows more examples of how you can use the **ROUND** function, using cell A1, which contains the number **62.5512**.

▼ **Table 20.4** Ways of using the ROUND function

Function	Result of rounding	What it does
=ROUND(A1,2)	62.55	Rounds the contents of A1 to two decimal places
=ROUND(A1,1)	62.6	Rounds the contents of A1 to one decimal place. Note that the second figure 5 in 62.5512 has forced the previous figure to be rounded up
=ROUND(A1,0)	63	Rounds the contents of A1 to 0 decimal places. Note that the first figure 5 in 62.5512 has forced the previous figure to be rounded up
=ROUND(A1, −1)	60	Rounds the contents of A1 to the nearest 10. The negative value for decimal places allows this function to round numbers in tens, hundreds, etc.
=ROUND(A1, −2)	100	Rounds the contents of A1 to the nearest 100. Note that the figure 6 has forced the previous figure to be rounded up from 0 to 1

Save and print a copy of the spreadsheet showing the average number of hours worked displayed as an integer value. Print a copy of the spreadsheet showing the average number of hours worked rounded to the nearest whole hour.

Activity 20b

Create a new spreadsheet model to calculate:
» the whole number part of 375.56411
» 375.56411 rounded to two decimal places
» 375.56411 rounded to the nearest whole number
» 375.56411 rounded to the nearest ten
» 375.56411 rounded to the nearest hundred
» 375.56411 rounded to the nearest thousand.

Task 20i

Open the file **project.csv**. This file lists some workers and below each worker is the number of jobs they have still to finish for a project.

Place a formula in cell A22 to count the number of workers that still have jobs to be finished for the project. Place a formula in cell A24 to count the number of workers on the project.

COUNT

For this task you will need to use functions that count different values. It is possible to count the number of numeric (number) values in a list using the **COUNT** function. Open the file, place the cursor in cell A22 and enter the formula **=COUNT(A2:A19)**. This will look at the range A2 to A19 (notice that you have not counted cell A1, which contains the title, nor cell A20, which may be used for something else later) and count only the cells with numbers in them. It will not count any blank spaces and should give the value 7.

COUNTA

The **COUNTA** function works in a similar way to the COUNT function. Rather than counting just the number of numeric values, this function counts the number of numeric or text values displayed in the cells. It will not count any blank cells within the range. There is no count function for just text values in *Excel*, so the COUNTA and COUNT functions will both be used to calculate the number of workers on the project. Place the cursor in cell A24 and enter the formula =COUNTA(A2:A19)–COUNT(A2:A19). This will look at the range A2 to A19 and count the cells with text or numbers in them, then subtract the number of cells with numbers in to leave only the cells with text in them, in other words the names of the employees. It should give the value 9 and look like this.

21	Number of workers who have not finished
22	=COUNT(A2:A19)
23	Number of workers on the project
24	=COUNTA(A2:A19)-COUNT(A2:A19)

▲	A
1	Project 142
2	Laila Aboli
3	4
4	Sri Paryanti
5	7
6	David Watson
7	2
8	Graham Brown
9	12
10	John Reeves
11	
12	Brian Sargent
13	6
14	Dan Bray
15	
16	Thirumalar Asokmani
17	3
18	Lea Cabusbusan
19	2
20	
21	Number of workers who have not finished
22	7
23	Number of workers on the project
24	9

Activity 20c

Open the file **classlist.csv**. This spreadsheet lists all the students in a class. If a student has attended any clubs during the year, the number of times they have attended is recorded in the cell below their name.

Place a formula in cell A71 to count the number of students in the class. Place a formula in cell A74 to count the number of students who have attended extra clubs this year. Save the spreadsheet.

Task 20j

Open the file **staff.csv**. This file lists some workers on another project and lists each worker's job. Place formulae in cells B24 to B28 to count how many of each type of worker are employed on the project. Place a formula in cell B31 to count the number of employees with less than five years' experience.

Place a formula in cell B32 to count the number of employees with ten or more years' experience.

COUNTIF

For this task, you need to count how many people have each type of job. Open the file and place the cursor in cell B24. The function needed for this task is **COUNTIF**, which looks at the cells within a given range and counts the number of cells in that range that meet a given condition. The condition is placed in the function and can be a number, text, an inequality or a cell reference. There are a number of ways the COUNTIF function can be used: any of the formulae given in Table 20.5 can be entered in cell B24 and will give the correct result.

▼ **Table 20.55** Alternative formulae using the COUNTIF function

Function	What it does
=COUNTIF($B$3:$B$21,"Director")	Counts the number of cells in the range B3 to B21 that contain the word 'Director'
=COUNTIF(Job,"Director")	Counts the number of cells in the named range Job (B3 to B21) that contain the word 'Director'. This only works if cells B3 to B21 have been named 'Job'
=COUNTIF($B$3:$B$21,A24)	Counts the number of cells in the range B3 to B21 that contain the same text as the contents of cell A24
=COUNTIF(Job,A24)	Counts the number of cells in the named range Job (B3 to B21) that contain the same text as the contents of cell A24. This only works if cells B3 to B21 have been named 'Job'

Advice

Note in examples 1 and 3 in Table 20.5 that the range $B$3:$B$21 has been set as an absolute reference so that this range is always in the same place if the formula is replicated. Also note that examples 3 and 4 have cell A24 set as a relative reference so that it will look for the next job title when the formula is replicated. Named ranges are absolute references, but you must show screenshot evidence that you have named the range correctly.

Replicate the function in cell B24 into cells B25 to B28. As these cells are to be replicated, methods three and four in Table 20.5 are the most efficient, as you do not have to edit each formula with a different name for each row. If a question asks you to show evidence of absolute and relative referencing, then method 3 would be the most appropriate. If named ranges are required, or absolute and relative referencing are not asked for in the question, method 4 is the most efficient.

To count the number of employees with less than five years' experience, place the cursor in cell B31 and enter the formula =COUNTIF($C$3:$C$21,"<5"). This will look at the range C3 to C21 and count the cells with a number value of less than 5. The speech marks around the <5 are needed to tell *Excel* that it is dealing with another formula (in this case an inequality), rather than searching for the symbols <5. The spreadsheet should show the value 7.

To count the number of employees with ten or more years' experience, place the cursor in cell B32 and enter the formula =COUNTIF($C$3:$C$21,">=10"). The value calculated should be 5. Save your spreadsheet as **task20j**.

Activity 20d

Open the file that you saved in Activity 20c. This spreadsheet lists all the students in a class. Next to each student's name is the colour of the house that they are in.

Place formulae in cells E2 to E5 that use both absolute and relative referencing to count the number of students in each house.

Place a formula in cell E7 to count the number of students with less than five clubs.

Place a formula in cell E8 to count the number of students with 12 or more clubs.

Save the spreadsheet.

IF

An **IF** function contains a pair of brackets and, within the brackets, three parts, each separated by a comma. An example of an **IF** function is:

=IF(A1=5,A2*0.05,"No discount")

The first part is a condition; in this example, it is testing to see if cell A1 contains the number 5. The second part is what to do if the condition is met, and the third part is what to do if it is not met. If the condition is met, a number or label could be placed in the cell, or a reference made to another cell, or even a calculation performed. The same range of options applies if a condition is not met. In this example, if the condition is met, the result of multiplying the contents of cell A2 by the number 0.05 is displayed in this cell. If the condition is not met this cell will display the text 'No discount'.

> ### Task 20k
>
> Open the file that you saved in Task 20j.
>
> Add a new label 'Category' into cell D2.
>
> Place formulae in cells D3 to D21 to display 'Very experienced' for employees with ten or more years' experience, otherwise to display 'Not experienced'.

Open the file and place the cursor in cell D2. Enter the label 'Category'. Place the cursor in cell D3 and enter the formula =IF(C3>=10,"Very experienced","Not experienced"). The reason that C3>=10 is used rather than C3>9 (which in many circumstances would be a more efficient formula), is because one employee has 0.2 years' experience. As the data does not only contain whole numbers, there could be an employee with 9.5 years' experience so C3>9 would not work for all data. Do not use absolute referencing in this formula as the reference to cell C3 needs to change when you replicate the formula. Replicate this formula so it is copied into cells D4 to D21. Save your spreadsheet as **task20k**. Your spreadsheet should look similar to this. ────

	A	B	C	D
1	**Project 153**			
2	Name	Job	Years experience	Category
3	Laila Aboli	Programmer	3	Not experienced
4	Greg Mina	Programmer	2	Not experienced
5	Sri Paryanti	Analyst	12	Very experienced
6	Bishen Patel	Sales	5	Not experienced
7	Rupinder Singh	Engineer	7	Not experienced
8	Sergio Gonzalez	Programmer	5	Not experienced
9	Rupinder Vas	Sales	6	Not experienced
10	Henri Ramos	Sales	10	Very experienced
11	John Mortlock	Programmer	14	Very experienced
12	Cameron Garnham	Analyst	7	Not experienced
13	Brian Guthrie	Director	3	Not experienced
14	Julia Frobisher	Engineer	6	Not experienced
15	Dan McNevin	Programmer	9	Not experienced
16	Patrick O'Malley	Engineer	11	Very experienced
17	Thirumalar Asokmani	Sales	10	Very experienced
18	Sean O'Byrne	Programmer	2	Not experienced
19	Lea Cabusbusan	Programmer	1	Not experienced
20	Brian O'Driscoll	Programmer	0.2	Not experienced
21	Wim Van Hoffmann	Engineer	2	Not experienced

> ### Activity 20e
>
> Open the file that you saved in Activity 20d. Add a new label 'New students' into cell F1. Place formulae in cells F2 to F6 to display 'Add to this house' if the number of students in this house is less than 6 or to display 'Full' if the number is 6 or more.

20.1.12 Use nested functions

Nested functions means having one function inside another one. Sometimes nested functions could contain several functions within each other. If the nested functions include a number of **IF** statements, be careful to work in a logical order. Work from smallest to largest or vice versa (depending on the question). Do **not** start with middle values; this will give incorrect results. Other functions, apart from the IF function, can also be nested. This is illustrated in the next task.

Task 20l

Open the file that you saved in Task 20k.

Change the formulae in cells D3 to D21 to display 'Not experienced' if they have less than five years' experience, 'Experienced' if they have five or more years' experience and 'Very experienced' for employees with ten or more years' experience.

For this task, three conditions exist. If the value for experience is:

>=10 then display 'Very experienced'
>=5 then display 'Experienced'
<5 then display 'Not experienced'.

Place the cursor into cell D3 and change the formula so that it becomes
=IF(C3>=10,"Very experienced",IF(C3>=5,"Experienced","Not experienced")).

Advice

Note that as the conditions are all 'greater than', they have been placed in reverse order. If they were placed in a different order the calculation would not work. For example, if the person had 40 years' experience, and the condition >=5 was placed first, and then the condition >=10: the first condition >=5 would be true, so the result displayed would be 'Experienced'; it would never get as far as the test for >=10.

Notice how the second part of the formula (highlighted in yellow) has been placed as a 'No' condition within the first formula. Be careful to get the brackets correct: each condition has one open and one closed bracket. When you work through this formula, it checks whether the value is greater than or equal to 10 first; if so, it displays the correct text. Then, if it were not true, it would check if the value is greater than or equal to 5 next; if so, it displays the correct text. As there are no other conditions that could occur, rather than having another nested statement the resulting text has been placed.

Replicate this formula into cells D4 to D21. Save your spreadsheet as **task20m**. Your spreadsheet should look similar to this.

	A	B	C	D
1	**Project 153**			
2	Name	Job	Years experience	Category
3	Laila Aboli	Programmer	3	Not experienced
4	Greg Mina	Programmer	2	Not experienced
5	Sri Paryanti	Analyst	12	Very experienced
6	Bishen Patel	Sales	5	Experienced
7	Rupinder Singh	Engineer	7	Experienced
8	Sergio Gonzalez	Programmer	5	Experienced
9	Rupinder Vas	Sales	6	Experienced
10	Henri Ramos	Sales	10	Very experienced
11	John Mortlock	Programmer	14	Very experienced
12	Cameron Garnham	Analyst	7	Experienced
13	Brian Guthrie	Director	3	Not experienced
14	Julia Frobisher	Engineer	6	Experienced
15	Dan McNevin	Programmer	9	Experienced
16	Patrick O'Malley	Engineer	11	Very experienced
17	Thirumalar Asokmani	Sales	10	Very experienced
18	Sean O'Byrne	Programmer	2	Not experienced
19	Lea Cabusbusan	Programmer	1	Not experienced
20	Brian O'Driscoll	Programmer	0.2	Not experienced
21	Wim Van Hoffmann	Engineer	2	Not experienced

Activity 20f

Open the file that you saved in Activity 20e. Change the formulae in cells F2 to F6 to display 'Add to this house' if the number of students in this house is less than six, 'Ideal number' if there are between six and ten students, or to display 'Full' if the number is more than ten.

Task 20m

Open the file that you saved in Task 20l.

Insert the label 'Total experience for:' in cell A34, the label 'Programmer' in cell A35 and 'Engineer' in cell A36.

Insert a formula in cell B35 that uses both absolute and relative referencing to calculate the number of years' experience for the programmers.

Insert a formula in cell B36 that uses both absolute and relative referencing to calculate the number of years' experience for the engineers.

SUMIF

SUMIF works in a similar way to **COUNTIF**. It compares each value in a range of cells and, if the value matches the given condition, it adds the value in another related cell to form a running total.

Add the labels as required by the task into cells A34, A35 and A36. Move the cursor into cell B35 and enter the formula =SUMIF($B$3:$B$21,A35,$C$3:$C$21). The total for this cell starts at 0. This looks at the contents of each row in the range B3 to B21 and compares the value in each cell to the contents of cell A35 (which contains the text 'Programmer'). If these two items are identical it adds the value from the same row within the range C3 to C21 to the total. When all rows in this range have been checked the total is displayed in this cell. This happens within a fraction of a second as you press the <Enter> key or change any value within these ranges.

To calculate the number of years' experience for the engineers, place in cell B36 the formula =SUMIF($B$3:$B$21,A36,$C$3:$C$21). Save the spreadsheet as **task20m**. The results of these formulae should look like this. ➡

34	Total experience for:	
35	Programmer	36.2
36	Engineer	26

Advice

You could use named ranges rather than absolute referencing for cells B3 to B21 and C3 to C21. One alternative formula in cell B35, which uses the named range 'Job' created earlier in the chapter, is =SUMIF(Job,A35,$C$3:$C$21).

Activity 20g

Open the file **clubs.csv**.

Insert a formula in cell B37 that uses both absolute and relative referencing to calculate the number of clubs attended by students in red house.

Replicate this formula in cells B38 to B40 for each house colour. Place your name in one of the cells.

Use lookups

The term 'look up', as used in questions, means to look up from a list. It does not mean that you should use the LOOKUP function, as there are three variations of the LOOKUP function that can be used within *Excel*. These are: **LOOKUP**, **HLOOKUP** and **VLOOKUP**.

LOOKUP

LOOKUP is used to look up a value using data in the first row or the first column of a range of cells and returns a relative value. For our purposes, this is probably the least useful of the three formulae.

HLOOKUP

HLOOKUP is a function that performs a horizontal look up of data. This should be used when the values that you wish to compare your data with are stored in a single **row**. The values to be looked up are stored in the rows below these cells.

> ## Task 20n
>
> Open the file **jobs.csv**.
>
> Insert formulae in the Description column to look up and display the JobTitle using the JobCode as the look-up value.

Open the file jobs.csv and click the left mouse button to place the cursor in cell C6. Enter the formula =HLOOKUP(B6,$B$2:$H$3,2) into this cell. This formula will look up and compare the contents of cell B6 with the contents of each cell in the top (horizontal) row of the range B2 to H3. When it finds a match, it will take the value or label stored in the second row, which is directly under the matched cell. The '2' at the end of the formula tells *Excel* to look in the second row of the given range. Replicate this formula into cells C7 to C27. Save the spreadsheet as **task20n**. The results should look similar to this.

	A	B	C	D
1	**Project 160**			
2	JobCode	1	2	3
3	JobTitle	Director	Engineer	Analyst S
4				
5	**Name**	JobCode	Description	
6	Laila Aboli	5	Programmer	
7	Greg Mina	5	Programmer	
8	Sri Paryanti	3	Analyst	
9	Bishen Patel	4	Sales	
10	Rupinder Singh	2	Engineer	
11	Sergio Gonzalez	5	Programmer	

VLOOKUP

VLOOKUP is a function that performs a vertical look up of data. This should be used when the values that you wish to compare your data with are stored in a single **column**. The values to be looked up are stored in the columns to the right of these cells. The look up data can be stored either in the same file or in a different file.

20.1.13 Use external data sources within functions

> ## Task 20o
>
> Open the file **tasks.csv**
>
> Insert formulae in the CurrentTask column to look up the client, using the TaskCode for the look up value and the file **client.csv**. Make sure that you use both absolute and relative referencing within your function.

Open the file tasks.csv and click the left mouse button to place the cursor in cell C3. The task instructs you to use the file client.csv for the look up. Open this file in a new spreadsheet. Examine the layout of this file to decide which type of look up formula to use. The file client.csv looks like this.

	A	B
1	TaskCode	Client
2	1	Rootrainer
3	2	Quattichem
4	3	Hothouse Design
5	4	Avricom
6	5	Binnaccount
7	6	LGY
8	7	Rock ICT

Because it is stored with the look up data in vertical columns, a **VLOOKUP** is the most appropriate formula to use. Enter the formula =VLOOKUP(B3,client.csv!$A$2:$B$8,2,FALSE) into this cell. This formula will look up and compare the contents of cell B3 with the contents of each cell in the left (vertical) column of the range A2 to B8 within the file client.csv. When entering this formula, you can add the yellow highlighted section of the formula by moving the cursor into this file and dragging it to highlight all of the cells in both columns, so it includes the look up value and the result. The number '2' in the formula tells *Excel* to look in the second column of this range. The 'False' condition in the formula tells *Excel* to only display the match if it is an exact match. If you set this to 'True' it will find the nearest approximate match. When it finds a match, it will take the value or label in the second column of the range A2:B8, which is to the right of the matched cell. Replicate this formula into cells C4 to C24. Save the spreadsheet as **task20o**. The first few results should look similar to this.

	A	B	C
1	Current client list		
2	Name	TaskCode	CurrentTask
3	Laila Aboli	6	LGY
4	Greg Mina	4	Avricom
5	Sri Paryanti	6	LGY
6	Bishen Patel	6	LGY
7	Rupinder Singh	3	Hothouse Design
8	Sergio Gonzalez	5	Binnaccount
9	Rupinder Vas	1	Rootrainer
10	Bryan Revell	1	Rootrainer
11	Henri Ramos	7	Rock ICT

Advice

Experiment with these settings. Change the value in cell B24 to 5.2. See the result of this change. Now change the exact match condition from False to True in cell C24. See the result of this change. Try other numbers, like 5.9 in B24, to see what happens.

XLOOKUP

XLOOKUP is a new function in *Excel* that can be used to perform either a horizontal or a vertical look up of data. This is similar to HLOOKUP and VLOOKUP, but is more powerful and flexible than either of these. It will also reference data stored in rows/columns before the lookup value. It therefore allows backward referencing within an array. The values to be looked up can be stored to either the right or left or above or below the lookup array. The look up data can be stored either in the same file or in a different file.

Advice

XLOOKUP and the following task can only be attempted with the latest versions of *Excel*. If you have older software skip this section and move onto Activity 20h.

Task 20p

Open the file **tasks.csv**.

Insert formulae in the CurrentTask column to look up the client, using the TaskCode for the look up value and the file client1.csv. Make sure that you use both absolute and relative referencing within your function.

Open the file tasks.csv and click the left mouse button to place the cursor in cell C3. The task instructs you to use the file client1.csv for the look up. Open this file in a new spreadsheet. Examine the layout of this file to decide which type of look up formula to use. The file client1. csv looks like this.

	A	B
1	Client	TaskCode
2	Rootrainer	1
3	Quattichem	2
4	Hothouse Design	3
5	Avricom	4
6	Binnaccount	5
7	LGY	6
8	Rock ICT	7

At first glance, because it is stored with the look up data in vertical columns, a VLOOKUP may appear the correct function, but the TaskCode column is to the right of the Client column and VLOOKUP cannot do backwards referencing. Therefore, the most appropriate function to use for this task would be **XLOOKUP**. Enter the formula =XLOOKUP(B3,client1.csv!$B$2:$B$8,client1.csv!$A$2:$A$8,"Not found",0,1) into this cell. This formula will look up and compare the contents of cell B3 with the contents of each cell in the range B2 to B8 within the file client1.csv. When entering this formula, you can add the yellow highlighted section of the formula by moving the cursor into this file and dragging it to highlight all the cells in this range, so it includes only the TaskCodes (the lookup array). You can also add the blue highlighted section of the formula by moving the cursor into this file and dragging it to highlight all the cells in this range, so it includes only the names of the clients (the return array). The text "Not found" is displayed if the TaskCode is not found during the look up. The number 0 is the match mode, the 0 tells the function that we want an exact match only. The final number 1 instructs the function to search through the items first to last as the TaskCodes are in ascending order in the source file. When it finds a match, it will take the value or label in the

	A	B	C
1	Current client list		
2	Name	TaskCode	CurrentTask
3	Laila Aboli	6	LGY
4	Greg Mina	4	Avricom
5	Sri Paryanti	6	LGY
6	Bishen Patel	6	LGY
7	Rupinder Singh	3	Hothouse Design
8	Sergio Gonzalez	5	Binnaccount
9	Rupinder Vas	1	Rootrainer
10	Bryan Revell	1	Rootrainer
11	Henri Ramos	7	Rock ICT

return array which is the range A2:A8. Replicate this formula into cells C4 to C24. Save the spreadsheet as task20p. The first few results should look similar to this.

Activity 20h

Open the file **tutors.csv**. This lists a number of students and the initials for their personal tutor. Insert formulae in the Tutor Name column to look up the tutor's name using the file **teachers.csv**.

Insert formulae in the Room Number column to look up the room number using the file **rooms.csv**.

Make sure that you use both absolute and relative referencing within all of your functions. Save your spreadsheet.

20.2 Manipulate data

20.2.1 Search and select data

Searching for data means getting *Excel* to search through data held in a spreadsheet to extract only rows (or columns) where the data matches your search criteria.

Search using text filters

> **Task 20q**
>
> Open the file that you saved in Task 20o.
>
> Select from all the data only the employees who are currently working on jobs for Binnaccount.

Open the file that you saved in Task 20o and highlight cells A2 to C24. Select the **Data** tab and find the **Sort & Filter** section. Click on the **Filter** icon. ————

Sort & Filter

This displays an arrow in the top right corner of each column, like this. ————

When you click on the **CurrentTask** arrow, a small drop-down menu appears like this. ————

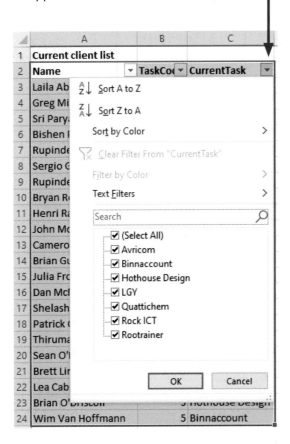

	A	B	C
1	Current client list		
2	**Name** ▾	**TaskCo**▾	**CurrentTask** ▾
3	Laila Aboli	6	LGY
4	Greg Mina	4	Avricom
5	Sri Paryanti	6	LGY
6	Bishen Patel	6	LGY
7	Rupinder Singh	3	Hothouse Design
8	Sergio Gonzalez	5	Binnaccount
9	Rupinder Vas	1	Rootrainer
10	Bryan Revell	1	Rootrainer
11	Henri Ramos	7	Rock ICT
12	John Mortlock	2	Quattichem
13	Cameron Garnham	2	Quattichem
14	Brian Guthrie	1	Rootrainer
15	Julia Frobisher	5	Binnaccount
16	Dan McNevin	1	Rootrainer
17	Shelash O'Leary	1	Rootrainer
18	Patrick O'Malley	5	Binnaccount
19	Thirumalar Asokmani	5	Binnaccount
20	Sean O'Byrne	3	Hothouse Design
21	Brett Ling	2	Quattichem
22	Lea Cabusbusan	7	Rock ICT
23	Brian O'Driscoll	3	Hothouse Design
24	Wim Van Hoffmann	5	Binnaccount

In the check box section of the menu, click on the tick box for (Select All) which will remove all of the ticks from every box. Find, then tick, only the Binnaccount box, before clicking on [OK]. This will display only the five selected rows like this.

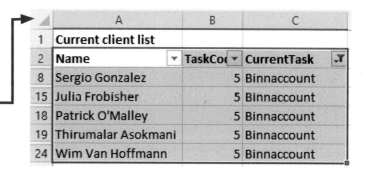

The same method can be used to select more than one company from the list. By selecting different drop-down menu options, searches can be made using different criteria in different columns. Save the spreadsheet as **task20q**.

Search using number filters

> ### Task 20r
>
> Open the file that you saved in Task 20o.
>
> Select from all the data only the employees where the task code is between 3 and 6 inclusive.

Open the file and set the AutoFilter arrows for cells A2 to C24 as in the previous task. This time the search will be performed on the TaskCode column. Select the drop-down menu for this column using the arrow followed by Number Filters.

This opens a sub-menu; it should look like this.

Select Custom Filter...
to get this Custom AutoFilter window.

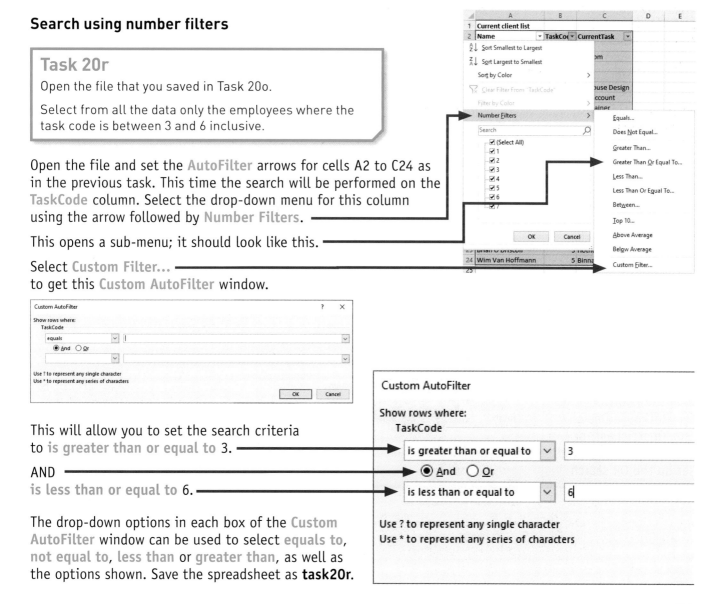

This will allow you to set the search criteria to is greater than or equal to 3.

AND

is less than or equal to 6.

The drop-down options in each box of the Custom AutoFilter window can be used to select equals to, not equal to, less than or greater than, as well as the options shown. Save the spreadsheet as **task20r**.

Advice

The method shown here is an alternative to selecting only the boxes for 3, 4, 5 and 6. Even though it may seem easier to click on the tick boxes for this question, you will need to use the **Custom AutoFilter** window when a number of options are required. The **Custom AutoFilter** window also allows you to select **Is not equal to** and to perform wildcard searches.

Search using two or more criteria

> ### Task 20s
>
> Open the file that you saved in Task 20o.
>
> Select from the data all the employees who are currently working on jobs for Quattichem or Hothouse Design, except John Mortlock and Sean O'Byrne.

Open the file and set the **AutoFilter** arrows for cells A2 to C24 as in the previous task. This time the search will be performed on both the **Name** and **CurrentTask** columns. Select the drop-down arrow for the **Name** column, **Text Filters** and then select **Does not equal** from the sub-menu. This opens the **Custom AutoFilter** window; enter the initial letter 'J' in the right box (this speeds up the search). When you click on the arrow for the drop-down list, it will show you all the Names starting with 'J', so select 'John Mortlock' from the list.

Select the AND operator and repeat the process for Sean O'Byrne, selecting **Does not equal** in the left box and typing 'S' to find Sean O'Byrne, selecting his name from the list in the right box. Click on ⟦ OK ⟧.

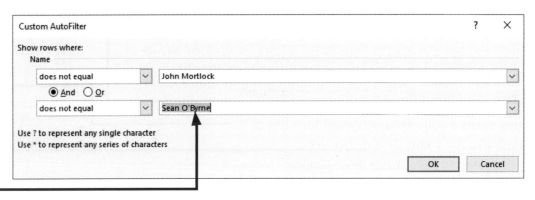

Select the search arrow for the **CurrentTask** column. Select from this menu only the two tick boxes for 'Hothouse Design' and 'Quattichem', or select **Text Filters** and set up the OR search like this.

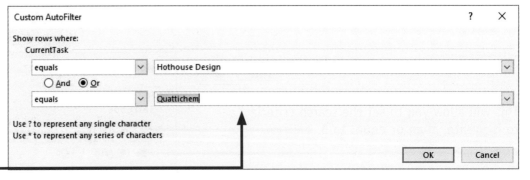

Save the spreadsheet as **task20s**. The results of this task should look like this.

	A	B	C
1	**Current client list**		
2	**Name**	**TaskCode**	**CurrentTask**
7	Rupinder Singh	3	Hothouse Design
13	Cameron Garnham	2	Quattichem
21	Brett Ling	2	Quattichem
23	Brian O'Driscoll	3	Hothouse Design

Activity 20i

Open the file that you saved in Activity 20h. Select from all the data:
» all the students with a tutor called Chris Scott
» all the students who will be using rooms numbered between 22 and 74 inclusive
» all the students except Kiah and Hartati with a tutor called Kate Morrissey or Mike Arnott.

Search using wildcards

A wildcard is a character that is used as a substitute for other characters. The * (asterisk) character is often used to show a number of characters (including 0), while the ? (question mark) is often used to show a single character. *Excel* uses these wildcard characters but AutoFilter also contains other features that simplify some of these searches.

Task 20t

Open the file that you saved in Task 20o.

Select from all the data only the employees who have a name that starts with the letter 'S'.

Open the file and set the AutoFilter arrows for the cells A2 to C24 as in the previous task. This time the search will be performed on the Name column. Click on the drop-down arrow for this column and select Text Filters followed by Begins with... from the sub-menu. This opens the Custom AutoFilter window. Enter the initial S in the right box like this and click on ☐ OK ☐. ────

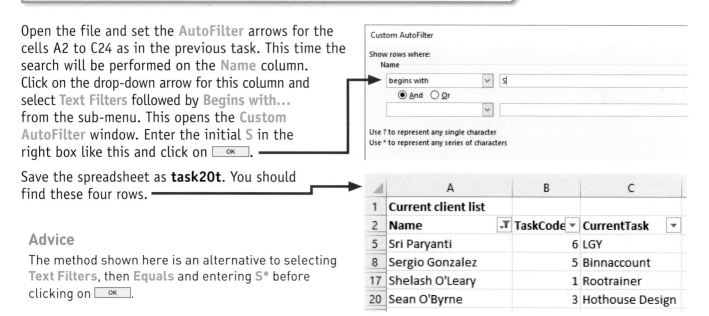

Custom AutoFilter

Show rows where:
Name

begins with | S

⦿ And ○ Or

Use ? to represent any single character
Use * to represent any series of characters

Save the spreadsheet as **task20t**. You should find these four rows. ────

	A	B	C
1	**Current client list**		
2	**Name**	**TaskCode**	**CurrentTask**
5	Sri Paryanti	6	LGY
8	Sergio Gonzalez	5	Binnaccount
17	Shelash O'Leary	1	Rootrainer
20	Sean O'Byrne	3	Hothouse Design

Advice

The method shown here is an alternative to selecting Text Filters, then Equals and entering S* before clicking on ☐ OK ☐.

Task 20u

Open the file that you saved in Task 20o.

Select from all the data only the employees who have a name that ends with the letter 'a'.

This is a similar process to the previous task. Use the same process, this time selecting the Text Filters from the menu, then the Ends with... option to obtain the Custom AutoFilter window. Enter the letter a in the right box like this and click on [OK].

Save the spreadsheet as **task20u**. You should find this single row.

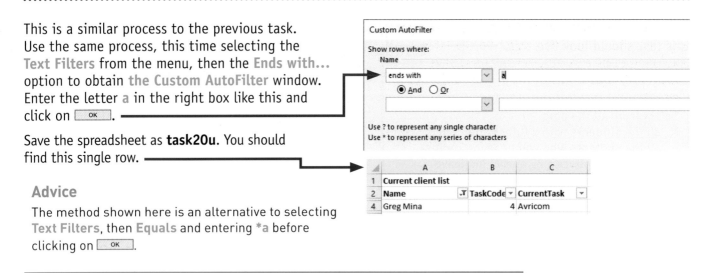

Advice

The method shown here is an alternative to selecting Text Filters, then Equals and entering *a before clicking on [OK].

Task 20v

Open the file that you saved in Task 20o.

Select from all the data only the employees who have a name that contains the two characters O', for example, Brian O'Driscoll.

Again, select the Text Filters from the drop-down menu in the Name column. This time select the Contains... option, enter the letter O followed by an apostrophe in the right box and click on [OK].

Save the spreadsheet as **task20v**. You should find these four rows.

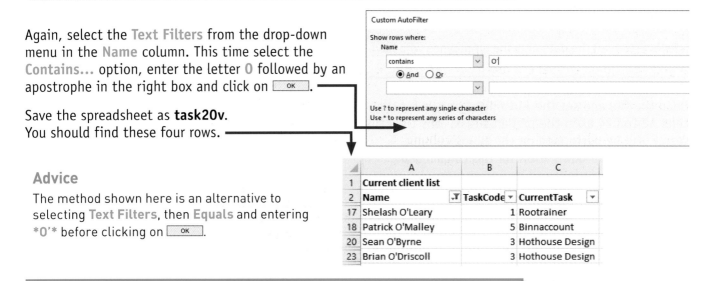

Advice

The method shown here is an alternative to selecting Text Filters, then Equals and entering *O'* before clicking on [OK].

Task 20w

Open the file that you saved in Task 20o.

Select from all the data only the employees who have a first name that has the second and third letters 'ea'.

Using the same methods as the previous searches, select the Text Filter from the drop-down menu in the Name column. This time select the Begins with... option and add the characters ?ea to the right box before clicking on [OK].

This tells *Excel* that the first letter can contain any character. Then there must be the letters 'ea' followed by any other characters. Save the spreadsheet as **task20w**. You should find these two rows. ━━━━━━━➤

◢	A	B	C
1	**Current client list**		
2	**Name** ⊤	**TaskCode** ▾	**CurrentTask** ▾
20	Sean O'Byrne	3	Hothouse Design
22	Lea Cabusbusan	7	Rock ICT

Advice

The method shown here is an alternative to selecting Text Filters, then Equals and entering ?ea* before clicking on ⬚ OK ⬚.

Activity 20j

Open the file that you saved in Activity 20h. Select from the data:
» all the students with a forename that starts or ends with the letter 'R'
» all the students with a forename that contains the letters 'eth'
» all the students with a forename that contains the letters 'Jam' and who have a tutor who uses room 60.

20.2.2 Sort data

Before you try to sort any data, make sure that you select **all** of the data for each item to be sorted. One common error is to select and sort on a single column. If you were to do this, the integrity of the data would be lost. Table 20.6 gives an example showing correct and incorrect sorting on the student's name for a spreadsheet containing test results in Maths and English. The yellow shaded cells show the areas selected for the sort. Note how the results for each person have been changed when sorting without highlighting all the data.

▼ **Table 20.6** Correct and incorrect data selection for sorting

Original data			Sorted correctly with all data selected			Sorted with only the name column selected (this is an example of lost data integrity–the correct test scores no longer match the students)		
Name	Maths	English	Name	Maths	English	Name	Maths	English
Sheila	72	75	Karla	52	75	Karla	72	75
Marcos	64	34	Marcos	64	34	Marcos	64	34
Vikram	61	44	Sheila	72	75	Sheila	61	44
Karla	52	75	Vikram	61	44	Vikram	52	75

Task 20x

Open the file **salary.csv**. Sort the data into ascending order of surname, then ascending order of forename.

Open the file **salary.csv**. Highlight all the cells in the range A2 to C43. Do not highlight row 1 because if you do the column headings will also be sorted within the employee names. Select the **Home** tab and find the **Editing** section. Click on the **Sort & Filter** icon to obtain the drop-down menu.

Select **Custom Sort...** to open the **Sort** window. In the **Sort** by box select **Surname** from the drop-down list.

This will be the primary sort for this task. Make sure that the **Order** box contains **A to Z** to sort the data into ascending order.

To add the secondary sort to this data you need to add a second level to the **Sort** window. To add the second sort level, click on the **Add Level** button.

In the **Then by** box select **Forename** from the drop-down list. Again, make sure that the **Order** box contains **A to Z** to sort the data into ascending order. Click on OK to perform the sort. Save the spreadsheet as **task20x**. The data should look like this.

Advice

You can sort into descending order rather than ascending order by selecting **Z to A** rather than **A to Z** in the **Order** box.

Activity 20k

Open the file that you saved in Activity 20h.

Sort the data into descending order of tutor name, then ascending order of student forename.

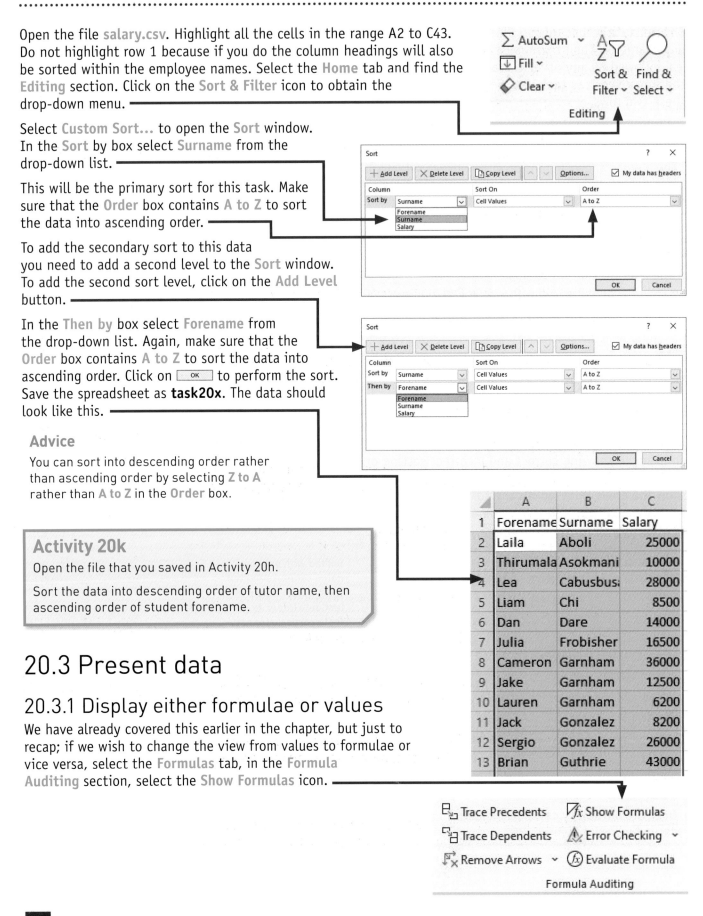

20.3 Present data

20.3.1 Display either formulae or values

We have already covered this earlier in the chapter, but just to recap; if we wish to change the view from values to formulae or vice versa, select the **Formulas** tab, in the **Formula Auditing** section, select the **Show Formulas** icon.

Select data for display

Many of the features described in this section can be applied to an individual cell, a range of cells, to one or more rows or columns, or to the entire spreadsheet. To apply the feature to the entire spreadsheet, click in the top left-hand corner of the sheet.

To select a row or rows, click on the number or numbers to the left of the row and it will select all the cells in that row.

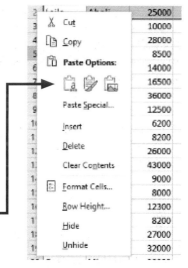

To select a column or columns, click on the column letter or letters to select all the cells in the column or columns.

To select a single cell, click in that cell.

To select a range of cells, drag the cursor to highlight a range of cells. If you need to select different cells or ranges from different parts of the sheet at the same time, hold down the <Ctrl> key while making your selections.

20.3.2 Adjust rows and columns

Adjust row height/column width

Earlier you learned how to expand column widths using the drag handle to make sure that all data in the spreadsheet is visible. Row heights can be adjusted in exactly the same way.

The settings for row heights can also be changed by right clicking the mouse button on the row number on the left to obtain this drop-down menu.

Hide a row/column

The row can be hidden from view by selecting the Hide option, or can have a different row height set using the Row Height... option.

This option opens the Row Height window, where you can adjust the height setting before clicking on OK.

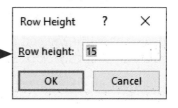

The column width can be hidden or adjusted in a similar way. To get the drop-down menu, click the right mouse button on the column heading at the top of the column.

Use this ability to change the row height and column width to **always** make sure that the contents of all cells (whether they contain values or formulae) are fully visible.

Advice

To unhide a row or column, select the rows/columns on both sides of the hidden one/s. Click the right mouse button on the selection and choose the Unhide option.

20.3.3 Wrap text within a cell

Refer to Section 20.1.7, where you learned to wrap text within a cell and practised this in Task 20d. This skill is useful when you are required to fit everything on a single page width, yet, because some of the text in the cells is quite lengthy, it does not fit. Cells in a row can always be 2,3, or even 4 times as high as the rest of the cells to assist in improving page layout.

Task 20y

Open the file **clothing.csv**. Merge cells A1 to C1 and set the text height of this cell to 36 point. Merge cells A3 to C3. Set all other text to 14 points high. Format the spreadsheet to look like this:

Print your spreadsheet so that it fits on a single A4 portrait page. Save the spreadsheet as task20y.

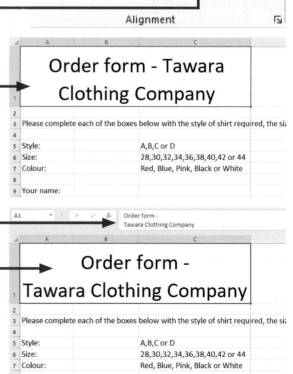

Open the file. Merge cells A1 to C1 using the methods learned in Section 20.1.7. Set the text in this merged cell to be 36 point. Use the Home tab, locate the Font section, then select the Font Size icon.

You can either use the drop-down list of sizes (shown by the arrow) or overtype the value of 11 with the value 36. Select this cell and from the Home tab, in the Alignment section, select the Wrap Text icon.

Set the row height of row 1 to 100 pixels and widen or narrow the columns so that the text in this cell wraps. The text will not wrap to match the task. It may look similar to this.

We must force a line break after the hyphen to make the cell look like the image in the task. To do this, click within the cell, then in the Formula Bar.

Place the cursor immediately before 'Tawara'. Hold down the <Alt> key and press <Enter> to change the wrapping to look like this.

Highlight all cells between A2 and C9 and set the Font Size to 14.

Merge cells A3 to C3. Set the row height of row 3 to 60 pixels. To set row 2 to be smaller than the other rows (as shown in the Task) select the row and change the Row Height from its current setting (mine is 18.75 pixels) to a value around half of that, so in this case 9 pixels. Rather than repeating this for row 4 and 8, a shortcut is to click the mouse button on the number for row 4 then hold <Ctrl> and click <Y>. Repeat for row 8. This repeats the previous action so only works if setting the original row height was the last action that you took within the spreadsheet. The spreadsheet should look like this.

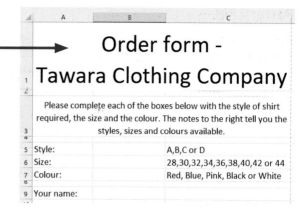

20.3.4 Enhance a spreadsheet

To enhance data, first select the data to be enhanced. All of the enhancement features are located using the Home tab.

Bold, italic and underline

The Font section contains icons that allow you to set the cell contents to be **bold**, *italic* (sloping), or <u>underlined</u>.

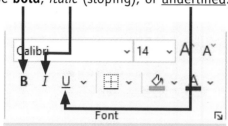

For this task the text in cells A5 to A9 must be bold, so highlight these cells then click on the Bold icon.

> **Advice**
>
> <Ctrl> <B> is the keyboard shortcut for bold, <Ctrl><I> for italic and <Ctrl><U> for underline.

Background colour

You have already changed the font size (which can also be used as an enhancement). Cells can also be enhanced using different colours for the background of the cell. Again, highlight the area to be coloured, in this case the merged cell A1:C1, then select the drop-down menu from the Fill Color icon. The drop-down menu looks like this.

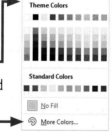

There are a number of standard colours as well as colours selected by *Excel* (called Theme Colors) for the current colour schemes. If the colour that you want is not there, click on the colour palette icon.

Select a dark blue colour to match the task. When you are selecting colours, ensure that the foreground and background colours contrast and can be seen easily when printed. Do not use green and red, to help people who are colour blind.

Font colour

The text colour of a cell (the font colour) can be selected in the Font section. The Font Color icon is to the right of the Fill Color icon. The drop-down menu from this icon is the same as the menu for the background colour. Select a yellow font colour from this palette. The spreadsheet now looks like this.

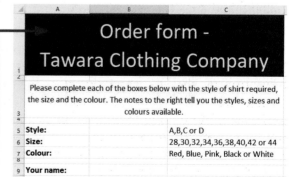

Pattern Fill

To produce the cell shading/pattern fill for cells A5 to A7, highlight all three cells together, then select the font settings arrow to open the Format Cells window.

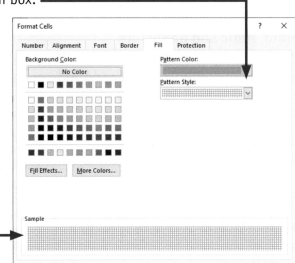

Choose the Fill tab along the top: this gives more options than the Fill Color icon. Select the Pattern Style: drop-down box. You can use this and the Pattern Color: to select the style of shading required, like this.

Click [OK] to apply this patterned background.

Text orientation

The Format Cells window is useful for many other enhancements. After highlighting the cell/s to be formatted, selecting the Alignment tab will let you change the way the text fits into a cell/s, either by rotating the text direction (by dragging the red handle in the Orientation panel).

This is not used in this task. However, this window also gives an alternative method for merging cells or wrapping text within a cell.

Borders and gridlines

Gridlines are often added to the whole spreadsheet but can be used as borders to some cells to give emphasis, as in this task. Highlight cells A5 to B7 inclusive. From the Home tab, in the Font section, select the Borders icon to get the drop-down menu.

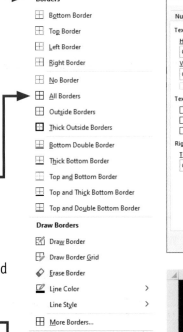

Select All Borders for the highlighted cells.

Select cells A9 to B9. Repeat the steps above to set all borders for these cells. Save and print the spreadsheet, adjusting the column widths so that all data is visible and the spreadsheet fits on a single portrait A4 page. The spreadsheet will now look like this.

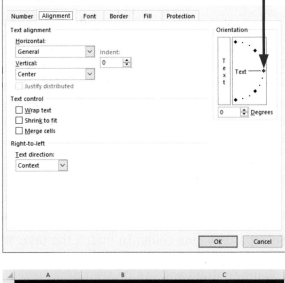

20.3.5 Format numeric data

Formatting cells containing numbers changes the way a cell is displayed but does not change the values held within it.

Task 20z

Create a spreadsheet model that looks like this.

Place a formula in cell C2 that multiplies the contents of cell A2 by the contents of cell B2. Format cell A2 as an integer.

	A	B	C
1	First	Second	Product
2	1.2	5	6

Create the spreadsheet as shown. In cell C2 enter the formula =A2*B2. The spreadsheet will look like this.

	A	B	C
1	First	Second	Product
2	1.2	5	6

Format to a specified number of decimal places

To format cell A2 as an integer, place the cursor in this cell and select the Home tab. In the Number section, click on the arrow in the bottom right corner.

This opens the Format Cells window.

When this window opens, it should have the Number tab selected. The Format Cells window will allow you to format cells in different currencies, into percentages or even as dates or times.

For this task, you need to format this cell as a number. In the Category: section, select Number from the list.

Change the cell formatting to 0 Decimal places: so that the window looks like this.

Click on OK to set the formatting. The spreadsheet will now look like this.

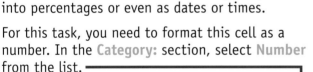

	A	B	C
1	First	Second	Product
2	1	5	6

If you compare the two views of the spreadsheet, you can see that cell A2 has changed. The actual content of cell A2 remains as 1.2 but in the second view it displays as 1. For this reason the answer for the product appears to be incorrect in the second view.

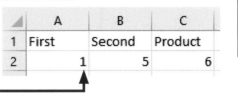

Original

	A	B	C
1	First	Second	Product
2	1.2	5	6

Formatted

	A	B	C
1	First	Second	Product
2	1	5	6

Use the **INT** or **ROUND** function to force a cell to contain whole numbers. Formatting a cell does not change the value of the cell, so it does not always appear to give the correct answer.

Task 20aa

Open the file **costs.csv**.

Format cells A1, D1, D3 and G3 so that the font is bold and 14 point.

Format all numeric cells in row 2 into their respective currencies to three decimal places.

Format all numeric cells in columns C and D into pounds sterling with two decimal places.

Format the cells E5 to E15 into Euros with two decimal places.

Format the cells F5 to F15 into Japanese Yen with zero decimal places.

Format all cells between G5 and G15 into percentage values with no decimal places.

Open the file costs.csv. Click in cell A1. Select the Home tab, find the Font section, then use the drop-down list to change the size of this cell to 14 point. Click the mouse on the Bold icon to set this cell to bold. Locate the Clipboard section, then click on the Format Painter icon and then click in cell D1.

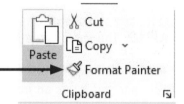

Click on Format Painter again and then click in cell D3, then Format Painter again and click in cell G3. This process should copy the formatting from cell A1 into these other three cells.

Move the cursor into cell E2. In the Number section, click on the arrow in the bottom-right corner to open the Format Cells window in the Number tab. In the Category: section, select Currency. Set the number of decimal places to 3.

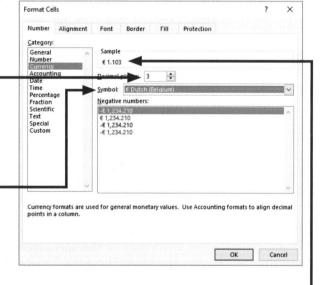

Although this is not the correct number of decimal places for Euro, it was specified in the task.

Format different currency symbols

In the Symbol: section, select an appropriate Euro format from the list.

You may need to scroll down the list of available currencies to find it. The Sample area will show you what the formatting of the cell will look like when you click on OK.

When you have checked this formatting, click on OK.

Repeat this process for cell F2, but this time selecting Japanese Yen. Some currencies, such as the Japanese Yen, have no decimal places (so would normally need to be formatted to zero decimal places) but in this task you were told to set this cell to three decimal places. The Format Cells window should look like this.

Click on ☐ OK ☐.

To format all the numeric cells in columns C and D, highlight all cells in the range C5 to D15. Then open the Format Cells window and set the Category: to Currency, the number of Decimal places: to 2 and the Symbol: to pounds sterling (£). Repeat this process for cells E5 to E15, selecting Euro with two decimal places, and for cells F5 to F15 with Japanese Yen set to zero decimal places (which are the appropriate formats for both of these currencies).

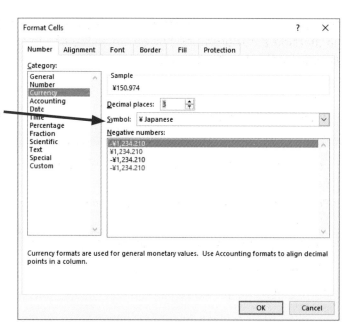

Advice

If the currency symbol that you are looking for (for example, ¥) does not appear in the drop-down list, there are a number of text options available. In this case you can select JPY, which is the international standard code for Japanese Yen.

Format cells as percentage values

To format all cells between G5 and G15 into percentage values, highlight this range then, in the Format Cells window, set the Category: to Percentage. Set the number of Decimal places: to 0. Resize each column, as necessary. The finished spreadsheet should look like this.

	A	B	C	D	E	F	G
1	**Current jobs**			**Exchange**	Europe	Japan	
2					€1.103	¥150.974	
3	Customer	Job reference	Estimate	**Cost**			**Increase**
4				UK	Europe	Japan	% Increase
5	Avricom	4023	£2,940.00	£4,200.00	€4,633.86	¥634,091	43%
6	LGY	4122	£192,000.00	£240,000.00	€264,792.00	¥36,233,760	25%
7	Hothouse Design	4123	£1,050.00	£1,500.00	€1,654.95	¥226,461	43%
8	Binnaccount	4125	£320.00	£475.00	€524.07	¥71,713	48%
9	Rootrainer	4126	£16,240.00	£23,200.00	€25,596.56	¥3,502,597	43%
10	Rock ICT	4128	£12,250.00	£17,500.00	€19,307.75	¥2,642,045	43%
11	Quattichem	4129	£1,400.00	£2,000.00	€2,206.60	¥301,948	43%
12	LGY	4130	£10,800.00	£12,000.00	€13,239.60	¥1,811,688	11%
13	Hothouse Design	4131	£720.00	£720.00	€794.38	¥108,701	0%
14	Binnaccount	4132	£1,680.00	£2,400.00	€2,647.92	¥362,338	43%
15	Hothouse Design	4133	£4,500.00	£5,000.00	€5,516.50	¥754,870	11%

Advice

An alternative to this for percentage values with no decimal places is to highlight the cell/s, select the Home tab, locate the Number section, then click on the Percent Style icon.

20.3.6 Conditional formatting

Conditional formatting is used to change the display format (usually the font or background colour within a cell), depending on the contents of the cell. There are many different methods for completing this: using rules that you apply (rather than the spreadsheet's default settings) is the recommended method and will enable you to attempt anything that may be asked at IGCSE level.

Open the file task20m. In previous tasks you have highlighted the range of cells to be formatted (in this case D3 to D21). This question has asked for column D, so click on the column heading (the letter D) to highlight the entire column. Select the Home tab, find the Styles section, then select the Conditional Formatting icon, which will open this drop-down menu.

Choose New Rule....

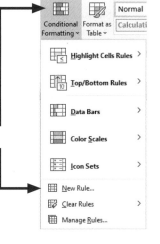

This opens the New Formatting Rule window.

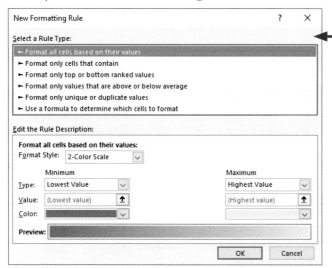

Select the second option for Format only cells that contain and the window will change to look like this.

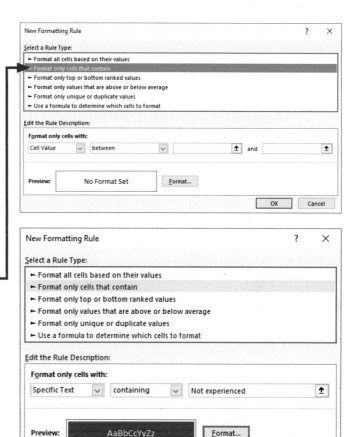

In the Edit the Rule Description: section, in the left Format only cells with: box use the drop-down box on the left to choose Specific text (as the cells all contain labels). In the right dialogue box enter the text 'Not experienced'. Click on the Format button, select the Fill tab and a red background colour, then, from the Font tab select an appropriate foreground colour, then [OK]. You can see what the font will look like at each stage. In this case we have chosen a white font as this gives good contrast.

When you are happy that this looks good, click [OK].

Repeat this process for the other two items of text. Be careful with the 'Experienced' one – use beginning with 'Experienced', not that contain 'Experienced', or all cells will become amber. This section of the completed sheet looks like this.

20.3.7 Adjust page orientation

You may need to change the page orientation from portrait to landscape, especially when displaying the formulae that you have used. To change this, select the Page Layout tab and find the Page Setup section. Click on the Orientation icon, then select either Portrait or Landscape from the drop-down menu.

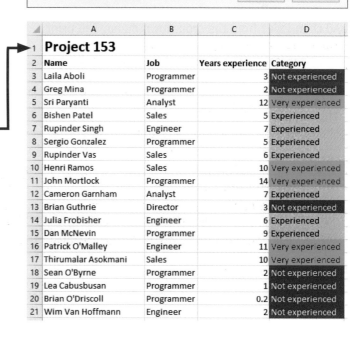

	A	B	C	D
1	**Project 153**			
2	**Name**	**Job**	**Years experience**	**Category**
3	Laila Aboli	Programmer	3	Not experienced
4	Greg Mina	Programmer	2	Not experienced
5	Sri Paryanti	Analyst	12	Very experienced
6	Bishen Patel	Sales	5	Experienced
7	Rupinder Singh	Engineer	7	Experienced
8	Sergio Gonzalez	Programmer	5	Experienced
9	Rupinder Vas	Sales	6	Experienced
10	Henri Ramos	Sales	10	Very experienced
11	John Mortlock	Programmer	14	Very experienced
12	Cameron Garnham	Analyst	7	Experienced
13	Brian Guthrie	Director	3	Not experienced
14	Julia Frobisher	Engineer	6	Experienced
15	Dan McNevin	Programmer	9	Experienced
16	Patrick O'Malley	Engineer	11	Very experienced
17	Thirumalar Asokmani	Sales	10	Very experienced
18	Sean O'Byrne	Programmer	2	Not experienced
19	Lea Cabusbusan	Programmer	1	Not experienced
20	Brian O'Driscoll	Programmer	0.2	Not experienced
21	Wim Van Hoffmann	Engineer	2	Not experienced

Activity 20o

Open the file that you saved in Activity 20m.

Add coloured backgrounds to show the colour of each house, that are dependent on the cell contents. Apply appropriate foreground colours to this text.

Print your spreadsheet showing the values. Take screenshot evidence of the rules used to apply this formatting.

20.3.8 Control the page layout for printing

Display gridlines for printing

You may be required to display gridlines for the whole spreadsheet, rather than just borders to specific cells (as seen earlier). If borders were set for specific cells these will also appear, usually slightly thicker than the gridlines, when printed. To display gridlines when printing select the Page Layout tab. Locate the Sheet Options section and tick the check box in the Gridlines area for Print.

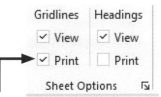

To hide gridlines when printing (except those set as enhancements), simply remove this tick.

Display row and column headings for printing

You may be required to display row and column headings when printing. To do so select the Page Layout tab. Locate the Sheet Options section and tick the check box in the Headings area for Print.

To hide row and column headings when printing, simply remove this tick.

Prepare to print

When preparing your spreadsheet for printing, you can adjust the layout of the spreadsheet on the printed page/s before you print. To do this, select the File tab and then Print from the drop-down menu. The print preview will be shown to you along with options to change the Page Setup and Printer Properties.

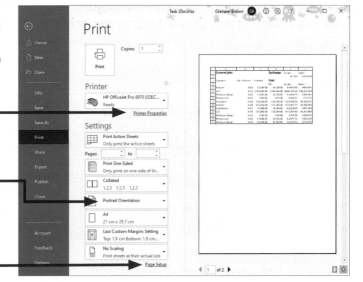

Advice

This window can be used as another way of changing the page orientation.

If you need to make adjustments most can be made using the Page Setup link, which opens the Page Setup window.

You can change the number of pages wide or tall in the printout. Use the **Fit to:** radio button in the **Scaling** section and select the number of pages.

If you set a printout to a single page wide, ensure that all the formulae/values and labels can be seen clearly. If the font size is so small that it is not clearly readable, you may not get recognition of your work for that section. When you have changed the page settings, click on ⬚ OK ⬚. If the question asks for two pages wide and does not say how many pages tall, just set the width and clear the tall box. Do not set this manually to 1 as, if this is a formulae print, the font is likely to be so small it would be unreadable.

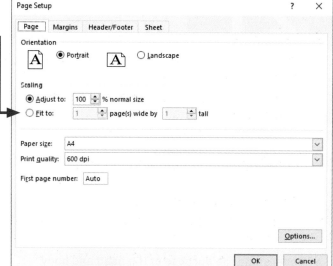

Print a specified print area

If you are required to print a specified part of the spreadsheet, first highlight that part only. Then select the **File** tab and then **Print** from the drop-down menu. In the **Settings** section use the top button, select from the drop-down menu the option for **Print Selection**.

Save and print data

Save your work regularly. As recommended before, it is a good idea to save different versions, at all times each with a different version number. If you make a mistake and corrupt a file, you can always go back and redo a small part of the task without losing too much time. When printing your spreadsheets, make sure that you have adjusted all column widths and row heights to ensure that your printouts show all:

>> labels in full
>> formulae in full
>> data in full.

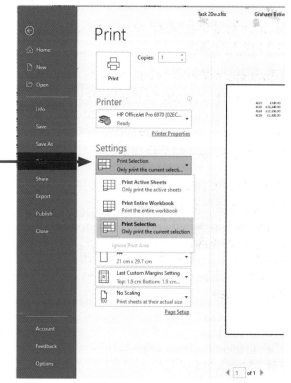

Do not forget to submit printouts showing the formulae used; check that you have worked through the section on displaying formulae near the start of the chapter. You can use screenshots to show how you achieved your results. Make sure that all printouts contain your name, candidate and Centre number.

To print, select the **File** tab followed by **Print** from the menu. Check your work to make sure that all the all data/formulae are fully visible before you select the **Print** button.

You may be required to export your spreadsheet data into different formats. In *Excel*, this is done by selecting the **File** tab followed by **Export**. If you select **Change File Type** it will allow you to export the data into common text formats like .txt (text format) and .csv (comma separated values). Although other export features exist, these should be sufficient for most tasks.

21 Website authoring

Before starting this chapter you should have studied:
★ Chapter 12 Images

In this chapter you will learn how to:
★ understand the three development layers used in web page creation
★ understand the purpose of the content layer
★ understand the purpose of the presentation layer
★ understand the purpose of the behaviour layer
★ use the content layer to create the web page structure
★ understand the purpose of the head and body sections
★ apply tags to text in the content layer to display pre-defined styles
★ open an existing web page
★ place appropriate content in the body section
★ print web pages
★ understand the reason for using tables to structure elements within a web page
★ insert a table
★ headers and footers in tables
★ use embedded CSS in HTML
★ set table and cell sizes in terms of pixels
★ set table and cell sizes in terms of % values
★ apply styles to tables
★ adjust cells to span more than one table column
★ adjust cells to span more than one table row
★ insert an image
★ adjust an image size
★ insert a video file

★ insert an audio file
★ apply styles to elements within a web page
★ apply styles to a list
★ create a bookmark
★ create a hyperlink
★ understand the need to use relative file paths
★ use the head section
★ insert a page title
★ understand the function of metatags
★ use metatags
★ set a default target window
★ apply styles and classes to the HTML
★ understand the characteristics of cascading style sheets
★ understand CSS syntax
★ save styles in cascading style sheet format
★ attach an external stylesheet to a web page
★ understand the use of relative file paths for attached stylesheets
★ add comments to a stylesheet
★ specify CSS text
★ specify font properties
★ specify background properties
★ specify table properties
★ styles and classes
★ create and apply a class
★ specify CSS tables.

For this chapter you will need these source files:
★ brick.css
★ brick.png
★ bricknblocktopia.htm
★ class1.css
★ colourcodes.htm
★ htmltips.htm
★ ptct.jpg
★ remora.htm
★ remora.jpg
★ style1.css
★ style2.css
★ subscript.htm
★ sun.png
★ task21al.png
★ task21am.css

★ task21x.css
★ turtle.jpg
★ turtlelogo.gif
★ wall.png
★ webpage1.htm
★ webpage2.htm
★ webpage3.htm
★ webpage4.htm
★ webpage5.htm
★ webpage6.htm
★ webpage7.htm
★ webpage8.htm
★ webpage9.htm
★ whale.mp3
★ wreck.mp4

21.1 Web development layers

What is a website?

A **website** is a collection of individual but related **web pages** that are often stored together and hosted by **a web server**. Web pages can include different objects such as text, sound, video and still images.

A web page is created using three layers. Each of these layers has a different purpose in the development of a web page. These are:

>> the **content layer**
>> the **presentation layer**
>> the **behaviour layer**.

21.1.1 The content layer

This layer is where the content of the web page, such as text and images, are placed. It is also where the page structure, such as frames, tables, hyperlinks, etc. are placed. This layer is sometimes called the structure layer. You will develop the content/structure layer of your web pages in a language called **HTML**.

What is HTML?

HTML is an abbreviation for HyperText Markup Language. It is a text-based language used to develop the content layer of websites. Files are written in HTML using a simple **text editor** (or a **web-authoring package** such as *Adobe Dreamweaver* or *Microsoft Expression Web*). Files are written in text format and are usually saved with an .htm (or .html) file extension. These files are recognised by **web browsers** such as *Microsoft Edge, Internet Explorer, Google Chrome* or *Mozilla Firefox* as web pages. You are going to develop your own web pages using a simple **text editor**.

21.1.2 The presentation layer

This layer is where the visual impact of the web page is created and contains the styles to be used, such as colour themes, fonts, etc. You will develop the presentation layer of your web pages using **CSS**.

What is CSS?

CSS is an abbreviation for cascading stylesheet, another text-based language. **Styles** are created and added to web pages. CSS can be written (embedded) into HTML but it is usually created in a separate file saved with a .css file extension. The stylesheet is then attached to a web page. Many websites have one or more common stylesheets attached to every page in the website. This makes all the pages have a similar appearance, with the same font styles and colour schemes, etc. You will also develop your own stylesheets using a simple **text editor**.

21.1.3 The behaviour layer

This layer is where all actions, such as controlling elements (except hyperlinks), on a web page are created. These are usually created using scripting languages like *JavaScript*, but we will not cover the practical programming of this at this level.

21.2 Create a web page

Getting started

A good technique for working on web pages is to tile four windows on the screen at the same time: 'tile' means to fit them side by side like tiles. Whenever you do any work in HTML and CSS, it is recommended that you open two copies of a text editor, a web browser and a list of your files in their storage folder.

Locate the taskbar (usually at the bottom of your screen) and place the cursor in the Search box. Enter the text Notepad into the search box. ———

Click on the app to open it. ———

Resize this window so that it fills a quarter of the screen. Place this in the top left corner of your screen. Repeat this so that two copies of *Notepad* are opened at the same time. Place and resize the second copy so it fills the lower left quarter of the screen. These text editors will be where we create the content layer (the HTML) and the presentation layer (the Cascading Style Sheet) for each web page.

Open the File Explorer window by pressing the <Windows> and <E> keys together. Place the File Explorer window in the lower right corner of the screen and resize it to fill about half the width and a quarter of the height of the screen.

Click the left mouse button to select the drive that you will use as your work area. Then click on the New folder icon.

Name this folder Chapter 21. The location of this will depend on the structure of the system you are using. Go into this folder and create new subfolders for each task in this chapter. Call these folders Task21a to Task21z, and Task21aa to Task21aq. There should be 43 folders in total. You must save all the files for each task in this chapter in the correct folder. Make sure you are in the folder Task21a. This is where all the work from the first part of this chapter will be stored. The window should look similar to this. ———

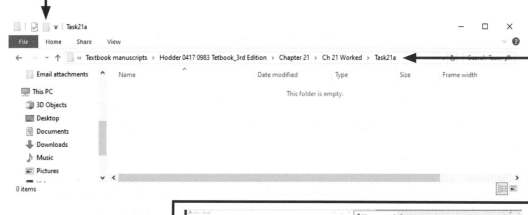

Open your web browser and resize this window so that it fills the remaining area of your screen. Make sure that the windows fit together and do not overlap. The screen will look similar to this. ———

Although many people refer to HTML as a programming language, that is not strictly true. It is a markup language that uses a set of markup **tags** to describe a web page to the browser.

21.2.1 Use the content layer to create a web page structure

Use HTML in the content layer

HTML tags are shown using angle brackets around them like this:

<html>

The angle brackets tell the browser that this is a markup tag and not text to be placed on the web page. The browser does not display the HTML tags, but uses them to display the content of the page. Most HTML commands have two tags: one to open the command and one to close it. Each tag has a pair of angle brackets around it.

All HTML web pages start with a <!DOCTYPE html> declaration and, although it has angle brackets, it is not an HTML tag. This is always the first thing in your markup. The <!DOCTYPE html> declaration is an instruction to the browser to tell it that the page is written in HTML rather than another markup language. The first tag that will usually appear in any web page will be <html>. This tag tells the browser that the markup following this tag will be written in hypertext markup language. The tag </html> tells the browser that this is the end of this markup language and appears at the end of the markup. The forward slash shows that it is a closing tag. All other HTML tags, and all web page content, will appear between these tags.

> **Advice**
>
> Note that, with the exception of the DOCTYPE statement, all text in HTML tags should be in lower case.

21.2.2 The head and body sections of a web page

Each web page has two clearly defined sections: the **head** and the **body**.

The head section

The head section starts with <head> and closes with </head>. Objects between these tags are **not usually displayed** by the web browser. Only a few tags are universally accepted within the head section of a web page; these are: <base>, <link>, <meta>, <title>, <style> and <script>. The head section should always contain a title. This is the name displayed in the browser toolbar. It is the page title used if a page is added to your 'favorites' in your browser and is the title displayed in search engine results. We will study the head section in more detail later in the chapter.

The body section

The body section starts with `<body>` and closes with `</body>` and objects between these tags **are usually displayed** in the web page. The basic structure of any web page should therefore include these tags.

Insert tags for the head section here. ──────

Insert objects to be displayed by the browser in the body section here. ──────

HTML markup

```
<!DOCTYPE html>
<html>
<head>
<title>Web page name</title>
</head>
<body>
</body>
<!-- This is a comment -->
</html>
```

Add comments to your HTML markup

Comments can be added to your markup if there are notes that you wish to make but not display on the web page. This is very useful for making sure that your name, Centre number and candidate number are on every web page, even if you are not instructed to display them. Comments start with `<!--` and end with `-->`. As the comments do not affect the markup, they can be placed in the head or body sections and before or after any tags. Comments look like this. ──────

21.2.3 Apply tags to text in the content layer to display pre-defined styles

Text is organised into paragraphs, with the paragraph style applied. Headings usually have different styles to the paragraph style. All text added to a web page should have a tag telling the browser what text style should be applied. There are a number of predefined styles available for use in a web page. The normal paragraph style is obtained using `<p>` and ended with `</p>`. Likewise, six heading styles are available and are defined with the style names `<h1>` to `<h6>`. Each item in a bulleted or numbered list can be defined with the `<li>` tag and finished with `</li>`; there are more details on lists later in this chapter.

Task 21a

Create and save a new web page showing paragraph and heading styles.

Click the cursor into the top text editor. Type the following markup into the editor, replacing MY NAME HERE with your name. Always remember to add your name, centre number and candidate number to all of your printouts.

Advice

It is essential that the text is typed exactly as shown here. One typing error may cause the web page not to function as expected.

Advice

It is acceptable to use capital letters in the text that is displayed on the page, but not in the HTML tags.

```
<!DOCTYPE html>
<html>
<!-- Markup created on 06/01/2022 -->
<head>
<title>Task 21a</title>
</head>
<body>
<p>My first web page by MY NAME HERE</p>
<h1>This is style h1, the largest heading style</h1>
<h2>This is style h2</h2>
<h3>This is style h3</h3>
<h4>This is style h4</h4>
<h5>This is style h5</h5>
<h6>This is style h6, the smallest heading style</h6>
<p>This is style p, the paragraph style</p>
</body>
</html>
```

When this has been entered and carefully verified (by checking this original document against your typed copy), you must select **File** followed by **Save As...**, which will open the **Save As** window.

Click on the folder names until you find the Task21a folder created earlier in this chapter.

You need to enter a filename for the web page. This filename **must** be saved with an .htm extension. If you do not use a .htm file extension, this will operate as a text file rather than as a web page. Enter the filename **task21a.htm** and click on `Save`.

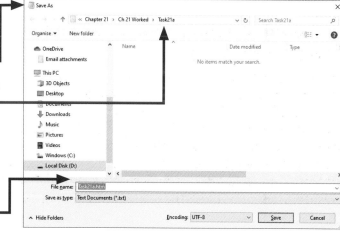

The file should appear in the **File Explorer** window and may look similar to this.

If the file cannot be seen, move into the Task21a folder. Make sure that the file displays the browser (usually the 🌐, 🌀, 🧭, or 🔴) symbol to show that this is a web page and not a text document with a 🗎 symbol. The text document symbol only appears if you forget to add the .htm extension to the filename.

Select the file **task21a.htm** from the File Explorer window and drag this file (holding the left mouse button down) into the browser window.

The screen should now look similar to this.

The browser view now contains your first web page.

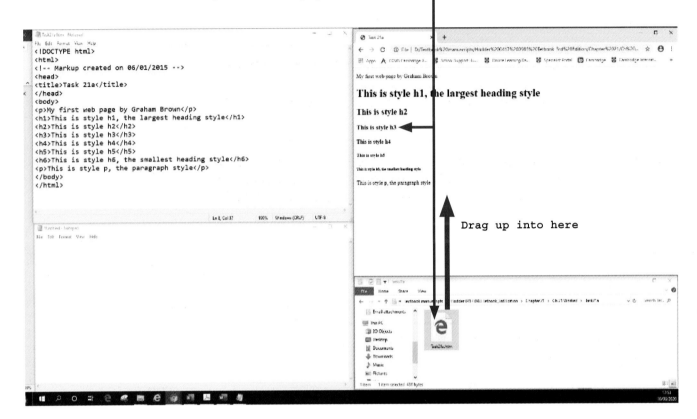

Advice

Some browser settings will make this open in a new browser window, rather than the one that you have just opened.

21.2.4 Open an existing web page

To open an existing web page in both the text editor and the web browser you must find the web page in the File Explorer window. For all web page files, it is advisable to copy the files into a subfolder of your HTML directory before starting.

Task 21b

Open the file **webpage1.htm** and view this web page in both the text editor and browser.

Improve this web page by setting the '3' in x^3 as superscript and setting the '2' in H_2O as subscript.

Copy the file **webpage1.htm** into your Task21b folder. Drag this file from the File Explorer window into the top text editor. Drag another copy of this file from the File Explorer window into your browser. The screen should look like this.

Advice

Editing is easier if you ensure that the word wrap is selected in Notepad. To do this, use the **Format** menu and check that the **Word Wrap** option is ticked.

21.2.5 Place appropriate content in the body section

There are different ways of placing appropriate content in the body section of a web page. Usually this is completed when the structure of the web page has been created, and we will use different methods later in the chapter. It is also important to add enhancements like superscript and subscript to text in a web page should this be appropriate.

Superscript and subscript

Move the cursor into the text editor window and make the following changes to the markup:

» Replace Graham Brown with your name.
» Place the tags ^{and} around the number '3'.
» Place the tags _{and} around the number '2'.

You may notice that all text within the head and body sections is indented to make it easier to identify where each starts and finishes.

Advice

If you prefer you can click the mouse on the browser window and then press the function key <f5> to refresh the browser view each time you have saved the file.

```
<!DOCTYPE html>
<html>
  <head>
    <title>Task 21b</title>
  </head>
  <body>
    <p>My first web page by Graham
Brown</p>
    <h2>Text can be enhanced in
different ways. Here are some of those
ways.</h2>
    <p>Text cannot be underlined in
later versions of html because it looks
like the text is a hyperlink</p>
    <p>Text can be superscripted like
x<sup>3</sup></p>
    <p>Text can be subscripted like
H<sub>2</sub>O</p>
  </body>
</html>
```

When you have made all these changes to the web page, save the page by selecting the text editor, followed by **File**, **Save As...**, selecting the **Task21b** folder and entering the filename **task21b.htm** before clicking on [Save]. Test the web page works by dragging this new filename from the **Documents** window into the browser window. The new browser view should look like this.

21.2.6 Print web pages

From time to time, you will be required to print different views of your web pages. You must ensure that your name is included on the web page before it is sent to the printer, in whichever view is specified. Printing the HTML view is often required. Even if you are using a WYSIWYG (what you see is what you get) package, such as *Adobe Dreamweaver* or *Microsoft Expression Web*, you will need to open the web page in a text editor to print the HTML.

If you are printing from a web browser, make sure that your name and candidate details are fully visible on the printout. If you are using a WYSIWYG package, make sure that you test the web page in a browser and not just within the package. Some products will display what appears to be the browser view, but it is only a development tool and does not necessarily display the page as it will be seen. Make sure that there is clear evidence that this is a browser and that the URL is visible (or the file name and path are visible instead of the URL). Use screenshots of your pages, taken using the <Print Screen> button on your keyboard, to copy the screen contents into the clipboard. Then paste the clipboard into another package (often a word processor) to present evidence of your work.

Activity 21a

Open the file **subscript.htm** and view this web page in both the text editor and browser. Replace the text MY NAME HERE with your name.

Set the '2' in 10 meters 2 and the '3' in 500 cm3 as superscript and set the '2' in CO2 as subscript. Set the text 'Enhancing Text' into style h1. Print your web page as HTML and as it is viewed in your browser.

21.2.7 The reason for using tables to structure elements within a web page

Tables can be used to create the basic structure of many web pages. They can be used to organise page layout and are often used in web pages even though their borders may not be visible. In more recent versions of HTML, tables have been replaced by **semantic elements** and other more complex structures (including CSS structures) to layout full pages, but at this level we will use simple tables to create our structures.

21.2.8 Insert a table

If you need to create a table within a web page, it is always worth planning it on paper before starting to create the markup.

Task 21c

Create a new web page that looks like this and has the caption 'Colours':

Red	36%
Green	23%
Blue	41%

Basic table structure

Tables in HTML always start with a `<table>` tag and end with `</table>`. Start by adding these tags in the body section of the markup. Make sure you replace the text 'your name' with your own name. It should look similar to this.

Advice

It would be much easier to use **WYSIWYG** software to create your tables. However, this section is designed to ensure that you understand how to create and edit tables, and the markup used to define tables. To begin with, this may be difficult for you if you decide to use a WYSIWYG package to develop your tables.

```
<!DOCTYPE html>
<html>
    <!-- Task 21c by your name -->
<head>
    <title>Task 21c</title>
</head>
<body>
    <table>
    </table>
</body>
</html>
```

Everything between these tags will be included in the table, except for the caption. This is added using the `<caption>` and `</caption>` tags, which allows you to display a caption (usually centre aligned) above the table. If a caption is used it **must** be the first HTML tag after the `<table>` tag.

```
<body>
  <table>
  <caption>Colours</caption>
  <tr>
  </tr>
  <tr>
  </tr>
  <tr>
  </tr>
  </table>
</body>
```

Each table is split into rows.

Row 1	Red	36%
Row 2	Green	23%
Row 3	Blue	41%

For this task, the table you need to create has three table rows. The tag for a table row is `<tr>`. Create the three blank rows between the caption and the end of the table like this.

Each table row will contain two cells of table data. The tag for table data is `<td>`. A row can have one or more `<td>` tags. Between each `<tr>` and `</tr>` tag, place start table data `<td>` and end table data `</td>` tags like this.

Each table row has two pieces of table data. A table cell can contain text, images, other tables, lists, paragraphs, forms, horizontal rules, and so on.

Advice

It is sometimes quicker to create one complete table row first with the table data cells included, then copy this row a number of times using copy and paste.

```
<body>
<table>
  <caption>Colours</caption>
<tr>
  <td>
  </td>
  <td>
  </td>
</tr>
<tr>
  <td>
  </td>
  <td>
  </td>
</tr>
<tr>
  <td>
  </td>
  <td>
  </td>
</tr>
</table>
</body>
```

The data can now be added to each cell like this. ────────────────────────

Your table will look similar to this.

Colours

Red   36%

Green   23%

Blue   41%

Table borders

This table has been created but does not have a visible border. The word 'border' is an **attribute**. To show the table gridlines you must add a border attribute with a value of "1". An attribute is something that is added to one of the markup commands to give further information/instructions to the browser. Attributes should be in lower case and attribute values should always be enclosed in quotes.

Change your markup like this. ──────────

The only valid border values in HTML5 are "1" and "":

» "1" makes the border visible. ─────────
» "" hides the table border, yet allows the table to control the structure of the page.

Save this web page as **task21c.htm** in your Task21c folder.

> **Advice**
>
> HTML5 is the latest standard used by all modern web browsers. This is different from earlier versions of HTML where "0" hid the border.

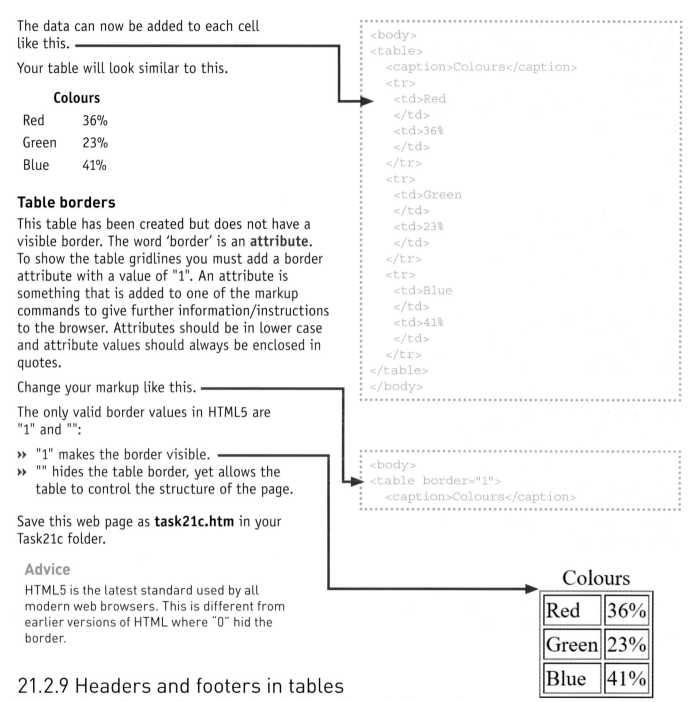

```
<body>
<table>
  <caption>Colours</caption>
  <tr>
   <td>Red
   </td>
   <td>36%
   </td>
  </tr>
  <tr>
   <td>Green
   </td>
   <td>23%
   </td>
  </tr>
  <tr>
   <td>Blue
   </td>
   <td>41%
   </td>
  </tr>
</table>
</body>
```

```
<body>
<table border="1">
  <caption>Colours</caption>
```

21.2.9 Headers and footers in tables

Tables can have three sections: a header, a body section and a footer. These are defined using the <thead>, <tbody> and <tfoot> tags, and closed with </thead>, </tbody> and </tfoot> respectively. Notice how these all begin with t (for table).

Task 21d

Create a new web page that looks like this and has the caption 'Fruit sales'.

Fruit	Price
Apple	$1230
Orange	$780
Pear	$240
Banana	$4235
Lemon	$75
Total	$6560

To create this web page you need to first create the open table and close table tags within the body section of the markup. Place the caption tags between these in the same way that you did when you completed Task 21c. The initial markup for this section should look like this.

```
<body>
  <table border="1">
   <caption>Fruit sales</caption>
  </table>
</body>
```

Before continuing with the markup it is worth planning the table using a hand-drawn sketch similar to this.

This will help you work out the structure needed for the markup. For this table, you will need three sections to the table.

These three sections need to be created within the markup. The header section is created using the table head tags, with `<thead>` to start the section and `</thead>` to finish the section. The footer section uses the tags `<tfoot>` and `</tfoot>`, and the body is defined with `<tbody>` and `</tbody>`. In HTML you must define the table header, footer and then body (in that order) if all three sections are to be included. Create the three sections within the table of your markup like this.

Caption

	Fruit	Price	
Table Header	Fruit	Price	1 table row with 2 table header cells.
Table Body	Apple	$1230	5 table rows, each with 2 cells of table data.
	Orange	$780	
	Pear	$240	
	Banana	$4235	
	Lemon	$75	
Table Footer	Total	$6560	1 table row with 2 cells of table data.

```
<body>
  <table border="1">
  <caption>Fruit sales</caption>
   <thead>
   </thead>
   <tfoot>
   </tfoot>
   <tbody>
   </tbody>
  </table>
</body>
```

Within each section add the correct number of table rows, using the notes you made on your sketch to help you.

You can add the table data sections to the footer and body of the table using the tags `<td>` and `</td>`. Do not use these tags in the table header. At each stage, save your web page and check that the markup that you have written gives you the results that you expected.

In the table header, create heading cells (which are bold and centre aligned) using the tags `<th>` and `</th>` rather than the table data tags. These will set the column headings in heading style. Heading cells can be used inside the table body and table footer sections and are useful in the left column of a table if row headings are required. Do not forget to replace the text 'your name' with your own name.

Place the contents (in this case text) of the header section in the header cells and place the contents of the body and footer sections in the relevant cells. The finished markup should look like this. ──

The resulting web page should look like this. ──

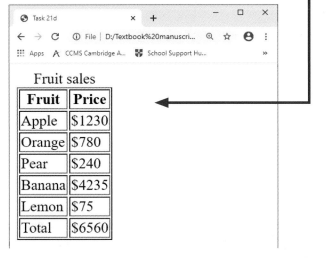

Save this web page as **task21d.htm** in your Task21d folder. Save copies of this page as **task21e.htm** in your Task21e folder, as **task21f.htm** in your Task21f folder, and as **task21i.htm** in your Task21i folder.

Activity 21b

Create a new web page with a table that looks like this and has the caption 'Hours of sunshine last week'. Make sure the top row of the table is in the header section and the bottom row is in the footer section. Print your web page as HTML and as it is viewed in your browser.

Day	Hours
Monday	6
Tuesday	4.5
Wednesday	8
Thursday	7
Friday	3.5
Saturday	5
Sunday	6
Weekly total	40

```
<!DOCTYPE html>
<html>
<!-- Task 21d by Graham Brown -->
<head>
   <title>Task 21d</title>
</head>
<body>
   <table border="1">
   <caption>Fruit sales</caption>
     <thead>
       <tr>
         <th>Fruit</th>
         <th>Price</th>
       </tr>
     </thead>
     <tfoot>
       <tr>
         <td>Total</td>
         <td>$6560</td>
       </tr>
     </tfoot>
     <tbody>
       <tr>
         <td>Apple</td>
         <td>$1230</td>
       </tr>
       <tr>
         <td>Orange</td>
         <td>$780</td>
       </tr>
       <tr>
         <td>Pear</td>
         <td>$240</td>
       </tr>
       <tr>
         <td>Banana</td>
         <td>$4235</td>
       </tr>
       <tr>
         <td>Lemon</td>
         <td>$75</td>
       </tr>
     </tbody>
   </table>
</body>
</html>
```

21.2.10 Use embedded CSS in HTML

Although this section introduces the use of styles into your web page, this will not be covered in detail until Section 21.3.

Styles can be applied to tables and other HTML elements by placing CSS instructions in a style attribute within the HTML tag. This is called embedded CSS.

21.2.11 Set table and cell sizes in terms of pixels

> **Task 21e**
>
> Open the file **task21e.htm**. Set the table to be 400 pixels wide and each row to be 50 pixels high. Set the left column to be 280 pixels wide.

Resize a table

Open the file task21e.htm. You have seen that each table grows to fit the data in each cell. In order to avoid this, each table, as well as each row/column within the table, can be set to a fixed width or a width related to the size of the browser window. For this task an attribute is added to either the table <table>, table row <tr> or table data <td> tags. This attribute is an embedded CSS style attribute. In the table tag add a second attribute named style with the embedded CSS property value width:400px, like this.

```
<body>
<table border="1" style="width:400px">
<caption>Fruit sales</caption>
<thead>
```

The width of the table will now be fixed to 400 pixels. If the browser window is resized, this table size will not change; if the window is made smaller than 400 pixels the browser will display scroll bars.

> **Advice**
>
> Use px for pixels and do not put a space between the digits and px.

Use similar style attributes in all seven table row tags to set the row height like this.

In the first table header cell add a similar attribute to set the CSS width property of the first column to 280px, like this.

```
<thead>
<tr style="height:50px">
<th style="width:280px">Fruit</th>
<th>Price</th>
```

> **Advice**
>
> The syntax for CSS elements is the property name, colon, the value to be applied, for example, name:value
>
> If more than one property is to be applied these are separated with semicolons, for example, name1:value; name2:value

These two style attributes only need to be applied once per row or column; all other cells in the row/column will match the attribute set. The finished table looks like this.

Save this web page as **task21e.htm** in your Task21e folder.

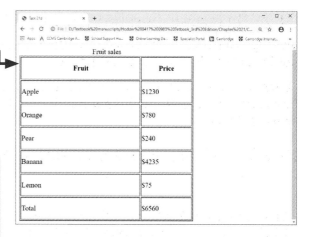

21.2.12 Set table and cell sizes in terms of % values

Task 21f

Open the file **task21f.htm**. Set the table to fit to 80% of the browser window and the left column to be 75% of the width of the table. Set the top row to be 60 pixels high and the bottom row to be 40 pixels high. Align the table in the centre of the browser window. Set the names of the fruit to be centre aligned and the prices in the right column to be right aligned.

Open this web page. Set a style attribute for the table tag with the width property and a value of 80%. Use a similar 75% property for the style attribute in any table data (or table header) tag in the left column, like this.

```
<body>
  <table border="1" style="width:80%">
    <caption>Fruit sales</caption>
    <thead>
      <tr>
        <th style="width:75%">Fruit</th>
        <th>Price</th>
```

21.2.13 Apply styles to tables

Centre align a table in a window

To centre align the table within the window, two more style properties must be used with the table tag. These are to set the margin to the left to automatic and the margin to the right to automatic. In CSS, if more than one property is used, the semicolon (;) is used between one property and value and the next.

The extra properties for the table style attribute will look like this.

```
<body>
  <table border="1" style="width:80%; margin-left:auto; margin-right:auto;">
    <caption>Fruit sales</caption>
```

The table is now centre aligned inside the browser. If the browser is resized the table still has the same relative size and alignment like this.

Set the row height of the table header (the first row) to 60 pixels and the bottom row to 40 pixels. Use **<tr style="height: 60px">** and **<tr style="height: 40px">** like this. ———

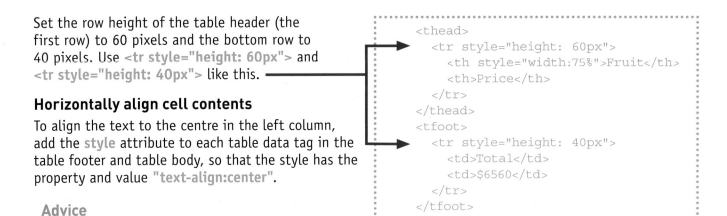

```
<thead>
  <tr style="height: 60px">
    <th style="width:75%">Fruit</th>
    <th>Price</th>
  </tr>
</thead>
<tfoot>
  <tr style="height: 40px">
    <td>Total</td>
    <td>$6560</td>
  </tr>
</tfoot>
```

Horizontally align cell contents

To align the text to the centre in the left column, add the **style** attribute to each table data tag in the table footer and table body, so that the style has the property and value **"text-align:center"**.

Advice

Note the American spelling of 'center' rather than the English spelling 'centre'.

To align the text to the right in the right column, add the **style** attribute to the table data for each cell in this column (except the table header) so that the style has the property and value **"text-align:right"**. The web page will now look like this. ———

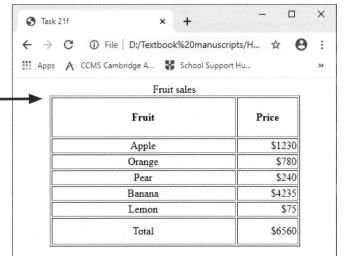

Advice

Colgroup tags to align cell elements are no longer supported in HTML5.

Save this web page as **task21f.htm** in your Task21f folder. Save copies of this page as **task21g.htm** in your Task21g folder and **task21o.htm** in your Task21o folder.

Activity 21c

Create a new web page with a table that looks like this and has the caption 'SupaHols visitors 2016'.

Country	Visitors
Egypt	440
India	2000
Jamaica	140
United Arab Emirates	420
Total visitors	3000

Make the company name, SupaHols, bold. Make sure the top row of the table is in the header section and the bottom row is in the footer section. Set the table to fit to 70% of the browser window and the left column to be 100 pixels wide. Set the top row to be 60 pixels high. Align the table in the centre of the browser window. Set the contents of row 1 and the names of the countries to be centre aligned and the number of visitors to be right aligned. Print your web page as HTML and as it is viewed in your browser.

Table borders

You have already studied how to set the table borders on or off with a border attribute for the table tag. To set table borders to appear as you want them you can change the border settings in the whole table or parts of the table. You will notice that all of the tables that you have created so far have a double border because the table and the table header/table data parts have separate borders.

Create a single table border

Task 21g

Open the file **task21g.htm**. Display the table with a single, solid border 4 pixels wide, and with internal gridlines 2 pixels wide.

Open this web page in *Notepad*. Set a **style** attribute for the table tag with the **border-collapse** property and a value **collapse**, like this.

```
<body>
  <table border="1" style="width:80%; margin-left:auto; margin-right:auto;
  border-collapse:collapse;">
  <caption>Fruit sales</caption>
```

The table will now look like this.

Set table border widths

Table borders can be set using the embedded CSS **style** attribute with the **border** property and values.

To set the outside border of a table, the **style** attribute is added to the **table** tag. The values assigned to this tag must set the **border** to **solid** and to **4px**. To set internal gridlines style, attributes are added to the **<th>** and **<td>** tags; each of these tags must have the style attribute with **border:solid 2px**.

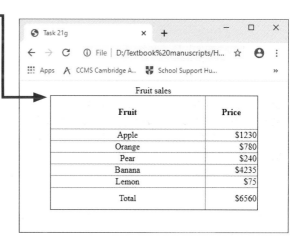

```
<!DOCTYPE html>
<html>
<!-- Task 21g by Graham Brown -->
<head>
  <title>Task 21g</title>
</head>
<body>
  <table border="1" style="width:80%; margin-left:auto; margin-right:
auto; border-collapse:collapse; border:solid 4px;">
  <caption>Fruit sales</caption>
    <thead>
      <tr style="height:60px">
        <th style="border:solid 2px; width:75%;">Fruit</th>
        <th style="border:solid 2px;">Price</th>
```

```
      </tr>
    </thead>
    <tfoot>
      <tr style="height:40px">
        <td style="border:solid 2px; text-align:center;">Total</td>
        <td style="border:solid 2px; text-align:right;">$6560</td>
      </tr>
    </tfoot>
    <tbody>
      <tr>
        <td style="border:solid 2px; text-align:center;">Apple</td>
        <td style="border:solid 2px; text-align:right;">$1230</td>
      </tr>
      <tr>
        <td style="border:solid 2px; text-align:center;">Orange</td>
        <td style="border:solid 2px; text-align:right;">$780</td>
      </tr>
      <tr>
        <td style="border:solid 2px; text-align:center;">Pear</td>
        <td style="border:solid 2px; text-align:right;">$240</td>
      </tr>
      <tr>
        <td style="border:solid 2px; text-align:center;">Banana</td>
        <td style="border:solid 2px; text-align:right;">$4235</td>
      </tr>
      <tr>
        <td style="border:solid 2px; text-align:center;">Lemon</td>
        <td style="border:solid 2px; text-align:right;">$75</td>
      </tr>
    </tbody>
  </table>
</body>
</html>
```

Advice

Table border settings in CSS are different from the border attribute for the table, which is only used to show if borders are visible or invisible.

Save your web page as **task21g.htm** in your Task21g folder. The finished table will look like this.

Later in this chapter you will learn how to fix styles for all table cells without repeatedly entering the same style attribute for each tag.

Fruit sales

Fruit	Price
Apple	$1230
Orange	$780
Pear	$240
Banana	$4235
Lemon	$75
Total	$6560

Activity 21d

Edit the web page you created for Activity 21c so that: the table has a single border of 6 pixels, the table header and footer have a single border of 4 pixels, and the table data has a single border of 2 pixels. Print your web page as HTML and as it is viewed in your browser.

Vertically align table cell contents

Data held in table cells can be vertically aligned with embedded CSS so that it fits in the top, middle or bottom of the cell. The **style** attribute is added to the **<td>** tag with a property of **vertical-align** and a value of **top**, **middle** or **bottom**.

Task 21h

Create a new web page that looks like this. Set both row heights to 60 pixels. Centre align the contents of all cells. Vertically align to the top, centre and bottom of the cell as shown.

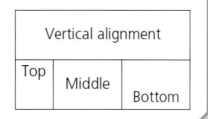

Advice

If you need to vertically align to the centre of the cell, always set the property value to middle.

Create a new web page that has a table with two rows. In the top row include one piece of table data and, in the second row, include three pieces of table data. Save this in your Task21h folder. It should look like this. ──────

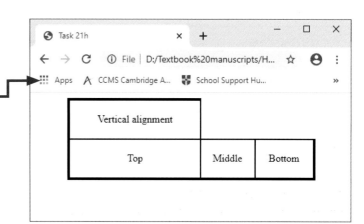

Find the three table data <td> tags in the second row and add the following attributes to them.

```
<tr style="height:60px; text-align:center;">
  <td style="border:solid 2px; vertical-align:top">Top</td>
  <td style="border:solid 2px; vertical-align:middle">Middle</td>
  <td style="border:solid 2px; vertical-align:bottom">Bottom</td>
</tr>
```

Save your web page as **task21h.htm** in your Task21h folder. The text will now align in the table like this. —————

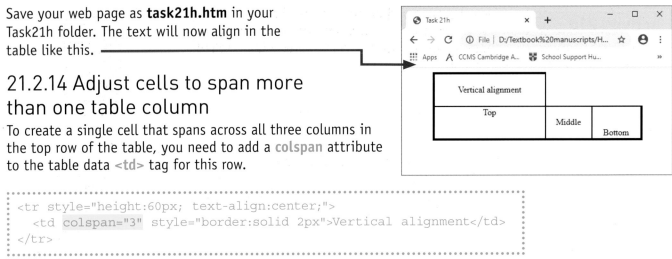

21.2.14 Adjust cells to span more than one table column

To create a single cell that spans across all three columns in the top row of the table, you need to add a colspan attribute to the table data <td> tag for this row.

```
<tr style="height:60px; text-align:center;">
   <td colspan="3" style="border:solid 2px">Vertical alignment</td>
</tr>
```

Save your web page as **task21h.htm** in your Task21h folder. The completed table should look like this. —————

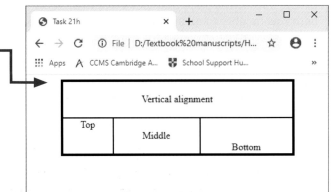

21.2.15 Adjust cells to span more than one table row

To merge cells vertically use the rowspan attribute in the same way as you used colspan in the previous task.

Activity 21e

Create a new web page to look like this. Table and header borders must be 6 pixels and all other gridlines must be 3 pixels. The right column must be 50% of the width of the table.

Class 11A Exam Results		
Amir	96	
Belle	96	Students who have
Cai	94	performed extremely well.
Denise	92	
Eric	66	
Fiona	23	Must do better.

Cell padding

Cell padding is the space between the cell contents and the border of the cell. It can be applied to both the table tag <table> and/or to each item of table cell using table data <td> or table header <th>.

Task 21i

Open the file **task21i.htm**. Copy the table so that there are three tables, one above the other, on the page. Change the captions from 'Fruit Sales' to 'No padding' for the top table, 'Padding set to 25 pixels' for the middle table and 'Variable padding' for the lower table. Set the cell padding of the middle table to 25 pixels and the padding of the lower table to have a top padding of 25 pixels, bottom padding of 20 pixels and left and right padding of 15 pixels.

Open the file **task21i.htm**. Copy the table and paste it twice. Place a `<br>` tag between each table to set a line break. The `<br>` tag does not have a close tag. Add an ID attribute to each table so we can identify them: they will be called top, middle and bottom. For example:

```
<br>
<table border="1" id="middle" style="padding:25px">
<caption>Padding set to 25 pixels</caption>
```

In the `<table>` tag for the middle table, add the single CSS style **padding** property with a value of 25 pixels like this.

For the bottom table we can set the different padding by stating all four values, starting at the top and rotating clockwise like this.

```
<br>
<table border="1" id="bottom" style="padding:25px 15px 20px 15px;">
<caption>Variable padding</caption>
```

Advice

This is a shortened version of the CSS padding properties. Where padding should be specified in full, for each side it will look like this. ➤

```
padding-top:25px;
padding-bottom:20px;
padding-right:15px;
padding-left:15px;
```

The web page now looks like this.

This has only set the padding for the table borders. To change each cell the same style attributes, properties and values will need copying and pasting into every `<th>` and `<td>` tag. This will change the middle and bottom tables to look like this.

Save your web page as **task21i.htm** in your Task21i folder, and a copy of your page as **task21j.htm** in your Task21j folder.

Task 21j

Open the file **task21j.htm**. Set the top table to have a horizontal border spacing of 20 pixels and a vertical border spacing of 10 pixels.

Border spacing

The spacing between the borders (**border spacing**) of individual cells is set in the `<table>` tag. The **style** attribute is used with the **border-spacing** property. Two values can be passed to this property: the horizontal spacing first, then the vertical spacing, like this.

```
<body>
<table border="1" id="top" style="border-spacing:20px 10px;">
<caption>No padding</caption>
```

No padding

Fruit	Price
Apple	$1230
Orange	$780
Pear	$240
Banana	$4235
Lemon	$75
Total	$6560

Padding set to 25px

Fruit	Price
Apple	$1230
Orange	$780
Pear	$240
Banana	$4235
Lemon	$75
Total	$6560

Variable padding

Fruit	Price
Apple	$1230
Orange	$780
Pear	$240
Banana	$4235
Lemon	$75
Total	$6560

Padding set to 25px

Fruit	Price
Apple	$1230
Orange	$780
Pear	$240
Banana	$4235
Lemon	$75
Total	$6560

Variable padding

Fruit	Price
Apple	$1230
Orange	$780
Pear	$240
Banana	$4235
Lemon	$75
Total	$6560

The top table of the web page will look like this. ─────

Advice

If the horizontal and vertical border spacing are the same, you can use a single value.

Fruit	Price
Apple	$1230
Orange	$780
Pear	$240
Banana	$4235
Lemon	$75
Total	$6560

No padding

Activity 21f

Open your finished web page from Activity 21b. For each table cell, set the padding to have a top value of 8 pixels, bottom of 12 pixels, a left value of 20 pixels and a right value of 16 pixels. Set internal and border spacing for the table to 20 pixels.

Task 21k

Create a new web page with a table that looks like this and has the caption 'Sales team'. The image that you require is called turtle.jpg.

	Expenses		
Turtle Travel	Lee	Amir	Maxine
Travel	$162.20	$285.75	$150.00
Hotel	$240.00	$182.40	$322.00
Food	$146.50	$102.10	$104.50

Plan the table using a hand-drawn sketch similar to this.

Caption

Table Header	Image here 1 cell 2 rows deep	1 cell three columns wide		
		Lee	Amir	Maxine
Table Body	Travel	$162.20	$285.75	$150
	Hotel	$240	$182.40	$322
	Food	$46.50	$62.10	$64.50

2 table rows with 4 columns, top 2 cells in first column merged, 3 right cells in the top row merged, 3 table heading cells.

3 table rows, each with 1 heading cell and 3 table data cells.

Shading shows cells with a heading format rather than table data format.

Create the basic markup as you did with the earlier tasks, starting with the table tags, the table attributes to show the borders, the caption, the header and body sections of the table, then insert the table rows. The markup so far will look like this.

```
<body>
  <table border="1" style="border-collapse:collapse; border:solid 1px;">

    <caption>Sales team</caption>
    <thead>
      <tr>
      </tr>
      <tr>
      </tr>
    </thead>
```

```
      <tbody>
        <tr>
        </tr>
        <tr>
        </tr>
        <tr>
        </tr>
      </tbody>
    </table
  </body>
```

Advice

When creating a new table like this, it is wise to add a single letter as the contents of each cell when you create it. In this case a single letter 'A' has been added to the top left cell, the letter 'B' to the next cell and so on. This is because some web browsers do not display a table cell if it is empty. By adding these single letters it allows you to test the table as you are creating it.

The top row of the table header has only two cells. The first of these is a cell that covers two rows. For this you use a **rowspan** attribute to tell the browser this cell is going to span the first two rows. The markup for this cell will look like this.

The second cell in the top row is a cell that covers three columns. Use the **colspan** attribute to tell the browser that this cell is going to span three columns. This cell was identified in the sketch as a being a heading cell, so the **colspan** attribute is used within the table heading tag. The markup for this cell will look like this.

```
  <thead>
    <tr>
      <td rowspan="2" style="border:solid 1px" >A</td>
      <th colspan="3" style="border:solid 1px" >B</th>
    </tr>
```

Using the sketch to work from, add the cells to each row of the table. In the body of the table, set the first cell of each row as a table heading and the next three cells as table data. This section of the table will look like this.

The table structure should now look like this.

```
        <th colspan="3" style="border:solid 1px">B</th>
      </tr>
      <tr>
        <th style="border:solid 1px">C</th>
        <th style="border:solid 1px">D</th>
        <th style="border:solid 1px">E</th>
      </tr>
  </thead>
  <tbody>
    <tr>
      <th style="border:solid 1px">F</th>
      <td style="border:solid 1px">G</td>
      <td style="border:solid 1px">H</td>
      <td style="border:solid 1px">I</td>
    </tr>
    <tr>
      <th style="border:solid 1px">J</th>
      <td style="border:solid 1px">K</td>
      <td style="border:solid 1px">L</td>
      <td style="border:solid 1px">M</td>
    </tr>
    <tr>
```

Sales team

A	B		
	C	D	E
F	G	H	I
J	K	L	M
N	O	P	Q

```
      <th style="border:solid 1px">N</th>
      <td style="border:solid 1px">O</td>
      <td style="border:solid 1px">P</td>
      <td style="border:solid 1px">Q</td>
    </tr>
  </tbody>
  </table>
</body>
</html>
```

Enter all the text and currency values into the correct cells in the table. The web page should look like this. ⌐➔

Sales team

A	Expenses		
	Lee	**Amir**	**Maxine**
Travel	$162.20	$285.75	$150.00
Hotel	$240.00	$182.40	$322.00
Food	$146.50	$102.10	$104.50

Save your web page as **task21k.htm** in your Task21k folder.

21.2.16 Insert an image

Images (such as pictures or icons) are often used in web pages and are often used for hyperlinks. To complete the web page for Task 21k, you need to replace the letter 'A' in the top left cell of the table with the image **turtle.jpg**. To do this you have to tell the web browser the name of the **image source**, which should be stored in the same folder as your web page. Make sure that you have copied the file **turtle.jpg** into your Task21k folder. Add the following to the markup. As some browsers may not display the image, you can tell the browser to replace the image with alternative text. This usually describes the image so that the user can still understand what is being shown even though they cannot see the image. The markup will look like this.⌐➔

```
<thead>
  <tr>
    <td rowspan="2" style="border:solid 1px"><img src="turtle.jpg" alt="Company
Logo"></td>
    <th colspan="3" style="border:solid 1px">Expenses</th>    </tr>
```

Where to store an image

Images must be stored in the same folder as the web page. This is called the current folder. Notice in the markup shown above how the filename **turtle.jpg** is given as the image source. This does not contain any reference to which folder the image is stored in. Because there is no absolute reference to a folder, the browser automatically looks in the current folder for the image. This means that if this web page is opened on another computer, as long as the image is stored in the same folder as the web page, it will work properly.

If an absolute reference had been used for a file, for example:

```
      <img src="C:/My websites/My pictures/turtle.jpg" alt="Company
      Logo"></td>
```

This would prevent the file being found unless the folders in all the computers were structured in this way. If the file **turtle.jpg** is not in the current folder, the web page will look like this.

Sales team

	Expenses		
Company Logo	Lee	Amir	Maxine
Travel	$162.20	$285.75	$150.00
Hotel	$240.00	$182.40	$322.00
Food	$146.50	$102.10	$104.50

Apply alternate text

The image has been replaced by the text 'Company Logo' defined by the alt text attribute to tell the user what the missing image should be. This text is also used in some browsers by text readers. An image (`<img>`) tag must have an alternative (`alt=""`) text attribute added for all browsers to display the image as expected. This must have a 'value' attached to it within quotation marks, even if this is left empty (although it is bad practice to leave it empty). For any image that you place on a web page it is advisable to always include the alt attribute.

Copy the image into your Task21k folder. When the image file is stored in the current folder, this will be displayed.

Save the web page as **task21k.htm** in your Task21k folder and save a copy as **task21m.htm** in your Task21m folder.

Sales team

	Expenses		
Turtle Travel	Lee	Amir	Maxine
Travel	$162.20	$285.75	$150.00
Hotel	$240.00	$182.40	$322.00
Food	$146.50	$102.10	$104.50

Advice

A common mistake made is to use absolute pathways for files, such as images, stylesheets, etc.

File types for images

Raster or bitmap graphics
There are three common file types for **bitmap** images used in websites. These are **JPEG** files, **GIF** files or **PNG** files. You can use a graphics package such as *Adobe Photoshop* or *GIMP* to change images from one format to another by opening them and using Save As... to change the file format for the new image.

Vector graphics
Another file type that is growing in popularity is the **SVG** file type. This is a **vector graphic** rather than a raster graphic and is created in another markup language called XML, so images can be created without the use of a graphics package (although many people use packages such as *Inkscape* to create them). These are fully scalable, so there is no loss of quality if they are expanded. This can make it easier for the visually impaired when using zoom features as the graphics do not become pixelated. Many other vector graphics formats do not work in web pages.

Advice

Image files added to web pages are usually in bitmap graphics formats such as .jpg, .gif or .png format. Many other image formats, for example, vector graphics such as .tif, will not work in a web page.

Activity 21g
Create a new web page with a table that looks like this and has the caption 'Last week'. The image that you require is called **ptct.jpg**. Print your web page as HTML and as it is viewed in your browser.

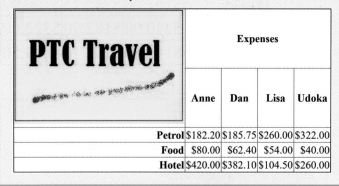

	Expenses			
	Anne	**Dan**	**Lisa**	**Udoka**
Petrol	$182.20	$185.75	$260.00	$322.00
Food	$80.00	$62.40	$54.00	$40.00
Hotel	$420.00	$382.10	$104.50	$260.00

21.2.17 Adjust an image size

Images can be resized using two methods:

» The first method is to change the size of the displayed image in the markup. This is the easier of the two methods, but often uses large image files, which are slower to upload and can delay the display of a completed web page.

» The second method is to physically resize the image in a graphics package. You did this in Task 12b. This method has the advantage of being able to reduce the file size of an image so that a web page will be displayed more quickly. It has the disadvantage of using lower-resolution images, which can appear pixelated, particularly if you wish to enlarge them.

Task 21l

Open the file **webpage2.htm**. Use both methods to resize this image to 80 pixels wide and compare the relative file sizes of the two images. Save both versions of your web page.

Link

For more on resizing images see Chapter 12.

Adjust an image size in the markup

Copy the web page and supporting files **remora.htm**, **remora.jpg** and **turtle.jpg** into your Task21l folder. To change the size of an image in the markup use either the width or height attributes within the image tag. For this task the width needs setting to 80 pixels.

Image aspect ratio

If you change the width of the image to 80 pixels and do not specify a height for the image, it will maintain its **aspect ratio**. This means that it will keep the same proportions. Sometimes you may be asked to distort an image to give a different effect within a web page. This is done by specifying both width and height but not keeping the aspect ratio of the original image. Find the markup for the image **remora.jpg**, in the file **webpage2.htm**, which looks like this.

```
<tr>
  <td rowspan="3"><img src="remora.jpg" alt="Remora"></td>
  <td colspan="3"><h1>Image alignment</h1></td>
```

Add a new attribute to the image tag to specify the new width of the remora image, like this.

```
<tr>
  <td rowspan="3"><img src="remora.jpg" alt="Remora"
style=width:80px></td>
  <td colspan="3"><h1>Image alignment</h1></td>
```

Save the web page which will change from this to this.

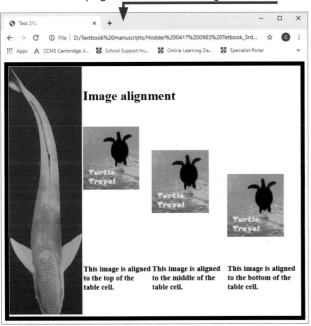
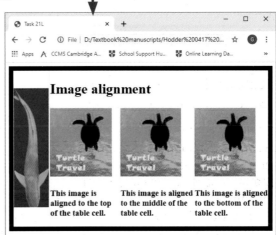

Although the vertical alignment of all three turtle images has not been changed in the markup, the effect is to make the images appear to have the same vertical alignment. This is because the row height has been reduced to fit with the new row height for the image of the remora.

Adjust an image size an external package

You have already completed this in Task 12b. Copy the image that you resized and called **remora1.jpg** from your Task12b folder into your Task21l folder. When using this technique it is useful to have a small, low-resolution image (called a thumbnail) on a web page. If the user wants to see more detail, they can click on the image and a new window will open containing a high-resolution version of the same image. The web page needs to be amended so that the width attribute is no longer present, and the source attribute within the image tag points to the new filename.

```
<tr>
  <td rowspan="3"><img src="remora1.jpg" alt="Remora"></td>
  <td colspan="3"><h1>Image alignment</h1></td>
```

Save your amended web page with the filename **task21l.htm**.

Comparing the two methods

Open the File Explorer window and navigate to the Task21l folder.

This folder contains the two image files and shows you the difference in file sizes between the two methods. Your image sizes may vary from this depending on the resolution you selected when you saved the file. As can be seen here, in this case the new image should load in about 60 per cent of the time the original will take.

Insert an animated image

There are two different methods used to place an animated image on a web page. If the file is an animated GIF, the method is the same as inserting a still image.

> ### Task 21m
>
> Edit the web page saved in Task 21k to replace the image with the moving image **turtlelogo.gif**.

Copy the file **turtlelogo.gif** into your Task21m folder. In Task 21k you saved the completed web page in your Task21m folder. Open this file in *Notepad*. Change the image source from turtle.jpg to **turtlelogo.gif**, like this.

```
<td rowspan="2" style="border:solid 1px">
<img src="turtlelogo.gif" alt="Animated Company Logo">
</td>
```

Save the web page as **task21m.htm** in your Task21m folder. The resulting web page will look like this.

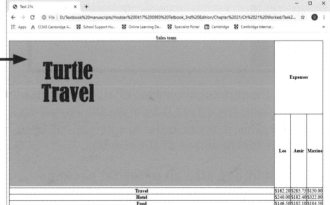

21.2.18 Insert a video file

Videos can be placed in a web page using the `<video>` and `</video>` tags. You must include width and height attributes within the `<video>` tag, so that the correct space is saved on the page for the video. The controls attribute shows the video controls and allows the user to control (start/pause/maximise/adjust volume, etc.) the video.

The video source is different from other HTML elements as it uses a `<source>` tag as well as the src attribute. In the `<source>` tag the type attribute tells the browser the file type of the video to be shown. You must include text between the `<video>` and `</video>` tags for browsers that do not support HTML5 or videos of this type.

> ### Advice
>
> Accepted video formats are .mp4, .webm and .ogg. Many other video formats, such as .wmv, will not work with the <video> tag.

Task 21n

Open the file **webpage3.htm** and save this as task21n.htm. Replace the text *Place video here* with the video **wreck.mp4**. Replace the text *Place audio here* with the sound **whale.mp3**.

Copy the files **wreck.mp4** and **whale.mp3** into your Task21n folder. Open **webpage3.htm** in *Notepad*. Replace the text *Place video here* with this HTML.

```
<video width="400" height="224" controls>
   Your browser does not support this type of video.
   <source src="wreck.mp4" type="video/mp4">
</video>
```

Save the web page as **task21n.htm** in your Task21n folder. The resulting web page will look like this.

At the moment this video will play when the controls are used, clicking on here will start the video.

Video controls and autoplay

To remove the controls from the video simply remove the controls attribute from the video tag. To 'autoplay' the video so that it runs as soon as it has loaded onto the web page, replace the controls attribute with the autoplay attribute. As many browsers refuse to autoplay, unless the video is muted, we must also add the muted attribute to this tag. To get the video to play in a continuous loop, the loop attribute is used. To autoplay the video the markup looks like this.

```
<video width="400" height="224" autoplay loop muted>
   Your browser does not support this type of video.
   <source src="wreck.mp4" type="video/mp4">
</video>
```

21.2.19 Insert an audio file

Audio files, sometimes called sound clips, can be placed in a web page using the <audio> and </audio> tags.

The controls attribute works in a similar way to the video controls. It allows the user to control the sound clip.

The audio source works in a similar way to the video source. In the <source> tag the type attribute tells the browser the file type of the audio to be played.

You must include text between the <audio> and </audio> tags for browsers that do not support HTML5 or files of this type.

Replace the text *Place audio here* with this HTML.

```
<audio controls>
   Your browser does not support this type of audio file.
   <source src="whale.mp3" type="audio/mpeg">
</audio>
```

Save and test the web page. It should look like this. ———➤

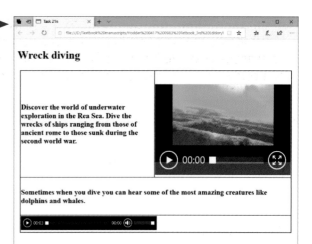

21.2.20 Apply styles to elements within a web page

We have already applied some styles to the tables we created. Colour is important in web page design for both text and backgrounds.

Colour – part 1

Colour is always defined in CSS, either embedded in the HTML or within an attached stylesheet (which you will meet later in the chapter). One method is to use colour names as the property values, such as red, green and blue within the HTML code. There are currently only 16 colour names accepted as web standards in CSS and by the World Wide Web Consortium (known as W3C). These are: aqua, black, blue, fuchsia, gray (note the American spelling), green, lime, maroon, navy, olive, purple, red, silver, teal, white and yellow. Other colour names are, however, accepted by some browsers. A table showing these colours and their names is included in the file **colourcodes.htm** and is available with the source files. You can open this web page and use these colours in your own stylesheets attached to your web pages.

It is not always easy to remember the names of the colours, and many web designers prefer to use hexadecimal codes (often referred to as hex codes) to define the colour of text, backgrounds or objects. Hexadecimal is a counting system where counting is done in 16s (rather than in the tens used in the decimal system). Because we do not have 16 different characters for numbers, we use letters and numbers as shown in Table 21.1.

▼ **Table 21.1** The hexadecimal counting system

Decimal	1	2	3	4	5	6	7	8	9	10	11	12	13	14	15	16	17	18	19	20	21	22	23	24	25	26	27	...
Hexadecimal	1	2	3	4	5	6	7	8	9	A	B	C	D	E	F	10	11	12	13	14	15	16	17	18	19	1A	1B	...

Decimal	...	152	153	154	155	156	157	158	159	160	161	162	163	164	165	166	167	168	169	170	171	172	...
Hexadecimal	...	98	99	9A	9B	9C	9D	9E	9F	A0	A1	A2	A3	A4	A5	A6	A7	A8	A9	AA	AB	AC	...

Advice

Check this table to help you work out which hex codes are useful.

The largest number that can be stored in a single byte (8 bits) of information is the decimal number 255, which is FF in hexadecimal.

Each pixel (dot) on a monitor or projected on to a screen is made up of three different colours. The primary colours when using light (which is very different from the primary colours used in painting) are red, green and blue. All other colours can be made from combinations of these three colours. You will notice that the initial letters are RGB, hence RGB monitors. Each of these colours can be off, partially on or fully on. In hexadecimal, if a colour is off it is set to 00 and if it is fully on it is set to FF. To create the colour for any pixel you must tell the computer how much red, green and blue light to show. This means that all colour codes have six characters, the first two being red, the next two green and the final two blue. This example uses the hex code for red, as the red component is fully on (FF), the green component is off (00) and the blue component is also off (00).

```
<h1 style="color:#ff0000">This is red</h1>
```

Advice

Note the American spelling of 'color', rather than the English 'colour'.

Advice

The hash symbol (#) tells the browser that the number is in hexadecimal.

All of the different combinations of red, green and blue allow more than 16 million different colours to be used.

▼ **Table 21.2** Using hex codes to create different colours

Amount of light (colour)	Hex code	Example (red only)	Colour
Fully on	FF	FF0000	
¾ on	C0	C00000	
½ on	80	800000	
¼ on	40	400000	
Off	00	000000	

The web page **colourcodes.htm** contains the hex codes (as well as the names) for the most popular colours. It is interesting to note that, when working with light, mixing red and green gives yellow, mixing green and blue gives cyan, and mixing red and blue gives magenta. If all three colours are fully on, the result is white. If no colour is on, the result is black.

21.2.21 Specify background properties

Set the background colour

Hexadecimal colour codes can be used with background and foreground colours. For example, in CSS text colours can be changed using the **style** attribute with a **color** property. You must set the background colour using the CSS property **background-color**.

Task 21o

Open the file **task21o.htm**. Edit the web page to look like this. The colour codes you will need are #32879B for the header, #92CDDC for the footer and #B6DDE8 for the table body.

Fruit sales

Fruit	Price
Apple	$1230
Orange	$780
Pear	$240
Banana	$4235
Lemon	$75
Total	$6560

Open the file **task21o.htm** in *Notepad*. Add a **style** attribute to the **<thead>** tag like this.

```
<thead style="background-color:#32879b">
```

Add a **style** attribute to the **<tfoot>** tag like this.

```
<tfoot style="background-color:#92cddc">
```

Add a **style** attribute to the **<tbody>** tag like this.

```
<tbody style="background-color:#b6dde8">
```

Because the footer area has coloured text we will add a second **style** attribute to the **<tfoot>** tag. Note that both style properties are within the quotes and that a semicolon separates the **background-color** and **color** properties (and their values) like this.

```
<tfoot style="background-color:#92cddc; color:#ff0000">
```

21.2.22 Apply styles to a list

You can include on a web page either a numbered list, which is an **ordered list**, or a bulleted list, which is an **unordered list**. Bulleted (unordered) lists can also be nested (placed one inside the other) to give you more flexibility in the design of your web pages. Items to be placed in a list start with the markup **<li>** and close with **</li>**. These are used in the same way as the style definitions for headings (styles h1 to h6) and paragraph styles. Each item in the list must have the list tags around it. The way each of these lists is displayed can be changed using CSS. An example of an item placed in a list would look like this.

```
<li>This is one item from a bulleted or numbered list</li>
```

Numbered lists

Numbered lists are ordered lists in HTML because they are in number order. Place the tag **<ol>** at the start of the numbered list and the tag **</ol>** at the end.

> ### Task 21p
> Create a web page containing the heading 'Fruit' and a numbered list for the following items: Apple, Orange, Pear, Banana and Lemon.

Enter this markup into your text editor. ⟶

Save the web page, as **task21p** in your Task21p folder, which should look like this in your browser.

```
<!DOCTYPE html>
<html>
<!-- Task 21p by your name -->
<head>
<title>Task 21p</title>
</head>
<body>
<h1>Fruit</h1>
<ol>
<li>Apple</li>
<li>Orange</li>
<li>Pear</li>
<li>Banana</li>
<li>Lemon</li>
</ol>
</body>
</html>
```

Bulleted lists

Bulleted lists are called unordered lists in HTML. Place the tag `<ul>` at the start of the numbered list and the tag `</ul>` at the end.

Task 21q

Create a web page containing the heading 'Colours' and a bulleted list for the following items: Red, Yellow, Blue, Green and Cyan.

Enter this markup into your text editor. ⟶

Save the web page, as **task21q** in your Task21q folder, which should look like this in your browser.

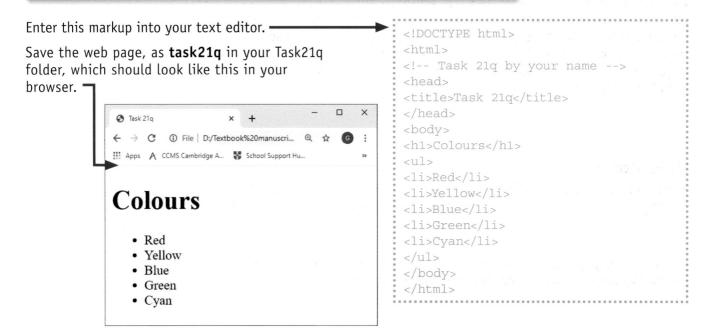

```
<!DOCTYPE html>
<html>
<!-- Task 21q by your name -->
<head>
<title>Task 21q</title>
</head>
<body>
<h1>Colours</h1>
<ul>
<li>Red</li>
<li>Yellow</li>
<li>Blue</li>
<li>Green</li>
<li>Cyan</li>
</ul>
</body>
</html>
```

Nested lists

> ### Task 21r
>
> Create a web page containing the names of two resorts as a bulleted list. These resorts are Ellmau in Austria and Sharm El Sheikh in Egypt. For each resort, list the main activities.

Bulleted lists can be nested by having sub-lists. These are created by placing one unordered list within another list.

Enter this markup into your text editor to create the primary list.

```
<!DOCTYPE html>
<html>
<!-- Task 21r by your name -->
<head>
<title>Task 21r</title>
</head>
<body>
<ul>
<li>Ellmau</li>
<li>Sharm El Sheikh</li>
</ul>
</body>
</html>
```

After each resort, enter a new sub-list that contains the activities offered in each of these places. Note that the sub-list fits between the list item name and the close tag for that item. The finished markup will look like this.

```
<!DOCTYPE html>
<html>
<!-- Task 21r by your name -->
<head>
<title>Task 21r</title>
</head>
<body>
<ul>
<li>Ellmau</li>
<ul>
<li>Skiing</li>
<li>Snowboarding</li>
<li>Sledging</li>
<li>Mountaineering</li>
</ul>
<li>Sharm El Sheikh</li>
<ul>
<li>Scuba diving</li>
<li>Snorkelling</li>
</ul>
</ul>
</body>
</html>
```

Save the web page, as **task21r** in your Task21r folder, which should look like this in your browser.

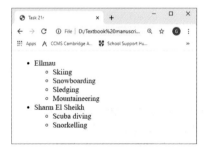

> ### Activity 21h
>
> Create a new web page containing the heading 'Winter sports', a brief introduction and an unordered list of the following winter sports: skiing, tobogganing and snowboarding. For each winter sport, make a sub-list of the items of clothing and equipment required. Set these sub-lists as unordered lists. Print the web page as viewed in your browser and as HTML.
>
> Change these sub-lists to ordered lists. Again, print the web page as viewed in your browser and as HTML.

Bookmarks

A **bookmark** is a named reference point in an electronic document. It is often used to hyperlink to that point from other locations. Bookmarks can be useful if a web page is very long. Links can then be created to the bookmark and when a link is clicked the page will scroll down or up to the bookmark location. You can also add links to bookmarks on other pages. A bookmark can be added to most HTML elements. We will use bookmarks later in the chapter to navigate around our pages using hyperlinks.

Hyperlinks

A **hyperlink** is a method of accessing another document or resource from your current application. Hyperlinks do not just relate to web pages: other application software can also use them. Hyperlinks are often used to create menu options with web pages, using either text or images. When you select a hyperlink (usually by clicking the left mouse button), the hyperlink will perform an action. It may move your position within a page, open another page either locally or on the internet, or open your email editor so that you can send an email to a specified place or company. The colour of the hyperlink gives us information about its use. All browsers, using their default settings, display links like this:

» blue and underlined – a link that has not yet been used
» purple – a link that has been previously used
» red – an active link.

Division tags

The <div> tag is short for a division or section of an HTML document or page. It is also used as a container for HTML elements that can be styled with CSS (or manipulated with JavaScript, but this will not be covered in this textbook). A division starts with a <div> tag and ends with a </div> tag. Any content can be placed in a <div> tag.

> **Advice**
> Browsers place a line break before and after the <div> element.

Anchors

An anchor is used to create a hyperlink to allow you to navigate within the page or navigate to an external page. An anchor starts with an <a> tag and closes with an </a> tag. Although there are many attributes that can be used with anchors, we will only use the href attribute with tells the browser where to create a hyperlink to, and the target attribute which tells the browser in which window to open the linked document or page. You will use these in the next section.

21.2.23 Create a bookmark

Task 21s

Edit the web page **webpage4.htm** so that each new section contains an anchor. Use these anchors to create hyperlinks from the appropriate text in the first paragraph. Make the word 'top' in the last line a hyperlink to the top of the page. Make the words 'W3schools website' a hyperlink to the website www.w3schools.com and the words 'W3C website' a link to the website www.w3.org.

To start this task you must first identify all the sections to be linked to. Copy the file webpage4.htm in your Task21s folder. Open the web page in your text editor and in your web browser. Viewing the page in the browser sometimes makes it easier to see where the bookmarks need to be placed. Each section needs a bookmark with a different name. The bookmark is created using the id attribute.

You should always choose short yet meaningful names for each ID. For this web page you will give each division an ID (identifier). These will be called top, 21a, 21b, 21c, 21d, 21e and 21f, as these relate directly to the sections within the web page. It is sensible to place all the bookmarks into the document before creating the hyperlinks to each bookmark. Each bookmark is created like this.

```
<h1 id="top">Chapter 21</h1><hr>
```

You can see that the id attribute is inside the tag defining the style for the text. The value for this attribute (the bookmark name) is placed in speech marks. This ID will be used in all hyperlinks to navigate this point. The <hr> tag used in this example is another single tag (it does not have a closing tag) that draws a horizontal line across the page. This is not part of the bookmark. Add the other bookmarks to the markup, one for each section of the document, like this.

```
<hr>
<h2 id="21a">21a Understand what html is</h2>
<p>Many students sit the practical examinations without …
```

```
<hr>
<h2 id="21b">21b Problems with WYSIWYGs</h2>
<p>There are many well designed WYSIWYG packages on the …
```

```
<hr>
<h2 id="21c">21c Use the correct terms</h2>
<p> Over the past few years, as the practical examinations …
```

Advice

If the anchor name is visible in the browser view of the page it often means that you have made a syntax error (an error in the structure of the markup, often in the opening or closing speech marks around the value).

Add divisions for 21d, 21e and 21f with similar markup.

21.2.24 Create a hyperlink

Hyperlinks within a web page

In the final sentence, find the word 'top'. This will be used to create a hyperlink to the bookmark with the name 'top' that you created earlier. The hyperlink is created using an anchor. The two anchor tags are placed each side of the word 'top'. The markup includes a hyperlink reference (the markup attribute for this is href) and the name of the destination anchor. This anchor name is always inside speech marks and preceded by the # symbol, like this.

```
<p>Back to the <a href="#top">top</a></p>
```

In the first paragraph find the text 'what is HTML?' Edit the markup for this text so that it creates a hyperlink to the anchor with the ID 21a. It will look like this.

```
<h3>Here is advice to try to help you succeed; if you follow
this you are likely to create better web pages. First you
need to know,<a href="#21a"> what is HTML? </a> Once you have
a sound understanding of HTML, it is worth considering the
use of WYSIWYGs and the potential problems of using these
packages...
```

Add the other hyperlinks to this paragraph like this.

```
<h1>Advice for practical web page creation</h1>
<h3>Here is advice to try to help you succeed; if you follow
this, you are likely to create better web pages. First you
need to know <a href="#21a"> what is HTML?</a> Once you have a
sound understanding of HTML, it is worth considering the use
of <a href="#21b"> WYSIWYGs</a> and the potential problems of
using these packages. Make sure that you <a href="#21c"> use
the right terms</a> to describe what you have done, are doing
or could be asked to do. Learn how to <a href="#21d">create
and attach stylesheets </a> to your web pages. Make sure that
you can <a href="#21e"> work with tables</a>. These provide a
fundamental structure to web pages and seem to be replacing
frames in many areas. Look for <a href="#21f">other resources</
a> to help you prepare for the practical examinations.</h3>
```

Now that the hyperlinks have been created, each one needs testing. Save the web page and refresh your browser, then try each hyperlink in turn and make sure that it directs you to the correct place in the web page. If the name that you have used in the hyperlink reference does not exist, your browser will go to the top of the page and the browser does not show you that there is an error.

Hyperlinks to other web pages

Hyperlinks can be created to another web page stored locally, usually in the same folder as the current web page, or to an external website on the internet. The markup for both of these links has the same syntax (structure). The only difference is the address of the web page that the hyperlink is to go to.

To complete Task 21s, two hyperlinks need to be added to external web addresses. These follow a similar format, with the URL for the web address appearing as the hyperlink. The markup for these two hyperlinks is shown here.

```
<h2 id="21f">21f Other useful links</h2>
<p>There are other places that can be used to gain valuable
information that may help. These include the <a href="https:
//www.w3schools.com/"> W3schools website</a> and the
<a href="https://www.w3.org/">W3C website</a>.</p>
<p><a href="#top">Back to the top</a></p>
```

Add these hyperlinks to the last section of your markup and save your web page as **task21s.htm** in your Task21s folder, and as **task21t.htm** in your Task21t folder. Test the hyperlinks to make sure they work as you expected.

References to pages stored in the same folder as your web page just have an address without the URL. To link to a local file called 'next_page.htm', you would include a hyperlink reference like this.

```
<p><a name="next _ page.htm">Click here for the next page</a>.</p>
```

21.2.25 The use of relative file paths

When creating a hyperlink reference to another file, particularly one stored locally, it is really important to use a relative file path, such as:

```
<a href ="next _ page.htm">
```

This is better than using an absolute file path such as:

```
<a href ="C:my documents/my folder/html/next _ page.htm">
```

While either of these is likely to work on your computer, other computers are unlikely to have the same folder structure and filename. Therefore, if you used an absolute file path, the file next_page.htm would not be found on another computer system and the hyperlink would not work. The same reasoning applies to images and other objects included in your web page where relative references **must** be used rather than absolute references.

Activity 21i

Open the web page **htmltips.htm** and replace the text YOUR NAME with your name. Edit the web page so that each new section contains an anchor. Use these anchors to create hyperlinks from the appropriate text in the first section. Make the word 'top' in the last line a hyperlink to the top of the page.

Make the words 'Hodder Education' a hyperlink to the website www. hoddereducation.co.uk and the text 'W3C' a hyperlink to www.w3.org. Print the HTML view of this web page.

Open a web page in a new browser window

When a web page is opened, it may open in the current window or it may open in a new window. This is set using the target attribute. This attribute is part of the anchor and tells the browser which window to use for the web page that you are going to open. The target attribute can either be set as a default setting in the head section of the markup or as an individual setting for a hyperlink within the body section. If the target attribute is not used, the browser will decide where to open a web page. To set a target window for a single hyperlink, add the target attribute to the first anchor. Some target attributes have specific functions. If a target name of _blank is applied, this will open in a new browser window. If _self is applied it will open in the current window. Other target names, such as _parent and _top, are reserved and perform different functions with frames, which are beyond the scope of this book. Any other target name that you use will open the specified web page in a window with that target name, if it exists, or open it in a new window with that target name.

Task 21t

Using your web page **task21t.htm**, make the hyperlink you created to the W3C website open in the same window and the hyperlink to the W3schools website open in a new window called **_w3s**.

Open the web page task21t.htm in your text editor and in your web browser. Edit the markup for the last two hyperlinks to include the target attributes like this.

```
<p>There are other places that can be used to gain valuable
information that may help. These include the <a href="https:
//www.w3schools.com/" target="_w3s"> W3schools website</a> and
the <a href="https://www.w3.org/" target="_self">W3C website</
a>.</p>
<p><a href="#top">Back to the top</a></p>
```

Add these hyperlinks to the last section of your markup and save your web page as **task21t.htm** in your Task21t folder, and as **task21w.htm** in your Task21w folder. Test the hyperlinks to make sure that they work as you expected, checking the tabs at the top of the browser to see if a new target window has been opened.

Use a hyperlink to send an email message

Hyperlinks from web pages, other applications packages or documents can be used to open an email editor and prepare a message to be sent to another person or company. This is very useful in a website, where you can set up your email address and subject line within the markup, instruct the browser to open the email editor and insert these details into a new message when the hyperlink is selected.

The format for this is very similar to the hyperlinks shown earlier in this section. In place of the URL or path of a web page, the mailto: instruction is placed within the hyperlink reference of the anchor. This is followed by the email address of the recipient. To include the subject line for the message, this is included by specifying subject= followed by the text for the subject line. The whole hyperlink reference is enclosed within speech marks.

Task 21u

Create a new web page that contains a hyperlink to prepare an email message to be sent to graham.a.brown@hotmail.co.uk with the subject line 'IGCSE Book'.

For this task you need to prepare the following new markup in your text editor:

```
<p><a href="mailto:graham.a.brown@hotmail.co.uk?subject=IGCSE%20Book">
Click here to contact us page</a></p>
```

Save this in your Task21u folder and try it in your browser. When you click on the hyperlink it will open your email editor; place the address in the To: section and the text 'IGCSE Book' in the Subject: line.

Note how the space in the text 'IGCSE Book' has been replaced in the markup with %20. This is the hex value for the ASCII character 32, which represents a space. There should not be any spaces inside the speech marks for the hyperlink reference.

Advice

Body text could also be added by adding '&body=Add%20the%20body%20text' as an extra value at the end of the mailto property.

Create a hyperlink from an image

Task 21v

Open the file **task21v.htm**. Make the image in this web page a hyperlink to the web page **remora.htm**.

Copy all the files from your Task21l folder to your Task21v folder. Rename task21l.htm as **task21v.htm**. Open the file task21v.htm in *Notepad*.

Images can be used as hyperlinks in the same way as text. To create a hyperlink to the web page **remora.htm**, add this anchor tag with its `href` attribute and value so that it surrounds the image tab like this.

```
<tr>
  <td rowspan="3">
<a href="remora.htm"> <img src="remora.jpg" alt="Remora"></a></td>
  <td colspan="3"><h1>Image alignment</h1></td>
```

This hyperlink will open the partially constructed web page called remora.htm. Test the hyperlink and save the web page.

21.2.26 The head section

At the start of the chapter we stated there are two parts to every web page, the head section and the body section. The head section is a container for all the head elements, such as titles, stylesheets and metadata. The word metadata means data about other data. The head section is always placed between the <html> tag and <body> tag. The metadata about the HTML document is not displayed in the browser. We will study some of the tags used for the metadata later in this chapter – these are called metatags.

21.2.27 Insert a page title

This is added to the web page to define the title for the page. You have already added this to all of the web pages you have worked on so far, but have not explained what it does. It can contain only text and is displayed in the web page tab or the browser's title bar when the page is opened by a web browser. For example, when we created task 21a, we included the title tag in the HTML like this.

```
<head>
   <title>Task 21a</title>
</head>
```

This places the text 'Task 21a' so that it is displayed in the browser like this.

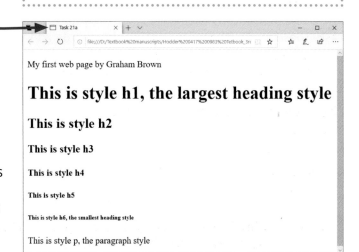

21.2.28 The function of metatags

Metatags are not displayed in the browser but hold important information that the browser requires, such as specifying the character set, page description, keywords, author of the document, and the viewport settings. These functions tell browsers how to display the page and they tell search engines about keywords, which helps them list the page in the results of relevant searches. Further explanation of all these follow.

21.2.29 Use metatags

As we have already learned, a metatag is a tag that holds metadata. It uses the `<meta>` tag to open it and the `</meta>` tag to close it. We will use only three attributes with the `<meta>` tag, these are: **charset**, **name** and **content**.

Metatag attributes – charset

To define the character set used by a web page, we use the charset attribute. This specifies the type of characters (called the character encoding) that are displayed. There are hundreds of character sets, but no browser can contain them all, so we will use only one of two common examples that are used for English. These are UTF-8, which is for Unicode, and ISO-8859-1, which is for the Latin alphabet.

Task 21w

Open the file **task21w.htm**. Place, into the appropriate section of the HTML, metadata to:
» define the character set used to UTF-8
» include your name as the author of the web page
» add a description of the web page
» set the keywords to be the words **HTML**, **web page creation**, **web development**, **stylesheet**, and **WYSIWYG**
» set the viewport to match the width of the device and the initial scaling to 1.

Set the web page so that any hyperlink from the page will open in a new window or tab.

Open task 21w.htm. Move to the head section. Within the head section add the following metadata.

```
<head>
    <title>Task 21w</title>
    <meta charset="UTF-8">
    <style>
```

This has set the character set to that specified in the task. This metatag can be placed anywhere in the head section, except between other tags. For example, it cannot be placed between the <style> and </style> tags, or between <title> and </title>.

Metatag attributes – name

The name attribute is used to specify the four other elements required for this task, these are: **author**, **description**, **keywords** and **viewport**. Each of these name attributes is followed by a content attribute.

Metatag attributes – content

The content attribute is used with the name attribute and contains the value assigned to the name. This value is in the form of text.

Define the author

To include the name of the author of the web page you must use both the name and content attributes. Within the head section add the following metadata, changing the content so that it contains your name rather than Graham Brown.

```
<head>
    <title>Task 21w</title>
    <meta charset="UTF-8">
    <meta name="author" content="Graham Brown">
    <style>
```

Web page description

To include a suitable description of the web page, the name attribute will contain 'description' and the content will contain an appropriate description, such as 'Advice for practical web page creation'. Within the head section add the following metadata.

```
<meta charset="UTF-8">
<meta name="author" content="Graham Brown">
<meta name="description" content="Advice for practical web page creation">
<style>
```

Keywords for a search engine

The keywords are used by search engines to try and find websites that match a user's search string. The more relevant keywords your website contains, the better the chance of it appearing near the top of the search results. It is therefore better to have lots of keywords in your metadata, using the sorts of words or phrases that a user may type into their search engine. Some examples also include common misspellings of the words and phrases – for example if **HTML** was to be included you may also add **.htm**, **HTM** and **.html**.

For this task you are given the keywords to be used as content in the metadata: these are **HTML**, **web page creation**, **web development**, **stylesheet**, and **WYSIWYG**, so you will include only those in the content section. As more than one keyword will be added to the content attribute, each value must be separated with a comma. Within the head section add the following metadata.

```
<meta name="author" content="Graham Brown">
<meta name="description" content="Advice for practical web page creation">
<meta name="keywords" content="HTML, web page creation, web development, stylesheet, WYSIWYG">
<style>
```

Viewport settings

The viewport is the user's visible area of the web page. Using the viewport setting can make a significant difference when using a smaller display size to view a web page, for example, on a mobile phone or tablet. There are two content parts to the viewport, the first is the width, which should normally be set to the width of the device, and the second part is the initial scaling for the web page, which would usually be set to 1.0. For this task (and probably for most web pages) these settings are required, so in the head section add the following metadata.

```
<meta name="author" content="Graham Brown">
<meta name="description" content="Advice for practical web page creation">
<meta name="keywords" content="HTML, webpage creation, web development, stylesheet, and WYSIWYG">
<meta name="viewport" content="width=device-width, initial-scale=1.0">
<style>
```

Save your web page. Unfortunately, you cannot test these elements (apart from viewport if you publish the web page and then load it onto different devices) to make sure that you have made no errors, so carefully visually verify that you have made no typing errors.

21.2.30 Set a default target window

You have already studied how to use the target attribute within an anchor tag to open a web page in a new browser window, or in the same window, etc. If you have a web page with several hyperlinks that require the same type of action (same target window/tab or a new window/tab) you can make this the default setting for the page. To complete the task, you must set the web page so that any hyperlink from the page will open in a new window or tab. The default settings for this are also in the head section and are added using the `<base>` tag. In the head section add the following base tag.

```
    <meta name="author" content="Graham Brown">
    <meta name="description" content="Advice for practical web page creation">
    <meta name="keywords" content="HTML, webpage creation, web development,
stylesheet, and WYSIWYG">
    <meta name="viewport" content="width=device-width, initial-scale=1.0">
    <base target="_blank">
    <style>
```

When you save and test the web page, each time that you click on a hyperlink it will open a new tab/window to display the new content.

Activity 21j

Edit the web page that you saved for Activity 21g. Set the background colour for the table to #FFFF00 and an outside border of 4 pixels, so it looks like this.

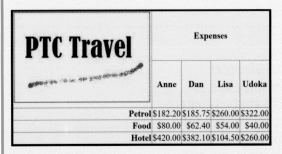

Make the image a hyperlink to send an email message to ptc_travel@outlook.com with the subject line 'Expenses' and the body text 'Please send me updated expenses details.' Place meta data to:

» define the character set used to ISO-8859-1
» include your name as the author of the web page
» set the keywords to the words **PTC**, **travel**, and **expenses**
» set the viewport to match the width of the device and the initial scaling to 2.

Set the web page so that any hyperlink from the page will open in the same window or tab.

Print your web page as HTML and as it is viewed in your browser.

21.2.31 Apply styles and classes to the HTML

Task 21x

Edit the html in the file **webpage5.htm** so that:

» the text Chapter 21 is set in style h1
» each paragraph style with an ID is set in style h2
» the hyperlinked items between 'What is HTML?...' and '...Other resources' becomes a bulleted list and this bulleted list is indented by 50 pixels from the left edge
» each occurrence of the text 'HTML', after the bulleted list, is set to the class called red
» the final sentence is set in style h3
» the whole table is formatted to be centre aligned.

Copy the files **webpage5.htm** and **task21x.css** into your Task21x folder. From your Task21x folder, open the file **webpage5.htm** in *Notepad*. Locate, at the start of the body section, the markup for the text 'Chapter 21'. Change the style from paragraph style **<p>** and **</p>** to style **h1** so that it looks like this.

```
<body>
    <h1>Chapter 21</h1><hr>
    <p id="top">Advice for practical webpage creation</p>
```

Locate throughout the document each paragraph tag that has an ID attribute, like this. For each of these six opening and closing tags, change the style from paragraph style **<p>** and **</p>** to style **h2** so that it looks like this.

```
<body>
    <h1>Chapter 21</h1><hr>
    <h2 id="top">Advice for practical webpage creation</h2>
```

Locate the hyperlinked items in paragraph tags between 'What is HTML?...' and '...Other resources'. Change each of these items from paragraph style to list style by replacing the **<p>** and **</p>** tags with **<li>** and **</li>** tags like this.

```
<li><a href="#21a">What is HTML?</a></li>
<li><a href="#21b">WYSIWYGs</a></li>
<li><a href="#21c">Use the right terms</a></li>
<li><a href="#21d">Create and attach stylesheets</a></li>
<li><a href="#21e">Work with tables</a></li>
<li><a href="#21f">Other resources</a></li><body>
```

Use the <div> tag to apply a style

When this is saved and opened in a browser the bulleted list appears over to the left of the body text and you have been instructed to indent this bulleted list by 50 pixels from the left edge. This could be completed by adding a style attribute to each <li> tag, but that would require you to enter the style information six times. Rather than do this repeatedly, you can use a single division <div> tag. Place the <div> and </div> tags around the bulleted list and add the style attribute, its declaration (margin-left:) and value (50px) to the <div> tag like this.

```
<div style="margin-left:50px">
<li><a href="#21a">What is HTML?</a></li>
<li><a href="#21b">WYSIWYGs</a></li>
<li><a href="#21c">Use the right terms</a></li>
<li><a href="#21d">Create and attach stylesheets</a></li>
<li><a href="#21e">Work with tables</a></li>
<li><a href="#21f">Other resources</a></li>
</div>
```

Apply a class to elements within a web page

To set each occurrence of the text HTML to the class called red we cannot use the <div> tag, as this would place a line break in the text and each time the text 'HTML' appears it is within a sentence. Find the first 'HTML' in the document like this.

```
<h2 id="21a">21a Understand what HTML is</h2>
```

To make the text go red, place anchor tags <a> and </a> around 'HTML' and use the class attribute followed by the class name red, like this.

```
<h2 id="21a">21a Understand what <a class="red">HTML</a> is</h2>
```

The finished text looks like this.

21a Understand what HTML is

Advice

In **Notepad** you can use the **Edit** tab, then **Find** and **Find Next** to locate the items you are looking for.

Locate the final sentence and change the tags from paragraph tags to style h3 like this.

```
<h3>Click on this link to go <a href="#top">Back to the top</a></h3>
```

To format the whole table to be centre aligned, use the `<div>` and `</div>` tags and place these around the entire table. Add the following tags to the markup to the start of the table and to the end of the table, like this.

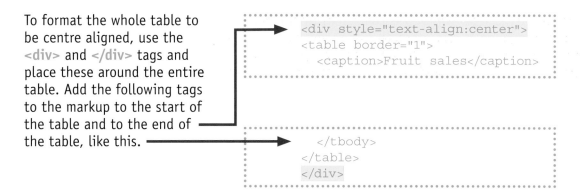

```
<div style="text-align:center">
<table border="1">
  <caption>Fruit sales</caption>
```

```
  </tbody>
 </table>
</div>
```

21.3 Use stylesheets

Using **styles** in your web pages helps you to be consistent in the way the pages look. Using styles is much quicker and easier than applying individual settings – such as font face, font size, text alignment and font colours – to every piece of text in each web page that you create.

You have already met the heading styles, h1 to h6, and the paragraph style, p, earlier in the chapter. When you used these styles the web browser did not find any of these style definitions in your HTML markup, so it used its own default settings. However, you can set your own definitions for each style and the web browser will attempt to apply these styles to the page.

Styles are not only set for text, but can also be used to define page layout, colour schemes and default settings for other objects and links on the page. Using a consistent style is often important to give a 'corporate feel' to a website. Particular elements, such as colour schemes, table presentation, logos and font faces, are often used to aid recognition of well-known companies or brands.

While styles can be set with HTML tags, normally they are defined in the presentation layer of the web page in CSS format. You have already embedded some presentation layer elements in the HTML using the `style` attribute. These are called in-line styles. Styles may also be defined in the head section of a web page or defined in an external **stylesheet**. If stylesheets are used, the stylesheet is attached to the web page in the **head** section of the markup. As we have already seen, styles can be applied individually to each page, but it is more efficient to write, edit and attach one or more common stylesheet/s to all the pages in a website. This collection of styles is saved in a different file in a **cascading stylesheet** (.css) format.

21.3.1 The characteristics of a cascading stylesheet

A cascading stylesheet is a simple way of adding style (for example, fonts, colours, spacing) to web pages.

One or more of these cascading stylesheets can be attached to a web page, and the styles in the stylesheet will be applied to that page. Where more than one web page is used, the styles only have to be defined once and then attached to all the web pages. In-line styles, defined within the HTML, usually override styles attached from an external stylesheet. This allows companies to develop different stylesheets for specific items such as colour schemes, text styles and styles for a particular document or set of documents. If more than one stylesheet is attached to a web page at the same time, those attached later in the markup have priority over earlier ones. If a style has more than one declaration of the same property, the last value is used for the property.

21.3.2 CSS syntax

CSS rules have a selector and a declaration block like this.

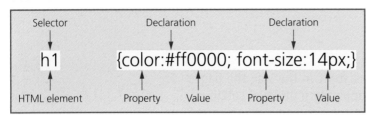

>> Each element has one or more declarations, each separated by a semicolon.
>> Each declaration has a property name and a value, separated by a colon.
>> Each declaration block is surrounded by curly brackets.

To make the CSS easier to read, you can put one declaration on each line, like this.

```
h1      {color:#ff0000;
         font-size:14px;}
```

Task 21y

Open a copy of the web page that you saved in Task 21g. Add an external stylesheet to this page to define the table header and table data so that they each have a solid border 4 pixels wide.

Open the web page task21g.htm in *Notepad*. Save it as **task21y.htm** in your Task21y folder. Copy one line of the embedded CSS from the table header and paste it in your second *Notepad* window (for the stylesheet) like this.

Edit this so the stylesheet looks like this.

The element name/s, in this case **td** and **th**, are followed by curly brackets {}. In this example: you have set each piece of table data and each table header so that its border property has a solid border that is 4 pixels thick. By defining the two elements td and th at the same time, you have saved yourself extra work.

```
td style="border:solid 2px;
```

```
td,th {border: 4px solid #000000;}
```

21.3.3 Save styles in cascading stylesheet format

Save this file using the filename **tablestyle.css** in the same folder as your web page. The saved file should look like this when viewed in File Explorer. ━━━

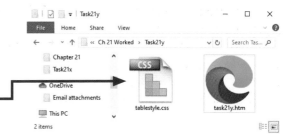

Advice

Make sure that you use the .css file extension and not .htm or .txt.

Go back to the *Notepad* window for the HTML of **task21y.htm** and remove all the border properties and values from each of the style tags in the table header and the table body. This example shows the first ones removed. ━━━━━━━━━➤

```
<thead>
<tr style="height:60px">
<th style="width:75%;">Fruit</th>
<th>Price</th>
```

21.3.4 Attach an external stylesheet to a web page

In the HTML window, add this line of text below the title tags in the head section.

```
<link rel="stylesheet" type="text/css" href="tablestyle.css">
```

21.3.5 Use relative file paths for attached stylesheets

Make sure that you **do not** put an absolute address in a hyperlink reference, for example:

```
<link rel="stylesheet" type="text/css" href ="C:/my documents/my folder/
css/tablestyle.css">
```

as this is only likely to work on your computer. Other computers are unlikely to have the same folder structure and filename. The link (with the relative file path) is attached to the web page so when the page is opened or refreshed, the browser searches for the file tablestyle.css and applies the styles from this file to the web page. The filename in this line of markup **must** match the name of the CSS file that you saved.

The new markup should start like this.

```
<!DOCTYPE html>
<html>
<!-- Task 21y by your name -->
<head>
  <title>Task 21y</title>
  <link rel="stylesheet" type="text/css" href="tablestyle.css">
</head>
```

Save this web page. View this web page in your browser; it should have changed from this to this.

Fruit	Price
Apple	$1230
Orange	$780
Pear	$240
Banana	$4235
Lemon	$75
Total	$6560

Fruit sales

Fruit	Price
Apple	$1230
Orange	$780
Pear	$240
Banana	$4235
Lemon	$75
Total	$6560

Fruit sales

Advice

Using external stylesheets saves you lots of time. One stylesheet can be attached to many web pages and one style can be attached to every element on those pages with little effort.

Activity 21k

Edit the web page that you saved for Activity 21j so that the styles in the head section are removed and edited to become a new external stylesheet called 21kstyles. Change all references for 21j to 21k. Attach this stylesheet to your web page. Print your stylesheet, and your web page, both as HTML and as it is viewed in your browser.

When you mark Activity 21k, check the answers carefully. Although both of the answers shown (in text format and as a screenshot) may meet the requirements of the question, you may not be credited with this work. Why?

Answer: your name, Centre number and candidate details are not visible on the print out.

21.3.6 Add comments to a stylesheet

Although you will often be told to place your name and candidate details as text on the web page, this is not as easy in a stylesheet. Text placed in a stylesheet will often stop the styles from working. Any text must have /* before it and */ after it, so that the browser knows to ignore it.

Task 21z

Open a copy of the web page and stylesheet that you saved in Task 21y. Add your name and a brief description of the stylesheet as comments to the stylesheet.

Edit the stylesheet so that it looks like this. ⟶

You can see that the comments can be on a single line or on more than one line. Only one /* and */ are required for each comment. Check that the stylesheet still works with the web page.

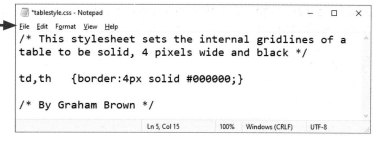

```
/* This stylesheet sets the internal gridlines of a
table to be solid, 4 pixels wide and black */

td,th    {border:4px solid #000000;}

/* By Graham Brown */
```

Advice

Whenever you edit a stylesheet, save it using Save As... and refresh the browser view of the web page to make sure that the changes you have made work correctly.

Task 21aa

Open a copy of the web page that you saved in Task 21a. Change the title of this page to Task 21aa. Apply the stylesheet **style1.css** to this page and save this web page. Change the attached stylesheet to **style2.css** and save this with a new filename.

Select the folder called Task21aa in your Documents window. Copy the file task21a.htm into this folder. Rename this file as **task21aa.htm**. Open this file in your text editor and in your web browser. Copy the files **style1.css** and **style2.css** into this folder.

Change the title of the web page to Task 21aa. To apply the styles from the stylesheet **style1.css**, you must attach it to the web page. Move the cursor to the text editor containing the HTML and add this line of text below the title tags in the head section of the markup, like this.

```
<html>
<head>
  <title>Task 21aa</title>
  <link rel="stylesheet" type="text/css" href="style1.css">
</head>
<body>
  <p>My first web page by MY NAME HERE</p>
  <h1>This is style h1, the largest heading style</h1>
  <h2>This is style h2</h2>
  <h3>This is style h3</h3>
  <h4>This is style h4</h4>
  <h5>This is style h5</h5>
  <h6>This is style h6, the smallest heading style</h6>
  <p>This is style p, the paragraph style</p>
</body>
</html>
```

Save this web page. View this web page in your browser. You will notice that your web page has changed from this to this.

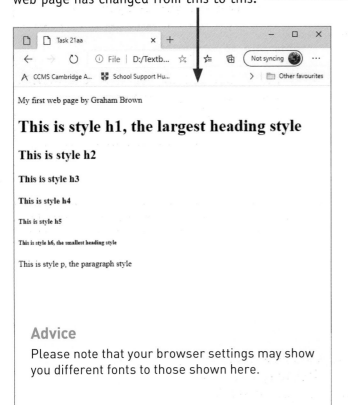

The page content has not changed but the styles applied to the page are very different. Notice that the font face, sizes, colours and alignment have all been specified in the stylesheet. This stylesheet is a poor example because it contains too many variations. If you change the markup to attach style2.css to the page rather than style1.css, you should see something like this.

This is the same web page again, but with the slightly improved stylesheet style2.css, which has a background colour defined in the stylesheet. You will discover how to create and amend these stylesheets later.

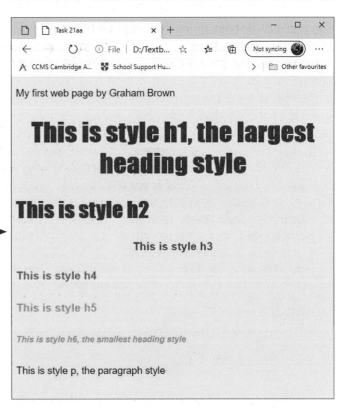

21.3.7 CSS text

It is very easy to create a cascading stylesheet in your text editor. The structure of a .css file has a few very simple rules. Stylesheets do not have tags in them as they are not a markup language. Each style has a style name, which is called a selector. The selector is followed by curly brackets {}. Inside these curly brackets are the property for the style, followed by a colon, then the property's value. For example, if you want to set the text in style h1 to be centre aligned, it would appear like this.

```
h1 {text-align: center}
```

Note the American spelling of 'center'.

Each style can have a number of properties and values. If there is more than one property then each property is followed by a semicolon. For example, if you want to set the text in style h1 to be centre aligned, 16-point high and bold, it must appear like this.

```
h1 {text-align: center;
font-size: 16pt;
font-weight: bold}
```

If a value within a style contains more than one word, it must be placed in speech marks like this.

```
h2 {font-family: "Times New Roman", serif}
```

Stylesheets are saved in .css format (in a similar way to saving in .htm format) from the text editor.

21.3.8 Specify font properties

Font families

Individual fonts can be specified, but these are not always available in all browsers, so there are a number of **generic font families**, including **serif** and **sans-serif** fonts, which can also be used. These font families include 'serif', 'sans-serif', 'cursive', 'fantasy' and 'monospace', which has proportional spacing.

The generic font family must always be listed after the other preferred font/s. The font-family property must contain a hyphen. In the example above, font-family is set so that the browser will look at the list of fonts installed in the machine and will try to find Times New Roman first (it is in speech marks in the stylesheet because there are spaces in the font name); if it cannot find it, it will find any generic serif font that is available. It is good practice to offer the browser two (or more) different font families and a generic font type. These are usually a *Windows* font, a *MAC OS* font and a generic font type. The order that these values are placed within the font-family declaration is important as the browser will try to locate the first font in the list. If that is not available in the system being used then it looks for the next font in the list, until, if none of the specified fonts are available, it will finally reach the generic font type. When this happens, the browser will display the font-family that it has stored for this generic font type.

Advice

A serif font is one that has small lines or strokes (called serifs) at the ends of characters, like this:

A font that does not contain serifs is known as a sans-serif font.

Task 21ab

Open a copy of the last web page that you saved in Task 21aa.

Create a new stylesheet called serif.css that sets all the styles as generic serif fonts. Apply this stylesheet to your web page. View the web page in your browser.

Change the generic settings in the stylesheet to a different generic font style. Save the stylesheet with a new name. Try all the generic style settings to see what each one looks like.

Copy the last web page you saved in your Task21aa folder into your Task21ab folder and rename it **task21ab.htm**. Open this file in your text editor and in your web browser. Edit the title of the web page so it becomes Task 21ab. To attach the stylesheet to the web page, you must edit the link line in the head section of the markup so that it becomes:

```
<link rel="stylesheet" type="text/css" href="serif.css">
```

Save the web page. You are going to create the stylesheet in the second copy of the text editor (*Notepad*). Enter the following style definitions into it.

Carefully verify your stylesheet by checking this original document with your typed copy. Save the file using the filename **serif.css**. Refresh your browser so that you can see the effect that this has on the web page.

```
h1 {font-family: serif}
h2 {font-family: serif}
h3 {font-family: serif}
h4 {font-family: serif}
h5 {font-family: serif}
h6 {font-family: serif}
p {font-family: serif}
td style="border:solid 2px;
```

Group style definitions

As all the styles have the same values for the **font-family** property, you can group all of the styles together and change the value only once. This stylesheet can be simplified to this single line.

```
h1,h2,h3,h4,h5,h6,p {font-family: serif}
```

Edit it and save it so that it replaces the old version. Refresh the browser to check that it still works.

Edit this stylesheet so that it sets the **font-family** to 'sans-serif'. Save this file using the filename **sans-serif.css**. Change the markup in the HTML to link to this file and save this web page. Repeat this process for each of the other generic font families.

Task 21ac

Open a copy of the web page that you saved in Task 21ab.

Create a new stylesheet called font.css that sets all the styles so that the font **Trebuchet MS** is used, if this is not available then set it so **Arial** is used, if this is not available then use the browser's default sans-serif font.

Copy the web page you saved in your Task21ab folder into your Task21ac folder and rename it **task21ac.htm**. Open this file in your text editor and in your web browser. Edit the title of the web page so it becomes Task 21ac. Edit the attached stylesheet so that it becomes:

```
<link rel="stylesheet" type="text/css" href="font.css">
```

Save the web page. You are going to create the stylesheet in the second copy of the text editor (*Notepad*). Enter the following grouped style definitions into it.

```
h1,h2,h3,h4,h5,h6,p        {font-family: "Trebuchet MS", Arial, sans-serif}
```

You will notice that the Trebuchet MS has been included in speech marks (as it is more than one word) and that there is a comma used to separate each value within the font-family declaration.

Carefully verify your stylesheet by checking this original document with your typed copy. Save the file using the filename **font.css**. Refresh your browser which may look like this.

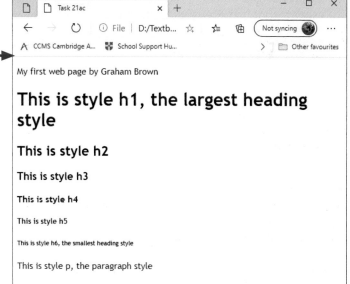

Font size

The font-size property must contain a hyphen and can be followed by absolute heights, by setting values relative to each other, or a mixture of both.

Absolute values can be used to set the number of **points**, **picas**, or **pixels** high, for each character. If point sizes are used, there are 72 points to an inch, so a 28-point font will be about 1 cm tall. This will not be affected by the size or resolution of the monitor. The sizes specified are set as numbers with 'pt' to show it is in points, for example an 18-point font is written as 18pt. Alternatively, font size can be measured in picas, which is abbreviated as 'pc' and is the equivalent of 12 points, so a two-pica font size is the same as a 24-point font. A pixel is one dot on a computer monitor. This means that pages will appear differently depending on the size and resolution of the monitor used. For older-style monitors, one pixel was often about the same size as one point, but high-definition (HD) monitors now mean that characters appear much smaller on these devices. The abbreviation for pixels is 'px'.

Other absolute values include 'in' to show the measurement in inches, 'cm' for centimetres or 'mm' for millimetres. Do not place a space between the number and the abbreviation: 24px sets a 24-pixel height, but 24 px will not set the value to pixels.

Task 21ad

Open a copy of the web page and stylesheet that you saved in Task 21ac.

Edit this stylesheet so that style h1 is 36 point, h2 is 24 point, h3 18 point, h4 16 point, h5 14 point, h6 12 point and the paragraph style is 12 point. Save this stylesheet as size.css.

Change these settings to try and get similar results using the settings for pixels (the number will depend on your monitor display settings), picas, inches centimetres and millimetres.

Copy the web page you saved in your Task21ac folder into your Task21ad folder and rename it **task21ad.htm**. Open this file in your text editor and in your web browser. Edit the title of the web page so it becomes Task 21ad.

Because all of the font settings are different in this case, it is more sensible to keep all of the settings for each style together. It is possible to produce a stylesheet giving these results like this.

```
h1,h2,h3,h4,h5,h6,p        {font-family: "Trebuchet MS", Arial, sans-serif}

h1                         {font-size: 36pt}
h2                         {font-size: 24pt}
h3                         {font-size: 18pt}
h4                         {font-size: 16pt}
h5                         {font-size: 14pt}
h6                         {font-size: 12pt}
p                          {font-size: 10pt}
```

This works, so does keeping the style definitions together like this.

```
h1 {font-family: "Trebuchet MS", Arial, sans-serif; font-size: 36pt}
h2 {font-family: "Trebuchet MS", Arial, sans-serif; font-size: 24pt}
h3 {font-family: "Trebuchet MS", Arial, sans-serif; font-size: 18pt}
h4 {font-family: "Trebuchet MS", Arial, sans-serif; font-size: 16pt}
h5 {font-family: "Trebuchet MS", Arial, sans-serif; font-size: 14pt}
h6 {font-family: "Trebuchet MS", Arial, sans-serif; font-size: 12pt}
p {font-family: "Trebuchet MS", Arial, sans-serif; font-size: 10pt}
```

Amend the markup for the web page to link to the new stylesheet size.css. Save this in your Task21ad folder. Save the new stylesheet as **size.css** in the same folder. Refresh your browser so that you can see the effect that this has on the web page.

It should look similar to this.

Try different absolute font sizes to see what they look like in different fonts.

Relative values are often based on previously defined values for the fonts, as defined by the default browser settings. Two values are shown using the abbreviations 'em' and 'ex'. One em is the same as the current font size; two em is twice the current font size, etc. One ex is about half the height of the current font size and is the measured height of the letter 'x'. This can be useful as it automatically selects the default fonts set by the user in other stylesheets or by the browser.

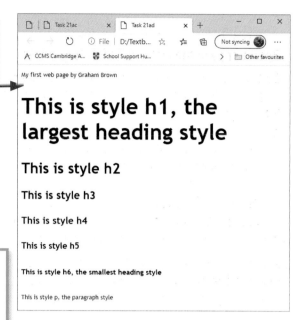

Task 21ae

Open a copy of the web page and stylesheet that you saved in Task 21ad.

Edit the stylesheet so that the paragraph style is 16 point. Set style h1 so that it is 3 em, h2 is 2 em, h3 is 1.5 em, h4 is 3 ex, h5 is 2 ex and h6 so that it is 1.5 ex. Save as size2.css

Open the web page saved in Task 21ad and edit this to attach the stylesheet size2.css to it. Save this as **task21ae.htm** in the Task21ae folder. Open the stylesheet size.css and edit it so that it changes the font sizes like this.

```
h1 {font-family: "Trebuchet MS", Arial, sans-serif; font-size: 3em}
h2 {font-family: "Trebuchet MS", Arial, sans-serif; font-size: 2em}
h3 {font-family: "Trebuchet MS", Arial, sans-serif; font-size: 1.5em}
h4 {font-family: "Trebuchet MS", Arial, sans-serif; font-size: 3ex}
h5 {font-family: "Trebuchet MS", Arial, sans-serif; font-size: 2ex}
h6 {font-family: "Trebuchet MS", Arial, sans-serif; font-size: 1.5ex}
p  {font-family: "Trebuchet MS", Arial, sans-serif; font-size: 16pt}
```

Save this stylesheet as **size2.css** in the task21ae folder. View the web page with this stylesheet attached. Notice the difference in the em and ex sizes.

Other relative values frequently used in cascading stylesheets are **percentage** values, for example, setting the font size to 200% would force the font to be twice the size of the current paragraph style.

There is also a set of predefined relative sizes that can be used. These are: 'xx-small', 'x-small', 'small', 'medium', 'large', 'x-large' and 'xx-large'. Other acceptable relative values are 'smaller' and 'larger', which can be useful if defining different classes within a style.

Task 21af

Open a copy of the web page and stylesheet that you saved in Task 21ae.

Edit this stylesheet so that style h1 is xx-large, h2 is x-large, h3 is large, h4 is medium, h5 is small, h6 is x-small and the paragraph style is xx-small. Save as size3.css.

Open the web page saved in Task 21ae and edit this so that the stylesheet size3.css is attached to it. Save this as **task21af.htm** in the Task21af folder. Open the stylesheet size2.css and edit this so that it changes the font sizes like this.

```
h1 {font-family: "Trebuchet MS", Arial, sans-serif; font-size: xx-large}
h2 {font-family: "Trebuchet MS", Arial, sans-serif; font-size: x-large}
h3 {font-family: "Trebuchet MS", Arial, sans-serif; font-size: large}
h4 {font-family: "Trebuchet MS", Arial, sans-serif; font-size: medium}
h5 {font-family: "Trebuchet MS", Arial, sans-serif; font-size: small}
h6 {font-family: "Trebuchet MS", Arial, sans-serif; font-size: x-small}
p  {font-family: "Trebuchet MS", Arial, sans-serif; font-size: xx-small}
```

Save this stylesheet as **size3.css** in the Task21af folder. View the web page with this stylesheet attached.

Align text

A font style (or class within a style) can be aligned in one of four different ways. You can use the text-align property to format text so that it is left aligned, centre aligned, right aligned or fully justified, as shown in this sample stylesheet. The text-align property must contain a hyphen like this.

```
h1 {text-align: left}
h2 {text-align: center}
h3 {text-align: right}
h4 {text-align: justify}
```

Advice

For centre aligned text, note the American spelling for center.

Task 21ag

Open the file you saved in Task 21b. At the top of the page add a new title 'Aligning text' in style h1. Set the heading style h1 to be centre aligned. Set style h2 to be right aligned. Set style p to be left aligned.

Open the web page saved in Task 21b and edit this by attaching a new stylesheet called align.css like this.

```
<link rel="stylesheet" type="text/css" href="align.css">
```

Add the title 'Aligning text' in style h1. Save this as **task21ag.htm** in your Task21ag folder. Create a new stylesheet like this.

```
h1 {text-align: center}
h2 {text-align: right}
p  {text-align: left}
```

Save this stylesheet as **align.css** in the Task21ag folder. Check that this works and that the styles have been applied correctly like this.

Advice

Carriage returns within the HTML have no effect on the layout of the web page.

Enhance text within a stylesheet

You have already used the color and background-color properties to enhance text in earlier tasks and we will study these enhancements in more detail later in the chapter. Other enhancements are available, including to embolden text (make it bold), italicise text (make it italic) and underscore (to underline text). Each of these uses a different property, but the default value for these three enhancements is set to normal. To get bold text, set the font-weight property to 'bold', like this.

To italicise text, set the font-style property to 'italic', like this.

To underline text, set the text-decoration property to 'underline', like this.

```
h1 {font-weight: bold;
    font-style: italic;
    text-decoration: underline}
```

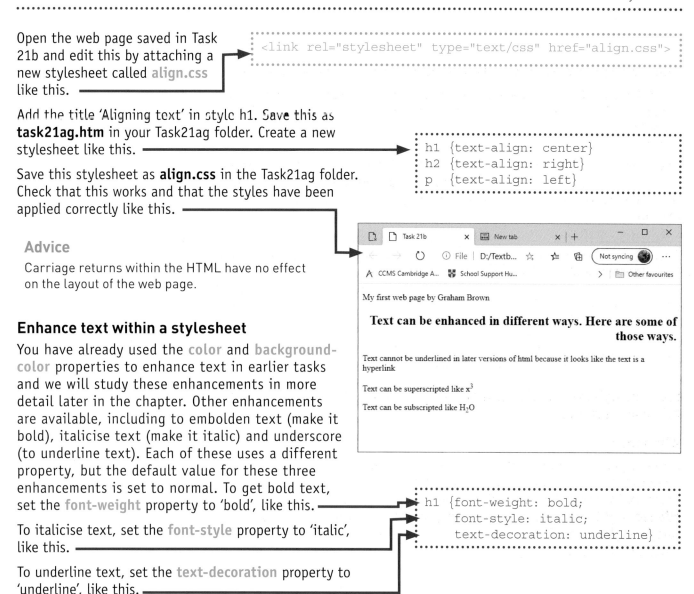

Advice

Although the underline command is no longer part of HTML, it can still be used by setting it within a style in the stylesheet.

Task 21ah

Create a new stylesheet called mystyle1.css and attach this to the web page called **webpage6.htm**. This stylesheet will set style h1 to a bold, italic, 18-point font. If 'Times New Roman' is available the browser will use that, otherwise it will choose 'Times', but if this is not available the browser's default serif font will be used. Make this text centre aligned.

Copy the file webpage6.htm into your Task21ah folder. Open this file in your web browser and text editor. Enter the following CSS and save it as a new stylesheet called **mystyle1.css** in the Task21ah folder. Refresh this file in your web browser.

```
h1      {font-family: "Times New Roman",Times,serif;
        font-size: 18pt;
        text-align: center;
        font-weight: bold;
        font-style: italic}
```

Advice

Notice that each property and its value/s are on a new line. This makes it easier to read and check for mistakes.

Activity 21l

Create a new stylesheet called mystyle2.css and attach this to the web page called **webpage7.htm**. This stylesheet will set:

» h1 as an italic, centre aligned, 24-point font – if 'Helvetica' is available the browser will use that, otherwise it will choose 'Arial Narrow' but, if this is not available, the browser's default sans-serif font will be used

» h2 as a bold, right aligned, 16-point font – if 'Courier Narrow' is available the browser will use that, otherwise it will choose 'Courier' but, if this is not available, the browser's default proportional spaced font will be used

» h3 as an underlined, left aligned, 16-point font – if 'Courier Narrow' is available the browser will use that, otherwise it will choose 'Courier' but, if this is not available, the browser's default proportional spaced font will be used

» p as a 14-point, left aligned, serif font.

Print evidence of your stylesheet, the HTML source and the browser view of the web page with the stylesheet attached.

Text colour

You can use the color property to change the colour of text within a style. Earlier in the chapter you changed text colour with an embedded CSS color property in the HTML. As mentioned earlier, it is usual to work with hex colour codes. These are always preceded by a hash (#) symbol.

Task 21ai

Edit your files for Task 21ah so that style h1 is red.

Copy both files from your Task21ah folder into the Task21ai folder. Open the stylesheet **mystyle1.css** in the text editor. Edit the stylesheet to add a new color declaration with the value #ff0000, like this.

The first two characters (ff) are red, 00 for green and 00 for blue. Save the stylesheet and test the web page in your browser.

```
h1      {font-family: "Times New Roman",Times,serif;
        font-size: 18pt;
        text-align: center;
        font-weight: bold;
        font-style: italic;
        color:#ff0000;}
```

Task 21aj

Edit your files for Task 21ai so that style h1 contains the following colour hexadecimal components: red 0, blue ff and green 00.

Copy both files from your Task21ai folder into the Task21aj folder. Open the stylesheet **mystyle1.css** in the text editor. Edit the **color** property to have a new value like this.

```
h1      {font-family: "Times New Roman",Times,serif;
         font-size: 18pt;
         text-align: center;
         font-weight: bold;
         font-style: italic;
         color:#0000ff;}
```

The value #0000ff is correct: the single 0 for the red component has been turned into 00, and the colours have been placed in the correct RGB (red-green-blue) order. Save the stylesheet and refresh the browser to test it.

Activity 21m

Copy the files saved in Activity 21l. Edit the stylesheet so that each style has the following colours. All values are in hexadecimal, and only hexadecimal codes should be used in your stylesheet:

» h1 is blue
» h2 has a full red component, green is 45 and blue is 0
» h3 has 8B blue, 3D green and 48 red
» h4 has 8B for red and blue, and 0 green
» p is half red and no other colour.

Print evidence of your stylesheet and the browser view of the web page with the stylesheet attached.

21.3.9 Specify background properties

Background colour

In Task 21o you set the background colour of a table using an in-line (embedded) CSS style. It is possible to do this for each element, but is much easier to define it once in an external stylesheet that can be applied to all pages and will set all elements on the page.

Copy both files from your Task21aj folder into the Task21ak folder. Open the stylesheet **mystyle1.css** in the text editor. Add a new selector to define the **body** section of the web page. Use the **background-color** property to have a new value like this.

The **background-color** property must contain a hyphen. Save the stylesheet and refresh the browser to test it.

The background colour can be applied to the whole page (like this), or to tables, table rows, headers or footers with a single definition in the stylesheet.

Task 21ak

Edit your files for Task 21aj so that the web page has a khaki (f0e68c) background colour.

```
body     {background-color:#f0e68c;}
```

Advice

The **background-color** declaration can also be used with other styles to give different effects. Try defining the CSS for different styles like this.

```
h1      {background-color:#0000ff;}
```

Activity 21n

Copy the files saved in Activity 21m. Edit the stylesheet so that the web page has a background colour with a red component of f2, a blue component of 8e, and e8 green. All values are in hexadecimal, and only hexadecimal codes should be used in your stylesheet. Print evidence of your stylesheet and the browser view of the web page with the stylesheet attached.

Background images

Background images can be applied to the body section of a web page using the **background-image** property with a value containing the **Uniform Resource Locator** (which is often shortened to **URL**) followed by the image's address or filename. This can be used to place either a single background image in the centre of the page or can be repeated to place lots of copies of an image tiled to make the background.

Task 21al

Edit your files for Task 21ak so that the web page has the file **task21al.png** as a single background image placed in the top right of the window.

Copy both files from your Task21ak folder into the Task21al folder. Copy the file **task21al.png** into your Task21al folder.

```
body    {background-color: #f0e68c;
         background-image: url("task21al.png");
         background-repeat: no-repeat;}
```

Add to the **body** section of the stylesheet **mystyle1.css** new **background-image** and **background-repeat** properties with these values.

Each of these properties must contain a hyphen. Save the stylesheet and refresh the browser to test it. The page will look like this.

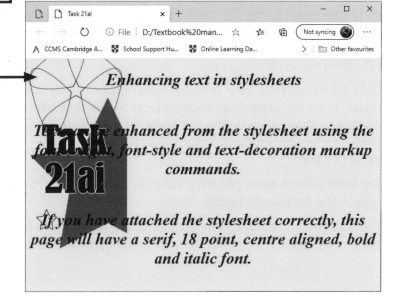

Tiled background images

Try changing the value for the **background-repeat** declaration to this.

```
background-repeat: repeat;}
```

Save the stylesheet. Test in your browser, maximised to fill the entire screen. What do you notice?

Also test out the values repeat-x and repeat-y with the background-repeat declaration to see what effects these have. Change the background-repeat declaration so that the image is no longer tiled. Save your web page and stylesheet in your Task21al folder.

Advice

In later browsers, more than one background-image declaration can be placed in a window at the same time.

Position a background image

A single background image can be positioned within the browser window. Add a new background-position declaration like this to the body style in task21al.css.

```
body    {background-color: #f0e68c;
         background-image: url("task21al.png");
         background-repeat: no-repeat;
         background-position: right top;}
```

Although this positions the image into the top right corner of the window, some of the text overwrites the background image. In some cases, this effect can be very useful (for example, a watermark) but in this case it is difficult to read all of the text, as shown here.

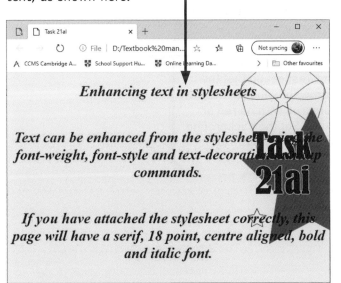 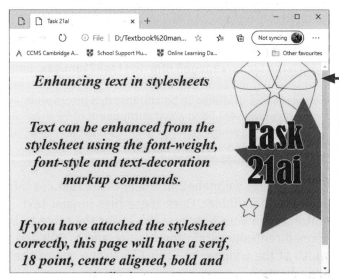

By adding a margin-right definition like this, you can force the contents away from the image. The page now looks like this.

```
body    {background-color: #f0e68c;
         background-image: url("task21al.png");
         background-repeat: no-repeat;
         background-position: right top;
         margin-right: 200px;}
```

Save and test the stylesheet.

Activity 21o

Open the stylesheet **brick.css** and the web page **bricknblocktopia.htm**. Edit the stylesheet so that the web page has a tiled background image using the file **brick.png**. Print evidence of your stylesheet and the browser view of the web page with the stylesheet attached.

Activity 21p

Copy the files saved in Activity 21o. Replace the background image with the file **wall.png**. Repeat this image down the left side of the web page only. Do not allow any of the text to overlap these images.

21.3.10 Specify table properties

You have already created and styled tables in the content layer earlier in this chapter. You embedded style attributes for the table, table rows, table headers, table footers and table data, including setting the padding and border spacing. To revise each of these skills and place the table properties in an external stylesheet you will try one more task on tables.

Task 21am

Open the files **webpage8.htm** and **task21am.css**. Edit the stylesheet so that the table is aligned centrally within, and 70% the width of the browser window. Set all borders and gridlines to be collapsed, 3 pixels wide and coloured with no red or green components and a red component of 99 in hexadecimal. Set the background colour for the whole table to ffff99. Set all text to be aligned centrally both horizontally and vertically within the table.

Copy the files webpage8.htm and task21am.css into your Task21am folder. Open these files in your text editor and in your web browser. To set the table to be aligned centrally within the window and to 70% the width of the window, add this CSS to the end of the stylesheet.

```
table       {width:70%;
             margin-left:auto;
             margin-right:auto;}
```

To set the borders to be collapsed add, in the table section, the border-collapse property and value like this.

Note how the closed curly bracket has now moved to the end of this declaration. To make sure that all other elements for the borders are applied to both the table and table data, create another block with two selectors and a shortcut border declaration like this.

```
table       {width:70%;
             margin-left:auto;
             margin-right:auto;
             border-collapse:collapse;}
```

```
table, td   {border: 3px solid #990000;}
```

If a table header was present this could also be added here, separated by another comma.

```
table, td    {border: 3px solid #990000;
              background-color: #ffff99;
              text-align:center;
              vertical-align:middle;}
```

The background-color property and properties to align text vertically and horizontally within the table can also be added, again making sure the curly brackets are **only** at the end of the final value, like this.

Save the stylesheet and refresh the browser. The finished web page should look like this.

21.3.11 Styles and classes

You have defined styles for elements within a web page, such as a paragraph. But suppose you wanted just one paragraph in a web page to have some additional formatting, such as different coloured text? You can easily do this using classes.

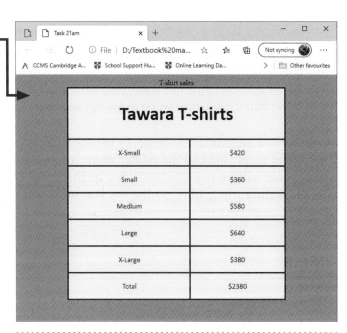

These are useful for adding to or changing styles without defining a completely new style. You can define a class in the stylesheet by using the dot or full stop (.) symbol. For example, this stylesheet defines the style h1 in the normal way.

It also defines a class called **right** that can be used with any style to change the colour and alignment of the style that it is applied to. This is also useful within tables as you may define the layout of all tables in the same way, using the table and td styles, yet add variations to this by adding a class.

```
h1              {text-align:left}
.right          {color:#0000ff;
                 text-align:right;}
```

21.3.12 Create and apply a class

> **Task 21an**
>
> Edit your files for Task 21am so that the right column of the table is right aligned and the bottom row of the table is coloured #a00000.

Copy the files task21am.htm and task21am.css into your Task21an folder. Rename these files **task21an.htm** and **task21an.css**. Open these files in your text editor and in your web browser. Edit the HTML so that the web page applies the correct stylesheet like this. ➜

```
<link rel="stylesheet" type="text/css" href="task21an.css">
```

You will create two new classes in the stylesheet. You will call these **red** and **right**. When you define a class it has a full stop at the start of the class name. Everything else in terms of structure and declarations is the same as a CSS style. In the stylesheet, add the following text.

```
.red            {color:#a00000;}
.right          {text-align:right;}
```

Save the stylesheet.

These two classes need to be applied to the HTML. We will start with setting the table footer as red text. (We could also apply these styles to the table row, or to the table data). It might appear easier to apply only one of these, to the <tr> tag, but as the right cell of this row will also need to be right aligned, we will apply the class separately to the table data. Edit the markup for the table footer to look like this.

```
<tfoot>
  <tr>
    <td><p class="red">Total</p></td>
    <td><p class="red">$2380</p></td>
  </tr>
</tfoot>
```

Advice

A common error is to include a full stop before the right, note that there is no full stop here, that is only used when defining the style.

Save the web page and test it works before moving on to the second class. Add the second class **right** to the HTML. When it is added to the right cell in the footer there will be two classes added to the same <p> (paragraph tag) and both are held within the quotes, so the markup looks like this.

```
<tfoot>
  <tr>
    <td><p class="red">Total</p></td>
    <td><p class="red right">$2380</p></td>
  </tr>
</tfoot>
<tbody>
  <tr>
    <td><p>X-Small</p></td>
    <td><p class="right">$420</p></td>
  </tr>
  <tr>
    <td><p>Small</p></td>
    <td><p class="right">$360</p></td>
  </tr>
  <tr>
    <td><p>Medium</p></td>
    <td><p class="right">$580</p></td>
  </tr>
  <tr>
    <td><p>Large</p></td>
    <td><p class="right">$640</p></td>
  </tr>
  <tr>
    <td><p>X-Large</p></td>
    <td><p class="right">$380</p></td>
  </tr>
</tbody>
```

The finished website looks like this.

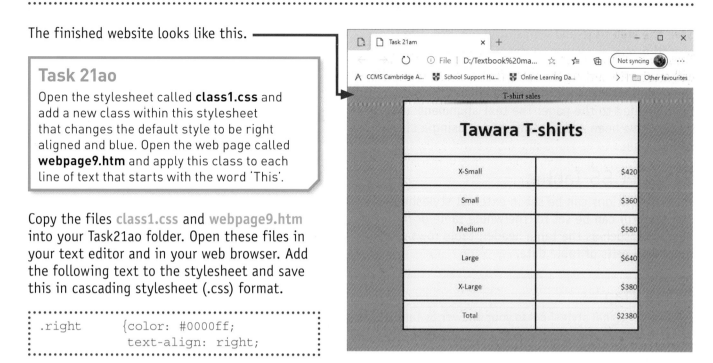

Task 21ao

Open the stylesheet called **class1.css** and add a new class within this stylesheet that changes the default style to be right aligned and blue. Open the web page called **webpage9.htm** and apply this class to each line of text that starts with the word 'This'.

Copy the files class1.css and webpage9.htm into your Task21ao folder. Open these files in your text editor and in your web browser. Add the following text to the stylesheet and save this in cascading stylesheet (.css) format.

```
.right      {color: #0000ff;
             text-align: right;
```

Enter the highlighted markup to the web page to add the **right** class sub-type to each line starting with the word 'This'. It should look like this.

```
<!DOCTYPE html>
<html>
  <head>
    <title>Task 21ao</title>
    <link rel="stylesheet" type="text/css" href="class1.css">
  </head>
  <body>
    <h1>Task 21ao</h1>
    <h1>Style h1 is a sans-serif, 20 point, centre aligned font.</h1>
    <h1 class="right">This is the subtype of h1 called .right</h1>
    <h2>Style h2 is a sans-serif, 14 point, left aligned font.</h2>
    <h2 class="right">This is the subtype of h2 called .right</h2>
    <h3>Style h3 is a sans-serif, 12 point, left aligned, italic font.</h3>
    <h3 class="right">This is the subtype of h3 called .right</h3>
    <p>Style p is a serif, 10 point, left aligned font.</p>
    <p class="right">This is the subtype of p called .right</p>
    <p>Last edited by YOUR NAME</p>
  </body>
</html>
```

Save the web page and refresh the browser. The screen should now look similar to this.

You can see from this printout that the original style definitions (except for the text alignment) have all been applied to the page. The text alignment and colour have been added to the styles using a class called 'right'.

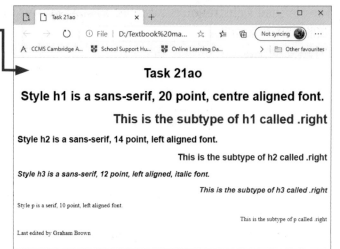

21.3.13 CSS Tables

Table definitions can be set in external stylesheets. The selector can be set for the whole table or for elements, such as the table header, table rows and individual cells of table data.

Task 21ap

Add an external stylesheet to your answer to Task 21d to set the following styles:

Selector	Property	Value
Web page	Background colour	#90ee90
Table	Background colour	#0000ff
Table cells	Background colour	#2eb757
Table header	Background colour	#cfcf00

All values are in hexadecimal. Show evidence of your method.

Copy the web page from your Task21d folder into your Task21ap folder. Open this file in your text editor. Add a new line to the head section to attach an external stylesheet to this web page, like this.

```
<link rel="stylesheet" type="text/css" href="table1.css">
```

In your second text editor window and in your Task21ap folder create a new stylesheet called **table1.css**. For the first style the selector says the whole web page. This is the same as the body section, so create a style definition like this.

```
body  {background-color: #90ee90;}
```

Save the web page and the stylesheet and test that this has worked. Add to the stylesheet the background colour for all of the table like this.

```
body  {background-color: #90ee90;}
table {background-color: #0000ff;}
```

Save the stylesheet and test the web page, which should now look similar to this. ———————

To change the table cells, add the **td** selector and a **background-color** property with a value of #2eb757 like this.

```
body     {background-color: #90ee90;}
table    {background-color: #0000ff;}
td       {background-color: #2eb757;}
```

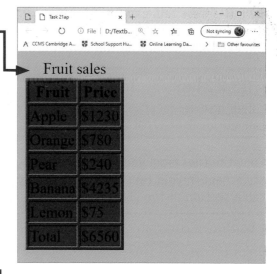

Save the stylesheet and test the web page, which should look similar to this.

You will see that the table background is still visible between the cells with the table data, but the table data is now a green colour. ———————

Now add the **thead** selector and a **background-color** property with a value of #cfcf00 like this.

```
body     {background-color: #90ee90;}
table    {background-color: #0000ff;}
td       {background-color: #2eb757;}
thead    {background-color: #cfcf00;}
```

When you have saved the stylesheet and tested it in the browser your web page should look similar to this. ———————

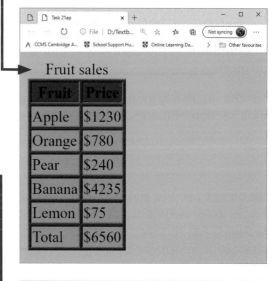

Advice

The technique used in this task – to do one small part, test it, correct it and test again (if needs be) before going on to the next part – is ideal for any web development (or programming).

Activity 21q

Copy the files saved in Activity 21b. Attach an external stylesheet to this web page that defines the web page with a background of ff8c00 and a table with a background colour of ff4500. The table header should have a background with ffd700 and all other cells in the table should have a background with ffff00. All values are in hexadecimal. Place a single image of a sun (using the file sun.png) in the top right corner of the web page and make sure no other elements on the page could overwrite this. Print evidence of your method.

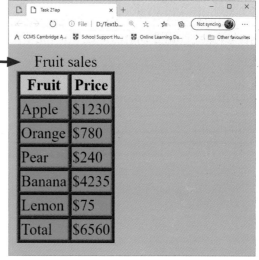

CSS table borders and gridlines

You may be asked to set internal gridlines and/or external table borders for tables. As you created tables earlier in the chapter, you will now be able to set the cell padding and spacing within a stylesheet as well as define table and cell borders within it. To set the border width of internal gridlines you must adjust the border width of the table data (or table header); for the external borders set the border for the table.

Task 21aq

Edit the external stylesheet for your answer to Task 21ap so that the table has single black external borders 4 pixels wide and internal gridlines 2 pixels wide.

Copy the files from your Task21ap folder into your Task21aq folder. Open the stylesheet in your text editor. For the external borders add these four lines to table section of the CSS.

```
table      {background-color: #0000ff;
            border-collapse: collapse;
            border-style: solid;
            border-width: 4px;
            border-color: #000000;}
```

Save the stylesheet and test the web page, which should change to this.

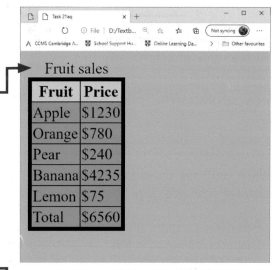

For the internal gridline width add this extra line to the table data section of the stylesheet.

```
td         {background-color: #2eb757;
            border-width: 2px;}
```

We do not need to add the border-collapse, border-style or border-color definitions as these are cascaded from the table settings. Again, save and test to see that the gridlines have changed in width like this.

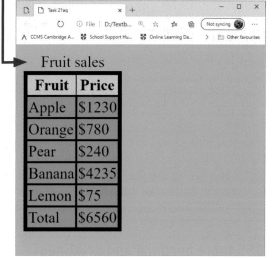

Experiment with other values for the border-style, such as dashed, dotted or double.

Activity 21r

Copy the files saved in Activity 21q. Edit this stylesheet so that the table has a solid red border 4 pixels wide and cell padding of 10 pixels. Align all text in the table to the centre of each cell. All values must be in hexadecimal. Print evidence of your method.

Index